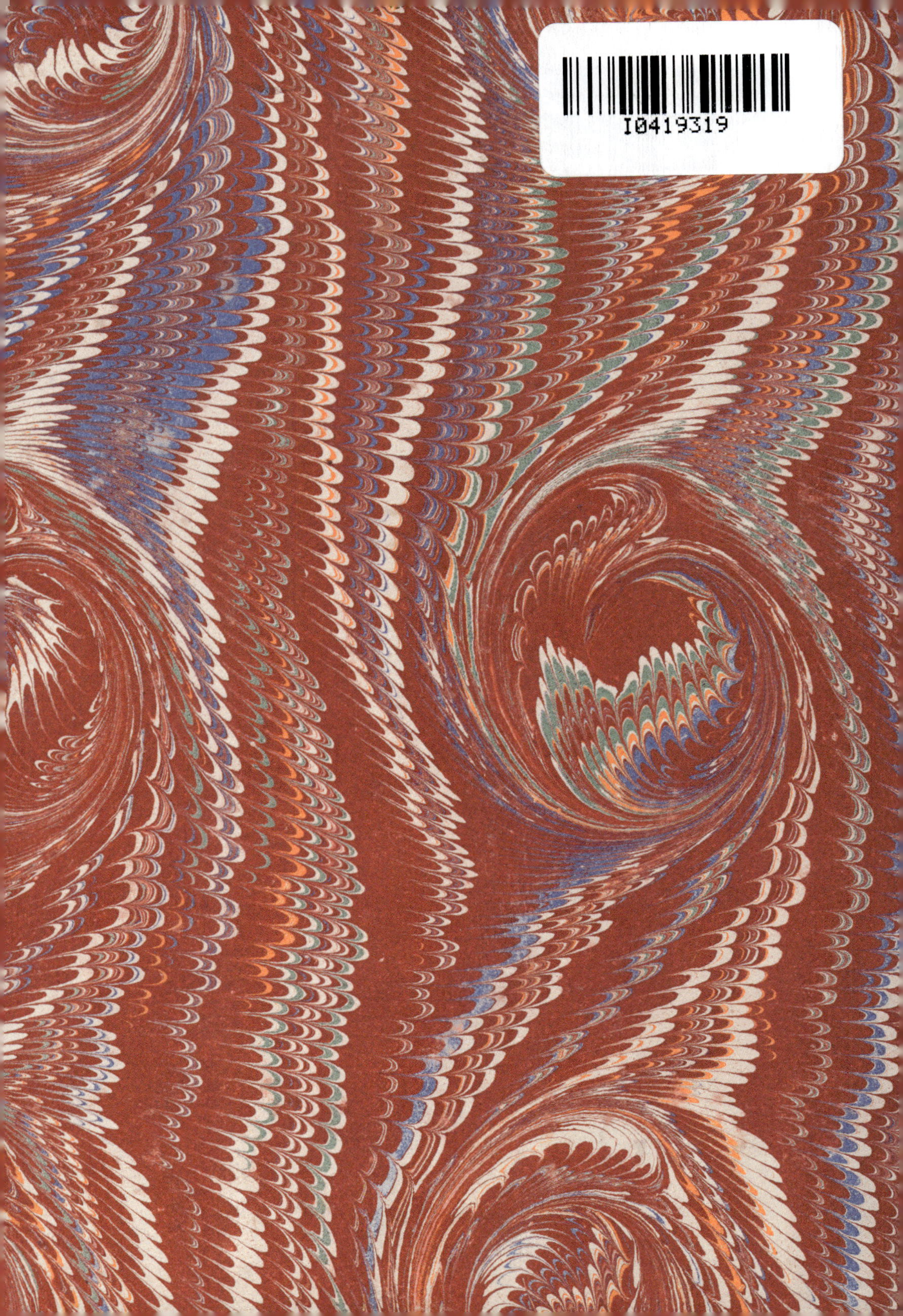
I0419319

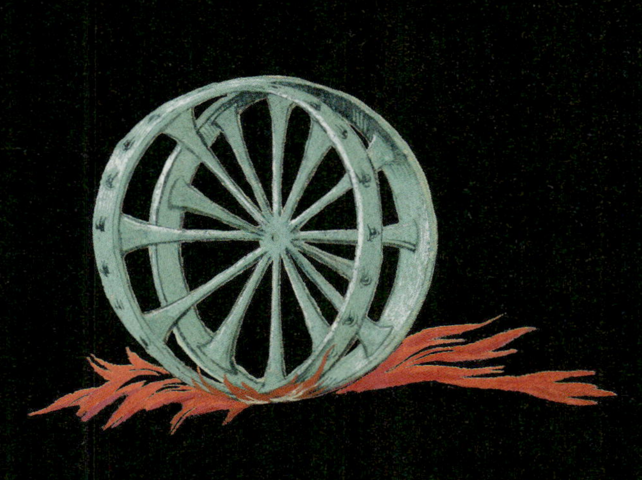

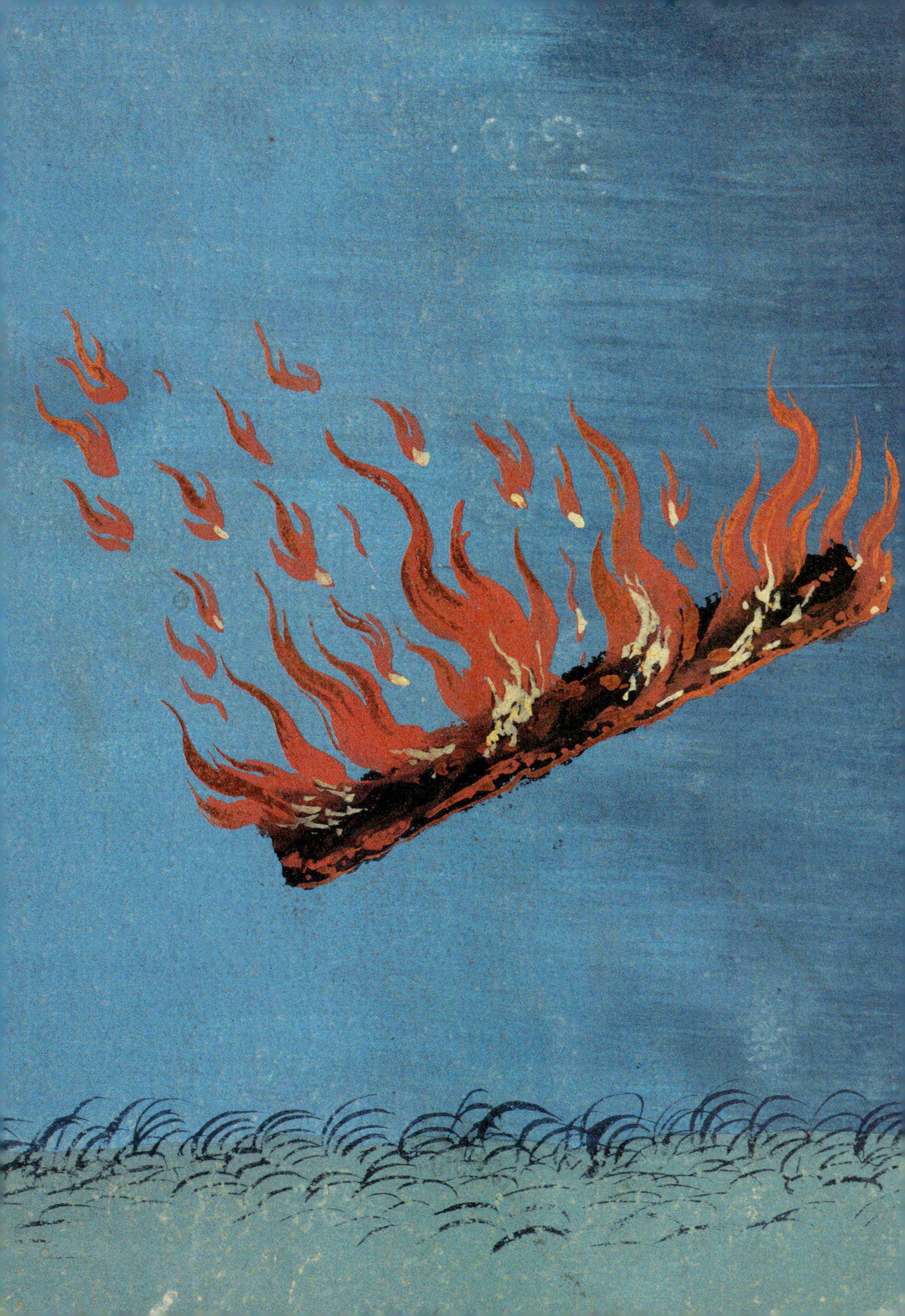

Till-Holger Borchert

The Book of MIRACLES

Das Wunderzeichenbuch
Le Livre des miracles

The Augsburg manuscript from the
Collection of Mickey Cartin

TASCHEN

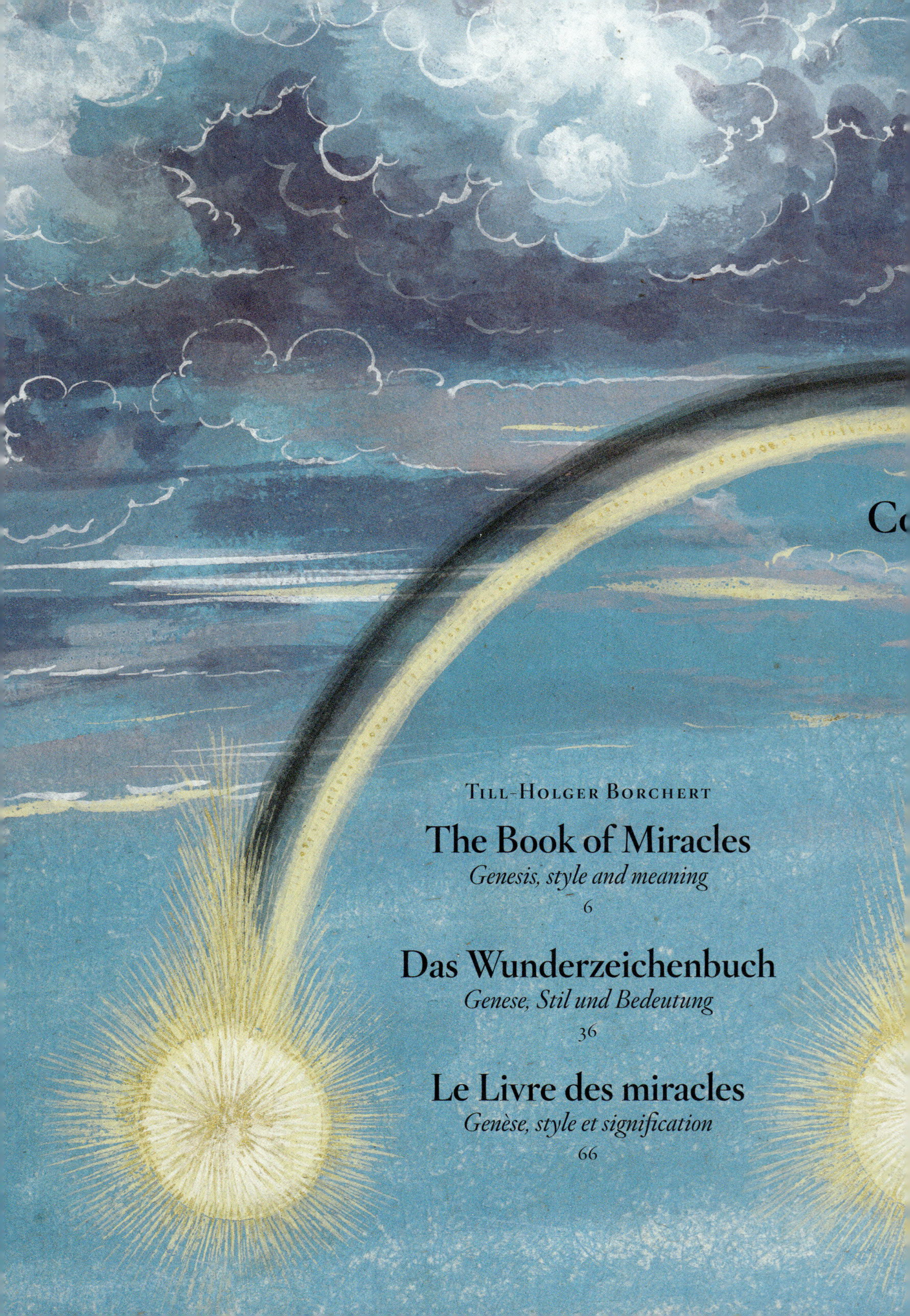

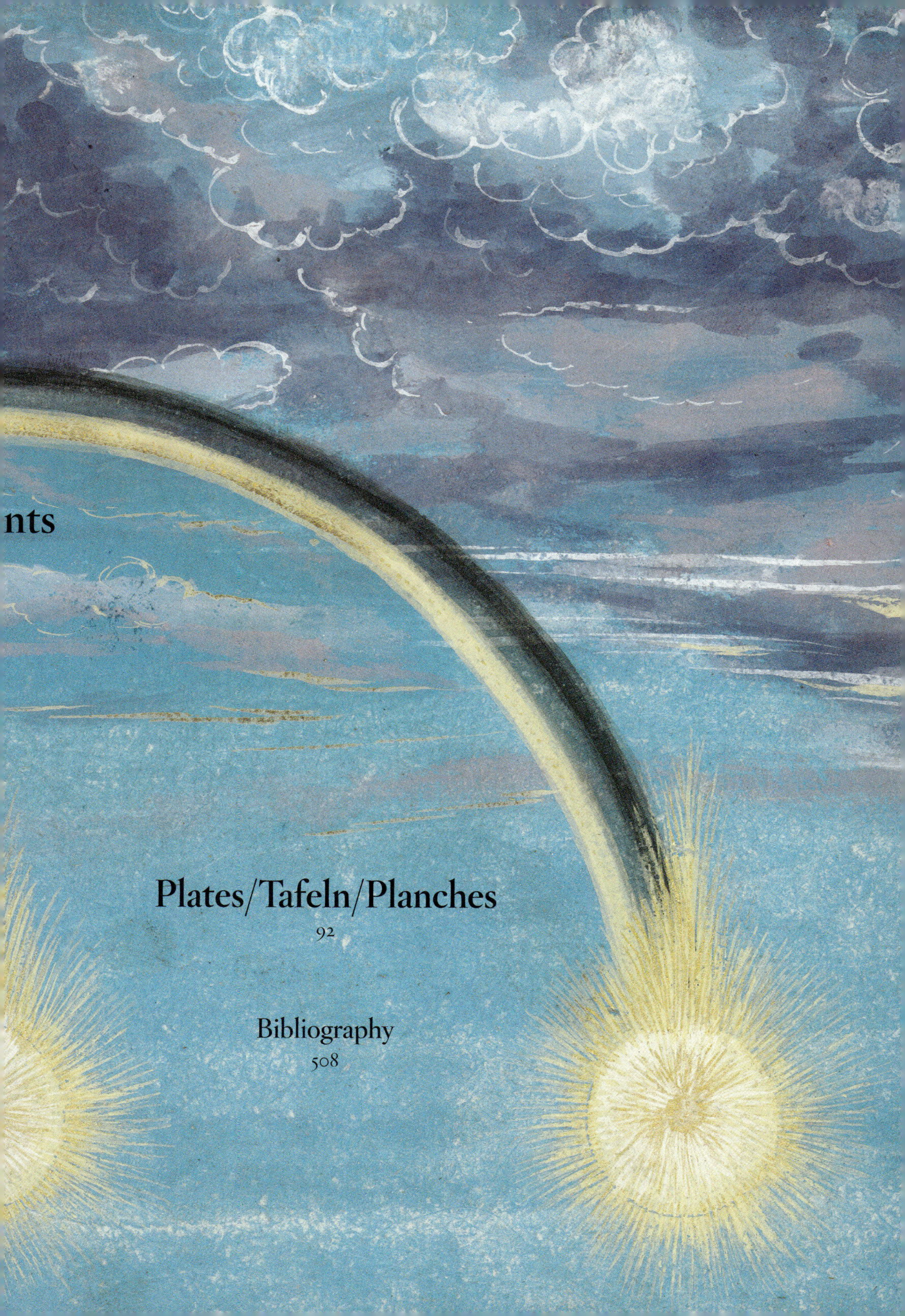

nts

TILL-HOLGER BORCHERT

The Book of Miracles

Genesis, style and meaning

The manuscript contains accounts and descriptions of miraculous signs that have been observed throughout history, starting in Old Testament times (fols. 1r–15r) and continuing through Antiquity (fols. 16r–30r), the Middle Ages and Late Middle Ages (fols. 32r–90r) right up to the middle of the 16th century (fols. 91r–171r). It concludes with the signs in the heavens seen by St John, as described in the Book of Revelation (fols. 172r–192r) and interpreted to announce the Second Coming of Christ, the Last Judgement and the future kingdom of God. The manuscript thus aims to be comprehensive in its scope, in so far as it covers miraculous signs not just from the time of the creation of humankind up to its own day but also those expected at the end of the world. With regard to the divine plan for Salvation, at least, it aims for completeness.

The Book of Miracles, with its comparatively lavish illustration, originally comprised 200 pages, each bearing an accomplished and artistic gouache representation of a scene and an accompanying text on one side of the sheet only. A number of the original pages was removed when the book was rebound in the 19th century, however, and the manuscript in its present form comprises only 167 original folia and 23 inserts. We were able to track down four of these detached folia and have included them in this edition. The pages in question are fols. 93r, 111r, 191r and 192r.

The original manuscript was probably produced in Augsburg (see below) and its contents compiled by an unknown patron or by a scholar commissioned with the task. It thus falls into entirely the same tradition as other more or less contemporary books of wonders. Its combination of Old Testament, historical and Apocalyptic miraculous signs lies at the heart of the *Histoires prodigieuses* (Paris 1560) by the Breton humanist Pierre Boaistuau (*c.* 1520–1566), for example, a book so popular that it was rapidly translated into English as *Certain Secrete Wonders of Nature, Containing a Description of Sundry Strange Things* (London 1569). And it also characterises the *Prodigiorum ac*

1496 – Tiber monster / Tibermonster / Monstre du Tibre
in: *Book of Miracles*, Augsburg, *c.* 1550–1552, fol. 90r (detail)
Private collection

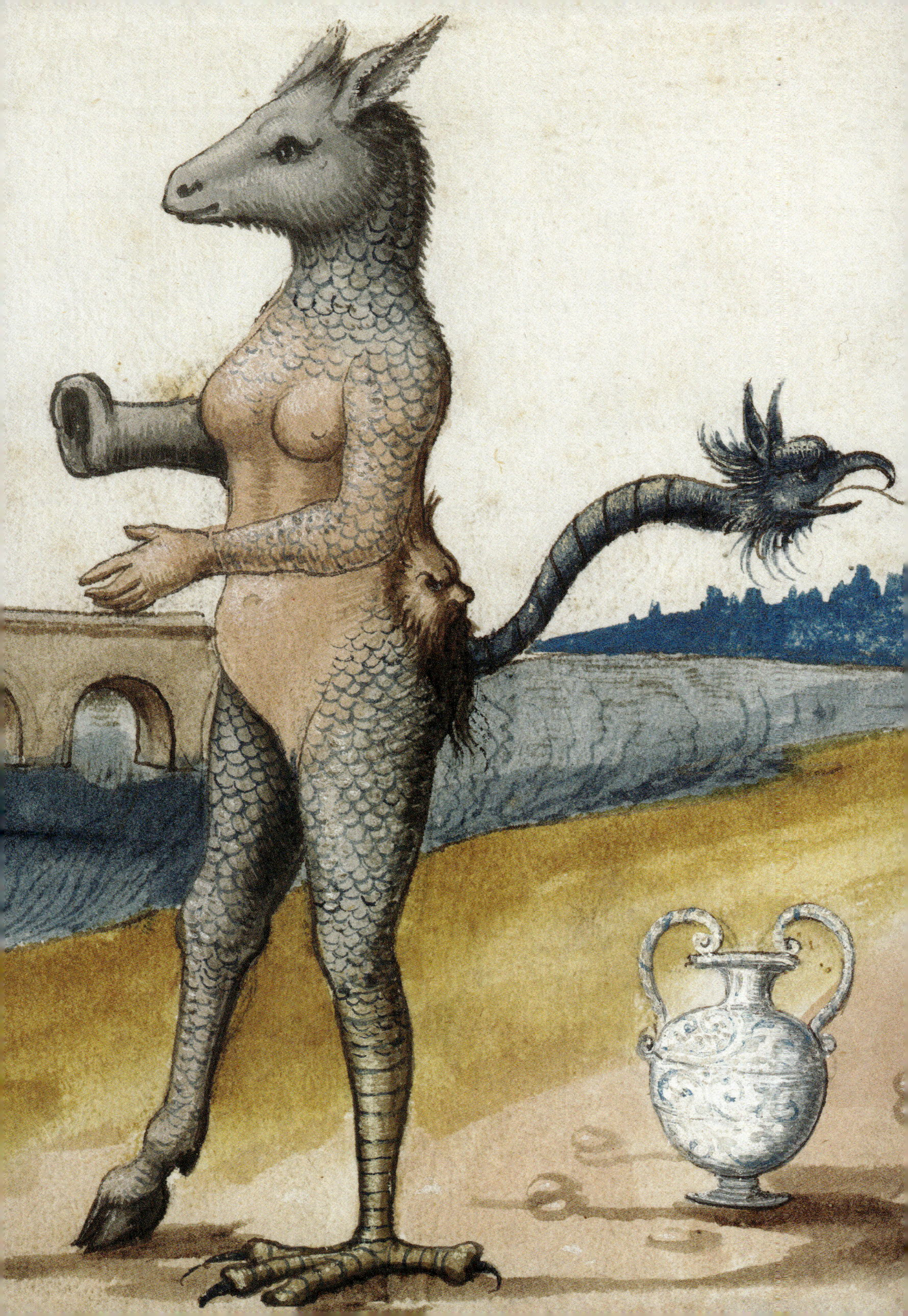

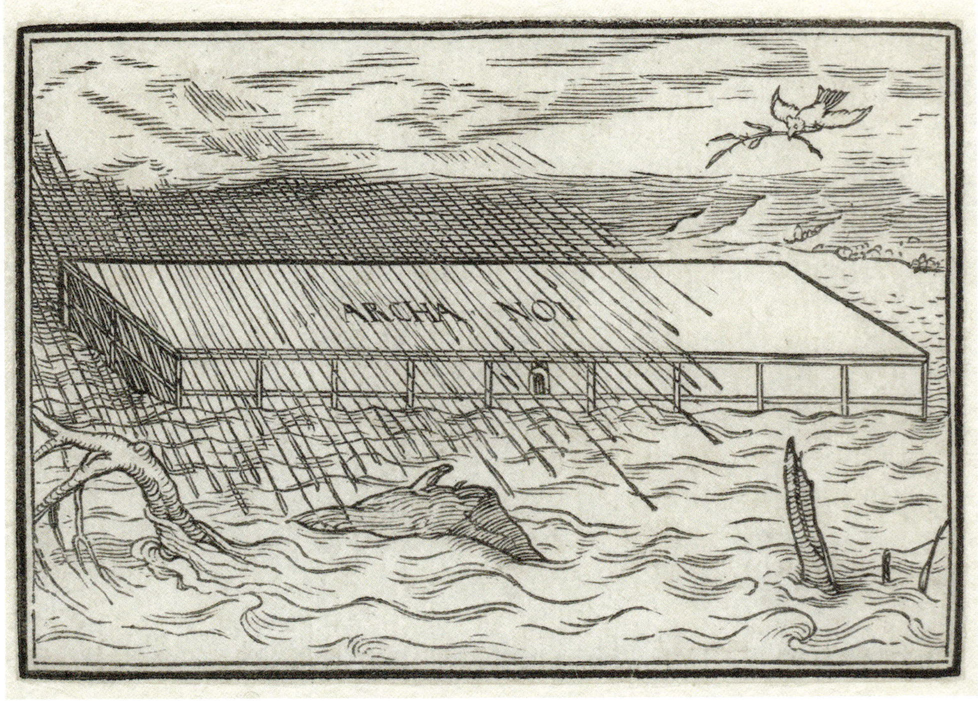

Ill. 1
Hans Holbein the Younger
The Deluge / Die Sintflut / Le Déluge
in: *Historiarum Veteris Instrumenti icones ad vivum expressae*, Lyons 1538
Basel, Kunstmuseum, Kupferstichkabinett

ostentorum chronicon (Chronicle of Prodigies and Portents; ill. 15) published in Basel in 1557 by the Alsatian universal scholar Conrad Lycosthenes. The present codex nevertheless claims a special place within the genre on account of its scope and skilfully rendered illustrations.

Miraculous signs from the Old Testament

The manuscript starts without an introduction of any kind: it has no dedication, preface or list of contents. It begins with a selection of Old Testament events that were interpreted as miraculous signs sent by God. In contrast to the illustrated chronicle by Lycosthenes, the more or less contemporary Book of Miracles does not begin with the Fall, but with the Deluge, God's punishment upon sinful humankind as recounted in Genesis, chapters 6–9 (fol. 1r). The magnificent miniature shows Noah's Ark battling through the flood, beneath darkened skies and the lashing rain, while people and animals fight for their lives in the waters flooding the landscape all around. The illustration occupies almost three-quarters of the sheet and is accompanied by a text of several lines under-

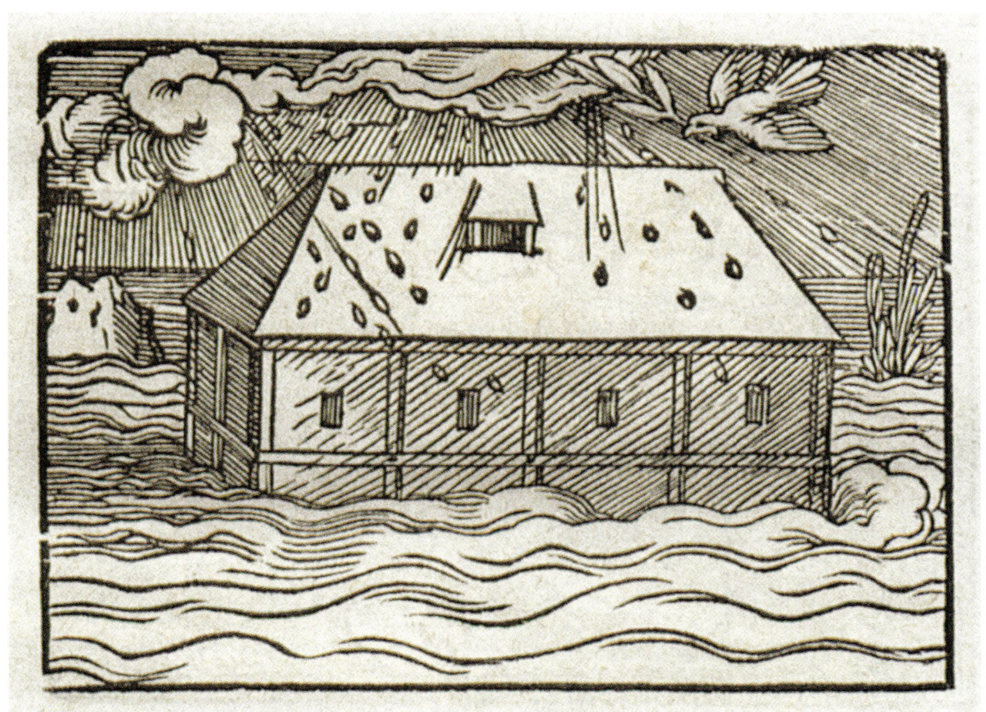

Ill. 2
Hans Sebald Beham
The Deluge / Die Sintflut / Le Déluge
in: *Biblicae historiae artificiosissime depictae. Biblische Historien figürlich fürgebildet*,
Frankfurt am Main 1537 (2nd ed.), fol. 3r. Munich, Bayerische Staatsbibliothek

neath. The heading, initial and decorative elements are executed in red, while the main body of the text is written in pen and black ink. Image and caption are framed within a black border. This layout is followed on every page of the Book of Miracles, with the exception of a handful of folia on which the text is divided into two columns (see below). The accompanying texts are written in German and adhere to the 1545 edition of the Luther Bible, the German-language translation of the Bible by Martin Luther.

Many of the illustrations in the opening, Old Testament section of the Book of Miracles are based on woodcuts by Hans Holbein the Younger or Hans Sebald Beham. In the case of the Deluge however, the illustration is more complex than the corresponding representations by these two artists (ills. 1, 2), and is not based directly upon the woodcut in the Luther Bible (ill. 28). Although parallels can undoubtedly be seen in the depiction of the downpour and the people drowning in the waters, the painter has here reduced the number of individual motifs in favour of a concentrated pictorial narrative – omitting, for example, the figures clambering up on to the rocks.

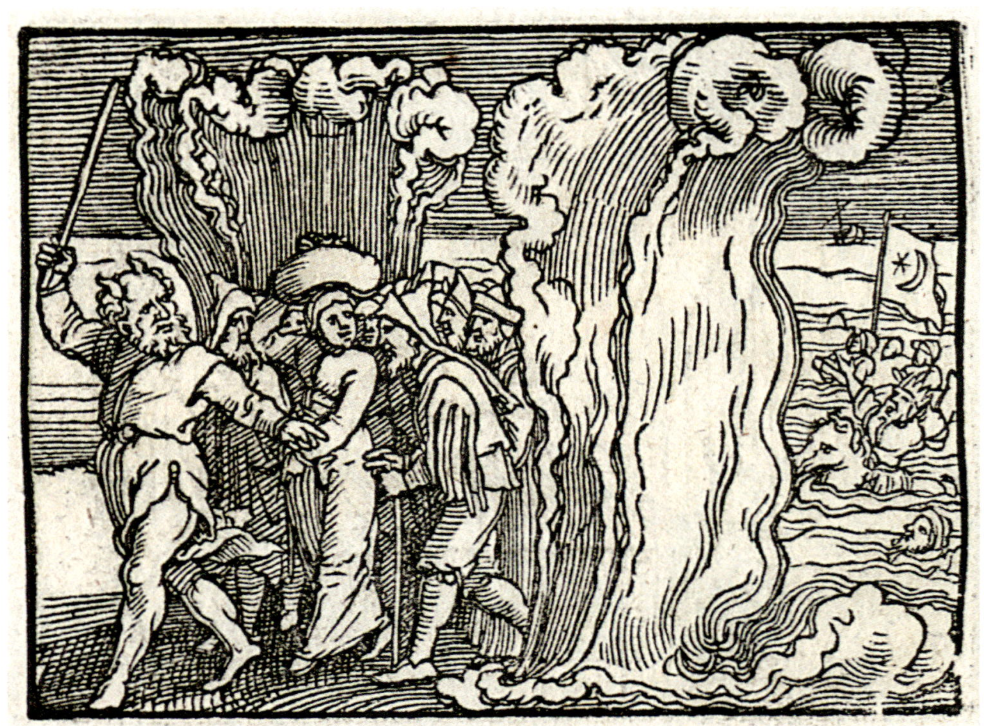

Ill. 3
Hans Sebald Beham
Moses and the Israelites crossing the Red Sea
Moses führt die Israeliten durch das Rote Meer / Le Passage de la mer Rouge
in: *Biblicae historiae artificiosissime depictae. Biblische Historien figürlich fürgebildet*, Frankfurt am Main 1537 (2nd ed.), fol. 10v. Munich, Bayerische Staatsbibliothek

The Deluge is followed on folio 2r by the appearance of the rainbow described in Genesis as the sign of God's covenant with humankind (Gen. 9:12–15). The double rainbow here is combined with figural representations of the twelve signs of the zodiac, six on either side. As allegories of the twelve months of the year, these symbolise the eternal course of time. The phenomenon of the double rainbow was evidently familiar to the artist from first-hand experience, since the paler inner arch is seen as white (as it can often appear) and the outer one as red, yellow and green. The overall effect of the illustration is particularly heightened by the use of gold, which has been applied with painstaking care.

Folio 4r shows the destruction of Sodom and Gomorrah (Gen. 19:24–26). In the context of prodigious events and miraculous signs, Lot and his daughters, with Lot's wife – turned into a pillar of salt – in the centre of the scene, are of secondary importance. Most of the image is taken up by the destruction of the two cities.

Having devoted its opening pages to natural phenomena as expressions of God's will, the Book of Miracles switches its focus in what follows: folio 5r shows Moses striding at the head of the Israelites as they escape from Egypt with Pharaoh in pursuit. While Moses parts the waters of the Red Sea before him, on the right of the scene the waves close up again over Pharaoh and his army. This illustration of the events from Exodus (14:27–29) draws our attention less to the miraculous parting of the Red Sea than to Moses and the Israelites. In this respect the painter has borrowed his composition from the woodcut in Hans Sebald Beham's *Biblicae historiae* (ill. 3).

It is unclear why the Book of Miracles, in contrast to other biblical cycles, omits the Sacrifice of Isaac and Jacob's Dream (of the ladder leading up to Heaven), and also does not show the plagues inflicted upon the land of Egypt (Exod. 7–11). The first two episodes are linked with divine manifestations in the form of celestial apparitions, while the biblical plagues to a certain extent represent archetypes of catastrophes that are most definitely ranked as miraculous events in the second half of the manuscript, such as hailstorms, rivers of blood and plagues of locusts.

The episode represented on folio 6r may likewise be seen as the biblical archetype of prodigious events included in the latter part of the manuscript as food miracles. According to the account in the Old Testament, God saved the people of Israel from starvation by sending down a shower of manna (Exod. 16:14–16). This "precipitation" is actually manna lichen – edible crustose lichen that is carried by the wind. The subject was considered a prefiguration of the Last Supper and the Sacrament of the Eucharist and was also included in Protestant pictorial cycles. The illustration is based on a woodcut from the *Icones*, a major cycle of illustrations to the Old Testament by Hans Holbein the Younger produced around 1525/26 (Müller 1997, pp. 285–286). The present artist has taken his figural motifs from Holbein's woodcut (ill. 17) and incorporated them into the pictorial landscape, their proportions correspondingly adjusted.

On folio 7r we look down from a slightly elevated viewpoint upon the group around Moses and Aaron, the latter in the robes of a priest. At their feet, the earth is opening up to swallow the rebellious Korah and his followers. Beyond them, our eye is led smoothly into the background, where a river meanders through the expansive landscape before flowing out into the sea. A tall conifer borders the left-hand edge of the composition, its scale underlining the distance separating foreground and background. Using comparatively simple means, the painter succeeds in achieving impressive atmospheric effects that testify to a good knowledge of the panel painting of the Danube School, Franconia and Swabia (ill. 29). The subsidiary scene on the right, in which riders are being consumed by fire from Heaven, shows the punishment of those who supported Korah the Levite and is part of the story of Korah related in the Book of Numbers. The accompanying text corresponds to Numbers 16:4–7, verses that cover the start of Korah's rebellion against Moses, but not the end. The viewer's understanding of the illustration does not follow directly from reading the text, but presupposes a more detailed knowledge of the Old Testament.

Folio 8r shows the prophet Elijah being taken up to Heaven in a chariot, as described in II Kings 2 in modern Bible editions. The heading above the text, however, gives the source as III Kings *(Regnum iii)* – the numbering system still employed in the Renaissance, during which the two Books of Samuel were counted as one of the Books of Kings. Underneath, the three-line text breaks off in mid-verse. The illustration is once again dependent for its composition upon the corresponding woodcut in Holbein's *Icones*.

The prophet Isaiah's vision of the Temple on folio 9r, which, contrary to the order of events in the Old Testament, here follows directly after Elijah's ascension, is an unusual subject. The caption (Isa. 1:1–3) refers solely to the prophet and contains no reference to his vision, which is not described in the Book of Isaiah until Chapter 6. Isaiah tells of seeing God enthroned in the clouds above a temple (pictured here as a centrally planned church) and surrounded by seraphim (Isa. 6:1–7). In terms of imagery, Isaiah's vision finds its New Testament counterpart in the Revelation of St John, with the present illustration being based in turn on Holbein's treatment of the subject in his *Icones*. While the following picture of the two sundials (fol. 10r, Isa. 38:8) also goes back to Holbein, the calling of the prophet Jeremiah on folio 11r is inspired by the corresponding Bible illustration by Hans Sebald Beham.

Daniel's vision of the four beasts (fol. 12r) is another reference to the end times (Dan. 7:1–7, the accompanying text here cites verses 1 to 4). While the four winds blow towards the centre from the four points of the compass, four monstrous beasts emerge out of the great sea. They embody four dominions that shall be vanquished by one king, whose own rule shall then be taken away and replaced by the everlasting kingdom of God. The artist has assigned each beast to one of the continents and thereby follows the illustration in the Luther Bible (ill. 18).

On the next sheet (fol. 13r), which is again based on the *Icones*, the Archangel Gabriel interprets the prophet Daniel's second eschatological vision of a ram and a goat (Dan. 8:1–12; in the accompanying text, only Dan. 8:1–4). In copying his source, however, the artist has committed an oversight by missing out a highly significant detail in Holbein's woodcut: he has failed to show the ram's broken horn – the symbolic feature identifying the ram with the first kingdom that four others will follow.

Medieval theologians saw in the story of Jonah and the whale an Old Testament prefiguration of the death and Resurrection of Christ. But although the text on folio 14r cites the end of Jonah 1, which describes Jonah being swallowed by the whale, the event itself appears only as a subsidiary scene taking place out at sea in the background. The main scene shows an episode related in chapters 3 and 4 in which Jonah, who is angry with God, is resting under a tree outside the gates of the city of Nineveh. God has made a giant gourd grow above his head in order to shade him from the sun. In the Luther Bible these two events from the life of Jonah are combined into a simultaneous picture (ill. 4), whereas Holbein's *Icones* woodcut (once again a source here), like Beham's, focused only upon Jonah's anger.

Holbein's depiction of Ezekiel's vision (ill. 30) is also the basis of the illustration on folio 15r, which in the Book of Miracles follows on directly from the story of Jonah, even though Ezekiel actually appeared before Daniel in contemporary Bible editions. The artist has modified the scale and proportions of his source to the manuscript's format, and the Majestas Domini, the four living creatures and the spherical wheel of fire are all smaller than in the original. In his nuanced treatment of the fire, smoke and clouds, the painter of the Book of Miracles once again shows himself to be an unusually talented colourist. The accompanying text cites the first three verses of

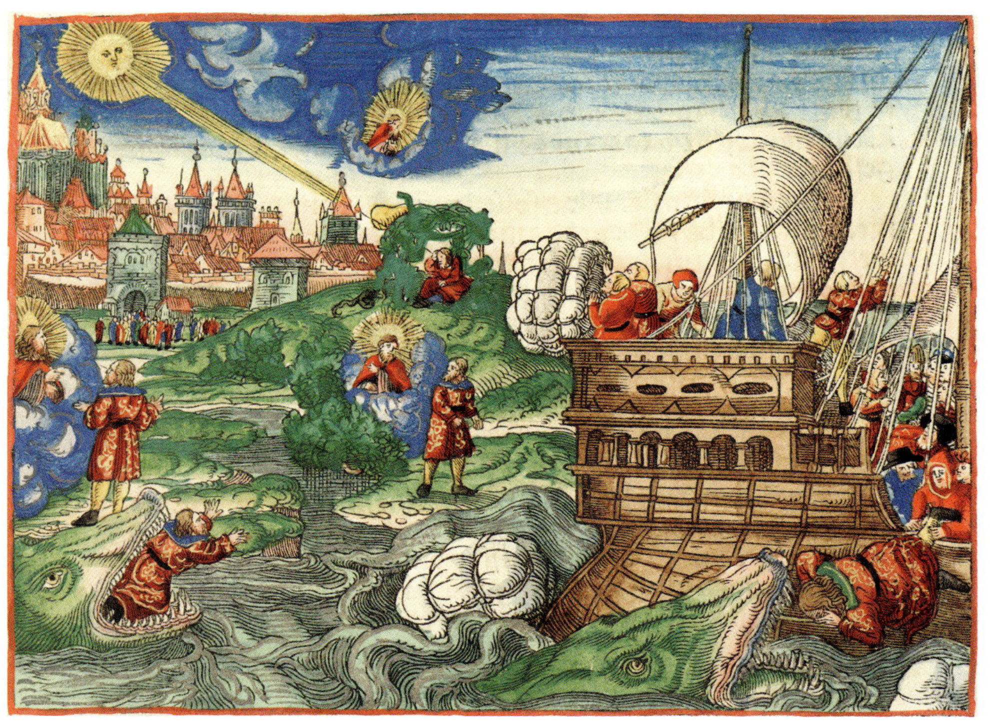

Ill. 4
Workshop of Lucas Cranach the Elder
Jonah and the whale / Jona und der Wal / Jonas et la baleine
in: *The Luther Bible*, Wittenberg 1534, fol. XXXVr. Weimar, Herzogin Anna Amalia Bibliothek

Ezekiel 1 and serves as an associative reference to the vision in question, which is described in detail in the verses that follow (Ezek. 1:4–28). Ezekiel's vision concludes the first part of the Book of Miracles, which contains a selection of divine punishments, miracles and visions from the Old Testament.

Miraculous signs from Antiquity to the present

The second part of the manuscript comprises 135 of the 167 surviving sheets and contains representations of miraculous signs spanning a period from Antiquity right up to the middle of the 16th century and the years leading up to the book's production.

These non-biblical events begin on folio 16r with a flood that occurred during the lifetime of Job. An ox was alleged to have risen up out of the floodwaters of a river that had burst its banks, ascended all the way up to Heaven and then plunged back down into the water. This miraculous vision led 'simple-minded people' to venerate the animal as a god. Even if it alludes to the animal worship mentioned in the Old Testament, the episode itself is not taken from the Bible but probably has its source in folio 29r of the *Chronicle of the World* by Hartmann Schedel, of 1493, or folio 17r of the 1531 chronicle by Sebastian Franck.

After a blank insert, the events represented on folia 18r and 19r are taken from *De bello Judaico* (*The Jewish War*) by Flavius Josephus (ill. 5). The two pictures and captions refer to signs and portents that preceded the ninth destruction of Jerusalem, which according to Josephus included a star resembling a sword that appeared in the skies over Jerusalem, a sacrificial cow that gave birth to a lamb, and a massively heavy gate in the inner temple that opened of its own accord. Folio 18r shows the cow and lamb outside the gates of the city, while a fiery sword hangs resplendent overhead. On the following sheet (fol. 19r), armies of knights in armour appear in the clouds over a city. According to Josephus, this vision was seen above all the cities of Judaea, so that the view does not necessarily show Jerusalem.

After these two events, set in the first century AD, we step back in time on the next two sheets to the year 73 BC. The illustration on folio 21r shows the miraculous sign on the left and the ensuing calamity on the right. From the caption we learn that blood is issuing out of the bread the men have broken during their meal and this miraculous flow of blood portends the hailstorm shown in the right half of the illustration, which raged for several days and destroyed the entire harvest.

Blood miracles, natural catastrophes and plagues of animals (for the latter, see fols. 87r, 109r, 141r) were understood as punishments from God even in Old Testament times and make up prominent categories of miraculous signs in the present manuscript. Comets, solar and lunar eclipses, haloes and polar lights had been considered heralds of disaster ever since Antiquity. Even in the middle of the 16th century, when the manuscript was produced, they were still thought to bring bad luck.

Celestial apparitions

The illustrations of celestial apparitions are particularly fascinating for the modern viewer, since the vividness and care with which they are depicted manifest an almost scientific interest that looks ahead to the future and that seems strangely contradictory in the context of portents and miraculous signs.

Represented with great precision on folio 26r are three suns that, following the murder of Julius Caesar, appeared in the reddish dawn sky above Rome and then merged to form a single sun. This miraculous sign was reported by Julius Obsequens in chapter 130 of his *Liber prodigiorum* (Book of Prodigies) and was also included in Schedel's *Chronicle of the World* (fol. 92v) and in Franck's chronicle (1531, fol. 127v), which appears to be the direct source of the inscription. The

Ill. 5
Master of the Munich Boccaccio
Zedechiah blinded and the Temple at Jerusalem destroyed by fire
Zedechias geblendet und der Tempelbrand in Jerusalem
Sédécias aveuglé et incendie du temple de Jérusalem
Bodycolour on parchment, 20.9 x 17.6 cm (8¼ x 7 in.)
in: Flavius Josephus, *Les Antiquités judaïques*, Paris/Tours, *c.* 1415/1420–1470
Paris, Bibliothèque nationale de France, Ms fr 247, fol. 213v

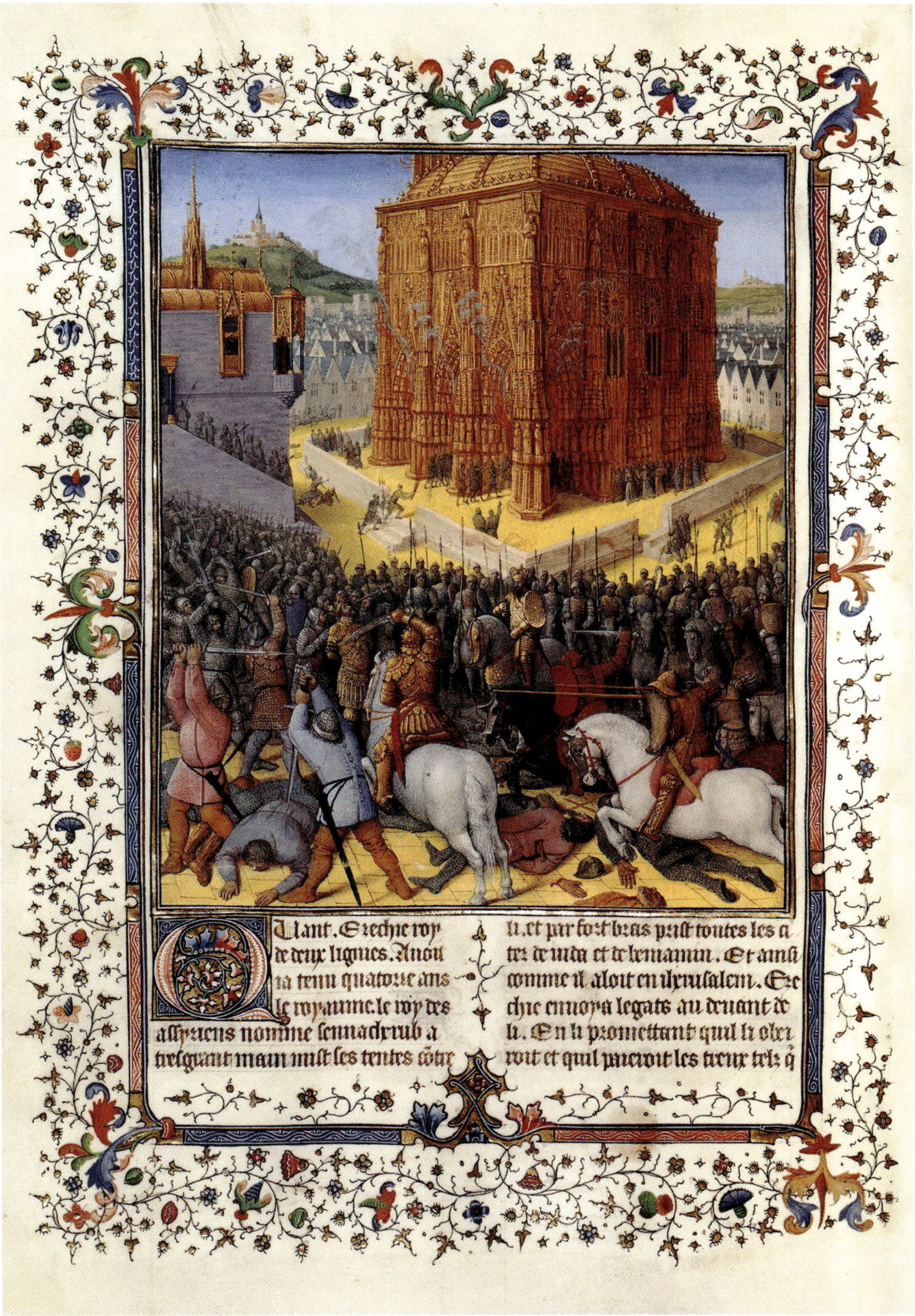
Quant. Ezechie roy
de deux lignies. Anou
ia tenu quatorze ans
le royaume. le roy des
assyriens nomme sennacherib a
tresgrant main mist les tentes cõtre
li. et par fort bras prist toutes les ci
tez de iuda et de beniamin. Et ainsi
comme il aloit en iherusalem. Eze
chie envoya legats au devant de
li. En li promettant quil li obei
roit et quil paieroit les treux tels q̃

appearance of mock suns, caused by refractions of light passing through tiny ice crystals in the air, is likewise documented on folio 45r. The two mock suns that appeared over Vienna in January 1520 (fols. 102r, 106r) belonged to a series of unusual celestial phenomena that were observed in the skies above the city over several days and nights (fols. 104r, 106r, 107r; cf. Fincel 1556, p. 68; ill. 6).

From the point of view of quality and originality, the atmospheric handling of colour that distinguishes the illustrations of these Vienna events is perhaps the most important artistic achievement within the Book of Miracles. In these pages we find a striking contrast between images of polar lights and solar aureoles set against a deep blue night sky, and illustrations in which subtle yellow and gold highlights in the clouds convey the play of light at sunrise to great effect.

Together with further phantom suns seen in combination with other celestial apparitions (fols. 112r, 113r, 139r), the rare phenomenon of mock moons is also illustrated (fol. 49r). On folio 62r three moons are shown in a night sky across which a comet is blazing. These are not mock moons but a particular constellation of stars that were mistaken for moons. According to the accompanying text, in 1304 three moons appeared around midnight for several months in "*welschen landen*" (Italy).

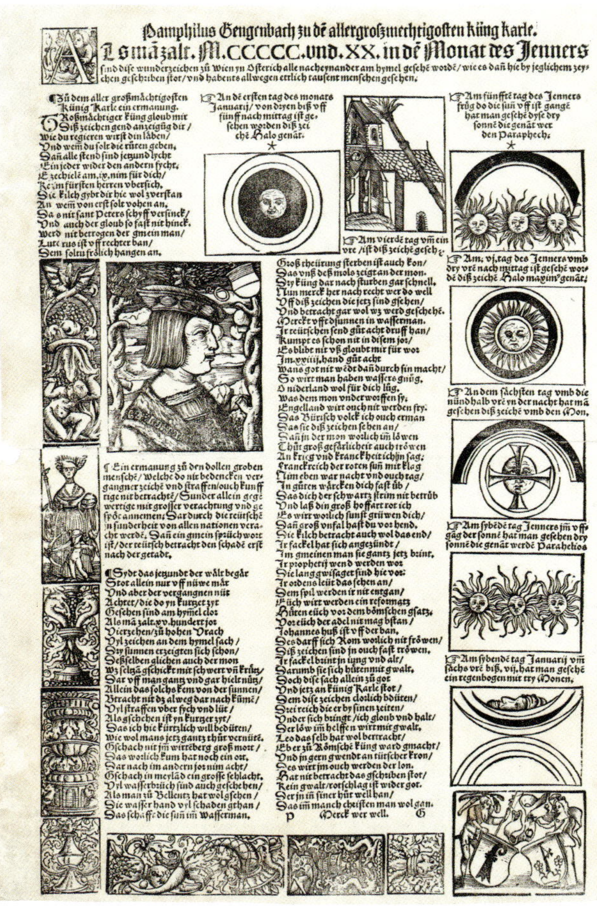
Pamphilus Gengenbach zu dē allergroszmechtigosten küng karle.
ALs mā zalt. M.CCCCC.vnd.XX. in dē Monat des Jenners
sind dise wunderzeichen zů Wien yn Osterich alle nacheynander am hymel geschē wordē / wie es dañ hie by jeglichem zeychen geschriben stot / vnd habents allwegen etlich tausent menschen gesehen.

Zů dem aller großmächtigosten küng Karle ein ermanung.
GRoßmächtiger küng gloub mir
Diß zeichen gend anzeigūg dir /
Wie du regieren wirst din läben /
Vnd wem du solt die růten geben.
Dañ alle stend sind jetzund lycht
Ein jeder wider den andern fycht.
Ezechielē am .iv. nim für dich /
Keim fürsten herren vbersich.
Die kilch gybt dir hie wol zverstan
An wem von erst solt vohen an.
Das nit sant Peters schyff versinck /
Vnd auch der gloub so fast nit hinck.
Werd nit betrogen der gmein man /
Luter rus ist vff rechter ban /
Dem soltu frölich hangen an.

An dē ersten tag des monats Januarij / von dryen biß vff fünff nach mittag ist gesehen worden diß zeichē Halo genāt.

Am vierdē tag vm̄ ein vre / ist diß zeichē gesehē.

Am fünfftē tag des Jenners frůg do die suñ vff ist gangē hat man geschē dyse dry sonnē die genāt wer den Paraphech.

Am vj. tag des Jenners vmb dry vrē nach mittag ist geschē wordē diß zeichē Halo mayim genāt.

An dem sächsten tag vmb die nündhalb vrē yn der nacht hat mā gesehen diß zeichē vmb den Mon.

Am sybēdē tag Jenners jm vffgāg der sonnē hat man gesehen dry sonnē die genāt werdē Parahelios

Am sybendē tag Januarij vm̄ sächs vrē biß. vij. hat man geschē ein regenbogen mit try Monen.

Groß theürung sterben ist auch kon /
Das vnß deß mols zeigt an der mon.
Dry küng dar nach sturben gar schnell.
Nun merck her nach recht wer do well
Vff diß zeichen die jetz sind gsehen /
Vnd betracht gar wol wz werd geschehē.
Merckt vfft dsunnen in wasserman.
Ir teütschen send gůt acht druff han /
Kumpt es schon nit in disem jor /
Es blibt nit vß gloubt mir für wor
Im .xxiiij. hand gůt acht
Wans got nit wēdt dañ durch sin macht /
So wirt man haben wassers gnůg.
O niderland wol für dich lůg.
Was dem mon vnder worffen sy.
Engelland wirt ouch nit werden fry.
Das Bürisch volck ich ouch erman
Das sie diß zeichen sehen an /
Dañ jn der mon worlich im̄ löwen
Thůt groß gefärlicheit auch tröwen
An krieg vnd kranckheit ich jm sag.
Franckreich der roten suñ mit klag
Nim eben war nacht vnd ouch tag /
In gůten wärcken dich fast üb /
Das dich der schwartz strim nit betrůb
Vnd laß din groß hoffart rot ich
Es wirt worlich sunst grüwen dich /
Dañ groß vnfal hast du vor hend.
Die kilch betracht auch wol das end /
Ir fackel hat sich angezündt /
Im gmeinen man sie gantz jetz brint.
Ir prophetij wend werden wor
Die lang gwisaget sind hie vor.
Ir ordens leüt das sehen an /
Dem spil werden ir nit entgan /
Küch wirt werden ein reformatz
Hüten eüch vor dem bömschen gsatz.
Vor eüch der adel nit mag bstan /
Johannes huß ist vff der ban.
Des darff sich Rom worlich nit fröwen /
Diß zeichen sind jn ouch fast tröwen.
Ir fackel brint jn jung vnd alt /
Darumb sie sich hůten mit gwalt.
Doch dise sach allein zů got
Vnd jetz an künig Karle stot /
Dem dise zeichen clorlich bdüten /
Drei reich die er by sinen zeiten /
Vnder sich bringt / ich gloub vnd halt /
Der löw im̄ helffen wirt mit gwalt.
Leo das selb hat wol bertracht /
Eb er zů Römschē küng ward gmacht /
Vnd jn gern gwendt an tütscher kron /
Des wirt jm ouch werden der lon.
Hat nit betracht das gschriben stot /
Kein gwalt / rotschlag ist wider got.
Der jn im̄ siner hůt well han /
Das im̄ manch christen man wol gan.
P Merck wer well. G

Ein ermanung zů den dollen groben menschē / Welche do nit bedencken vergangner zeichē vnd straffen / ouch kunfftige nit betrachtē / Sunder allein gegēwertige mit grosser verachtung vnd gespöt annemen. Dar durch die teütschē yn sunderheit von allen nationen veracht werdē. Dañ ein gmein sprůch wort ist / der teütsch betracht den schadē erst nach der getadt.

Sydt das jetzundt der wält begär
Stot allein nur vff nüwe mär
Vnd aber der vergangnen nüt
Achtet / die do yn kurtzer zyt
Gesehen sind am hymel clor
Als mā zalt .xv. hundert jor
Viertzehen / zů hohen Vrach
Vyl zeichen an dem hymel sach /
Dry sunnen erzeigten sich schon /
Deßselben glichen auch der mon
Wz seltzā gschickt mit schwert vñ krütz /
Dar vff man gantz vnd gar hielt nütz /
Allein das solchs kem von der sunnen /
Btracht nit dz alweg dar nach kūmē /
Vyl straffen vber fych vnd lüt /
Als gschehen ist yn kurtzer zyt /
Das ich hie kürtzlich will bedüten /
Wie wol mans jetz gantz thůt vernütē.
Gschach nit jm wirtēberg groß mort /
Das worlich kum hat noch ein ort.
Dar nach im andern jor nim acht /
Gschach in meylād ein grosse schlacht.
Vyl wasserbrüch sind auch geschehen /
Als man zů Bellentz hat wol gsehen /
Die wasser hand vyl schaden gthan /
Das schafft die suñ im̄ Wasserman.

Ill. 6
Pamphilus Gengenbach
Illustrated broadsheet on celestial phenomena over Vienna, January 1520
Flugblatt über ein Himmelsphänomen über Wien, Januar 1520
Feuillet illustré mentionnant un phénomène céleste au-dessus de Vienne, janvier 1520
Zurich, Zentralbibliothek, Graphische Sammlung, inv. PAS II, 9/14

The Book of Miracles carries many reports of unnatural colours seen in the skies being followed by catastrophe. A blood red moon, for example, announced a devastating earthquake in Italy (fol. 39r). In an illustration in which the artist has evoked an unnaturally sombre mood with minimal means, the black silhouette of the ruined town stands out clearly against the dark night sky. In the case of the red mood seen on folio 147r, it is only upon reading the caption that we discover it represents a lunar eclipse: "there was a darkening of the moon at night, so that the moon looked all bloody" ("*bei nacht ist ain finsternus des mons gewessen das der mon gantz blutig sach*").

The widespread belief that eclipses were portents of disaster is reflected in the manuscript's inclusion of several solar eclipses (fols. 64r, 69r, 70r, 87r, 149r). The event illustrated on folio 149r was witnessed in January 1544 in Augsburg, where the Book of Miracles was produced only shortly afterwards. The schematic nature of the illustration suggests, however, that the painter did not observe the eclipse at first hand.

The manuscript also includes figural apparitions that were sighted in the heavens (ill. 31) during the 16th century (fols. 124r, 126r, 134r, 144r, 150r, 157r). Broadsheets carried reports of such cloud pictures, which were interpreted at the time as signs of imminent war. As in the case of folio 157r, which depicts a celestial apparition seen in 1547 in Glarus, Switzerland, the illustrations usually derive from the popular prints through which such phenomena were publicised (ill. 19).

Comets

The pages of the Book of Miracles contain a great many comets. Together with an illustrated treatise on comets produced around 1587 in Flanders (Massing 1977; ill. 20), the manuscript contains probably the largest early collection of comet pictures. In Antiquity these celestial apparitions were considered portents of serious misfortune lasting several years. Although this attitude changed in the Middle Ages, when comets were viewed in a positive light as messengers from God, Reformation-minded Humanists subsequently returned to the gloomy interpretation of comets as bringers of bad luck. Comets are illustrated on no fewer than 26 sheets (fols. 32r, 34r, 35r, 37r, 46r, 50r, 58r, 61r, 62r, 64r, 65r, 67r, 74r, 79r, 83r, 92r, 100r, 101r, 110r, 120r, 121r, 122r, 125r, 128r, 142r, 146r). Despite the differentiated nature of these illustrations, we may search in vain for any attempt at scientific classification.

The manuscript originally contained further comet pictures, as revealed by one of the sheets later detached from the manuscript, which shows a blazing ball of light and an unsheathed sword, accompanied by small tongues of flame and swords (for the present edition the plate has been inserted in its original position as folio 111r; cf. Falk 2005).

In his endeavour to visualise the comets in a variety of different ways, the artist has drawn not only upon earlier, somewhat schematic woodcuts, some of which appeared in Lycosthenes's Book of Prodigies (ill. 32), but above all upon written accounts. The meteorite that fell to Earth in 1007 (fol. 34r) is surrounded by flames, while that in the year 1173 takes the form of a fiery shaft of light (fol. 46r). The comet seen over Rome in 684 (in Roman numerals, but incorrectly given in Arabic numerals as 1184; fol. 50r) is described as being the harbinger of a huge and devastating storm, just as the comet of 1300 (fol. 61r) portends an earthquake in the Eternal City.

Natural catastrophes

In a number of illustrations, comets appear in conjunction with devastating natural disasters and these make up another category of prodigious events represented in the Book of Miracles. Direct sources for them cannot, however, always be clearly identified. The events on folio 30r are probably taken from the chronicle by Franck and relate to an earthquake that destroyed the Temple in Jerusalem in AD 367. Such an event is described by the Syrian theologian Theodoret of Cyrus (393–468) in Book 3 of his *Historia ecclesiastica*, a volume devoted to the history of the early Christian Church under the Roman Emperor Julian. According to Theodoret, the pagan Julian ordered the Christian basilica built by Constantine the Great to be demolished and a heathen temple to be erected in its place. Even before the new building was complete, God sent an earthquake to destroy it. Underlying this literary account is a historical event that took place in AD 365, namely an earthquake in the Mediterranean that caused the destruction of Alexandria and a devastating tidal wave in Asia Minor.

Whatever the case, the illustration on folio 30r is one of the most impressive in the entire manuscript. A city burns in a fiery red glow at the left-hand edge of the picture as floodwaters beat in steep waves against a narrow strip of land before its gates. Extending to the right is a flooded plain, where further towns are disappearing beneath the water and people and animals are trying to swim back to the shore. The trees are dramatically bowed under the force of the storm and the painter has used irregular hatching to convey the impression of driving rain and hail. On the left, fire rains down on the city, some of whose towers have collapsed or begun to fall under the force of the earthquake. A huge column of fire and smoke rises above the rooftops and lends the mountains in the background a reddish hue.

Bent and broken towers recur throughout the manuscript as a potent symbol of the destructive power of earth tremors. They can be seen in the illustrations of the two earthquakes of 1119 (fol. 39r) and 1228 (fol. 52r), each represented by a ruined city in a landscape bathed in pale moonlight, the whole presenting a distinctly apocalyptic air. Somewhat untypical is the illustration of an earthquake that occurred in 1357 in Spain (fol. 68r): the foreground is dominated by a towering rock, beyond which we glimpse the ruins of the town and the devastation suffered by the landscape to the left and right.

The sole representation of a volcanic eruption is conceived in a similar fashion: Mount Vesuvius spews glowing magma into the sky in the foreground while Naples burns behind it (fol. 85r). The caption dates the event to 1482, while the text speaks of the destruction of towns and villages by streams of lava and also names Pliny – who indeed lost his life during the eruption of Vesuvius in 79 B. C. – among the victims. The scribe has evidently misinterpreted his source at this point: he has based his information on Franck's chronicle (fol. 270r), according to which Vesuvius erupted in 82 B. C.

Floods are another type of natural disaster appearing regularly in the volume and are often illustrated jointly with other weather events and catastrophes (fols. 28r, 30r, 47r, 55r, 73r, 75r, 86r, 116r, 118r, 119r). Floods had devastating long-term consequences since they destroyed crops and livestock across wide swathes of the countryside and posed a serious threat to human life. Being associated with the biblical Deluge, they were also considered examples of divine retribution *par excellence*.

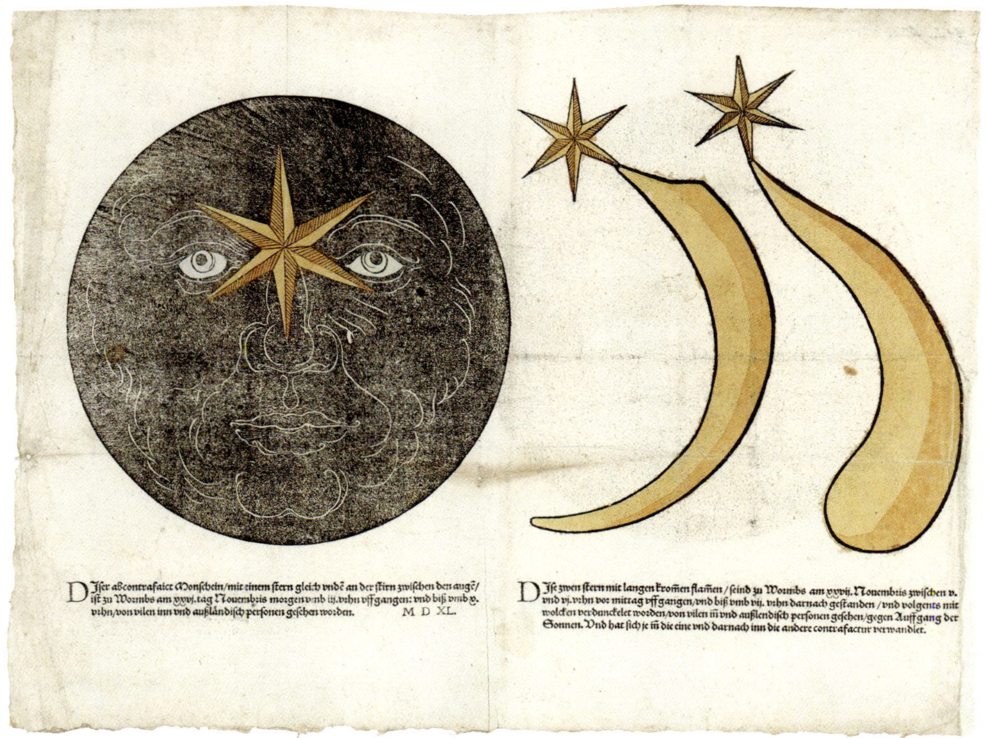

Ill. 7
Illustrated broadsheet reporting the appearance of a double comet over Worms, 26/27 November 1540
Flugblatt über das Erscheinen eines Doppelkometen über Worms, 26./27. November 1540
Feuillet illustré mentionnant l'apparition d'une double comète au-dessus de Worms, 26/27 novembre 1540
Nuremberg, Germanisches Nationalmuseum, Graphische Sammlung, inv. HB 2783

In order to convey an impression of the vast scale of these floods, the illustrations show a panoramic landscape in bird's-eye view. Mountains, forests and towns are dotted like islands amongst the floodwaters, which extend all the way to the horizon. People and animals can be seen desperately attempting to swim to safety. The perspective occasionally changes: while the inundation of A. D. 570 (in Roman numerals, but incorrectly given in Arabic numerals as 170; fol. 28r) is seen from a relatively high viewpoint, the flood that struck the city of Antioch (fol. 47r) is presented from a viewpoint only just above the horizon line.

In folio 86r the swollen rivers of the Tiber and Po in Italy and the Rhine and Danube in central Europe are condensed into a single picture, succinctly illustrating the widespread flooding that occurred, according to the caption, in November 1480 (the year 1482 written in red ink is a mistake on the part of the scribe). Two trees that have lost most of their leaves rise up from a narrow strip of land surrounded by water in the foreground, while floods cover virtually the whole of the

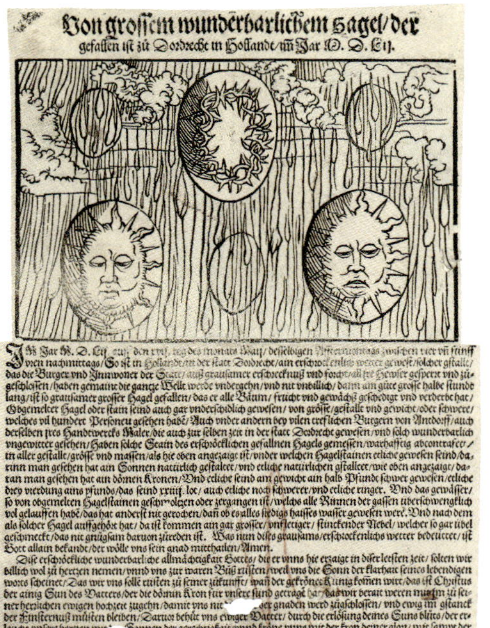

Von grossem wunderbarlichem Hagel/ der gefallen ist zů Dordrecht in Hollandt/ im Jar M. D. Lij.

IN Jar M. D. Lij. auff den xviij. tag des monats May/ desselbigen Affternmittags zwischen vier vñ fünff vren nachmittags/ So ist in Hollandt/ in der statt Dordrecht/ ain erschrockenlich wetter gewest/ solcher gstallt/ das die Burger vnd Innwoner der Statt/ auß grausamer erschreckhnuß vnd forcht/ all jre Hewser gespert vnd zůgeschlossen/ haben gemaint die gantze Wellt werde vndergehn/ vnd nit vnbillich/ dann ain gůte grosse halbe stunde lang/ ist so grausamer grosser Hagel gefallen/ das er alle Bäum/ frucht vnd gewächß geschedigt vnd verderbt hat/ Obgemelter Hagel oder stain seind auch gar vnderschidlich gewesen/ von grösse/ gestallt vnd gewicht/ oder schwere/ welches vil hundert Personeu gesehen habẽ/ Auch vnder andern bey vilen treflichen Burgern von Antdorff/ auch derselben jres Handtwercks Maler/ die auch zur selben zeit in der statt Dordrecht gewesen/ vnd solch wunderbarlich vngewitter gesehen/ Haben solche Stain des erschröcklichen gefallnen Hagels gemessen/ warhafftig abcontrafect/ in aller gestallt/ grösse vnd massen/ als hie oben angezaigt ist/ vnder welchen Hagelstainen etliche gewesen seind/ darinn man gesehen hat ain Sonnen natürlich gestaltet/ vnd etliche natürlichen gstallt/ wie oben angezaigt/ daran man gesehen hat ain dörnen Kronen/ Vnd etliche seind am gewicht ain halb Pfundt schwer gewesen/ etliche drey vierdung ains pfunds/ das seind xxiiij. lot/ auch etliche noch schwerer/ vnd etliche ringer. Vnd das gewässer/ so von obgemelten Hagelstainen geschmoltzen oder zergangen ist/ welchs alle Rinnen der gassen überschwengklich vol gelauffen habẽ/ das hat anderst nit gerochen/ dañ ob es alles siedigs haisses wasser gewesen werẽ. Vnd nach dem als solcher Hagel auffgehört hat/ da ist kommen ain gar grosser/ vnfletiger/ stinckender Nebel/ welcher so gar übel geschmeckt/ das nit gnůgsam daruon zůreden ist. Was nun dises grausams/ erschrockenlichs wetter bedeuttet/ ist Gott allain bekandt/ der wölle vns sein gnad mitthailen/ Amen.

Dise erschröckliche wunderbarliche allmächtigkait Gottes/ die er vnns hie erzaigt in diser letsten zeit/ solten wir billich wol zů hertzen nemen/ vnnd vns zur waren Bůß rüsten/ weil vns die Sonn der klarhait seines lebendigen worts scheinet/ Das wir vns söllẽ rüsten zů seiner zůkunfft/ wañ der gekrönet Künig komen wirt/ das ist Christus der ainig Sun des Vatters/ der die dörnin Kron für vnsere sünd getragẽ hat/ das wir berait weren mit jm zů seiner herrlichen ewigen hochzeit zugehn/ damit vns nit [illegible] der gnaden werd zůgeschlossen/ vnd ewig im gstanck der Finsternuß müsten bleiben/ Daruor behüt vns ewiger Vatter/ durch die erlösung deines Suns blůts/ der erleücht vnsere hertzen mit [illegible] Sonnen der gerechtigkait/ vnnd kröne vnns mit der kron deiner glori/ mit sampt der krafft des hailigen Gai[illegible]n.

landscape as far as the distant horizon. Tiny figures are being swept along by the current, their arms raised in a plea for help.

Folio 118r, meanwhile, shows the massive storm-tide that inundated the Flemish coast in November 1530. The painter has visualised the scene almost entirely as a waterscape, within which people are seeking refuge on two small hillocks rising above the waves or climbing trees to escape from drowning. A town lies half-submerged in water on the right, some of its towers snapped and broken. According to the accompanying text, this represents Vlissingen on the former island of Walcheren. The flood in question, which has since entered the history books as the Sint Felixvloed, struck the coast of Flanders and Zeeland in the first week of November 1530 and ultimately claimed almost 100,000 lives as a result of drowning, starvation and epidemics.

Flash floods, storm tides and earthquakes are regularly accompanied by lashing rain, snow and hail (ill. 8). But it was not uncommon for extreme meteorological phenomena such as hail, snow and ice to devastate crops and lead to famine and epidemics in their own right. The manuscript contains several hailstorms (fols. 21r, 27r, 47r, 78r, 115r, 171r) and snowstorms (fols. 44r, 51r, 54r). These innovative illustrations of the weather number among the earliest of their kind in German art.

Two sheets document particularly severe winters and their consequences. On folio 42r the artist conveys a drastic impression of the harsh winter of 1126, when temperatures plunged so low that crows were seen to freeze in mid-flight and fall to the earth. Although the caption on folio 56r likewise speaks of a famine caused by frost and cold in the winter of 1234, the artist has here illustrated the freezing of the waterways, along which only an ox and cart are making their way. On folio 44r the heavy snow that fell on Milan in 1162 is depicted. The capital of Lombardy is silhouetted in the distance on the far side of a plain blanketed in snow, as thick flurries continue to fall.

Ill. 8

Illustrated broadsheet reporting hail in Dordrecht, 1552
Flugblatt über Hagel in Dordrecht | *Feuillet illustré mentionnant une grêle à Dordrecht*
Zurich, Zentralbibliothek, Graphische Sammlung, inv. PAS II 1/32a

1552 – *Hail in Dordrecht* | *Hagel in Dordrecht* | *Grêle à Dordrecht*
in: *Book of Miracles*, Augsburg, *c.* 1550–1552, fol. 171r (detail). Private collection

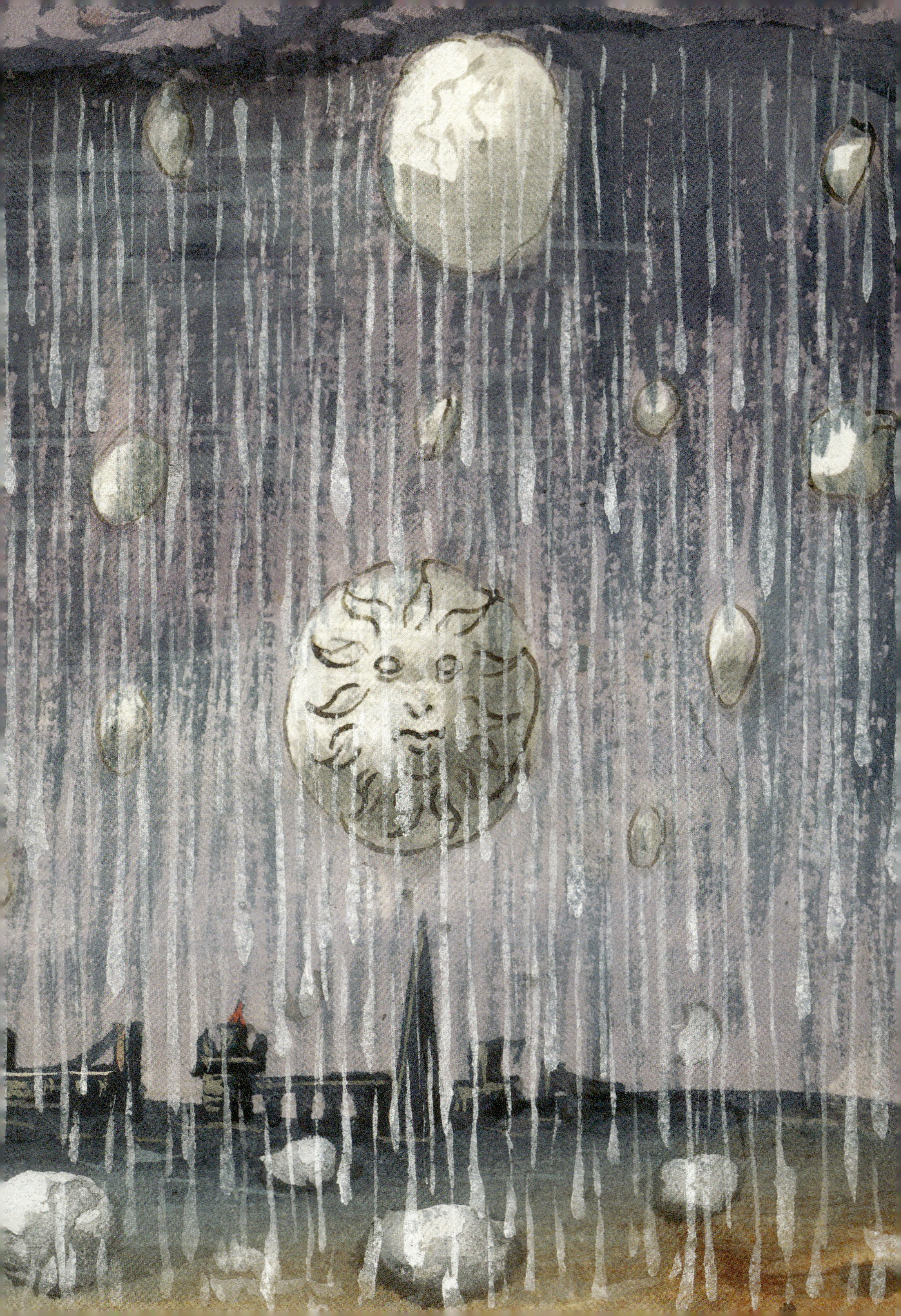

Blood and food miracles

Several pages of the manuscript are devoted to blood miracles, which in the Protestant sphere, in particular, were interpreted on the basis of prophecies in Revelation to signify the imminent ending of the world (fols. 21r, 28r, 36r, 38r, 51r, 54r, 71r, 81r, 119r, 167r). Waters that suddenly turn into blood (fol. 36r) or the discovery of a spring of blood (fol. 167r) are both depicted here. The majority, however, concern blood rain, a natural phenomenon greeted with terror ever since Antiquity and which is still seen today – it occurs when fine, reddish-yellow particles of desert sand, whipped up by storms and suspended in the air, fall back to earth as part of a rain shower. A rare variant of blood rain is the blood snow witnessed in Styria in 1226 (fol. 51r) and again in 1229 (fol. 54r) and which is here illustrated in the form of atmospheric wintry landscapes.

Related to blood rain are showers of bread and manna, such as the episode described in the Old Testament (fol. 6r). An interesting example is the representation of the shower of grain that fell on Klagenfurt on March 23, 1550 (fol. 166r). The illustration is based on an illustrated broadsheet produced in Nuremberg in 1550 and subsequently copied in Strasburg (ill. 22) and elsewhere.

Prodigies and freaks of nature

The Book of Miracles devotes a number of pages to prodigies and freaks of nature, ranging from animals born with two heads to a woman who apparently lived on air (fols. 88r, 90r, 97r, 117r, 133r, 145r, 158r). One of the pages in the original manuscript featured a rare human example, in this case conjoined twins; the sheet was later detached but probably appeared after folio 92r. The illustrations in this category differ from the others in the book both in their figural scale and in their renunciation of colour in the background. Moreover, almost all the prodigies and freaks of nature reproduced in the manuscript go back to existing prints, their motifs sourced from illustrated broadsheets as well as engravings by Dürer and Wenzel von Olmütz. In several cases two monstrous births are combined into one picture and their captions supplied in separate columns underneath. The text accompanying the representation of a still-born calf on folio 117r names the painter as Hans Burgkmair, and the same name also appears on a sheet, today preserved in Stuttgart, showing conjoined twins born in 1513 on the estate of Countess Lodron, the sister of Cardinal Matthias Lang (1468–1540), in Carinthia (in the present edition this plate has been inserted into its original position as folio 93r).

Folio 158r brings together three motifs that all go back to designs by Heinrich Vogtherr the Elder (1490–1556) and which were in circulation as broadsheets. A bunch of grapes infested with parasites on the left is accompanied by an unusual ear of wheat and, on the right, by the miracle of the young woman from Roth, who allegedly refused all food for a number of years and lived from donations – a popular form of benefit fraud in the Middle Ages (ills. 25, 26).

Ill. 9

Representation of several miraculous signs of the twelfth century, including blood rain, earthquake and fiery arrows / Darstellungen von Wunderzeichen des 12. Jhs., Blutregen, Erdbeben und Feuerblitze / Présentation de signes miraculeux du XIIe siècle, pluie de sang, tremblement de terre et éclairs flamboyants
in: Hartmann Schedel, *Das buch der Cronicken und gedechtnus wirdigern geschichten von anbegynn der werlt bis auf dise vnßere zeit*, Nuremberg 1493, fol. 198r. Weimar, Herzogin Anna Amalia Bibliothek

Sant Bernhart

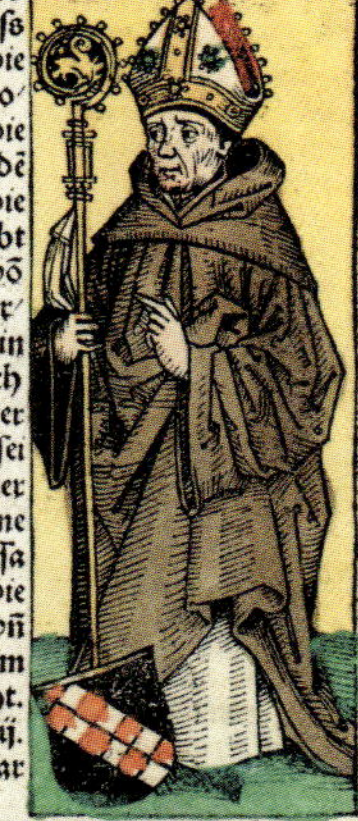

BErnhardus abbt zu claraualle ein Burgundier was auß Castellione dem edeln gschloß oder statt von edeln eltern pürtig. sein vater was ein gestrenger vnnd andechtiger ritter der statt defontanis bey diuione. So was sein müter vom gschloß montißbarri genant. Die hat en disen Bernhardum sunst fünff sün vnd ein tochter. die nachfolgend in ein closter kome gehabt. vnd dieselben ire kind mit gemayner vnd grober speyß (das sie got in den clöstern dest freyer dienen möchten) erzogen. Dieweil die müter disen iren sun im leib trüge. do sahe sie ein weiß hüntlein ein wenig rötlet auff dē rucken vnd pellende. zu künftiger anzaigung seins geschrayes vñ pellens dz er wid die nachred vñ entzieher d kirchē thun wurdt. Er kome in dē. xxij. iar seins alters mitsambt xxx. gesellen in das cistercienſisch closter. darum name er also zu das er in kürtzer weil võ seiner großen heilligkeit. schrifftlicher weißheit vnd lere wegen zu abbt in claraualle erkorn wardt. Dasselb closter hat er in großem rům vnd ere. xxxvi. iar verwesen. vnd in seinem leben hundert vnd sechtzig clöster seins ordens außgepawt. vnd die cristenlichen kirchen mit heiligkeit seins lebens. süeßigkeit seiner lere. vnd mit glori vnd rům der wunderzaichen erleüchtet. vnd neben seinem heilligen vnd löblichen lebē sunst auß seiner synnreichen geschicklichkeit vil heilliger inniger. andechtiger. süeßer. hönigfließēder schrift. bücher vnd lere gemacht vnnd hinder ime gelassen. Als bey den orientischen die statt Edissa den cristen entwendet worden was. do hat er die fürsten. prelaten. edeln vnd das volck in gallia vñ auch Cunraten den römischen könig zu gemaynem zug wider die vnglawbigen auffwegig gemacht. Nach vil geübten wunderzaichen starb er im. lxiij. iar seins alters selligclich. das was dz M. c. liij. iar des herrñ cristi.

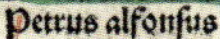

Petrus alfonsus

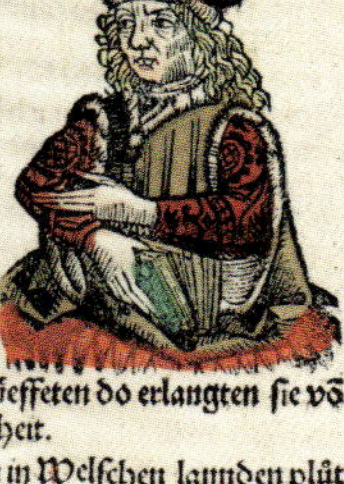

PEtrus alfonsus ein iud dauor moyses genāt verließ den irrsal der iudischeit vñ empfieng das sacrament des tawfs andechtigclich. vnd machet ein büch wider die iuden vnd hayden treffenlich disputirende. vnd wardt an sant Peters vnd Pauls tag getawft. vnd von alfonso dē könig hyspanie auß dem tawf gehebt. vnd des zu gedechtnus vnd sant Peter zu eren Petrus vnd mit dē zunamen alfonsus genant.

DIser zeit. als in dem. M. c. xxviij. iar warden ettliche menschen mit nidergang mit dem heiligē feür also angezündet dz inē ire glider wie die koln erschwartztē. Als sie aber in vnßer liebē frawen kirchen in derselben gegent lieffen vnd got anrüeffeten do erlangten sie võ got durch fürbette marie der iunckfrawen gesuntheit.

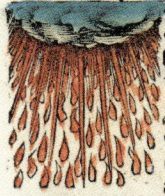

IN disem iar in dem monat Junij hat es an ettlichen enden in Welschen lannden plůt geregnet.

AIn saw gepare in der Liginensischen pfarr ein schweinlein das het menschēs antlitz. So wardt desselben iars ein vierfüßiges hünlein außgebrüret.

FEürige stralen oder spitzen erschynen am himel. die taylten sich durch den gantzē himel. So fieln stern auff die erden. so man wasser darauff goße so gaben sie einen hale.

ES was ein harter winter. dē volget er große tewrung nach. also das vil lewt vnd vih starben vnd die fögel sichselbs erwürgten.

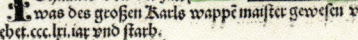

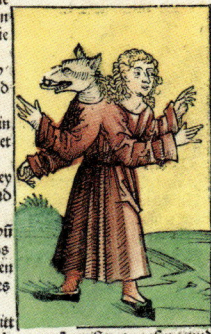

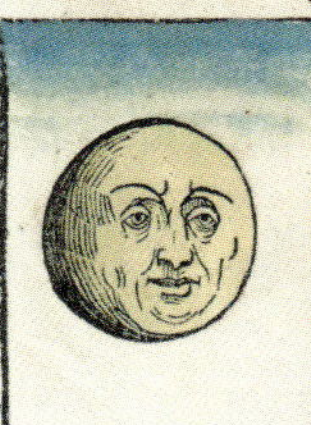

Johannes von d zeit

IN welschē landē wz ein erdbidē. xl. tag. der keret die dörffer vmb.

DEr mond wardt bey nacht verfinstert vnd plůtfar.

EIn weib gepare ein wunder gestalt zwifachs leibs. vornen eins menschen vnnd hindten eins hundes angesiht habende.

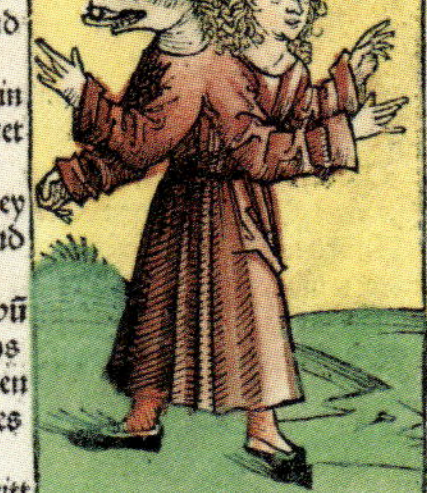

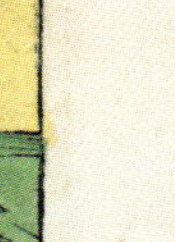

JOhannes von der zeitt was des großen Karls wappē maister gewesen vnnd lebet. ccc. lxi. iar vnd starb.

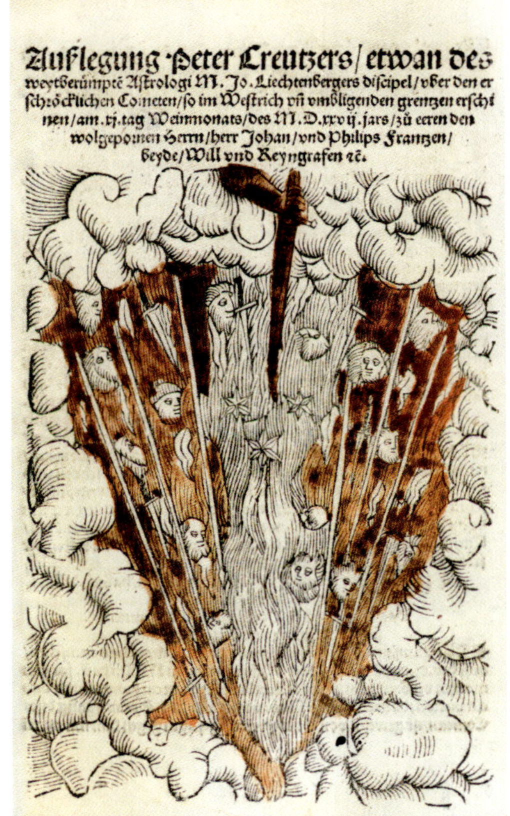
Außlegung Peter Creutzers/ etwan des
weytberümptē Astrologi M. Jo. Liechtenbergers discipel/ vber den er
schröcklichen Cometen/ so im Westrich vñ vmbligenden grentzen erschi
nen/ am. xj. tag Weinmonats/ des M. D. xxvij. jars/ zů eeren den
wolgepornen Herrn/ herr Johan/ vnd Philips Frantzen/
beyde/ Will vnd Reyngrafen ꝛc.

The Revelation of St John

The final section of the manuscript is devoted to signs from the Book of Revelation announcing the end of the world and the Second Coming of Christ. The particular interest felt by theologians, above all Reformation theologians, in the study of miraculous signs was linked with their conviction that these portended the end of the world. Seen from this perspective, the illustrations of the Apocalypse, which once again feature earthquakes, floods, fire raining down from the skies and other disasters, represent the inevitable consequence of the prodigious events documented in the preceding pages.

The eschatological vision received by John of Patmos is set out in the manuscript across a total of 19 surviving sheets. The illustrations lean heavily upon Beham's woodcut cycle *Typi in apocalypsi Ioannis depicti*, which was published in Frankfurt in 1539 and which in turn paraphrases Dürer's *Apocalypse* series from 1497/98 (ill. 14). As in the case of the Old Testament scenes at the beginning, adapting the source to suit the proportions of the manuscript and interpreting the resulting composition in colour constitute the chief areas of artistic originality, in which the painters once again demonstrate an extraordinary sensitivity. The pages follow the same sequence as Beham's *Apocalypse* cycle but leave out certain passages. The manuscript then seems to break off its coverage of Revelation surprisingly abruptly with the Heavenly Harvest.

Some of the illustrations from this final section of the manuscript are in fact missing. At least four other scenes from the Revelation of St John have been detached from the end of the book; in 2005 they were auctioned at Karl & Faber in Munich but their current whereabouts is unknown (folia 191r, 192r). The scenes show four events at the end of Revelation, including the Vision of the Twelve Gates that concludes the *Apocalypse* cycle by Beham.

Ill. 10
Title page of / Titelblatt von / Page de titre de
Peter Creutzer, *Außlegung […] uber den erschröcklichen Cometen so im Westrich und umbligenden grentzen erschinen*, Nuremberg 1528. Munich, Bayerische Staatsbibliothek

Dating, place of production and attribution

The manuscript was produced around the middle of the 16th century and can be localised to southern Germany on the basis of the vernaculars it employs. The hailstorm that visited the Netherlandish town of Dordrecht in 1552 (ill. 8), illustrated on folio 171r, is the most recent natural catastrophe to be included in the Book of Miracles and occurs immediately before the final section devoted to the Revelation of St John. 1552 can therefore be considered the *terminus post quem* for the composition of the codex, although it should also be noted that the work seems to have been produced in phases. The texts accompanying the biblical illustrations are based on the Luther Bible of 1545, which supports the argument that work only began after this date.

Analysis of the watermarks has confirmed that the sheets date from the period around 1550 and has also yielded clues as to their place of production. Two watermarks occur several times and both of them in two variants. 20 pages carry the watermark of a heraldic shield set within a quatrefoil and depicting a cross rising above a triple hilltop. This watermark, which is similar to nos. 154059 and 154082 in the Piccard watermark collection, measures almost four centimetres in height and thereby corresponds to Augsburg charters from the period between 1539 and 1559 (Bower 2009, pp. 26–27).

53 pages carry a watermark barely two centimetres high and showing a spider in a shield (similar to Piccard 42787, 42788, 42791 and 42792). This watermark is common in charters and records drawn up in the middle of the 16th century in a number of Swabian towns, including Lauingen, Dillingen, Ulm and Augsburg (Falk 2005; Bower 2009, p. 27). Two further sheets have fragments of a watermark (a six-pointed star over an anchor, similar to Piccard 119009) that surfaces in 16th-century Austrian and Upper Italian papers, but which is also found in a document issued in Augsburg in 1550 (cf. Bower 2009). Just as the watermarks lend weight to a dating of around 1550, the other documents in which they are found suggest that the manuscript was produced in Swabia.

A striking number of the historical events described took place in Augsburg and its vicinity (fols. 73r, 74r, 78r, 113r, 115r, 117r, 138r, 144r, 145r, 149r, 154r, 159r, 164r). This is particularly true in the case of the events closest in time to the date when the manuscript would appear to have been written (fol. 113r and following). For this reason, too, we may suspect that the manuscript was produced in Augsburg, which in the 16th century was a leading centre of the arts and sciences in South Germany.

This hypothesis is supported by various other factors. The caption describing the appearance of mock suns in 1541 on folio 139r, for example, states that "three suns in a triangle with a rainbow around them were seen here in Augsburg" ("*man [hatt] hie zu augspurg drey sonnen in driangel gesehen*"), establishing a direct link between the text and the event itself. The word "here" ("*hie* or *hier*") as a geographical specifier is used on three further occasions, and explicit references to Augsburg also appear in the captions to events in 1542 (fol. 144r) and 1547 (fol. 159r). Again, on folio 156r and folio 164r, the text states that the celestial apparitions in question were seen "here in the sky" ("*hie am hiemel*"), although it is not apparent from the text where these events took place. Viewed in the context of the manuscript, however, it is clear that "here" means Augsburg.

Another link between Augsburg and the book emerges from the description of two monstrous births recorded in the 16th century and connected with the Swabian towns of Langweid, Donauwörth (fol. 117r) and Dillingen (fol. 145r). If the manuscript was indeed produced in the Swabian capital, that might well explain why, on these two pages, the captions specifically mention artists who were active in Augsburg or who were profoundly shaped by its influence. According to the caption on folio 145r, the illustration of a chick born with deformities in 1543, seen here alongside a monk-fish, is based on a design by the court painter to the Dillingen-based Bishop of Augsburg (ill. 11). The bishop in question was perhaps Christoph von Stadion (1478–1543), who relocated the episcopal residence to Dillingen; it is more likely, however, to have been Otto Truchsess von Waldburg (1514–1573), who became Bishop of Augsburg in 1543 and was an active patron of Counter-Reformation art during his 30-year tenure. It remains, however, to be disovered who held the position of court painter to the bishop in 1543, and indeed whether such a formal post existed at that time.

Folio 117r provides an example of two separate incidents of monstrous births, in this case two calves, illustrated on a single page. The calf on the left was still-born on January 14, 1529 in Langweid, near Augsburg; the other was born alive in 1532 near Donauwörth. On this page we also find the name of an Augsburg artist: in the caption beneath the calf on the left it says: "and I, Hans Burgkmair, painter, bought the skin for half a guilder from a parchment-maker, who had bought it for only six kreuzer". This remarkable statement – the only passage in the entire manuscript to use the first person singular (besides the text on fol. 118r, which takes the first person from a published source) – links the Book of Miracles with the name of Hans Burgkmair.

We have already encountered this name in conjunction with the woodcut that provided the basis for the illustration, on a page subsequently detached from the book, of the front and rear views of conjoined twins born in 1513 (Falk 2005; fol. 93r). The artist in question can be named as Hans Burgkmair the Elder, the celebrated Augsburg painter and printmaker who was entrusted with, among other things, designs for Emperor Maximilian's triumphal procession and who, together with Hans Holbein the Elder (*c.* 1465–1524), executed the Basilica cycle of paintings for the Dominican convent in Augsburg (Krause 2002, pp. 290f.). Hans Burgkmair the Elder can be ruled out as the creator of the volume, however, on the basis that he died some twenty years before it was produced.

The "Hans Burgkmair, painter" named on folio 117r was therefore probably his son, Hans Burgkmair the Younger, who was officially admitted to the Augsburg guild of painters on October 15, 1531 and who took over his father's workshop upon the latter's death. He had learned his trade from his father and after completing his apprenticeship stayed on as a member of the paternal workshop. Hans Burgkmair the Younger's few documented commissions include 12 paintings of heraldic shields for the funeral of Emperor Maximilian and decorations for the funeral of Emperor Charles V in 1559. Apart, however, from a few drawings and prints with the monogram HB, his other activities as an artist are unknown. Documents show that his financial circumstances were at times precarious (cf. Selig 1997, pp. 217–218; Seidl 2012, pp. 22–28). Despite the difficult period between the wave of Protestant iconoclasm in 1537 and the Peace of Augsburg concluded in 1555, however, his workshop must nevertheless have flourished, since he took on apprentices in 1536, 1548, 1549 and 1559.

Certain of the woodcuts, etchings and drawings attributed to Hans Burgkmair the Younger are based directly on works by his father, but those which are not fall short of the latter's artistic and technical skill. In a number of tournament books illustrated by his hand, for example, the younger Burgkmair has sourced his designs from his father's preliminary drawings for the triumphal procession of Emperor Maximilian (Vienna 2012). The oldest of these tournament books (Munich, Staatliche Graphische Sammlung) was produced for William IV, Duke of Bavaria (1493–1550), and is considered to be a joint work by father and son. Closely related to this first tournament book is a second one (Bayerische Staatsbibliothek, Cod. Icon 403) that was probably completed around 1540 and can thus be ascribed wholly to the younger Burgkmair (ill. 12). Hans Burgkmair the Younger's signature also shows him to be the author of the final section of a three-part tournament book (Sigmaringen, Hofbibliothek, HS 63) produced around the middle of the 16th century (Reuter 2010; Seidl 2012). This final section, dated 1553 and again partially dependent on designs for Maximilian's triumphal procession, is illustrated with pen and bodycolour drawings that display an impressive feel for colour and testify to a thorough mastery of gouache similar to that found in the Book of Miracles. In particular the subtle handling of gold and silver in the illustrations of jousting scenes recalls the carefully applied gold and silver highlights in the present manuscript's comet pictures.

The younger Burgkmair is also thought to have executed the majority of the etchings on iron accompanying what is known as the Augsburg Book of Nobles (in German, the *Ernwertes Geschlechter Buch der löblichen deß Heiligen Reichs Statt Augspurg Patricorium*). This project was conceived in the wake of the decision in 1538 to increase the number of patrician and noble families

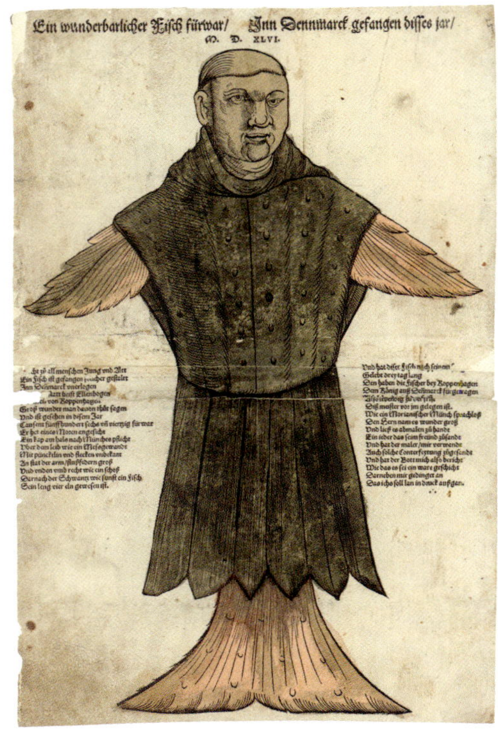

Ill. 11

Illustrated broadsheet on a wondrous fish in 1546
Flugblatt über einen wundersamen Fisch im Jahr 1546
Feuillet illustré mentionnant un poisson merveilleux en l'an 1546
Zurich, Zentralbibliothek, Graphische Sammlung, inv. PAS II 1/3

eligible to take part in the political running of the city, and was intended to record the coats of arms of Augsburg's patriciate. According to the frontispiece of the edition originally planned for 1545 but only published in 1618, the engravings were made by Hans Burgkmair and Heinrich Vogtherr, a name that has been interpreted to refer to Heinrich Vogtherr the Elder by some and to his son Heinrich Vogtherr the Younger (1513–1568) by others (Falk in Augsburg 2011, pp. 190–192; Seidl 2012). A volume returned to the Stuttgart Staatsgalerie in 2010 contains 44 pen drawings and 53 proofs for this Augsburg Book of Nobles, including autograph works by Burgkmair (cf. Seidl 2012). Given their exclusively graphic nature, however, these drawings and etchings provide no points of stylistic comparison with the atmospheric, painterly illustrations in the Book of Miracles.

The fact that the younger Burgkmair collaborated with either the older or the younger Heinrich Vogtherr on the Augsburg Book of Nobles is none the less sufficient to make us prick up our ears, since some of the illustrations in the present manuscript go back to designs by Heinrich Vogtherr the Elder. The three motifs on folio 158r, for example, are based on broadsheets made from woodcuts by the Dillingen artist (ills. 25, 26). The sheet is unique within the manuscript for combining three motifs on a single page. The fact that all three can be traced back not just to the same artist but to one who was Swabian by birth raises the question as to whether Heinrich Vogtherr the Elder could have been involved in the illustration of the Book of Miracles.

Heinrich Vogtherr the Elder was born in Dillingen in 1490, and attended the grammar school there before training as a painter in Augsburg. The son of a surgeon and eye doctor, he pursued an extremely varied career as a painter, designer, publisher and an eye doctor himself, which led him via Erfurt (1510), Leipzig (1514), Augsburg (1518) and Wimpfen on the River Neckar (1522) to Strasbourg, where in 1526 he was granted citizenship. Having already supplied designs on a regular basis to publishers in Augsburg and Basel, in 1536 Vogtherr set up his own printing press and one year later published the *Kunstbüchlin*, the very first pattern book to appear in print. This 'art booklet' contained 700 illustrations, including specimen designs for faces, hands, suits of armour, side-arms and ornaments (ill. 34). Vogtherr senior produced the *Kunstbüchlin* with his son Heinrich, whose portrait medallion appears on the title page alongside that of his father (ill. 35). The printing press soon ran into financial difficulties, however, and it closed in 1540. Continuing lack of business, due not least to the Reformation, resulted in the younger Vogtherr leaving the paternal workshop the following year and moving to Augsburg, where he set himself up at the end of March as an independent master.

In 1542 Heinrich Vogtherr the Elder travelled from Strasbourg to the Diet of Speyer and then on to Augsburg, where he stayed with his son for a few months. In 1543 he continued on via Basel to Zurich, where he worked as an illustrator. He paid a last visit to Augsburg during the Diet of

Ill. 12
Hans Burgkmair the Younger
Jousting on the field in armour** / **Das Lanzenstechen in stählerner Rüstung** / **La joute en armure de métal
in: *Turnierbuch*, Augsburg, *c.* 1540, fol. 7r. Watercolour and bodycolour on paper,
40.5 x 27.5 cm (16 x 10¾ in.). Munich, Bayerische Staatsbibliothek, Cod. Icon 403

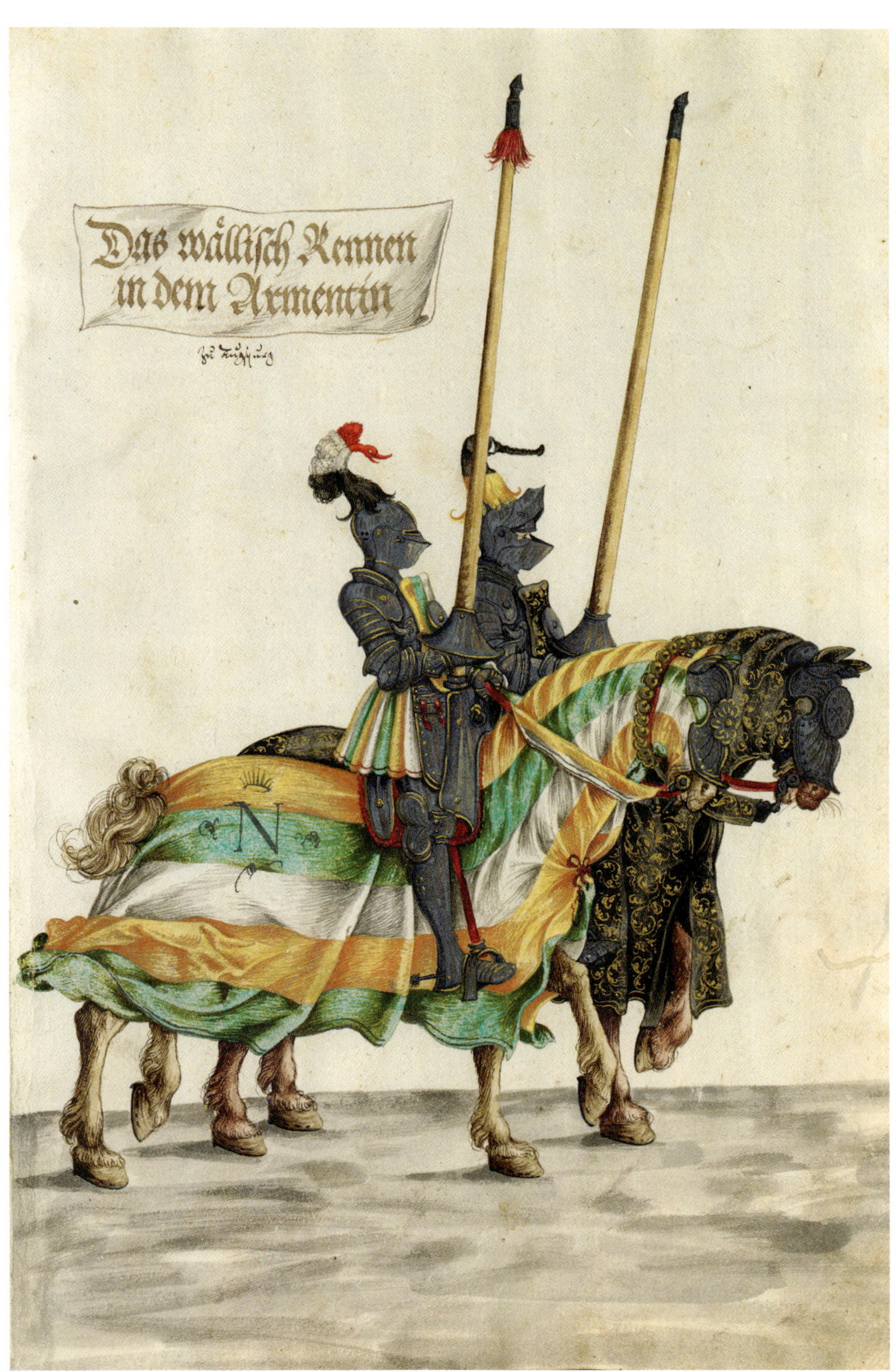
Das wällisch Rennen
in dem Armentin
zu Augspurg

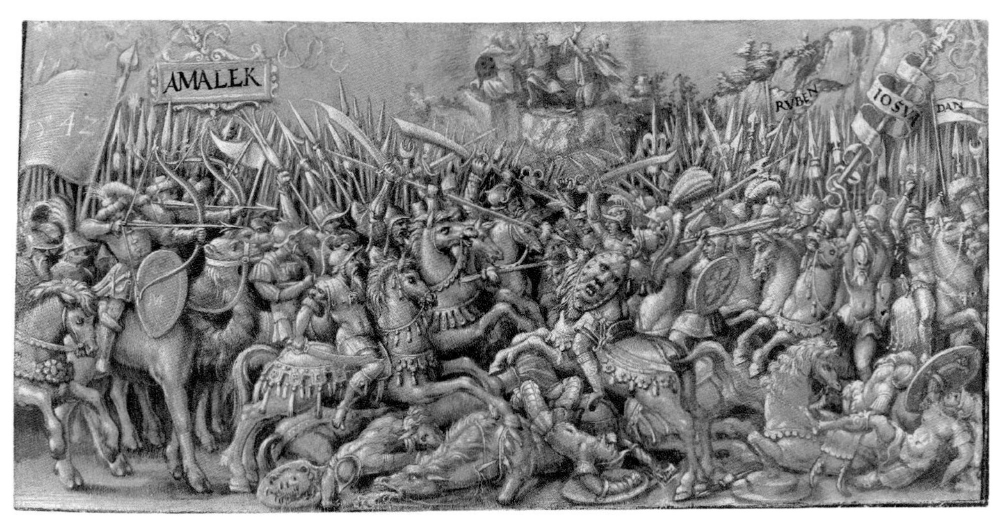

Ill. 13
Heinrich Vogtherr the Younger
Battle between the Amalekites and the Israelites / Kampf zwischen Amalekitern und dem Volk Israel / Le combat entre les Amalécites et le peuple d'Israël
Brush drawing in grey wash, heightened with white bodycolour, on grey-blue prepared paper, 15 x 29.8 cm (5⅞ x 11¾ in.). London, British Museum, Department of Prints and Drawings, inv. PD 1921, 0614.5

1547/48. Possibly hoping for a position at the court of Ferdinand I, at the end of his life Vogtherr moved to Vienna, where he was active as an artist and an eye doctor up to his death in 1556.

Given Heinrich Vogtherr the Elder's travels and multiple changes of residence, it is unlikely that he could have been involved to any great extent with the Book of Miracles, which was produced largely between 1545 and 1552 in Augsburg. It is possible, however, that his son collaborated on the project, operating out of his own Augsburg workshop and using his father's designs as a source of inspiration. In a similar fashion to the younger Burgkmair, who almost never stepped out of his father's shadow, Heinrich Vogtherr the Younger's style was also a continuation of his own father's, making it difficult to separate their individual hands. With regard to the Augsburg Book of Nobles and the attribution of the drawings and etchings, it has thus recently been argued that Hans Burgkmair the Younger cooperated not with Heinrich Vogtherr the Elder but with his son (Seidl 2012).

Heinrich Vogtherr the Younger lived and worked in Augsburg from spring 1541 to the end of 1554. He ran a successful workshop in which three apprentices learned the painter's trade, including Antonius Breu, son of the painter Jörg Breu the Younger (*c.* 1510–1547), who joined the workshop in 1547. In 1555 Vogtherr junior travelled to Vienna to be with his dying father, albeit retaining his Augsburg citizenship. There he was commissioned by the Habsburg court to produce designs for coins, banners and heraldic paintings. He also completed a copy drawing of Maximilian's tomb and contributed to the decorations for the funeral of Emperor Ferdinand I in 1564.

As in the case of the younger Burgkmair, the extent of Heinrich Vogtherr the Younger's involvement cannot be gauged according to stylistic criteria. The differences in their media alone make it impossible to compare the illustrations in the manuscript with Vogtherr's known woodcuts and etchings. Just two of his studies exhibit analogies with the illustrations in the book. The first is a watercolour and bodycolour drawing of a fish's head (ill. 36), authenticated by the monogram HV as the work of the younger Vogtherr and bearing the date 1564, which means it must have been produced in Vienna. The sheet demonstrates a masterly handling of gouache and at the same time reveals an almost scientific curiosity, not unrelated to Dürer's nature studies, that ultimately also characterises many of the illustrations in the manuscript.

The second study is a brush drawing on greyish-blue prepared paper that has been systematically highlighted in white (ill. 13). The drawing, which was formerly attributed to Heinrich Vogtherr the Elder (Rowlands 1993; Müller 1997), shows the battle between the Amalekites and the people of Israel, as recounted in Exodus (17:8–16). The drawing carries the monogram HVE on the left and the date 1542 and was produced in the younger Vogtherr's Augsburg workshop. Giulia Bartrum was the first to point out the analogies between this study and the illustrations in the Book of Miracles (Day & Faber 2010). Parallels can indeed be seen between the figures in the drawing and the horse and rider on folio 126r, and between Vogtherr's use of white highlights and the treatment of certain clouds (e.g. fols. 102r, 124r, 126r).

The realities of workshop practice in the early modern era meant that other painters besides Vogtherr and Burgkmair also contributed to the decoration of the manuscript – a fact reflected in the heterogeneous quality of the illustrations. These range from carefully elaborated figures to simple "matchstick" men, from richly varied landscapes receding into the far distance to spectacular images of comets and celestial phenomena, and include cities seen in schematic outline, condensed representations of the natural world and the multiple repetition of individual motifs. The uneven standard of quality of the book's illustrations points to the involvement of workshop members and apprentices who were working under supervision and who had to employ stock designs.

It is highly unlikely that the volume was produced in a single burst. It is possible that the scenes from the Old Testament at the start of the manuscript and from the Revelation of St John at the end were only conceived as self-contained cycles after work on the miraculous signs in the lengthy middle section had already begun. Placing a homogeneous stamp upon the manuscript as a whole was evidently a major concern, and care was taken to ensure that the biblical pictorial cycles did not deviate significantly from the format of the other illustrations.

Differences in the handwriting and layout of the captions suggest that the Book of Miracles is the work of a number of scribes, who were possibly involved on the manuscript at different times. Taking into account changes in the script and layout of these accompanying texts, we can distinguish at least three phases of production.

The bulk of the captions were written out by a single scribe, whose contribution includes all the texts in the Old Testament section and the majority of the texts in the second part of the

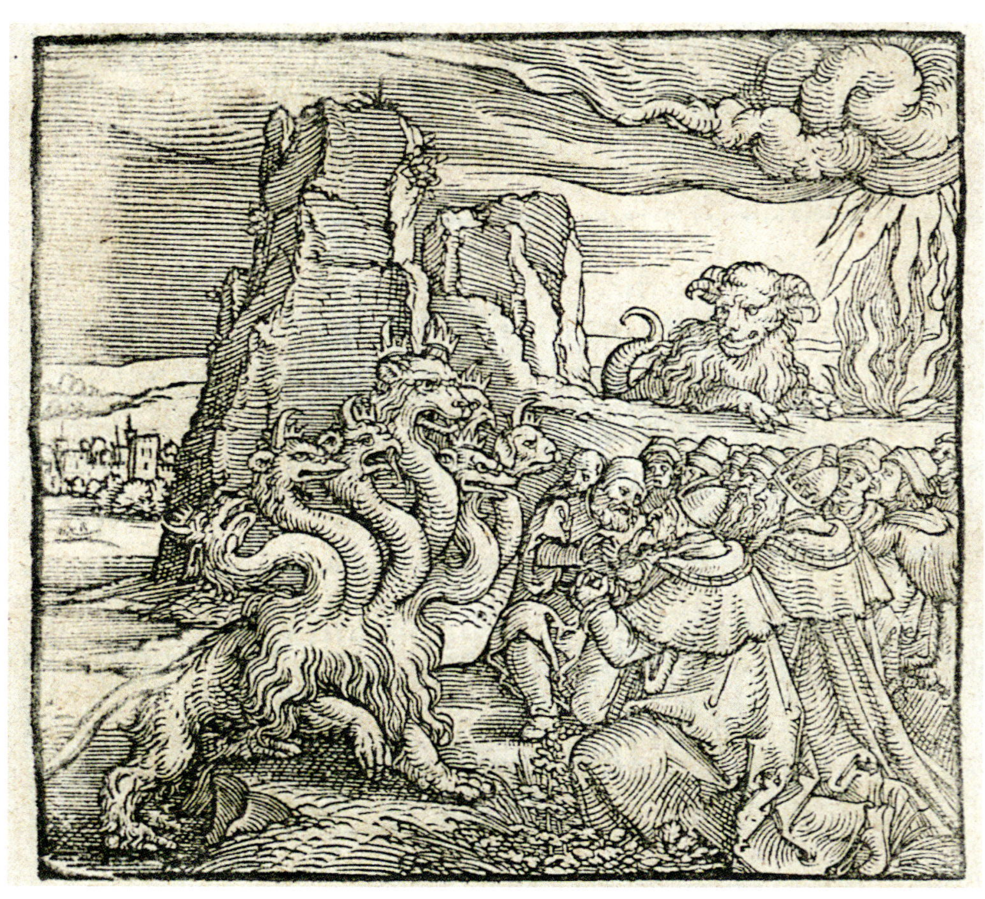

Ill. 14
Hans Sebald Beham
The sea monster and the beast with the lamb's horn / Das Meerungeheuer und die Bestie mit zwei Hörnern wie ein Lamm / La créature marine et la Bête à la corne d'agneau
in: *Typi in apocalypsi Ioannis depicti vt clarivs vaticinia Ioannis intelligi possint*, Frankfurt am Main 1539, fol. 11r. Munich, Bayerische Staatsbibliothek

manuscript. The Revelation of St John section can probably also be ascribed to the same individual in view of the similarity of the handwriting (which also calls to mind the writings by the Augsburg city clerk Clemens Jäger; cf. Munich 2010, pp. 32–35), even though the scribe has here fitted considerably more text on to the page. Folio 154r, whose caption employs the same layout even if it is clearly written by a different hand, and the separate page featuring the illustration of conjoined twins after Burgkmair the Elder and today housed in Stuttgart (fol. 93r), are also both related to the main bulk of the manuscript in this respect.

A second production phase can be recognised in a group of sheets whose captions are written out in two columns. The script is similar to that of the bulk of the manuscript but was possibly written by another hand and perhaps indicates a change of plan that was then abandoned. Captions in two columns are found between folio 94r and folio 107r (with the exception of fol. 100r and fol. 101r, which keep the conventional layout) and again on folia 117r, 145r and 158r. The first group begins on folio 94r with a celestial phenomenon recorded in 1513 and includes the sightings of polar lights and mock suns over Vienna in January 1520, originally shown on six separate sheets (see above). The remaining pages with texts in two columns are devoted to illustrations of prodigies and freaks of nature, whose motifs go back to designs by Burgkmair, Vogtherr and the court painter to the Bishop of Augsburg in Dillingen (see above).

The sheets added in the final phase of production can be identified through their different handwriting. They include several pages at the end of the second part of the manuscript, immediately before the Revelation of St John. The text, which here reverts to the single-column layout, uses a comparatively fancy lettering which can be clearly distinguished from the other captions above all by its decorative, calligraphic flourishes. The sheets in this group begin with an event from the year 1533 on folio 129r, which appears between two pages from the main group. Like the next sheet from this last phase (fol. 144r), it was probably introduced only during the final editing. After folio 153r and folio 157r, the third group then concludes with illustrations of the most recent miraculous signs in the manuscript (fols. 160r to 170r). These relate to events from the years 1549 to 1551 and possibly represent a later supplement.

The manuscript was thus a product of almost exactly the same time as a magnificent volume of the *Eclipses luminarium* by the Augsburg scholar Cyprian Leowitz (1524–1574). In this work, which was produced in 1555 and likewise in Augsburg, dedicated to the later Emperor Ferdinand I, Leowitz calculated all the solar and lunar eclipses up until 1605. This astronomical treatise includes scientific illustrations and genre scenes in the guise of pictures of the months (ill. 37). While it is true that the illustrations to the *Eclipses luminarium* are not directly dependent upon the Book of Miracles and its artists, they nevertheless make it clear that the illustrations in the present manuscript belong to a pictorial tradition about which our knowledge remains sketchy, and at the same time seem to be establishing a new genre of scientific illustration.

Pages 34–35
The sea monster and the beast with the lamb's horn
Das Meerungeheuer und die Bestie mit zwei Hörnern wie ein Lamm
La créature marine et la Bête à la corne d'agneau
in: *Book of Miracles*, Augsburg, *c.* 1550–1552, fol. 187r (detail)
Private collection

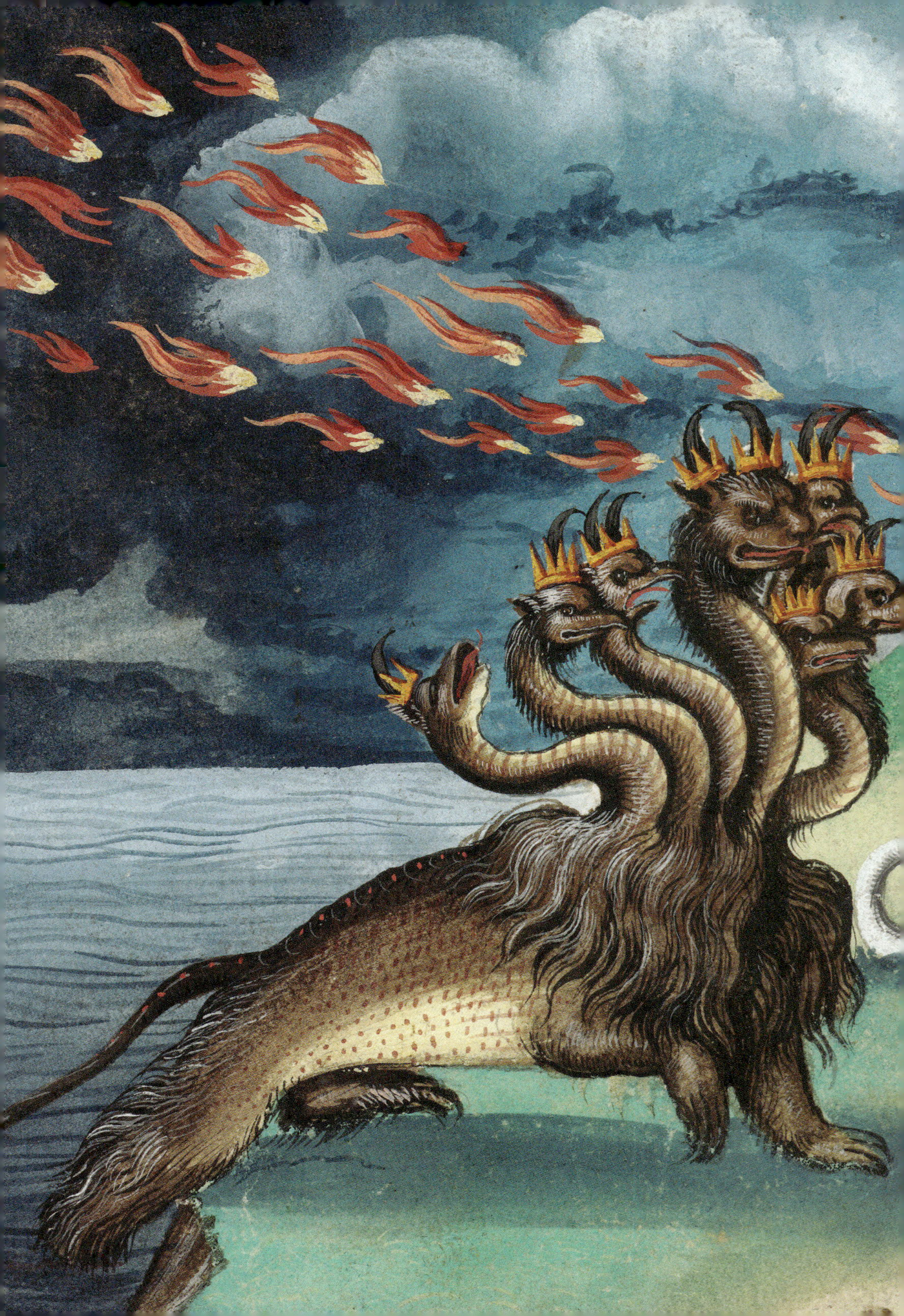

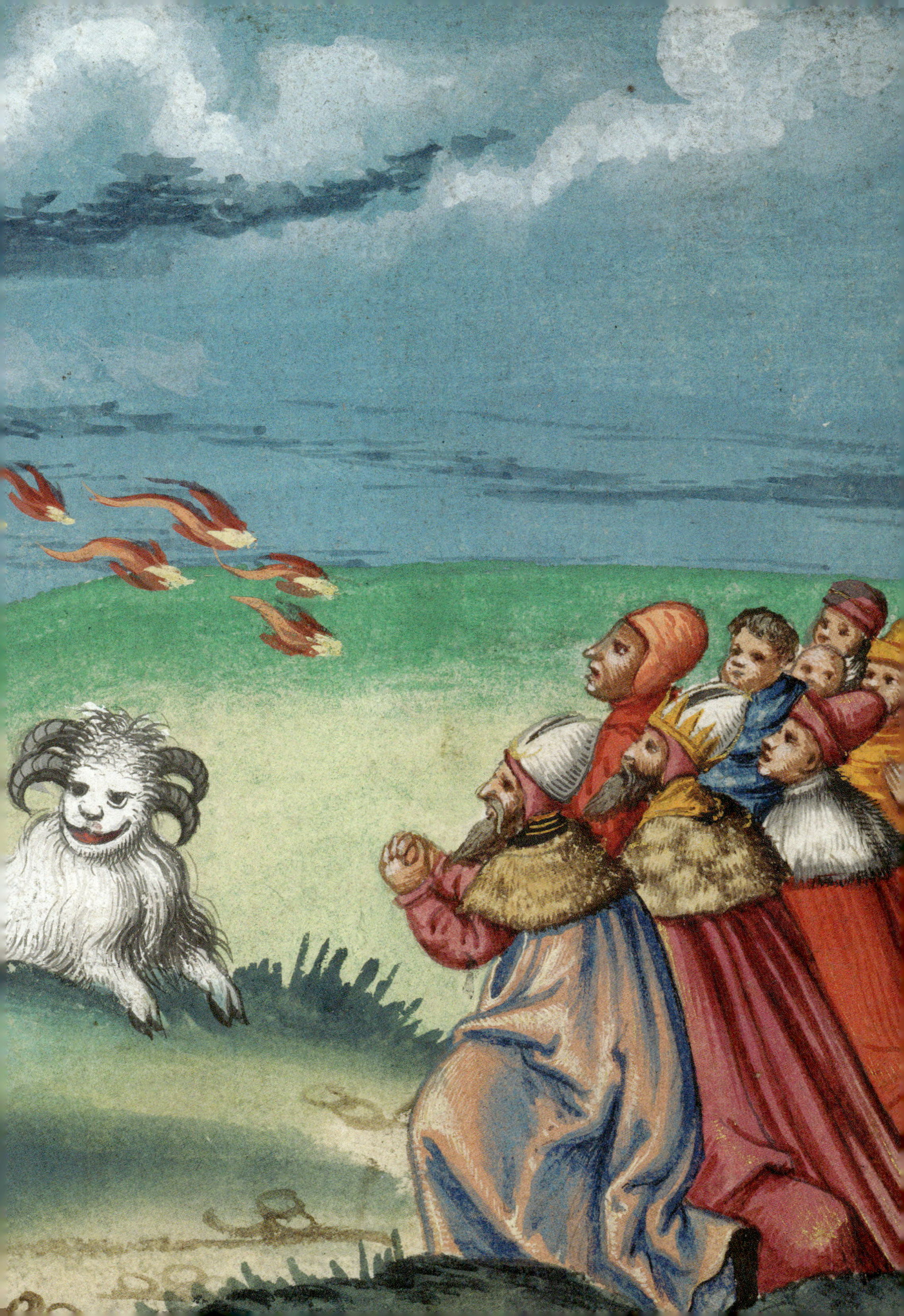

TILL-HOLGER BORCHERT

Das Wunderzeichenbuch

Genese, Stil und Bedeutung

Das Manuskript enthält Berichte und Aufzeichnungen von Wunderzeichen, die sich seit alttestamentlichen Zeiten (fol. 1r–15r) über die Antike (fol. 16r–30r), das Mittelalter und Spätmittelalter (fol. 32r–90r) bis gegen Mitte des 16. Jahrhunderts hin ereignet haben (fol. 91r–171r). Es schließt mit Schilderungen der in der Offenbarung des Johannes beschriebenen Himmelszeichen (fol. 172r–192r), welche die Wiederkunft Christi, das Jüngste Gericht und das künftige Gottesreich ankündigen sollen. Es ist in seinem Anspruch also insofern umfassend, als es Berichte über Wunderzeichen von der Erschaffung der Menschheit bis in die eigene Gegenwart hinein enthält und diese bis zum erwarteten Weltenende fortsetzt. Im Hinblick auf die Vollendung des göttlichen Heilsplans ist Vollständigkeit angestrebt.

Die mit ihren kunstvollen Gouachen vergleichsweise aufwendig illustrierte Prodigienhandschrift bestand ursprünglich aus knapp 200 einseitig mit Text und Illustrationen versehenen Blättern und weist in ihrem heutigen Zustand noch 167 originale folia sowie 23 Einlagen auf. Letztere ersetzen die Originalseiten, die während einer Neubindung im 19. Jahrhundert herausgelöst wurden. Vier der herausgelösten folia konnten wir ausfindig machen und haben sie in diese Ausgabe eingebaut. Es handelt sich um die folia 93r, 111r, 191r und 192r.

Die vermutlich von einem unbekannten Auftraggeber oder einem hiermit betrauten Gelehrten verantwortete Zusammenstellung der wohl in Augsburg entstandenen Handschrift (siehe unten) ist mit anderen Vorzeichensammlungen des 16. Jahrhunderts durchaus vergleichbar. So liegt auch den beiden etwa gleichzeitig mit dem Manuskript entstandenen Prodigienchroniken, den *Histoires prodigieuses* (Paris 1560), des bretonischen Humanisten Pierre Boaistuau (um 1520–1566) und dem *Prodigiorum ac ostentorum chronicon* (Basel 1557; Abb. 15), des elsässischen Universalgelehrten Conrad Lycosthenes die Kombination von alttestamentlichen, historischen sowie endzeitlichen

1527 – Plague of locusts in Poland / Heuschreckenplage in Polen / Invasion de locustes en Pologne
in: *Book of Miracles*, Augsburg, *c.* 1550–1552, fol. 109r (detail)
Private collection

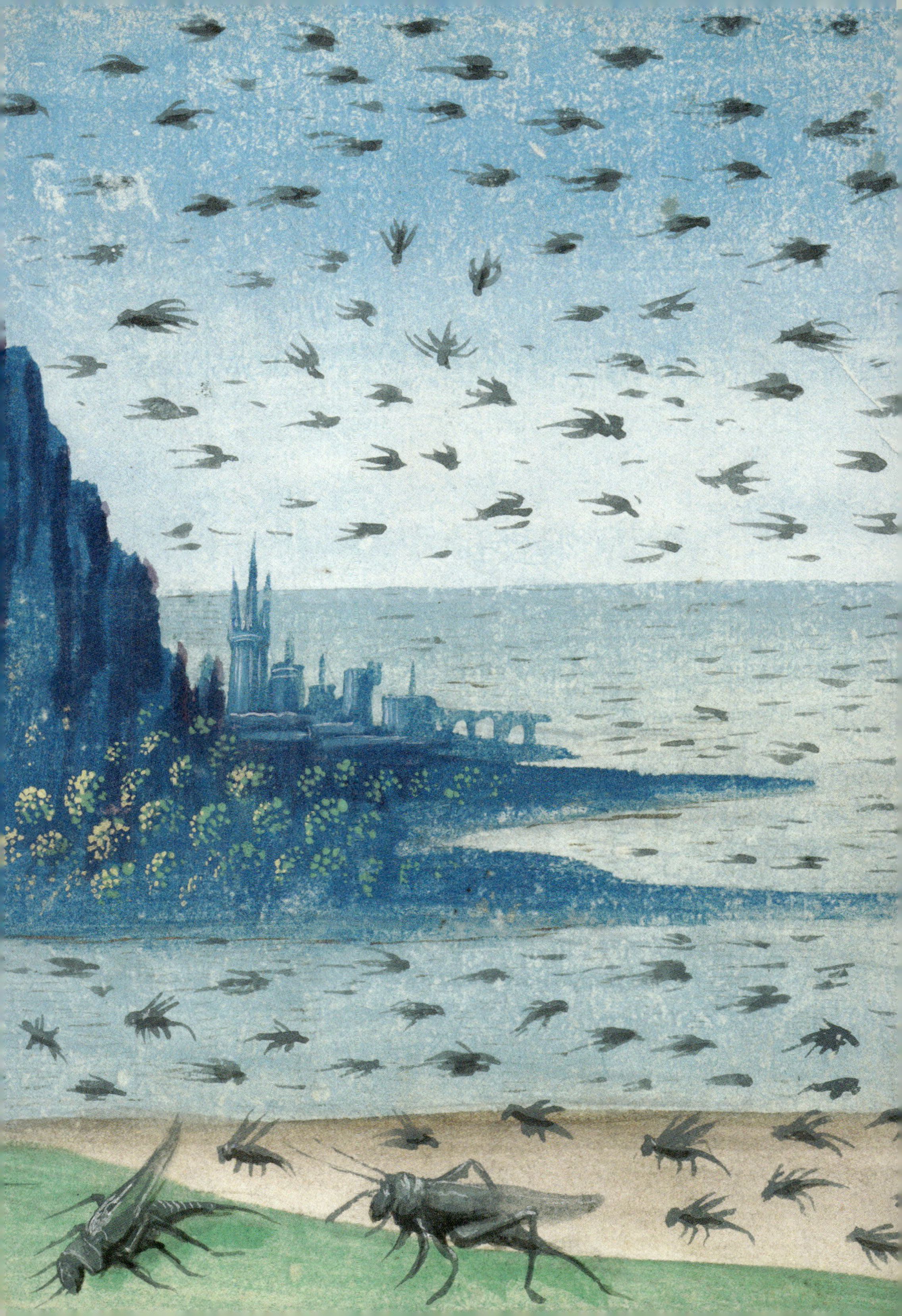

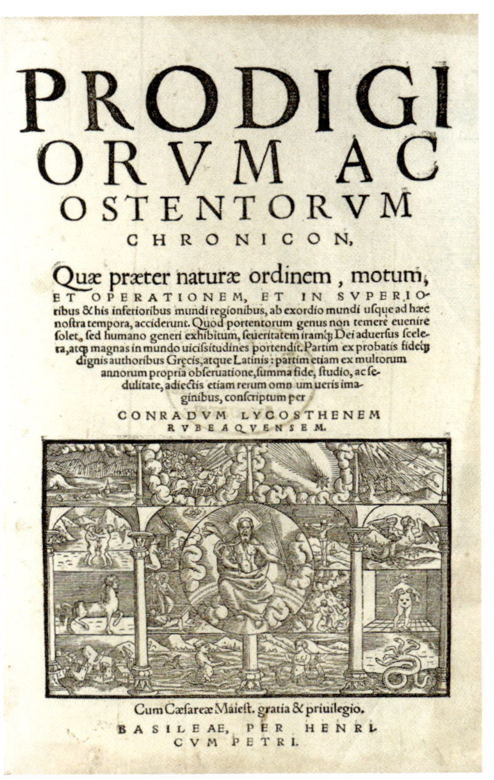
PRODIGI
ORVM AC
OSTENTORVM
CHRONICON,

Quæ præter naturæ ordinem, motum, et operationem, et in superioribus & his inferioribus mundi regionibus, ab exordio mundi usque ad hæc nostra tempora, acciderunt. Quod portentorum genus non temere euenire solet, sed humano generi exhibitum, seueritatem iramq; Dei aduersus scelera, atq; magnas in mundo uicissitudines portendit. Partim ex probatis fideq; dignis authoribus Græcis, atque Latinis: partim etiam ex multorum annorum propria obseruatione, summa fide, studio, ac sedulitate, adiectis etiam rerum omn um ueris imaginibus, conscriptum per

CONRADVM LYCOSTHENEM RVBEAQVENSEM.

Cum Cæsareæ Maiest. gratia & priuilegio.

BASILEAE, PER HENRI CVM PETRI.

Wunderzeichen zugrunde. Aufgrund seiner kunstvollen Illustrationen und seines Umfangs behauptet der vorliegende Codex jedoch eine Sonderstellung innerhalb der Gattung.

Die Wunderzeichen des Alten Testaments

Unvermittelt, d. h. ohne Widmung, Vorwort oder Inhaltsverzeichnis, setzt das Wunderzeichenbuch mit einer Auswahl jener im Alten Testament beglaubigten Ereignisse ein, die man als Fingerzeige Gottes bzw. als Wunderzeichen begreifen konnte. Im Unterschied zu der illustrierten Chronik der Wunder- und Vorzeichen von Lycosthenes beginnt das etwa zur selben Zeit verfertigte Wunderzeichenbuch nicht mit dem Sündenfall, sondern mit der göttlichen Menschheitsstrafe der Sintflut (fol. 1r). Die prachtvolle Miniatur zeigt Noahs Arche vor einer regnerisch-düsteren Wasserlandschaft inmitten wilder Fluten treibend, während Mensch und Tier schwimmend ums Überleben kämpfen.

Die Illustration nimmt fast drei Viertel des Blattes ein. Eine mehrzeilige Beischrift befindet sich am unteren Blattrand. Überschrift, Initiale und Ornamente des Textes sind mit roter Farbe gestaltet, der Text selbst ist in schwarzer Feder ausgeführt. Beischrift und Bild werden durch eine schwarze Einfassung gerahmt. Diese Anordnung von Text und Bild wird auf allen Blättern des Wunderzeichenbuches beibehalten, lediglich der Textspiegel variiert auf einigen folia (siehe unten).

Die deutschen Beischriften folgen der Luther'schen Bibelübersetzung in der Ausgabe von 1545. Während die Illustrationen zum Alten Testament im Wunderzeichenbuch regelmäßig auf

Ill. 15
Title page of / Titelblatt von / Page de titre de
Conrad Lycosthenes, *Prodigiorum ac ostentorum chronicon*, Basel 1557 (2nd ed.)
Göttingen, Niedersächsische Staats- und Universitätsbibliothek

Ill. 16
Margaretha Bruch of Leidringen marked with the instruments of the Passion
Margaretha Bruch von Leidringen mit den Leidenswerkzeugen
Margaretha Bruch von Leidringen avec les instruments de la Passion
in: Jakob Mennel, *De signis, portentis atque prodigiis tam antiquis quam novis cum eorundem typis et figuris*, Freiburg 1503, fol. 18v. Vienna, Österreichische Nationalbibliothek

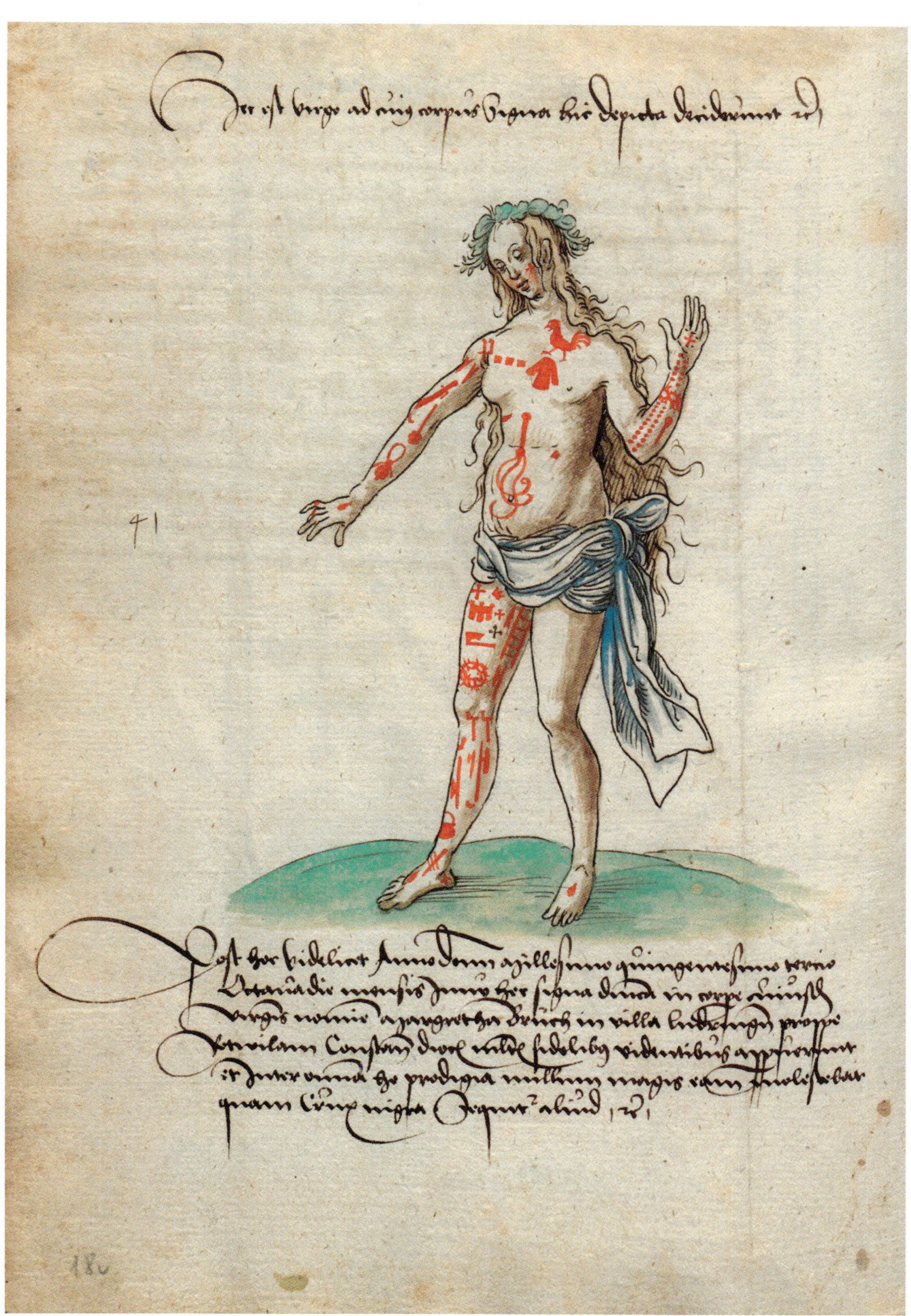

Hec est virgo ad cuius corporis figuram hec depicta deciderunt etc.

41

Post hec videlicet Anno domini millesimo quingentesimo tercio [illegible] die mensis Junii hec signa deciderunt in corpore cuiusdam virginis nomine Margarethe [illegible] in villa [illegible] prope [illegible] Constantiensis diocesis [illegible] fidelibus videntibus apparuerunt et dicte virgini hec prodigia nullum magis [illegible] [illegible] [illegible] aliud etc.

18v

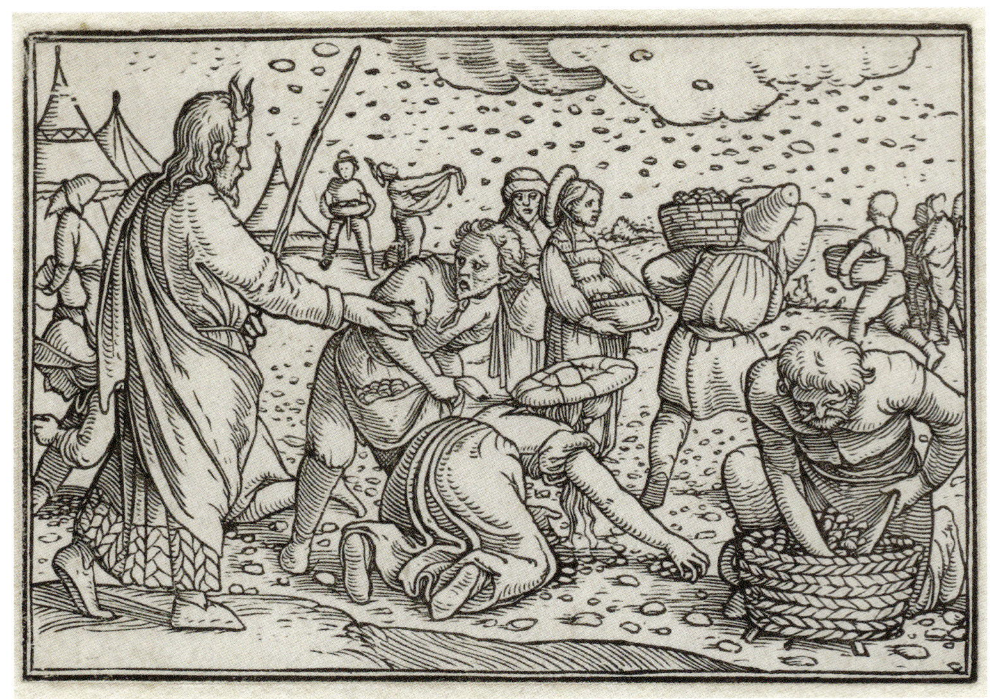

Ill. 17
Hans Holbein the Younger
The Fall of manna / Mannaregen / La manne tombée du ciel
in: *Historiarum Veteris Instrumenti icones ad vivum expressae*, Lyons 1538
Basel, Kunstmuseum, Kupferstichkabinett

Holzschnitten von Hans Holbein dem Jüngeren oder Hans Sebald Beham gründen, ist die *Sintflut* komplexer als die entsprechenden Darstellungen beider Künstler (Abb. 1, 2). Der Holzschnitt der Lutherbibel ist in der Darstellung des Wolkenbruchs sowie der in den Fluten Ertrinkenden durchaus verwandt, diente dem Maler aber wohl kaum als unmittelbare Vorlage (Abb. 28): Die Zahl der Einzelmotive ist hier zugunsten einer konzentrierten Bilderzählung begrenzt, was im Verzicht auf die sich an die Felsen klammernden Gestalten anschaulich wird.

Auf die Sintflut folgt auf folio 2r die Darstellung eines Regenbogens, der im Buch Genesis als Zeichen des göttlichen Bundes mit der Menschheit beschrieben wird (Gen. 9,12-15). Ein doppelter Regenbogen wird links und rechts mit Darstellungen der zwölf Tierkreiszeichen verknüpft, die als Sinnbilder der zwölf Monate des Jahres den immerwährenden Lauf der Zeiten symbolisieren. Das Phänomen des doppelten Regenbogens war dem Maler offenbar aus eigener Anschauung bekannt, denn der hellere innere Bogen ist korrekt weiß, der äußere dagegen rot, gelb und grün gestaltet; äußerst behutsam wurde Gold appliziert, was die Wirkung der Darstellung besonders steigert.

Auf folio 4r folgt die Zerstörung von Sodom und Gomorra (Gen. 19,24–26). Lot und seine Töchter sowie die zur Salzsäule erstarrte Frau des Lot, im Zentrum der Darstellung, sind im Kontext von Prodigien und Wunderzeichen von sekundärem Belang. Im Mittelpunkt steht die Zerstörung der beiden Städte.

Konzentrieren sich die ersten Darstellungen des Wunderzeichenbuches auf Naturphänomene als Ausdruck göttlichen Willens, so ändert sich dies im Folgenden: Folio 5r zeigt Moses, der den aus Ägypten ausziehenden Israeliten voranschreitet. Während er links das Meer teilt, schließen sich rechts hinter ihm die Fluten über dem Pharao und seinem Heer. Die Illustration des Buches Exodus (14,27–29) lenkt das Augenmerk weniger auf die Wasserscheidung als vielmehr auf Moses und die Israeliten: Der Maler entlehnte die Komposition dem Holzschnitt aus Hans Sebald Behams *Biblicae historiae* (Abb. 3).

Unklar ist, warum das Wunderzeichenbuch, im Gegensatz zu anderen Bibelzyklen, auf das Opfer des Isaak oder auf Jakobs Vision der Himmelsleiter verzichtet und auch die Landplagen nicht abbildet (Ex. 7–11). Die ersten beiden Ereignisse sind mit göttlichen Manifestationen in Form von Himmelserscheinungen verbunden, während es sich bei den biblischen Landplagen gewissermaßen um Urbilder von Katastrophen handelt, denen man – wie Hagel, Blutflüsse oder Heuschreckenplagen im zweiten Teil der Handschrift zeigen – durchaus den Rang von Wunderzeichen zubilligte.

Die Darstellung auf folio 6r darf gleichfalls als biblisches Urbild jener Prodigien gelten, die im zweiten Teil der Handschrift als Nahrungswunder aufgenommen wurden. Durch den im Buch Exodus (16,14–16) beschriebenen Mannaregen bewahrt Gott das Volk Israel vor dem Verhungern. Bei dem „Niederschlag" handelt es sich um die sogenannte Mannaflechte, eine essbare Krustenflechte, die der Wind verbreitet. Das Thema galt als Präfiguration des Letzten Abendmahls und des Eucharistiesakraments und fand auch Eingang in protestantische Bildzyklen. Die Abbildung gründet auf einem Holzschnitt aus den um 1525/26 entworfenen *Icones* von Hans Holbein dem Jüngeren (Müller 1997, S. 285–286); von dieser Vorlage (Abb. 17) stammen die figürlichen Motive, die man dann unter Berücksichtigung der veränderten Proportionen in die Bildlandschaft eingefügt hat.

Auf folio 7r blickt man auf die Gruppe um Moses und den als Priester gewandeten Aaron herab, vor deren Füßen die Erde aufbricht und den rebellischen Korach und sein Gefolge verschlingt. Von dort aus gleitet der Blick in den Hintergrund, in dem sich ein Fluss in mehreren Kurven durch die weite Landschaft schlängelt und ins Meer mündet; links schließt die Komposition mit einem Nadelbaum ab, dessen Maßstab die Distanz zum Hintergrund verdeutlicht. Dem Maler gelingt es, mit vergleichsweise einfachen Mitteln eindrucksvolle atmosphärische Effekte zu erzielen, die von einer tieferen Kenntnis der Tafelmalerei der Donauschule, Frankens und Schwabens zeugen (Abb. 29). Die Nebenszene rechts, in der Reiter von Himmelsflammen vernichtet werden, zeigt die Bestrafung der geflüchteten Anhänger des Leviten Korach und ist Teil der Geschichte des Korach. Das Ereignis wird im Buch Numeri behandelt, die Beischrift der Handschrift gibt die Verse 4 bis 7 von Kapitel 16 wieder, die allein den Beginn von Korachs Auseinandersetzung mit Moses beschreiben, nicht aber das Ende. Das Verständnis der Abbildung ergibt sich nicht unmittelbar aus der Lektüre der Beischrift, sondern setzt vielmehr nähere Kenntnisse des Alten Testaments voraus.

Hieran schließt auf folio 8r die im 2. Kapitel des 2. Buchs der Könige beschriebene Himmelfahrt des Propheten Elia an; die Überschrift des dreizeiligen Textes, der mitten im Bibelvers abbricht, spricht allerdings vom 3. Buch der Könige und knüpft dabei an die noch in der Renaissance geläufige Zählung an, in der beide Bücher Samuel zu den Büchern der Könige gerechnet wurden. Die Abbildung ist abermals von Holbeins Holzschnitt der *Icones* abhängig, der die Komposition vorwegnimmt.

Die Tempelvision des Propheten Jesaja, die auf folio 9r entgegen der damals schon üblichen Ordnung des Alten Testaments unmittelbar auf Elias Himmelfahrt folgt, ist ein ungewöhnliches Sujet. Die Bildunterschrift (Jes. 1,1-3) bezieht sich ausschließlich auf den Propheten und hat keinen Bezug zur Vision, die erst im 6. Kapitel beschrieben wird. Die Bildhaftigkeit der Erscheinung – mit der in den Wolken thronenden Gestalt Gottes über einem hier als Zentralbau aufgefassten Tempel und der ausführlichen Beschreibung der Seraphim (Jes. 6,1-7) – fand ihren Widerhall in der Johannesoffenbarung. Als Vorlage wurden wiederum Holbeins *Icones* herangezogen. Während auch die folgende Darstellung der zwei Sonnenuhren (fol. 10r, Jes. 38,8) auf Holbein zurückgeht, gründet die auf folio 11r anschließende Berufung des Propheten Jeremia wiederum auf der entsprechenden Bibelillustration von Hans Sebald Beham.

Daniels Vision von den vier Tieren (Dan. 7,1-7 – in der Beischrift sind die ersten vier Verse wiedergegeben; fol. 12r) ist erneut eine Endzeitvision. Während die vier Winde aus den vier Himmelsrichtungen gegeneinanderblasen, steigen vier monströse Tiere aus den Fluten auf. Sie verkörpern vier Weltreiche, die erst durch einen Weltenherrscher vernichtet werden, bis dessen Herrschaft dann durch das ewige Gottesreich überwunden sein wird. Die Darstellung verbindet die vier Kontinente mit einer der Bestien und folgt hierin diesmal der Illustration der Lutherbibel (Abb. 18).

Die Darstellung des nächsten Blatts (fol. 13r), auf dem der Erzengel Gabriel dem Propheten Daniel dessen neuerliche Endzeitvision vom Widder und Ziegenbock deutet (Dan. 8,1-12, in der Beischrift lediglich Dan 8,1-4), folgt abermals den *Icones*. Beim Kopieren der Vorlage unterläuft dem Maler jedoch ein Irrtum. Das auf Holbeins Darstellung geborstene Horn des Ziegenbocks (Dan. 8,21-22) entgeht ihm und damit der Symbolgehalt des Details, wonach jener Ziegenbock für das erste von vier künftigen Königreichen steht.

Mittelalterlichen Theologen galt die Geschichte von Jona und dem Wal als Präfiguration von Tod und Auferstehung Christi. Der Text unterhalb der Darstellung auf folio 14r zitiert die Schlussverse des ersten und die Anfangsverse des zweiten Kapitels des Buches Jona, auf die sich die Nebenszene im Hintergrund bezieht. Die Hauptszene zeigt ein im dritten und vierten Kapitel beschriebenes Ereignis. Vor den Toren der Stadt Ninive ruht der Gott zürnende Jona unter einem Baum, während ein riesiger Kürbis über seinem Haupt wächst, um ihn vor der Sonne zu schützen. Während die Lutherbibel beide Ereignisse aus dem Leben des Jona in einem Simultanbild illustriert (Abb. 4), hatten sowohl Beham als auch Holbein in seinen auch hier als Vorlage dienenden *Icones* allein den Zorn des Jona abgebildet.

Holbeins Vision des Hesekiel (Abb. 30) ist auch die Vorlage für die Abbildung auf folio 15r, die im Wunderzeichenbuch unmittelbar an die Geschichte Jonas anschließt, obschon das Buch Hesekiel in zeitgenössischen Bibelausgaben vor den Büchern Daniels steht. Maßstab und

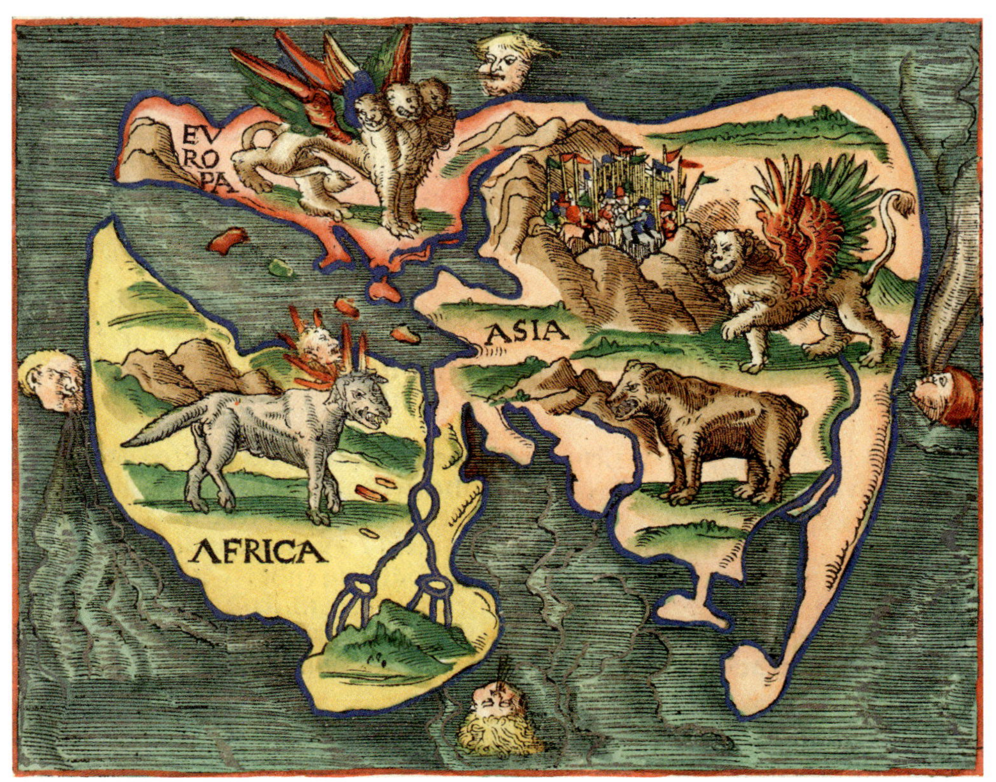

Ill. 18
Workshop of Lucas Cranach the Elder
Daniel's Dream* | *Traum Daniels* | *Le songe de Daniel
in: *The Luther Bible*, Wittenberg 1534, fol. XIIIIr. Weimar, Herzogin Anna Amalia Bibliothek

Proportionen werden an das Blattformat angepasst. Die Erscheinung Gottvaters wird gegenüber der Vorlage ebenso verkleinert wie die vier Lebewesen und das kugelförmige Feuerrad. Erneut erweist sich der Maler des Wunderzeichenbuches als ein außerordentlich talentierter Kolorist, der Feuer, Rauch und Wolken nuanciert gestaltet. Die Beischrift zitiert die ersten drei Verse des 1. Kapitels des Buches Hesekiel und fungiert als ein assoziativer Verweis auf die dargestellte Vision, die ausführlich in den späteren Versen beschrieben wird (Ez 1,4-28). Die Vision des Hesekiel beendet den Eingangsteil des Wunderzeichenbuches, der eine Auswahl von Gottesstrafen, Wundern und Visionen des Alten Testaments enthält.

Die Wunderzeichen von der Antike bis in die Gegenwart

Der zweite Teil der Handschrift umfasst 135 der 167 erhaltenen Blätter und enthält Darstellungen von Wunderzeichen, die von der Antike bis unmittelbar in die Entstehungszeit des Buches gegen Mitte des 16. Jahrhunderts reichen.

Die nichtbiblischen Ereignisse setzen auf folio 16r mit einer Überschwemmung ein, die sich noch zu Lebzeiten von Hiob zutrug. Aus den Fluten des über die Ufer getretenen Flusses sei ein Ochse entstiegen, der gen Himmel aufgefahren und sodann wieder ins Wasser abgetaucht sei; „einfältige Leute“ hätten das Tier als Gott verehrt. Wenngleich es hier um die im Alten Testament erwähnten Tierkulte geht, wird kein biblisches Ereignis illustriert. Die Quelle ist wahrscheinlich Schedels *Weltchronik* von 1493 (fol. 29r) oder die Chronik von Sebastian Franck von 1531 (fol. 17r).

Die nach einem leeren Einlageblatt auf folio 18r und folio 19r dargestellten Ereignisse entstammen der Schrift *De bello Judaico* des Flavius Josephus (Abb. 5).

Beide Darstellungen und Beischriften beziehen sich auf die bei Flavius Josephus erwähnten Vorzeichen, welche der neunten Zerstörung Jerusalems vorausgingen. Penibel stellt der Maler die in Josephus' Text erwähnten Einzelmotive dar: ein schwertähnlicher Stern über Jerusalem; ein Opferrind, das ein Lamm gebar; ein schweres Tor des inneren Tempelbezirks, das sich von selbst öffnete. Rind und Lamm werden dabei vor den Toren der Stadt Jerusalem dargestellt, über der ein feuriges Schwert prangt (fol. 18r). Auf dem folgenden Blatt (fol. 19r) erscheinen bewaffnete Ritterheere in den Wolken über einer Stadt. Flavius Josephus zufolge war diese Erscheinung über allen Städten Judäas zu sehen, sodass die Silhouette nicht unbedingt Jerusalem bedeutet.

Während diese beiden Ereignisse aus dem ersten nachchristlichen Jahrhundert datieren, so handelt es sich bei den nachfolgenden Geschehnissen um Begebenheiten aus dem Jahr 73 v. Chr. Folio 21r bildet das Vorzeichen gemeinsam mit dem daraus resultierenden Unheil ab. Aus der Beischrift geht hervor, dass Blut aus dem Brot quillt, welches die Männer während eines Mahles brechen. Das Blutwunder ist das Vorzeichen des auf der rechten Seite der Abbildung dargestellten Hagelsturms, der tagelang wütete und die gesamte Ernte vernichtete.

Blutwunder, Naturkatastrophen und Tierplagen (fol. 87r, 109r, 141r) wurden bereits im Alten Testament als Gottesstrafen verstanden und sind in der Handschrift prominente Kategorien von Zeichen. Kometen, Sonnen- und Mondfinsternisse, Haloerscheinungen und Polarlichter galten schon in der Antike als Vorboten von Unheil und wurden noch während der Entstehung der Handschrift als Unglücksbringer gedeutet.

Himmelserscheinungen

Vor allem die Darstellungen von Himmelserscheinungen faszinieren den modernen Betrachter, da sich in ihrer sorgfältig bildhaften Gestaltung ein geradezu naturwissenschaftliches Interesse manifestiert, das in die Zukunft weist und im Kontext von Vor- und Wunderzeichen merkwürdig zwiespältig wirkt.

Präzise werden auf folio 26r drei Sonnen dargestellt, die nach der Ermordung Cäsars am geröteten Morgenhimmel von Rom erschienen sein und sich zu einer einzigen Sonne zusammengezogen haben sollen. Bereits Julius Obsequens berichtet in seinem *Liber prodigiorum* (Kapitel 130) von diesem Wunderzeichen, das auch in Schedels *Weltchronik* (fol. 92v) und Francks Chronik (fol. 127v) Eingang fand. Letztere scheint die direkte Textquelle zu sein. Wiederholt finden sich Abbildungen solcher Nebensonnen, die durch Lichtbrechungen von winzigen Eiskristallen in der Luft erzeugt werden (fol. 45r). Die beiden Phantomsonnen, die im Januar 1520 am Himmel über Wien

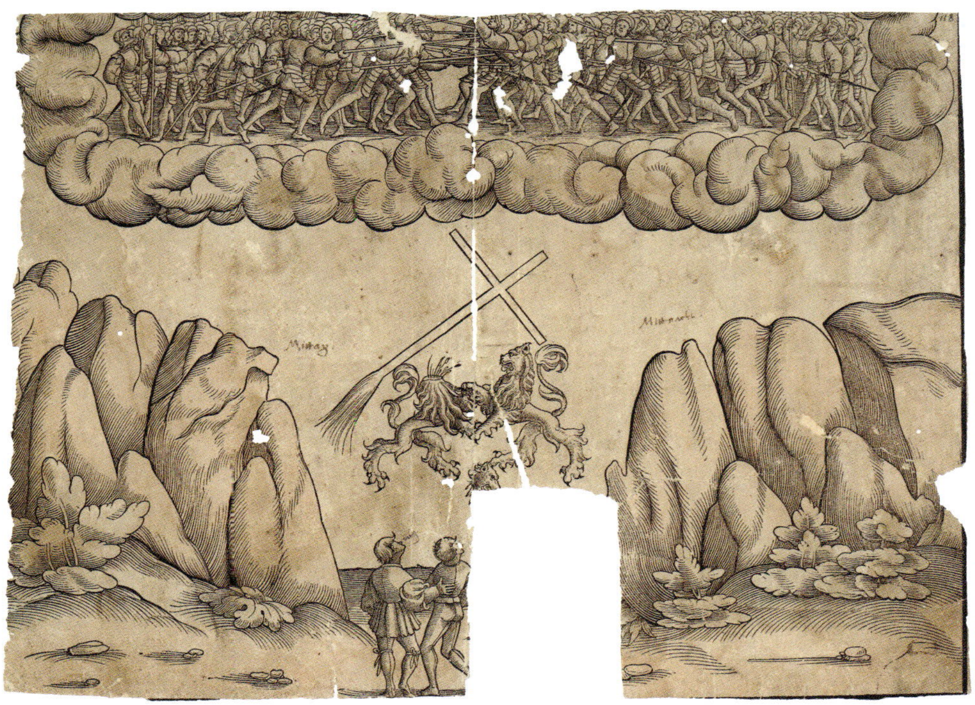

Ill. 19
Strange cloud phenomenon over the Sernf Valley, Glarus, 22 July 1547
Merkwürdige Wolkenerscheinung über dem Glarner Sernftal, 22. Juli 1547
Étrange formation nuageuse au-dessus de la vallée du Sernf, Glarus, 22 juillet 1547
Illustrated broadsheet, 1547. Zurich, Zentralbibliothek, Graphische Sammlung, inv. PAS II 1/31

erschienen (fol. 102r, 106r), gehörten dabei zu einer Reihe außergewöhnlicher Himmelsphänomene, die sich damals innerhalb weniger Tage und Nächte über Wien zeigten (fol. 104r, 106r, 107r; vgl. Fincel 1556, S. 68; Abb. 6).

Die Darstellungen der Wiener Ereignisse zeichnen sich durch ihr stimmungsvolles Kolorit aus, das als die vielleicht bedeutendste künstlerische Eigenleistung innerhalb des Wunderzeichenbuchs gelten kann. Subtile Gelb- und Goldhöhungen in den Wolken bilden das Lichtspiel der Morgendämmerung effektvoll ab und formen einen markanten Kontrast zum tiefblauen Nachthimmel, an dem Polarlichter und Sonnenaureolen erscheinen.

Neben weiteren Phantomsonnen, die in Kombination mit anderen Himmelserscheinungen auftauchen (fol. 112r, 113r, 139r), wird auch das seltene Phänomen von Nebenmonden abgebildet (fol. 49r). Auf folio 62r tauchen drei Monde am Nachthimmel auf, der von einem Kometen durchzogen wird. Hier handelt es sich nicht um Nebenmonde, sondern um eine spezielle Sternenkonstellation, die man für Monde hielt. Laut Beischrift erschienen im Jahr 1304 in „welschen Landen" (Italien) über Monate hinweg drei Monde um Mitternacht.

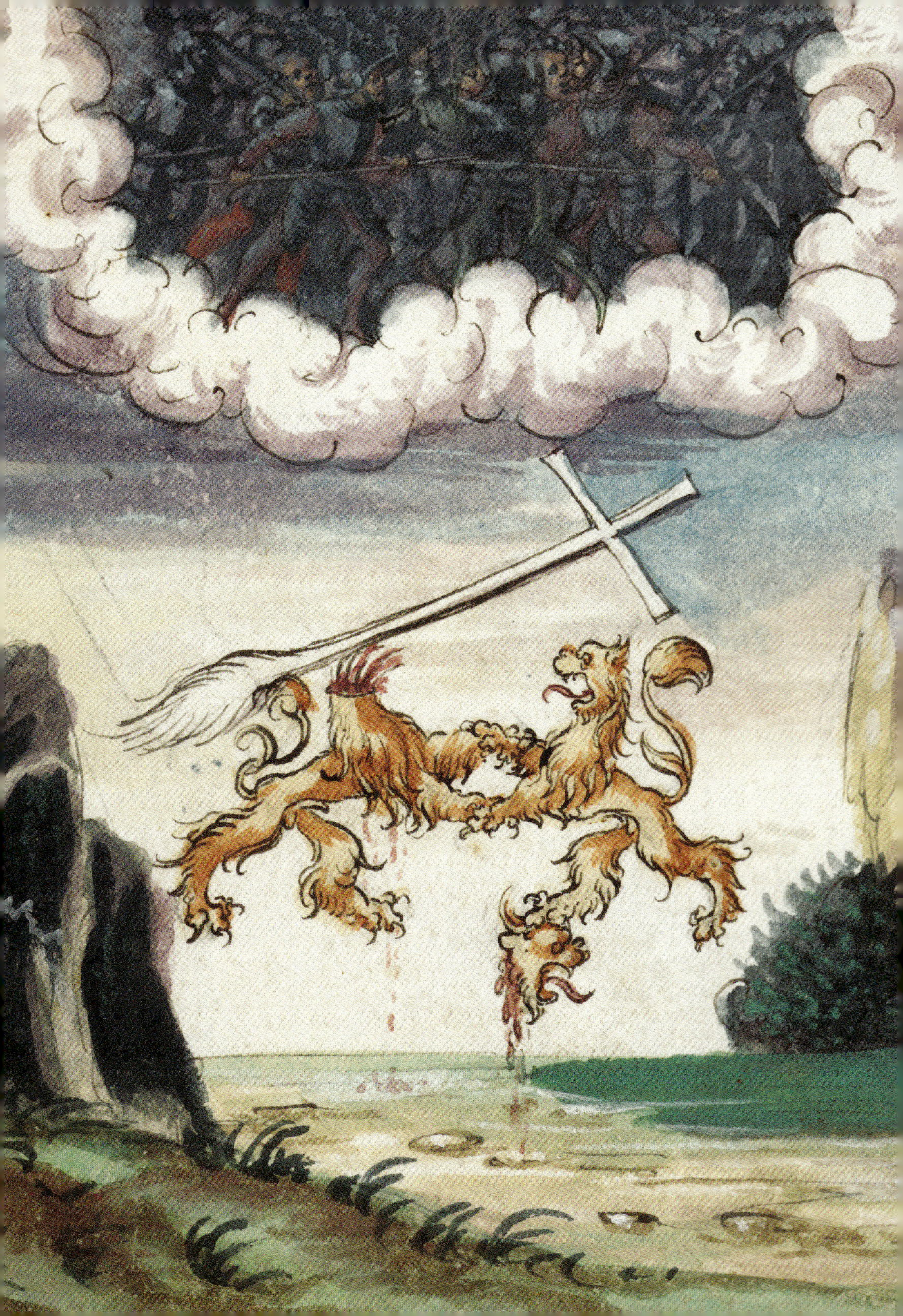

Das Wunderzeichenbuch berichtet oft von seltsamen Himmelsfärbungen, die Unheil nach sich ziehen. Ein blutroter Mond kündigt ein verheerendes Erdbeben in Italien an (fol. 39r), wobei mit minimalen Mitteln eine unwirklich düstere Stimmung erzeugt wird und sich die schwarze Trümmersilhouette deutlich vor dem dunklen Nachthimmel abzeichnet. Allein der Beischrift ist zu entnehmen, dass der rote Mond auf folio 147r eine Mondfinsternis illustriert: „bei nacht ist ain finsternus des mons gewessen das der mon gantz blutig sach."

Mehrere Sonnenfinsternisse bekräftigen die verbreitete Vorstellung, dass Eklipsen Vorboten von Unglück seien (fol. 64r, 69r, 70r, 87r, 149r). Das auf folio 149r illustrierte Ereignis fand im Januar 1544 in Augsburg statt, wo kurz darauf das Wunderzeichenbuch entstand. Die Darstellung bleibt indes schematisch und scheint keineswegs auf der Erfahrung des Malers zu gründen.

In die Handschrift sind ferner figürliche Erscheinungen am Firmament aufgenommen (Abb. 31), die man während des 16. Jahrhunderts gesichtet hatte (fol. 124r, 126r, 134r, 144r, 150r, 157r). Flugblätter verbreiteten die Kunde von solchen Wolkenbildern, die Zeitgenossen als Zeichen bevorstehender Kriege begriffen. Wie im Falle der 1547 im Schweizer Kanton Glarus gesichteten Himmelserscheinung (fol. 157r), gehen die Illustrationen meist auf einschlägige Einblattholzschnitte zurück (Abb. 19).

Kometenbilder

Zahlreich sind Kometendarstellungen im Wunderzeichenbuch vertreten. Zusammen mit einem um 1587 in Flandern illustrierten Kometenbüchlein (Massing 1977; Abb. 20) enthält es die wohl umfangreichste frühe Sammlung von Kometenbildern. Schon der Antike galten diese Himmelserscheinungen als regelrechte Unglücksbringer mit Jahre währender Wirkung. Diese düstere Haltung teilten reformatorisch gesinnte Humanisten, nachdem das Mittelalter Kometen durchaus positiv als Boten Gottes gedeutet hatte. Auf nicht weniger als 26 Blättern werden Kometenerscheinungen illustriert (fol. 32r, 34r, 35r, 37r, 46r, 50r, 58r, 61r, 62r, 64r, 65r, 67r, 74r, 79r, 83r, 92r, 100r, 101r, 110r, 120r, 121r, 122r, 125r, 128r, 142r, 146r), doch trotz der differenzierten Abbildungen sucht man Ansätze einer Klassifizierung vergeblich. Das Wunderzeichenbuch enthielt ursprünglich weitere Kometendarstellungen, denn eines der später aus dem Konvult ausgelösten Blätter zeigt ebenfalls die imposante Erscheinung eines geschweiften Lichtballs mit gezücktem Schwert (für unsere Ausgabe wurde das Blatt an seiner ehemalige Stelle als folio 111r eingebaut; vgl. Falk 2005).

Im Rückgriff auf schematische Kometenholzschnitte, denen man etwa in den Prodigienausgaben des Lycosthenes begegnet (Abb. 32), wird die Erscheinungsvielfalt im Wunderzeichenbuch vor allem auf Basis der Textüberlieferung visualisiert. Der auf die Erde stürzende Meteor des Jahres 1007 (fol. 34r) ist von Flammen umgeben, während die Erscheinung des Jahres 1173 (fol. 46r) die Form eines feurigen Holzbalkens erhält. Der Komet des Jahres 684 (in römischen Ziffern, aber fälschlich mit 1184 in arabischen Ziffern datiert; fol. 50r) über Rom wird als Vorbote eines

1547 – Celestial battle, lions over Glarus
Himmelsschlacht, Löwen über Glarus / Combat céleste, lions dans le ciel de Glarus
in: *Book of Miracles*, Augsburg, *c.* 1550–1552, fol. 157r (detail). Private collection

gewaltigen und zerstörerischen Gewitters beschrieben, wie auch der Komet des Jahres 1300 (fol. 61r) Vorbote eines Erdbebens in der Ewigen Stadt ist.

Naturkatastrophen

In einigen Illustrationen erscheinen Kometen zusammen mit verheerenden Katastrophen, die im Wunderzeichenbuch ebenfalls vertreten sind. Nicht immer sind die Quellen eindeutig zu identifizieren. Die Ereignisse auf folio 30r entstammen wohl Francks Chronik und umkreisen ein Erdbeben, das den Tempel in Jerusalem im Jahre 367 zerstörte. Der Darstellung liegen historische Geschehnisse zugrunde, nämlich die Erdbeben im Mittelmeerraum, welche 365 die Zerstörung Alexandrias sowie einen verheerenden Tsunami in Kleinasien zur Folge hatten. Ein solches Ereignis beschreibt der syrische Theologe Theodoret von Cyrus (393–468) im 3. Buch seiner *Historia ecclesiastica*, das dem römischen Kaiser Julian gewidmet ist. Kaiser Julian ließ die von Konstantin dem Großen erbaute christliche Basilika abreißen, um an deren Stelle einen Tempel zu errichten. Bereits während des Baus zerstörte Gott das heidnische Bauwerk durch ein Erdbeben.

Die Darstellung auf folio 30r gehört zu den eindrucksvollsten der Handschrift. Vor den Toren der am linken Bildrand im Widerschein des Feuers leuchtenden Stadtansicht trifft das Flutwasser in hohen Wellen auf einen schmalen Landstreifen. Dahinter fällt der Blick auf eine überflutete Ebene, in deren Hintergrund Städte im Wasser versinken und Mensch und Vieh sich schwimmend an Land zu retten suchen. Die Bäume vermitteln einen anschaulichen Eindruck von der Kraft des Sturms. Mit unregelmäßigen Schraffuren erzeugt der Maler den Eindruck gewaltiger Regen- und Hagelmassen. Links regnet Feuer auf die Stadt, deren Türme durch das Erbeben regelrecht einknicken. Eine gewaltige Feuer- und Rauchsäule steigt über den Dächern auf und färbt das Gebirge im Hintergrund rot.

Eingeknickte Türme veranschaulichen stets die zerstörerische Kraft der Beben: Apokalyptisch wirkt die zerstörte Stadt in einer in fahles Mondlicht getauchten Landschaft, die Erdbeben im Jahre 1119 (fol. 39r) und im Jahre 1228 (fol. 52r) illustriert. Eher untypisch ist die Abbildung eines Erdbebens in Spanien im Jahre 1357 (fol. 68r). Die Verheerungen werden links und rechts hinter einem Felsen sichtbar.

Die einzige Darstellung eines Vulkanausbruchs ist ähnlich aufgefasst: Der Vesuv schleudert feuriges Magma aus, und im Hintergrund erkennt man das brennende Neapel (fol. 85r). Die Überschrift datiert das Ereignis auf das Jahr 1482. Der Text berichtet von der Zerstörung von Städten und Dörfern durch Lavaströme und zählt Plinius zu den Todesopfern, der tatsächlich 79 v. Chr. beim Ausbruch des Vesuvs ums Leben kam. Offensichtlich unterlief dem Schreiber hier ein Missverständnis, als er die entsprechende Angabe aus Francks Chronik (fol. 270r) übernahm, derzufolge der Ausbruch im Jahr 82 v. Chr. stattfand.

Ill. 20
Treatise on Comets, Brussels (?) 1547
Kometentraktat, Brüssel (?) / *Traité sur les comètes*, Bruxelles (?)
Bodycolour on paper, 11.5 x 13.6 cm (4½ x 5⅜ inches)
London, The Warburg Institute, FMH 1290, fol. 27r

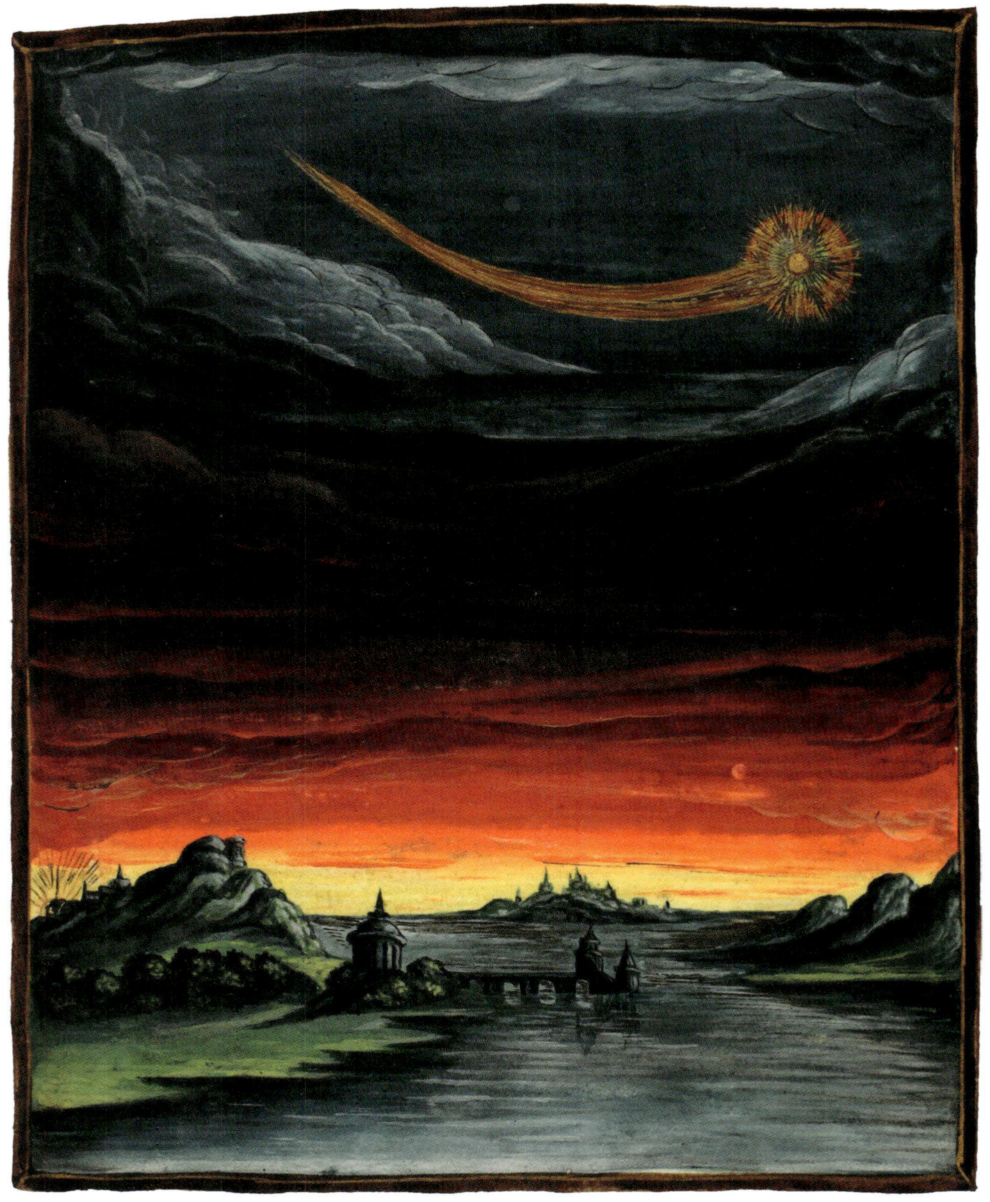

Ain wunderbarlich erschrockenlich gesicht/ so auff den vierdten tag des Mayens dises xxxxiij. Jars in dem dorff Zessenhausen zwů Meyl von Pfortzhaim gesehen worden/ wie dise figur außweißt.

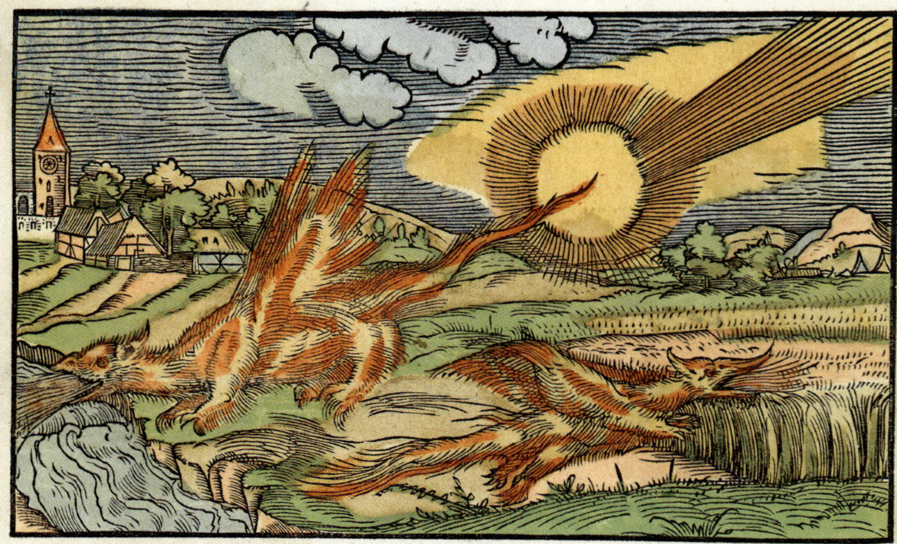

WIr haben Luce am ain vnd zwaintzigsten / Johelis am anderen/ Ezechielis am acht vnnd dreyssigsten/ Osee am zehenden/ Apocalipsi am sechsten. Es werden zaichen geschehen an der Sonnen vnd Mon / vnd Sternen/ vnd auff erden wirt den leüten angst sein / das sy nit wissen wa hinauß ꝛc. Auff das wir brieuen vnd gar war nemen / was Gott allweg hab wöllen würcken / So da Gott nye hatt wöllen die welt von jrem übel straffen / Er hab dann vorher Zaichen / Wunderbarliche gesicht an dem himel / oder auff Erden erscheinen lassen ꝛc. So hatt sich inn dem Jar / als man hatt zelt / Tausent/ fünff hundert/ vnnd drey vnd viertzig/ Auff den vierdten tag May / zwischen vier vnd fünff vrn gegen der nacht/ in ainem Dorff/ zwů meil von Pfortzhaim / Zessenhausen genandt / am himel gesehen worden/ ain Stern mit ainem langen Schwantz / inn der mit so groß wie ain Mülstain/ Auff das hatt sich von dem himel herab gelassen ain feür / die Bauren sagen / es sey ain feüriner Drack gewesen/ welches nur Erhalatio ist / in ainen fliessenden Bach gelassen/ vnd denselbigen Bach gar außgetrücknet / vnd sich widerumb auß dem bach gethon/ mit ainer grausamen vngestüme/ vnd auff ain Gersten acker gelassen / vnd denselbigen acker fünfftzehen schůch weyt sauber verbrendt / vnd darnach hat es sich wider übersich gezogen dem Stern zů/ vnd mit ainander verschwunden/ Es sagen die Bauren inn der selbigen gegend/ es sey das feür so grausam kommen/ vnnd sey dise Erhalation so groß geweßt / das man in den nächsten Dörffern darbey gelegen / hab die Sturm geschlagen/ Sy mainen auch/ die es gesehen haben/ wann es sich in das Dorff hinein hett gezogen/ es hets sauber verbrendt/ das hab ich selbs von fünff Bauren vnd andern glaubwürdigen leüten gehört / die gar grausam daruon sagen / die daselbst dahaimen seind/ vnnd selber gesehen haben/ sy haben sich auch verwegen gehabt jres lebens. Also ist auch gesehen worden inn dem jar/ als man zelt hatt/ Tausent/ fünff hundert/ vnnd zwaintzig/ zů Kaiser Maximilianus zeyten/ ain feüriner langer strom/ als ain Wißbaum. Vnd ist herab gehangt von himel biß auff die erden/ vnd hat sich mit der weil widerūb hinauf geschwungen/ vnd an ain zirckel gelegt/ was geschach im jar darnach/ zoch der Türckisch Kaiser in aigner person das Vngerland zů überfallen/ vñ Kriechischen Weissenburg/ mit etlichen Stetten vnd Schlössern durch verräterey eingenōmen ꝛc. Darumb wie oben anzaigt / seind vns Christen warnungen / darmitt wir von vnnserm sündigen leben abstehn/ vnnd vnns zů Gott keren/ will er vnnser genädiger Gott sein/ wie er dann genaigt ist / Amen.

1543.

Häufig tauchen auch Überschwemmungen in der Handschrift auf. Oft erscheinen sie gemeinsam mit anderen Wetterereignissen und Katastrophen im Bild (fol. 28r, 30r, 47r, 55r, 73r, 75r, 86r, 116r, 118r, 119r). Fluten hatten verheerende Langzeitfolgen, da sie in weiten Gebieten die Ernte und das Vieh vernichteten und eine ernste Bedrohung für Menschen darstellten; außerdem galten sie als „Sündfluten", d.h. als Gottesstrafe par excellence.

Um einen Eindruck von dem Ausmaß der Wassermassen zu vermitteln, zeigen die Abbildungen ein weites Landschaftspanorama in Aufsicht. Berge, Wälder und Städte erscheinen wie Inseln inmitten der sich bis an den Horizont erstreckenden Fluten, in denen Menschen und Tiere sich verzweifelt schwimmend ans Ufer zu retten suchen. Mitunter gibt es Perspektivwechsel: Wird die Überschwemmung des Jahres 570 (in römischen Ziffern, aber fälschlich mit 170 in arabischen Ziffern datiert; fol. 28r) von einem hohen Standpunkt aus gesehen, so wird die Überflutung der Stadt Antiochia (fol. 47r) von einem nur geringfügig oberhalb der Horizontlinie liegenden Punkt aus wiedergegeben.

Lakonisch wird die Überschwemmung der italienischen Flüsse Tiber und Po sowie der mitteleuropäischen Ströme Rhein und Donau ins Bild gesetzt, die laut Bildunterschrift im November 1480 – die mit roter Tinte aufgebrachte Jahreszahl 1482 ist ein Irrtum des Schreibers – stattfand (fol. 86r). Auf einer vom Wasser umspülten Landzunge stehen zwei entlaubte Bäume, während die Fluten beinahe das ganze Land bis an den Horizont überschwemmen. In der reißenden Strömung erkennt man winzige Figuren, die ihre Arme hilfesuchend aus dem Wasser recken.

Auf folio 118r wird indes eine Sturmflut abgebildet, die im November des Jahres 1530 die flämische Küste heimsuchte. Der Maler fasst das Ereignis als regelrechte Wasserlandschaft auf: Menschen retten sich aus den Fluten auf Hügel, die aus den Wassermassen herausragen, oder erklimmen Bäume, um dem Ertrinken zu entgehen. Rechts ist eine im Wasser versunkene Stadt zu sehen, deren Türme eingestürzt sind. Der Beischrift zufolge ist hier die Stadt Vlissingen auf Walcheren gemeint. Es handelt sich um die sogenannte Sint Felixvloed, die kurz nach Allerheiligen die Küsten von Flandern und Zeeland traf und nahezu 100.000 Todesopfer durch Ertrinken, Verhungern oder Seuchen forderte.

Überschwemmungen, Sturmfluten und Erdbeben werden im Wunderzeichenbuch regelmäßig von Dauerregen, Schnee und Hagel begleitet (Abb. 8). Doch auch für sich genommen hatten extreme Wetterphänomene wie Hagel, Schnee und Eis nicht selten Missernten, Hungersnöte und Seuchen zur Folge. Es finden sich gleich mehrere Hagelstürme (fol. 21r, 27r, 47r, 78r, 115r, 171r) und Schneestürme (fol. 44r, 51r, 54r) in der Handschrift. Diese innovativen Darstellungen gehören zu den frühesten Beispielen von Wetterillustrationen.

ILL. 21
Illustrated broadsheet reporting a ball-lightning over Zaisenhausen, 4 May 1543
Flugblatt zur Erscheinung eines Kugelblitzes bei Zaisenhausen, 4. Mai 1543
Feuillet illustré mentionnant l'apparition d'une boule de feu au-dessus de Zaisenhausen, 4 mai 1543
Nuremberg, Germanisches Nationalmuseum,
Graphische Sammlung, inv. HB 2784

Auf zwei Blättern werden schwere Winterjahre und deren Folgen beschrieben. Drastisch setzt der Maler auf folio 42r einen harten Winter im Jahre 1126 ins Bild, der so kalt war, dass Krähen am Himmel erfroren und zur Erde fielen. Während die Beschreibung des Winters im Jahre 1234 (fol. 56r) ebenfalls von einer durch Frost und Kälte verursachten Hungersnot spricht, illustriert der Maler hier das Zufrieren der Wasserwege, auf denen nun Ochsenkarren fahren. Auf folio 44r wird der heftige Schneefall, der im Jahre 1162 Mailand heimsuchte, dargestellt. Durch dichtes Schneegestöber hindurch ist in der Ferne die Silhouette der lombardischen Hauptstadt in einer schneebedeckten Ebene zu sehen.

Blut- und Nahrungswunder

Mehrere Blätter widmen sich der Schilderung von Blutwundern, die vor allem von protestantischer Seite aufgrund der Prophezeiungen der Johannesoffenbarung als Vorzeichen des bevorstehenden Weltuntergangs gedeutet wurden (fol. 21r, 28r, 36r, 38r, 51r, 54r, 71r, 81r, 119r, 167r). Gewässer, die sich Wasser plötzlich in Blut wandeln (fol. 36r), oder die Entdeckung einer blutigen Quelle (fol. 167r) werden gezeigt. Die meisten Darstellungen beziehen sich indes auf Blutregen, ein noch stets vorkommendes Naturphänomen, das auf der Verbreitung von rotgelbem Wüstensand in der Atmosphäre beruht und seit der Antike für Schrecken sorgte. Eine Variante des Blutregens bildet der seltene Blutschnee, der 1226 in der Steiermark (fol. 51r) und erneut 1229 (fol. 54r) belegt und hier in Form stimmungsvoller Winterlandschaften abgebildet ist.

Verwandt mit dem Phänomen des Blutregens ist der Brot- und Mannaregen, so wie er bereits im Alten Testament bezeugt ist (fol. 6r). Ein interessantes Beispiel ist die Darstellung des Kornregens, der am 23. März des Jahres 1550 in Klagenfurt niederging (fol. 166r). Die Handschrift greift einen Einblattholzschnitt auf, der 1550 in Nürnberg entstand und unter anderem in Straßburg kopiert wurde (Abb. 22).

Missgeburten

Die Abbildungen auf den folia 88r, 90r, 97r, 117r, 133r, 145r und 158r zeigen tierische Missgeburten und andere Missbildungen. Nur eine einzige ursprünglich zum Wunderzeichenbuch gehörige Darstellung einer menschlichen Missgeburt ist bekannt, die wohl auf folio 92r folgte. Die tierischen Darstellungen weichen durch ihren Figurenmaßstab von den übrigen Illustrationen der Handschrift ab und verzichten zudem auf eine farbige Gestaltung des Hintergrundes. Nahezu alle der im Manuskript abgebildeten Missgeburten gehen auf Vorlagen aus der Druckgrafik zurück. Einblattholzschnitte, aber auch Kupferstiche von Albrecht Dürer und Wenzel von Olmütz dienten als Motivquellen. Mehrfach werden zwei Missgeburten auf einem einzigen Blatt dargestellt und in einer zweispaltigen Beischrift erläutert. In der Beischrift der Darstellung eines tot geborenen Kalbes auf folio 117r wird Hans Burgkmair als Künstler genannt. Der Name kommt auch auf dem heute in Stuttgart befindlichen Blatt mit den siamesischen Zwillingen vor, die 1513 auf dem Gut der Gräfin Lodron, der Schwester des Kardinals Matthias Lang (1468–1540), in Kärnten zur Welt kamen (für unsere Ausgabe wurde das Blatt an seiner ursprünglichen Stelle als folio 93r eingefügt).

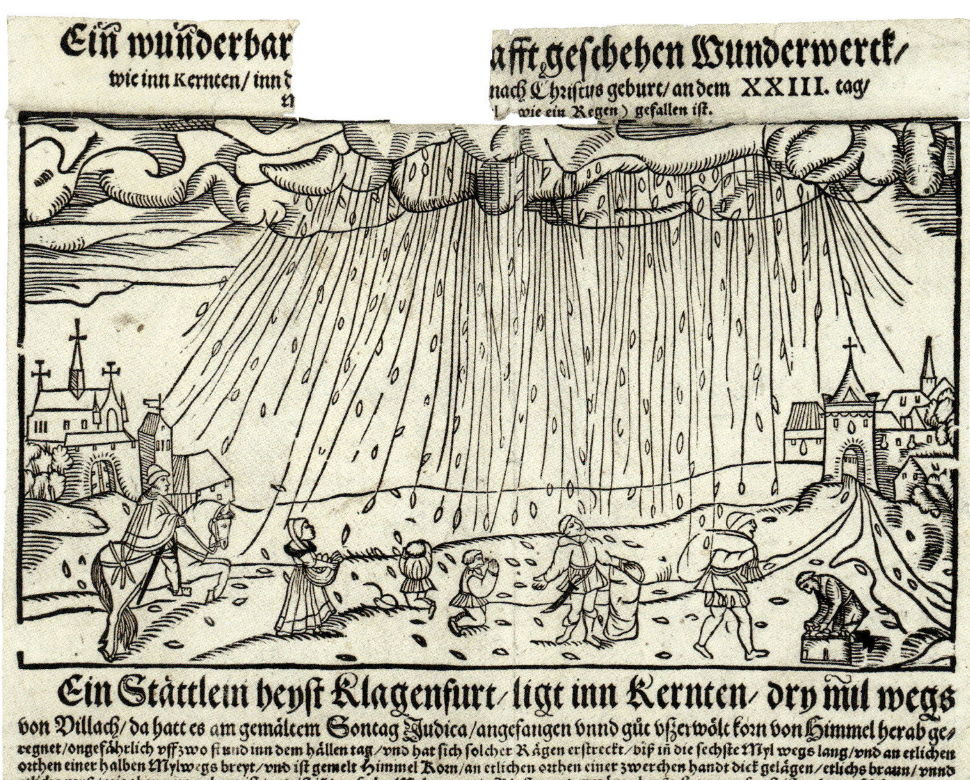

Ein wunderbar … afft geschehen Wunderwerck/
wie inn Kernten/ inn … nach Christus geburt/ an dem XXIII. tag/
… wie ein Regen) gefallen ist.

Ein Stättlein heyst Klagenfurt/ ligt inn Kernten/ dry mil wegs von Villach/ da hatt es am gemältem Sontag Judica/ angefangen vnnd güt vßzerwölt korn von Himmel herab geregnet/ ongefährlich vff zwo stund inn dem hällen tag/ vnd hat sich solcher Rägen erstreckt/ biß in die sechste Myl wegs lang/ vnd an etlichen orthen einer halben Mylwegs breyt/ vnd ist gemelt Himmel Korn/ an etlichen orthen einer zwerchen handt dick gelägen/ etlichs braun/ vnnd etlichs wyß/ wie oben verzeychnet ist/ vnd ist in den sechs Mylen nur ein Kloster vnderwägen heyßt Fytrung/ sunst ist es lutter schön wißmat nach dem aber der Rägen vergangen/ ist das Landtvolck kummen/ Vnd inn grossem wunder das Himmel Korn vffgehaben (wie die Kinder von Israel/ das Himmelbrot inn der Wüsten) vnnd haben das gemalen vnnd nachmals zü güttem wolgeschmacktem Brot gebachen/ ouch ist nachmals solchs Himmelkorn/ hin vnnd wider in vil Landt von einem güten Fründt zü dem anderen/ für ein groß Wunderwerck Gottes/ geschickt worden/ Was aber solchs Himmelkorn bedüt/ ist Gott allein bewüßt/ Dem sy lob/ Eer vnd pryß/ inn allen dingen/ AMEN.

Getruckt nach dem Exemplar/ zü Nürenberg durch Stephan Hamer Brieffmaler vff der Schmeltzhütten/ vßgangen den XX Junij

Ill. 22

A wondrous miracle that truly took place in Carinthia ... when grain fell (like rain) on the 23rd day of March / Ein wunderbar[lich und warh]afft geschehen Wunderwerck wie inn Kernten ... an dem XXIII. Tag [Martij Korn von dem Himme]l (wie ein Regen) gefallen ist / Un miracle merveilleux et vraiment arrivé en Carinthie... le XXIIIe jour de mars, du blé est tombé du ciel (comme de la pluie)

Illustrated broadsheet, Nuremberg 1547

Zurich, Zentralbibliothek, Graphische Sammlung, inv. PAS II 2/23

Gleich drei Motive, die jeweils auf Entwürfe von Heinrich Vogtherr den Älteren (1490–1556) zurückgehen und auf Flugblättern zirkulierten, werden auf folio 158r zusammengeführt. Eine von einem Schmarotzer befallene Weinrebe steht neben einem besonderen Weizenkorn, daneben wird das Wunder des Mädchens aus Roth beschrieben, das angeblich über mehrere Jahre die Nahrungsaufnahme verweigerte und von Spenden lebte – eine beliebte Form mittelalterlichen Sozialbetrugs (Abb. 25, 26).

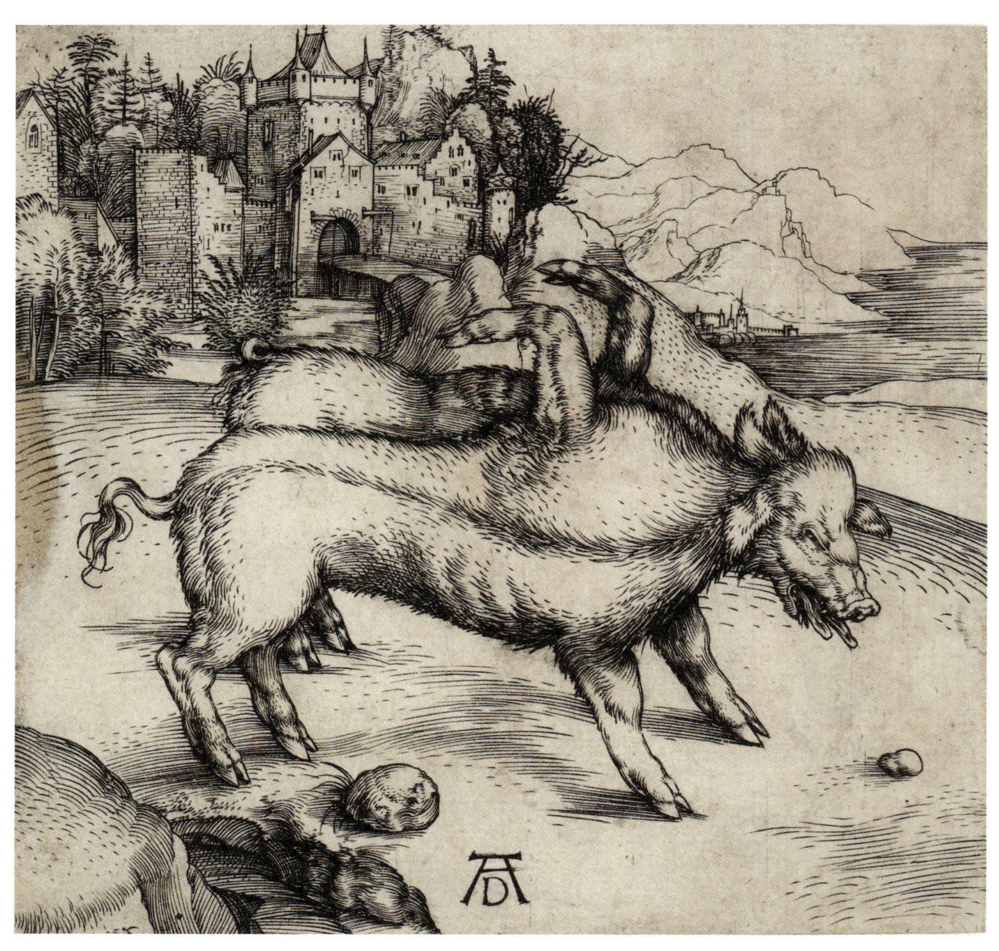

Ill. 23
Albrecht Dürer
Monstrous Pig of Landser, c. 1496
Die wunderbare Sau von Landser / Le monstrueux cochon de Landser
London, British Museum, inv. E,2.157

Die Offenbarung des Johannes

Der Schlussteil des Wunderzeichenbuches widmet sich jenen Zeichen, die in der Offenbarung des Johannes das Ende der Zeiten und das zweite Kommen Christi ankündigen. Das besondere Interesse vor allem reformatorischer Theologen am Studium der Wunderzeichen hing mit deren Überzeugung zusammen, dass sie das Weltenende anzeigten. Unter dieser Prämisse müssen die Darstellungen der Apokalypse, in denen ja nun nochmals Feuerregen, Erdbeben, Überschwemmungen und andere Katastrophen vorkommen, eigentlich als zwangsläufige Konsequenz der Aufzeichnungen von Prodigien gelten, so wie sie in der Handschrift vorgenommen wurden.

Auf heute noch 19 erhaltenen Blättern breitet die Handschrift die Endzeitvision des Johannes aus. Die Darstellungen lehnen sich an den 1539 in Frankfurt publizierten Zyklus *Typi in apocalypsi Ioannis depicti* des Hans Sebald Beham an, der seinerseits wiederum Dürers Apokalypse von 1497/98 paraphrasiert (Abb. 14). Wie im Falle der alttestamentarischen Ereignisse liegt auch hier der wesentliche gestalterische Beitrag in der Anpassung der Bildvorlage an die veränderten Bildproportionen der Handschrift sowie in der farbigen Gestaltung, die noch einmal das herausragende koloristische Gespür der Schöpfer der Wunderzeichenbuch-Illustrationen veranschaulicht.

Die Abfolge der dargestellten Ereignisse folgt dem Beham'schen Apokalypsezyklus, lässt aber einige Passagen aus. Überraschend abrupt scheint das Manuskript die Darstellung der Offenbarung mit dem Fall der Himmlischen Ernte abzubrechen. Doch tatsächlich sind die in der Handschrift überlieferten Illustrationen der Apokalypse unvollständig. Mindestens vier weitere Darstellungen der Johannesoffenbarung wurden am Ende der Handschrift herausgelöst; sie wurden 2005 bei Karl & Faber in München versteigert, ihr Verbleib ist bis auf zwei Blätter (fol. 191r, 192r) unbekannt. Es handelt sich um vier Ereignisse, die am Schluss der Offenbarung stehen, darunter auch die Vision der zwölf Pforten, mit denen der Beham'sche Apokalypsenzyklus schließt.

Datierung, Entstehungsort und Zuschreibung

Die Handschrift entstand Mitte des 16. Jahrhunderts und ist aufgrund des verwendeten Dialektes in Süddeutschland zu lokalisieren. Der auf folio 171r abgebildete Hagelsturm, der die niederländische Stadt Dordrecht 1552 heimsuchte (Abb. 8), ist die jüngste der im Wunderzeichenbuch aufgenommenen Naturkatastrophen und steht unmittelbar vor dem letzten, den Ereignissen der Johannesoffenbarung gewidmeten Teil des Manuskripts.

1552 kann daher als *terminus post quem* für die Vollendung des Codex gelten, der freilich in Phasen verfertigt zu sein scheint. Dass die Beischriften der Bibelillustrationen auf dem Text von Luthers Bibel von 1545 basieren, spricht dafür, den Beginn der Arbeiten danach anzusetzen. Die Datierung der Blätter in die Zeit um 1550 wird durch die Analyse der Wasserzeichen bestätigt, die auch Hinweise auf den Entstehungsort liefert. Zwei Wasserzeichen kommen mehrfach in je zwei Varianten vor. Auf zwanzig Blättern befindet sich ein in einen Vierpass eingestelltes Wappenschild mit einem Kreuz über drei Bergkuppen. Das beinahe vier Zentimeter große Wasserzeichen (ähnlich Piccard 154059/154082) korrespondiert dabei mit Augsburger Urkunden aus der Zeit zwischen 1539 und 1559 (Bower 2009, S. 26–27).

53 Blätter der Handschrift zeigen ein kaum zwei Zentimeter großes Wasserzeichen mit einer Spinne auf einem Schild (ähnlich Piccard 42787, 42788, 42791, 42792). Dieses Wasserzeichen ist Mitte des 16. Jahrhunderts auf Urkunden und Archivalien gängig, die in verschiedenen schwäbischen Städten wie Lauingen, Dillingen, Ulm und Augsburg entstanden (Falk 2005; Bower 2009, S. 27). Auf zwei weiteren Blättern finden sich Fragmente eines Wasserzeichens (ein sechszackiger Stern über einem Anker, ähnlich Piccard 119009), das in österreichischen und oberitalienischen Dokumenten des 16. Jahrhunderts auftaucht, aber auch in einem 1550 in Augsburg ausgestellten

Dokument nachweisbar ist (vgl. Bower 2009). Bekräftigen die Wasserzeichen eine Entstehung in den Jahren um 1550, so suggerieren die Referenzurkunden, dass die Handschrift in Schwaben geschaffen wurde.

Bemerkenswert häufig werden Ereignisse beschrieben, die sich in Augsburg und Umgebung zutrugen (fol. 73r, 74r, 78r, 113r, 115r, 117r, 138r, 144r, 145r, 149r, 154r, 159r, 164r). Dies trifft vor allem auf Geschehnisse zu, die sich zeitnah zur Entstehung der Handschrift ereigneten (fol. 113r und folgende). Auch darum liegt es nahe, den Ursprung der Handschrift in Augsburg zu vermuten, einem im 16. Jahrhundert auf dem Gebiet der Wissenschaften und Künste führenden Handelszentrum in Süddeutschland.

Mehrere Indizien bestätigen diese Hypothese: So spricht die Beischrift einer Erscheinung von Nebensonnen im Jahre 1541 (fol. 139r), „man [habe] hie zu augspurg drey sonnen in driangel gesehen“, was den direkten Zusammenhang zwischen dem Text und dem abgebildeten Ereignis herstellt. Lediglich an drei weiteren Stellen taucht das Wort „hie/hier“ als Ortszusatz auf, und die Beschreibungen von Ereignissen in den Jahren 1542 (fol. 144r) und 1547 (fol. 159r) nehmen erneut explizit auf Augsburg Bezug. Auch auf folio 156r und folio 164r ist anlässlich von Himmelserscheinungen davon die Rede, dass diese „hie am hiemel“ gesehen worden seien, allerdings geht aus dem Text nicht hervor, wo die Ereignisse stattfanden. Im Kontext der Handschrift betrachtet ist freilich deutlich, dass „hie“ erneut Augsburg meint.

Der Bezug zur schwäbischen Reichsstadt geht auch aus der Beschreibung zweier Missgeburten des 16. Jahrhunderts hervor, die mit schwäbischen Orten wie Langweid, Donauwörth (fol. 117r) und Dillingen (fol. 145r) in Verbindung gebracht werden. Die Entstehung der Handschrift in Augsburg kann erklären, warum ausgerechnet auf diesen beiden Blättern Künstler Erwähnung finden, die in der Stadt tätig waren oder von dort wesentliche Impulse empfingen. Die auf folio 145r neben der Abbildung eines Mönchfischs überlieferte Darstellung eines Kükens, das 1543 mit Missbildungen zur Welt kam, geht der Beischrift zufolge auf eine Vorlage zurück, die vom Hofmaler des in Dillingen residierenden Augsburger Bischofs stammt (Abb. 11). Möglicherweise war hiermit Bischof Christoph von Stadion (1478–1543) gemeint, der die Bischofsresidenz nach Dillingen verlegt hatte. Vermutlich aber handelte es sich um Otto Truchsess von Waldburg (1514–1573), der 1543 den Augsburger Bischofsthron bestieg und sich während seines 30-jährigen Episkopats um die Förderung gegenreformatorischer Kunst in Schwaben bemühte. Wer indes 1543 als bischöflicher Hofmaler fungierte und ob dieses Hofamt damals formal überhaupt bestand, ist fraglich.

Auf folio 117r sind zwei missgestaltete Kreaturen auf einer einzigen Seite abgebildet. Eines der missgebildeten Kälber kam am 14. Januar 1529 in Langweid bei Augsburg tot zur Welt, das andere wurde 1532 nahe Donauwörth lebend geboren. Auch auf diesem Blatt taucht der Name eines Augsburger Künstlers auf. In Bezug auf das erste Tier heißt es in der Beischrift: „vnnd ich hanns Bur: ckmair maler hab die haut vmb ein halben gulden kaufft von einem biermenter [Pergamentmacher], der sie nur vmb vi kreuzter kauff hat“. Mit dieser auch formal bemerkenswerten Aussage – es ist die einzige Textpassage der gesamten Handschrift, in der die Ich-Form verwendet wird (abgesehen von fol. 118r, wo der Quellentext in der ersten Person verfasst ist) – wird das Wunderzeichenbuch mit dem Namen Burgkmair verknüpft.

Bereits im Zusammenhang mit dem aus dem Buch herausgelösten Blatt mit Vorder- und Rückenansicht siamesischer Zwillinge aus dem Jahre 1513 war von Hans Burgkmair die Rede, auf dessen Vorlage die Abbildung beruht (siehe oben, Falk 2005; fol. 93r). Hans Burgkmair der Ältere, der berühmte Augsburger Künstler, der unter anderem mit Entwürfen für den Triumphzug Kaiser Maximilians betraut worden war und mit Hans Holbein dem Älteren (um 1465–1524) die Basilikabilder für das Augsburger Dominikanerkloster schuf (Krause 2002, S. 290ff.), ist als Schöpfer der ja erst Jahrzehnte nach seinem Tod entstandenen Handschrift auszuschließen.

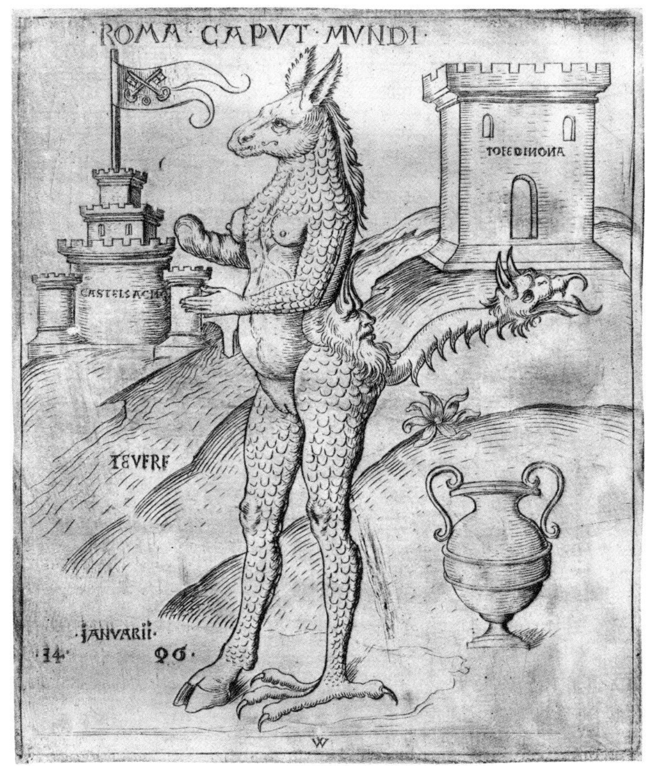

Vermutlich handelt es sich bei dem auf folio 117r erwähnten Maler um dessen Sohn Hans Burgkmair den Jüngeren, der am 15. Oktober 1531 offiziell in die Augsburger Malerzunft aufgenommen wurde und die Werkstatt des damals verstorbenen Vaters übernahm. Seine Ausbildung hatte er im väterlichen Atelier durchlaufen, in dem er nach der Lehrzeit beschäftigt blieb. Zu den wenigen beurkundeten Arbeiten zählen zwölf Wappenmalereien, die er für die Totenfeier Kaiser Maximilians schuf, sowie seine Beteiligung an den Dekorationen der Trauerfeierlichkeiten für Kaiser Karl V. im Jahre 1559; daneben sind von ihm einige mit dem Monogramm HB bezeichnete Zeichnungen und Grafiken bekannt. Ansonsten liegt sein Wirken im Dunkeln, Urkunden bezeugen mitunter prekäre wirtschaftliche Verhältnisse (vgl. Selig 1997, S. 217–218; Seidl 2012, S. 22–28). Da er 1536, 1548, 1549 und 1559 Lehrlinge aufnahm, dürfte seine Werkstatt trotz der schwierigen Periode zwischen dem protestantischen Bildersturm im Jahre 1537 und der Verkündung des Augsburger Religionsfriedens im Jahre 1555 floriert haben.

Ill. 24
Wenzel von Olmütz
Roma caput mundi, *c.* 1496–1500
Engraving, 12.4 x 10.4 cm (4⅞ x 4⅛ in.)
London, British Museum, inv. E,1.15

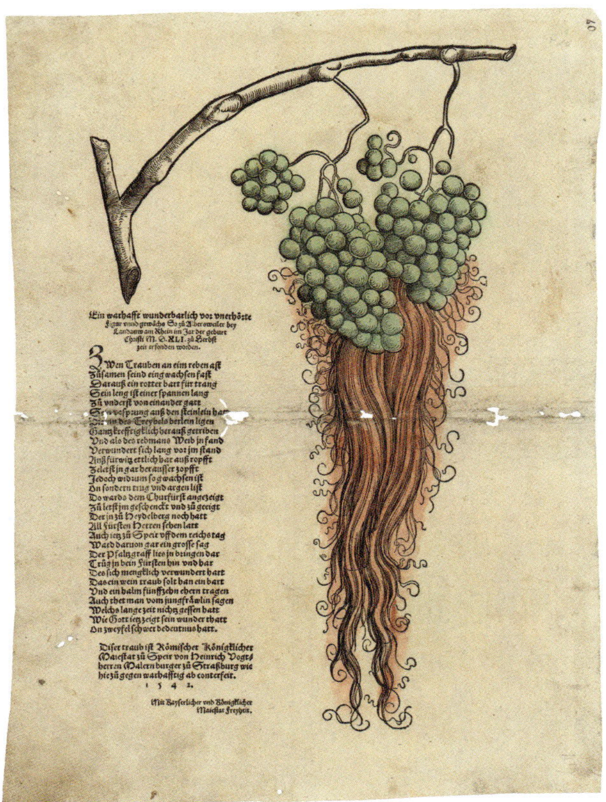

Die ihm zugeschriebenen Holzschnitte, Radierungen und Zeichnungen sind entweder unmittelbar vom Schaffen und von Vorlagen des Vaters abhängig oder werden als künstlerisch wie technisch minder versiert eingestuft. In gleich mehreren Fassungen sind Turnierbücher mit Illustrationen von seiner Hand überliefert, die er auf Grundlage der väterlichen Vorzeichnungen für den Triumphzug Kaiser Maximilians I. anfertigte (Wien 2012). Das älteste dieser Turnierbücher (München, Staatliche Graphische Sammlung) gilt als eine von Vater und Sohn gemeinsam ausgeführte Handschrift für Herzog Wilhelm IV. von Bayern (1493–1550). Eng verwandt ist ein zweites Turnierbuch (Bayerische Staatsbibliothek, Cod. Icon 403), das vermutlich um 1540 entstand und daher wohl integral dem jüngeren Burgkmair zuzuweisen ist (Abb. 12). Durch Signatur als sein Werk beglaubigt ist der letzte, 1553 datierte Abschnitt eines dreiteiligen, partiell wiederum von der Triumphzugsfolge abhängiges Turnierbuch in Sigmaringen (Hofbibliothek, HS 63), das um die Mitte des 16. Jahrhunderts entstand (Reuter 2010; Seidl 2012). Die mit Deckfarben kolorierten Federzeichnungen zeigen ein beeindruckendes Gespür für Farbgebung und zeugen von der souveränen Beherrschung der Gouachetechnik, ähnlich wie die Illustrationen des Wunderzeichenbuches. Insbesondere die nuancierte Applikation von Gold und Silber in den Turnierbuchillustrationen erinnert an die behutsam in Gold und Silber angebrachten Glanzlichter auf den Kometenillustrationen der Handschrift.

Ill. 25
Heinrich Vogtherr the Elder
A truly wondrous ... figure and plant found in autumn in the year ... 1541 at Albersweiler near Landau on the Rhine / Ein warhafft wunderbarlich ... figur unnd gewächs So zu Albersweiler bey Landauw am Rhein im Jar ... 1541 zu Herbstzeit erfonden worden / Une forme végétale vraiment merveilleuse découverte à Albersweiler près de Landauw sur le Rhin en l'automne de l'an... 1541
Illustrated boardsheet, 1541. Zurich, Zentralbibliothek, Graphische Sammlung, inv. PAS II 12/25

Auch die Eisenradierungen des *Ernwertes Geschlechter Buch Der löblichen deß Heiligen Reichs Statt Augspurg Patricorium* werden großenteils dem jüngeren Burgkmair zugeschrieben. Wie man dem Frontispiz der ursprünglich für 1545 geplanten Ausgabe entnimmt, stammen die Radierungen von Hans Burgkmair und Heinrich Vogtherr, wobei man sowohl an Heinrich Vogtherr den Älteren als an dessen Sohn (1513–1568) dachte (Falk in Augsburg 2011, S. 190–192; Seidl 2012). Ein 2010 an die Stuttgarter Staatsgalerie restituierter Sammelband mit 44 Federzeichnungen und 53 Probedrucken des Augsburger Geschlechterbuchs enthält eigenhändige Arbeiten Burgkmairs (vgl. Seidl 2012). Die Entwürfe entstanden, nachdem 1538 die Anzahl der Patrizier- und Adelsfamilien in Augsburg erhöht worden war, die an der politischen Gestaltung der städtischen Geschicke teilhaben durften (Geschlechtervermehrung). Sie liefern aufgrund ihres ausschließlich zeichnerischen Charakters allerdings keine stilistischen Anhaltspunkte, mit denen sich die malerisch-atmosphärisch aufgefassten Illustrationen des Wunderzeichenbuches vergleichen ließen.

Freilich lässt die Kooperation zwischen dem jüngeren Burgkmair und Vogtherr aufhorchen, denn auch das Wunderzeichenbuch enthält Abbildungen, die auf Entwürfe von Heinrich Vogtherr den Älteren zurückgehen. So wurden die drei Motive auf folio 158r Einblattholzschnitten entnommen, die nach Vorlagen des aus Dillingen stammenden Künstlers produziert worden waren (Abb. 25, 26). Dass die innerhalb der Handschrift einzigartige Kombination von drei Motiven auf einem einzigen Blatt zugleich auf einen einzigen Künstler zurückgeführt werden kann, der noch dazu aus Schwaben stammt, wirft Fragen in Bezug auf eine etwaige Beteiligung Heinrich Vogtherrs des Älteren an den Illustrationen der Handschrift auf.

Der 1490 in Dillingen geborene Künstler, der dort die Lateinschule besuchte und anschließend in Augsburg zum Maler ausgebildet wurde, war der Sohn eines Wund- und Augenarztes und durchlief selbst eine äußerst wechselvolle Karriere als Maler, Entwerfer, Verleger und Augenarzt. Sie führte ihn über Erfurt (1510), Leipzig (1514), Augsburg (1518) und Wimpfen am Neckar (1522) nach Straßburg, wo er 1526 das Bürgerrecht erwarb. Zwischen 1536 und 1540 betrieb Vogtherr, der bereits zuvor als Entwerfer von Holzschnitten regen Kontakt zu Verlegern in Augsburg und Basel unterhalten hatte, in Straßburg eine eigene Presse, in der er 1537 das erste gedruckte Musterbuch veröffentlichte. Auf insgesamt 700 Abbildungen illustrierte das *Kunstbüchlin* u. a. Vorbilder für Gesichter, Hände, Hieb- und Stichwaffen, Rüstungen, Ornamente (Abb. 34). Entworfen hatte sie der ältere Vogtherr gemeinsam mit seinem Sohn Heinrich, dessen Porträtmedaillon neben dem des Vaters auf dem Titelblatt des Kunstbüchleins erschien (Abb. 35). Aufgrund finanzieller Probleme schloss die Presse 1540, und der nicht zuletzt durch die Reformation bedingte Mangel an Aufträgen führte dazu, dass der jüngere Vogtherr die väterliche Werkstatt im folgenden Jahr verließ und nach Augsburg zog, wo er sich Ende März 1541 als Freimeister niederließ.

Heinrich Vogtherr der Ältere reiste 1542 von Straßburg zum Reichstag nach Speyer und sodann nach Augsburg, um dort für einige Monate bei seinem Sohn zu verbleiben. Die Reise führte ihn 1543 über Basel nach Zürich, wo er als Illustrator wirkte. Ein letzter Aufenthalt in Augsburg erfolgte während des dortigen Reichstags von 1547/48. Womöglich mit Aussicht auf eine Anstellung am Hofe Ferdinands I. zog Vogtherr am Ende seines Lebens nach Wien, wo er bis zu seinem Tode als Künstler und Augenarzt tätig war.

Aufgrund der für den älteren Vogtherr bezeugten Lebensstationen ist dessen umfassende persönliche Mitarbeit an dem größtenteils zwischen 1545 und 1552 in Augsburg entstandenen Wunderzeichenbuch nicht plausibel. Möglich erscheint dagegen eine Mitarbeit von Heinrich Vogtherr dem Jüngeren, der in seiner Augsburger Werkstatt auf Bildvorlagen des Vaters zurückgreifen konnte. Ähnlich wie im Falle des jüngeren Burgkmair, dessen Wirken kaum je aus dem väterlichen Schatten hervortritt, erschließt sich auch das Schaffen von Heinrich Vogtherr dem Jüngeren als Fortsetzung der väterlichen Kunst, ohne dass die jeweilige Autorschaft von Vater und Sohn abschließend geklärt wäre. So wurde zuletzt in Bezug auf die Zuschreibungen der Zeichnungen und Radierungen des Augsburger Geschlechterbuchs argumentiert, dass Hans Burgkmair der Jüngere hier keineswegs mit Heinrich Vogtherr dem Älteren kooperiert habe, sondern vielmehr mit dessen Sohn (Seidl 2012).

Heinrich Vogtherr der Jüngere wirkte zwischen Frühjahr 1541 und Ende 1554 dauerhaft in Augsburg. Hier leitete er eine erfolgreiche Werkstatt, in der drei Lehrlinge das Malerhandwerk erlernten, darunter seit 1547 Antonius Breu, der Sohn des Malers Jörg Breu des Jüngeren (um 1510–1547). 1555 begab sich Heinrich Vogtherr der Jüngere unter Beibehaltung seines Augsburger Bürgerrechts zu seinem im Sterben liegenden Vater nach Wien, wo er im Auftrag des habsburgischen Hofes unter anderem mit Entwürfen für Münzen, Banner und heraldische Malereien betraut war, eine Nachzeichnung des Maximiliangrabes anfertigte und an den Dekorationen zur Totenfeier Kaiser Ferdinands I. im Jahre 1564 beteiligt wurde.

Wie im Falle des jüngeren Burgkmair ist es unmöglich, die Mitarbeit von Heinrich Vogtherr dem Jüngeren am Wunderzeichenbuch stilistisch zu prüfen. Die Vogtherr zugeschriebenen Holzschnitte und Radierungen sind schon aufgrund unterschiedlicher Bildmedien nicht mit der Handschrift vergleichbar. Lediglich zwei seiner Studienblätter weisen Analogien zu den Illustrationen auf: Das Deckfarbenbild eines Fischkopfes (Abb. 36) ist durch das Monogramm HV als Werk des jüngeren Vogtherr beglaubigt, trägt die Jahreszahl 1564 und entstand demnach in Wien. Das Blatt zeigt die souveräne Beherrschung der Gouachetechnik und veranschaulicht zugleich eine den Naturstudien Albrecht Dürers verwandte, beinahe wissenschaftlich anmutende Neugier, die letztlich auch viele Illustrationen des Wunderzeichenbuches auszeichnet.

Die andere Studie ist eine auf graublau grundiertem Papier ausgeführte Pinselzeichnung, über die systematisch Weißhöhungen aufgebracht wurden (Abb. 13). Die früher Heinrich Vogtherr dem Älteren zugeschriebene Zeichnung (Rowlands 1993; Müller 1997) zeigt den im Buch Exodus beschriebenen Kampf zwischen Amalekitern und dem Volk Israel (Ex. 17,8-16). Die links mit HVE monogrammierte Zeichnung trägt die Jahreszahl 1542 und entstand in der Augsburger Werkstatt des jüngeren Vogtherr.

Zuerst wies Giulia Bartrum auf Analogien zwischen dieser Zeichnung und den Illustrationen des Wunderzeichenbuches hin (Day & Faber 2010). Tatsächlich sind Parallelen erkennbar, so sind zum Beispiel Pferd und Reiter der auf folio 126r abgebildeten Himmelserscheinung mit der Figurenauffassung der Zeichnung vergleichbar, und die dort sichtbaren Weißhöhungen ähneln in ihrem Auftrag den Wolkendarstellungen im Wunderzeichenbuch (zum Beispiel fol. 102r, 124r, 126r).

Ein wunderbarlich Mirackel von einem Meidlin von Rod

in Speirer Bistum/so in zwölff wochen vnd zweien jaren sich on leiblich speis enthalten/noch in obgemeltem Dorff bey Vater vnd Můtter in leib vnd leben ist.

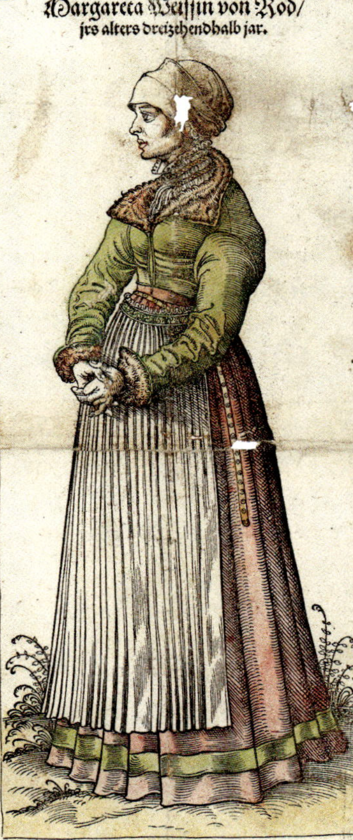

Margareta Weissin von Rod/
jrs alters dreizehendhalb jar.

EIn warhafftig Contrafactur
Hie angezeigt/auch recht figur/
Eins junckfrewlins Margreta gnant/
So in dem Bistum Sper vnd landt
Geboren in eim dorff heist Rod/
Durch Götlich fürsehung vnd gnad
Im tausent fünff hundert XXIX. jar
Durch Seufrid Weyssen/das ist war/
Barbara heist jr Můtter frum/
Vnd hat neun kind in einer sum/
So noch in leib vnd leben sind:
Hans heist das erstgeboren kind/
Margret das ander jr gepurt/
So alhie angezeiget würdt/
Wendel das drit/ Barbel das vierdt/
Heinrich der fünfft geheissen würdt/
Das sechste kindt heist Katarein/
Der sibend Claus ein knab gar fein/
Der acht heist Jacob wie ich sag/
Des neundten sie im kindtbet lag/
Als diss Margret ab ward gemalt
In rechter leng/form/vnd gestalt/
Wie oben die schwartz ling vnd strich/
Jr rechte leng thůt weysen dich/
So du der VIII. hast in der zal/
Hast jr gantz lenge vberal:
Kam auff Laurenti in die welt.
Vnd als man dreissig neune zelt/
Nemlichen auff den Weinacht tag
Sie fürterhin keinr speis mer pflag/
Biss Pfingsten aber tranck sie noch/
Darnach ist sie abgstanden och
Von aller leiblichn speis vnd tranck/
Vnd sechs vnd zweintzig monat langk
Nichts zů noch von jr gangen gar/
Allein durch Gottes gwalt fürwar
Erhalten vnd erneret würdt/
Auch gantz kein arglist hie gespürt/
Dann Könighliche Maiestat
Das jungfrewlin probiret hat
In der stat Speir auff dem Reichstag
Zwölff gantzer tag lang/wie ich sag/
Durch seinen Doctor/ Gerhart gnant/
Auch Heinrich Starcken wol erkant/
So in der zeit nie von jm gwichen
Im tag vnd nacht steiff nachgestrichen/
Vnd gleich sein gwand gezogen ab/
Damit es gar nichts bey jm hab/
Hand jm new kleider angethon/
So jm der König hat machen lon/
Ein braunen Rock mit Atlas bleit/
Wie dann hie gründtlich conterfeit/
Grün Atlas vbermůder zwar
Mit rotem beltz gefütert gar.
Vnd als Köngliche Maiestat
Den waren ernst gesehen hat/
Vnd gantz kein trug noch list gespürt/
Hat er zu der kleidung vnd zierd
Ein müntz zehen Ducaten schwehr
Auch ein gantz Lündsch tůch zu verehr
Dem Vater geben/das er sich
Sein Weib vnd Kinder kleid geleich/
Sind auch von Cur vnd Fürsten wert
Begabt vnd gantz reichlich verehrt/
Auch weils der Köng verwaret hat
Auff dem tag zu Speir in der stat.
Ist aus gunst vnd sonder gnad
So K. Kön. Maiestat bewilget hat
Durch meister Heinrichen Vogther
Auch Hansen Schiesser sein Vetter
Das Meidlin war abconterfeit/
Sein grös/sein leng sampt seinem kleidt
Vnd so gantz eigentlicher gstalt
Gantz vleissig auff ein Thůch gemalt/
Könglicher Maiestat zu lob
Durch sie verehrt zu einer gab.
Darumb der König sie gefreyt/
Daß jn niemant in langer zeyt
Dise Figur nachdrücken sol/
Was aber Gott zu disem mal
Anzeigen wöl durch solch geschicht
Kein mensch auff erd mag wissen nicht/
Dann gwiß würt solch mirakel groß
Etwas mitbringen solcher maß/
Das vns erschrecken würt schwerlich/
Drumb bitten Gott von Himelreich/
Das er vns vergeb allensamen/
Das helff vns Gott/nu sprechet Amen.
J. W. Z. C.

Mit Keiserlicher vnd Königlicher May. freyheit/auff zehen jar nicht nach zudrucken/bey peen vnd straff zehen marck lötigs golds.

Also zu drucken gefertiget/durch Hansen Schiessern Maler zu Wormbs/ im jar nach der gepurt Christi M. D. XLII. vnd volendt am XXI. tag Martij.

ILL. 26
After Heinrich Vogtherr the Elder
A wondrous miracle of a young maid / Ein wunderbarlich Mirackel von einem Meidlin
Un miracle prodigieux au sujet d'une jeune fille
Illustrated boardsheet, 1542. Zurich, Zentralbibliothek, Graphische Sammlung, inv. PAS II 12/23

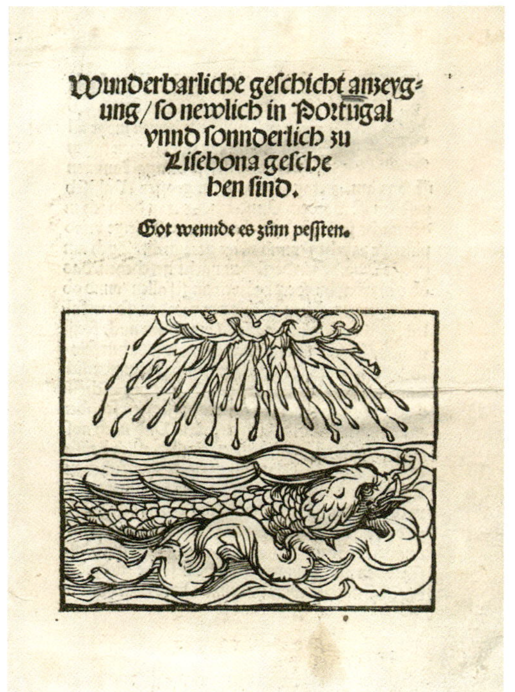

Wunderbarliche geschicht anzeyg-
ung/ so newlich in Portugal
vnnd sonnderlich zu
Lisebona gesche
hen sind.

Got wennde es zum pessten.

Dass außer Vogtherr und Burgkmair noch weitere Maler an der Ausstattung des Wunderzeichenbuches beteiligt waren, entspricht nicht nur den Realitäten frühneuzeitlicher Werkstattpraxis, sondern erschließt sich auch aus der heterogenen Qualität der Illustrationen. Das Spektrum reicht dabei von sorgsam ausgearbeiteten Figuren bis hin zu regelrechten Strichmännchen, umfasst abwechslungsreiche, tief gestaffelte Landschaftsräume und spektakuläre Himmels- und Kometenbilder, aber auch schematisch aufgefasste Stadtsilhouetten, reduzierte Naturdarstellungen und Motivwiederholungen. In den qualitativen Diskrepanzen offenbart sich die Mitwirkung von Mitarbeitern und Lehrlingen, die unter Aufsicht wirkten und auf Vorlagen im Atelierverband zurückgreifen mussten.

Höchstwahrscheinlich entstand das Wunderzeichenbuch nicht in einem Zug. Die Szenen des Alten Testaments am Beginn der Handschrift und die am Ende stehenden Bilder zur Johannesoffenbarung wurden womöglich erst als selbstständige Zyklen konzipiert, als die Arbeit an den Wunderzeichen des umfangreichen Mittelteiles schon begonnen worden war. Ganz offensichtlich wurde Wert auf ein einheitliches Erscheinungsbild der Handschrift gelegt, und es wurde Sorge getragen, dass die biblischen Bildzyklen nicht wesentlich von den übrigen Illustrationen abwichen.

Aufgrund von Differenzen im Schriftbild und deutlichen Veränderungen im Textspiegel der Beischriften darf man vermuten, dass das Wunderzeichenbuch von verschiedenen Schreibern verfasst wurde, die womöglich während unterschiedlicher Phasen in die Ausstattung der Handschrift involviert waren. Unter Berücksichtigung von Schriftwechsel und Differenzen im Textspiegel lassen sich mindestens drei Phasen unterscheiden.

Ill. 27
Title page of the pamphlet** | **Titelblatt von der Flugschrift** | **Page de titre de l'opuscule
Wunderbarliche geschicht anzeygung, so newlich in Portugal vnnd sonnderlich zu Lisebona geschehen sind,
Augsburg 1531. Munich, Bayerische Staatsbibliothek, inv. Rar. 271, Beibd. 2

Pages 64–65
1534 – Sea creature** | **Meeresgeschöpf** | **Créature marine
in: *Book of Miracles*, Augsburg, *c.* 1550–1552, fol. 133r (detail). Private collection

Das Manuskript wurde weitestgehend von einem Schreiber ausgeführt; sein Beitrag umfasst den alttestamentarischen Teil sowie den überwiegenden Teil der Beischriften im zweiten Teil der Handschrift. Das an die Schriften des Augsburger Ratsschreibers Clemens Jäger (vgl. München 2010, S. 32–35) gemahnende Schriftbild auf den Blättern der Johannesapokalypse ähnelt den Beischriften dieses Kerns und stammt vermutlich von demselben Schreiber, der hier allerdings wesentlich mehr Text einzupassen hatte. Mit diesem Kernbestand ist auch die Beischrift auf folio 154r verwandt, die demselben Textspiegel folgt, aber ganz offensichtlich von einem anderen Schreiber stammt, sowie die heute separat in Stuttgart aufbewahrte Darstellung siamesischer Zwillinge nach Burgkmair dem Älteren (fol. 93r).

Eine zweite Gruppe umfasst Blätter mit zweispaltig konzipierten Beischriften. Die Schriftzüge der Texte ähneln denen der Kernblätter, stammen aber möglicherweise von einer anderen Hand und deuten womöglich eine aufgegebene Planänderung an. Zweispaltige Beischriften finden sich zwischen folio 94r und folio 107r (mit Ausnahme von fol. 100r und fol. 101r, die den konventionellen Textspiegel wahren) sowie abermals auf den folia 117r, 145r und 158r. Der erste Teil setzt mit einer Himmelserscheinung im Jahre 1513 ein und umfasst die auf ursprünglich wohl sechs Blätter verteilten Erscheinungen von Polarlichtern und Nebensonnen über Wien im Januar des Jahres 1520 (siehe oben); die übrigen zweispaltig angelegten Blätter sind Darstellungen von Missgeburten und Ähnlichem gewidmet, die auf Vorlagen von Burgkmair, Vogtherr sowie dem Hofmaler des Augsburger Bischofs zu Dillingen zurückgehen (siehe oben).

Die in der Schlussphase der Handschrift hinzugefügten Blätter sind durch Abweichungen im Schriftbild zu erkennen. Diese Phase umfasst mehrere Blätter am Ende des zweiten Teils der Handschrift, unmittelbar vor der Johannesoffenbarung. Der hier nun wieder einspaltige Text ist mit einer vergleichsweise verschnörkelten Schrift niedergeschrieben, die sich vor allem in den dekorativ-kalligrafischen Verzierungen wesentlich von den übrigen Beischriften unterscheidet. Die aus dieser Phase der Entstehung der Handschrift stammenden Blätter setzen mit einem Ereignis des Jahres 1533 auf folio 129r ein, das sich zwischen zwei Blättern der Kerngruppe befindet. Es wurde ebenso wie das folgende aus dieser Endphase stammende Blatt (fol. 144r) womöglich erst in der abschließenden Redaktion der Handschrift eingefügt. Weitere Einzelblätter aus dieser Kampagne folgen auf folio 153r und 157r. Dann schließen sich auf folio 160r bis 170r die zeitlich jüngsten Darstellungen von Wunderzeichen in der Handschrift an, die sich auf Ereignisse der Jahre 1549 bis 1551 beziehen und möglicherweise Teil eines später hinzugefügten Nachtrags sind.

Die Handschrift entstand damit zeitlich und örtlich in unmittelbarer Nähe zu einem 1555 gleichfalls in Augsburg geschaffenen, dem späteren Kaiser Ferdinand I. zugeeigneten Prachtband von Cyprian Leowitz' (1524–1574) *Eclipses luminarium,* in dem der in Augsburg wirkende Gelehrte alle Sonnen- und Mondfinsternisse bis zum Jahre 1605 berechnet hat. Die wissenschaftlichen Illustrationen dieses astronomischen Traktats sowie die hierin enthaltenen Genreszenen (Abb. 37), welche die auch in Augsburg verbreitete Tradition von Monatsbildern aufgreifen, sind zwar nicht vom Wunderzeichenbuch und dessen Künstlern unmittelbar abhängig, sie veranschaulichen aber, dass die Illustrationen der Prodigienhandschrift innerhalb einer heute nur noch schwer fassbaren Bildtradition stehen und zugleich ein neues Genre der wissenschaftlichen Illustration zu begründen scheinen.

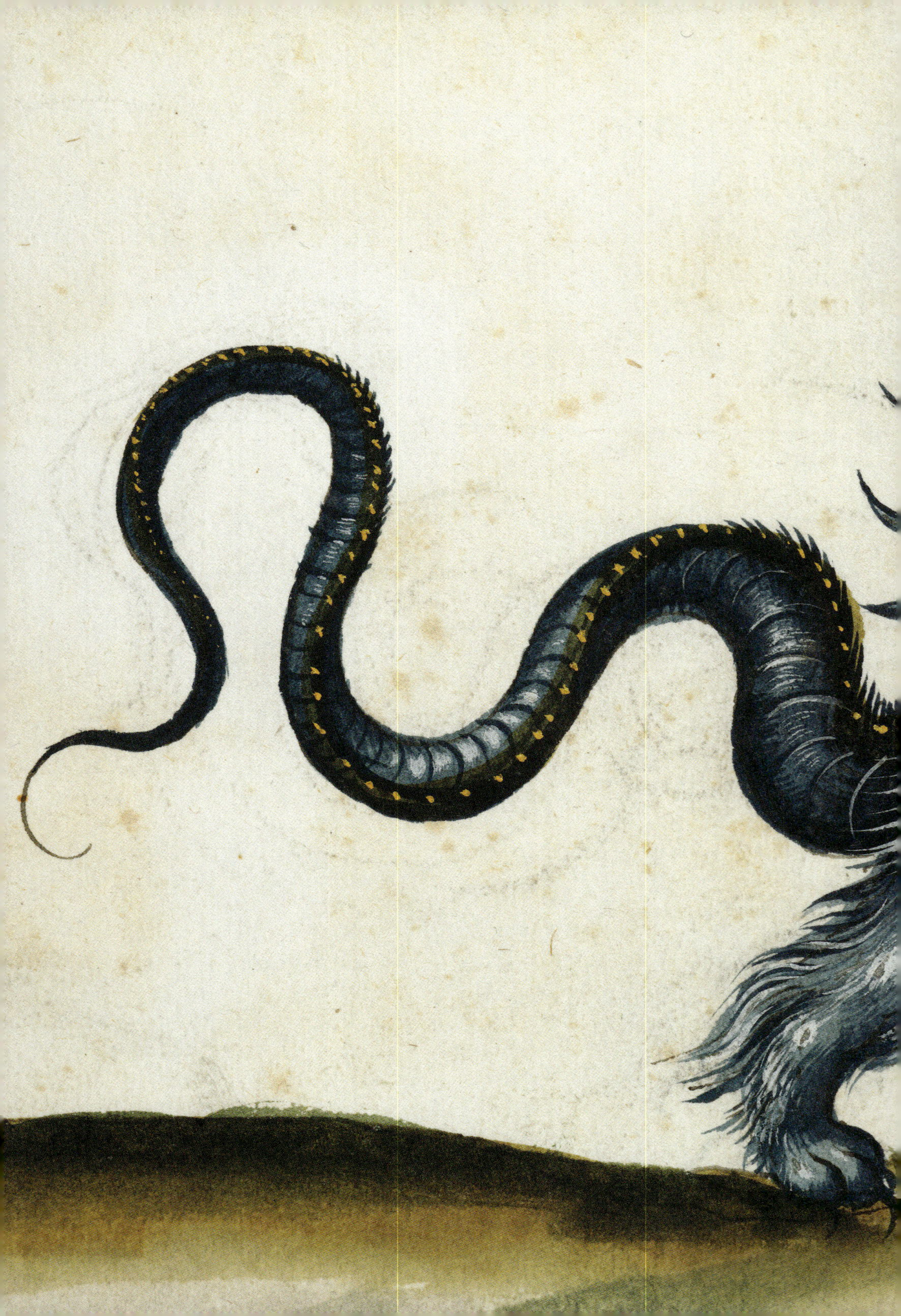

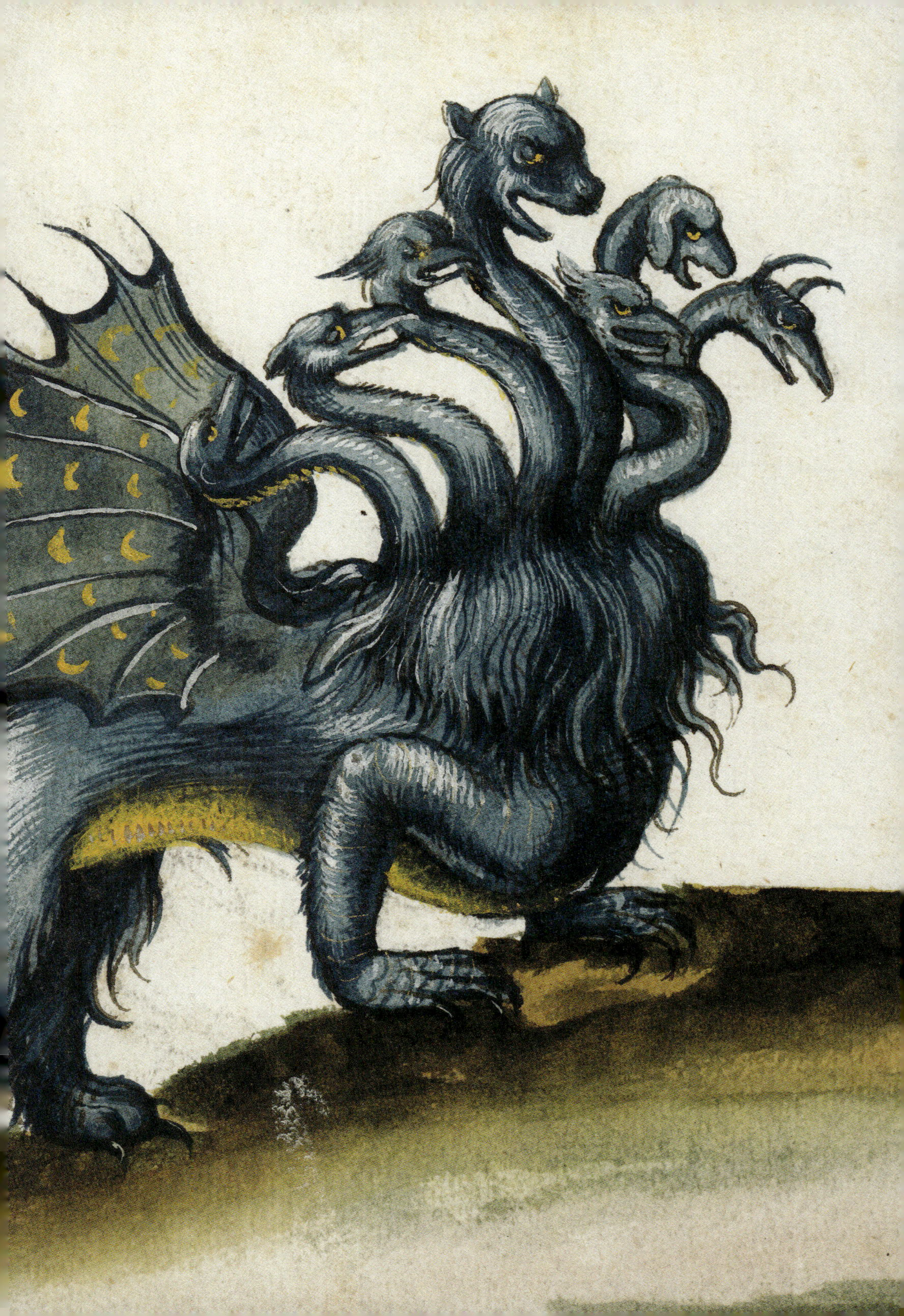

TILL-HOLGER BORCHERT

Le Livre des miracles

Genèse, style et signification

Ce manuscrit rassemble des récits et des reproductions de faits miraculeux survenus à l'époque vétérotestamentaire (fol. 1r–15r) au milieu du XVIe siècle (fol. 91r–171r) en passant par l'Antiquité (fol. 16r–30r), le Moyen Âge et le bas Moyen Âge (fol. 32r–90r) jusqu'au XVIe siècle (fol. 91r–171r). Il s'achève sur des illustrations de phénomènes célestes décrits dans l'Apocalypse de Jean (fol. 172r–192r), qui annoncent le retour du Christ, le Jugement dernier et le royaume de Dieu à venir. Ce manuscrit vise donc à un traitement complet des signes miraculeux, dans la mesure où il ne s'intéresse pas seulement à la période qui va de la création de l'humanité à l'époque contemporaine de l'ouvrage, mais aussi aux signes annoncés pour la fin du monde. Il a l'ambition de l'exhaustivité, au moins en ce qui concerne le salut envisagé par Dieu.

Illustré d'images assez somptueuses, le Livre des miracles comptait initialement 200 pages, chacune composée d'une scène représentée à la gouache, et d'un texte d'accompagnement, figurant uniquement au recto. Aujourd'hui encore, il comporte 167 folia originels et 23 annexes qui remplacent les pages originales détachées lors de la reliure des feuillets au XIXe siècle. Cette édition comporte quatre des folia disparus, dont nous avons retrouvé la trace. Il s'agit des folia 93r, 111r, 191r et 192r.

Vraisemblablement commanditée par un inconnu, ou un érudit à qui la tâche avait été confiée, cette compilation a vu le jour à Augsbourg (voir ci-après). Elle est en tous points comparable à d'autres recueils de présages réalisés au XVIe siècle, le manuscrit présentant la même combinaison de miracles vétérotestamentaires, historiques et eschatologiques que les *Histoires prodigieuses* (Paris 1560) de l'humaniste breton Pierre Boaistuau (v. 1520-1566) et que le *Prodigiorum ac ostentorum chronicon* (Bâle 1557 ; ill. 15), du savant alsacien Conrad Lycosthenes. Le présent codex se distingue toutefois des autres par son ampleur et la qualité de ses illustrations.

1550 – Rain of grain in Klagenfurt / Kornregen in Klagenfurt / Pluie de grain à Klagenfurt
in: *Book of Miracles*, Augsburg, *c.* 1550–1552, fol. 166r (detail)
Private collection

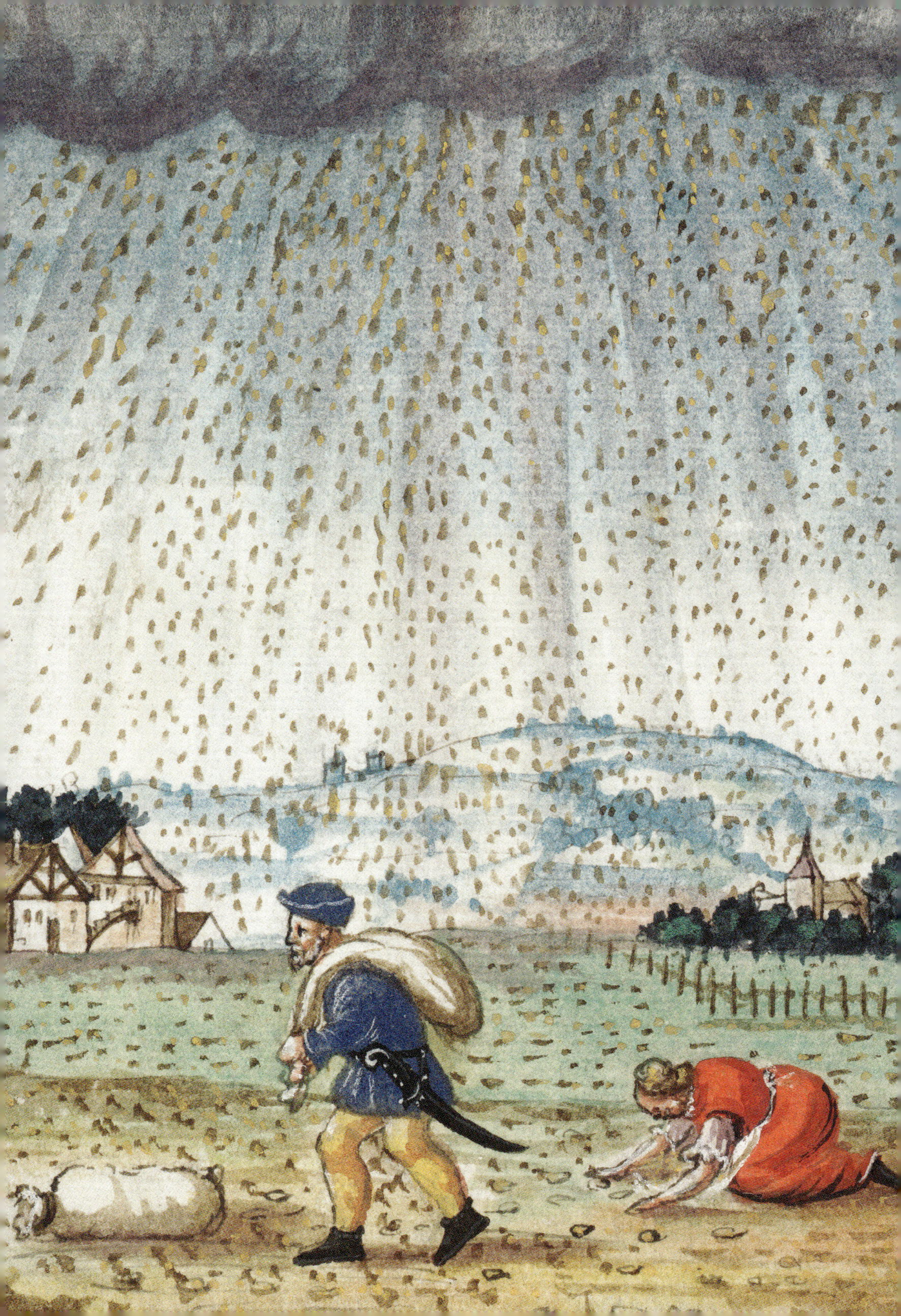

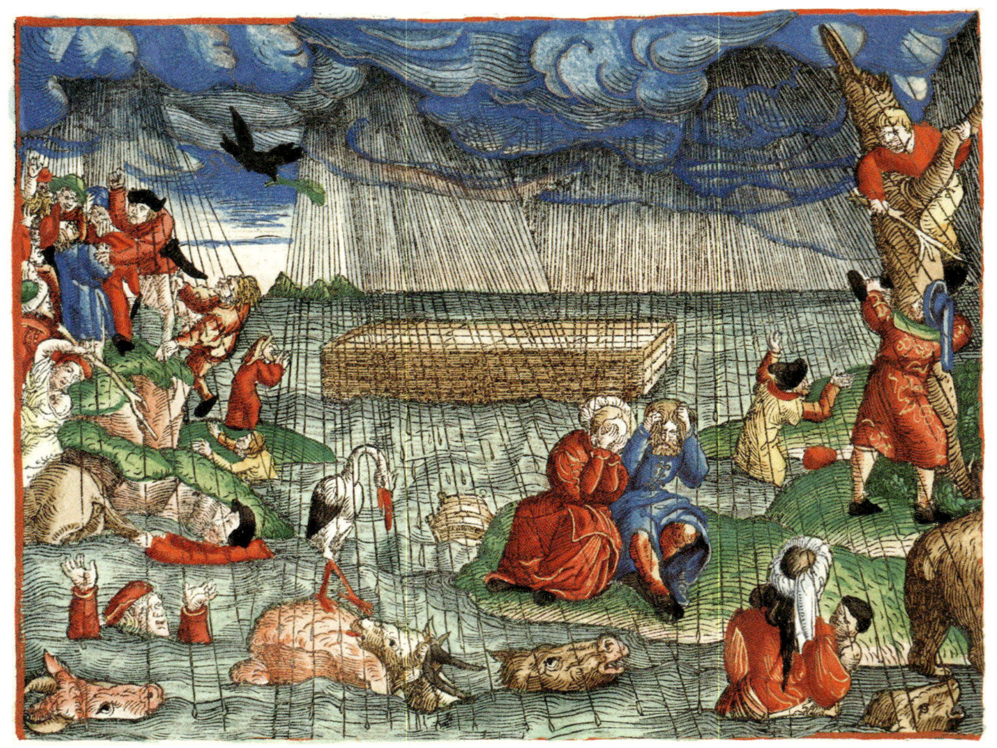

Ill. 28
Workshop of Lucas Cranach the Elder
The Deluge / Die Sintflut / Le Déluge
in: *The Luther Bible*, Wittenberg 1534, fol. IVv. Weimar, Herzogin Anna Amalia Bibliothek

Les miracles de l'Ancien Testament

Dépourvu de dédicace, d'avant-propos et de sommaire, le Livre des miracles s'ouvre abruptement sur une sélection de faits attestés dans l'Ancien Testament, et dans lesquels on pouvait voir une manifestation divine, ou un « prodige ». Contrairement à la Chronique des miracles et présages de Conrad Lycosthenes, le Livre des miracles, réalisé environ à la même époque, ne commence pas par la Chute originelle, mais par le Déluge initié par Dieu pour châtier les hommes (fol. 1r). Une superbe miniature montre l'Arche de Noé naviguant sur des flots agités dans un paysage sombre et pluvieux. L'arche est entourée d'hommes et d'animaux perdus au milieu des vagues et s'efforçant de sauver leur vie.

L'enluminure occupe près des trois quarts de la page. La partie inférieure présente une inscription sur plusieurs lignes. Le titre, la lettrine et les ornements sont en rouge, le texte à l'encre noire, le tout encadré de noir. Cet agencement se retrouve dans presque tout l'ouvrage, seul le corps de texte varie sur quelques folia (voir ci-après).

Les inscriptions en allemand sont conformes à la traduction de la Bible par Luther dans l'édition de 1545. Alors que les illustrations de l'Ancien Testament dans le Livre des miracles s'inspirent souvent de gravures sur bois de Hans Holbein le Jeune ou de Hans Sebald Beham, la représentation du Déluge est plus complexe que celles des deux artistes (ill. 1, 2). La gravure de la Bible de Luther lui est certes apparentée – du fait du traitement de la pluie torrentielle et de la noyade –, mais n'a pas dû servir de modèle direct au peintre (ill. 28), car le nombre de motifs isolés est limité au profit d'une narration picturale concentrée. L'artiste a d'ailleurs renoncé à représenter les personnages se cramponnant aux rochers.

Le Déluge est suivi de la représentation d'un arc-en-ciel (fol. 2r) décrit dans la Genèse comme un signe de l'alliance entre Dieu et les hommes (Gen. 9:12-15). Les douze signes du zodiaque figurés de part et d'autre du double arc symbolisent les douze mois de l'année et le temps qui s'écoule perpétuellement. Il semblerait que le peintre a bien observé la nature, puisqu'il représente correctement le premier arc en blanc et l'arc externe en rouge, jaune et vert. Les minutieuses applications d'or rehaussent tout particulièrement la composition.

Le folio 4r, qui décrit la destruction de Sodome et Gomorrhe (Gen. 19:24-26) montre Lot et ses filles ainsi que sa femme transmuée en statue de sel (au centre). Ils ne jouent cependant qu'un rôle secondaire dans le contexte des prodiges et des miracles, puisque la destruction des deux villes occupe le premier plan.

Si les premières pages du Livre des miracles dépeignent des phénomènes naturels considérés comme l'expression de la volonté divine, il en va autrement par la suite : le folio 5r montre Moïse conduisant les Hébreux hors d'Égypte. À gauche il fend les eaux, à droite les flots se referment sur le pharaon et son armée. Cette illustration de l'Exode (14:27-29) est moins axée sur le partage des eaux que sur Moïse et les Hébreux. Le miniaturiste a emprunté la composition à une xylographie des *Biblicae historiae* de Hans Sebald Beham (ill. 3).

On ignore pourquoi le Livre des miracles, contrairement aux autres cycles bibliques, ne comporte ni le Sacrifice d'Isaac ni l'Échelle de Jacob et ne traite pas les Dix plaies d'Égypte (Ex. 7-11). Les deux premiers événements sont associés à des manifestations divines sous forme d'apparitions célestes, alors que dans le cas des Plaies d'Égypte, il s'agit en quelque sorte d'archétypes de catastrophes auxquelles on concédait le rang de miracles, ainsi que le montrent la grêle, l'eau des rivières changée en sang et les averses de locustes évoquées dans la seconde partie du manuscrit.

La scène du folio 6r aussi peut être assimilée à l'archétype biblique de ces prodiges, intégrés dans la seconde partie du manuscrit en tant que « nourriture miraculeuse ». Décrite dans l'Exode (16:14-16), la manne tombée du ciel nourrit les Hébreux et leur sauve la vie. Cette « couche de rosée » est une concrétion comestible dispersée par le vent. Également évoqué dans les cycles bibliques protestants, le sujet était considéré comme la préfiguration de la Cène et du sacrement de l'Eucharistie. La composition est reprise à une estampe des *Icones* conçues vers 1525/1526 par Hans Holbein le Jeune (Müller 1997, p. 285-286). C'est de ce modèle (ill. 17) que proviennent les motifs figuratifs insérés dans le paysage dans le respect des nouvelles proportions.

Le folio 7r présente depuis une hauteur un groupe suivant Moïse et Aaron vêtu en prêtre ; la terre s'ouvre sous leurs pieds et engloutit Coré, le Lévite rebelle, et sa suite. Le regard du spectateur se dirige vers l'arrière-plan et suit une rivière qui serpente à travers le vaste paysage avant de se jeter dans la mer. À gauche, la composition est fermée par un conifère dont la taille sert de référence pour illustrer la distance séparant le groupe de l'arrière-plan. À l'aide de moyens relativement simples, l'artiste réussit à obtenir des effets atmosphériques impressionnants qui témoignent d'une connaissance approfondie de la peinture sur panneau de l'école du Danube, de Franconie et de Souabe (ill. 29). La scène secondaire, à droite, où nous voyons des cavaliers anéantis par le feu céleste, fait partie de l'histoire de Coré. Elle illustre le châtiment des partisans de Coré qui ont pris la fuite, événement relaté dans le Livre des Nombres. L'inscription du manuscrit mentionne les versets 4 à 7 du chapitre 16 qui décrivent le début de l'altercation entre Coré et Moïse, mais pas la fin. Or l'inscription ne suffit pas pour comprendre l'illustration, une connaissance approfondie de l'Ancien Testament est nécessaire.

Le folio 8r décrit l'ascension du prophète Élie (deuxième Livre des Rois). Le titre du texte de treize lignes, qui s'interrompt abruptement au milieu d'un verset de la Bible, mentionne le troisième Livre des Rois, renouant ici avec l'usage – encore courant à la Renaissance – de compter les Livres de Samuel avec les Livres des Rois. La composition est une fois de plus tributaire de l'estampe des *Icones* de Holbein.

La Vision au temple du prophète Isaïe qui, contrairement à l'ordre de l'Ancien Testament déjà coutumier à l'époque, suit directement sur le folio 9r l'Ascension d'Élie, est un sujet inhabituel. La légende (Is. 1:1-3) fait exclusivement référence au prophète. Elle est sans rapport avec la vision, abordée au sixième chapitre seulement. La qualité picturale de l'apparition – Dieu trônant dans les nuages au-dessus d'un temple ressemblant à un imposant bâtiment et le traitement minutieux des séraphins (Is. 6:1-7) – trouve un écho dans l'Apocalypse de saint Jean. Une fois encore, les *Icones* de Holbein ont servi de modèle.

Alors que les deux cadrans solaires représentés ensuite (fol. 10r, Is. 38:8) tiennent aussi de Holbein, la Vocation du prophète Jérémie, au folio 11r, se base sur une illustration de Hans Sebald Beham.

La vision des quatre bêtes de Daniel (fol. 12r; Dan. 7:1-7 – seuls les quatre premiers vers accompagnent l'illustration) est une fois encore d'ordre eschatologique. Tandis que les vents des points cardinaux soufflent sur la mer, quatre animaux monstrueux sortent des flots. Ils incarnent quatre royaumes qui seront anéantis par un souverain mondial avant que le règne de ce dernier soit balayé par le royaume des cieux éternel. La miniature associe chacun des continents à l'une des bêtes, suivant cette fois l'illustration de la Bible de Luther (ill. 18).

La feuille suivante (fol. 13r), qui montre l'archange Gabriel interpréter la vision du bélier et du bouc devant Daniel (Dan. 8 :1-12, Dan. 8:1-4 seulement dans la légende), doit encore aux *Icônes*. Le miniaturiste a toutefois commis une erreur en copiant le modèle. Il omet la corne brisée du bouc sur la représentation de Holbein (Dan. 8:21-22), or ce dernier symbolise le premier royaume qui sera suivi de quatre autres.

Pour les théologiens médiévaux, le récit de Jonas et de la baleine préfigure la mort et la résurrection du Christ. La légende du folio 14r cite les derniers vers du premier chapitre et les premiers vers du second chapitre du Livre de Jonas qui se réfère à la scène secondaire illustrée à l'arrière-plan.

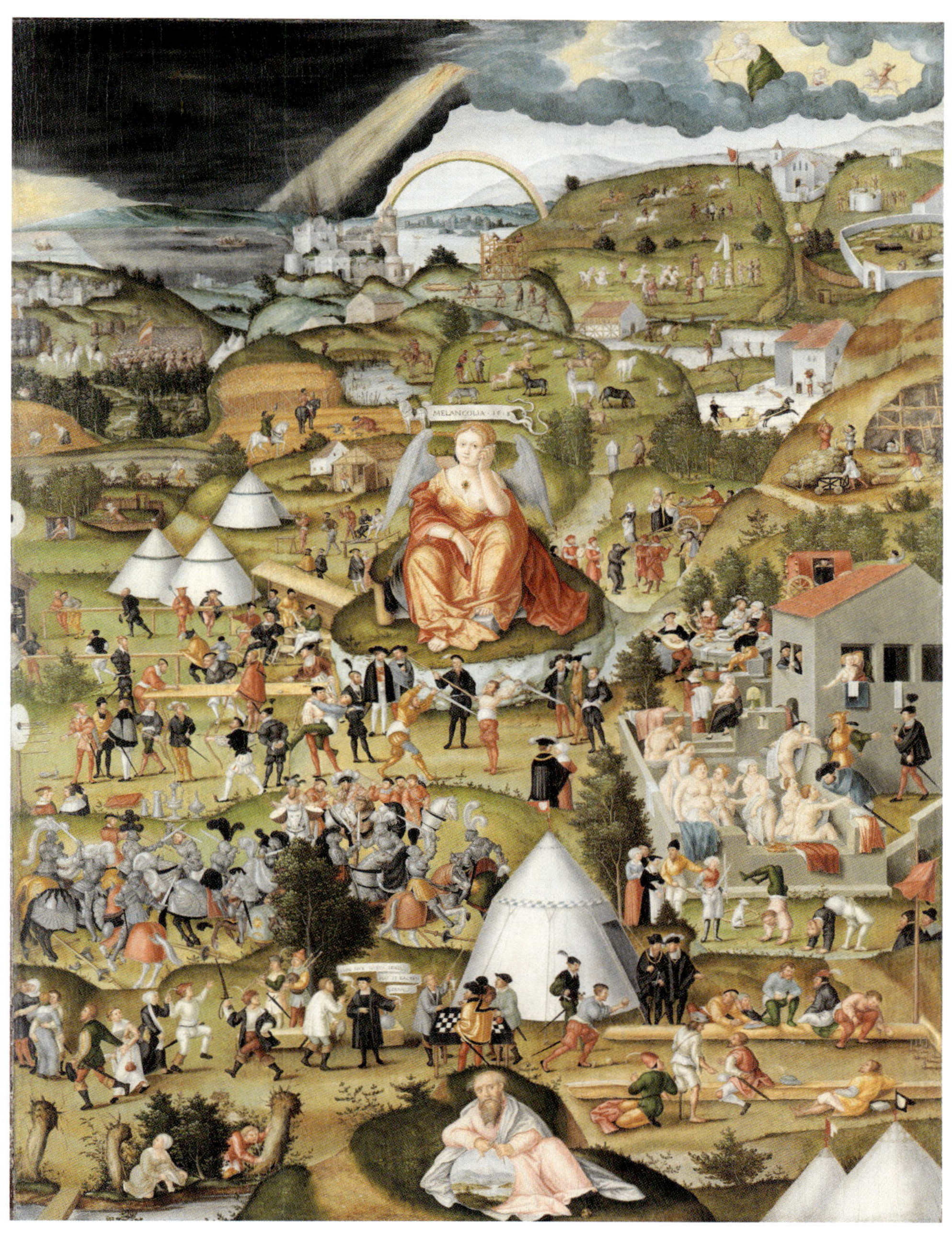

Ill. 29
Matthias Gerung
Melancholia, 1558 / *Melancholia* / *Mélancolie*
Oil on panel, 88 x 68 cm (34⅝ x 26¾ inches). Karlsruhe, Staatliche Kunsthalle

La scène principale montre un événement décrit dans le troisième et le quatrième chapitre. Irrité par l'attitude de Dieu, Jonas se repose sous un arbre aux portes de Ninive. Une courge gigantesque pousse au-dessus de sa tête pour le protéger du soleil. Tandis que la Bible de Luther traite les deux événements de la vie de Jonas de manière simultanée (ill. 4), Beham et Holbein, dont les *Icones* servent ici aussi de modèle, se sont contentés de représenter la colère de Jonas.

La Vision d'Ézéchiel par Holbein (ill. 30) sert aussi de modèle à la scène illustrée au folio 15r, qui suit directement l'histoire de Jonas dans le présent ouvrage, alors que le Livre d'Ézéchiel précède celui de Daniel dans les bibles éditées à l'époque. L'échelle et les proportions ont été adaptées aux dimensions de la feuille ; Dieu le père apparaît en plus petit, à l'instar des quatre créatures ailées et des deux roues imbriquées dans le feu. Une fois de plus, le peintre du Livre des miracles s'avère un coloriste de grand talent, capable de rendre les nuances du feu, de la fumée et des nuages. La légende cite les trois premiers versets du premier chapitre du Livre d'Ézéchiel, et sert de référence à la vision décrite en détail aux versets suivants (Éz. 1:4-28). La Vision d'Ézéchiel clôt la première partie du Livre des miracles qui comprend une sélection de châtiments divins, de miracles et de visions extraits de l'Ancien Testament.

Les signes miraculeux de l'Antiquité à nos jours

La seconde partie du manuscrit rassemble 135 des 167 feuilles conservées et offre des représentations de miracles survenus depuis l'Antiquité jusqu'à l'époque où le livre a été réalisé, dans le courant du XVIe siècle.

La représentation d'événements non bibliques commence au folio 16r par une inondation qui eut lieu du vivant de Job. Un bœuf, jailli de la rivière sortie de son lit, serait monté vers le ciel avant de replonger dans les flots et « les simples d'esprit » l'auraient vénéré comme un dieu. Même si nous avons affaire ici aux cultes rendus à des animaux mentionnés dans l'Ancien Testament, l'événement représenté n'est pas biblique. Il s'inspire probablement de la *Chronique du monde (Liber chronicorum)* de Hartmann Schedel, parue en 1493 (fol. 29r), ou bien du folio 17r tiré de la Chronique de 1531 de Sebastian Franck.

Les événements représentés aux folia 18r et 19r après une feuille intercalaire vierge sont issus de *De bello Judaico* (La guerre des juifs) de Flavius Josèphe (ill. 5).

Les deux illustrations et les textes qui les accompagnent se réfèrent aux signes annonciateurs ayant précédé la neuvième destruction de Jérusalem mentionnée par Flavius Josèphe. Le peintre décrit avec une grande minutie les différents motifs évoqués par l'historiographe : une étoile en forme d'épée au-dessus de Jérusalem, une vache amenée pour le sacrifice, qui a donné le jour à un agneau, la lourde porte du temple intérieur qui s'ouvrit d'elle-même. Ici, la vache et l'agneau sont représentés aux portes de la ville au-dessus de laquelle un glaive de feu attire les regards (fol. 18r). Sur la feuille suivante (fol. 19r), des troupes de chevaliers armés se profilent dans les nuages au-dessus de la ville. Flavius Josèphe avance que cette apparition était visible dans toutes les villes de Judée, ce qui signifie que la ville représentée n'est pas forcément Jérusalem.

Si les deux scènes décrivent des événements survenus au Ier siècle apr. J.-C., les incidents qui suivent se sont déroulés en 73 av. J.-C. Sur le folio 21r, le présage est représenté avec le malheur

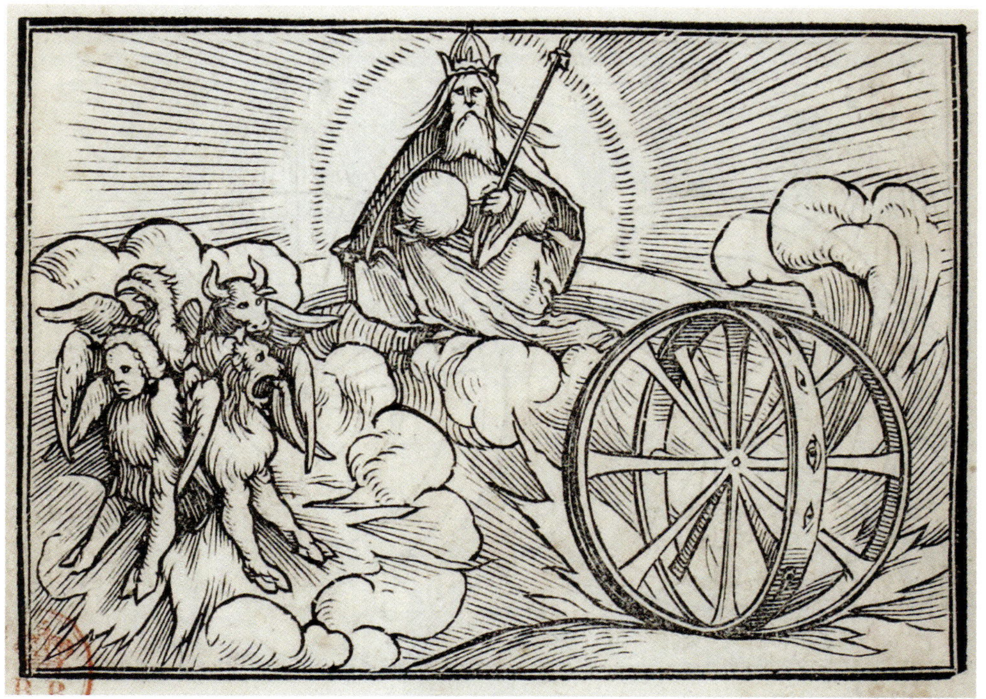

Ill. 30
Hans Holbein the Younger
Ezekiel's vision / Vision des Hesekiel / Vision d'Ézéchiel
in: *Historiarum Veteris Instrumenti icones ad vivum expressae,* Lyons 1539 (2nd ed.), fol. XXXIXv
Paris, Bibliothèque nationale de France

qui en résulte. Le texte nous apprend que du sang suinte du pain que les hommes rompent pendant le repas. Ce prodige annonce la tempête de grêle représentée à droite qui durera plusieurs jours et détruira toute la récolte.

Déjà considérés dans l'Ancien Testament comme un châtiment divin, les miracles sanglants, les catastrophes naturelles et les invasions d'animaux (fol. 87r, 109r, 141r) occupent une place éminente dans le manuscrit. Les peuples de l'Antiquité croyaient que les comètes, les éclipses solaires et lunaires, les phénomènes lumineux comme les halos et les aurores boréales annonçaient des calamités. Ils étaient encore censés porter malheur à l'époque de la création du manuscrit.

Phénomènes célestes

Les représentations de phénomènes célestes ont de quoi fasciner le lecteur d'aujourd'hui, tant leur minutie dénote un intérêt pour ainsi dire scientifique – un intérêt d'une part orienté vers l'avenir et d'autre part étrangement ambivalent dans le contexte des présages et des miracles.

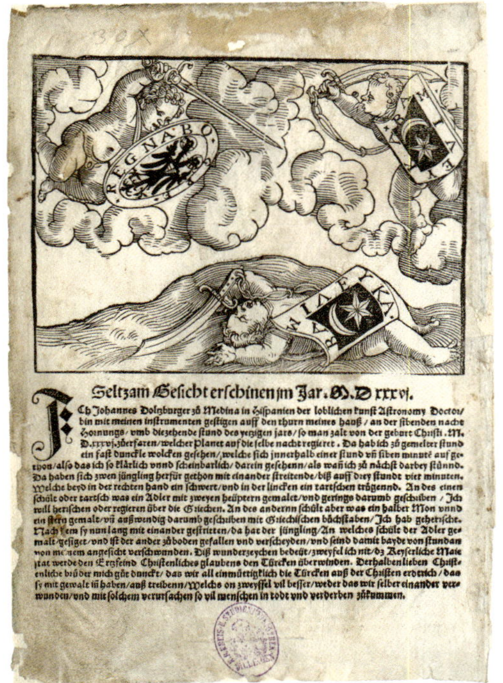

Seltzam Gesicht erschinen im Jar. M.D.xxxvj.

Ich Johannes Dolzburger zů Medina in Hispanien der loblichen kunst Astronomy Doctor/ bin mit meinen instrumenten gestigen auff den thurn meines hauß / an der sibenden nacht Hornungs/ vmb die zehende stund des yetzigen jars/ so man zalt von der geburt Christi .M.D.xxxvj. zů erfaren/ welcher Planet auf die selbe nacht regieret. Da hab ich zů gemelter stund ein fast dunckle wolcken gesehen/ welche sich innerhalb einer stund vñ siben minutẽ auf gethon/ also das ich so klärlich vnnd scheinbarlich/ darein gesehenn/ als wañ ich zů nächst darbey stůnnd. Da haben sich zwen jüngling herfür gethon mit einander streitende/ biß auff drey stundt vier minuten. Welche beyd in der rechten hand ein schwert/ vnd in der lincken ein tartschen trůgennd. An des einen schült oder tartsch was ein Adler mit zweyen heüptern gemalet/ vnd gerings darumb geschriben / Ich will herischen oder regieren über die Griechen. An des anderrn schült aber was ein halber Mon vnnd ein stern gemalt/ vñ außwendig darumb geschriben mit Griechischen bůchstaben/ Ich hab geherischt. Nach dem sy nun lang mit einander gestritten/ da hat der jüngling/ An welches schült der Adler gemalt/ gesiget/ vnd ist der ander zů boden gefallen vnd verscheyden/ vnd seind damit bayde von stundan von meinem angesicht verschwunden. Diß wunderzeychen bedeüt/ zweyfel ich nit/ dz Keyserliche Maiestat werde den Ertzfeind Christenliches glaubens den Türcken überwinden. Derhalben lieben Christenliche brůder mich gůt dunckt/ das wir all einmütigklich die Türcken auß der Christen erdtrich / das sy mit gewalt in haben/ auß treibenn/ Welchs on zweyffel vil besser/ weder das wir selber einander verwunden/ vnd mit solchem verursachen so vil menschen in todt vnd verderben zůkummen.

Le folio 26r dépeint avec précision trois soleils. Ces derniers apparurent après le meurtre de César dans le ciel matinal rougeoyant de Rome et s'assemblèrent jusqu'à ne faire plus qu'un. Julius Obsequens rapporta ce prodige à la fin du IVe siècle apr. J.-C. dans son *Liber prodigiorum* (chapitre 130), Schedel dans sa *Chronique du monde* (fol. 92v) et Franck dans sa Chronique (fol. 127v) – la légende s'inspirant directement de cette dernière.

La représentation de soleils secondaires générés par la réfraction de minuscules cristaux de glace dans l'air n'est pas unique (fol. 45r). Deux soleils fantômes observés en janvier 1520 dans le ciel de Vienne (fol. 102r, 106r) font partie d'une série de phénomènes célestes extraordinaires, qui se sont manifestés en l'espace de quelques jours et quelques nuits au-dessus de Vienne (fol. 104r, 106r, 107r ; *cf.* Fincel 1556, p. 68 ; ill. 6).

Les compositions en rapport avec les phénomènes de Vienne se caractérisent par des coloris fortement évocateurs, empreints de poésie, sans doute l'un des atouts artistiques majeurs du Livre des miracles. Des rehauts subtils de jaune et d'or dans les nuages restituent avec art le jeu de lumière de l'aurore et contrastent remarquablement avec le ciel bleu nuit sur lequel apparaissent les aurores boréales et les auréoles entourant le soleil.

Outre l'observation de soleils fantômes (fol. 112r, 113r, 139r), le peintre décrit d'autres phénomènes astronomiques rares comme l'apparition de doubles ou triples lunes (fol. 49r). Le folio 62r présente trois lunes dans un ciel nocturne traversé par une comète. Il ne s'agit pas de lunes secondaires mais d'une constellation que l'on a prise pour des lunes. Le texte précise qu'en 1304 apr. J.-C. trois lunes apparurent vers minuit dans les « welschen landen » (l'Italie) et que ce phénomène dura plusieurs mois.

Le Livre des miracles mentionne souvent l'observation d'un ciel aux couleurs étranges qui précède des calamités. Une lune sanglante annonce un terrible séisme en Italie (fol. 39r) – une atmosphère irréelle et sombre est ici générée avec des moyens très limités et les ruines noires

ILL. 31
Illustrated broadsheet reporting a celestial battle of three children which appeared in 1536
Illustriertes Flugblatt über eine Himmelsschlacht dreier Kinder im Jahr 1536
Feuillet illustré mentionnant un combat céleste de trois enfants apparu en 1536
Munich, Bayerische Staatsbibliothek, Einbl. V,58 m

se dessinent nettement dans la nuit. L'inscription nous apprend que la lune rouge représentée au folio 147r illustre une éclipse de lune : « La lune fut obscurcie la nuit, de sorte que la lune semblait ensanglantée. »

Plusieurs éclipses solaires étayent l'idée répandue selon laquelle les éclipses seraient les signes avant-coureurs du malheur (fol. 64r, 69r, 70r, 87r, 149r). L'événement illustré sur le folio 149r a eu lieu en janvier 1544 à Augsbourg, ville où fut réalisé le Livre des miracles peu après. La représentation reste toutefois schématique et ne semble pas du tout reposer sur l'expérience du peintre.

Le manuscrit accueille aussi des apparitions célestes figuratives (ill. 31) observées au XVIe siècle (fol. 124r, 126r, 134r, 144r, 150r, 157r). Des feuillets imprimés propagent la nouvelle de ces manifestations annonciatrices de guerres pour les contemporains. Comme dans le cas du phénomène observé en 1547 dans le canton de Glarus en Suisse (fol. 157r), les illustrations reposent la plupart du temps sur de simples gravures sur bois se rapportant à l'événement (ill. 19).

Les comètes

Les comètes sont amplement représentées dans le présent manuscrit qui renferme d'ailleurs la plus vaste collection d'anciennes images de comètes aux côtés d'un livret (Massing 1977 ; ill. 20) illustré en Flandre vers 1587. Déjà durant l'Antiquité, ces phénomènes célestes étaient censés provoquer un malheur de longue durée. Les humanistes orientés vers la Réforme aussi crurent à leur mauvais augure tandis le Moyen Âge voyait en elles un signe éminemment positif de la présence de Dieu. Le manuscrit livre des apparitions de comètes sur pas moins de 26 pages (fol. 32r, 34r, 35r, 37r, 46r, 50r, 58r, 61r, 62r, 64r, 65r, 67r, 74r, 79r, 83r, 92r, 100r, 101r, 110r, 120r, 121r, 122r, 125r, 128r, 142r, 146r), et les illustrations sont tellement diverses qu'il est vain de chercher à les classer.

Le Livre des miracles contenait à l'origine d'autres représentations de comètes, puisque l'une des feuilles détachées du contexte initial montre aussi l'apparition imposante d'une boule de feu chevelue brandissant une épée (dans cette édition, la feuille a retrouvé son emplacement initial au folio 111r ; *cf.* Falk 2005). Reprises à des gravures schématiques, rappelant plus ou moins les présages de Lycosthenes (ill. 32), les diverses représentations de comètes contenues dans le Livre des miracles doivent leur apparence aux textes transmis. Le météore qui fond sur la terre en 1007 (fol. 34r) est entouré de flammes, alors que l'apparition de 1173 (fol. 46r) prend l'aspect d'une poutre en feu. La comète observée à Rome en 684 (en chiffres romains dans le texte, la date titrant le folio 50r, 1184 apr. J.-C., est erronée) est décrite comme le présage d'un violent orage dévastateur, tout comme la comète de 1300 (fol. 61r) qui annonce un tremblement de terre dans la Ville Éternelle.

Les catastrophes naturelles

Sur certaines illustrations, les comètes apparaissent aux côtés de catastrophes dévastatrices, également représentées dans le Livre des miracles.

Il est parfois difficile d'identifier les sources. Les événements représentés sur le folio 30r proviennent sans doute de la Chronique de Franck et se rapportent à un tremblement de terre qui a détruit le temple de Jérusalem en 367 apr. J.-C. La représentation repose sur des faits historiques,

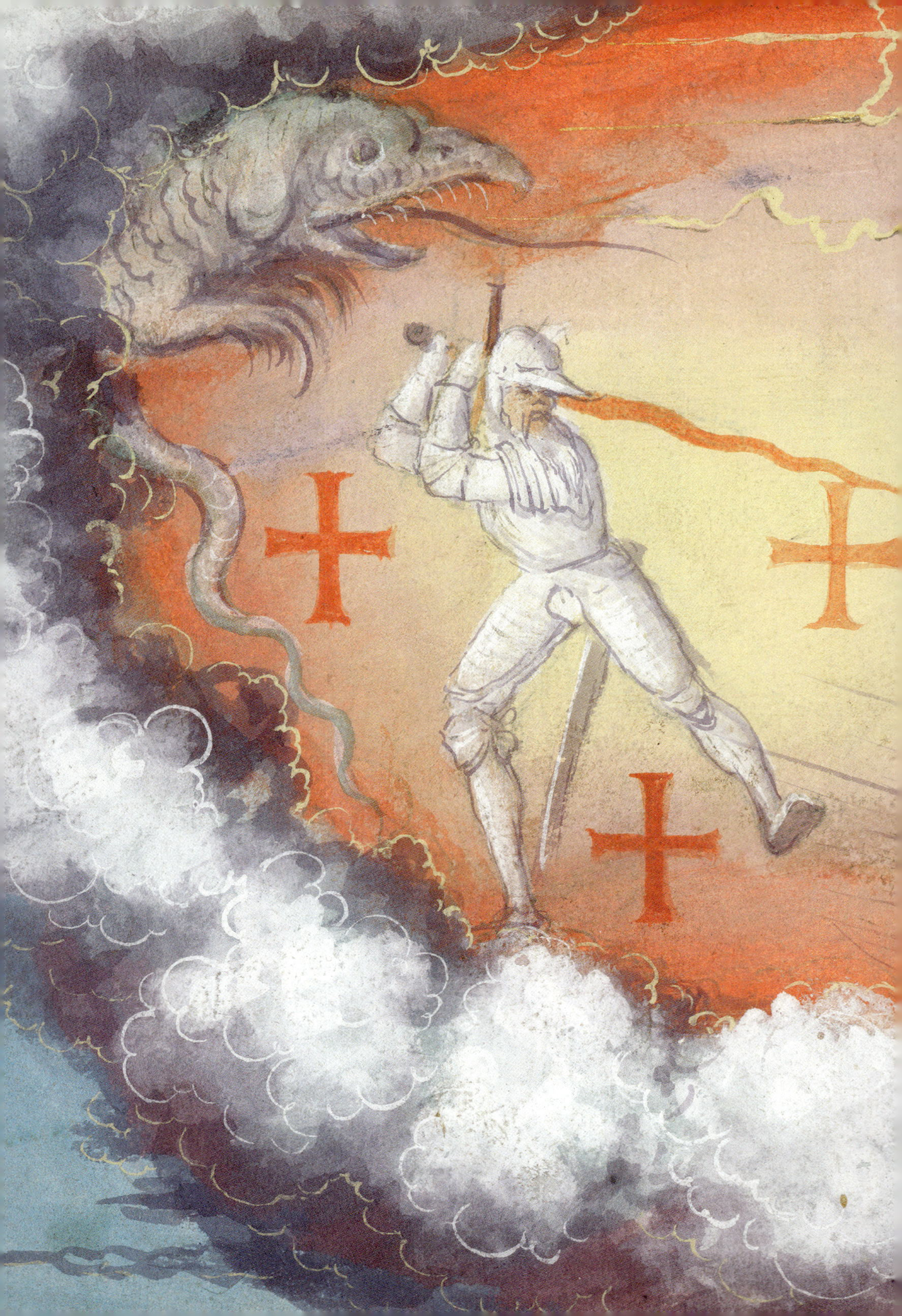

en l'occurrence les séismes survenus en 365 apr. J.-C. dans le bassin méditerranéen qui provoquèrent la destruction d'Alexandrie et un raz-de-marée dévastateur en Asie Mineure. Le théologien et historiographe syrien Théodoret de Cyr (393–468) mentionne un événement similaire dans le troisième livre de son *Historia ecclesiastica* dédiée à l'empereur romain Julien. Ce dernier fit démolir la basilique chrétienne construite par Constantin le Grand pour y édifier un temple. Le bâtiment païen n'était pas encore achevé que Dieu l'anéantit par le truchement d'un tremblement de terre.

Le folio 30r comporte l'une des illustrations les plus impressionnantes de l'ouvrage. Aux portes d'une ville éclairée par les flammes, en bas à gauche de l'image, de grandes vagues s'abattent sur une mince bande de terre. Une plaine inondée lui succède, et, au fond, des villes sombrent dans les flots tandis qu'hommes et animaux tentent de gagner la terre ferme à la nage. Les arbres au premier plan donnent une idée expressive de la force de la tempête. À l'aide de hachures irrégulières, le peintre génère l'impression d'une violente averse de pluie et de grêle. À gauche, une pluie de feu s'abat sur la ville dont les tours semblent se briser net sous l'effet du tremblement de terre. Un impressionnant couloir de feu et de fumée s'élève au-dessus des toits et teinte de rouge la montagne à l'arrière-plan.

Les tours qui s'écroulent sont un parfait indice de la force destructrice du séisme et la ville détruite illustrant les tremblements de terre de 1119 (fol. 39r) et de 1228 (fol. 52r) ressemble à une vision apocalyptique au clair de lune. En revanche, la description du séisme survenu en Espagne en 1357 (fol. 68r) est plutôt atypique : les ravages sont discrètement montrés de part et d'autre d'un rocher.

L'unique représentation d'éruption volcanique a été conçue de manière similaire. On voit le Vésuve en train de projeter une lave rougeoyante devant la ville de Naples en flammes (fol. 85r). Le titre date la catastrophe de l'année 1482. Le texte évoque la destruction de villes et de villages par des coulées de lave et mentionne parmi les victimes Pline l'Ancien, qui est effectivement mort en 79 av. J.-C. lors de l'éruption du Vésuve. Il est évident que le scribe s'est mépris en reprenant la date de la Chronique de Franck (fol. 270r), selon laquelle l'éruption aurait eu lieu en 82 av. J.-C.

Le manuscrit présente aussi plusieurs inondations, souvent associées à d'autres phénomènes atmosphériques et catastrophes (fol. 28r, 30r, 47r, 55r, 73r, 75r, 86r, 116r, 118r, 119r). Elles avaient des conséquences désastreuses sur le long terme, puisqu'elles anéantissaient les récoltes et le bétail sur de vastes surfaces et qu'elles représentaient une menace sérieuse pour les êtres humains. Elles étaient en outre, à l'image du Déluge, considérées comme le châtiment divin par excellence.

Afin de bien montrer l'ampleur du sinistre, les illustrateurs veillent à déployer un vaste paysage où montagnes, forêts et villes ressemblent à des îlots perdus au milieu des flots qui s'étendent à perte de vue et où hommes et animaux tentent désespérément de gagner la rive pour sauver leur vie. De temps en temps, la perspective change : l'inondation survenue en 570 apr. J.-C. (la date titrant le

1545 – Celestial battle over Poland
Himmelsschlacht über Polen / Bataille céleste dans le ciel de Pologne
in: *Book of Miracles*, Augsburg, *c.* 1550–1552, fol. 150r (detail). Private collection

fol. 28r, 170 apr. J.-C., est erronée) est observée d'une hauteur ; celle qui submerge la ville d'Antioche (fol. 47r) est rendue d'un point à peine plus élevé que la ligne d'horizon.

Le débordement du Tibre et du Pô, en Italie, ainsi que du Rhin et du Danube, en Europe centrale, est mis en scène de manière épurée (fol. 86r). L'inondation a eu lieu en novembre 1480 – l'année 1482 inscrite en lettres rouges par le copiste est une erreur. Deux arbres défeuillés se dressent sur une langue de terre entourée d'eau. Les flots ont englouti quasi tout le pays. Un courant violent entraîne avec lui de minuscules personnages en train de se noyer, agitant leurs bras hors de l'eau. Le folio 118r figure un raz-de-marée survenu en novembre 1530 sur la côte flamande. Le miniaturiste a élaboré un véritable paysage aquatique : des hommes gravissent des collines qui émergent des eaux ou grimpent aux arbres pour échapper à la noyade. À droite, une ville dont les tours s'effondrent s'enfonce dans les eaux. L'inscription indique qu'il s'agit de Vlissingen sur l'île de Walcheren. Cette inondation, dite de la Saint-Félix (Sint Felixvloed), ravagea les côtes de Flandre et de Zélande peu de temps après la Toussaint et causa près de 100 000 pertes – noyés, morts de faim et victimes d'épidémies.

Dans le Livre des miracles, inondations, raz-de-marée et tremblements de terre s'accompagnent régulièrement de pluie persistante, neige et grêle (ill. 8). Prises isolément du reste, ces intempéries extrêmes comme la grêle, la neige et le gel causaient souvent de mauvaises récoltes, famines et épidémies. Le manuscrit renferme plusieurs illustrations de tempêtes de grêle (fol. 21r, 27r, 47r, 78r, 115r, 171r) et de neige (fol. 44r, 51r, 54r) et ces représentations novatrices comptent parmi les plus anciens exemples du genre dans l'art allemand.

Deux feuilles sont consacrées aux conséquences des hivers rigoureux. Le folio 42r illustre de manière dramatique l'hiver 1126 durant lequel l'air était si froid que les grues gelaient en plein vol avant de s'écraser au sol. Tandis que le texte décrivant l'hiver 1234 (fol. 56r) évoque aussi la famine causée par le gel et le froid, le peintre figure les voies fluviales gelées où circulent alors des chars à bœufs. Le folio 44r décrit la violente chute de neige qui s'abattit sur Milan en 1162. À travers d'épais flocons, le lecteur distingue au loin les contours de la capitale lombarde sur une plaine enneigée.

Averses miraculeuses

Plusieurs feuilles sont consacrées à la description de miracles sanglants qui, en raison des prophéties de l'Apocalypse de saint Jean, ont surtout été interprétés par les protestants comme des signes de l'imminence de la fin du monde (fol. 21r, 28r, 36r, 38r, 51r, 54r, 71r, 81r, 119r, 167r). On voit des eaux se muer subitement en sang (fol. 36r) ; on assiste à la découverte d'une source sanglante (fol. 167r). La plupart des représentations se rapportent toutefois aux averses de sang, un phénomène naturel récurrent dû à la présence de sable rouge du désert dans l'atmosphère, pluie qui

Ill. 32
Representation of miraculous signs, such as hurricanes, rain and hailstorms, and earthquakes
Darstellung von Wunderzeichen wie Orkanwinde, Regen- und Hagelstürme, Erdbeben
Représentation de signes prodigieux tels des ouragans, des pluies torrentielles, des tempêtes de grêle et des séismes
in: Conrad Lycosthenes, *Prodigiorum ac ostentorum chronicon*, Basel 1557, fol. 355r
Göttingen, Niedersächsische Staats- und Universitätsbibliothek

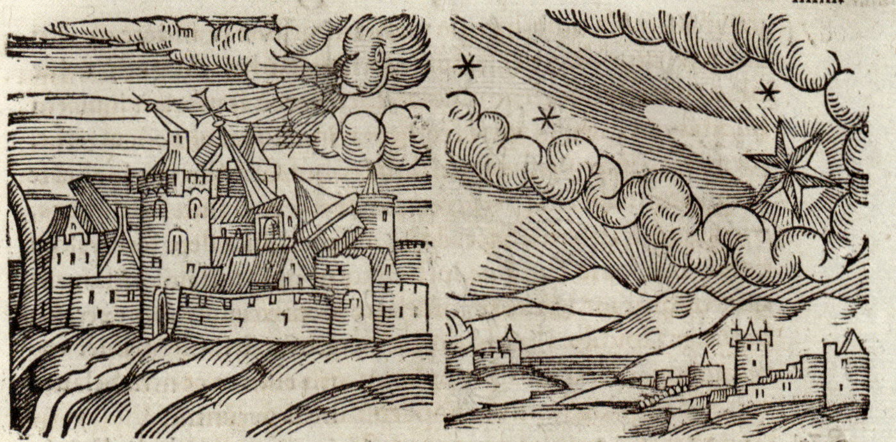

HAc tẽpestate grãdines, fulgetra, crebriores solitò territarunt 870
mortales: fruges, homines, pecudes afflixerunt. templum diui Petri Vangionum de cœlo tactum conflagrauit. Parietes solo æquati sunt. Tertio nonas Decemb. hora prima terra intremuit. Moguncíacũ euersum est. Lotharius Francorũ rex Romã ad Hadrianũ pontificem dum properat, ut se recõciliaret ei, ad sacram

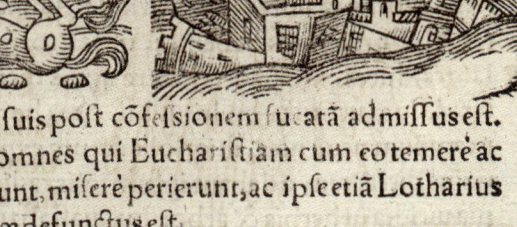

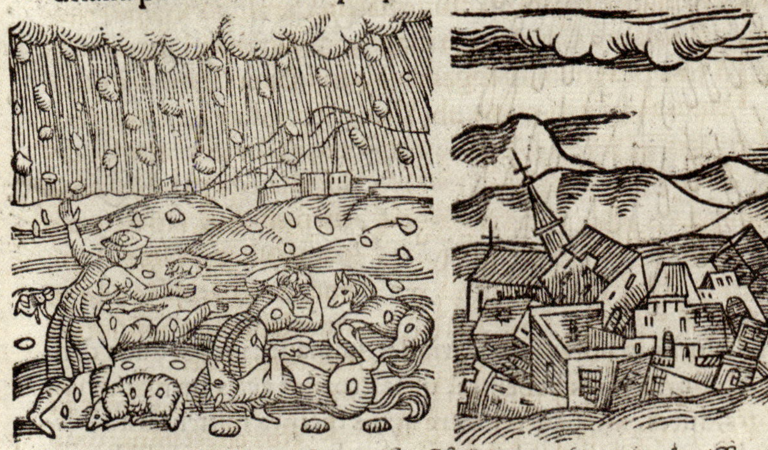

communionem cum suis post cõfessionem fucatã admissus est. Verum eodem anno omnes qui Eucharistiam cum eo temere ac fallaci animo acceperunt, misere perierunt, ac ipse etiã Lotharius in redeundo Placentiæ defunctus est.

Hh 2 Nu

effrayait les populations depuis l'Antiquité. Plus rare est la neige sanglante, repérée tout d'abord en 1226 en Styrie (fol. 51r) puis en 1229 (fol. 54r). Elle prend ici la forme de paysages hivernaux empreints de poésie.

Les averses de pain ou de manne, déjà évoquées dans l'Ancien Testament (fol. 6r), sont apparentées aux averses de sang. La représentation de la tempête de blé qui frappa Klagenfurt le 23 mars 1550 (fol. 166r) retient l'attention. Le manuscrit reprend une xylographie réalisée en 1550 à Nuremberg et qui fut copiée, entre autres, à Strasbourg (ill. 22).

Monstruosités

Les folia 88r, 90r, 97r, 117r, 133r, 145r et 158r dépeignent des animaux monstrueux et diverses malformations. À notre connaissance, une seule représentation d'être humain difforme apparaissait à l'origine dans le Livre des miracles, sans doute après le folio 92r. Ces dessins diffèrent des autres du fait de la proportion des personnages et de l'arrière-plan laissé vierge. Presque toutes les monstruosités du Livre des miracles sont reprises d'estampes. Les motifs s'inspirent de gravures sur bois et sur cuivre d'Albrecht Dürer et de Wenzel von Olmütz. On remarque la présence répétée d'animaux monstrueux sur une seule feuille, l'illustration étant accompagnée d'un texte sur deux colonnes. L'inscription qui accompagne la représentation d'un veau mort-né sur le folio 117r mentionne Hans Burgkmair comme artiste. Son nom se retrouve sur la feuille conservée aujourd'hui à Stuttgart et qui montre des frères siamois nés en 1513 dans la propriété de la comtesse Lodron, sœur du cardinal Matthias Lang (1468–1540), en Carinthie (dans cette édition, la feuille a retrouvé son emplacement initial au folio 93r).

Le folio 158r regroupe jusqu'à trois motifs tirés de dessins de Heinrich Vogtherr l'Ancien (1490–1556), qui circulaient sur des feuilles volantes. Une vigne infestée de parasites côtoie un grain de blé à l'aspect particulier. À côté se tient la fille de Roth dont on dit qu'elle cessa de s'alimenter plusieurs années durant, tout en vivant de dons – une forme appréciée de fraude sociale au Moyen Âge (ill. 25, 26).

L'Apocalypse de saint Jean

La dernière partie du Livre des miracles est consacrée aux signes annonçant la fin des temps et le second avènement de Jésus-Christ dans l'Apocalypse de saint Jean. L'intérêt particulier démontré par les théologiens réformistes pour l'étude des signes prodigieux va de pair avec leur conviction qu'ils annonçaient la fin du monde. Il découle de cette prémisse que les représentations de l'Apocalypse, avec ses averses de feu, tremblements de terre, inondations et autres catastrophes, doivent au fond être considérées comme la conséquence inévitable de la manifestation telle quelle de ces prodiges dans le manuscrit.

La vision eschatologique de saint Jean s'étend aujourd'hui encore sur 19 pages dans le manuscrit. Les illustrations s'appuient sur le cycle *Typi in apocalypsi Ioannis depicti* de Hans Sebald Beham, publié en 1539 à Francfort, lequel paraphrase l'Apocalypse gravée sur bois par Dürer en 1497/98 (ill. 14). Tout comme pour les événements de l'Ancien Testament, la qualité artistique première réside dans l'adaptation du modèle aux nouvelles proportions et dans la mise en couleurs qui prouve une fois

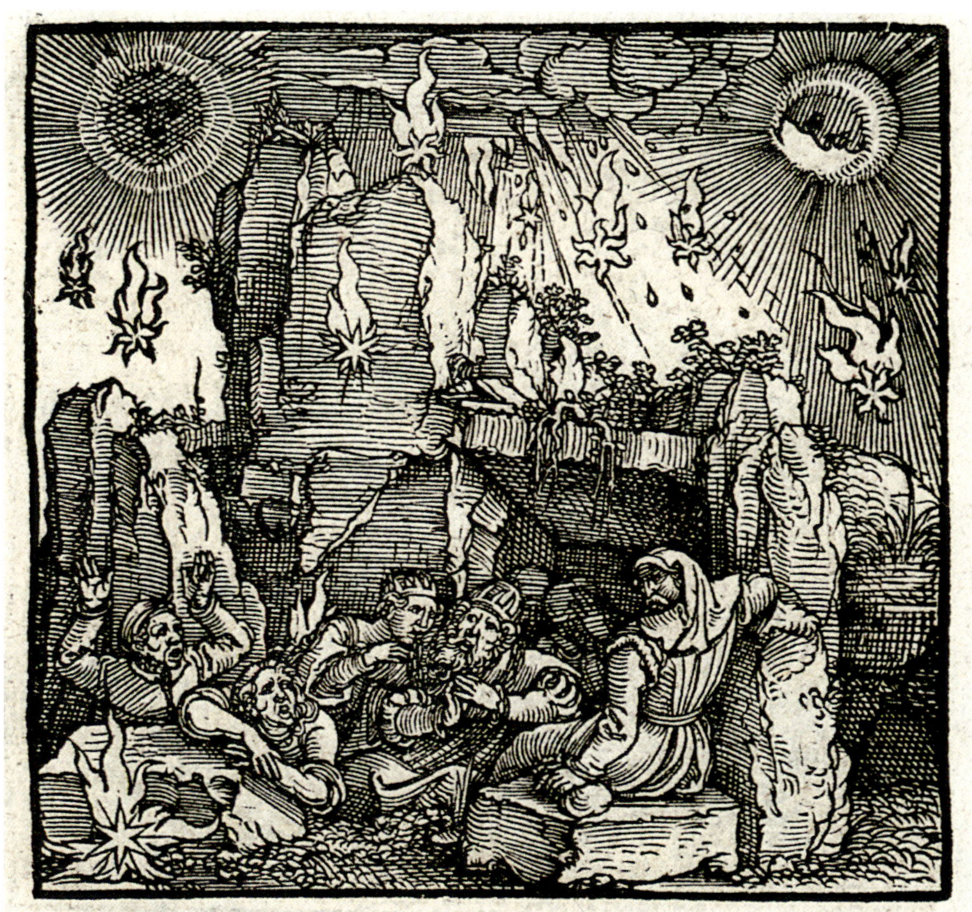

Ill. 33
Hans Sebald Beham
Opening of the sixth seal** / **Öffnung des sechsten Siegels** / **Ouverture du sixième sceau
in: *Typi in apocalypsi Ioannis depicti vt clarivs vaticinia Ioannis intelligi possint*,
Frankfurt am Main 1539, fol. 5r. Munich, Bayerische Staatsbibliothek

encore l'extraordinaire talent de l'enlumineur du Livre des miracles. Les événements illustrés se suivent comme dans le cycle de Beham, mais certains passages sont laissés de côté. La représentation de l'Apocalypse semble s'interrompre de manière étonnamment abrupte avec la récolte céleste.

En fait les représentations de l'Apocalypse contenues dans le manuscrit sont incomplètes. Au moins quatre autres feuilles illustrant le dernier livre du Nouveau Testament ont été détachées à la fin de l'ouvrage. Vendues aux enchères en 2005 à Munich chez Karl & Faber, on ignore leur lieu de conservation actuel (fol. 191r, 192r). Les quatre événements décrits se trouvent à la fin de l'Apocalypse et la vision des douze portes qui clôt le cycle de Beham en fait partie.

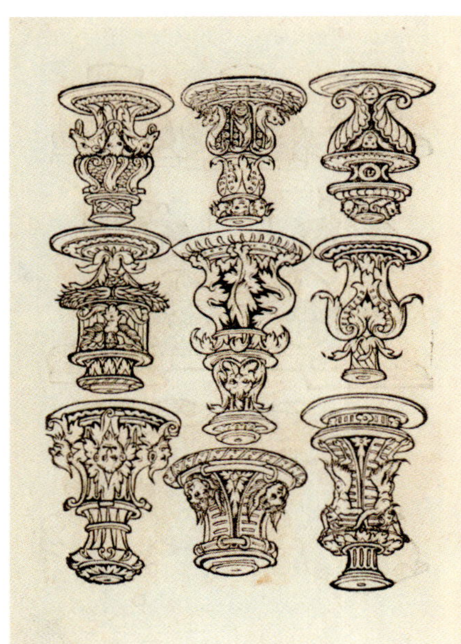

Datation, lieu d'origine et attribution

Le manuscrit a vu le jour au milieu du XVIe siècle, et le dialecte utilisé permet de le situer dans le sud de l'Allemagne. La tempête de grêle représentée au folio 171r, qui ravagea Dordrecht aux Pays-Bas en 1552 (ill. 8), est la catastrophe naturelle la plus récente insérée dans le Livre des miracles. Elle est placée juste avant la dernière partie du manuscrit consacré aux événements relatés dans l'Apocalypse de saint Jean.

Le codex n'a donc pu être achevé qu'à partir de 1552, même s'il semble avoir été réalisé par périodes. Le fait que les textes accompagnant les illustrations reposent sur la Bible de Luther de 1545 laisse penser que les travaux ont débuté après cette date. La datation des feuilles vers 1550 est confirmée par l'analyse des filigranes, qui livre aussi des indications sur le lieu d'origine. La présence de deux filigranes se répète sous deux variantes. Un écusson avec une croix au-dessus de trois montagnes, placé dans un quadrilobe, se trouve sur 20 feuilles de l'ouvrage. Le filigrane de près de quatre centimètres (semblable à Piccard 154059/154082) correspond à des documents écrits à Augsbourg entre 1539 et 1559 (Bower 2009, p. 26–27). 53 pages du manuscrit possèdent un filigrane d'à peine deux centimètres montrant une araignée sur un écu (semblable à Piccard 42787, 42788, 42791, 42792), filigrane répandu au milieu du XVIe siècle sur des documents et des pièces d'archives en provenance de villes de Souabe telles Lauingen, Dillingen, Ulm et Augsbourg (Falk 2005 ; Bower 2009, p. 27).

On observe sur deux autres feuilles les fragments d'un filigrane composé d'une étoile à six branches au-dessus d'une ancre (semblable à Piccard 119009), que l'on retrouve dans des documents provenant d'Autriche et d'Italie du Nord au XVIe siècle, mais également dans un document délivré en 1550 à Augsbourg (*cf.* Bower 2009). Si les filigranes confirment l'idée d'une origine située autour de l'an 1550, les documents de référence suggèrent que le manuscrit a été créé en Souabe.

Il est notable que les événements dépeints se rapportent à Augsbourg et à ses alentours (fol. 73r, 74r, 78r, 113r, 115r, 117r, 138r, 144r, 145r, 149r, 154r, 159r, 164r). Et notamment à des incidents survenus à l'époque de la genèse du manuscrit (fol. 113r et suivants). De ce fait, il convient aussi de supposer que le manuscrit a vu le jour à Augsbourg, centre de premier plan au XVIe siècle dans le domaine des sciences et des arts dans le sud de l'Allemagne.

ILL. 34
Heinrich Vogtherr the Elder and Heinrich Vogtherr the Younger
Study of column bases* / *Studie von Säulenbasen* / *Étude de bases de colonnes
in: *Ein frembdes und wunderliches Kunstbüchlin*, Strasbourg 1537 (ed. 1572), fol. 53v
Munich, Bayerische Staatsbibliothek

Plusieurs indices viennent confirmer cette hypothèse. Ainsi, le texte accompagnant l'apparition des soleils secondaires en 1541 sur le folio 139r dit : « trois soleils en triangle, entourés d'un arc-en-ciel, furent observés ici à Augsbourg », ce qui suggère une relation directe entre le texte et l'événement représenté. L'ajout du mot « ici » à trois autres endroits seulement, et les descriptions d'événements survenus en 1542 (fol. 144r) et 1547 (fol. 159r) se réfèrent de nouveau explicitement à Augsbourg. Sur les folia 156r et 164r, il est aussi mentionné à propos de phénomènes observés, qu'ils ont été vus « ici dans le ciel », sans que le texte indique le lieu où les événements se sont produits. Au vu du contexte, il est cependant clair qu'« ici » désigne de nouveau Augsbourg.

La référence à cette capitale culturelle et financière ressort aussi de la description de deux monstruosités apparues au XVIe siècle et mises en relation avec des localités de Souabe comme Langweid, Donauwörth (fol. 117r) et Dillingen (fol. 145r). Localiser la réalisation du manuscrit à Augsbourg permet d'expliquer pourquoi ces deux feuilles mentionnent justement des artistes actifs dans cette ville ou des artistes fondamentalement influencés par cette ville. Selon le texte accompagnateur, la représentation sur le folio 145r, à côté de celle d'une créature mi-moine mi-poisson, d'un poussin malformé venu au monde en 1543, est basée sur un modèle provenant du peintre de cour de l'évêque d'Augsbourg résidant à Dillingen (ill. 11). Il pourrait s'agir de l'évêque Christoph von Stadion (1478–1543) qui avait transféré la résidence épiscopale à Dillingen, mais tout aussi probablement d'Otto Truchness von Waldburg (1514–1573) nommé évêque à Augsbourg en 1543 et qui, durant les 30 années de son épiscopat, s'est attaché à promouvoir l'art de la Contre-Réforme en Souabe. On ignore qui était peintre à la cour épiscopale en 1543 – si tant est que cette charge ait existé à l'époque.

Le folio 117r regroupe sur une même page deux créatures monstrueuses. Un veau mort-né le 14 janvier 1529 à Langweid près d'Augsbourg, un autre qui survécut à sa propre naissance en 1532 près de Donauwörth. La feuille mentionne le nom d'un artiste d'Augsbourg : le texte se référant au premier animal dit en effet : « Et moi, Hans Burgkmair, peintre, en achetai la peau pour un demi-florin à un parcheminier, qui ne l'avait achetée que six kreuzers. » Cette indication marquante sur le plan formel – c'est le seul passage du manuscrit rédigé à la première personne (outre la légende du folio 118r, tirée d'une publication) – associe le Livre des miracles au nom de Hans Burgkmair. La feuille volante de 1513 montrant les frères siamois de face et de dos, mentionnait déjà un Hans Burgkmair qui aurait fourni le modèle de l'illustration (voir ci-dessus, Falk 2005 ; fol. 93r). Or, comme le manuscrit a été réalisé des décennies après sa mort, le célèbre artiste augsbourgeois Hans Burgkmair l'Ancien qui assura la réalisation de dessins pour le cortège triomphal de l'empereur Maximilien et qui créa avec Hans Holbein l'Ancien (vers 1465–1524) le cycle des basiliques pour les dominicaines du couvent à Augsbourg (Krause 2002, p. 290 et suiv.) ne peut l'avoir créé.

Le peintre évoqué au folio 117r est sans doute son fils Hans Burgkmair le Jeune qui intégra officiellement la guilde des peintres d'Augsbourg le 15 octobre 1531 et reprit l'atelier paternel. Formé dans cet atelier, il continua d'y travailler après son apprentissage. Douze peintures d'armoiries créées pour les funérailles de l'empereur Maximilien et des décorations réalisées pour la cérémonie mortuaire de Charles Quint en 1559 font partie de ses rares travaux documentés ; on connaît aussi quelques dessins et gravures signés de son monogramme HB. Sinon, ses activités restent obscures, des documents témoignent parfois d'une situation économique précaire (*cf.* Selig 1997, p. 217–218 ; Seidl 2012, p. 22–28). La présence d'apprentis dans son atelier en 1536, 1548, 1549 et en 1559 montre néanmoins que son atelier a dû prospérer malgré l'austérité des temps, entre les destructions iconoclastes protestantes en 1537 et l'annonce de la Paix d'Augsbourg en 1555.

Les gravures sur bois et sur métal et les dessins qui lui sont attribués reposent directement sur des créations et des modèles de son père ou sont classés dans la catégorie des œuvres mineures, aussi bien sur le plan technique qu'artistique. Plusieurs versions de livres des tournois illustrés de sa main nous sont parvenues. Il les a réalisés à partir de dessins créés par son père pour la Marche triomphale de l'empereur Maximilien Ier (Vienne 2012). Le plus ancien de ces ouvrages (Munich, Staatliche Graphische Sammlung) est considéré comme un manuscrit ayant été exécuté par le père et le fils pour le duc Guillaume IV de Bavière (1493–1550). Un second Livre des tournois (Bayerische Staatsbibliothek, Cod. Icon 403), probablement réalisé au cours de la décennie suivante et qu'il faut donc attribuer intégralement à Hans Burgkmair le Jeune, lui est étroitement apparenté (ill. 12). La dernière section d'un Livre des tournois en trois parties conservé à Sigmaringen (Hofbibliothek, HS 63), réalisé vers le milieu du XVIe siècle (Reuter 2010 ; Seidl 2012) et qui dépend une fois encore partiellement de la série de la Marche triomphale, est authentifiée par sa signature et datée de 1553. Les dessins à la plume coloriés à la gouache témoignent d'un sens impressionnant de la couleur et de sa maîtrise de la technique de la gouache ; ils rappellent les illustrations du Livre des miracles. L'application nuancée d'or et d'argent sur les enluminures du Livre des tournois évoque les accents lumineux d'or et d'argent délicatement placés sur les illustrations de comètes du présent manuscrit.

Les eaux-fortes de l'*Ernwertes Geschlechter Buch Der löblichen deß Heiligen Reichs Statt Augspurg Patricorium* (Livre des familles d'Augsbourg) sont elles aussi attribuées en grande partie à Burgkmair le Jeune. Ainsi que le signale le frontispice de l'édition prévue à l'origine pour 1545, les gravures ont été réalisées par Hans Burgkmair et Heinrich Vogtherr (Falk à Augsbourg 2011, p. 190–192 ; Seidl 2012) – on pensait ici aussi bien à Heinrich Vogtherr l'Ancien qu'à son fils (1513–1568).

Restitué en 2010 à la Staatsgalerie de Stuttgart, un recueil de 44 dessins à la plume et de 53 épreuves du Livre des familles d'Augsbourg comporte des travaux que Burgkmair a réalisés de sa main (*cf.* Seidel 2012). Les dessins ont vu le jour après 1538, année à partir de laquelle les familles nobles et patriciennes d'Augsbourg ont été plus nombreuses à participer à la vie politique dans la cité (accession accrue au patriciat). En raison de leur caractère purement graphique, ils ne livrent néanmoins aucun indice stylistique qui permettrait de les comparer aux illustrations pittoresques et poétiques du Livre des miracles.

Cependant, l'idée d'une collaboration entre Vogtherr et le jeune Burgkmair a de quoi surprendre, car le Livre des miracles contient lui aussi des illustrations tirées de dessins de Heinrich Vogtherr l'Ancien. Ainsi les trois motifs représentés sur le folio 158r ont été empruntés à des gravures sur bois dont le modèle a été fourni par l'artiste de Dillingen (ill. 25, 26). Le fait que la combinaison unique en son genre de trois motifs sur une seule feuille puisse être parallèlement attribuée à un seul artiste, qui plus est originaire de Souabe, remet en question l'éventuelle participation de Heinrich Vogtherr l'Ancien à l'illustration du manuscrit.

Né en 1490 à Dillingen, l'artiste fréquenta le collège avant de faire un apprentissage de peintre à Augsbourg. Fils d'un chirurgien et oculiste, on lui connaît un parcours très mouvementé puisqu'il sera peintre, décorateur, éditeur et oculiste. En 1526, il acquiert le droit de cité à Strasbourg après avoir vécu à Erfurt (1510), Leipzig (1514), Augsbourg (1518) et Wimpfen sur le Neckar (1522). Entre 1536 et 1540, Vogtherr qui entretenait déjà de bons contacts avec des éditeurs d'Augsbourg et de Bâle en tant que dessinateur de bois gravés, possède à Strasbourg une officine avec presse. Il y publiera le premier livre d'échantillons imprimés en 1537. Fort de 700 illustrations, le *Kunstbüchlin* présente notamment des modèles de visages, de mains, d'armes blanches, d'armures et d'ornements (ill. 34). Vogtherr l'Ancien les a conçus avec son fils Heinrich dont le portrait-médaillon est présent sur la page de titre à côté de celui de son père (ill. 35). En raison de difficultés financières, la boutique doit fermer en 1540 et le manque de commandes – l'influence de la Réforme se fait sentir –, fait que le jeune Vogtherr quitte l'atelier paternel l'année suivante et part à Augsbourg où il s'établit comme maître franc fin mars 1541.

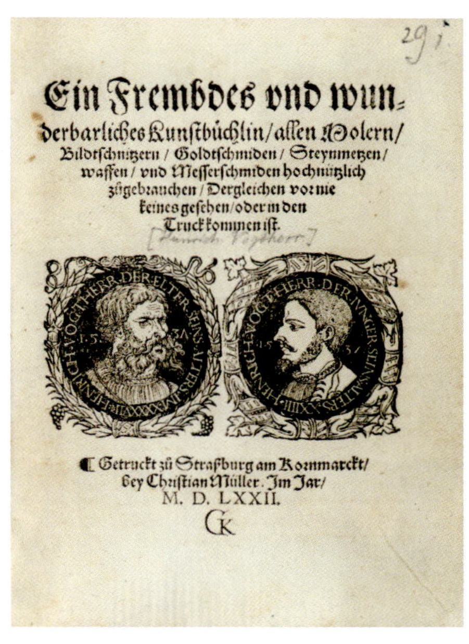

29 i.

Ein Frembdes vnd wunderbarliches Kunstbüchlin/allen Molern/ Bildtschnitzern/Goldtschmiden/Steynmetzen/ waffen/vnd Messerschmiden hochnützlich zügebrauchen/Dergleichen vor nie keines gesehen/oder in den Truck kommen ist.

[Heinrich Vogtherr]

Getruckt zü Straßburg am Kornmarckt/ bey Christian Müller. Im Jar/ M. D. LXXII.

GK

En 1542, Heinrich Vogtherr l'Ancien se rend à la Diète de Spire puis à Augsbourg. Il y restera plusieurs mois, séjournant chez son fils. Son voyage le conduit en 1543 à Bâle puis à Zurich où il travaille comme illustrateur. On le retrouve une dernière fois à Augsbourg pendant la Diète en 1547/1548. À la fin de sa vie, visant peut-être un emploi à la cour de Ferdinand 1er, Vogtherr s'installe à Vienne. Il y restera jusqu'à sa mort, travaillant comme artiste et oculiste.

En raison des nombreux déplacements attestés de Vogtherr l'Ancien au cours de sa vie, une collaboration personnelle importante au Livre des miracles, réalisé en majeure partie entre 1545 et 1552 à Augsbourg, n'est guère plausible. En revanche, celle de Heinrich Vogtherr le Jeune qui avait accès dans son atelier d'Augsbourg aux modèles de son père semble possible. À l'instar de celles de Burgkmair le Jeune, dont les activités ne sortent guère de l'ombre de son père, les créations de Heinrich Vogtherr le Jeune sont comprises comme le prolongement de l'art de son père, sans que l'on ne sache jamais lequel, du père ou du fils, est l'auteur des œuvres. Ainsi, à propos des attributions des dessins et gravures du Livre des familles d'Augsbourg, on a dernièrement argumenté que

Ill. 35
Heinrich Vogtherr the Elder and Heinrich Vogtherr the Younger
Frontispiece** | **Frontispiz** | **Frontispice
in: *Ein frembdes und wunderliches Kunstbüchlin*, Strasbourg 1537 (ed. 1572), fol. 29r
Munich, Bayerische Staatsbibliothek

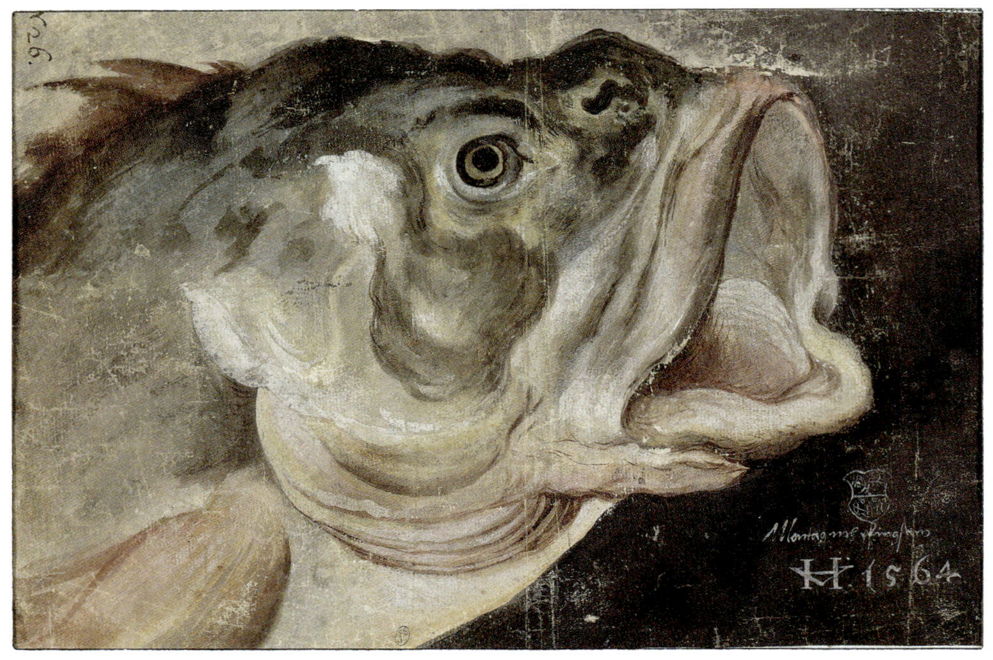

Ill. 36
Heinrich Vogtherr the Younger
Head of a fish, 1564 / *Fischkopf* / *Tête de poisson*
Watercolour and bodycolour on paper, 16.7 x 25.9 cm (6½ x 10¼ in.)
Paris, Musée du Louvre, inv. 18945

Hans Burgkmair le Jeune n'a pas du tout collaboré ici avec Heinrich Vogtherr l'Ancien mais avec le fils de celui-ci (Seidl 2012).

Heinrich Vogtherr le Jeune a été actif à Augsbourg en permanence entre le printemps 1541 et la fin 1554. Il y dirigeait un atelier réputé comptant trois apprentis peintres – dont Antonius Breu à partir de 1547, fils du peintre Jörg Breu le Jeune (vers 1510-1547). En 1555, tout en conservant son droit de cité à Augsbourg, Heinrich Vogtherr le Jeune se rendit à Vienne au chevet de son père mourant. La cour de Habsbourg lui confia alors le soin de concevoir des pièces de monnaie, des bannières et d'autres peintures héraldiques. Il dessina aussi une copie du tombeau de Maximilien et collabora au décor des funérailles de l'empereur Ferdinand Ier en 1564.

Comme dans le cas de Burgkmair le Jeune, une analyse du style ne livre aucune information sur la collaboration de Heinrich Vogtherr le Jeune au Livre des miracles. Les gravures sur bois et sur métal attribuées à Vogtherr ne peuvent être comparées aux images du manuscrit en raison de la différence de support. Seules deux de ses études présentent des analogies avec les illustrations. Tout d'abord une peinture à la gouache d'une tête de poisson (ill. 36) authentifiée par le monogramme HV comme une œuvre de Vogtherr le Jeune. Elle porte le sceau de l'année 1564 et a par conséquent vu le jour à Vienne. Cette feuille révèle une brillante maîtrise de la gouache et témoigne d'une curiosité similaire à celle qui transparaît dans les études de nature d'Albrecht Dürer, une curiosité que l'on pourrait presque qualifier de scientifique et qui caractérise aussi de nombreuses illustrations du Livre des miracles. L'autre étude est un dessin au pinceau sur un papier bleu-gris, avec des rehauts de blanc (ill. 13) appliqués méthodiquement. Autrefois attribué à Heinrich Vogtherr l'Ancien (Rowlands 1993 ; Müller 1997), il représente le combat entre les Amalécites et le peuple d'Israël, décrit dans la Bible (Ex. 17:8-16). Le dessin sur lequel on distingue à gauche le monogramme HVE, porte la date 1542 et a été réalisé dans l'atelier de Vogtherr le Jeune à Augsbourg.

Giulia Bartrum fut la première à signaler des analogies entre ce dessin et les illustrations du Livre des miracles (Day & Faber 2010). Il existe effectivement des similitudes, comme le montrent le cheval et le cavalier du folio 126r illustrant un phénomène céleste. Tous deux sont comparables dans leur conception aux personnages du dessin, dont les rehauts de blanc rappellent ceux des nuages du Livre des miracles (par exemple fol. 102r, 124r, 126r).

Le fait que d'autres peintres outre Vogtherr et Burgkmair aient contribué au décor du Livre des miracles ne correspond pas seulement à la réalité des pratiques d'atelier à la Renaissance. Cela explique également l'hétérogénéité des illustrations qui comportent aussi bien des personnages soigneusement élaborés que de grossiers « bonshommes », des espaces paysagers échelonnés en profondeur et des illustrations spectaculaires de phénomènes lumineux et de comètes que des vues schématiques de villes, des environnements d'une grande pauvreté et des répétitions multiples. Ces divergences qualitatives dénotent la participation de plusieurs collaborateurs et apprentis qui travaillaient sous surveillance et ont dû recourir à des modèles d'atelier.

Le Livre des miracles ne s'est fort vraisemblablement pas fait d'une seule traite. Il se peut que les scènes liminaires de l'Ancien Testament et que les illustrations finales de l'Apocalypse de saint Jean aient tout d'abord été conçues comme des cycles autonomes, alors que la volumineuse partie médiane était déjà en cours de réalisation. Les auteurs ont à l'évidence attaché de l'importance à l'aspect uniforme du manuscrit, veillant à ce que les cycles d'illustrations bibliques ne se distinguent pas significativement des autres illustrations.

Au vu des différences dans l'aspect du texte et de modifications distinctes dans le corps de texte, on peut supposer que le Livre des miracles a été rédigé par divers copistes, peut-être impliqués au cours des différentes phases de la réalisation du manuscrit. Si l'on prend en considération le changement d'écriture et les différences dans le corps de texte, on peut distinguer au moins trois périodes différentes.

La majeure partie du manuscrit est due à un copiste qui a réalisé la partie relative à l'Ancien Testament ainsi que la plupart des textes accompagnateurs de la seconde partie. L'aspect du texte sur les feuilles illustrant l'Apocalypse de saint Jean – on songe aux écrits de Clemens Jäger (*cf.* Munich 2010, p. 32–35), copiste au conseil d'Augsbourg – évoque celui de cette partie maîtresse et est probablement le fait du même copiste qui a dû cependant ici adapter des textes plus longs. L'inscription sur le folio 154r est, elle aussi, apparentée à cette partie centrale. Elle montre le même corps de texte mais provient manifestement d'un autre rédacteur. C'est aussi le cas de la représentation des frères siamois d'après Burgkmair l'Ancien (fol. 93r), conservée aujourd'hui séparément à Stuttgart.

Le second groupe concerne les feuilles dont les textes sont présentés sur deux colonnes. L'écriture ressemble à celle des feuilles de la partie maîtresse, mais il se peut qu'ils aient été écrits par une autre personne et indiqueraient ainsi l'abandon d'une modification de plan. Des textes à deux colonnes se retrouvent du folio 94r au folio 107r (à l'exception des folia 100r et 101r qui reflètent le canon appliqué aux autres) ainsi que sur les folia 117r, 145r et 158r. La première partie s'ouvre sur un phénomène céleste survenu en 1513 et comprend les apparitions d'aurores boréales et de soleils secondaires au-dessus de Vienne en janvier 1520 (voir ci-dessus), réparties à l'origine sur six feuilles. Les autres feuilles dont les textes sont agencés sur deux colonnes sont consacrées à la représentation de monstruosités et choses du même genre, basées sur des modèles de Burgkmair, de Vogtherr et du peintre de cour de l'évêque d'Augsbourg à Dillingen (voir ci-dessus).

Des différences dans l'aspect du texte permettent de reconnaître les feuilles ajoutées durant la phase finale de création. Plusieurs feuilles situées à la fin de la seconde partie du manuscrit sont concernées, juste avant l'Apocalypse de saint Jean. Le texte, réparti sur une seule colonne, présente une écriture relativement chargée en fioritures et se distingue surtout des autres inscriptions par ses ornements décoratifs et calligraphiques. Les feuilles issues de cette phase commencent par un événement de l'année 1533 au folio 129r intercalé entre deux feuilles du groupe principal. Tout comme la feuille suivante de cette phase finale (fol. 144r), il se peut qu'elle ait été ajoutée à la fin de la rédaction du manuscrit. D'autres feuilles isolées de cette période suivent aux folia 153r et 157r, puis du folio 160r au folio 170r, avec des représentations plus récentes de miracles, qui se réfèrent à des événements survenus de 1549 à 1551 et font peut-être partie d'un supplément ajouté plus tard.

Le manuscrit a par conséquent vu le jour sur le plan chronologique et géographique à proximité d'un magnifique ouvrage créé lui aussi en 1555 à Augsbourg et dédié au futur empereur Ferdinand Ier, l'*Eclipses luminarium* de Cyprian Leowitz (1524–1574), dans lequel l'érudit actif à Augsbourg a calculé toutes les éclipses de soleil et de lune jusqu'en 1605.

Même si les illustrations scientifiques de ce traité d'astronomie ainsi que les scènes de genre qu'il abrite (ill. 37) reprennent la tradition également répandue à Augsbourg des illustrations des mois de l'année et ne dépendent pas directement du Livre des miracles et de ses artistes, elles prouvent que les enluminures du Livre des miracles font partie d'une tradition difficilement saisissable aujourd'hui, qui semble en même temps poser les bases d'un nouveau type d'illustration scientifique.

Ill. 37
Cyprian Leowitz
Nocturnal masquerade with harlequins and sleigh-rides and the stars Scipia virginis and Regulus
Nächtlicher Mummenschanz mit Harlekinen und Schlittenfahrt und den Sternen Scipia virginis und Regulus
Mascarade nocturne avec arlequins et promenade en traîneau et les étoiles Scipia virginis et Regulus
in: *Eclipses luminarium*, Augsburg 1555, fol. 37r. Bodycolour on paper, 44.5 x 35.5 cm (17½ x 14 in.)
Munich, Bayerische Staatsbibliothek, Cod. Icon. 181

Pages 90–91
1551 – Five suns over Leipzig / Fünf Sonnen über Leipzig / Cinq soleils dans le ciel de Leipzig
in: *Book of Miracles*, Augsburg, *c.* 1550–1552, fol. 165r (detail). Private collection

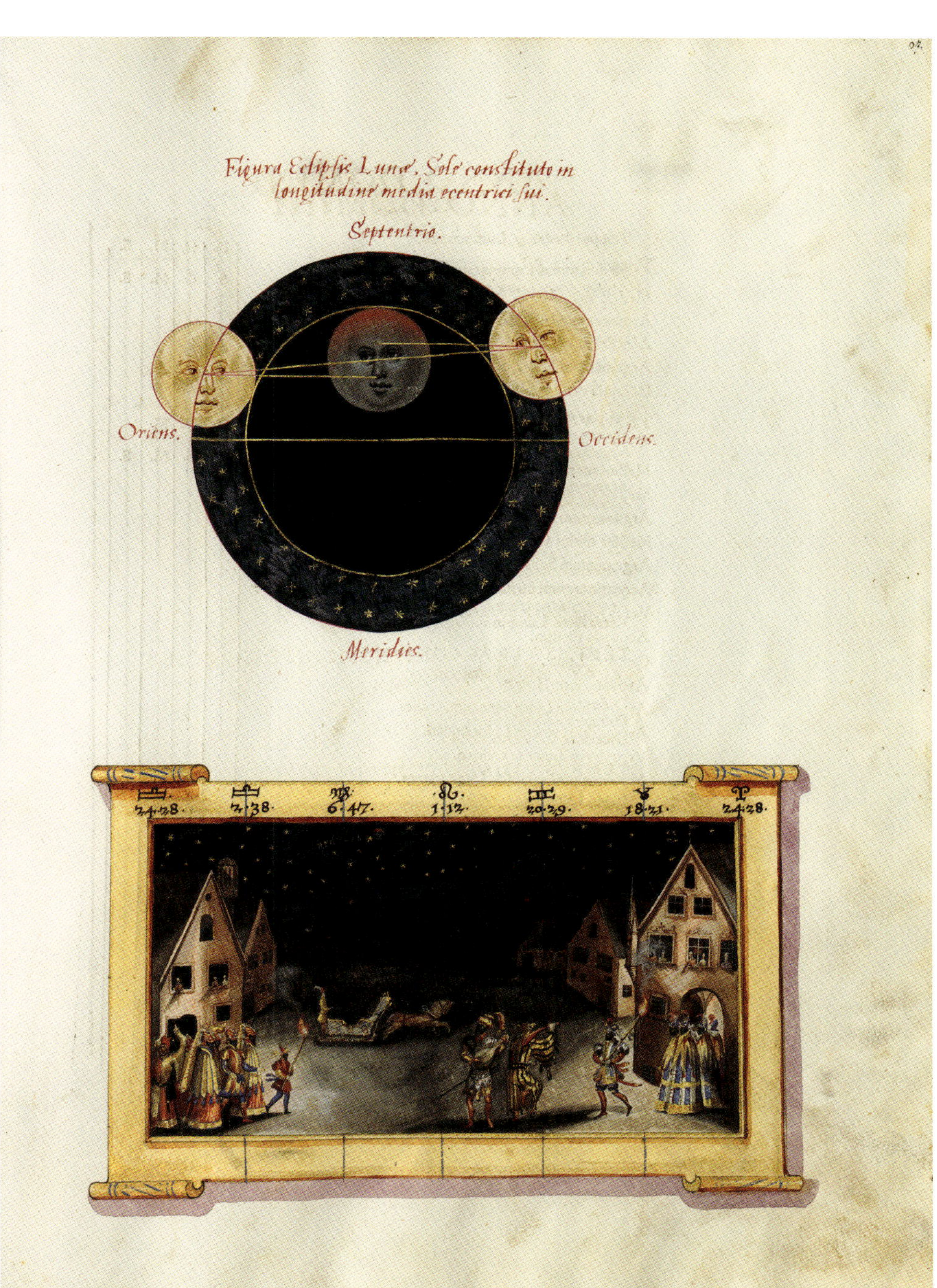
95.
Figura Eclipsis Lunæ, Sole constituto in longitudine media ecentrici sui.
Septentrio.
Oriens.
Occidens.
Meridies.
24.28.
7.38.
6.47.
1.12.
20.29.
18.21.
24.28.

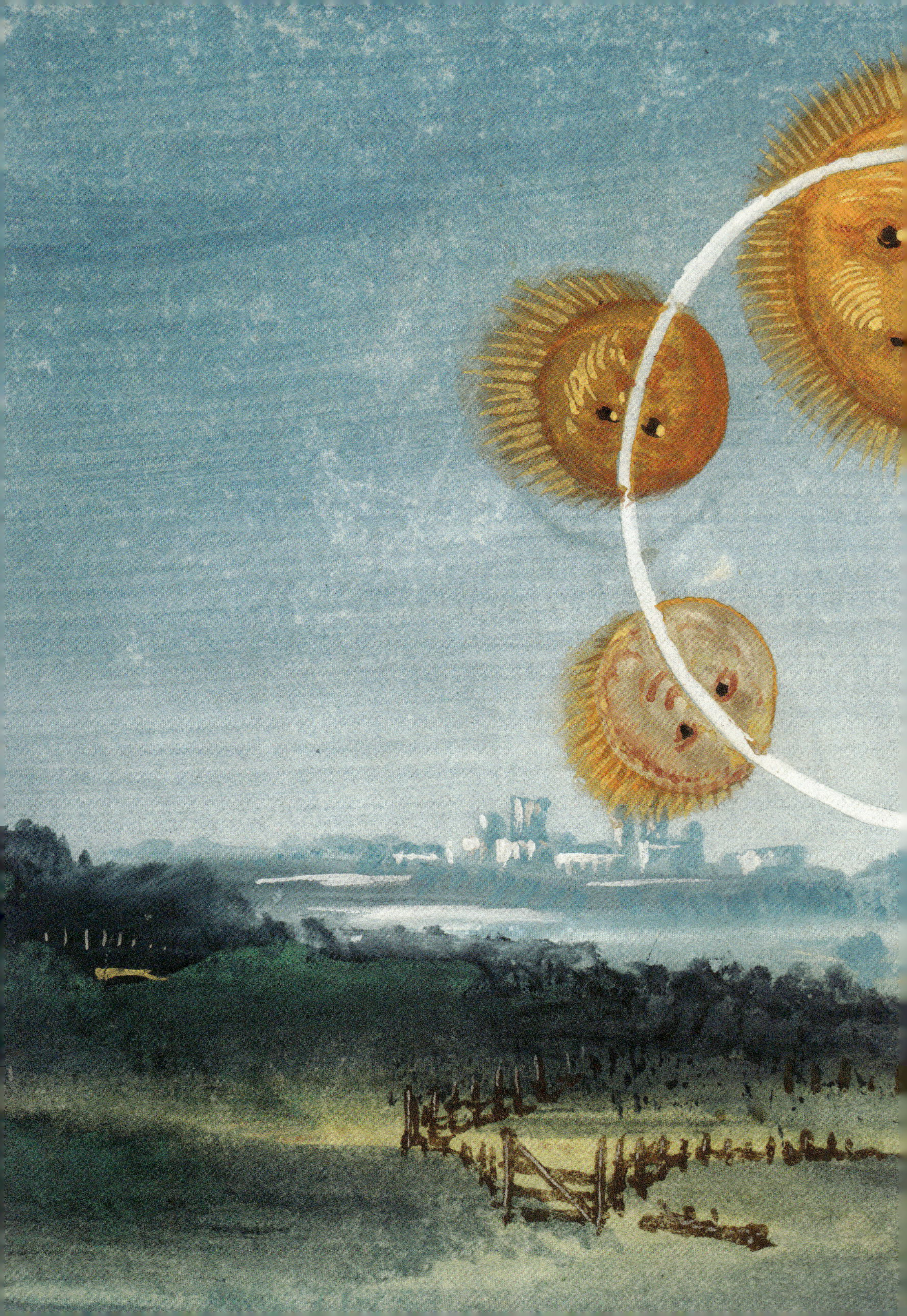

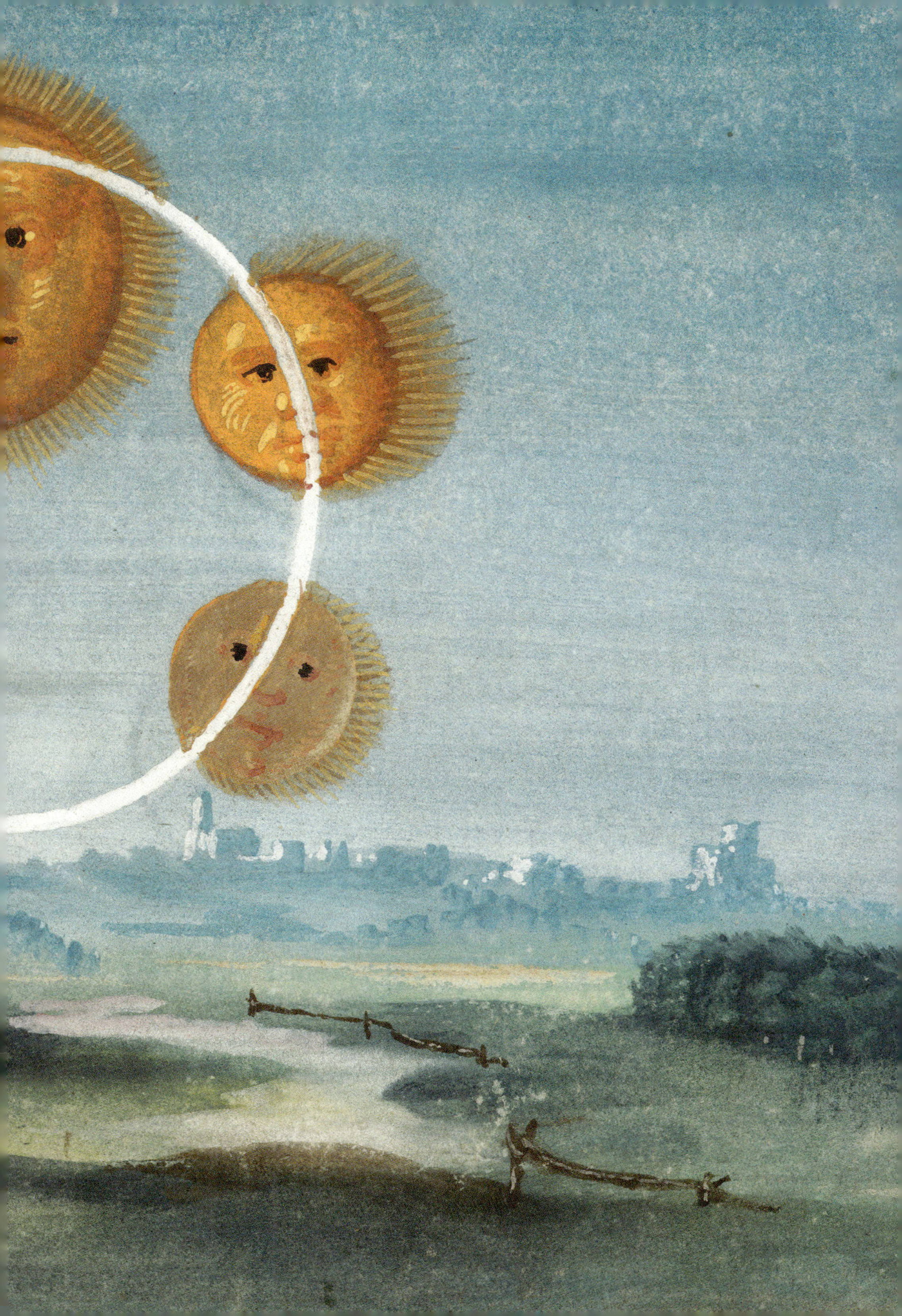

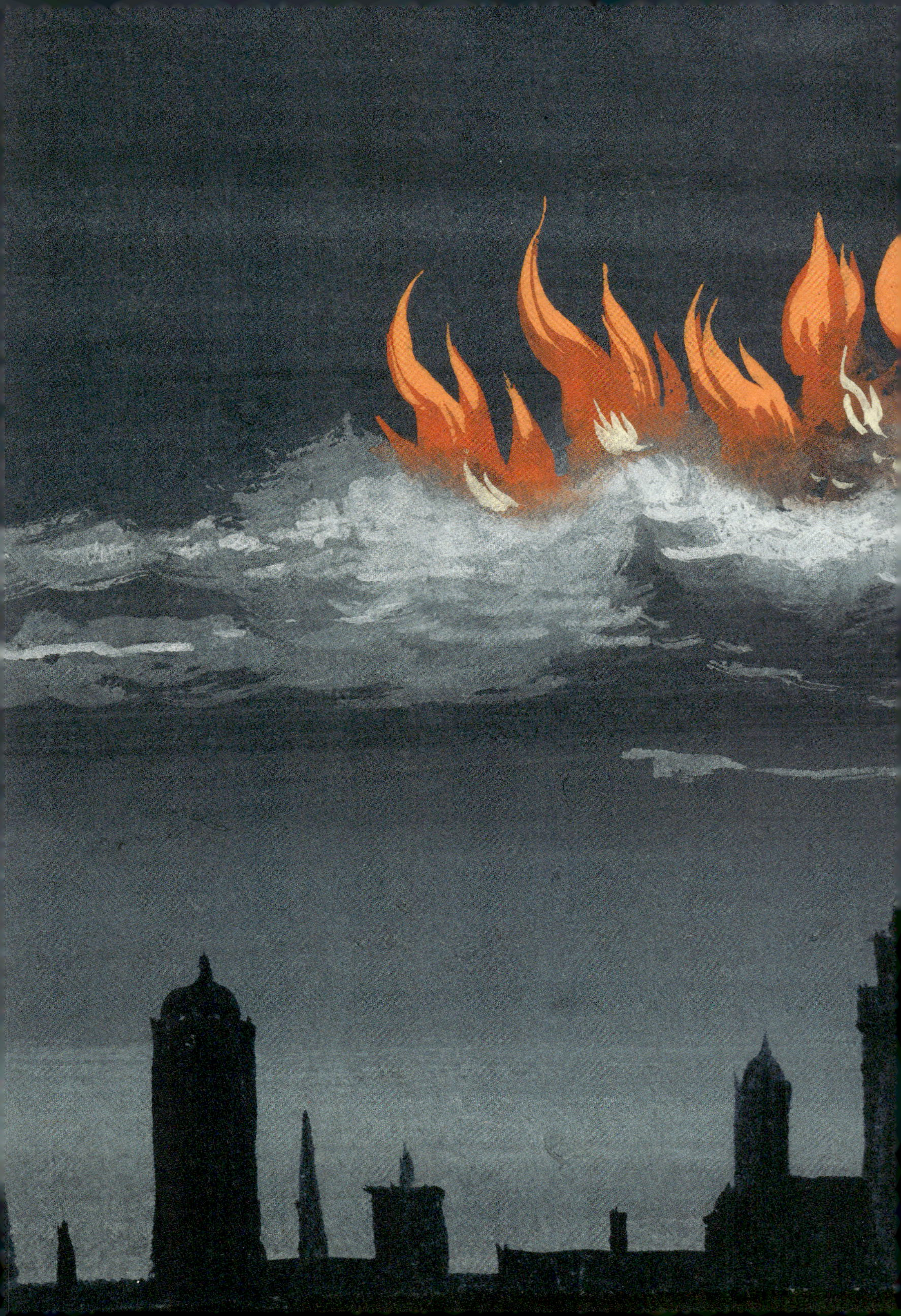

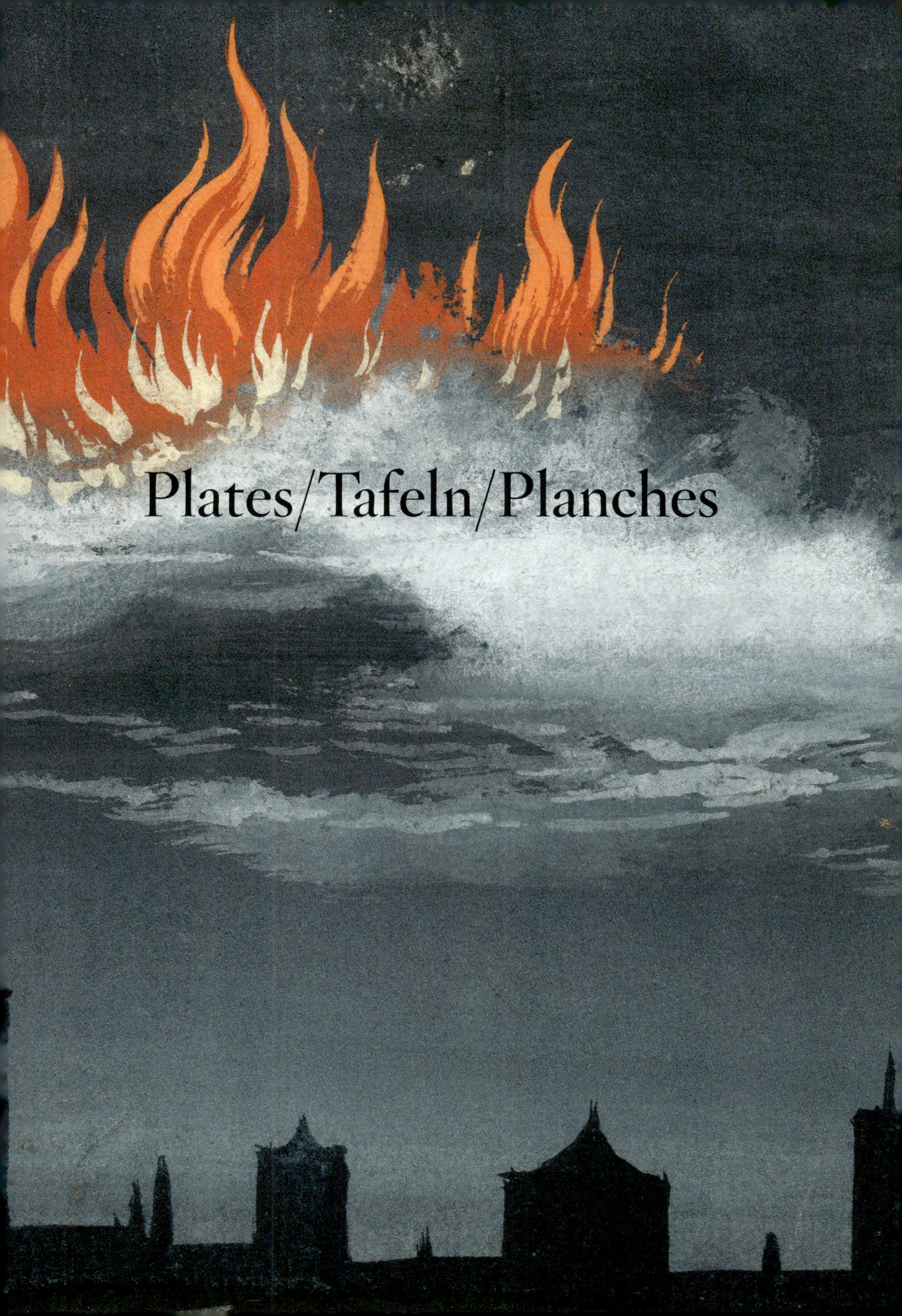

Plates/Tafeln/Planches

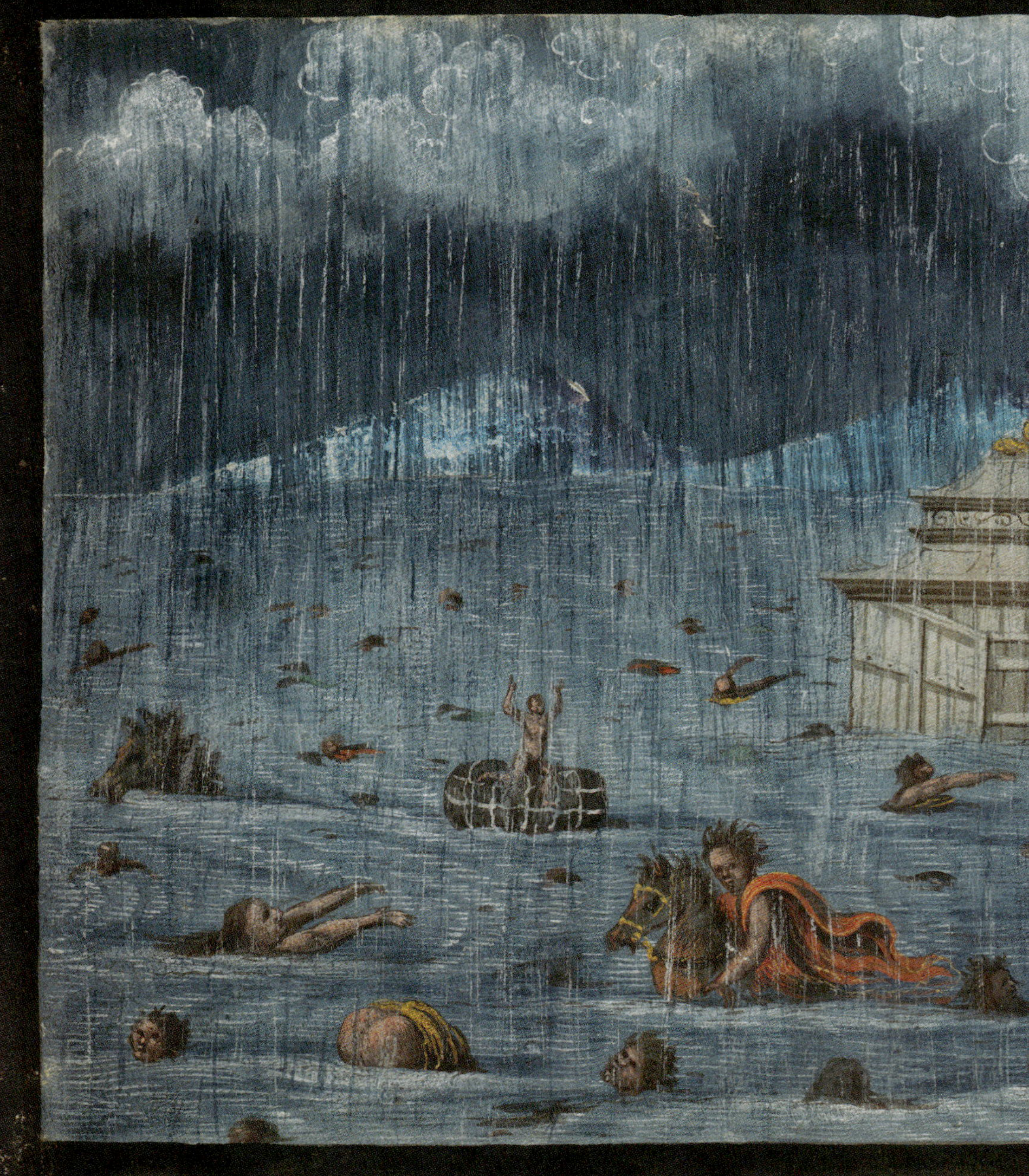

Genesi

In dem sechshünderten iar des alters Noah, am sieben zehend
tieffe vnnd thetten sich auff die fenster des himels vnnd ka
gieng Noah in den kasten mit Sem, Ham vnnd Japhet
aller ley gewürm das auff erden kreücht nach seiner art

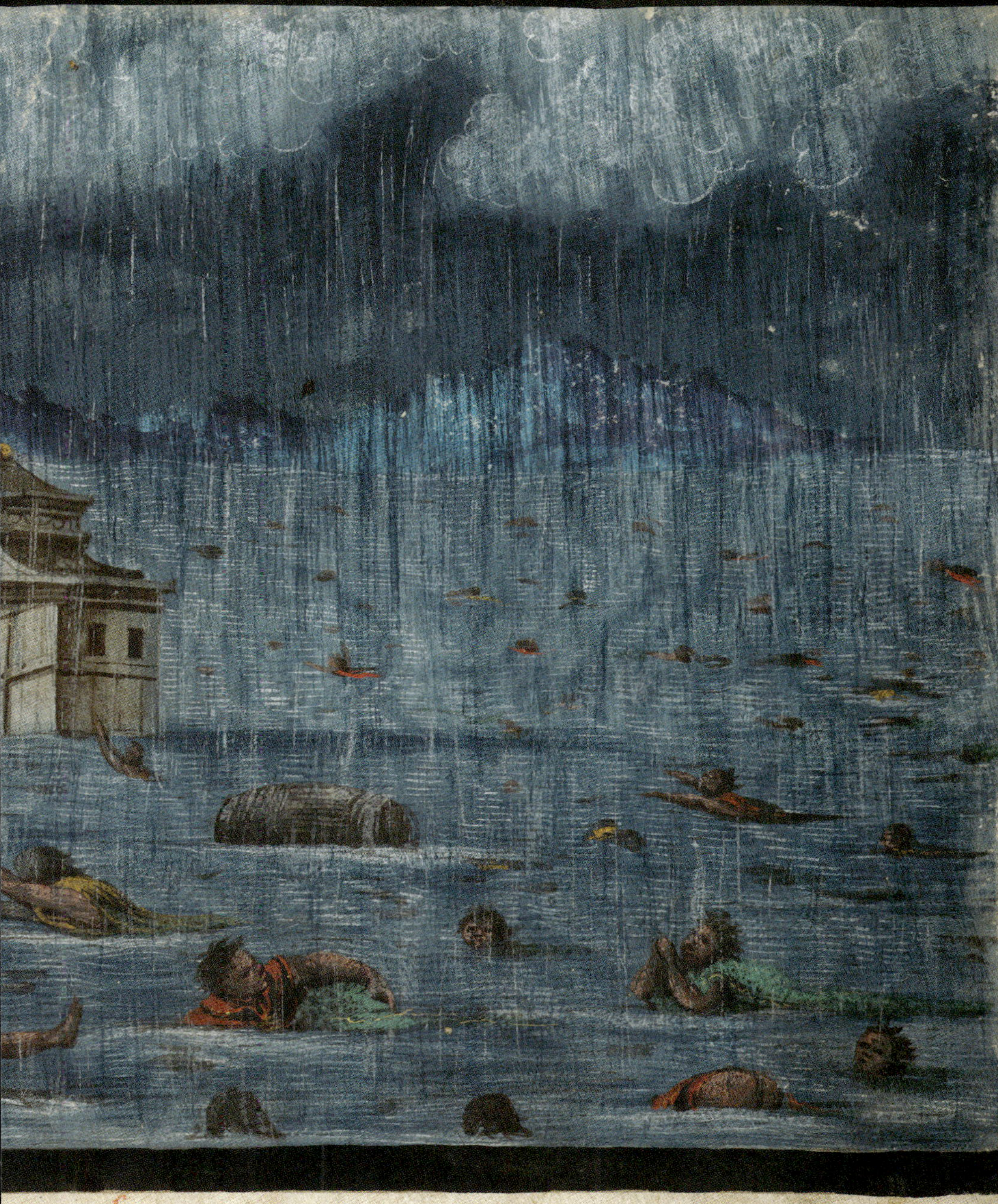

i capitel

s andern mondes, das ist der tag, da aufprachen alle brunen der grossen
en auf erden vierzig tage vnnd vierzig nachte. Eben am selben tage
nnen vnd mit seinem weibe dar zu allerley thier nach seiner art.
llerley gevogel nach irer art alles was fliegen kunt vnd alles was da.

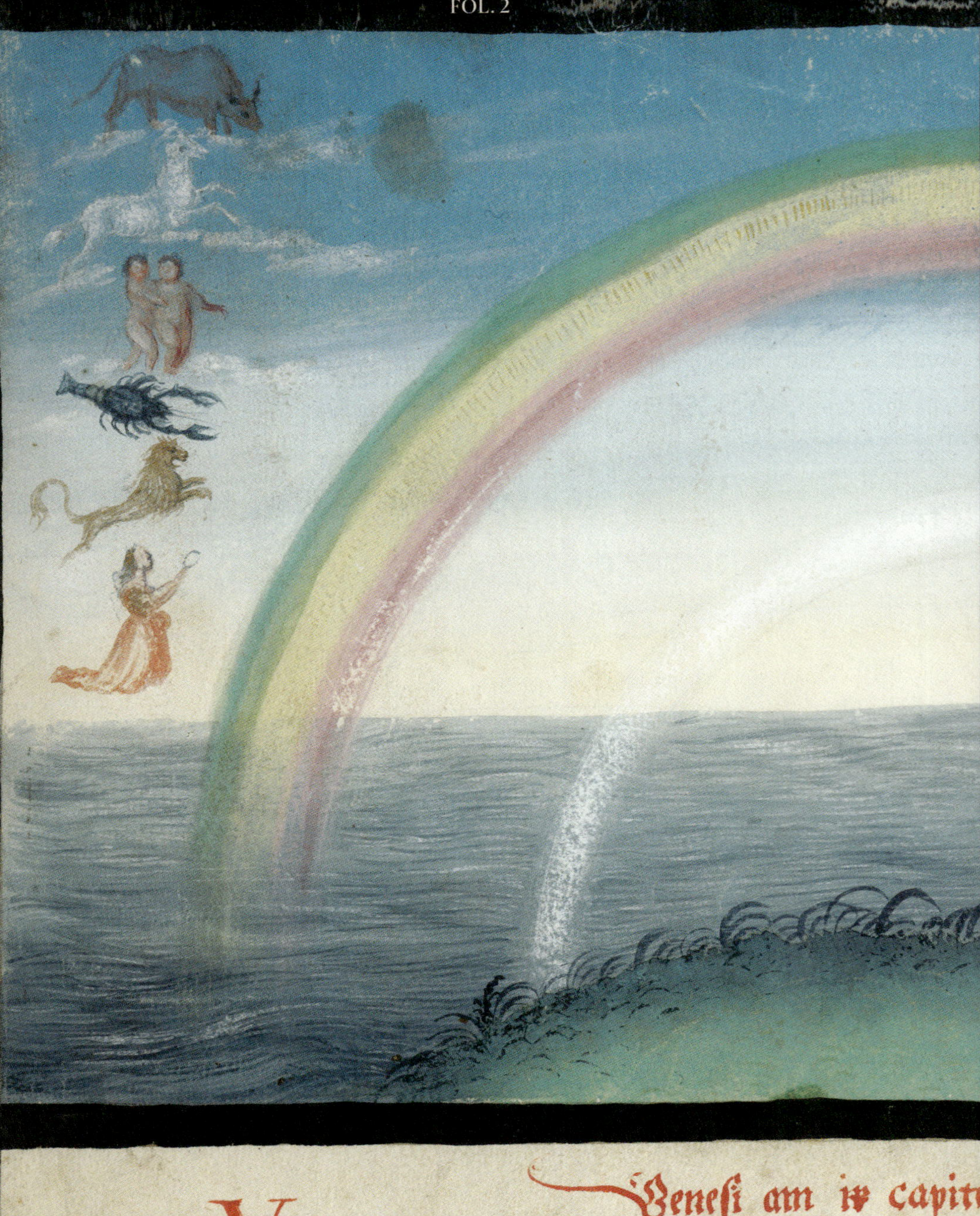

Genesi am ix capit

Vnd gott sprach/ das ist das zeichenn meins bunds/ den ich gemach
Ewigklich meinen bogen hab ich gesetzt in die wolcken d
Wen es kommett das ich wolcken vber die erden füre/ so
an meinen bunt

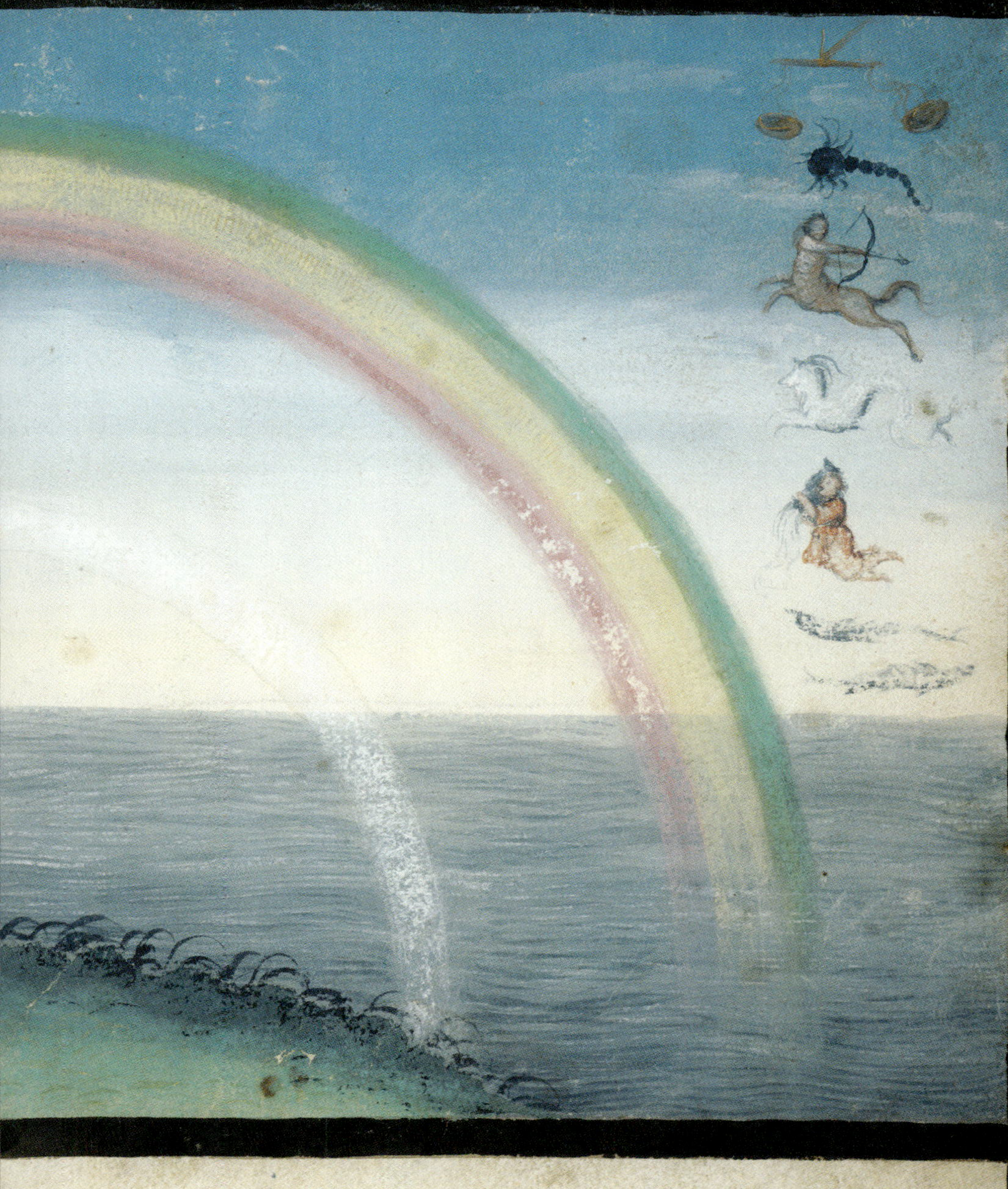

ischen mir vnnd euch vnd allem lebendigen thier bei euch hinfurt
s zaichen sein meins bunds zwischen mir vnnd der erden vnnd:
n meinen bogen sehen in den wolcken als den wil ich gedencken

FOL. 1

The Deluge | Die Sintflut | Le Déluge

Genesis 7:11–14 – 11 In the six hundredth year of Noah's life, in the second month, on the seventeenth day of the month, on that day all the fountains of the great deep burst forth, and the windows of the heavens were opened. 12 And rain fell upon the earth forty days and forty nights. 13 On the very same day Noah and his sons, Shem and Ham and Japheth, and Noah's wife and the three wives of his sons with them entered the ark, 14 they and every beast, according to its kind, and all the livestock according to their kinds, and every creeping thing that creeps on the earth, according to its kind, and every bird, according to its kind, every winged creature.

Genesis 7,11–14 – 11 In dem sechshundertsten Lebensjahr Noahs am siebzehnten Tag des zweiten Monats, an diesem Tag brachen alle Brunnen der großen Tiefe auf und taten sich die Fenster des Himmels auf, 12 und ein Regen kam auf Erden vierzig Tage und vierzig Nächte. 13 An eben diesem Tage ging Noah in die Arche mit Sem, Ham und Jafet, seinen Söhnen, und mit seiner Frau und den drei Frauen seiner Söhne; 14 dazu alles wilde Getier nach seiner Art, alles Vieh nach seiner Art, alles Gewürm, das auf Erden kriecht, nach seiner Art und alle Vögel nach ihrer Art, alles, was fliegen konnte, alles, was […].

Genèse 7:11–14 – 11 En l'an six cent de la vie de Noé, le second mois, le dix-septième jour du mois, ce jour-là jaillirent toutes les sources du grand abîme et les écluses du ciel s'ouvrirent. 12 La pluie tomba sur la terre pendant quarante jours et quarante nuits. 13 Ce jour même, Noé et ses fils, Sem, Cham et Japhet, avec la femme de Noé et les trois femmes de ses fils, entrèrent dans l'arche, 14 et avec eux les bêtes sauvages de toute espèce, les bestiaux de toute espèce, les bestioles de toute espèce qui rampent sur la terre, les volatiles de toute espèce, tout ce qui a des ailes.

FOL. 2

The sign of the covenant | Das Zeichen des Bundes | Le signe de l'alliance

Genesis 9:12–15 – 12 And God said, "This is the sign of the covenant that I make between me and you and every living creature that is with you, for all future generations: 13 I have set my bow in the cloud, and it shall be a sign of the covenant between me and the earth. 14 When I bring clouds over the earth and the bow is seen in the clouds, 15 I will remember my covenant […]."

Genesis 9,12–15 – 12 Und Gott sprach: Das ist das Zeichen des Bundes, den ich geschlossen habe zwischen mir und euch und allem lebendigen Getier bei euch auf ewig: 13 Meinen Bogen habe ich in die Wolken gesetzt; der soll das Zeichen sein des Bundes zwischen mir und der Erde. 14 Und wenn es kommt, dass ich Wetterwolken über die Erde führe, so soll man meinen Bogen sehen in den Wolken. 15 Als dann will ich gedenken an meinen Bund […].

Genèse 9:12–15 – 12 Et Dieu dit : « Voici le signe de l'alliance que j'institue entre moi et vous et tous les êtres vivants qui sont avec vous, pour les générations à venir : 13 je mets mon arc dans la nuée et il deviendra un signe d'alliance entre moi et la terre. 14 Lorsque j'assemblerai les nuées sur la terre et que l'arc apparaîtra dans la nuée, 15 je me souviendrai de l'alliance […]. »

FOL. 4

Sodom and Gomorrah | Sodom und Gomorrha | Sodome et Gomorrhe

Genesis 19:24–26 – 24 Then the LORD rained on Sodom and Gomorrah sulphur and fire from the LORD out of heaven. 25 And he overthrew those cities, and all the valley, and all the inhabitants of the cities, and what grew on the ground. 26 But Lot's wife, behind him, looked back, and she became a pillar of salt.

Genesis 19,24–26 – 24 Da ließ der HERR Schwefel und Feuer regnen vom Himmel herab auf Sodom und Gomorra 25 und vernichtete die Städte und die ganze Gegend und alle Einwohner der Städte und was auf dem Lande gewachsen war. 26 Und Lots Frau sah hinter sich und ward zur Salzsäule.

Genèse 19:24–26 – 24 Yahvé fit pleuvoir sur Sodome et sur Gomorrhe du soufre et du feu venant de Yahvé, depuis le ciel, 25 et il renversa ces villes et toute la plaine, tous ses habitants et la végétation du sol. 26 Or la femme de Lot regarda en arrière, et elle devint une colonne de sel.

FOL. 5

Moses parting the Red Sea
Moses teilt das Rote Meer | Moïse fend les eaux de la mer Rouge

Exodus 14:27–29 – 27 So Moses stretched out his hand over the sea, and the sea returned to its normal course when the morning appeared. And as the Egyptians fled into it, the LORD threw the Egyptians into the midst of the sea. 28 The waters returned and covered the chariots and the horsemen; of all the host of Pharaoh that had followed them into the sea, not one of them remained. 29 But the people of Israel walked on dry ground through the sea, the waters being a wall to them on their right hand and on their left.

Exodus 14,27–29 – 27 Da reckte Mose seine Hand aus über das Meer, und das Meer kam gegen Morgen wieder in sein Bett, und die Ägypter flohen ihm entgegen. So stürzte der HERR sie mitten ins Meer. 28 Und das Wasser kam wieder und bedeckte Wagen und Männer, das ganze Heer des Pharao, das ihnen nachgefolgt war ins Meer, sodass nicht einer von ihnen übrig blieb. 29 Aber die Israeliten gingen trocken mitten durchs Meer, und das Wasser war ihnen eine Mauer zur Rechten und zur Linken.

Exode 14:27–29 – 27 Moïse étendit la main sur la mer et, au point du jour, la mer rentra dans son lit. Les Égyptiens en fuyant la rencontrèrent, et Yahvé culbuta les Égyptiens au milieu de la mer. 28 Les eaux refluèrent et recouvrirent les chars et les cavaliers de toute l'armée de Pharaon, qui avaient pénétré derrière eux dans la mer. Il n'en resta pas un seul. 29 Les Israélites, eux, marchèrent à pied sec au milieu de la mer, et les eaux leur formèrent une muraille à droite et à gauche.

Note In the 19th century the following folia were removed:
3, 17, 22, 25, 31, 33, 40, 43, 53, 80, 89, 96, 105, 108, 130, 132, 140, 143, 148, 152, 162.

Genesi am xix capitel

Da lies der herr schwefel vnnd feiwer regnen von dem herren
ganzen gegent vnnd alle ein woner der stete vnnd wa
war zů einer salz seule

mel herab auff Sodama Gomora vnnd keret die stet vmb die
dem landt gewachsen war vnnd sein weib sahe hinder sich vnd

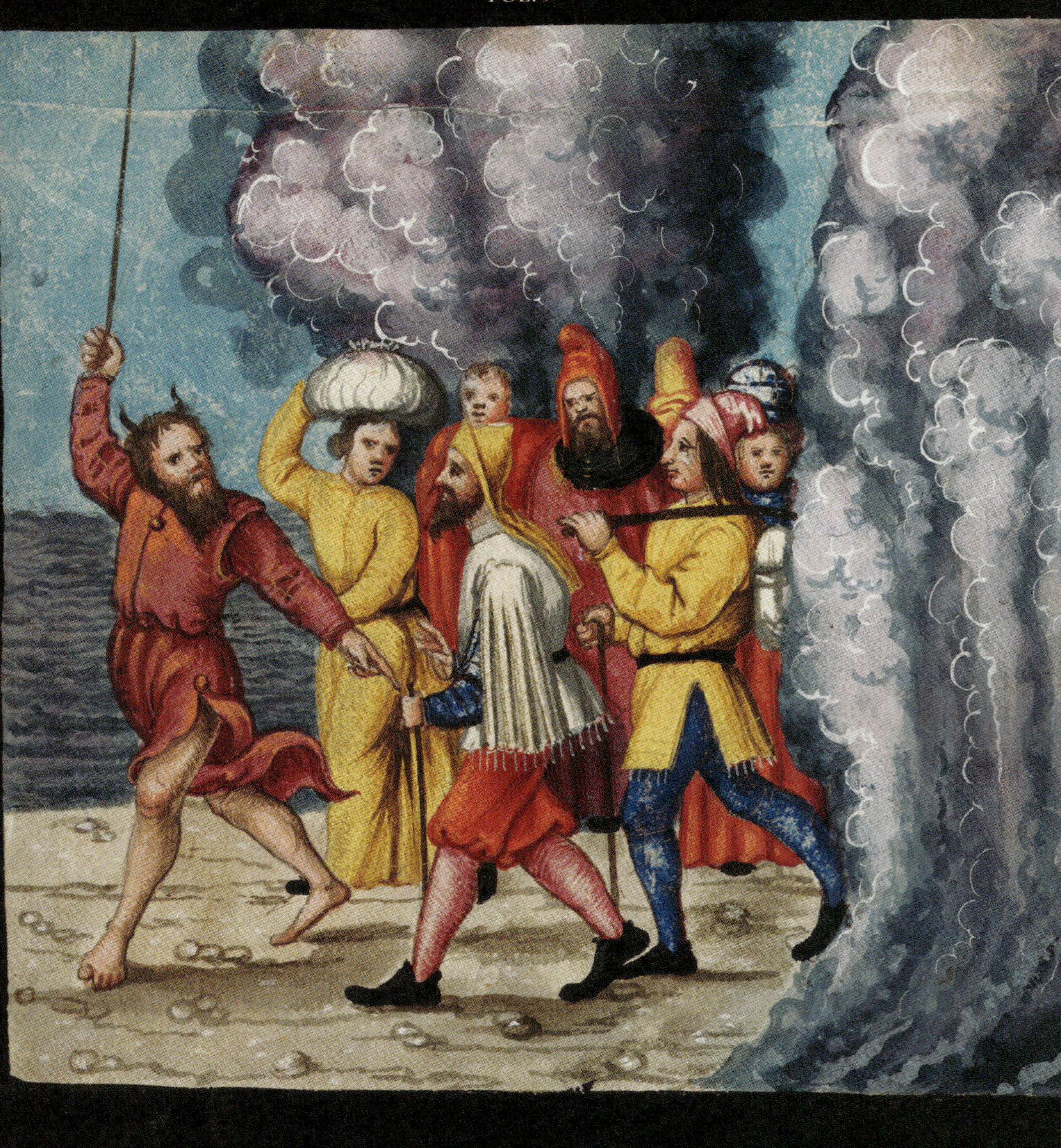

Exodi am xiiii capitel

Da recket mose sein hannd auf vber das meer vnnd das m
flohen im entgegen also sturtzet sy der herr mi
en vnnd reutter vnd alle macht des pharo die im n
bleib aber die kinder Israhel giengen trocken mit
rechten vnnd zur lincken

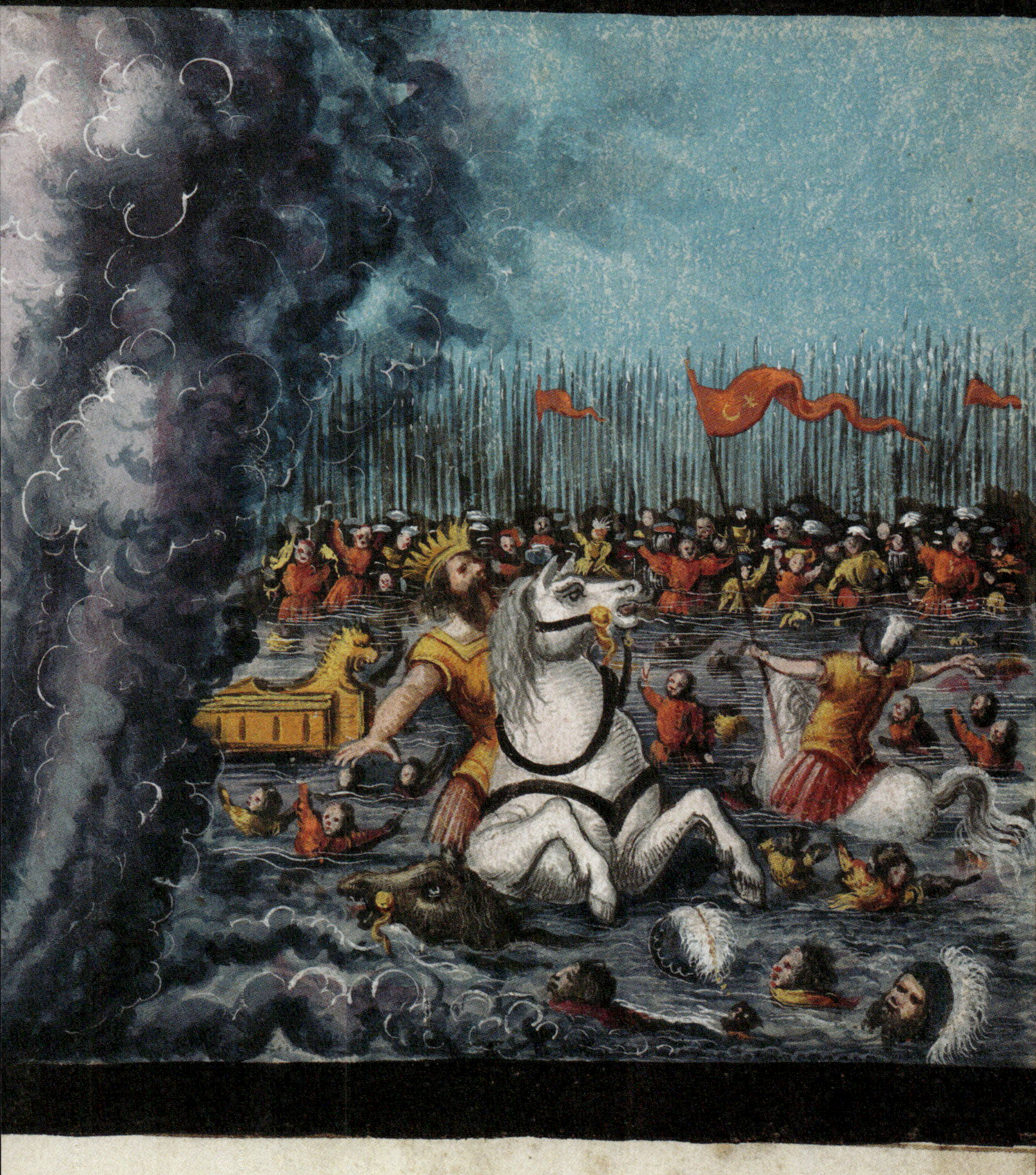

n wieder für morgens in seinen strom/ vnnd die Egiptter:
as meer das das wasser wieder kom/ vnnd bedecket wag:
volget waren ins meer das nit ainer aus inen vberr!
rchs meer vnnd das waser war in für mauren zur

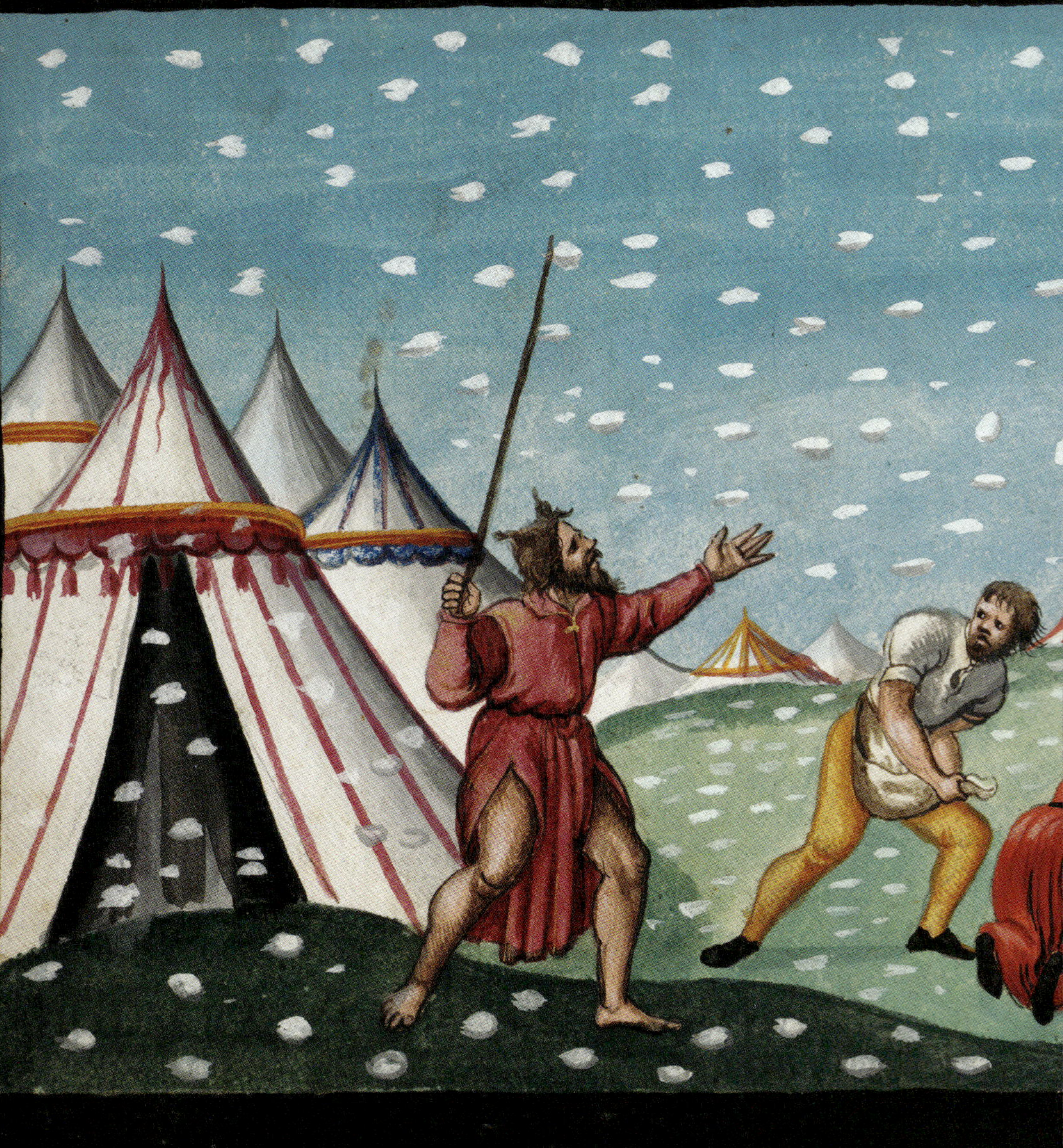

Exodi am xvi capitel

Vnnd als der taw gefallen wass siehe das lag etwas in
es die kinder Israhel sahen/ sprachens sy vnnder and
es ist das brot das euch der herr zu Essen gegeben
vil er fur sich isset vnnd neme ein Gomor auff

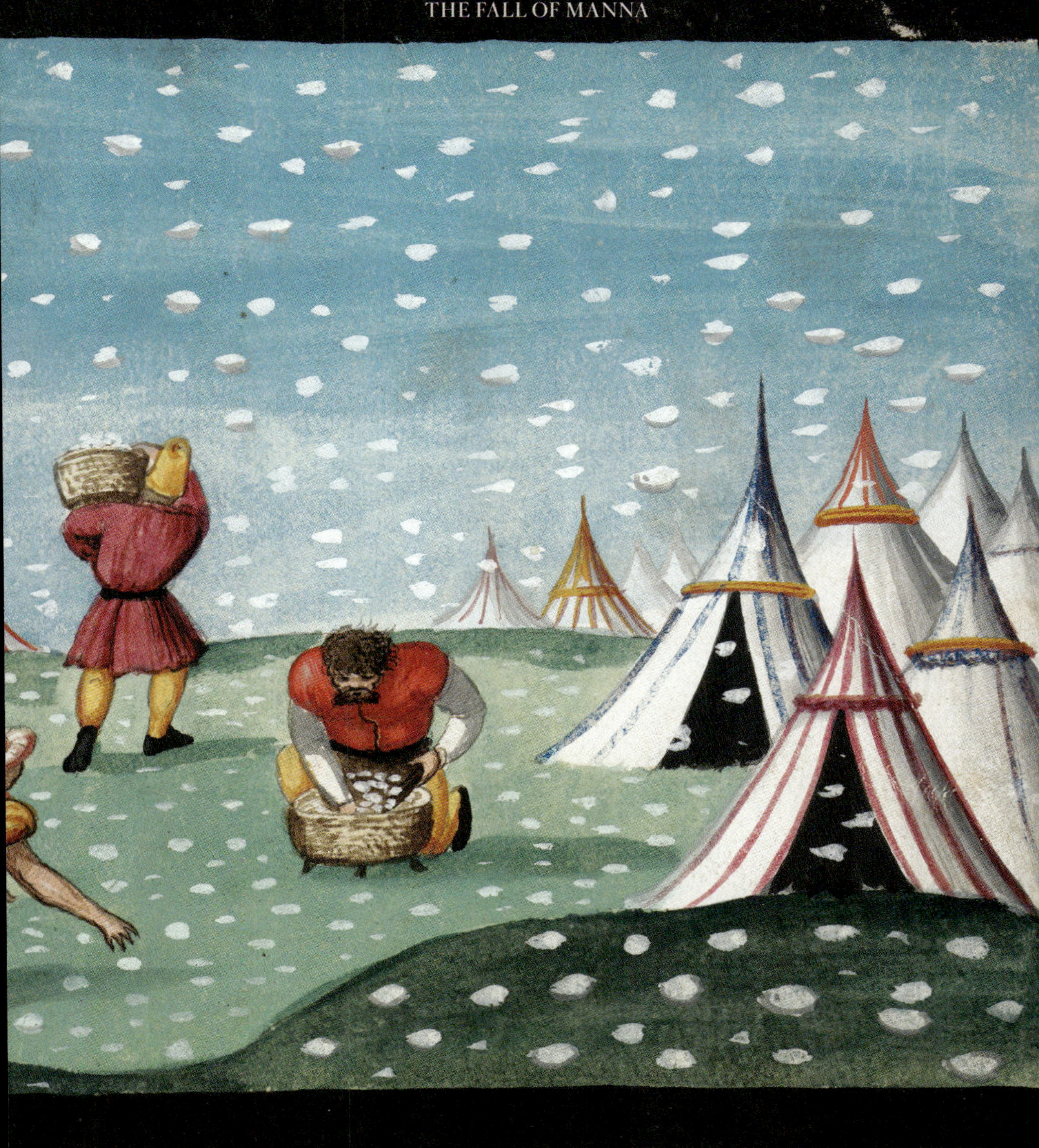

üſten dünne vnnd klain wie der reyffe auff dem land iſt/ vnnd da:
iſt man den ſi wüſten nicht waſ es war moſe aber ſprach zu:
as iſt aber das der herr gebotten hat/ ein yglicher ſamle des ſo:
eglich haupt nach der zal der ſelen in ſeiner hütten - - - -

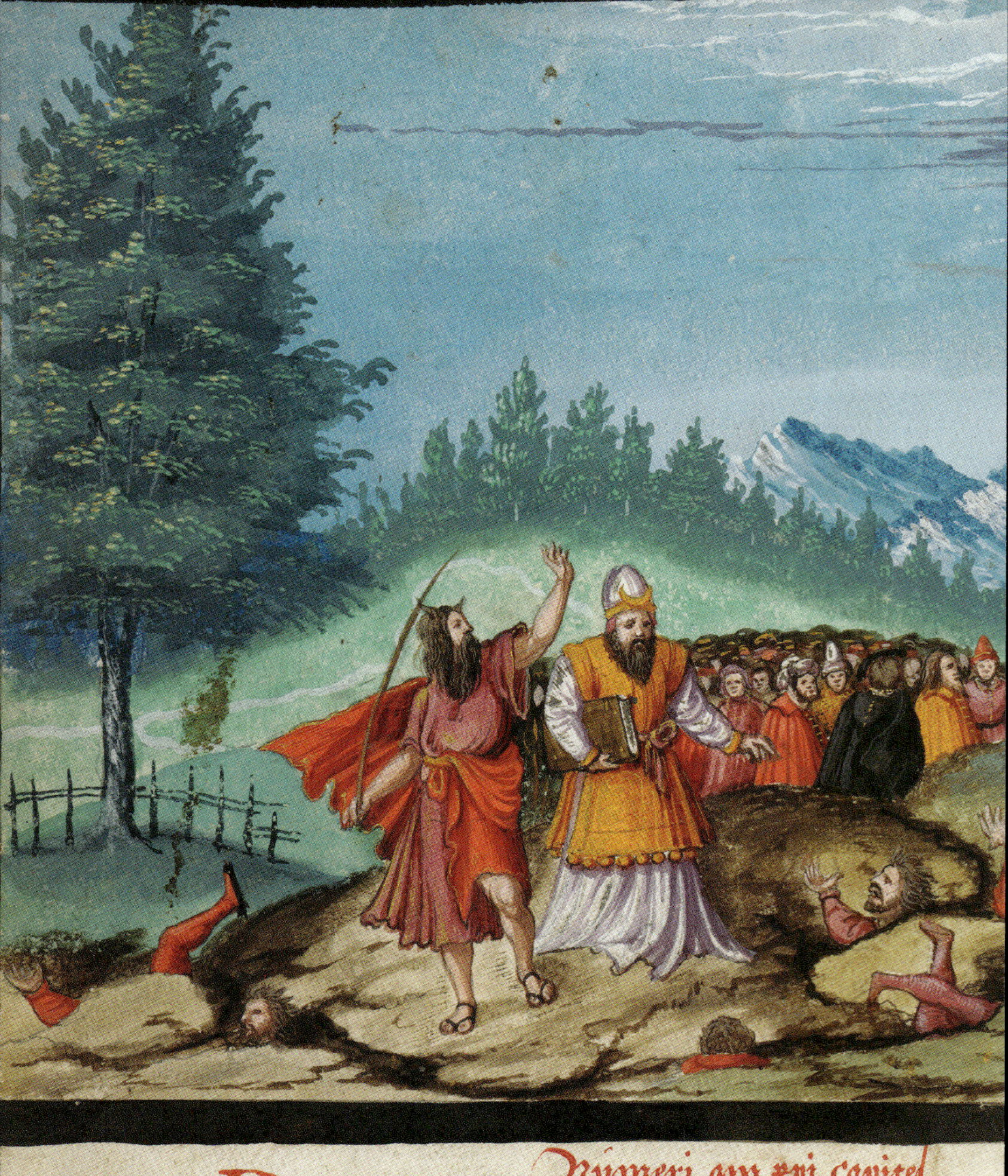

Numeri am xvi capitel

Da das mose horet: fil er auff sein angesicht vnnd sprach
kunt thůn wer sein sey wer heilige sey vnnd zu im
thůt nemet für euch pfannen korah vnnd sein gan
vor dem herren morgen welchen der herr erwoll

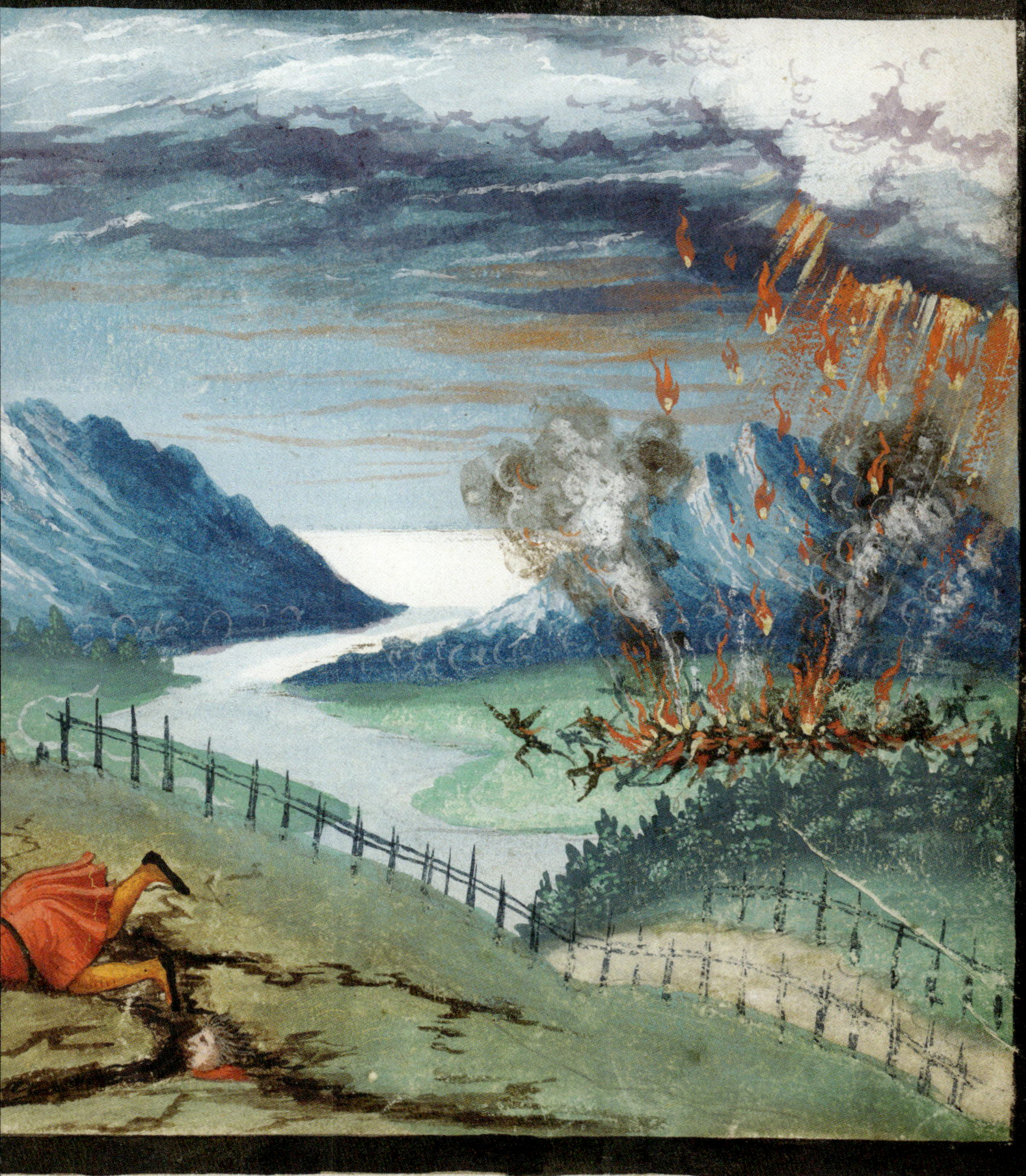

rah vnnd zů seiner gantzen rotte morgen wirt der herr
en soll wölchen er erwölet der söl sich zů im nahen das
otte vnnd legt feüer drein vnnd thůt reüchwerck drauf
r sey heylig ir machts zů vil ir kinder leui

FOL. 6

The fall of manna | Mannaregen | La manne tombée du ciel

Exodus 16:14–16 – 14 And when the dew had gone up, there was on the face of the wilderness a fine, flake-like thing, fine as frost on the ground. 15 When the people of Israel saw it, they said to one another, "What is it?" For they did not know what it was. And Moses said to them, "It is the bread that the LORD has given you to eat. 16 This is what the LORD has commanded: 'Gather of it, each one of you, as much as he can eat. You shall each take an omer, according to the number of the persons that each of you has in his tent.'"

Exodus 16:14–16 – 14 Und als der Tau weg war, siehe, da lag's in der Wüste rund und klein wie Reif auf der Erde. 15 Und als es die Israeliten sahen, sprachen sie untereinander: Man hu? Denn sie wussten nicht, was es war. Mose aber sprach zu ihnen: Es ist das Brot, das euch der HERR zu essen gegeben hat. 16 Das ist's aber, was der HERR geboten hat: Ein jeder sammle, soviel er zum Essen braucht, einen Krug voll für jeden nach der Zahl der Leute in seinem Zelte.

Exode 16:14–16 – 14 Une fois la couche de rosée évaporée, apparut sur la surface du désert quelque chose de menu, de granuleux, de fin comme du givre sur le sol. 15 Lorsque les Israélites virent cela, ils se dirent l'un à l'autre : « Qu'est-ce que cela ? » Car ils ne savaient pas ce que c'était. Moïse leur dit : « Cela, c'est le pain que Yahvé vous a donné à manger. 16 Voici ce qu'a ordonné Yahvé : Recueillez-en chacun selon ce qu'il peut manger, un gomor par personne. Vous en prendrez chacun selon le nombre des personnes qu'il a dans sa tente. »

FOL. 7

Moses and the sons of Levi
Moses und die Söhne Levis | Moïse et les fils de Lévi

Numbers 16:4–7 – 4 When Moses heard it, he fell on his face, 5 and he said to Korah and all his company, "In the morning the LORD will show who is his, and who is holy, and will bring him near to him. The one whom he chooses he will bring near to him. 6 Do this: take censers, Korah and all his company; 7 put fire in them and put incense on them before the LORD tomorrow, and the man whom the LORD chooses shall be the holy one. You have gone too far, sons of Levi!"

Numeri 16,4–7 – 4 Als Mose das hörte, fiel er auf sein Angesicht 5 und sprach zu Korach und zu seiner ganzen Rotte: Morgen wird der HERR kundtun, wer ihm gehört, wer heilig ist und zu ihm nahen soll; wen er erwählt, der soll zu ihm nahen. 6 Dies tut morgen: Nehmt euch Pfannen, Korach und seine ganze Rotte, 7 und legt Feuer hinein und tut Räucherwerk darauf vor dem HERRN. Wen dann der HERR erwählt, der ist heilig. Ihr geht zu weit, ihr Söhne Levi!

Nombres 16:4–7 – 4 Moïse, l'ayant entendu, tomba face contre terre. 5 Puis il dit à Coré et à tout son groupe : « Demain matin, Yahvé fera connaître qui est à lui, qui est l'homme consacré qu'il laissera approcher de lui. Celui qu'il fera approcher de lui, c'est celui-là qu'il choisit. 6 Voici ce que vous ferez : prenez les encensoirs de Coré et de tout son groupe, 7 mettez-y du feu et, demain, déposez dessus de l'encens devant Yahvé. Celui que choisira Yahvé, c'est lui l'homme consacré. Vous passez la mesure, fils de Lévi ! »

FOL. 8

Elijah and Elisha | Elija und Elischa | Élie et Élisée

2 Kings 2:11–12 – 11 And as they still went on and talked, behold, chariots of fire and horses of fire separated the two of them. And Elijah went up by a whirlwind into heaven. 12 And Elisha saw it and he cried, "My father, my father! The chariots of Israel [...]."

2. Könige 2,11–12 – 11 Und als sie miteinander gingen und redeten, siehe, da kam ein feuriger Wagen mit feurigen Rossen, die schieden die beiden voneinander. Und Elia fuhr im Wetter gen Himmel. 12 Elisa aber sah es und schrie: Mein Vater, mein Vater, du Wagen Israels [...].

Deuxième Livre des Rois 2:11–12 – 11 Or, comme ils marchaient en conversant, voici qu'un char de feu et des chevaux de feu se mirent entre eux deux, et Élie monta au ciel dans le tourbillon. 12 Élisée voyait et il criait : « Mon père ! Mon père ! Char d'Israël [...] ».

FOL. 9

Isaiah's vision | Vision des Jesaja | Vision d'Isaïe

Isaiah 1:1–3 – 1 The vision of Isaiah the son of Amoz, which he saw concerning Judah and Jerusalem in the days of Uzziah, Jotham, Ahaz and Hezekiah, kings of Judah. 2 Hear, O heavens, and give ear, O earth; for the LORD has spoken: "Children have I reared and brought up, but they have rebelled against me. 3 The ox knows its owner, and the donkey its master's crib, but Israel does not know, my people do not understand."

Jesaja 1,1–3 – 1 Dies ist die Offenbarung, die Jesaja, der Sohn des Amoz, geschaut hat über Juda und Jerusalem zur Zeit des Usija, Jotam, Ahas und Hiskia, der Könige von Juda. 2 Höret, ihr Himmel, und Erde, nimm zu Ohren, denn der HERR redet! Ich habe Kinder großgezogen und hochgebracht, und sie sind von mir abgefallen! 3 Ein Ochse kennt seinen Herrn und ein Esel die Krippe seines Herrn; aber Israel kennt's nicht, und mein Volk versteht's nicht.

Isaïe 1:1–3 – 1 Vision d'Isaïe, fils d'Amoç, qu'il reçut au sujet de Juda et de Jérusalem, au temps d'Ozias, de Yotam, d'Achaz et d'Ézéchias, rois de Juda. 2 Cieux écoutez, terre prête l'oreille, car Yahvé parle. « J'ai élevé des enfants, je les ai fait grandir, mais ils se sont révoltés contre moi. 3 Le bœuf connaît son possesseur, et l'âne la crèche de son maître, Israël ne connaît pas, mon peuple ne comprend pas. »

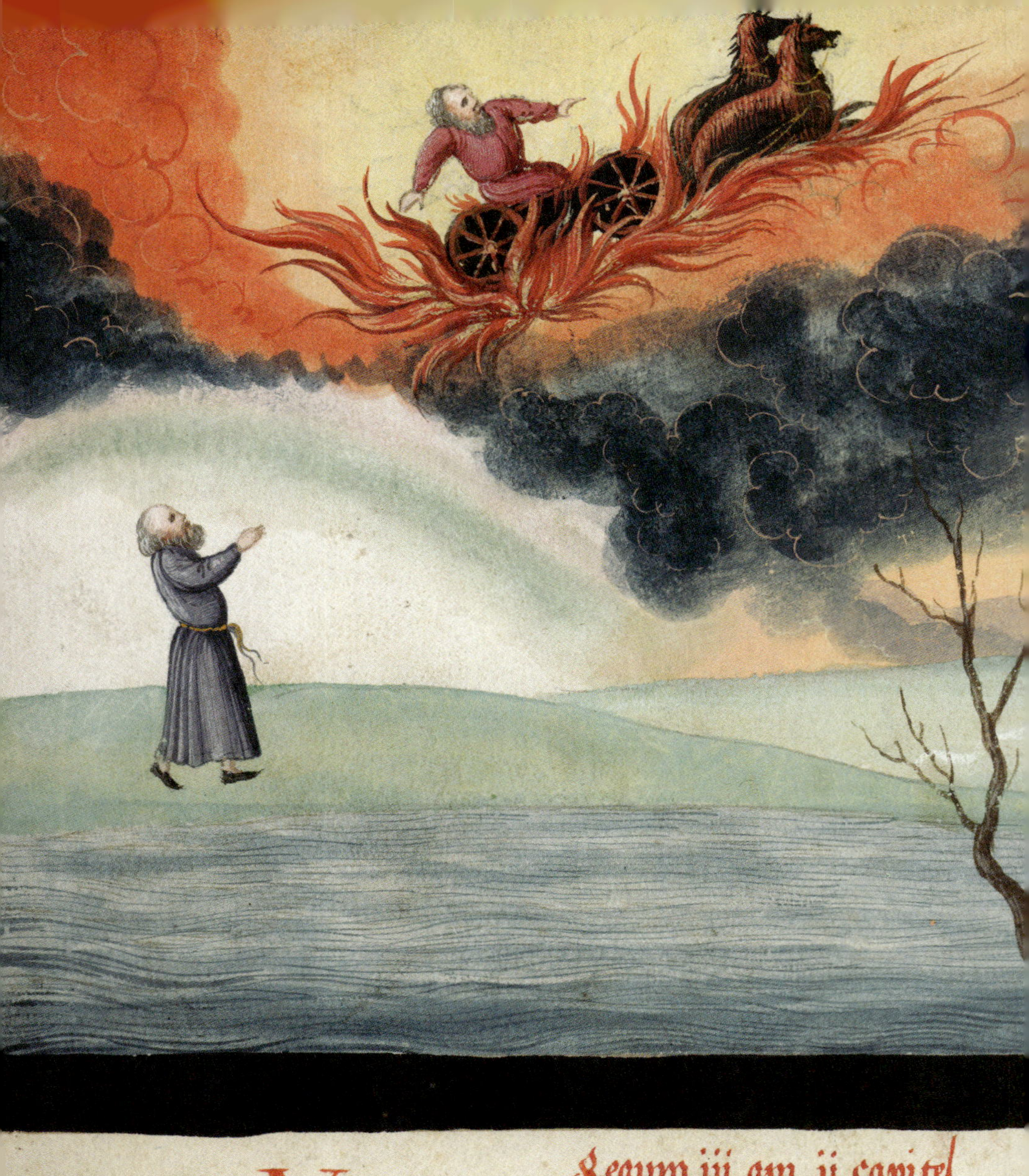

Regum iii am ii capitel

Vnnd da sie mit einander giengen vnnd
vnnd der wagen war auch gantz feürig
also im weter gen hiemel Elisa sahe es

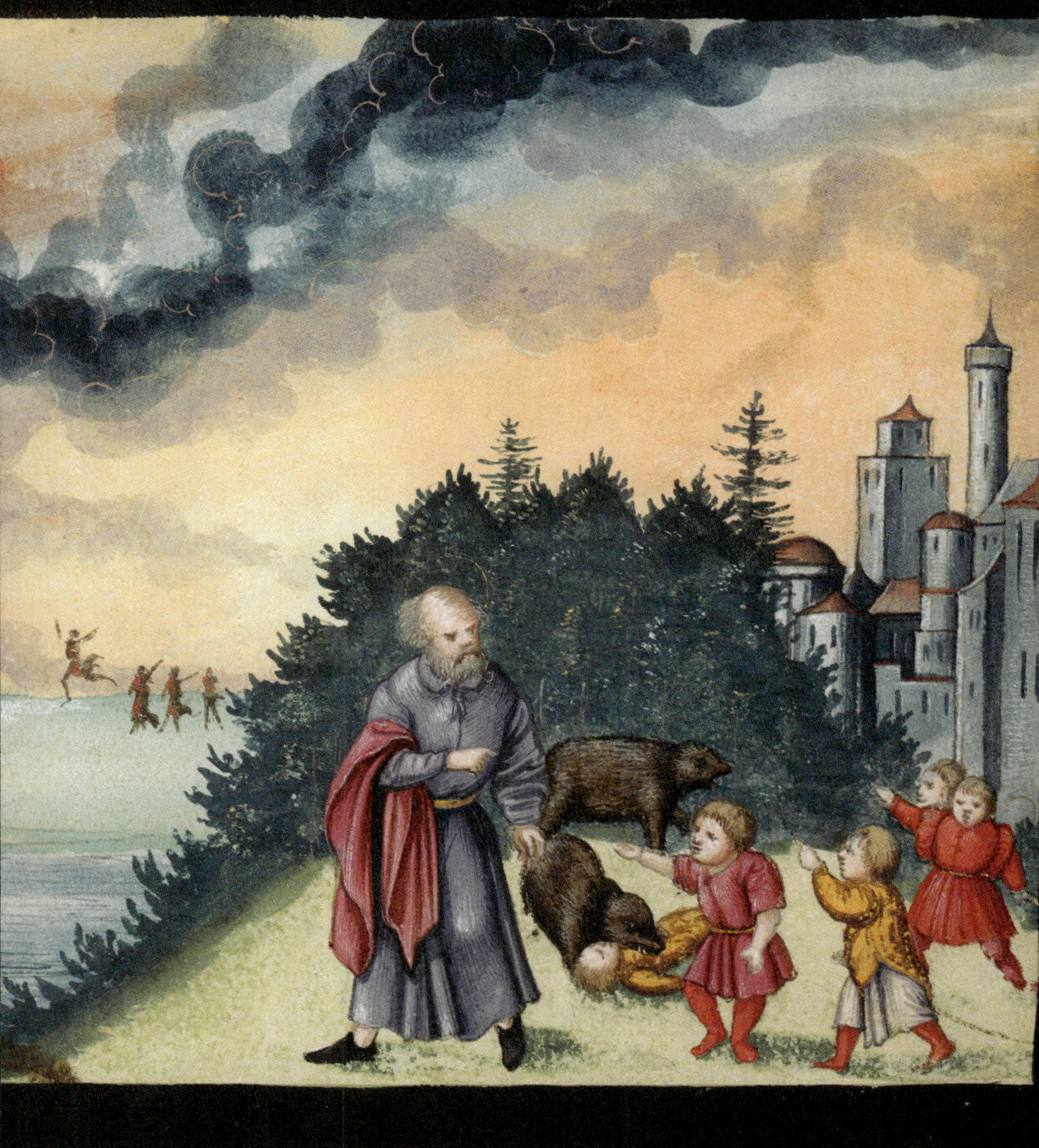

eten: siehe da kam ein wagen mit feürigen rossen
d schiedenten baid von ain ander vnnd Ellia für
schrei mein vatter: mein vatter: fürman Israhel

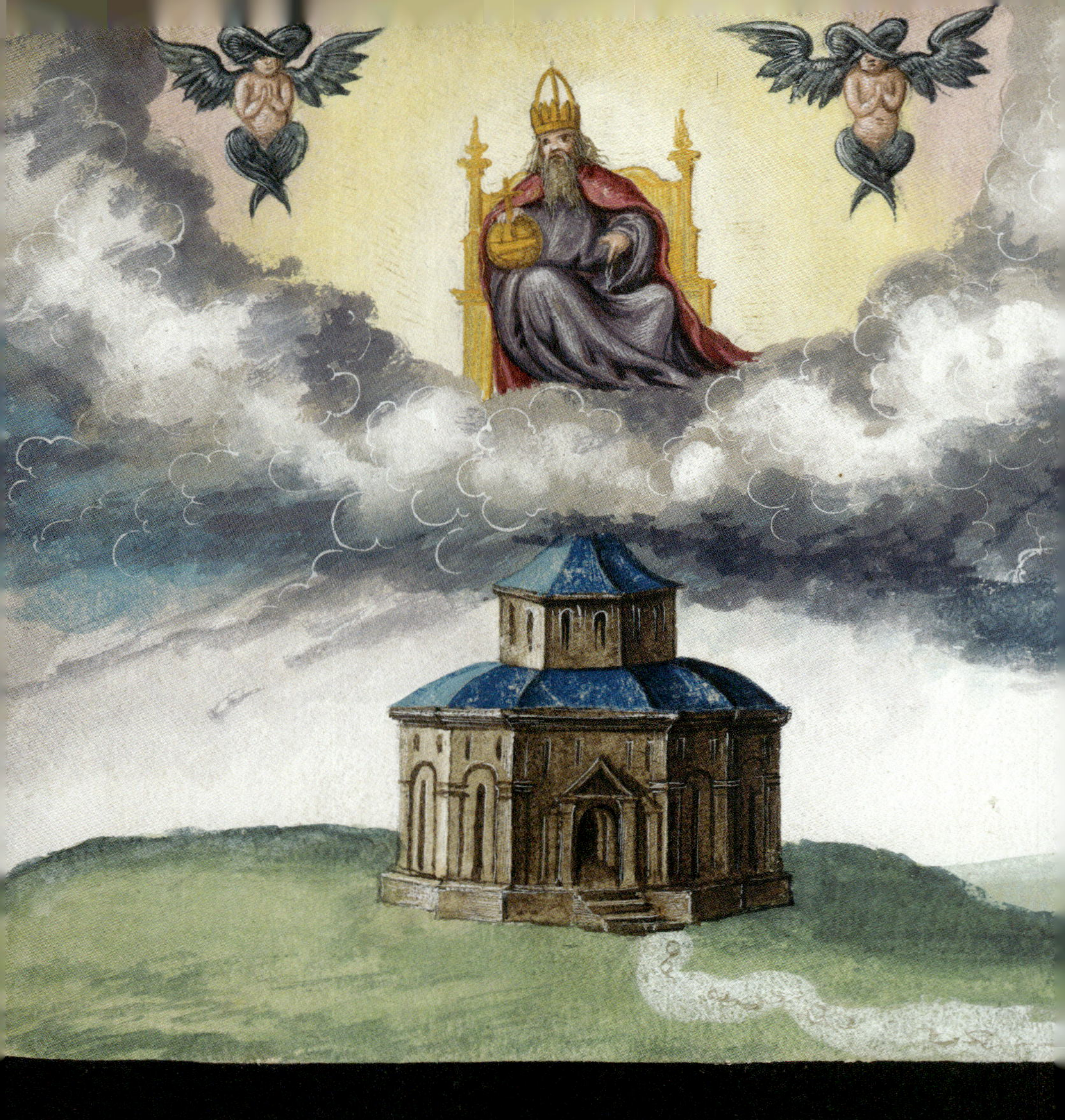

Prohet Jesaia, am ersten capitel

Dass ist das gesichte Jesaia des süns Amoz, welchs er sa
Jehiskia der konnige Juda, horet ir himel vnnd e
vnnd hoffet vnnd sie fallen mir ab. Ein ochse ken
Israhel kennets nicht vnnd mein volck ver nim

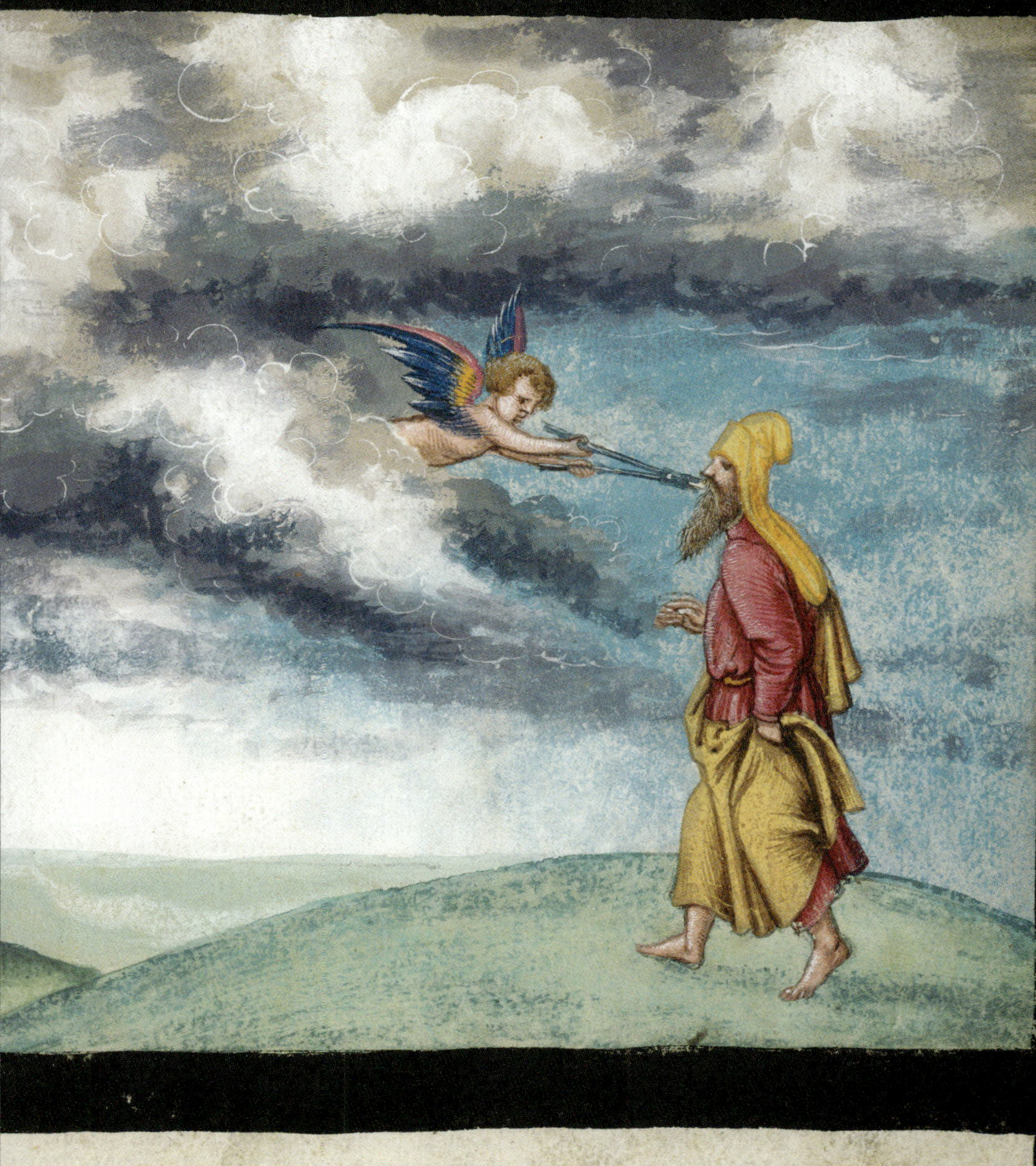

n Juda vnnd Jerusalem zur zeit Vsia Jotham Ahas vnnd:
ur zu oren den der herr redet ich hab kinder auff erzogen:
uiren herren vnnd ein esel die krippen seines herren aber
nicht .

Jesaia am xxxviii capitel

Da geschach das wort des heren zu Jesaia vnnd sprach geh
Dauit ich hab dein gebett erhort vnnd deine thren
Jar zu legen vnnd ich will dich sampt dieser statt e
diesse statt wol vertedingen vnnd hab dir das zu
wirt was er geredt hat/ siehe ich wil den schaten a
welchen gelauffen ist/ das die sonne zehen linien

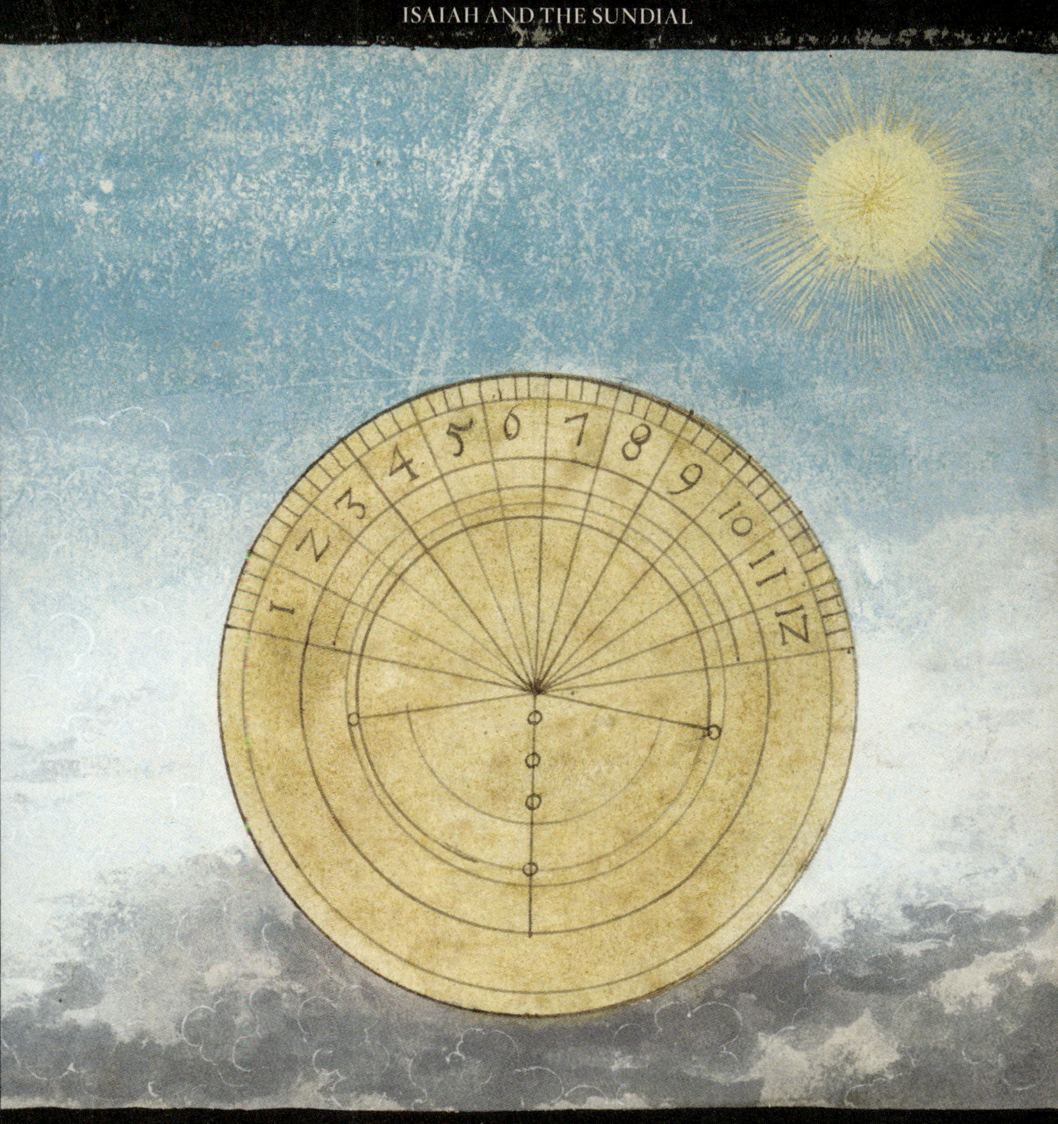

und ſag hiſkia So ſpricht der herr der got deines vatters
ſehen Siehe ich will deinen tagen noch fünff zehen :
en von der handt des konnigs zu aſſyrien/ den ich will
ichen von dem herren das der herr ſolchs thůn ::
enne zaiger ahas zehen linien zů ziehen vberr :
it lauffen ſol am zaiger vber welchen ſy gelauffen

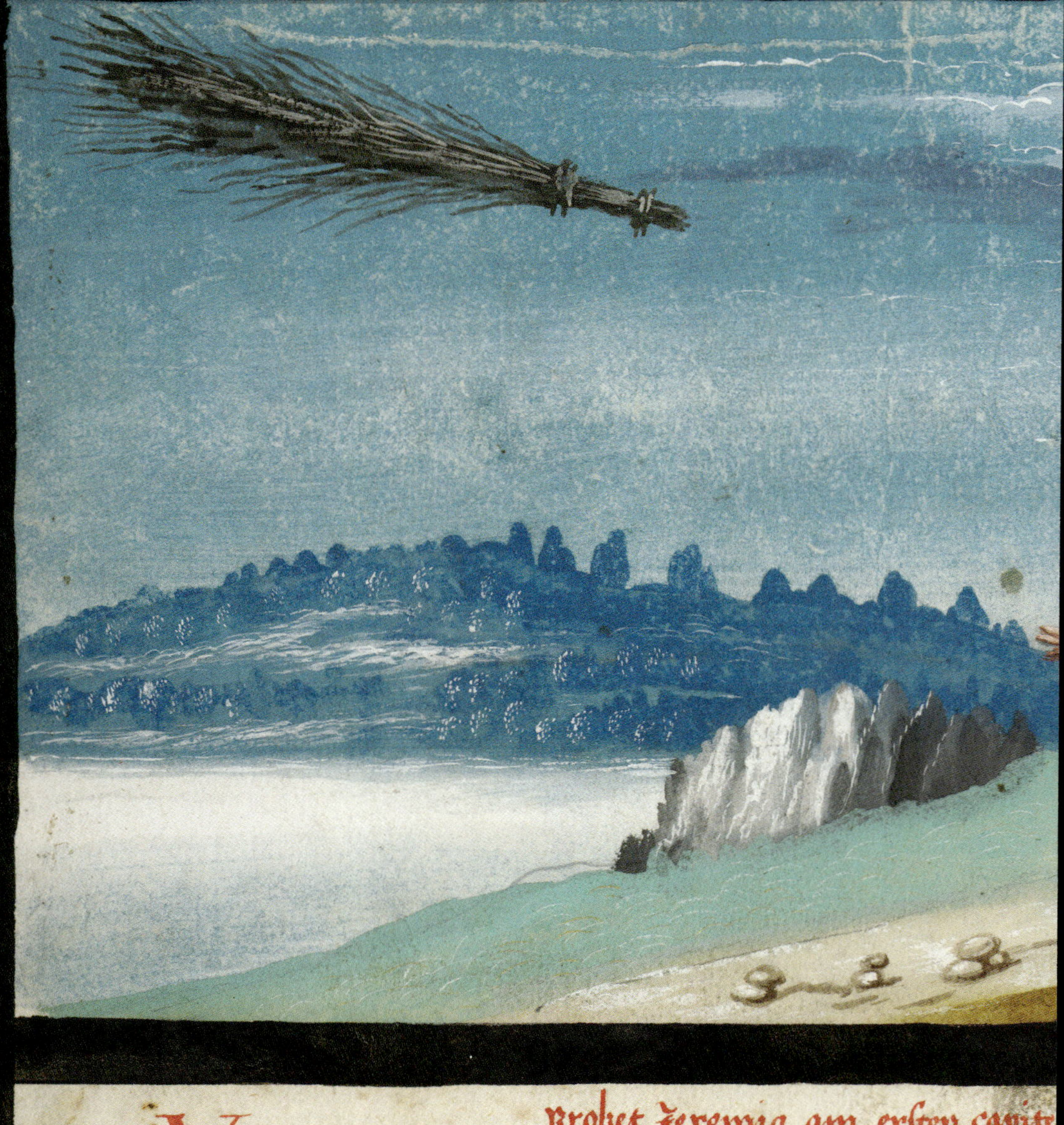

Prohet Jeremia am ersten capit

Vnnd es geschach des herrn wort zů mir/ vnnd sprach Jere
sprach zů mir/ du hast recht gesehen/ den ich will wacker s
M andern mal zů mir vnnd sprach/ was sihestu/ Ich spra
sprach zů mir von mitter nacht wirt das vnglück kom

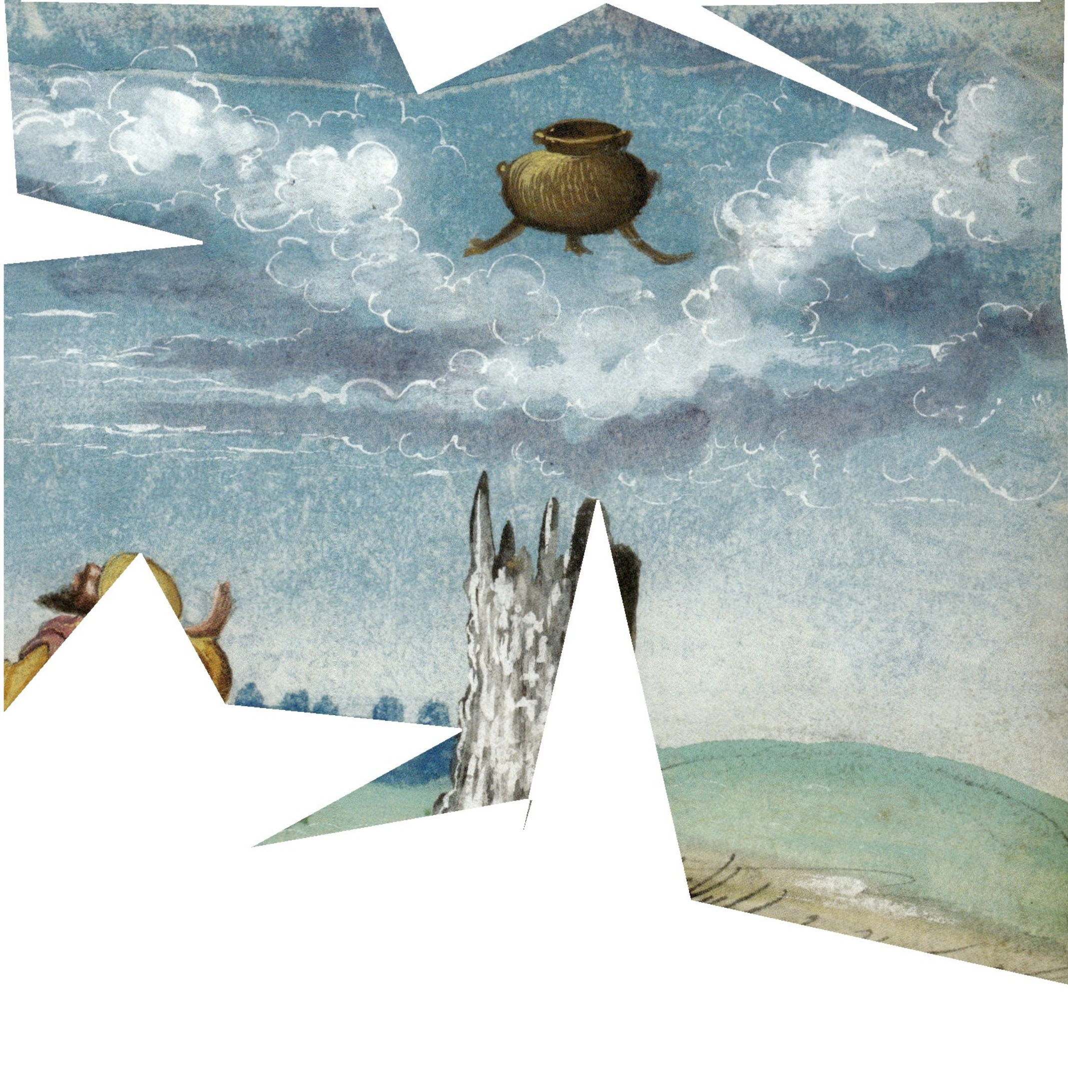

was siehestu ich sprach Ich siehe ein wackern stab: vnnd der herr:
er mein wort das ich thu: vnnd es geschach das herrn wort zum
siehe ein heiss siedend topffen von mitternacht her: vnnd der herr
ber die alle: die im lande wonen.

FOL. 10

Isaiah and the sundial

Jesaja und die Sonnenuhr | Isaïe et le cadran solaire

Isaiah 38:4–8 – 4 Then the word of the LORD came to Isaiah: 5 "Go and say to Hezekiah, Thus says the LORD, the God of David your father: I have heard your prayer; I have seen your tears. Behold, I will add fifteen years to your life. 6 I will deliver you and this city out of the hand of the king of Assyria, and will defend this city. 7 This shall be the sign to you from the LORD, that the LORD will do this thing that he has promised: 8 Behold, I will make the shadow cast by the declining sun on the dial of Ahaz turn back ten steps." So the sun turned back on the dial the ten steps by which it had declined.

Jesaja 38,4–8 – 4 Da geschah das Wort des HERRN zu Jesaja: 5 Geh hin und sage Hiskia: So spricht der HERR, der Gott deines Vaters David: Ich habe dein Gebet gehört und deine Tränen gesehen. Siehe, ich will deinen Tagen noch fünfzehn Jahre zulegen 6 und will dich samt dieser Stadt erretten aus der Hand des Königs von Assyrien und will diese Stadt beschirmen. 7 Und dies sei dir das Zeichen von dem HERRN, dass der HERR tun wird, was er zugesagt hat: 8 Siehe, ich will den Schatten an der Sonnenuhr des Ahas zehn Striche zurückziehen, über die er gelaufen ist. Und die Sonne lief zehn Striche zurück an der Sonnenuhr, über die sie gelaufen war.

Isaïe 38:4–8 – 4 Alors la parole de Yahvé se fit entendre à Isaïe : 5 « Va dire à Ézéchias : Ainsi parle Yahvé, Dieu de ton ancêtre David. J'ai entendu ta prière, j'ai vu tes larmes. J'ajouterai quinze années à ta vie. 6 Je te délivrerai, toi et cette ville, de la main du roi d'Assyrie, et je protégerai cette ville. 7 Voici, de la part de Yahvé, le signe qu'il fera ce qu'il a dit. 8 Voici que je vais faire reculer l'ombre des degrés que le soleil a descendus sur les degrés de la chambre haute d'Achaz – dix degrés en arrière. » Et le soleil recula de dix degrés, sur les degrés qu'il avait descendus.

FOL. 11

Jeremiah's vision | Vision des Jeremia | Vision de Jérémie

Jeremiah 1:11–14 – 11 And the word of the LORD came to me, saying, "Jeremiah, what do you see?" And I said, "I see an almond branch." 12 Then the LORD said to me, "You have seen well, for I am watching over my word to perform it." 13 The word of the LORD came to me a second time, saying, "What do you see?" And I said, "I see a boiling pot, facing away from the north." 14 Then the LORD said to me, "Out of the north disaster shall be let loose upon all the inhabitants of the land."

Jeremia 1,11–14 – 11 Und es geschah des HERRN Wort zu mir: Jeremia, was siehst du? Ich sprach: Ich sehe einen erwachenden Zweig. 12 Und der HERR sprach zu mir: Du hast recht gesehen; denn ich will wachen über meinem Wort, dass ich's tue. 13 Und es geschah des HERRN Wort zum zweiten Mal zu mir: Was siehst du? Ich sprach: Ich sehe einen siedenden Kessel überkochen von Norden her. 14 Und der HERR sprach zu mir: Von Norden her wird das Unheil losbrechen über alle, die im Lande wohnen.

Jérémie 1:11–14 – 11 La parole de Yahvé me fut adressée en ces termes : « Que vois-tu, Jérémie ? » Je répondis : « Je vois une branche de "veilleur". » 12 Alors Yahvé me dit : « Tu as bien vu, car je veille sur ma parole pour l'accomplir. » 13 Une seconde fois, la parole de Yahvé me fut adressée en ces termes : « Que vois-tu ? » Je répondis : « Je vois une marmite qui bouillonne : sa gueule regarde depuis le Nord. » 14 Alors Yahvé me dit : « C'est du Nord que va déborder le malheur sur tous les habitants du pays. »

FOL. 12

Daniel's vision | Vision Daniels | Vision de Daniel

Daniel 7:1–4 – 1 In the first year of Belshazzar king of Babylon, Daniel saw a dream and visions of his head as he lay in his bed. Then he wrote down the dream and told the sum of the matter. 2 Daniel declared, "I saw in my vision by night, and behold, the four winds of heaven were stirring up the great sea. 3 And four great beasts came up out of the sea, different from one another. 4 The first was like a lion and had eagles' wings. Then as I looked its wings were plucked off, and it was lifted up from the ground and made to stand on two feet like a man, and the mind of a man was given to it."

Daniel 7,1–4 – 1 Im ersten Jahr Belsazars, des Königs von Babel, hatte Daniel einen Traum und Gesichte auf seinem Bett; und er schrieb den Traum auf und dies ist sein Inhalt: 2 Ich, Daniel, sah ein Gesicht in der Nacht, und siehe, die vier Winde unter dem Himmel wühlten das große Meer auf. 3 Und vier große Tiere stiegen herauf aus dem Meer, ein jedes anders als das andere. 4 Das erste war wie ein Löwe und hatte Flügel wie ein Adler. Ich sah, wie ihm die Flügel genommen wurden. Und es wurde von der Erde aufgehoben und auf zwei Füße gestellt wie ein Mensch, und es wurde ihm ein menschliches Herz gegeben.

Daniel 7:1–4 – 1 En l'an I de Balthazar, roi de Babylone, Daniel vit un songe et des visions de sa tête, sur sa couche. Il rédigea le rêve par écrit. Début du récit : 2 Daniel dit : « J'ai contemplé des visions dans la nuit. Voici : les quatre vents du ciel soulevaient la grande mer ; 3 quatre bêtes énormes sortirent de la mer, toutes différentes entre elles. 4 La première était pareille à un lion avec des ailes d'aigle. Tandis que je la regardais, ses ailes lui furent arrachées, elle fut soulevée de terre et dressée sur ses pattes comme un homme, et un cœur d'homme lui fut donné. »

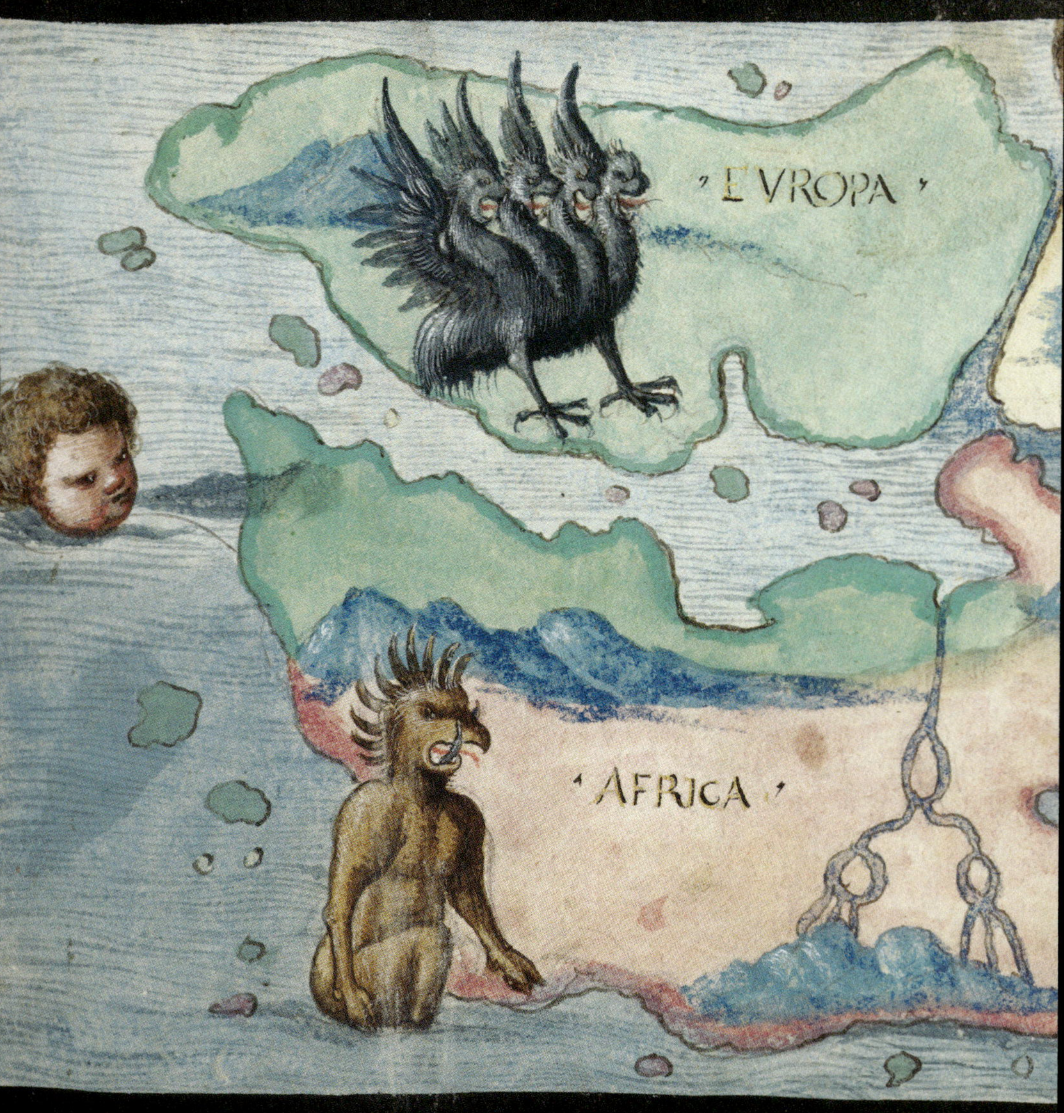

Daniel am vii capitel

Im ersten jar Belsazer des konigs zů Babel hatte dani
traum vnnd verfasset in also Ich daniel sahe ein gesicht
wider einander auff dem grossen meer vnnd vier g
ander das erste wie lewe vnnd hatte flugel wie ein
es ward von der erden genomen vnnd es stůnd auf

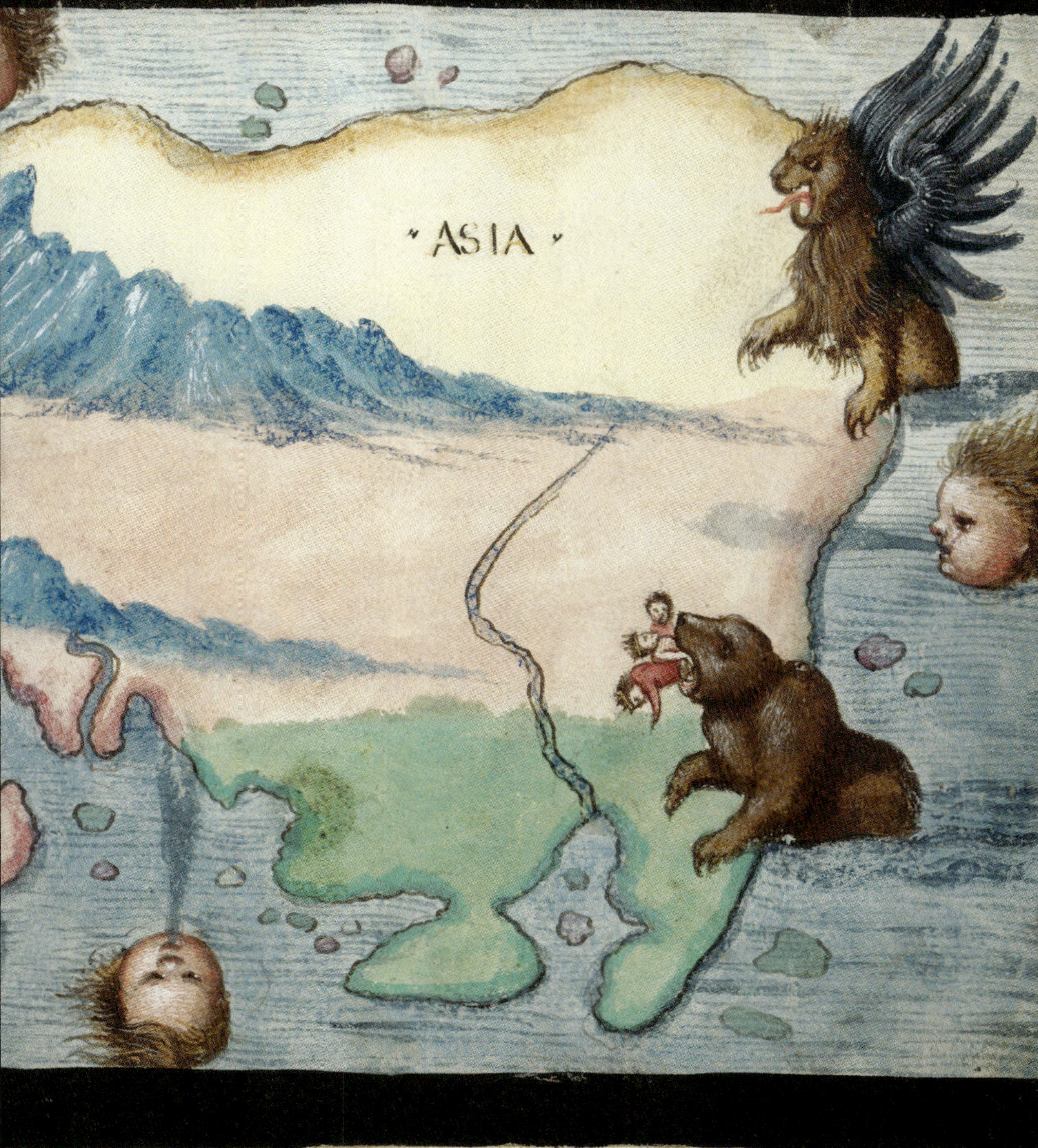
ASIA

n traum vnnd gesichte auff seinem bette / vnnd er schreib den selbigen
r nacht vnnd siehe die vier winde vnnder dem himmel stürmeten:
thier stiegen herauff auss dem meer eins ye anders den das:
ich sahe zu biss das im die flugel aus geraufft wurden / vnnd
en fuessen wie ein mensch vnd im ward ein menschlich hertz gebē

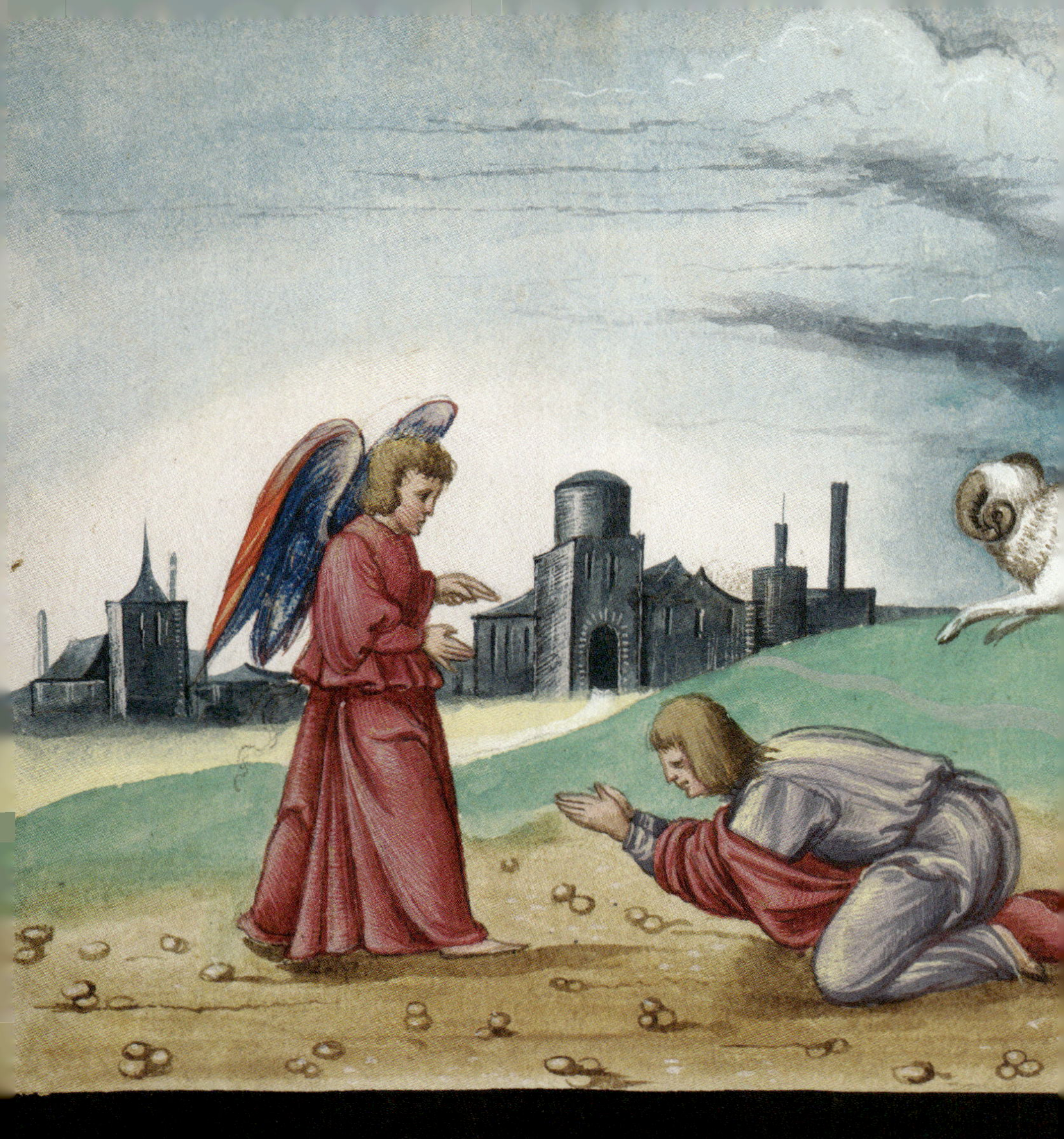

Daniel am viii capitel

a Im dritten iar des konigreichs des konig Belsazer erst
war / Ich war aber da ich solch gesicht sahe zu Susan
iii meine augen auff vnnd sahe vnnd siehe ein wieder
her den das ander vnnd das hohest wuchs am letsten
mitter nacht vnd gegen mittag / vnnd khain thier k

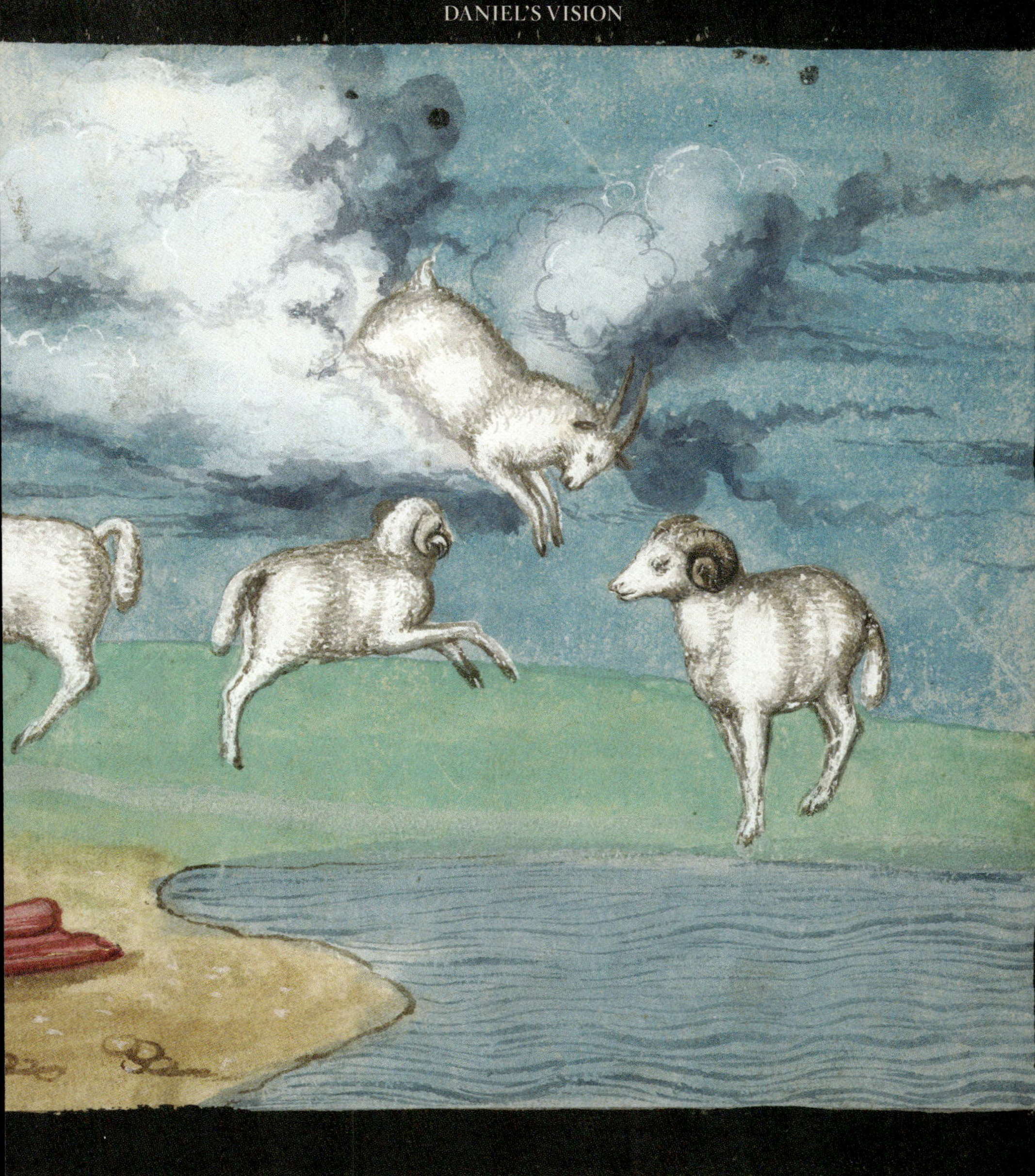

mir Daniel ein gesicht nach dem sonnir anversten erschinen
iub statt im lande Elam an wasser Ulai vnnd ich hub
für dem wasser der hatte zway hohe horner doch eines ho
che das der wider mit den hornern stiess gegen abent gegen
er im brsthen noch von seiner hand er rettet werdenn

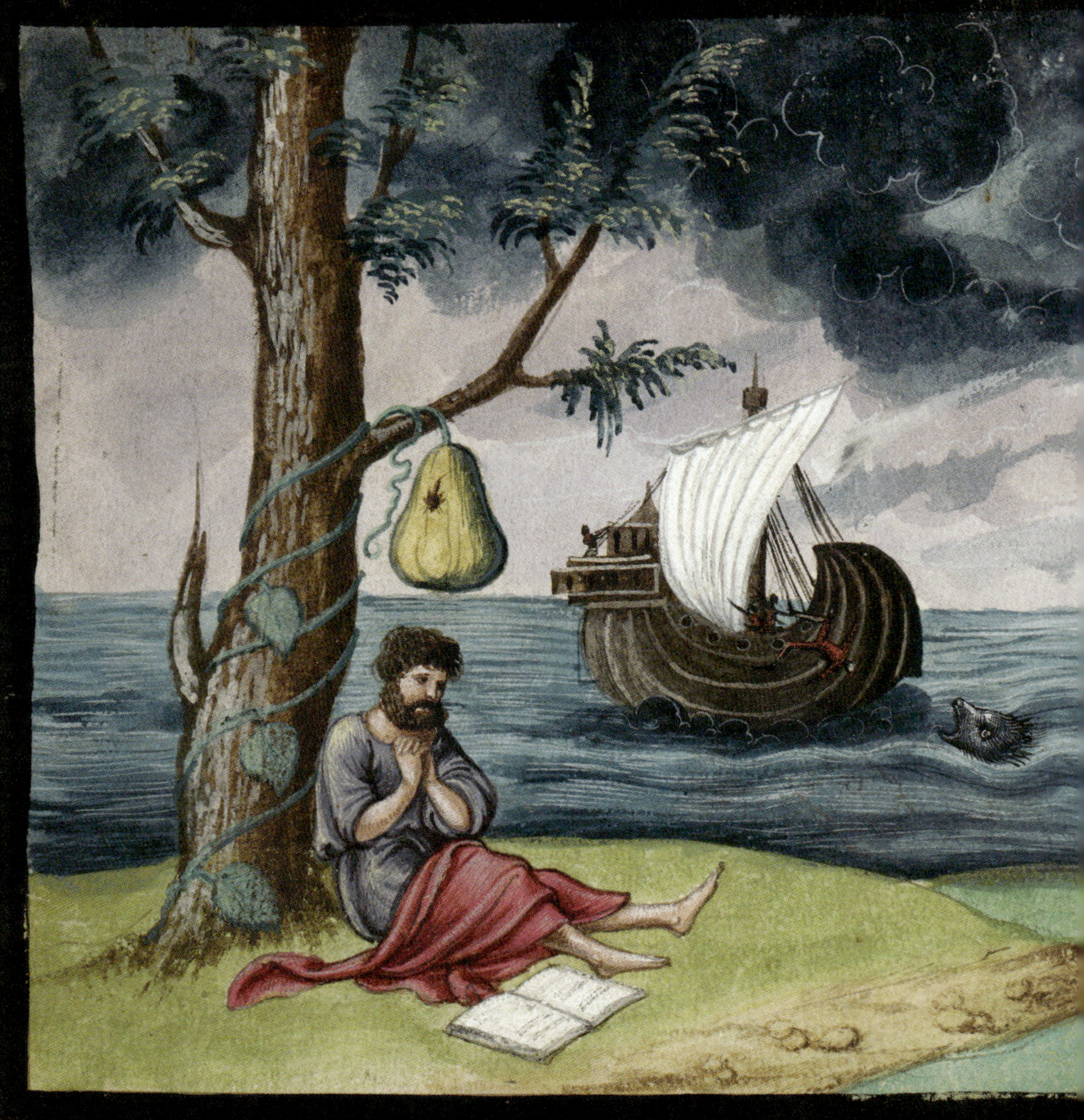

Jonna am ersten capitel

Vnnd sie namen Jonna vnnd würffen in ins
die leüt forchten den herren seer vnnd theten
afft ein grossenn visch Jona zu verschlinge
drey necht ..

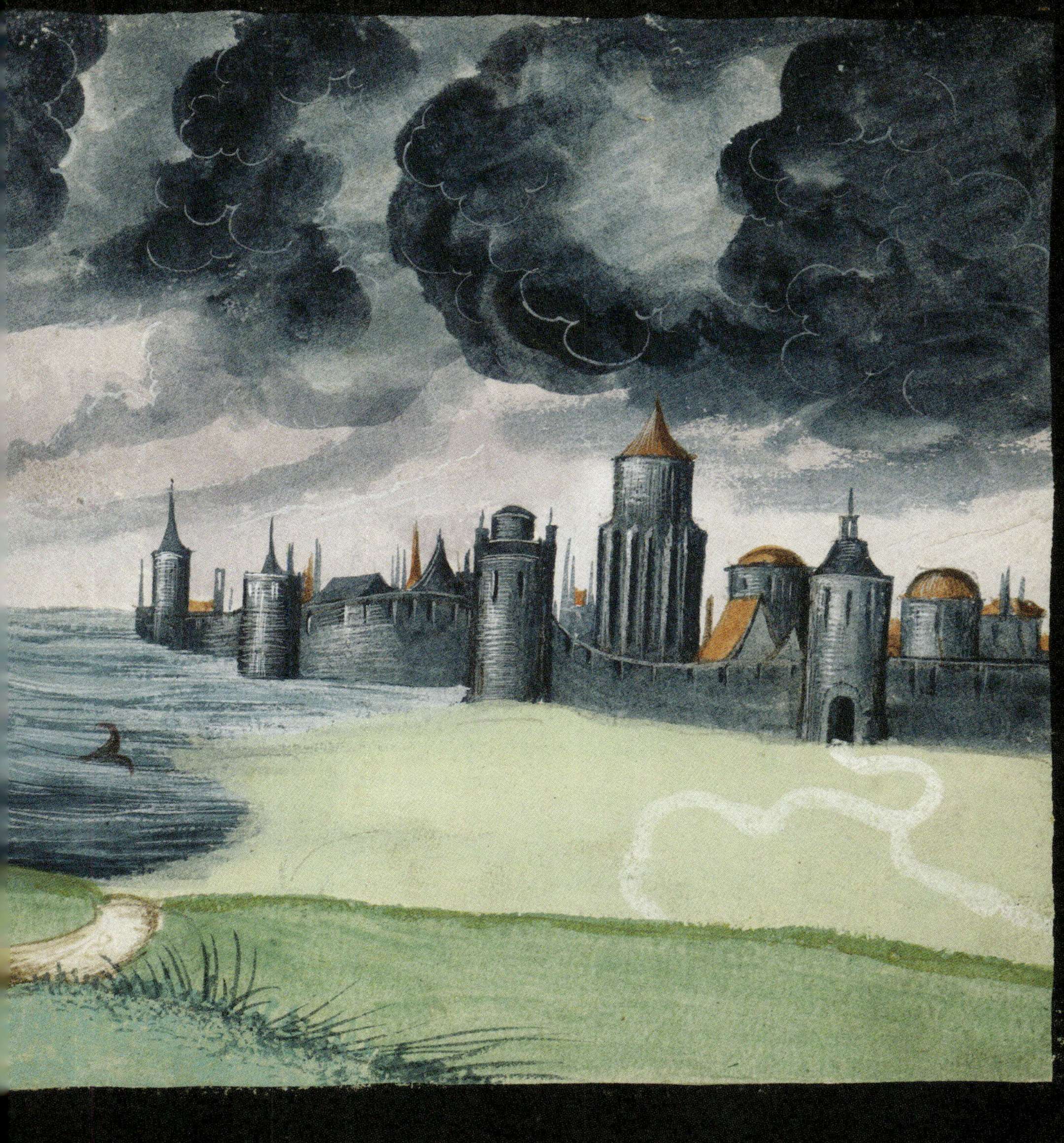

da stůnd das meer stil von seinem wůtten / vnnd
erren opffer vnnd gelübde aber der herr versch:
nd Jonna war im leibe des fisches drey tag vnnd

FOL. 13

Daniel's vision | Vision Daniels | Vision de Daniel

Daniel 8:1–4 – 1 In the third year of the reign of King Belshazzar a vision appeared to me, Daniel, after that which appeared to me at the first. 2 And I saw in the vision; and when I saw, I was in Susa the citadel, which is in the province of Elam. And I saw in the vision, and I was at the Ulai canal. 3 I raised my eyes and saw, and behold, a ram standing on the bank of the canal. It had two horns, and both horns were high, but one was higher than the other, and the higher one came up last. 4 I saw the ram charging westward and northward and southward. No beast could stand before him, and there was no one who could rescue from his power.

Daniel 8,1–4 – 1 Im dritten Jahr der Herrschaft des Königs Belsazar erschien mir, Daniel, ein Gesicht, nach jenem, das mir zuerst erschienen war. 2 Ich hatte ein Gesicht und während meines Gesichtes war ich in der Festung Susa im Lande Elam am Fluss Ulai. 3 Und ich hob meine Augen auf und sah, und siehe, ein Widder stand vor dem Fluss, der hatte zwei hohe Hörner, doch eins höher als das andere, und das höhere war später hervorgewachsen. 4 Ich sah, dass der Widder mit den Hörnern stieß nach Westen, nach Norden und nach Süden hin. Und kein Tier konnte vor ihm bestehen und vor seiner Gewalt errettet werden, [...]

Daniel 8:1–4 – 1 En l'an III du règne du roi Balthazar, une vision m'apparut, à moi Daniel, après celle qui m'était apparue en premier. 2 Je contemplais la vision, et tandis que je contemplais, je me trouvais à Suse, la place forte qui est dans la province d'Élam ; et, contemplant la vision, je me trouvais à la porte de l'Ulaï. 3 Je levai les yeux pour voir. Voici : un bélier se tenait devant la porte. Il avait deux cornes ; les deux cornes étaient hautes, mais l'une plus que l'autre, et la plus haute qui se dressa fut la seconde. 4 Je vis le bélier donner de la corne vers l'ouest, vers le nord et vers le sud. Nulle bête ne pouvait lui résister, rien ne pouvait lui échapper.

FOL. 14

Jonah and the whale | Jona und der Wal | Jonas et la baleine

Jonah 1:15–17 – 15 So they picked up Jonah and hurled him into the sea, and the sea ceased from its raging. 16 Then the men feared the LORD exceedingly, and they offered a sacrifice to the LORD and made vows. 17 And the LORD appointed a great fish to swallow up Jonah. And Jonah was in the belly of the fish three days and three nights.

Jona 1,15–17 – 15 Und sie nahmen Jona und warfen ihn ins Meer. Da wurde das Meer still und ließ ab von seinem Wüten. 16 Und die Leute fürchteten den HERRN sehr und brachten dem HERRN Opfer dar und taten Gelübde. 17 Aber der HERR ließ einen großen Fisch kommen, Jona zu verschlingen. Und Jona war im Leibe des Fisches drei Tage und drei Nächte.

Jonas 1:15–17 – 15 Et, s'emparant de Jonas, ils le jetèrent à la mer, et la mer apaisa sa fureur. 16 Les hommes furent saisis d'une grande crainte de Yahvé ; ils offrirent un sacrifice à Yahvé et firent des vœux. 17 Yahvé fit qu'il y eut un grand poisson pour engloutir Jonas. Jonas demeura dans les entrailles du poisson trois jours et trois nuits.

FOL. 15

Ezekiel's vision | Vision des Hesekiel | Vision d'Ézéchiel

Ezekiel 1:1–3 – 1 In the thirtieth year, in the fourth month, on the fifth day of the month, as I was among the exiles by the Chebar canal, the heavens were opened, and I saw visions of God. 2 On the fifth day of the month (it was the fifth year of the exile of King Jehoiachin), 3 the word of the LORD came to Ezekiel the priest, the son of Buzi, in the land of the Chaldeans by the Chebar canal, and the hand of the LORD was upon him there.

Hesekiel 1,1–3 – 1 Im dreißigsten Jahr am fünften Tage des vierten Monats, als ich unter den Weggeführten am Fluss Kebar war, tat sich der Himmel auf, und Gott zeigte mir Gesichte. 2 Am fünften Tag des Monats – es war das fünfte Jahr, nachdem der König Jojachin gefangen weggeführt war –, 3 da geschah das Wort des HERRN zu Hesekiel, dem Sohn des Busi, dem Priester, im Lande der Chaldäer am Fluss Kebar. Dort kam die Hand des HERRN über ihn.

Ézéchiel 1:1–3 – 1 La trentième année, au quatrième mois, le cinq du mois, alors que je me trouvais parmi les déportés au bord du fleuve Kebar, le ciel s'ouvrit et je fus témoin de visions divines. 2 Le cinq du mois – c'était la cinquième année d'exil du roi Joiakîn – 3 la parole de Yahvé fut adressée au prêtre Ézéchiel, fils de Buzi, au pays des Chaldéens, au bord du fleuve Kebar. C'est là que la main de Yahvé fut sur lui.

FOL. 16

An ox in the time of Job
Eine Ochse zur Zeit Hiobs | Un bœuf au temps de Job

In the time of Job, there occurred in Cassilia [according to Schedel: Thessaly] a great flood. And during this time there was a river in this area, out of which came an ox that went up into the air and then back down into the river so that the simple-minded people believed it to be a god.

Eine große Überschwemmung ist zu der Zeit Hiobs in Cassilia [laut Schedel: Thessalien] geschehen. Und zu der Zeit gab es einen Fluss in dieser Gegend, aus dem kam ein Ochse heraus und fuhr in die Luft und wieder herab in den Fluss, sodass ihn die einfältigen Leute für einen Gott hielten.

Au temps de Job, il y eut un grand déluge à Cassilia [en Thessalie, selon Schedel]. Et en ce temps, il y avait dans la région une rivière, d'où sortit un bœuf qui bondit dans les airs avant de redescendre dans la rivière, si bien que les simples d'esprit crurent voir un dieu.

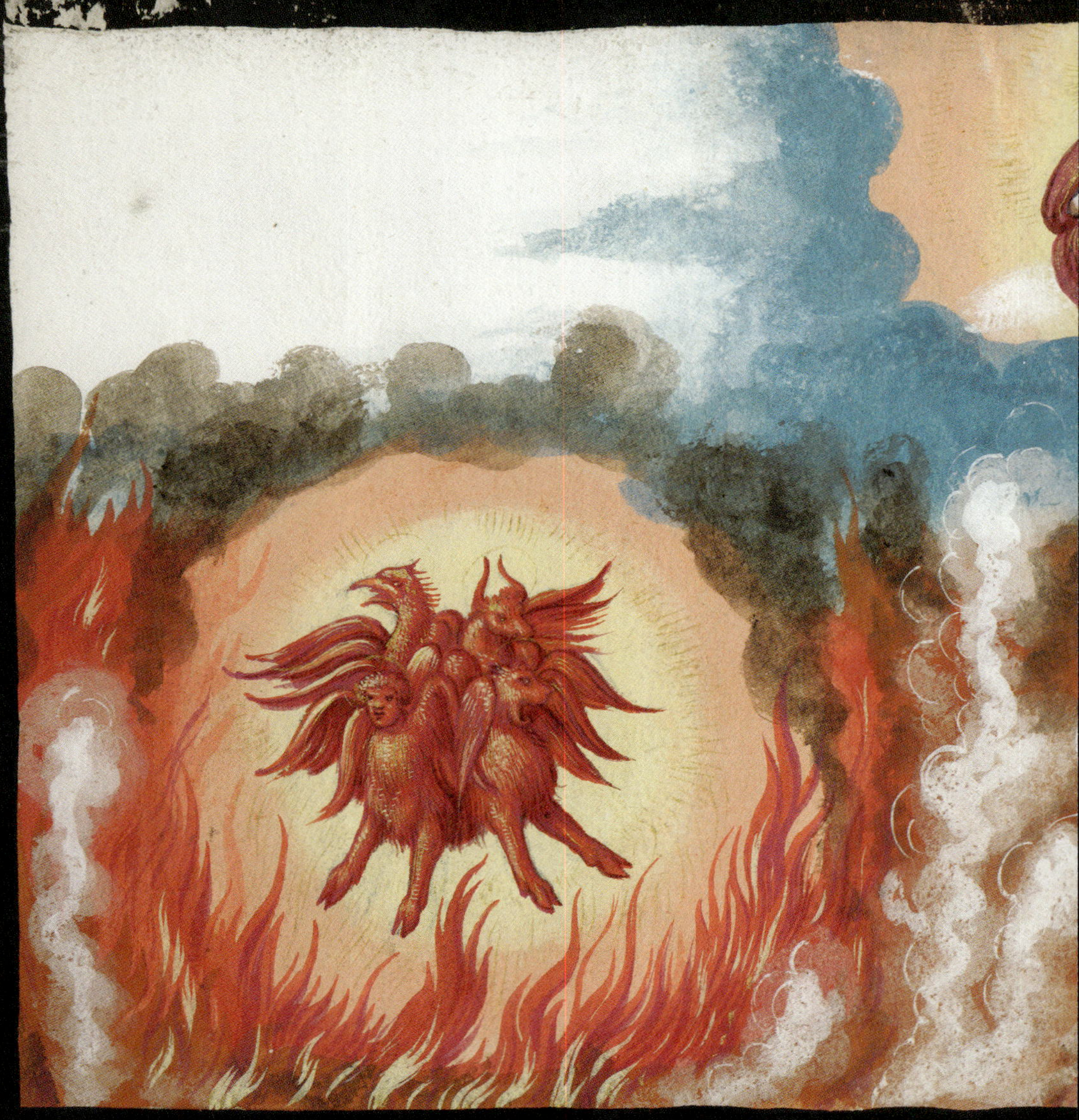

Prohet hesekiel am ersten ca

Im dreÿssigisten jar am funfften tage des vierden
himel auff / vnnd got zaigt mir gesichte / der selb funf
konnig juda gefanngen war weg gefurt / da geschach
Chaldeer / am wasser Chebar / daselbst kam des heren

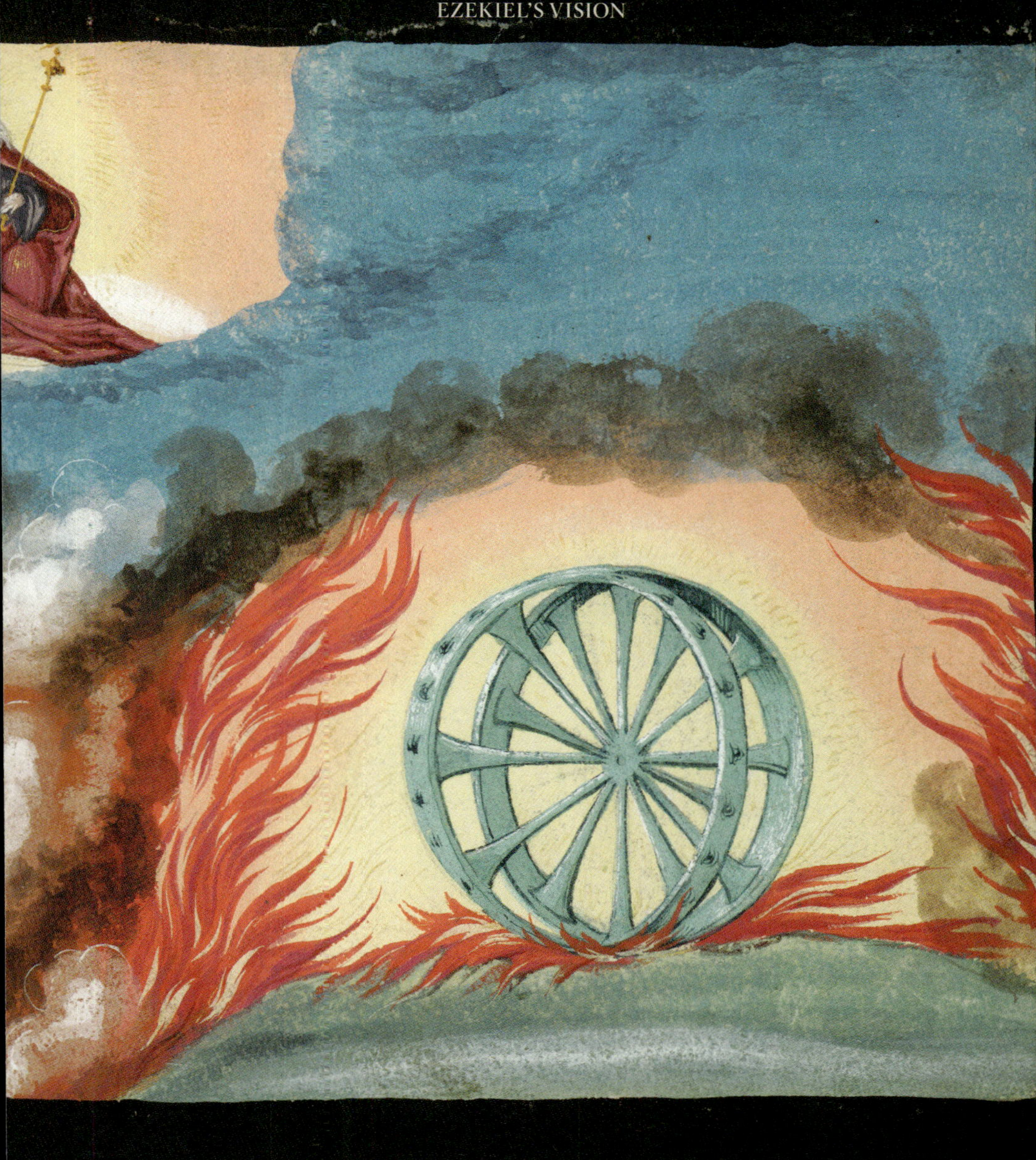

n/ da ich war vnder den gefangen am wasser Chebar/ thet sich der
ge des monden war eben im funfften jar nach dem Joachim der
rrn wort zu hesekiel dem sohn Busi/ des priesters im lande der
d vber in.

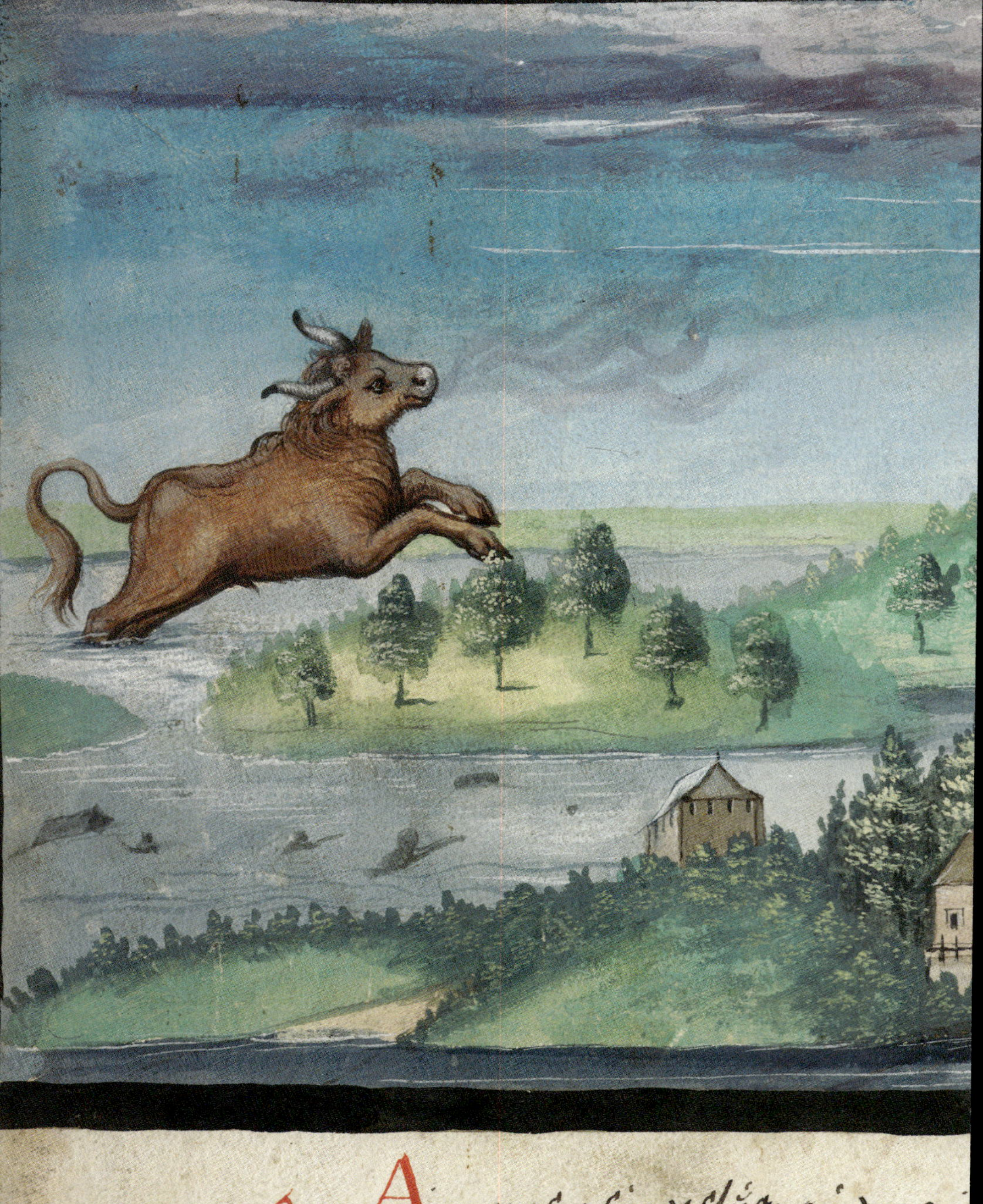

Ain groser sindtfluss zu der zei
was ein fluss in dirser gegent / da
wider her ab in den fluss / das i

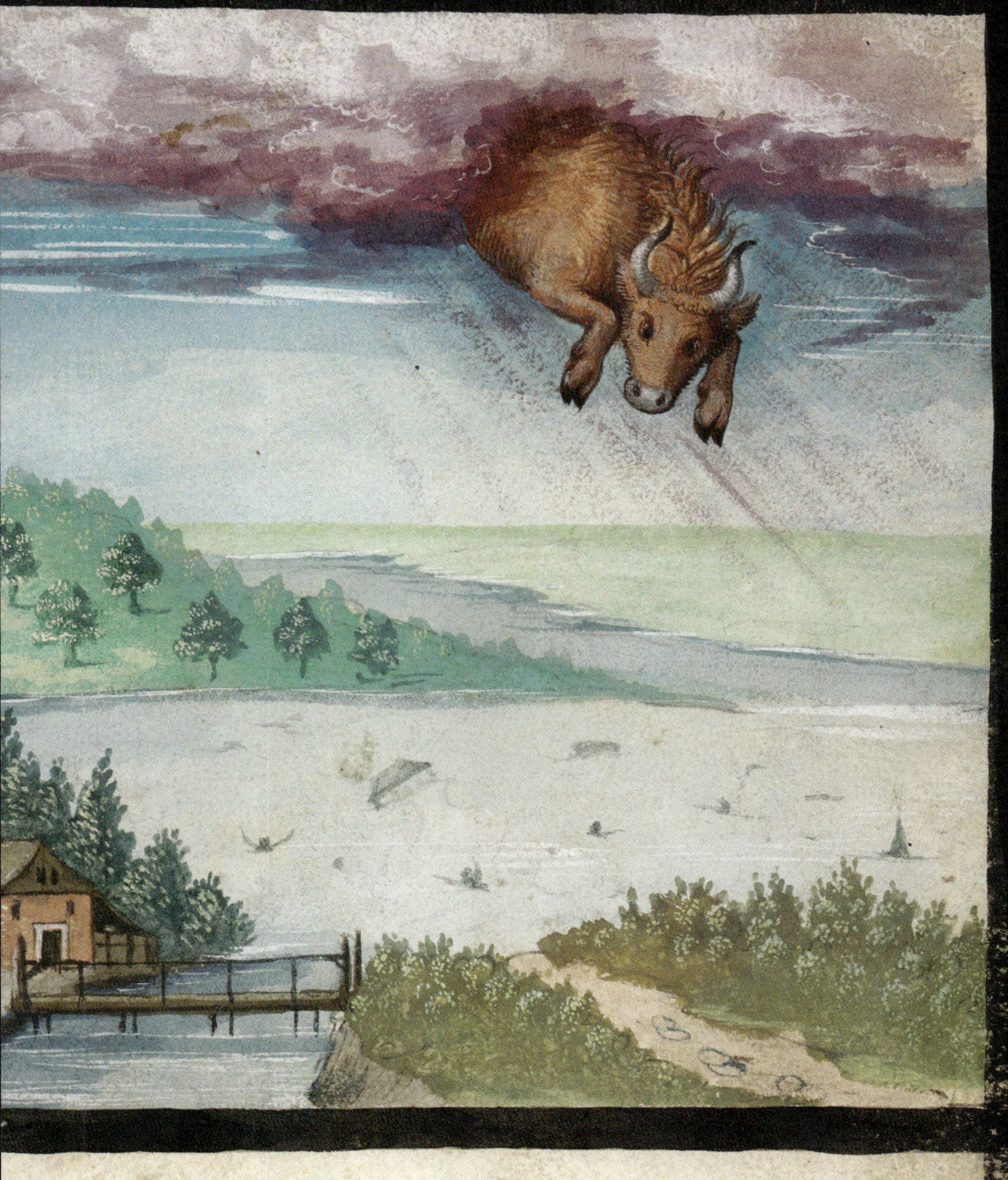

ist geschehen zu Cassilia / vnnd zu der zeit
gieng ein ochs / vnnd für in die lufft vnd
in feltigen leüt vür ein got hilltenn ~

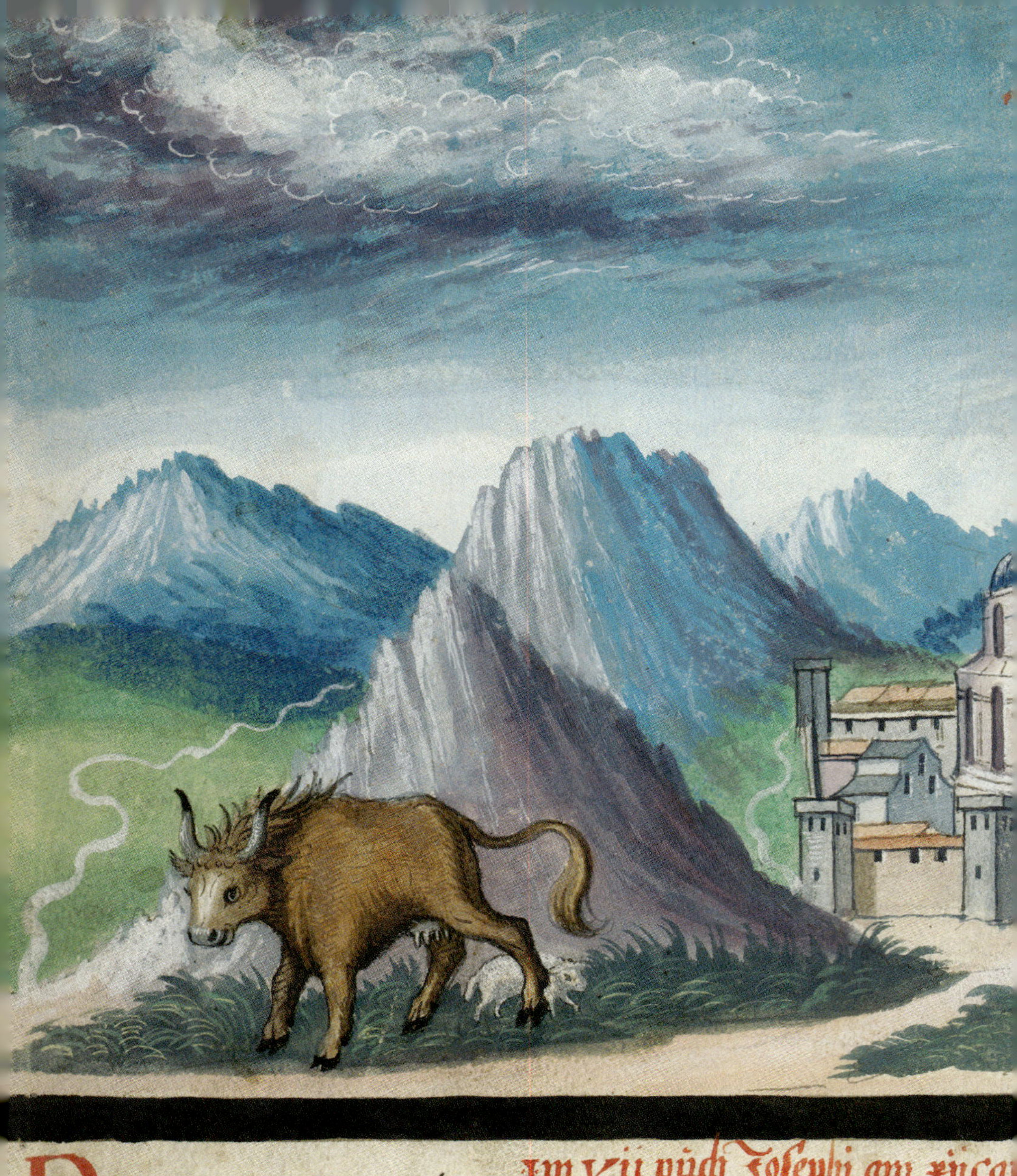

Im vii püch Josephi am xii ca

Dan ob der stat Iherusalem stünd ein gestirn gleich einem
als vor dem vnd schlag das volck zum österlichen tag zu s
in der nacht/ ward es so licht vmb den altar vnnd Temp
edt/ das die vnuerstendigen für ein gut zaichen hielten
legt worden/ am selben tag hat ein kü die zu opffer gefürt/

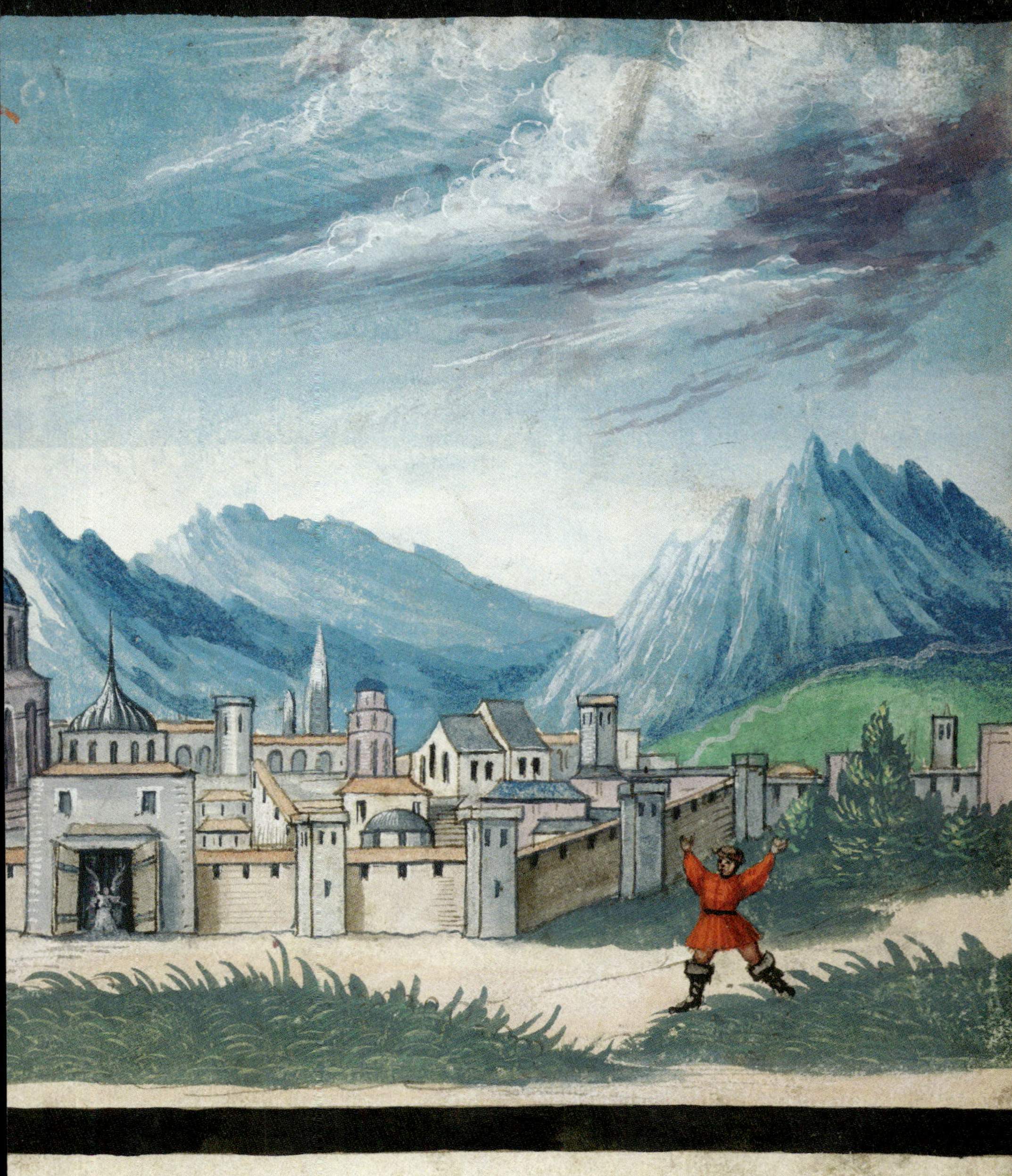

ert/ vnd werret ein gantz iar in gleichnis eines cometen vnd/
n kamen/ der dan was der acht tag der apprillen zu nein vrn
s oesterer tag gewesen werd/ vnd werret wol ein halbe stu
r ben den erfarnen ist es er dan es er gangen ist auff ge
n im Tempel ein lamb geworffen

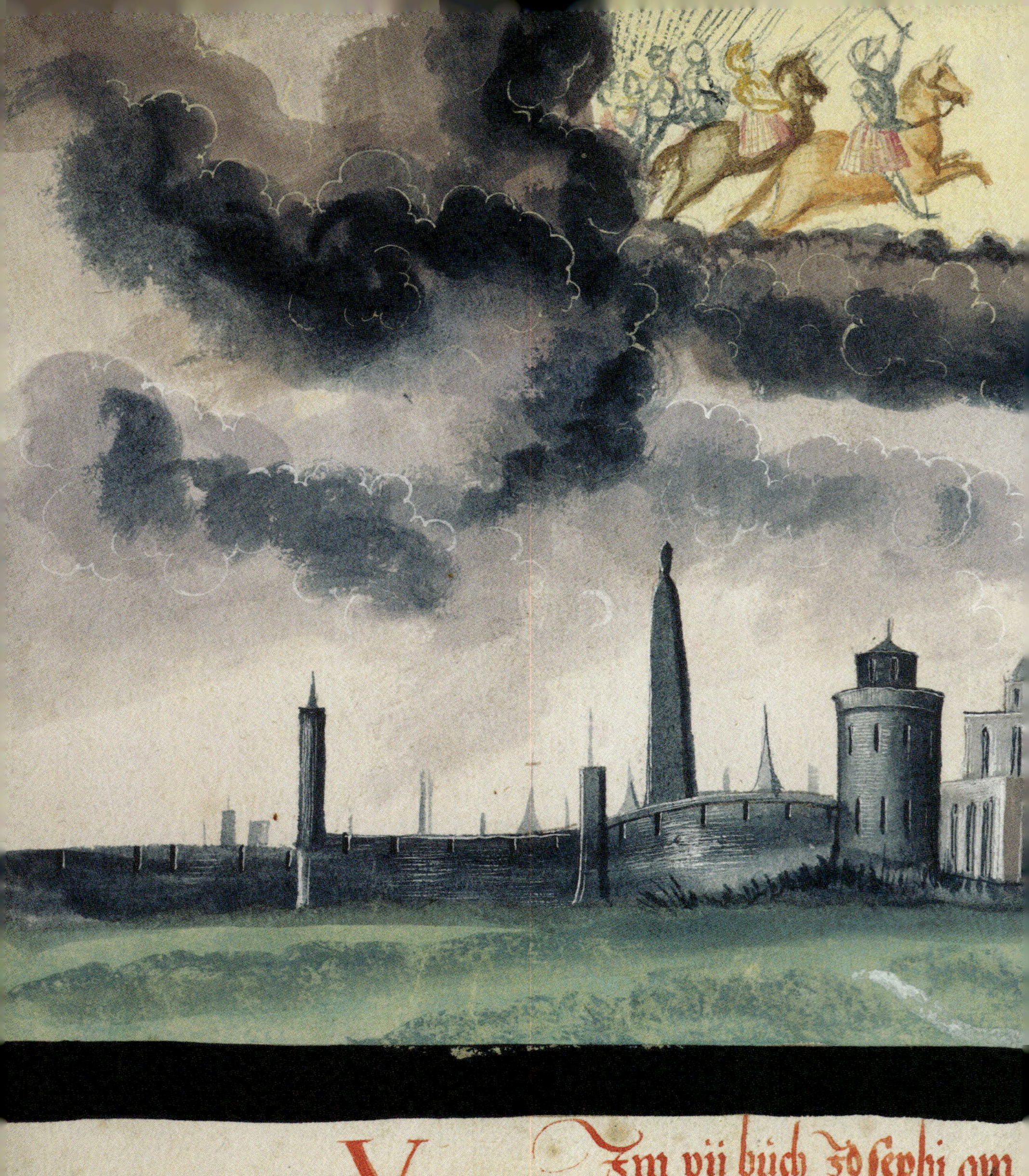

Jm vii büch Josephi am

Vor der neünten zerstörung hi
bildnus am himel gesehen w
ein gewapent heer in den lü
en/ am pfingstag haben sie ein

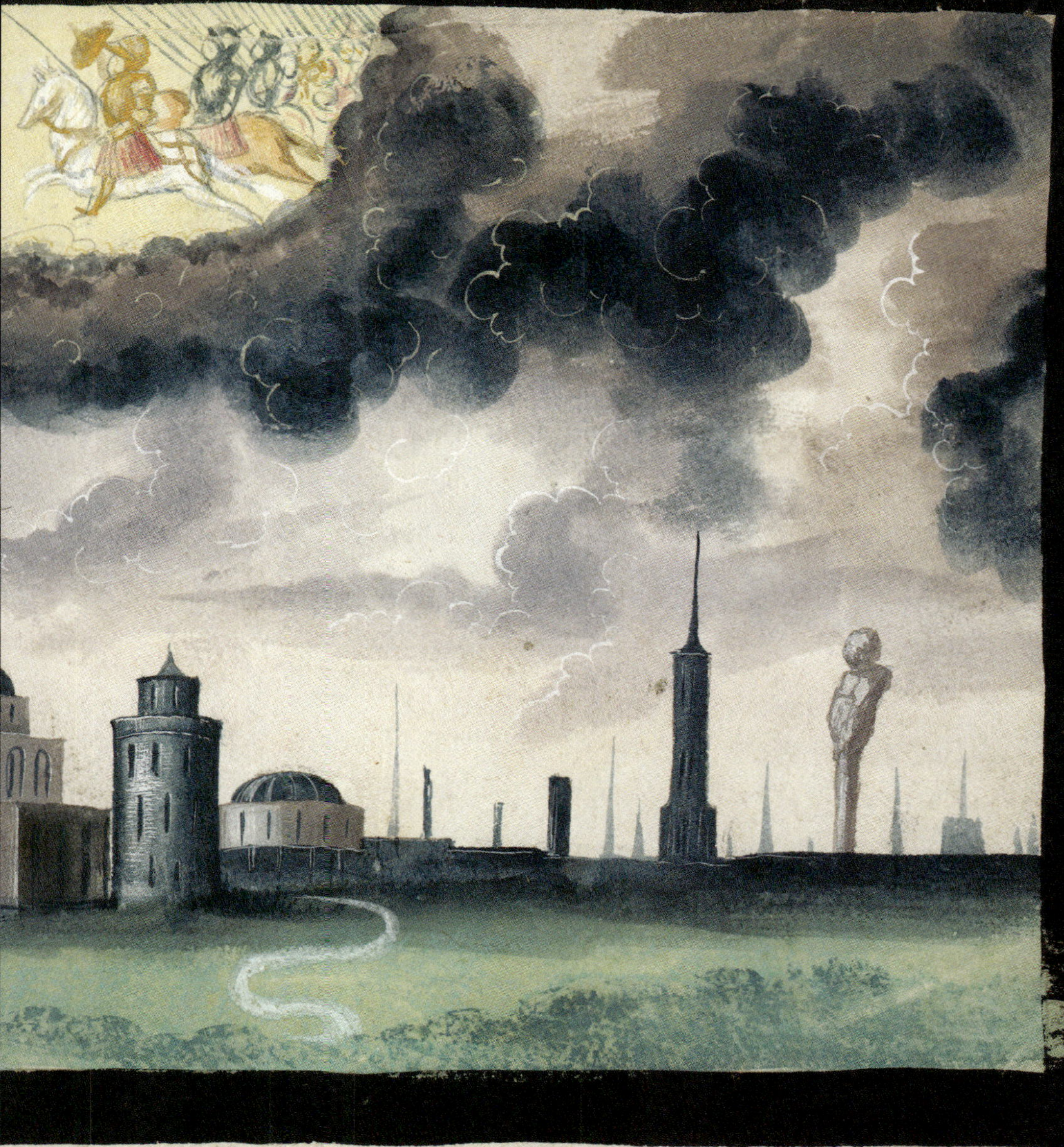

pitel

alrm von Titi vnd vespasiani ist dir

n vnnd vor nider gang der sonnen

n schwrben vnd vmb dir stadt herfar

shen erstlich gehort vnd dirser gesehen

FOL. 18

Jerusalem, sword-star and cow

Jerusalem, Schwertstern und Kuh | Jérusalem, étoile-épée et vache

In book VII of Josephus, from chapter XII – Then a star stood over the city of Jerusalem, resembling a sword, and stayed there for a whole year, like a comet. And when the people came together at the ninth hour in the night for the Paschal day, which was the eighth of April back then, it became so bright around the altar and the temple as if it were bright day, and it lasted for about half an hour, which the ignorant people thought to be a good sign. By the experienced people, however, it was interpreted before it had happened. On the same day, a cow, which was led to the sacrifice, brought forth a lamb in the middle of the temple.

Im VII. Buch Josephi, aus dem XII. Kapitel – Dann stand über der Stadt Jerusalem ein Stern, einem Schwert ähnelnd, und blieb ein ganzes Jahr, in Gestalt eines Kometen. Und als vor der Umkehr die Leute zum österlichen Tag, der damals der achte April war, zusammenkamen zur neunten Stunde in der Nacht, wurde es so hell um den Altar und den Tempel, als ob es heller Tag gewesen wäre, und es dauerte etwa eine halbe Stunde an, was die Unverständigen für ein gutes Zeichen hielten. Aber von den Erfahrenen ist es gedeutet worden, bevor es geschehen ist. Am selben Tag hat eine Kuh, die geopfert werden sollte, mitten im Tempel ein Lamm geworfen.

Dans le livre VII de Josèphe, chapitre XII – Puis, une étoile se tint au-dessus de la ville de Jérusalem, pareille à une épée, et y resta toute une année, comme une comète. Et lorsque les gens se rassemblèrent pour célébrer la fête du pain azyme à la neuvième heure de la nuit du jour pascal qui, à l'époque, était le huitième jour d'avril, elle brilla tellement autour de l'autel et du temple qu'on aurait dit qu'il faisait grand jour, et sa lumière persista pendant une demi-heure environ, en quoi les ignorants virent un bon augure. [...] Le jour même, une vache, qu'on avait conduite au sacrifice, mit bas un veau au beau milieu du temple.

FOL. 19

Celestial battle above Jerusalem

Himmelsschlacht über Jerusalem | Bataille céleste dans le ciel de Jérusalem

In book VII of Josephus, from chapter XII – Before the ninth devastation of Jerusalem by Titus and Vespasian, this image was seen in the sky and, before sunset, there appeared an armed host hovering in the air and circling the city. On the day of Pentecost, they heard for the first time a noise and saw this.

Im VII. Buch Josephi, aus dem XII. Kapitel – Vor der neunten Zerstörung Jerusalems durch Titus und Vespasian ist dieses Bild am Himmel gesehen worden und vor dem Untergang der Sonne ein gewappnetes Heer in den Lüften schweben und um die Stadt herumlaufen. Am Pfingsttag haben sie erstmals ein Rauschen gehört und dieses gesehen.

Dans le livre VII de Josèphe, chapitre XII – Avant la neuvième destruction de Jérusalem par Titus et Vespasien, cette image fut aperçue dans le ciel et, avant le crépuscule, apparut une armée de soldats qui volait dans les airs et encerclait la ville. Le jour de la Pentecôte, ils entendirent pour la première fois un bruit et virent ceci.

FOL. 20

73 B.C. — Tame animals return to the wild

Zahme Tiere gehen durch | Les animaux domestiques redeviennent sauvages

In the year 73 B.C. a terrible occurrence affected the animals and livestock in Italy most cruelly, such that all the animals that were tame – every donkey, ox, horse and sheep – suddenly returned to the wild and ran away into the wilderness, and completely forgot their previous nature.

Im Jahr 73 vor Christi Geburt hat sich in Italien ein grausames Wunder an den Tieren und dem Vieh ereignet, sodass alle Tiere, die zahm waren – alle Esel, Ochsen, Pferde und Schafe –, alle auf einmal wild wurden und in die Wildnis stürmten und ihre frühere Natur völlig vergaßen.

En l'an 73 avant J.-C., les animaux et le bétail de l'Italie furent victimes d'un événement terrible et des plus cruels par lequel tous les animaux domestiques – ânes, bœufs, chevaux et moutons – reprirent soudain leur état sauvage et s'enfuirent dans les régions sauvages, et oublièrent entièrement leur état antérieur.

FOL. 21

73 B.C. — Bleeding bread and hail

Blutendes Brot und Hagel | Le pain qui saigne, et grêle

In the year 73 B.C. people gathered together to drink but when they cut the bread blood came out of it as if out of a wound. There was also a hailstorm so terrible that rocks fell from the sky for seven days in succession, and therein too were pieces of real stones and plenty of sharp stones, so that the soil was destroyed by them.

Im Jahr 73 vor Christi Geburt floss dort, wo man miteinander zechte und Brot aß, Blut aus dem Brot wie aus einer Wunde. Auch gab es einen so grausamen Hagel, dass es sieben Tage hintereinander Steine schlug und Bruchstücke von richtigen Steinen darin gefunden wurden und recht spitze Steine, sodass davon das Erdreich zerstört wurde.

En l'an 73 avant J.-C., les gens se réunirent pour boire, mais quand ils rompirent le pain, du sang en coula comme d'une blessure. Il y eut aussi un orage de grêle si terrible que des pierres tombèrent du ciel pendant sept jours d'affilée et en celle-ci se trouvaient des morceaux de vraies pierres et beaucoup de pierres très acérées, lesquelles détruisirent la terre.

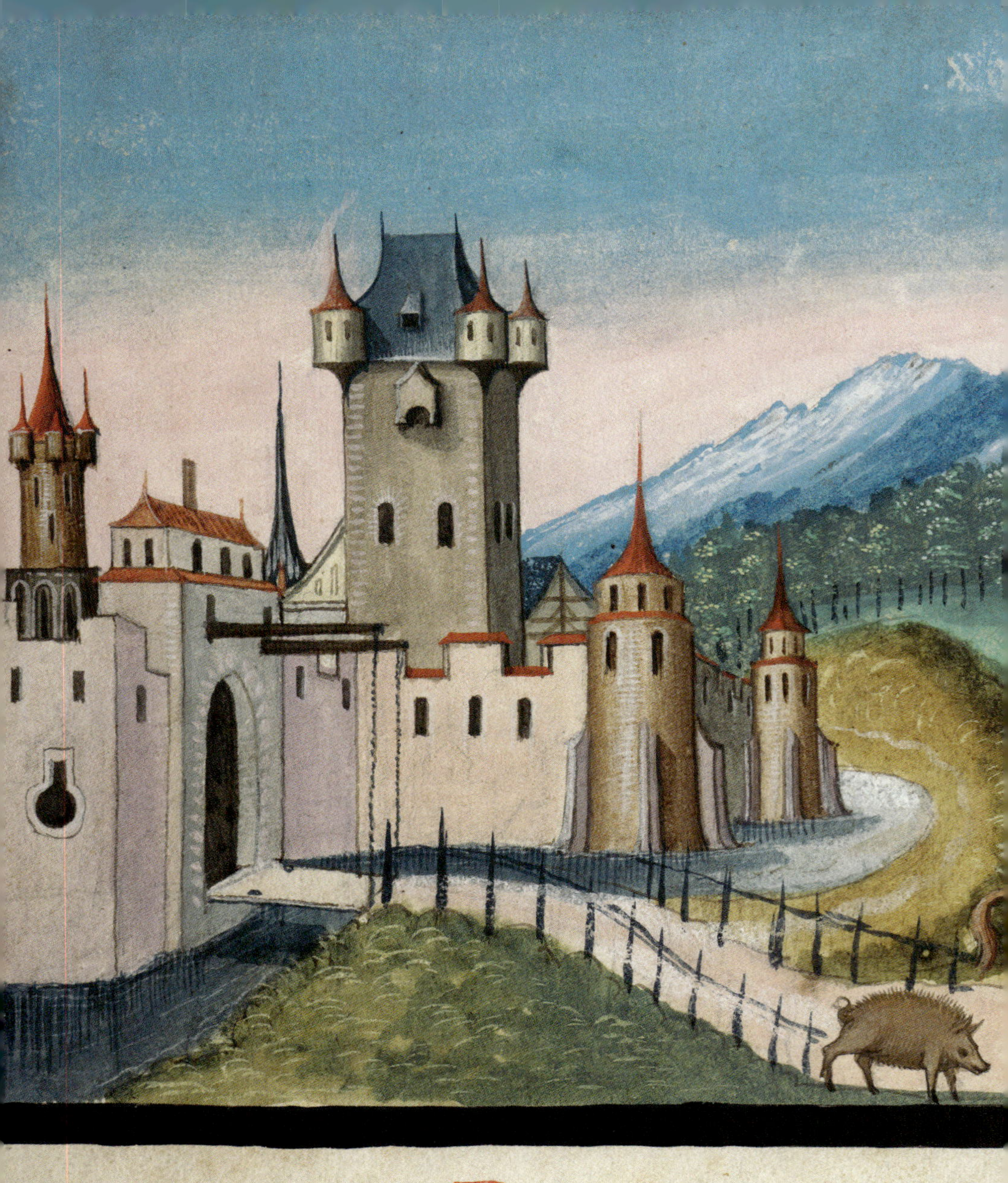

Da man zalt vor Christi get
den thieren vnnd vich er sch
M schaff alls auff ein mal wil
en vnnd irer vorigen art g

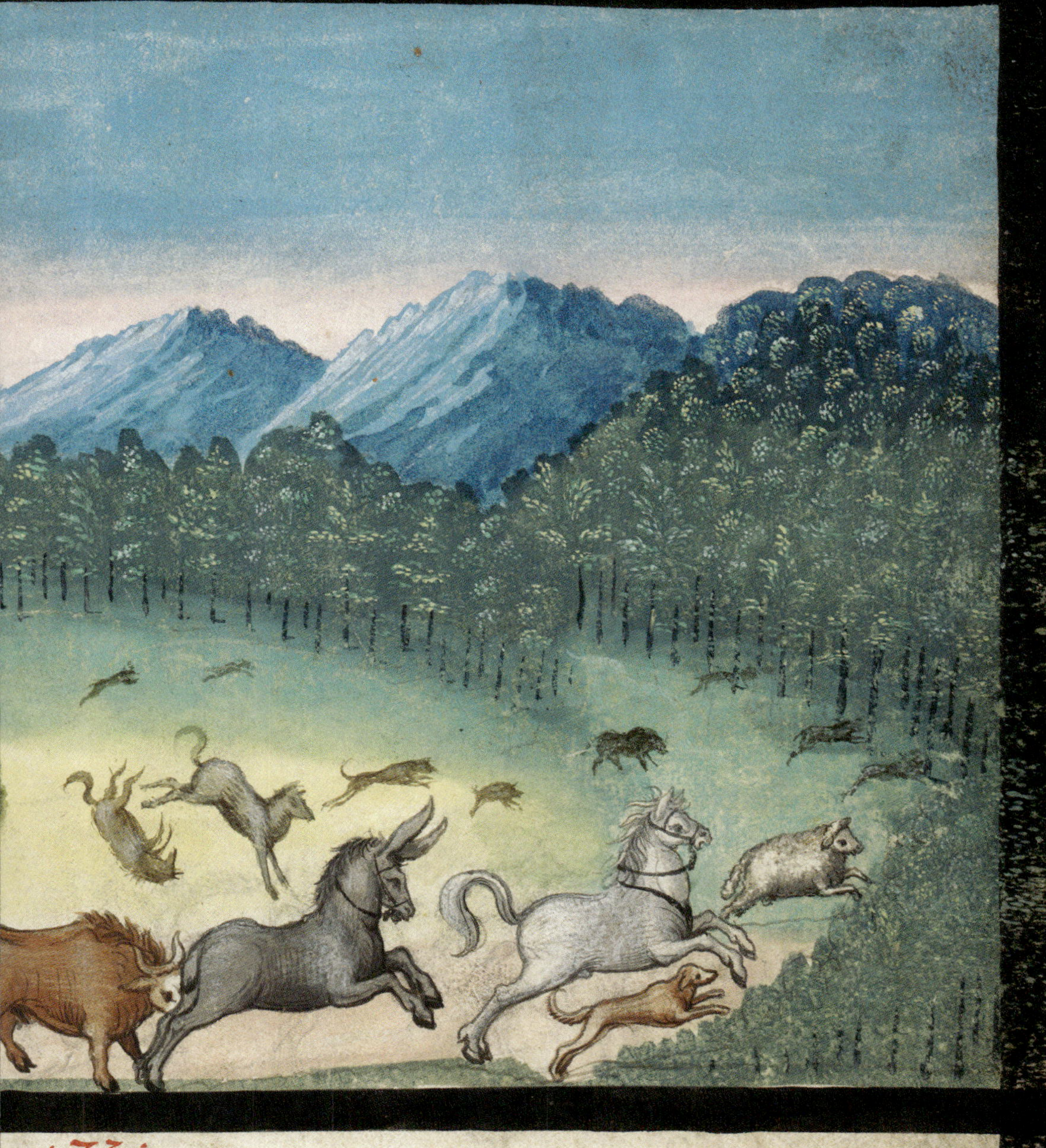

·73·

lxxiii iar ist in ittalia ain grausam wunder an:
, das alle thir die zam waren, alls esel ochsen ross
rd, vund mit ainem stürm in die wildnus liff:
r gessen

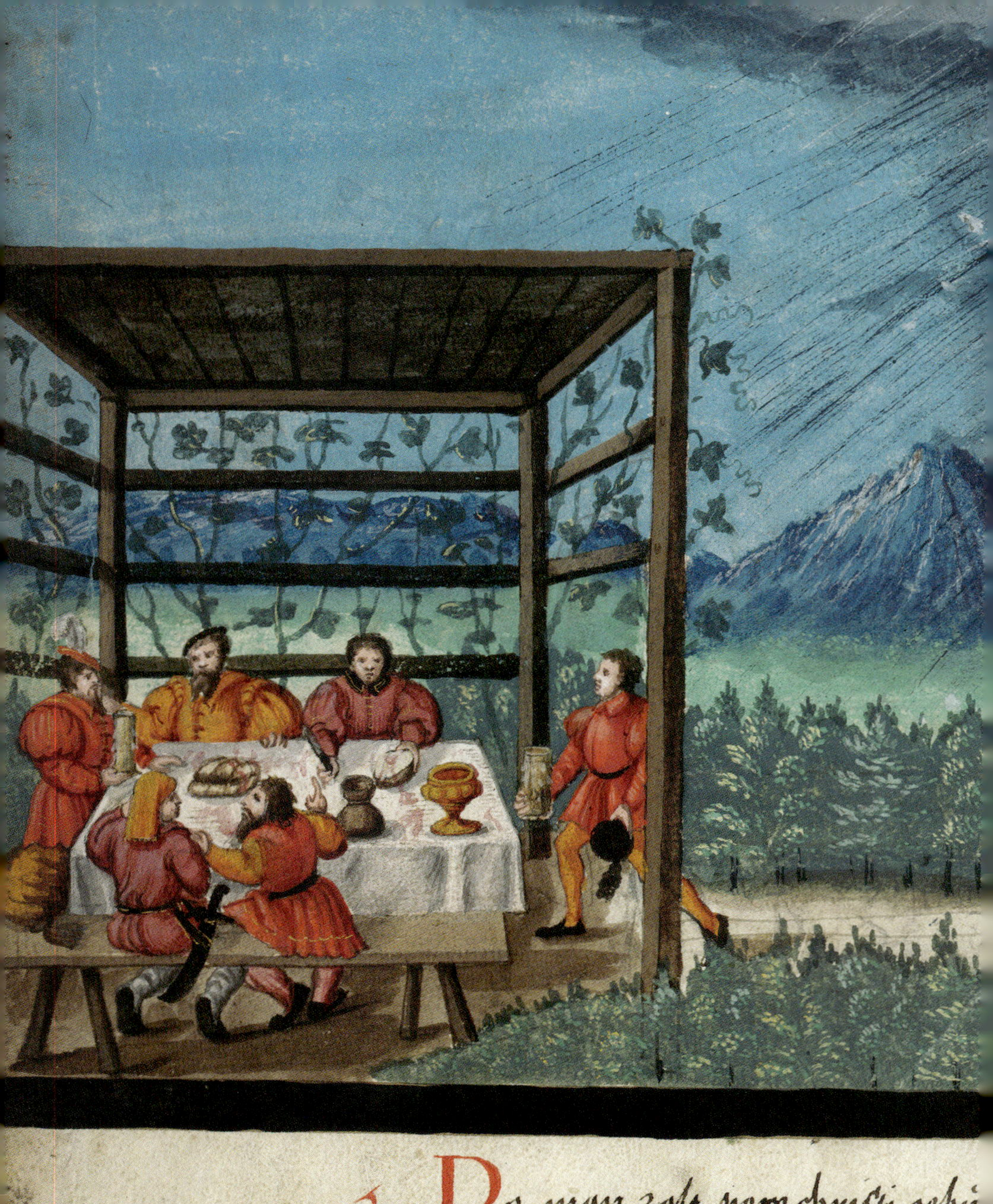

Da man zalt vorr christi gebu
brott schnitt so fluss das blůt
M hagel, das es siben tag an einan
men gefunden, vnd recht spirzi

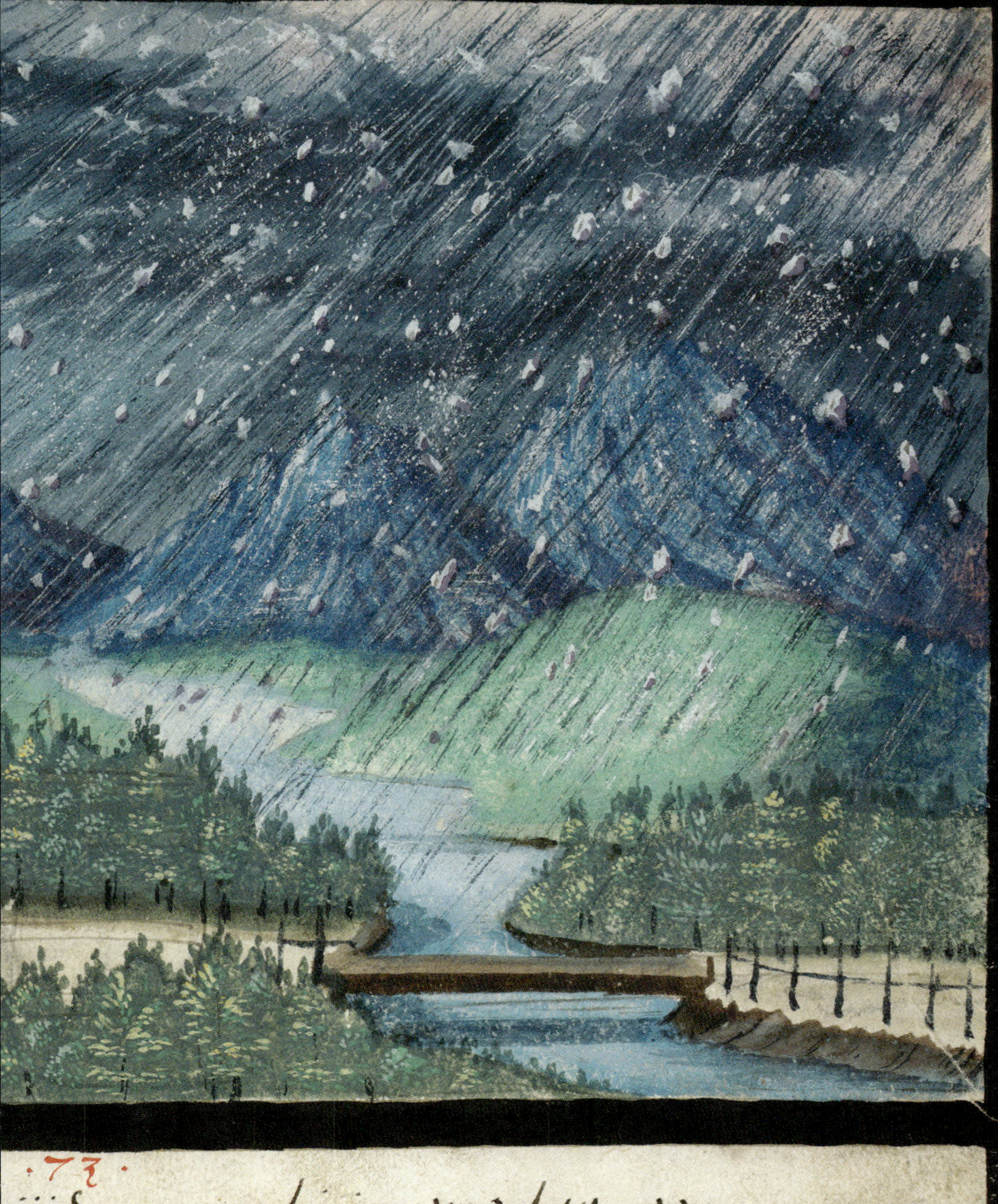

·77·

xiii Jar/ wa man bei ainander zerhet/ vnnd das
n/ wie auß einer wunden/ auch hett es so grausam
ain schlug vnnd darin scherben von rechten sta/
darin das das erdtrich dar von zu grunt ging

·73·

In der romer land lxxiii iar/ v
am himel die dan auff die erdt
in die lufft geflogen/ gegen a
bedeckt hatt/ darnach gefolget d

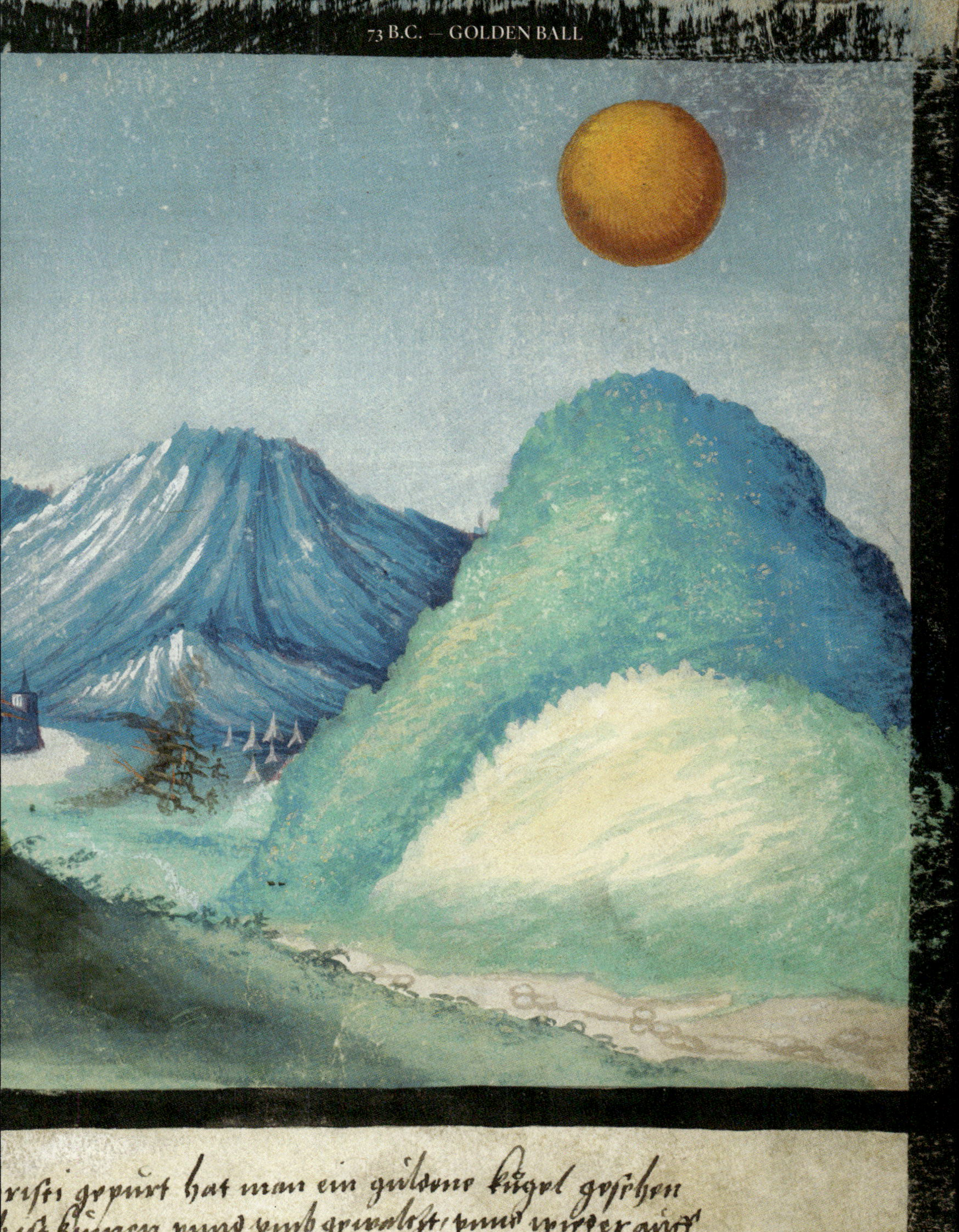

risti gepurt hat man ein guldene kugel gesehen
b ist kumen vnnd vmb gewalzt, vnnd wider auff
ang der sonnen: das sie mit irer grosse die sonne
ess romer krig·

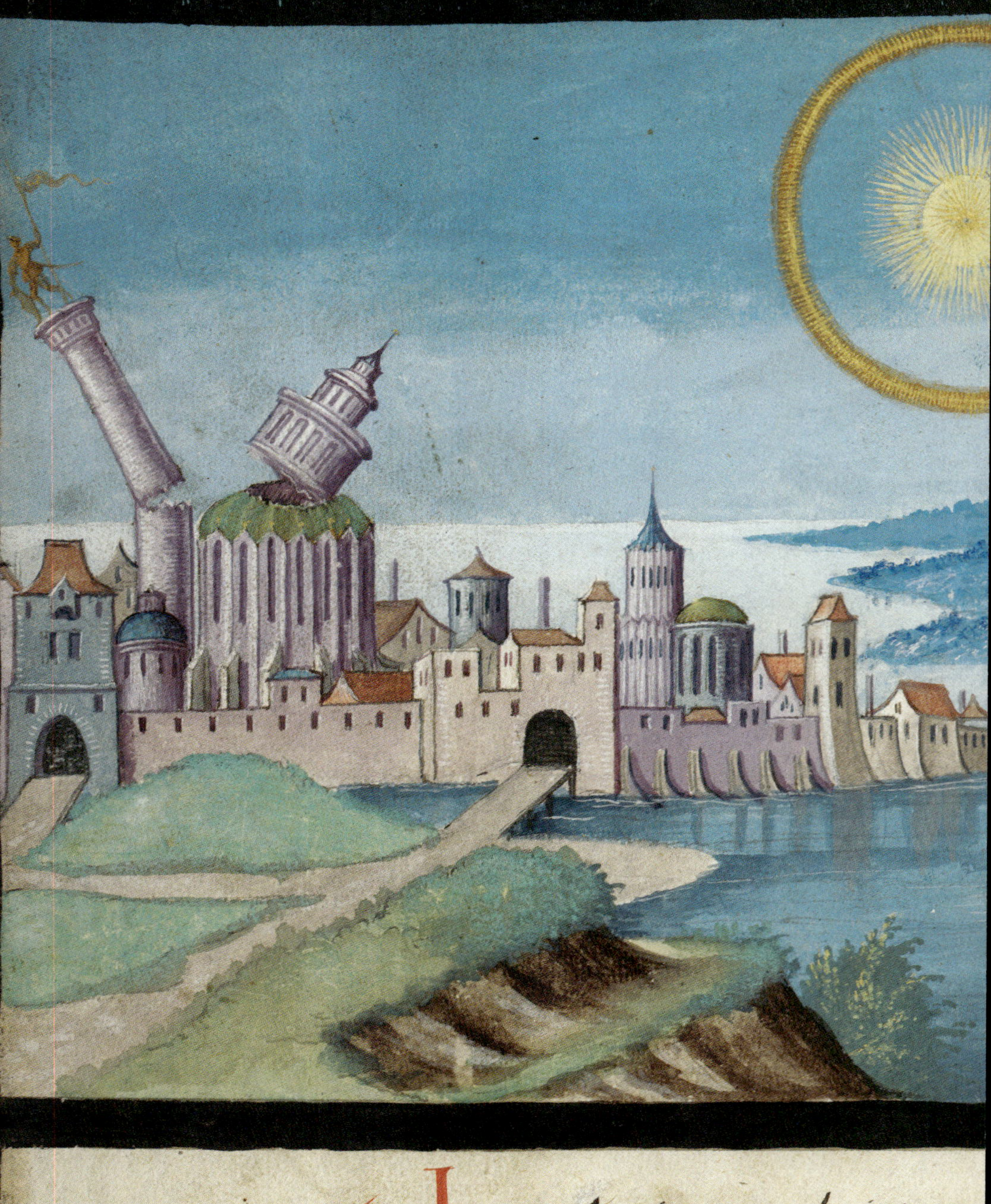

Im negsten iar vor Christus ge
entspringen vnnd den gantzen ta
ain güldener zirckel vmb die sun
ld sant rinnolij mit sampt dem tr
mercken das ainanderer herr vn

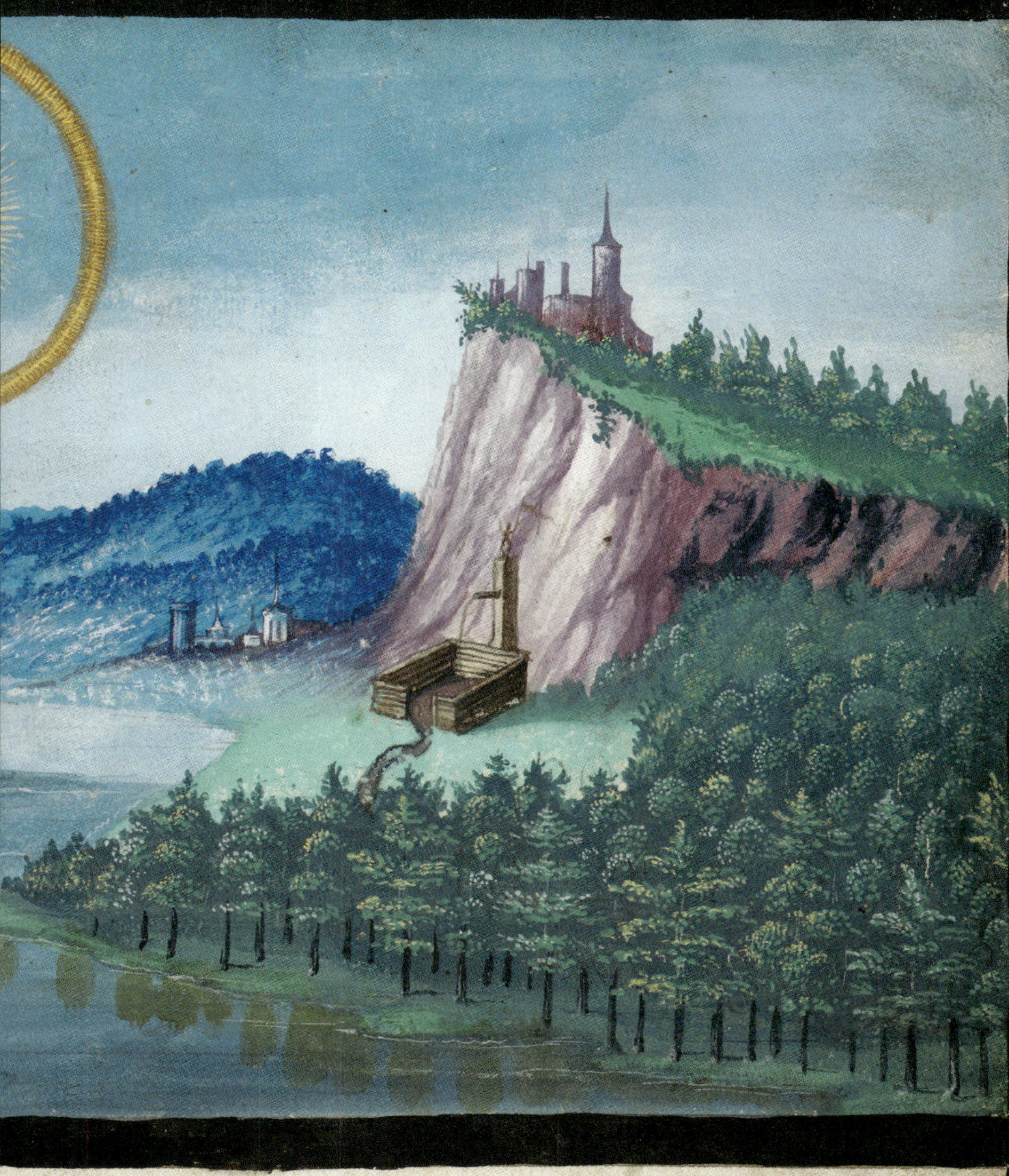

ist zu rom Jensit der tiber ain öll prun
chlich geloffen, und am tag der gepurt ist,
rschinen den gantzen tag, unnd ist die pi
l des frids zu grund gefallen, darbey ist zu
den ist gewesen

Am andern tag nach absterben kayser Julius
orient erschienen vnnd darnach genach zu s
zu der zeitt ein ochs zu rom in der vorstat
lich arbeit dan er wird vber klaine zeit me

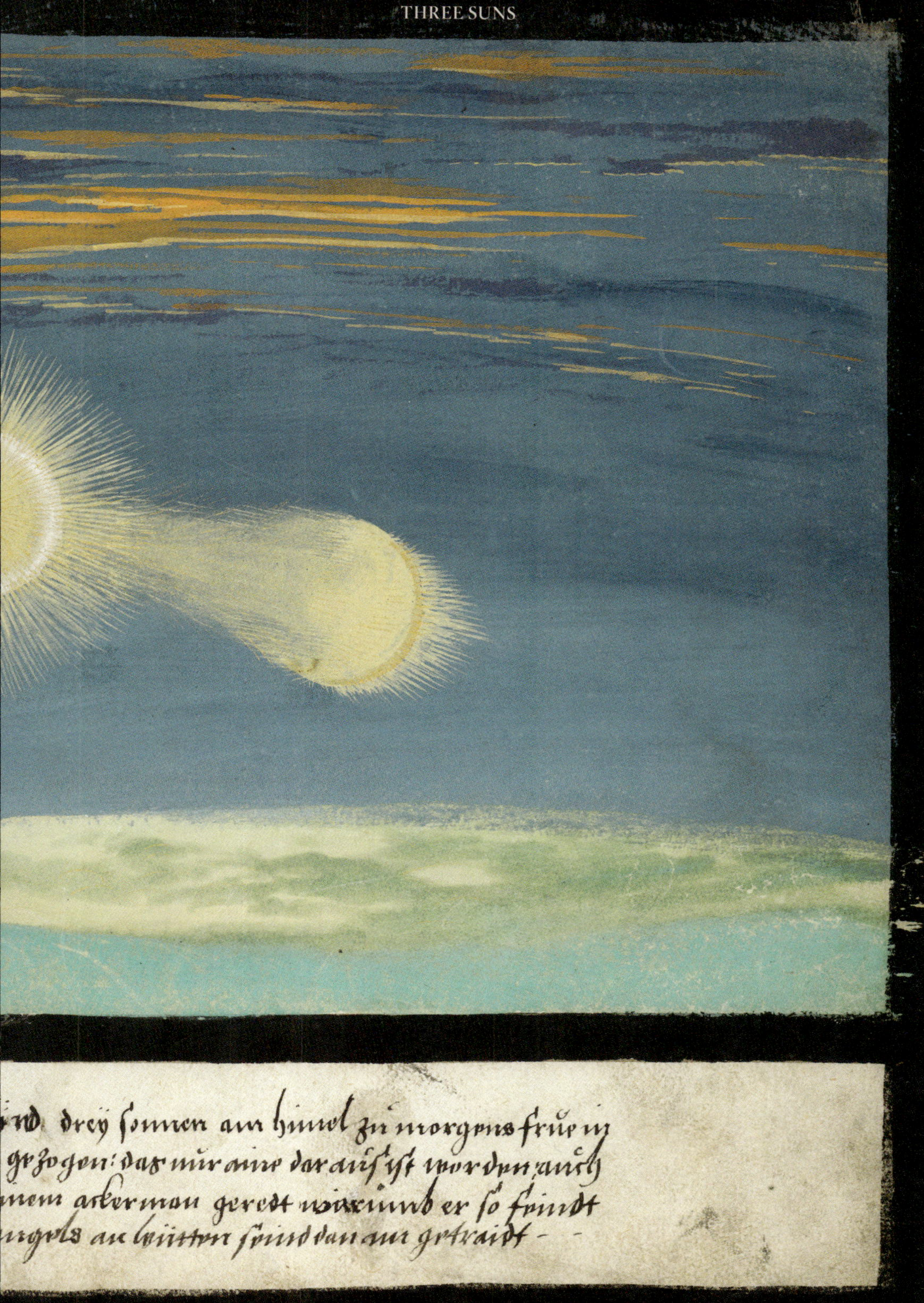
drey sonnen am himel zu morgens frue in
gezogen: das nur aine darauß ist worden, auch
ackerman geredt wie und er so feindt
an leütten seind dan am getraidt -

FOL. 23

73 B.C. — Golden ball | Goldene Kugel | Boule d'or

In the land of the Romans in the year 73 B.C. a golden ball was seen in the sky, which then came down to the earth and rolled about and flew back up into the air again, in the direction of the rising sun, so that its great size covered up the sun completely. This was followed by the great Roman war.

Im Land der Römer hat man 73 Jahre vor Christi Geburt eine goldene Kugel am Himmel gesehen, die dann auf die Erde herabgekommen und herumgerollt und wieder hinauf in die Luft geflogen ist, in Richtung des Aufgangs der Sonne, sodass sie mit ihrer Größe die Sonne verdeckt hat. Danach folgte der große Römerkrieg.

Au pays des Romains en l'an 73 avant J.-C., une boule d'or fut aperçue dans le ciel, qui descendit ensuite sur la terre et roula et repartit dans les airs, vers le levant, et recouvrit entièrement le soleil par sa grande taille. S'ensuivit la grande guerre romaine.

FOL. 24

1 B.C. — Golden circle around sun Goldener Sonnenring | Cercle doré autour du soleil

In the year before Christ was born an oilwell appeared near Rome, on the far bank of the Tiber, and oil flowed from it abundantly for the whole day. And on the day of the Nativity, a golden circle appeared around the sun for the whole day, and the statue of Romulus collapsed as did the Temple of Peace. It should be noted here that a different ruler was in place at that time.

Im Jahr vor Christi Geburt ist bei Rom jenseits des Tiber ein Ölbrunnen entsprungen und den ganzen Tag lang reichlich geflossen. Und am Tag der Geburt ist den ganzen Tag lang ein goldener Kreis um die Sonne erschienen und die Bildsäule des Romulus mitsamt dem Friedenstempel eingestürzt. Dabei ist zu bemerken, dass es einen anderen Herrn gegeben hat.

L'année précédant la naissance du Christ, un puits de pétrole apparut près de Rome sur la rive éloignée du Tibre et du pétrole en coula abondamment pendant toute une journée. Et le jour de la Nativité, un cercle d'or apparut autour du soleil pendant tout le jour, et la statue de Romulus s'effondra en même temps que le temple de la Paix. Ici, il faut noter que régnait un souverain différent.

FOL. 26

Three suns | Drei Sonnen | Trois soleils

On the day after the death of Julius Caesar three suns appeared in the East in the early morning sky which then moved towards each other so that they merged into one. Also at that time, an ox on the outskirts of Rome asked a farmer why he was working so hard, since before very long there would be more of a shortage of people than of grain.

Am anderen Tag nach dem Tod des Kaisers Julius sind drei Sonnen am Himmel in der Morgenfrühe im Osten erschienen und danach zusammengezogen, sodass daraus nur eine geworden ist. Auch hat zu der Zeit ein Ochse in der Vorstadt bei Rom einen Ackerbauern gefragt, warum er so heftig arbeite. Denn es würde über kurze Zeit mehr Mangel an Leuten geben als an Getreide.

Le lendemain de la mort de Jules César, trois soleils apparurent à l'est dans le ciel du petit matin et se rapprochèrent les uns des autres pour se fondre en un seul soleil. Au même moment, un bœuf dans les environs de Rome demanda à un fermier pourquoi il travaillait autant puisqu'il y aurait bientôt moins de bouches à nourrir que de grain.

FOL. 27

170 [in fact: 570] — Mountain in Gaul and hail
Berg in Gallien und Hagel | Montagne en Gaule et grêle

In the year A.D. 570, there came from a mountain in Gaul a great noise and screaming as if many people had been entombed inside it. There was also heavy hail for a long time.

Im 570. Jahr n. Chr. kam aus einem Berg in Gallien ein großer Lärm und Geschrei, als ob viele Leute darin verschüttet wären. Auch gab es eine lange Zeit starken Hagel.

En l'an 570 après J.-C., beaucoup de bruits et de hurlements sortirent d'une montagne de Gaule, comme si une foule y avait été ensevelie. Aussi, une forte grêle tomba pendant longtemps.

FOL. 28

170 [in fact: 570] — Rain of blood and flood
Blutregen und Überschwemmung | Pluie de sang et inondation

In the year A.D. 570, fiery arrows and drops of blood appeared in the sky over Italy. Afterwards, such a fierce rain fell there that many villages and towns were swept away and many people drowned. Also, there appeared in the water, from the waist up, several men and women with long hair.

Im 570. Jahr n. Chr. sind in Italien feurige Pfeile und Blutstropfen am Himmel erschienen. Danach ging ein solch grausamer Regen im welschen Land nieder, dass er viele Dörfer und Städte fortriss und viele Leute ertränkte. Auch erschienen im Wasser die Oberkörper von Männern und Frauen mit langen Haaren.

En l'an 570 après J.-C., des flèches enflammées et des gouttes de sang apparurent dans le ciel de l'Italie. Par la suite, une grêle si terrible s'y abattit que de nombreux villages et villes furent balayés et de nombreuses personnes noyées. Aussi, des hommes et des femmes portant de longs cheveux apparurent dans l'eau jusqu'au-dessus de la taille.

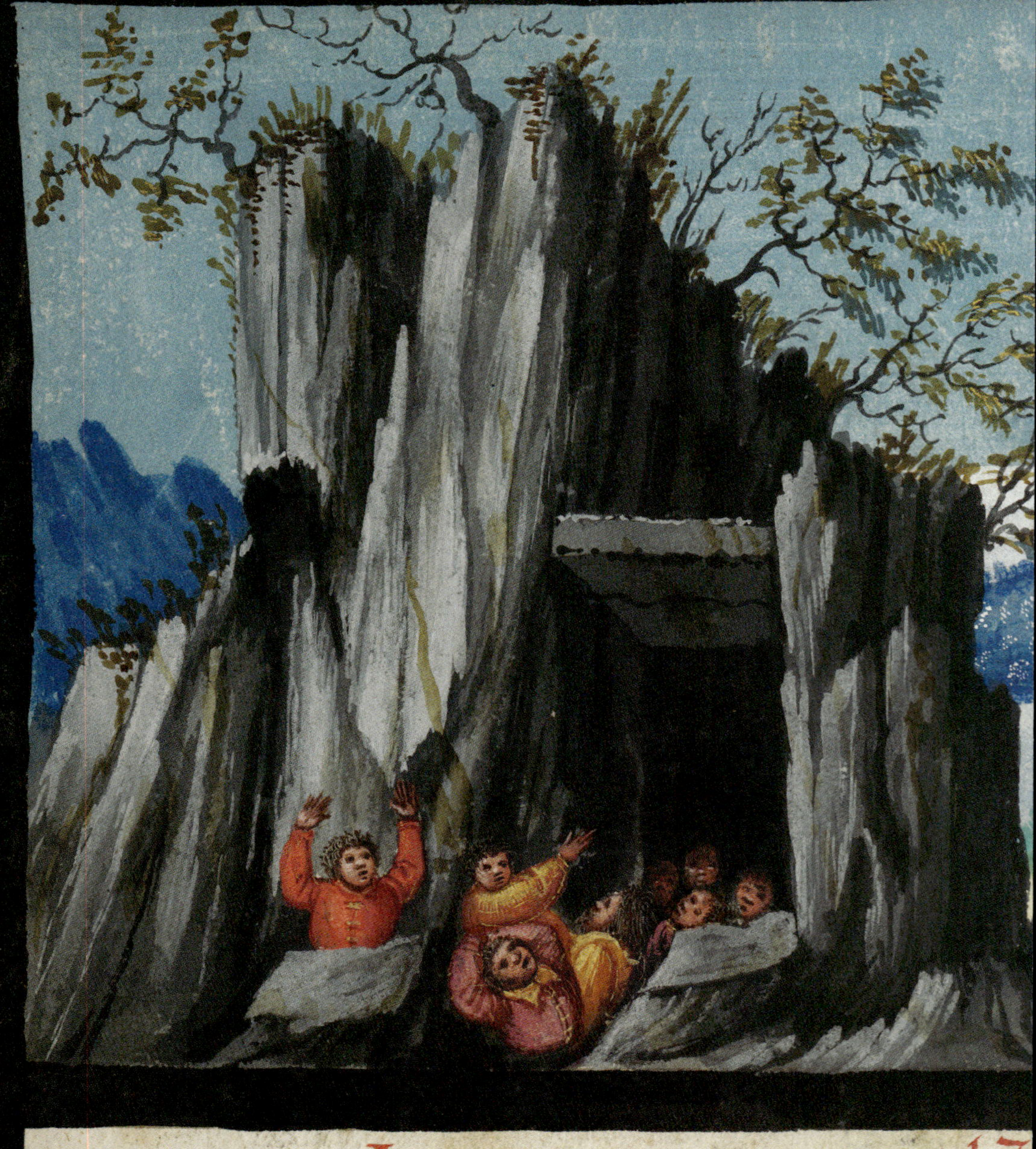

Im d lxx iar nach Cristi gepurt, wa
hall vnnd geschray alls ob vill leu
hagel ein lannge zeit gehabt

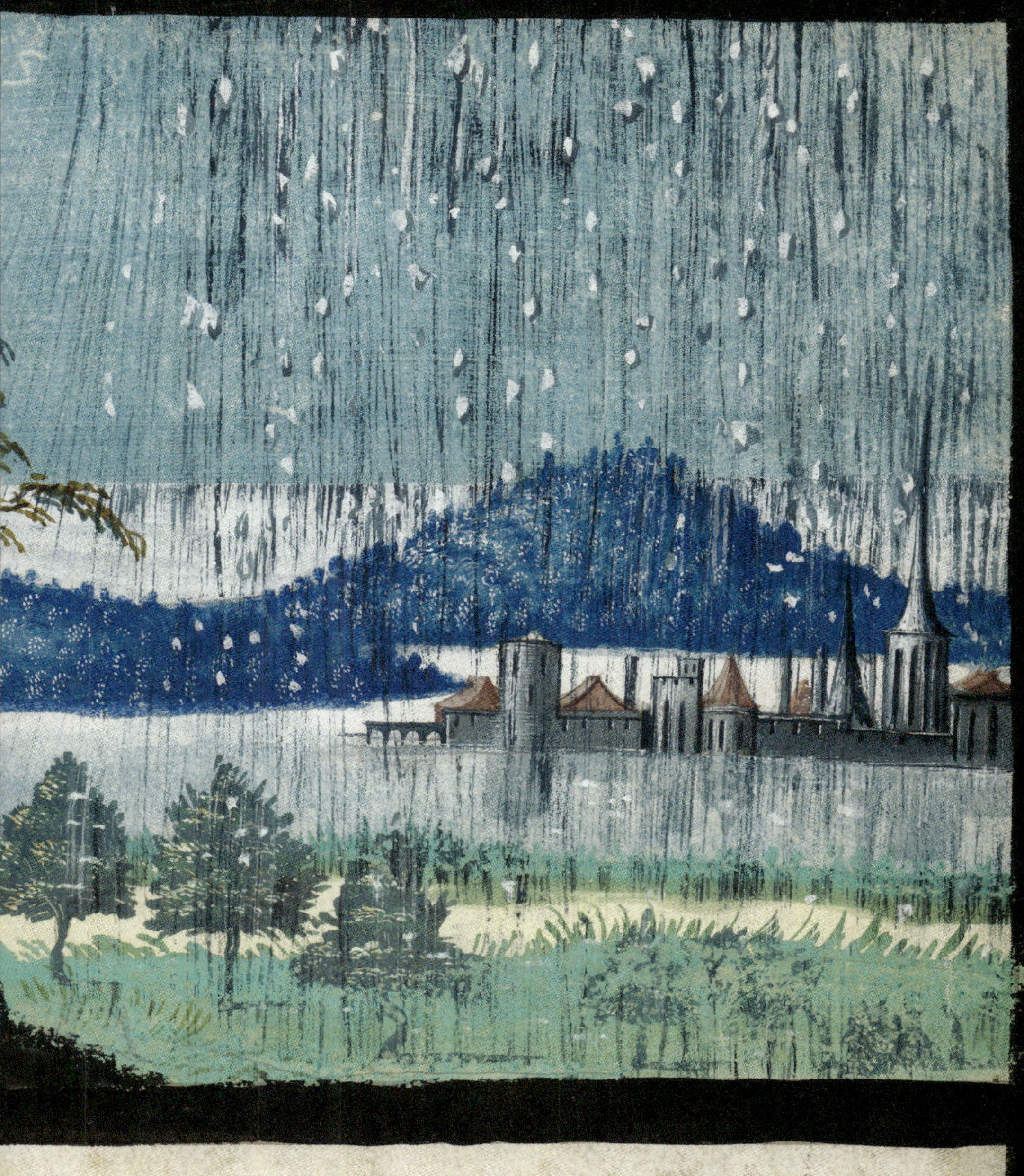

n perg in gallia · der gab ein grosen
r in ver fallen worn / auch grossin

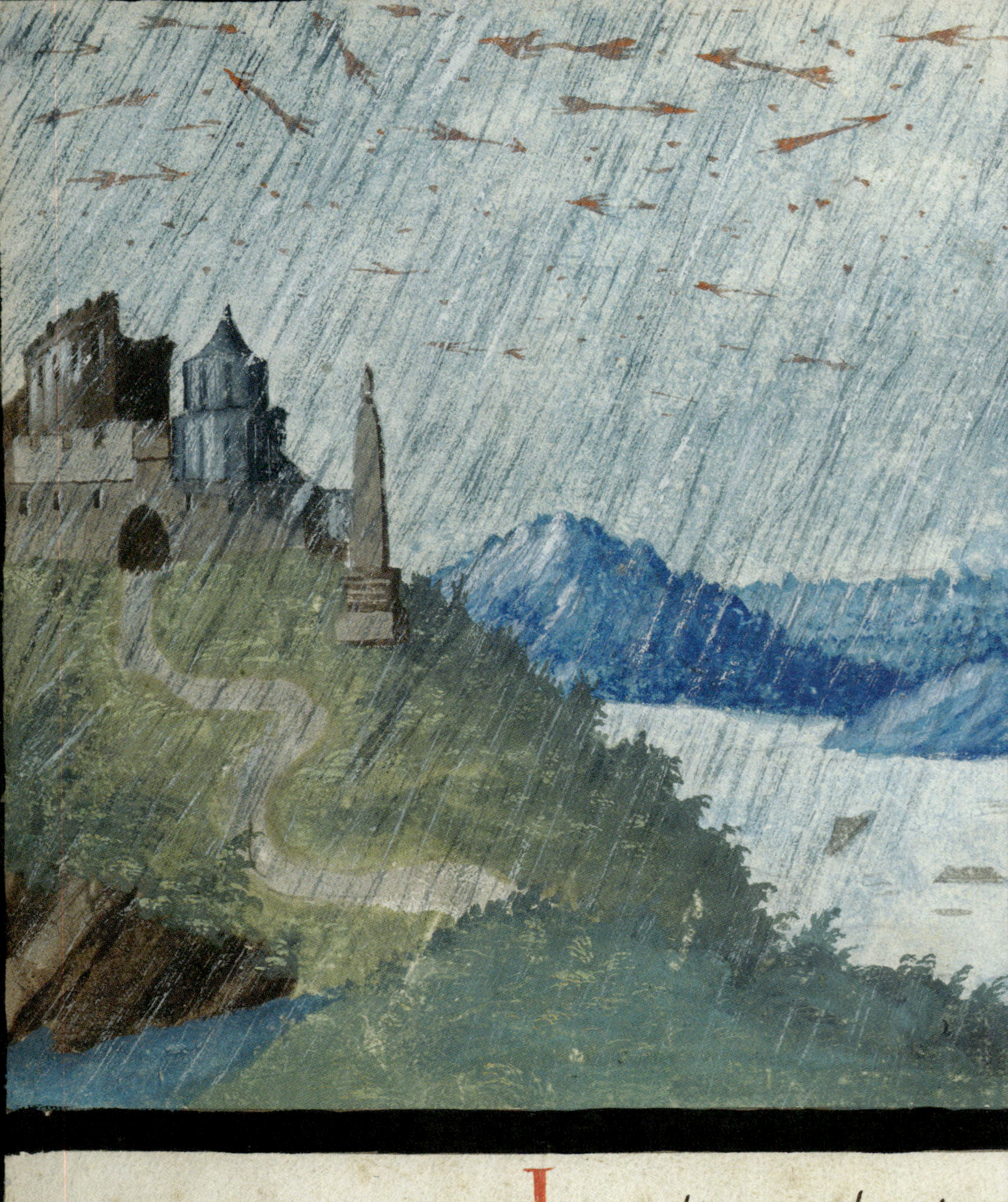

Im d lxx iar nach Cristi ge
am himel vnnd plůt trop
wesser dar nider in wolk
wert ristri vnnd vil volcks

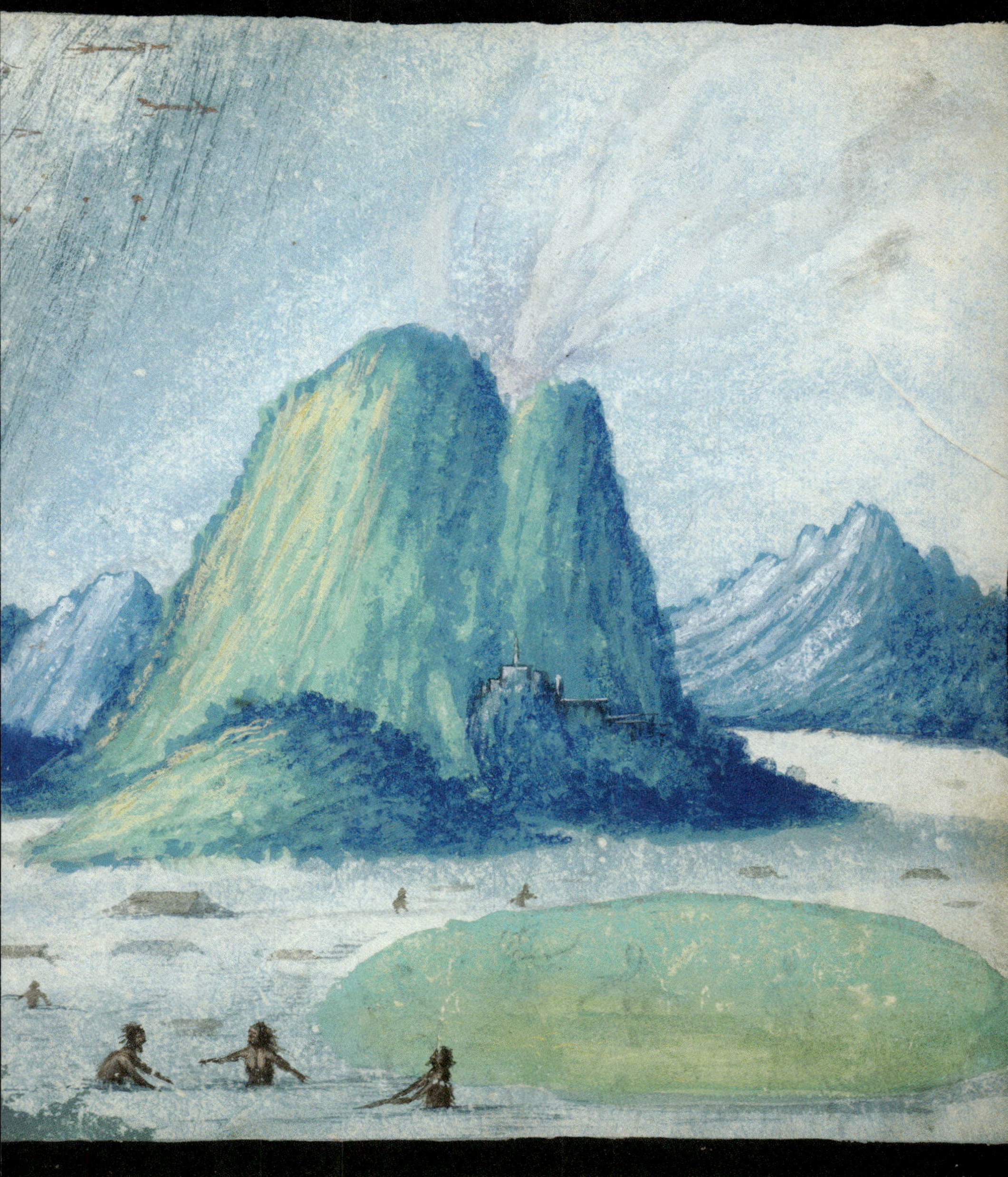

· 170 ·
send in welsch land feurige strel erschinen, weibs person
darbei, darnach ging ain solchs grausam gesim wasser mit
, das er vil dorffer vnnd schlosser hin, langen haar
rumckett hatt, auch erschinen man vnd oberhalb der gurt

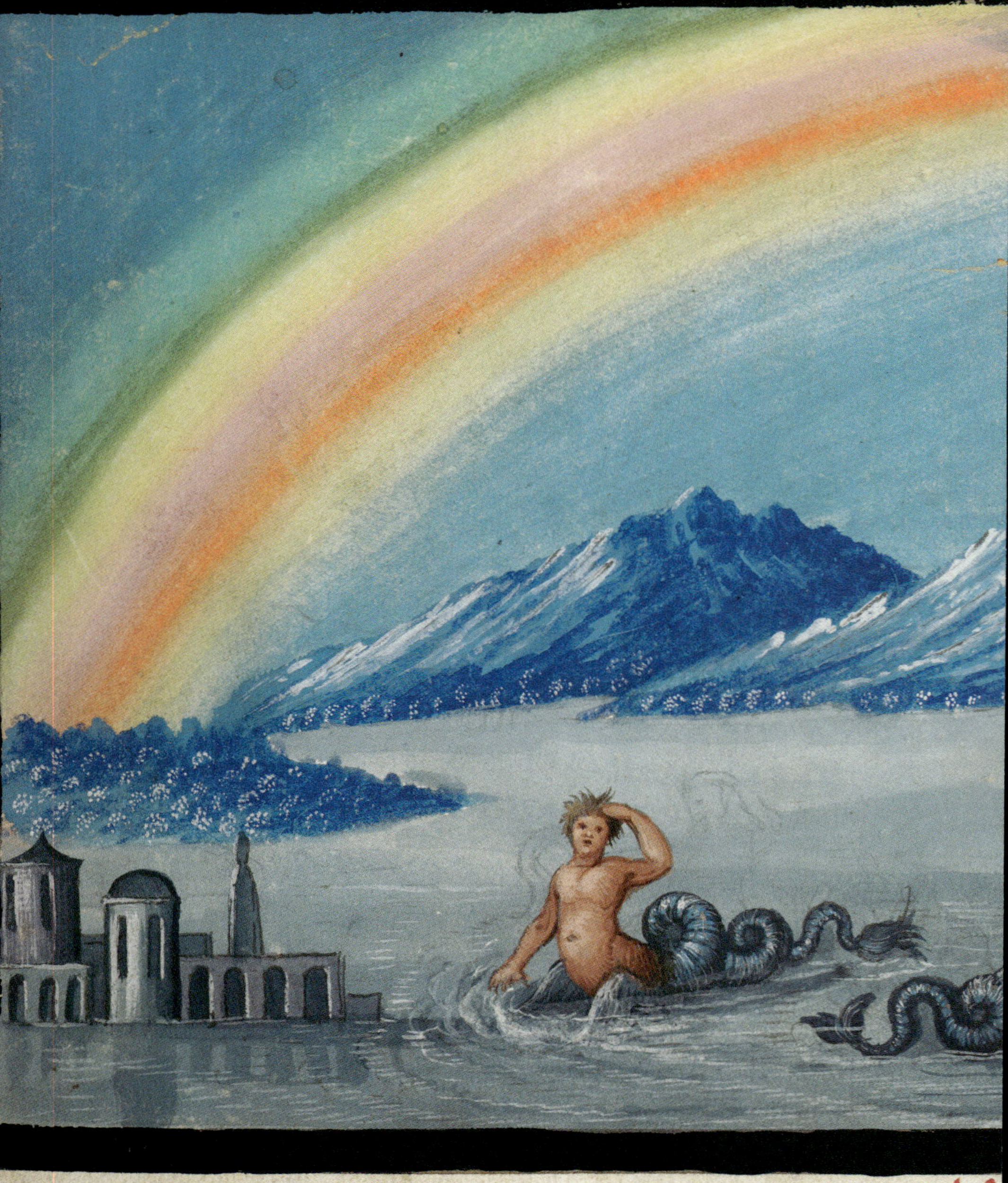

Im d lxxxxv iar nach Cristi gepurt: zu der zeit w ·19
in menschlicher gestalt gesehen, er vill auch frün
pogen, das die leut mainten es kem der iüngsta
hert wass worden darnach folget ain grosser peste

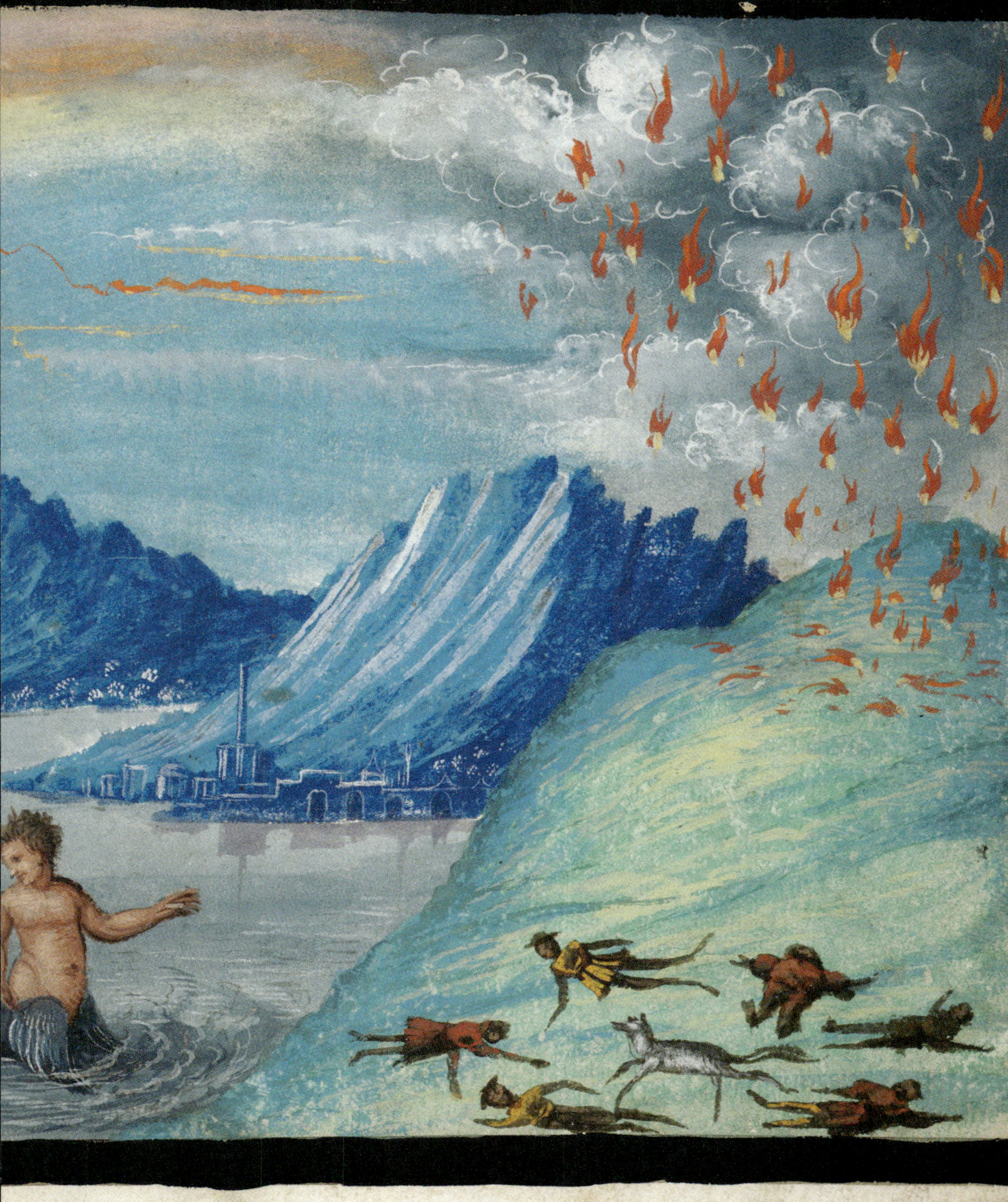

meti/ war in der insel delo zway merer wunder
n himel/ vnd er schin ain solcher heller regen
d thet so grausam donnerschleg das vor nie er/
hund nam vil folcks hin wegk

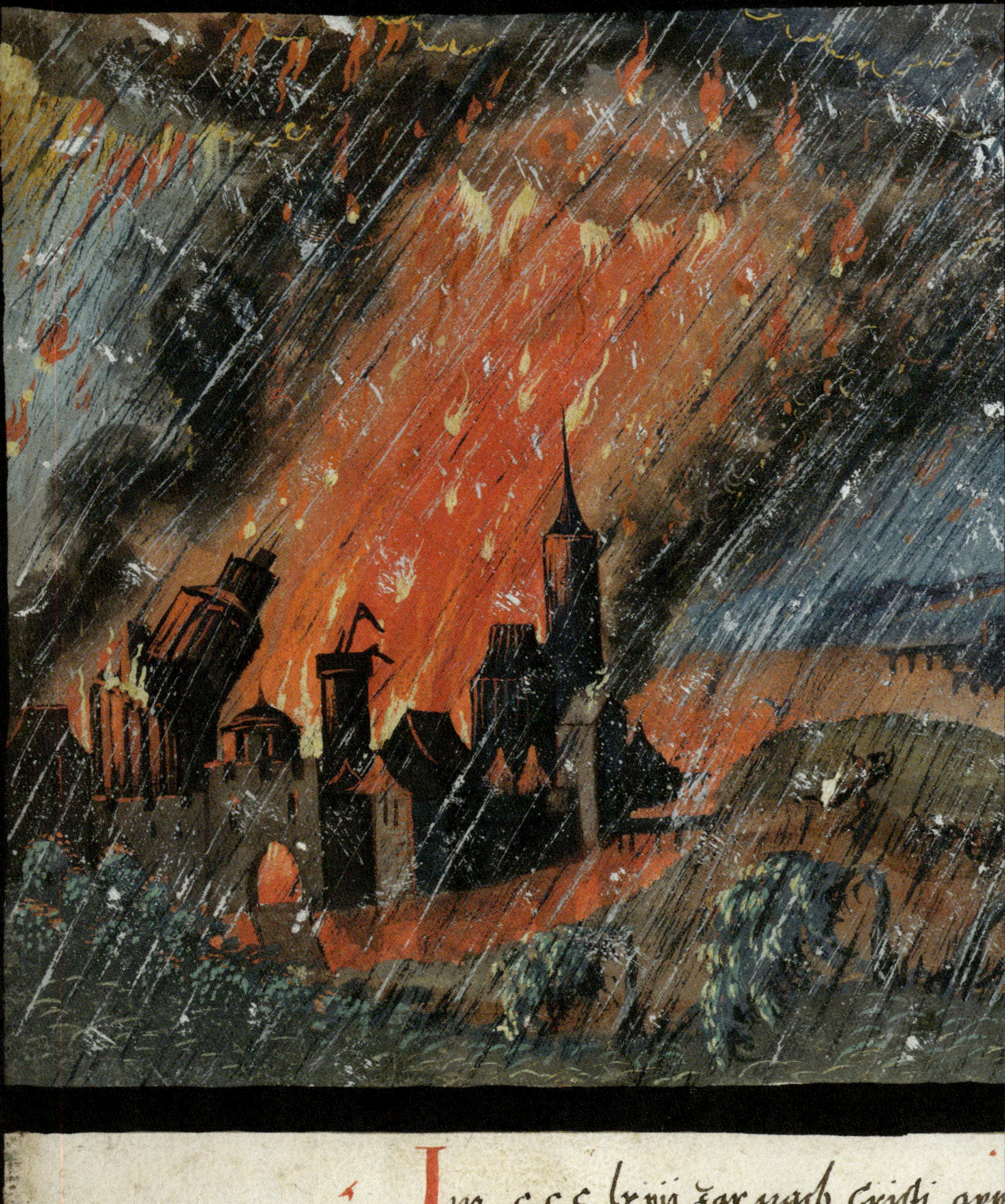

Im ccc lxvii Jar nach Cristi gr...
grausamer Erbidem gewesen / d...
M fallen dar nider zu poden / vnnd a...
gefallen / vnnd eissen vnnd stain
er drencket vnd vil leüt von hagel ...

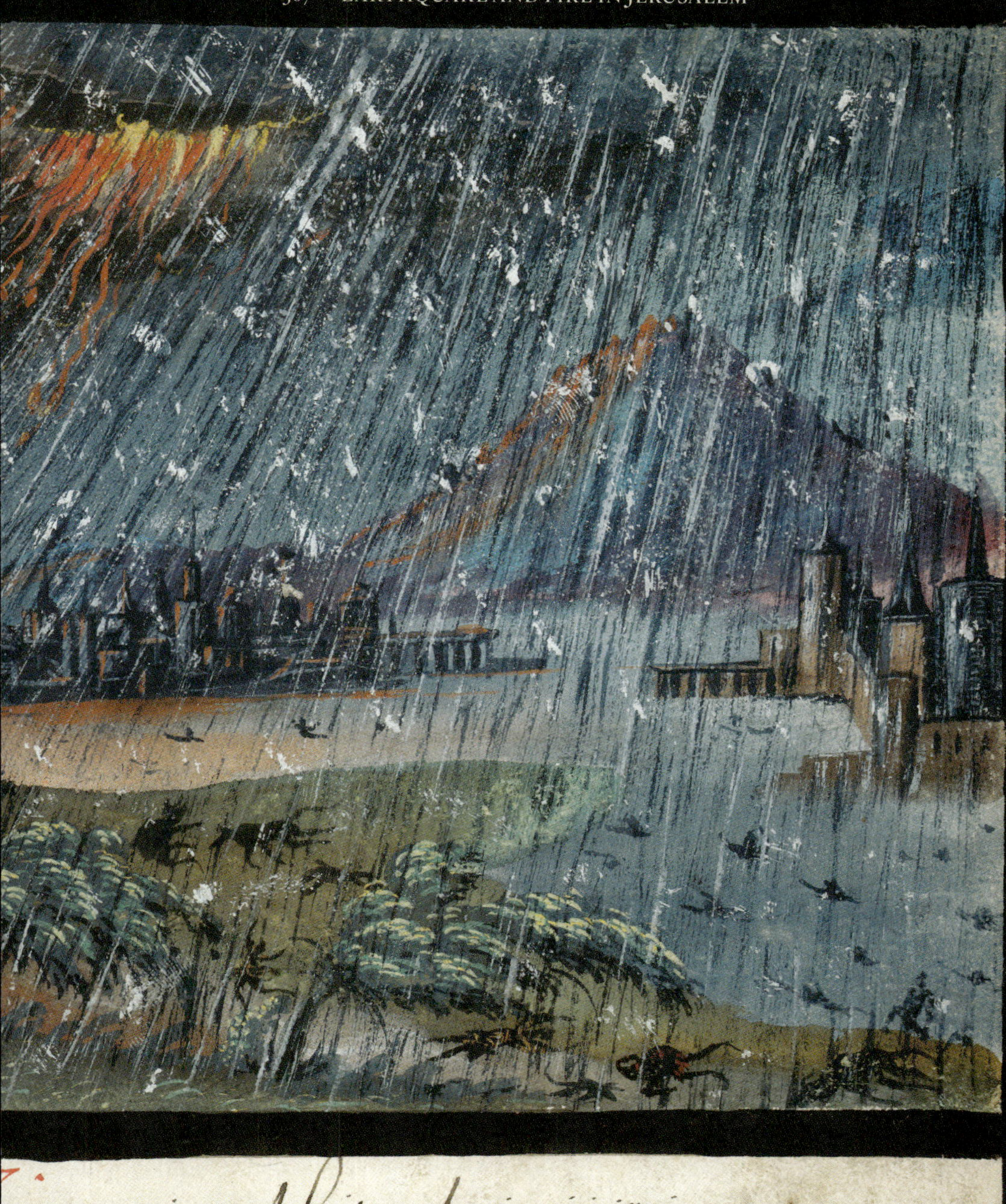

n andern iar nach kaiser valantiniani ist ein
r gantz welt. vnnd fiel der tempel zu jeru:
dem tag ist das feüer vom himel darauff
rrent vnd das meer die statt nicream gar
lagen vnd erdrenckt vnd hat gewert in asia

FOL. 29

195 [in fact: 595] — Rainbow and sea creatures

Regenbogen und Meeresgeschöpfe | Arc-en-ciel et créatures marines

In the year A.D. 595, in the time of Muhammad, two wondrous sea creatures having human form were seen off the island of Delos. Also, fire fell from the sky and a rainbow appeared of such brightness that the people thought Judgement Day had come. And there were peals of thunder more terrible than had ever been heard before. This was followed by a dreadful plague which carried off many people.

Im 595. Jahr n. Chr., zu der Zeit Mohammeds, wurden bei der Insel Delos zwei Meerwunder in menschlicher Gestalt gesehen. Es fiel auch Feuer vom Himmel, und es erschien ein solch heller Regenbogen, dass die Leute dachten, der Jüngste Tag käme. Und es gab so grausame Donnerschläge, wie sie vorher nie gehört worden waren. Danach folgte eine große Seuche und raffte viele Leute dahin.

En l'an 595 après J.-C., au temps de Mahomet, deux créatures merveilleuses à forme humaine furent aperçues au large de l'île de Délos. Aussi, des flammes tombèrent du ciel et un arc-en-ciel si éclatant apparut que l'on crut arriver le jour du Jugement dernier. Et il y eut des coups de tonnerre comme jamais on n'en avait entendu. S'ensuivit une horrible peste qui emporta beaucoup de gens.

FOL. 30

367 — Earthquake and fire in Jerusalem

Erdbeben und Feuer in Jerusalem | Tremblement de terre et incendie à Jérusalem

In the year A.D. 367, in the second year after the reign of the emperor Valentinian, an earthquake struck that was felt across the whole world, and the Temple in Jerusalem collapsed. And on the next day, fire fell upon it from the sky and destroyed its iron and stone. And the sea completely flooded the city of Nicaea and many people were slain by hail or drowned. And this spread right across the province of Asia.

Im 367. Jahr n. Chr. im zweiten Jahr nach Kaiser Valentinian hat sich ein Erdbeben auf der ganzen Welt ereignet. Und der Tempel zu Jerusalem stürzte ein. Und am nächsten Tag ist das Feuer vom Himmel darauf herabgefallen und hat Eisen und Stein zerstört. Und das Meer hat die Stadt Nicäa völlig überflutet, und viele Leute wurden von Hagel erschlagen und ertränkt. Und es hat sich über die Provinz Asia erstreckt.

En l'an 367 après J.-C., dans la deuxième année après le règne de l'empereur Valentinien, un tremblement de terre secoua le monde entier et le Temple de Jérusalem s'effondra. Et le lendemain, un déluge de feu s'abattit sur lui et en détruisit le fer et la pierre. Et la mer inonda entièrement la ville de Nicaea et beaucoup de gens furent tués par la grêle ou noyés. Et cela s'étendit à toute la province d'Asie.

FOL. 32

595 — Comet | Komet | Comète

In the year A.D. 595, in the time of Muhammad, something wondrous and fearsome appeared. At that time, a bright comet was seen over Constantinople for a whole year.

Im 595. Jahr nach Christus, zu der Zeit Mohammeds, erschien etwas Wunderbares und Furchtbares. Zu der Zeit wurde ein heller Komet zu Konstantinopel ein ganzes Jahr gesehen.

En l'an 595 après J.-C., au temps de Mahomet, un phénomène merveilleux et effrayant se produisit. À cette époque, une comète très brillante fut observée au-dessus de Constantinople pendant toute une année.

FOL. 34

1007 — Comet | Komet | Comète

In the year A.D. 1007, a wondrous comet appeared. It gave off fire and flames in all directions. As it fell to earth it was seen in Germany and Italy.

Im 1007. Jahr nach der Geburt Christi erschien ein wunderbarer Komet. Der gab Feuer und Flammen in alle Richtungen von sich. Dass er auf die Erde fiel, ist in Deutschland und Italien gesehen worden.

En l'an 1007 après J.-C., apparut une comète merveilleuse. En jaillissaient du feu et des flammes dans tous les sens. Alors qu'elle tombait sur la terre, elle fut observée en Allemagne et en Italie.

FOL. 35

1009 — Burning torch | Brennende Fackel | Torche enflammée

In the year A.D. 1009, the sun went dark and the moon was seen all blood-red and a great earthquake struck and there fell from the sky with a loud and crashing noise a huge burning torch like a column or a tower. This was followed by the death of many people and famine throughout Germany and Italy. More people died than remained alive.

Im 1009. Jahr nach der Geburt Christi wurde die Sonne verfinstert und der Mond ganz blutig gesehen und es geschah ein großes Erdbeben und es fiel eine große brennende Fackel wie eine Säule oder ein Turm mit lautem Lärm und Getöse vom Himmel. Darauf folgte ein großes Sterben und eine Teuerung in Deutschland und in Italien. Es starben mehr Leute, als am Leben blieben.

En l'an 1009 après J.-C., le soleil fut obscurci et on observa que la lune était rouge sang, et un grand tremblement de terre se produisit, et tomba du ciel en faisant grand bruit et vacarme une énorme torche enflammée ressemblant à une colonne ou une tour. S'ensuivit la mort de nombreuses personnes et la famine dans toute l'Allemagne et l'Italie. Il y eut davantage de morts que de survivants.

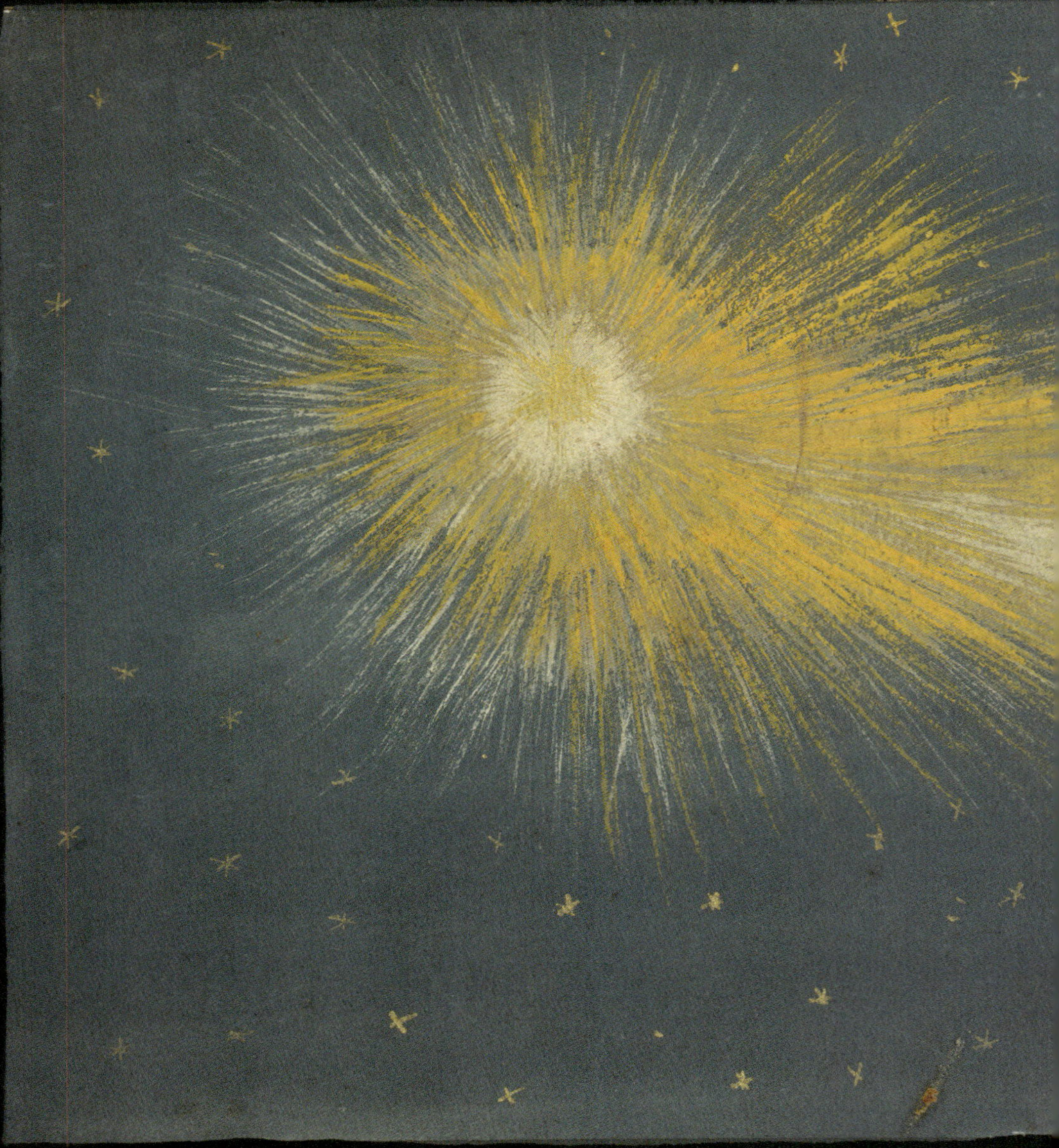

u

Im d lxxxxv iar nach
ein wunderberlich erschi
ain lichter comnet zu

5·95·

ti/ zů der zeit machometi erschein

lich ding zů sagen zů der zeit war

stantinopel ein gantz iar gesehen

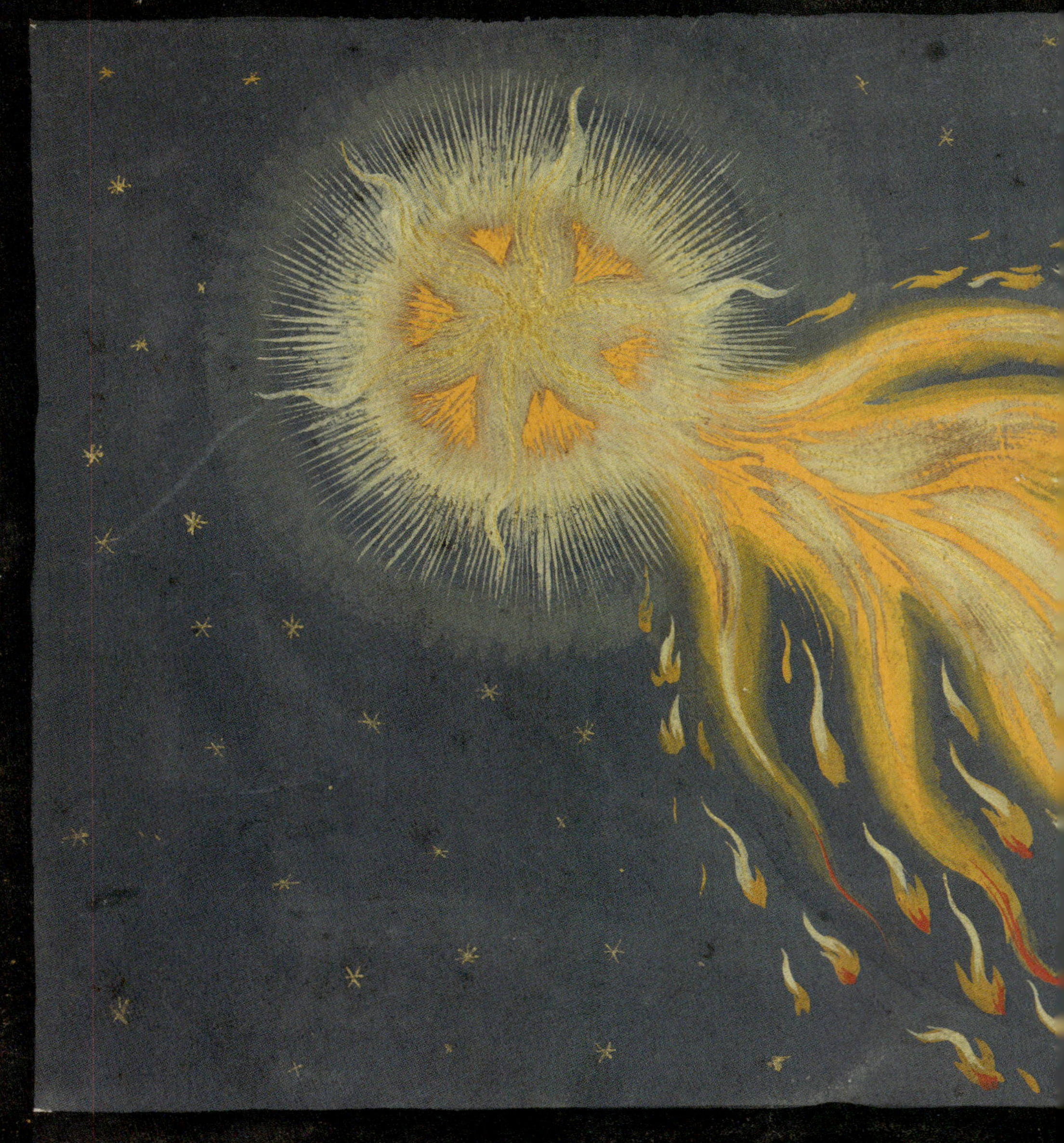

Im m vii iar nach de
Commet/ der gab feur
die erden fiell/ das g

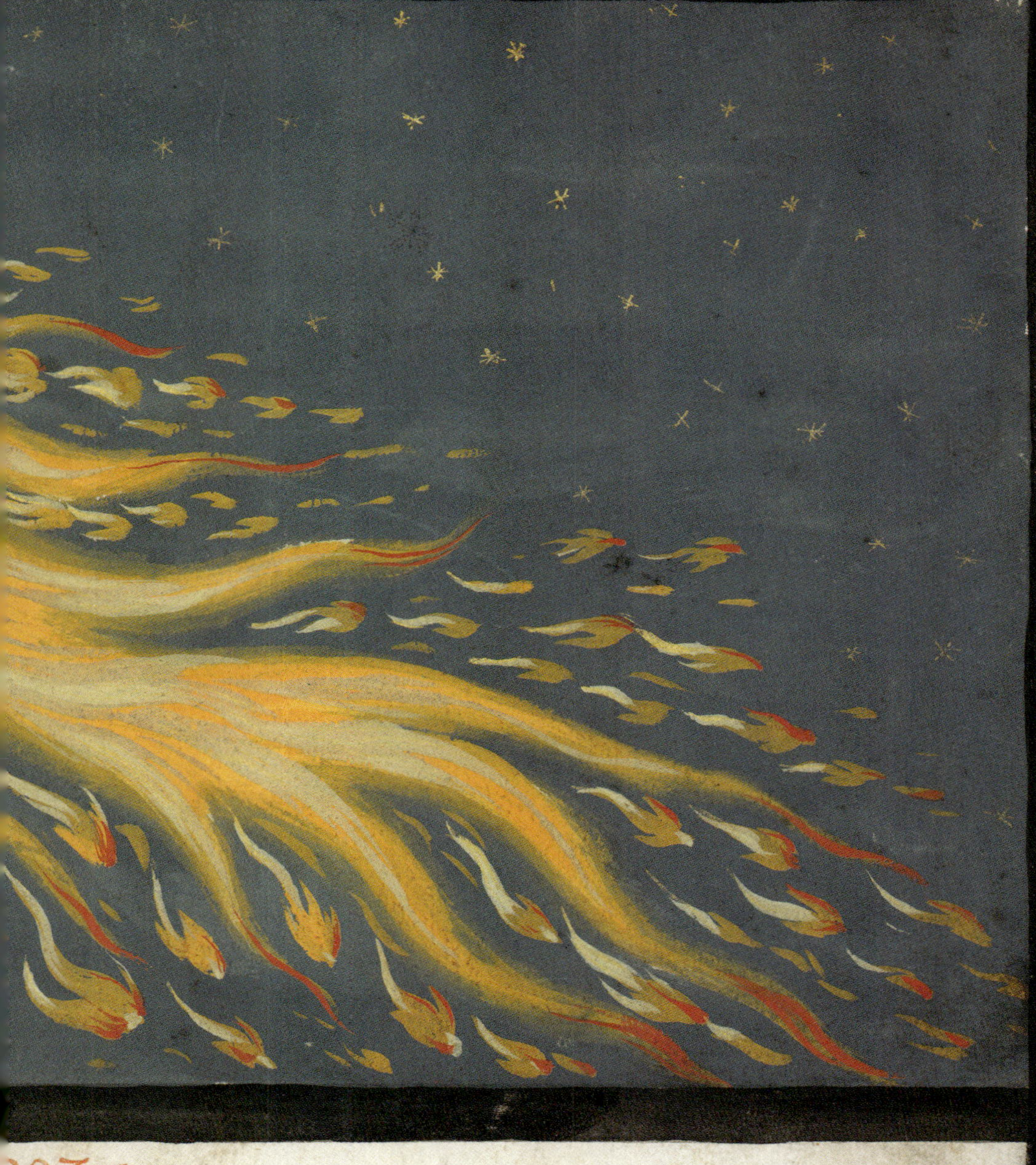
007
rt christi; erschin ein wunderbarlicher
rund her, von im flamen, das er auff
ist worden in deutschend welsch landt

10

Im m ix iar nach der gepurt christi
blüttig gesehen unnd geschach ein gr
wie ein saul oder thürn von hi
groser sterbet und trurung in deutsch

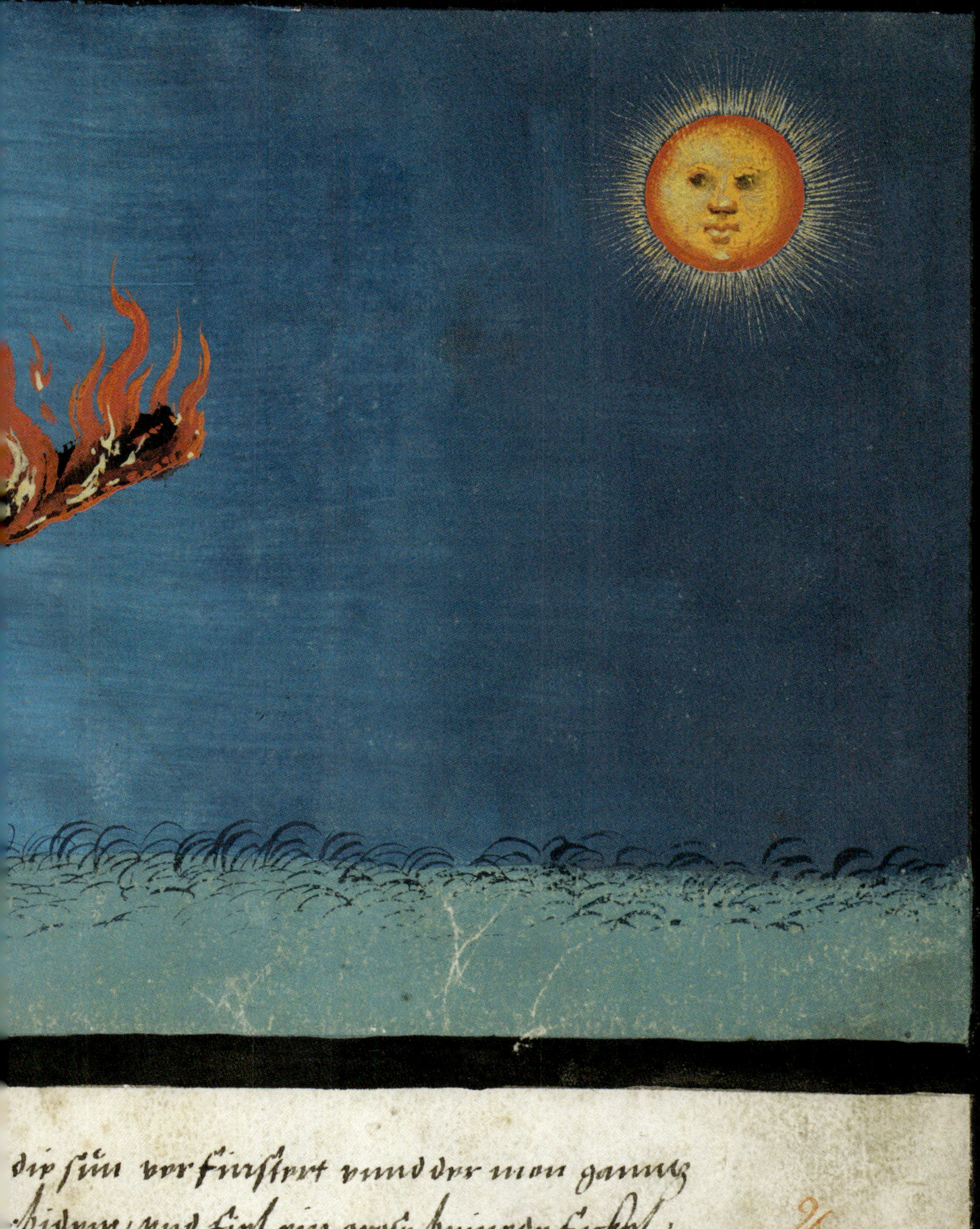
die sün verfinstert vnnd der mon gantz
bidem, vnd fiel ein grose brinende fackel;
in ainem grossen hall oder schal, dar auf
rsch land mer leut todt dan lebendig bliben

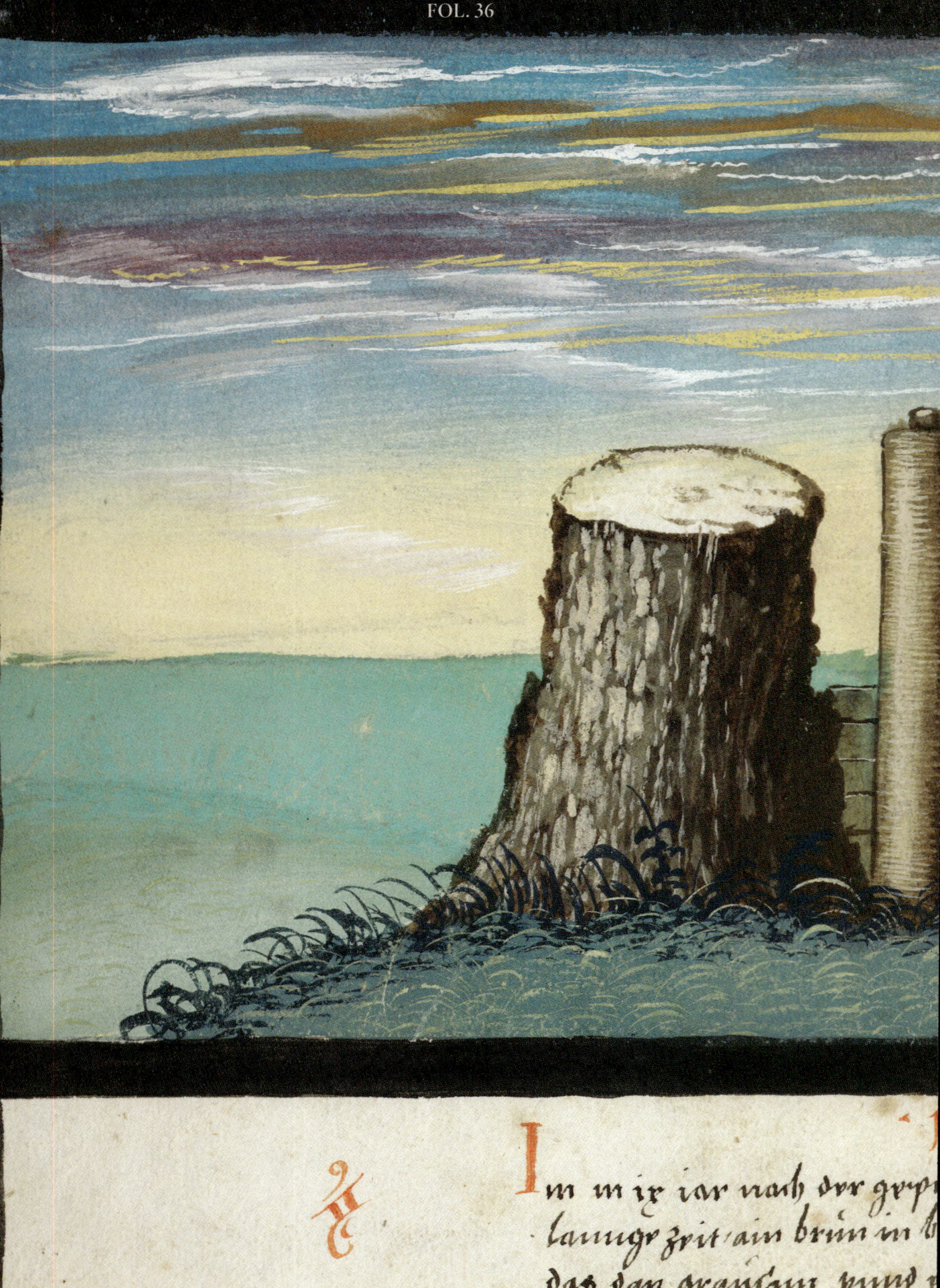
Im m ix iar nach der
lannge zeit ain brun in
das dan grausam vnnd

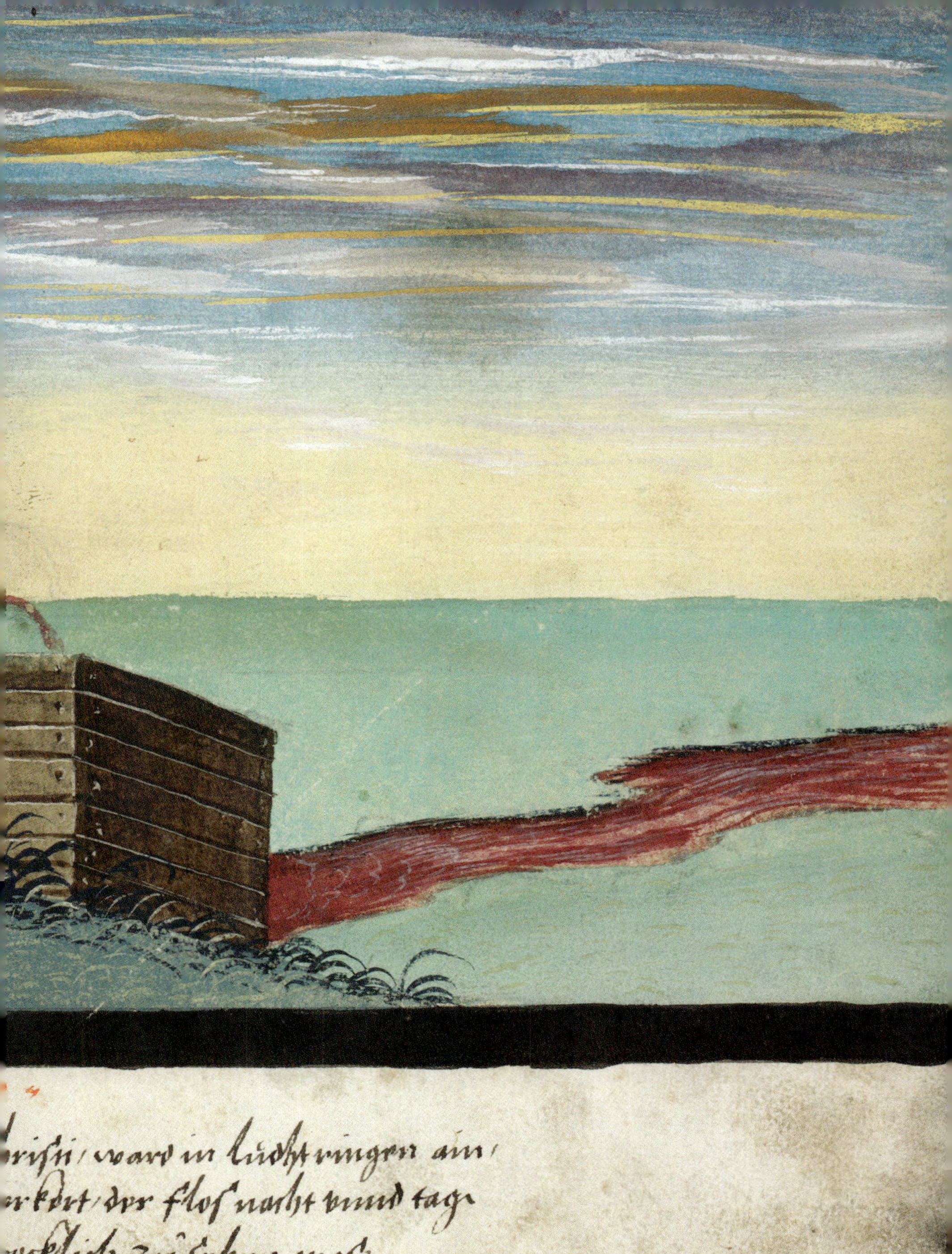

4

risti / ward in lüchtringen ain /
rkert / der flos nacht vnnd tag
rcklich zů sehen waß

Im m c iii iar nach der gepurt ch
vngewonlicher stern vmb dem abe
nchtet/ funff vnd zwaintzig tag als
palt nit gegen/ darnach am grünen

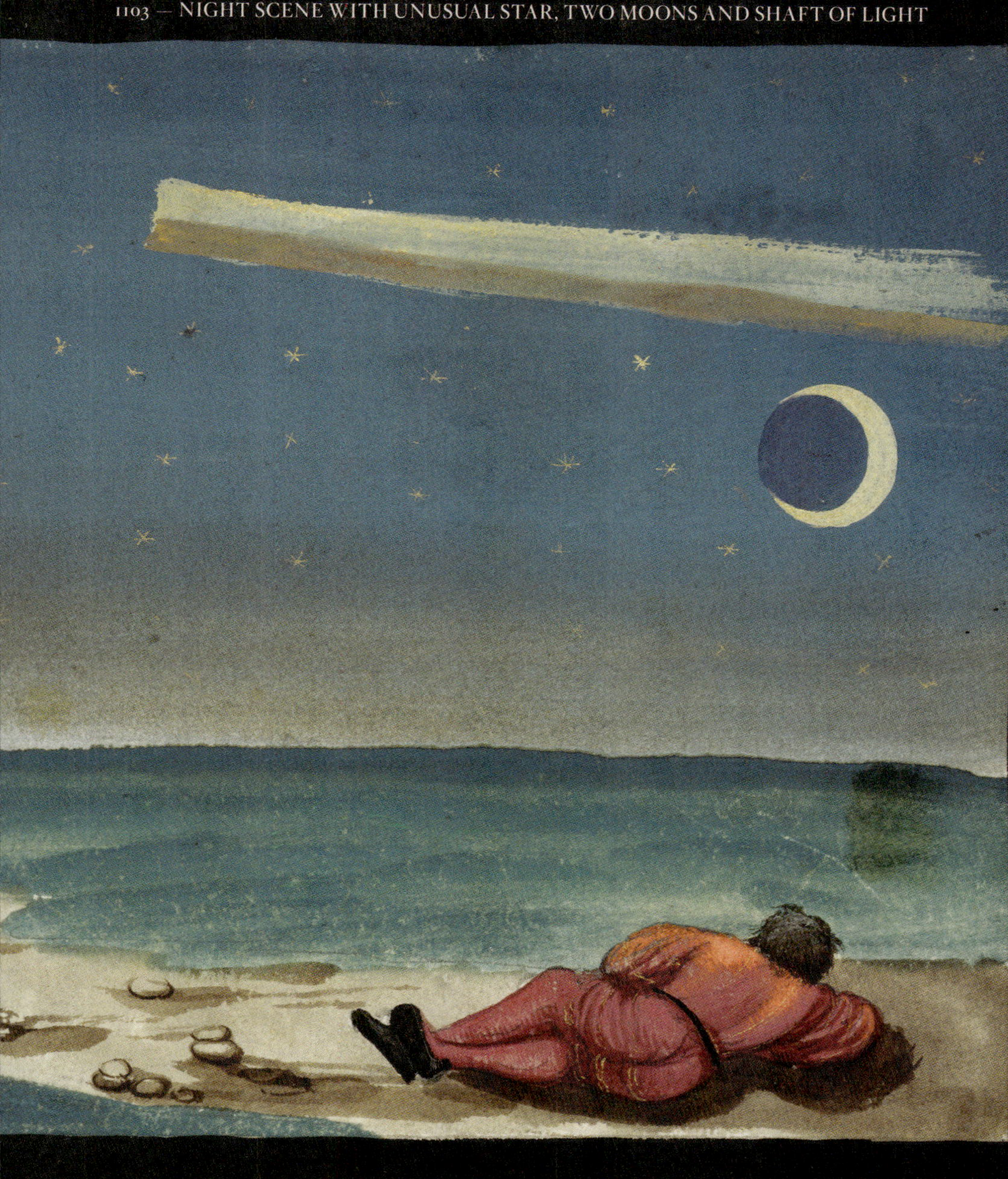

Z·
er schin am freitag in der ersten fast wochen ain
er stund gegen mittag vnnd nider gang· der le·
n der ainigen stund/gegen mittag lief ain groser·
rstag/waren zwen mon gesehen ainer im aufgāg

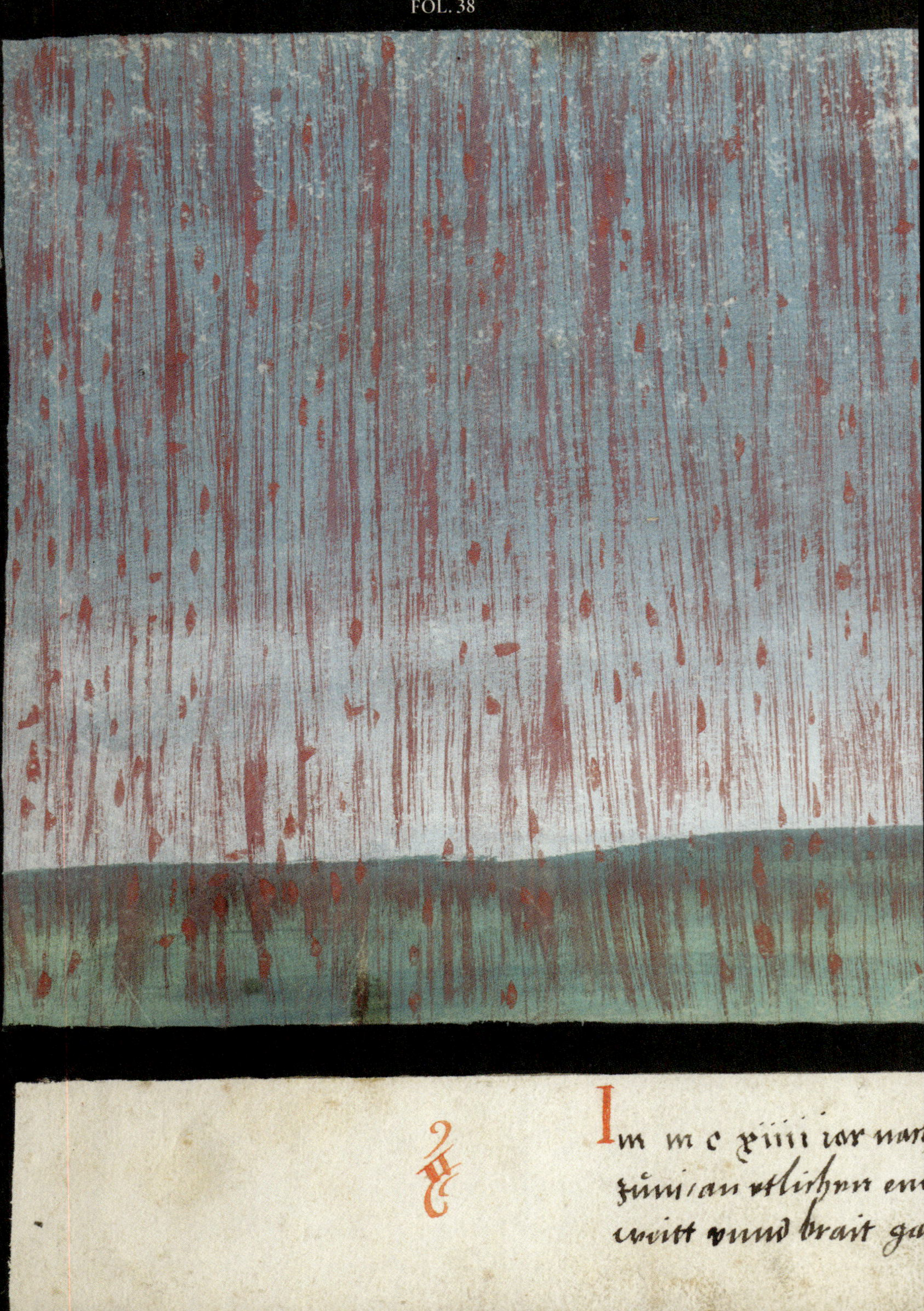

Im m c xiiii iar na
zuni/an etlichen en
weitt vnnd brait ga

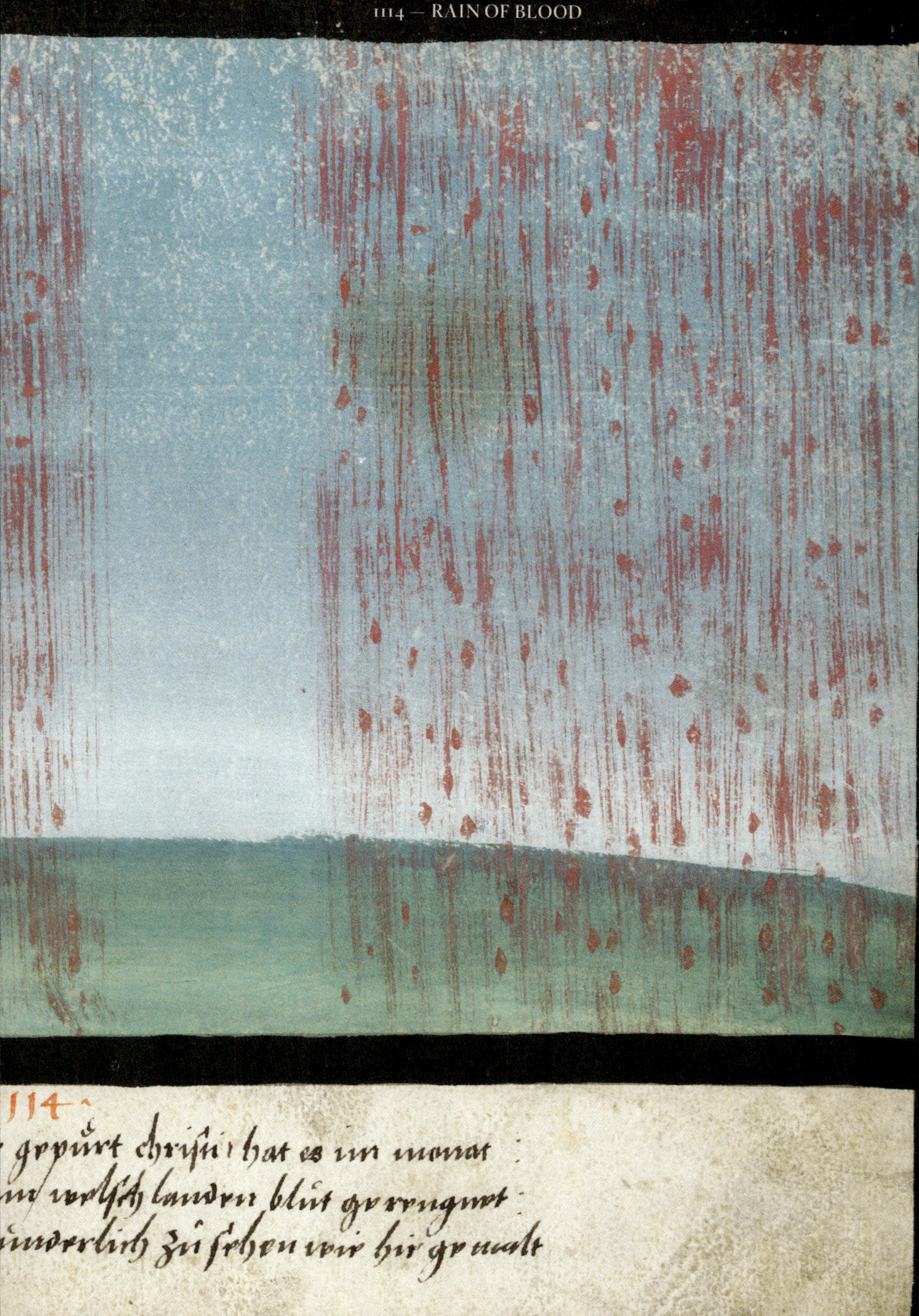
114.
gepůrt christi: hat es im monat
in welsch landen blůt geregnet
underlich zů sehen wie hie gemalt

FOL. 36

1009 — Bleeding well in Lorraine
Blutbrunnen in Lothringen | Puits de sang en Lorraine

In the year A.D. 1009, a well in Lorraine was changed into blood for a long time. It spilled out day and night, which was terrible and frightening to behold.

Im 1009. Jahr nach der Geburt Christi wurde in Lothringen lange Zeit ein Brunnen in Blut verwandelt. Der floss Tag und Nacht, was dann grausam und furchtbar anzusehen war.

En l'an 1009 après J.-C., l'eau d'un puits de Lorraine se changea en sang pendant une longue période. Elle jaillit jour et nuit, ce qui était terrible et effrayant à voir.

FOL. 37

1103 — Night scene with unusual star, two moons and shaft of light
Nachtszene mit ungewöhnlichem Stern, zwei Monden und Lichtbalken
Scène de nuit avec étoile inhabituelle, deux lunes et rai de lumière

In the year A.D. 1103, on the Friday of the first week of Lent, an unusual star appeared in the evening. It appeared in the south and in the west. It was visible for twenty-five days and always at the same hour. From the south, a great shaft of light moved towards it. After this, on Maundy Thursday, two moons were seen, one of them in the east.

Im 1103. Jahr n. Chr. erschien am Freitag in der ersten Fastenwoche ein ungewöhnlicher Stern um den Abend herum. Der stand in Richtung Süden und Westen. Er leuchtete fünfundzwanzig Tage immer zu der gleichen Stunde. Im Süden kam ein großer Lichtbalken entgegen. Danach, am Gründonnerstag, wurden zwei Monde gesehen, einer im Osten.

En l'an 1103 après J.-C., le vendredi de la première semaine de carême, une étoile inhabituelle apparut le soir. Elle apparut au sud et à l'ouest. Elle fut visible pendant vingt-cinq jours, toujours à la même heure. Venant du sud, un grand rai de lumière dirigea vers elle. Ensuite, le jeudi saint, on vit deux lunes, l'une d'elles à l'est.

FOL. 38

1114 — Rain of blood | Blutregen | Pluie de sang

In the year A.D. 1114, in the month of June, it rained blood in several places in Italy; it could be seen far and wide and in a very strange way, just as it is painted here

Im 1114. Jahr nach der Geburt Christi hat es im Monat Juni an etlichen Orten in Italien Blut geregnet; weit und breit auf ganz wunderliche Weise zu sehen, wie hier gemalt.

En l'an 1114 après J.-C., au mois de juin, il plut du sang en plusieurs lieux en Italie ; cela fut observé partout et sous une forme très étrange, comme dans cette peinture.

FOL. 39

1119 — Blood-red moon and earthquake
Blutroter Mond und Erdbeben | Lune ensanglantée et tremblement de terre

In the year 1119 the moon was seen the colour of blood and an earthquake lasted for nine days in Italy so that cities and villages collapsed.

Im 1119. Jahr wurde der Mond blutfarben gesehen, und ein Erdbeben dauerte neun Tage in Italien, sodass Städte und Dörfer zerstört wurden.

En l'an 1119 après J.-C., on vit la lune rouge sang, et un tremblement de terre eut lieu pendant neuf jours en Italie, qui provoqua l'effondrement de villes et de villages.

FOL. 41

1119 — Fiery arrows | Feurige Pfeile | Flèches enflammées

In the year A.D. 1119, fiery arrows or spears appeared in the sky, in all parts of the heavens. And stars fell from the sky and if water was poured over them, they screamed or made a noise.

Im 1119. Jahr n. Chr. erschienen feurige Pfeile oder Spieße am Himmel, überall am ganzen Himmel. Und es fielen Sterne vom Himmel, und wenn man Wasser darauf goss, dann gaben sie einen Laut oder Schrei von sich.

En l'an 1119 après J.-C., des flèches ou des lances enflammées apparurent dans le ciel, dans toutes ses parties. Et des étoiles tombèrent du ciel et si l'on versait de l'eau dessus, elles criaient ou faisaient un bruit.

FOL. 42

1126 — Frozen birds | Erfrorene Vögel | Oiseaux gelés

In the year A.D. 1126, the winter was so cold and severe that birds froze to death in mid-air. This was followed by such a famine that livestock and people died and birds killed each other in the air.

Im 1126. Jahr n. Chr. ereignete sich so ein harter und kalter Winter, dass die Vögel in der Luft erfroren. Darauf folgte eine solche Hungersnot, dass Vieh und Leute starben und die Vögel sich gegenseitig in der Luft töteten.

En l'an 1126 après J.-C., l'hiver fut si froid et si rude que les oiseaux mouraient gelés en plein vol. S'ensuivit une famine telle que le bétail et les gens périrent et que les oiseaux s'entretuèrent dans les airs.

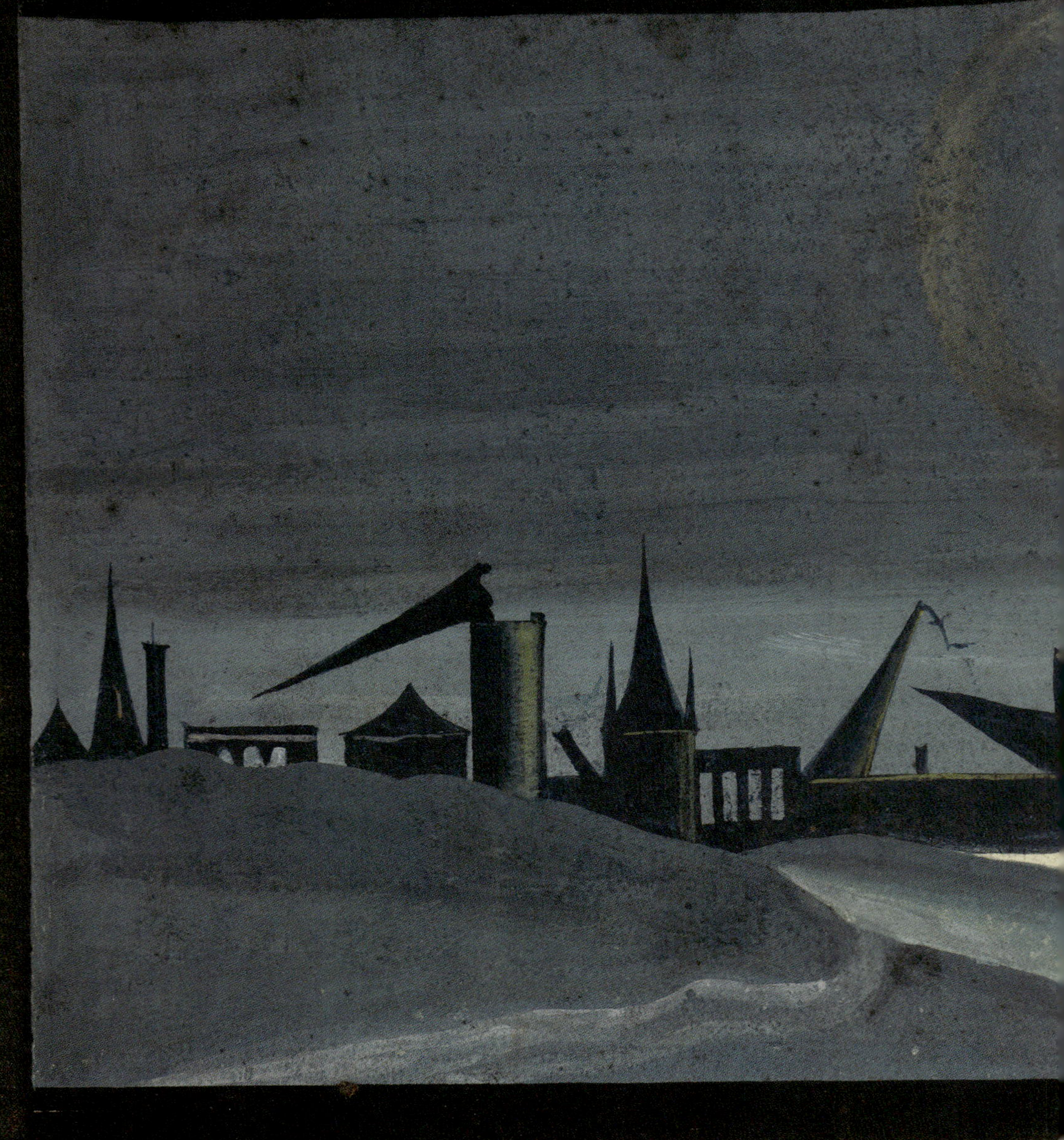

Im M c x ix iar ward der m
neün tag im welschland das

19 ·

lut farb gesehen · vnnd werrt ein erbidem
vnnd dorffer ein fiellen –

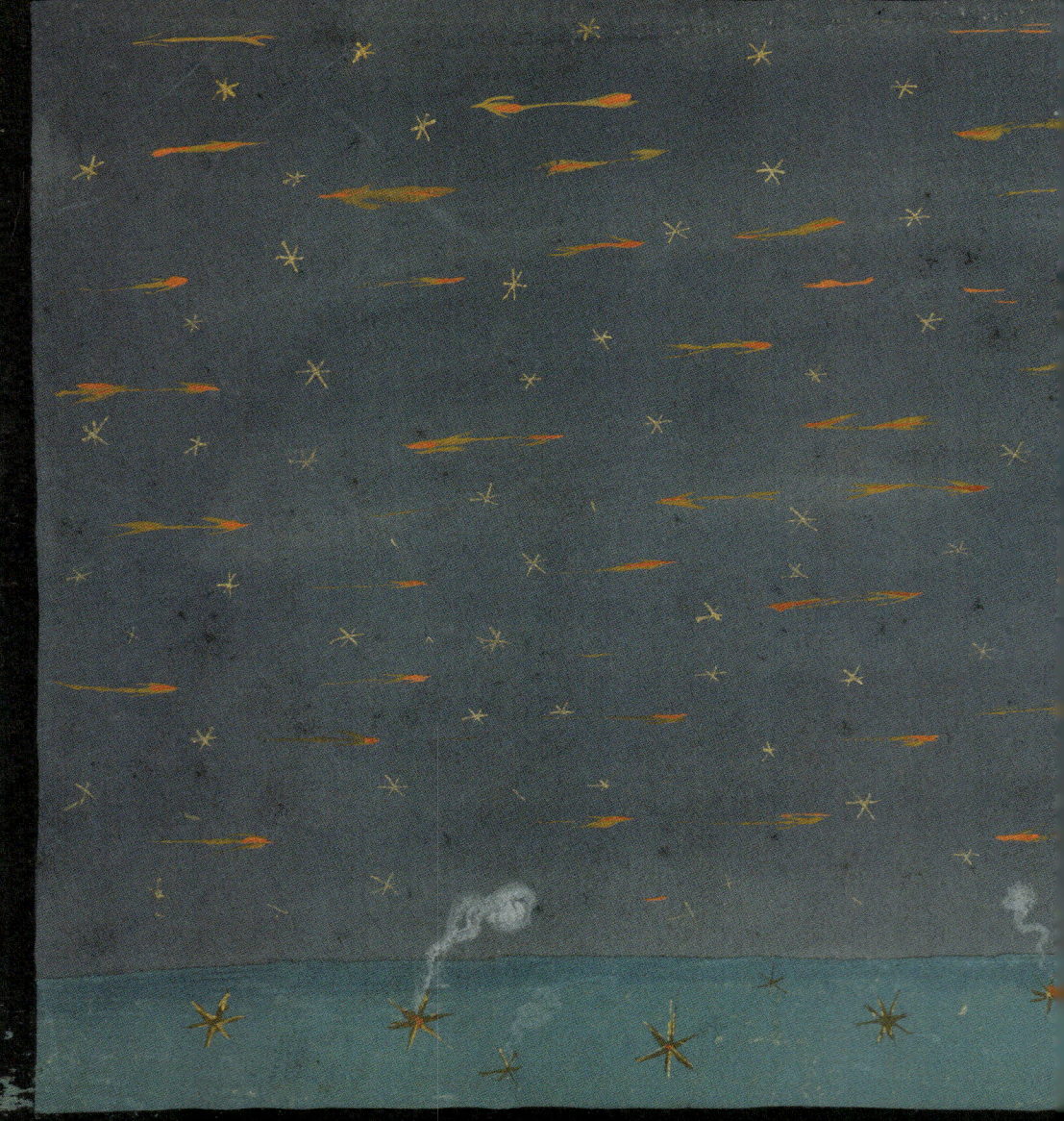

Im m c xix iar nach christi g
himel durch aus ain gantz
vnnd wan man wasser d

19

erschinen feurige strel oder spitz am
imel/ vnnd fiellen stern vom himel
tt gos so gaben sie ein hall oder schray

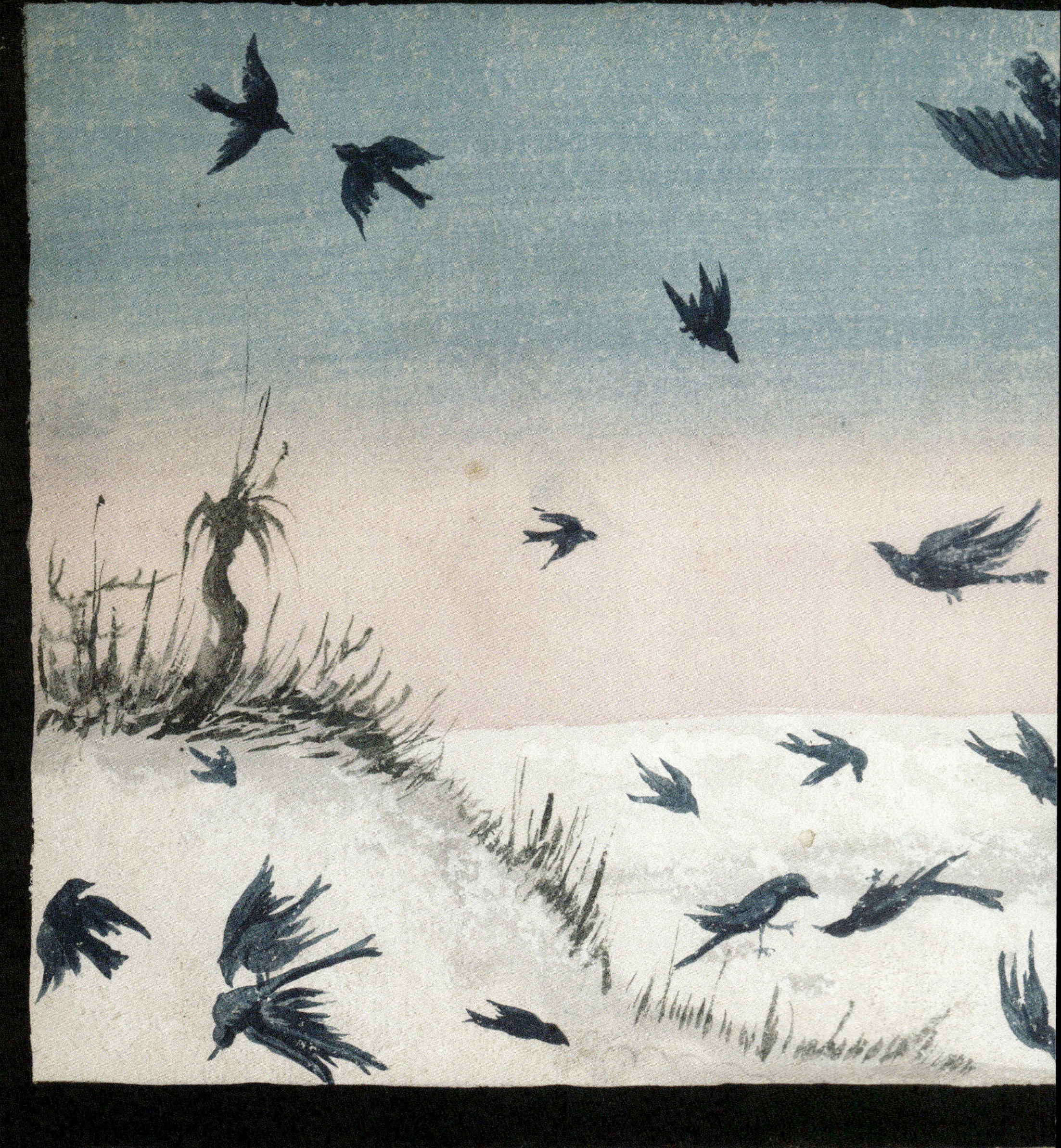

Im m c xxvi iar/ nach christ
winter/ das die fögel in luf
hunger das fich vnnd leut
ander in lufften

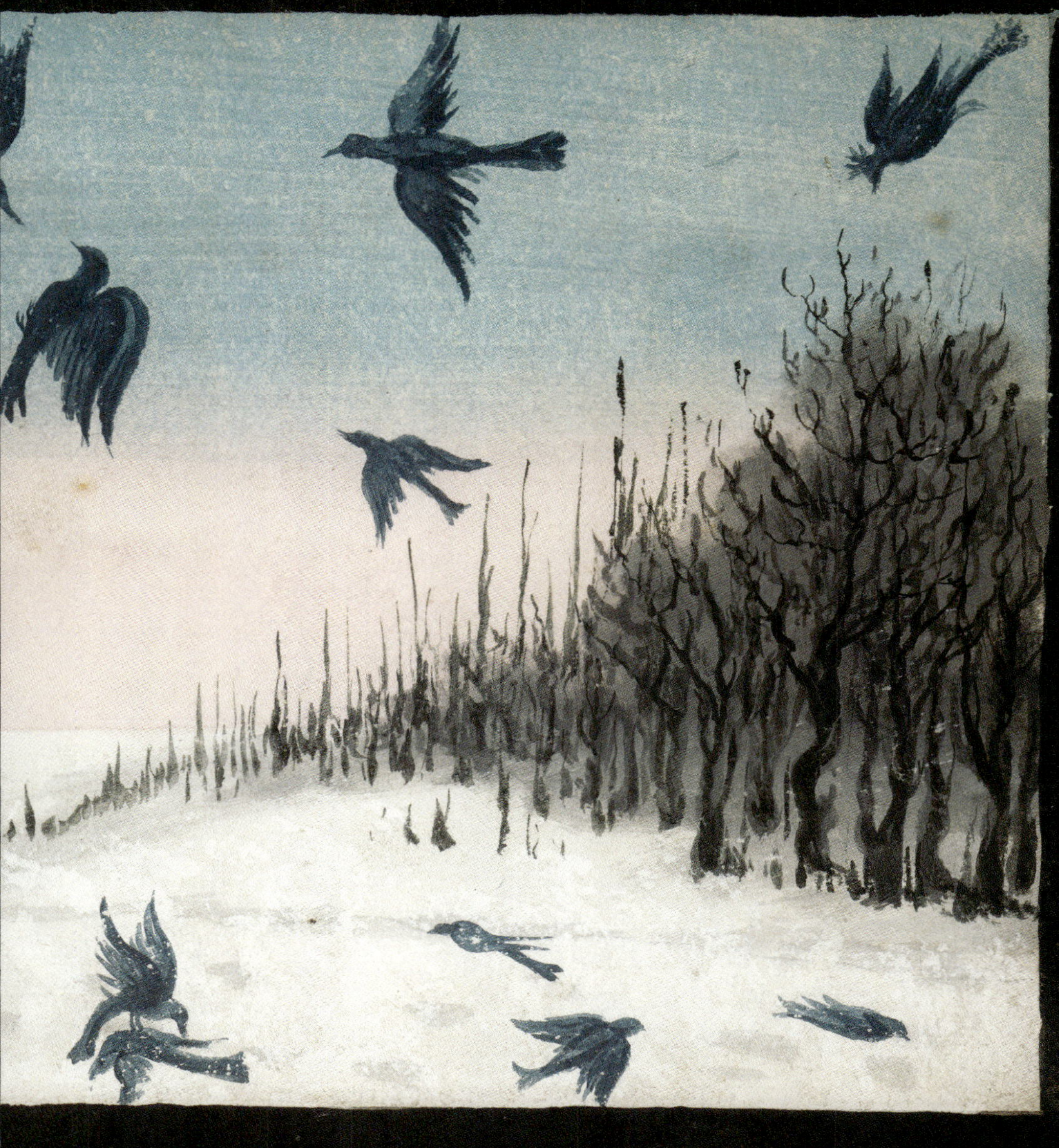

26r

ůrt/ ward so ein harter vnnd kalter
erfrůrren/ darauff kam ain solcher
ren/ vnd erwůrgten die vogel ein

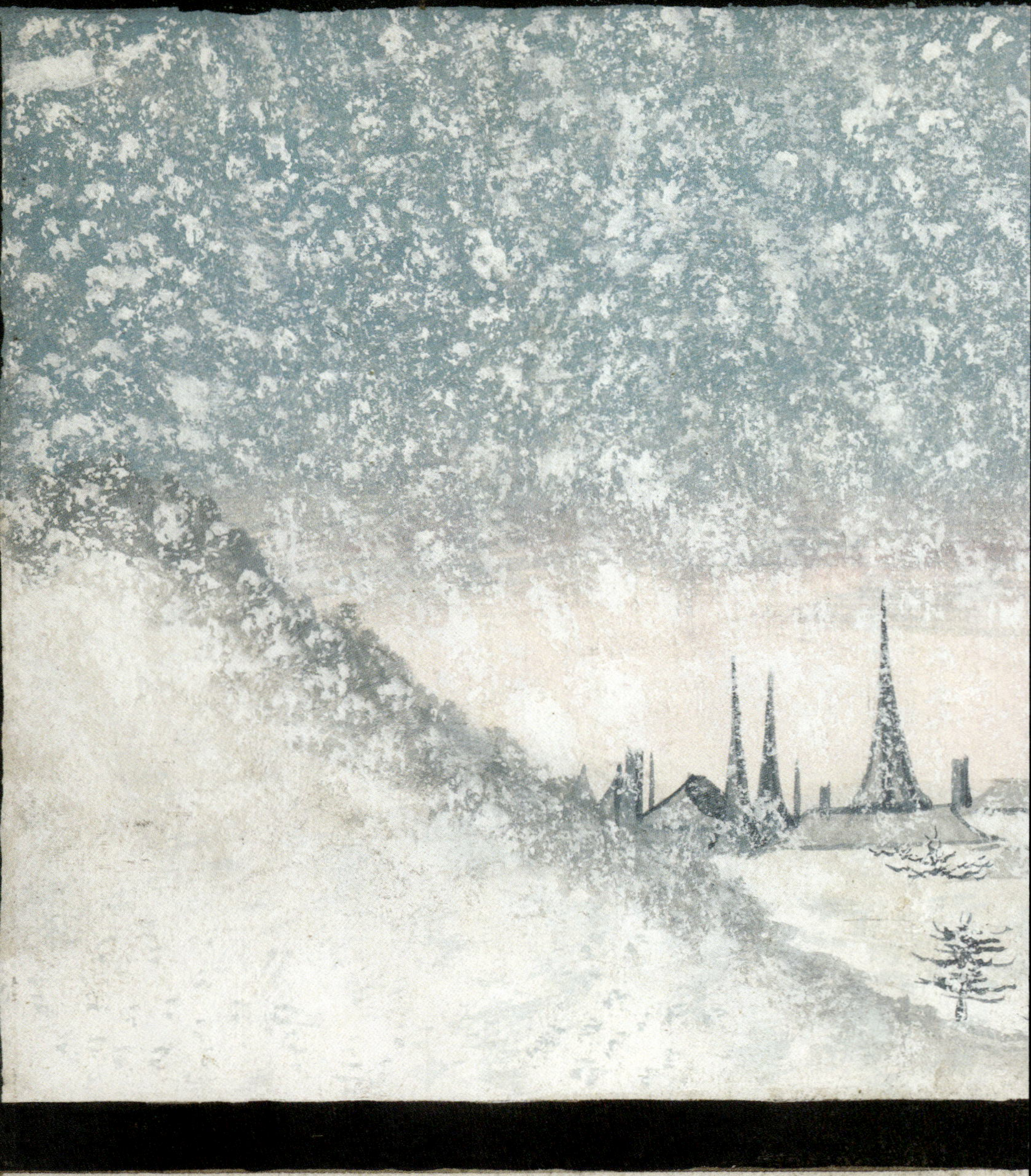

Im m c lxii iar nach der
vmb mailand/ das die leu
nt/ kumen/ vnnd der sch

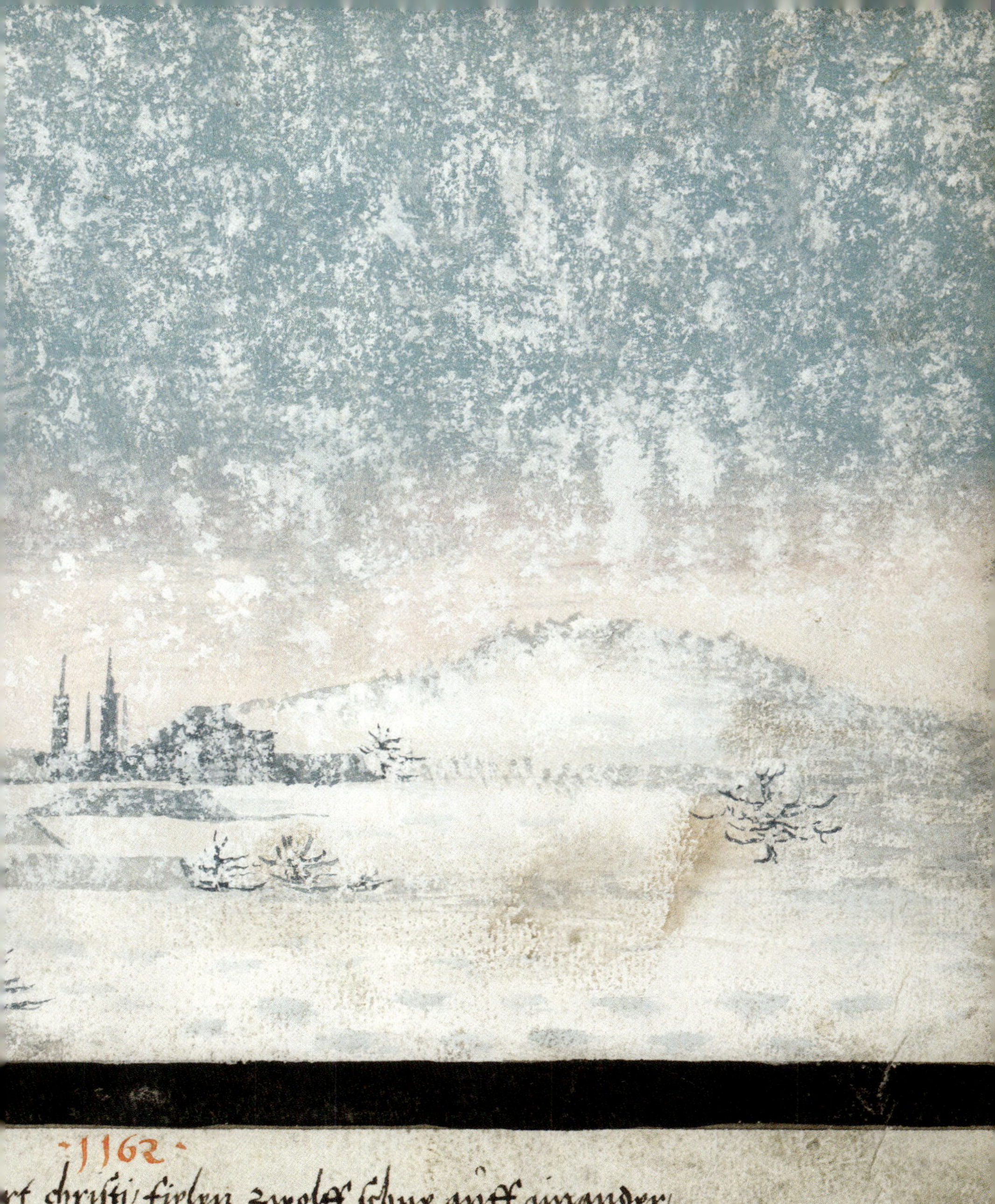

·1162·

rt christi/ fielen zwolff schne auff ainander/
r zagten/ vnnd niemandt zů dem andern ků/
ng vber etlich heüser vnnd beim er

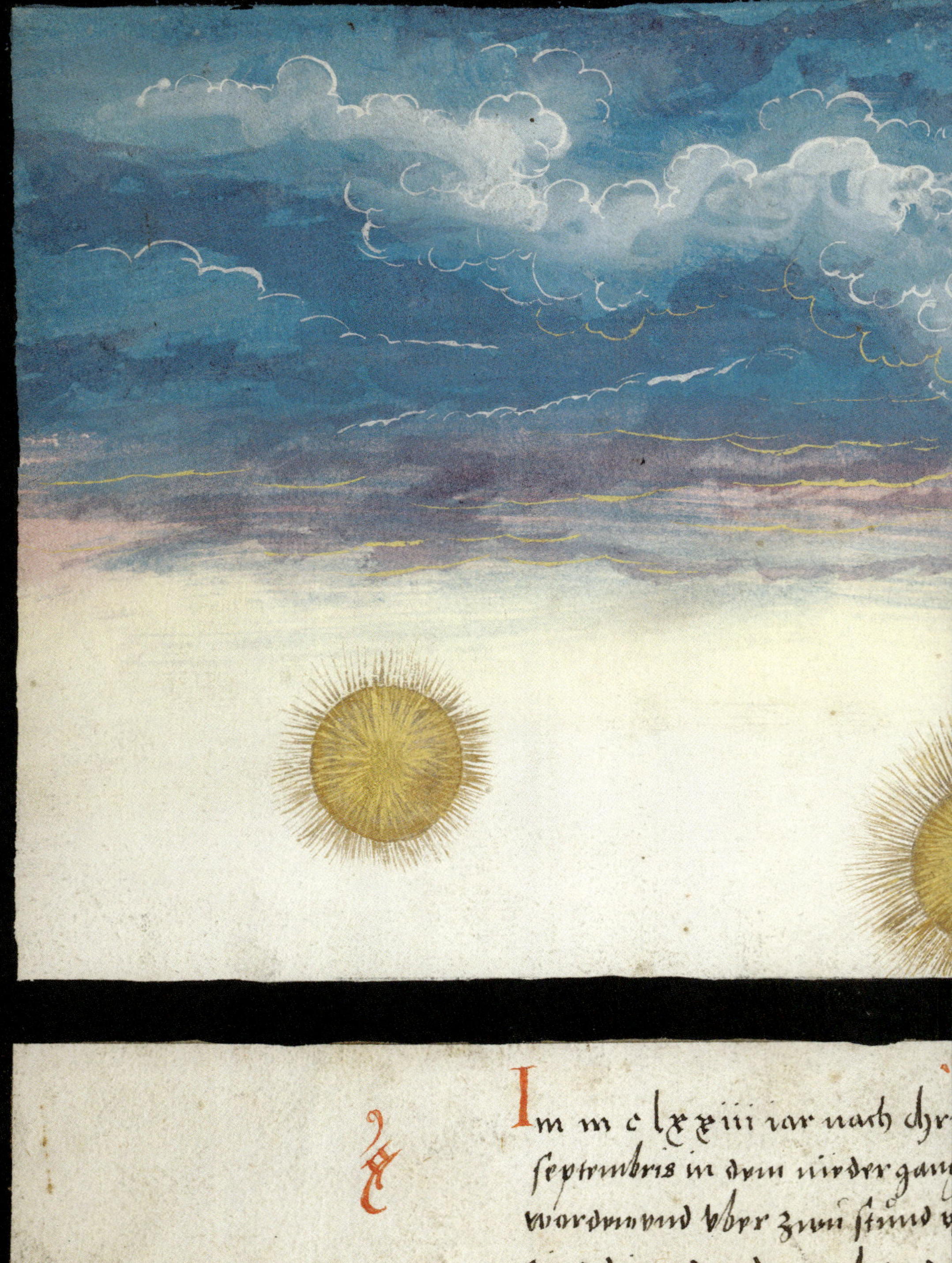
Im m c lxxiii iar nach
septembris in dem nider
worden vnd vber zwu stund
ging die ander darnach

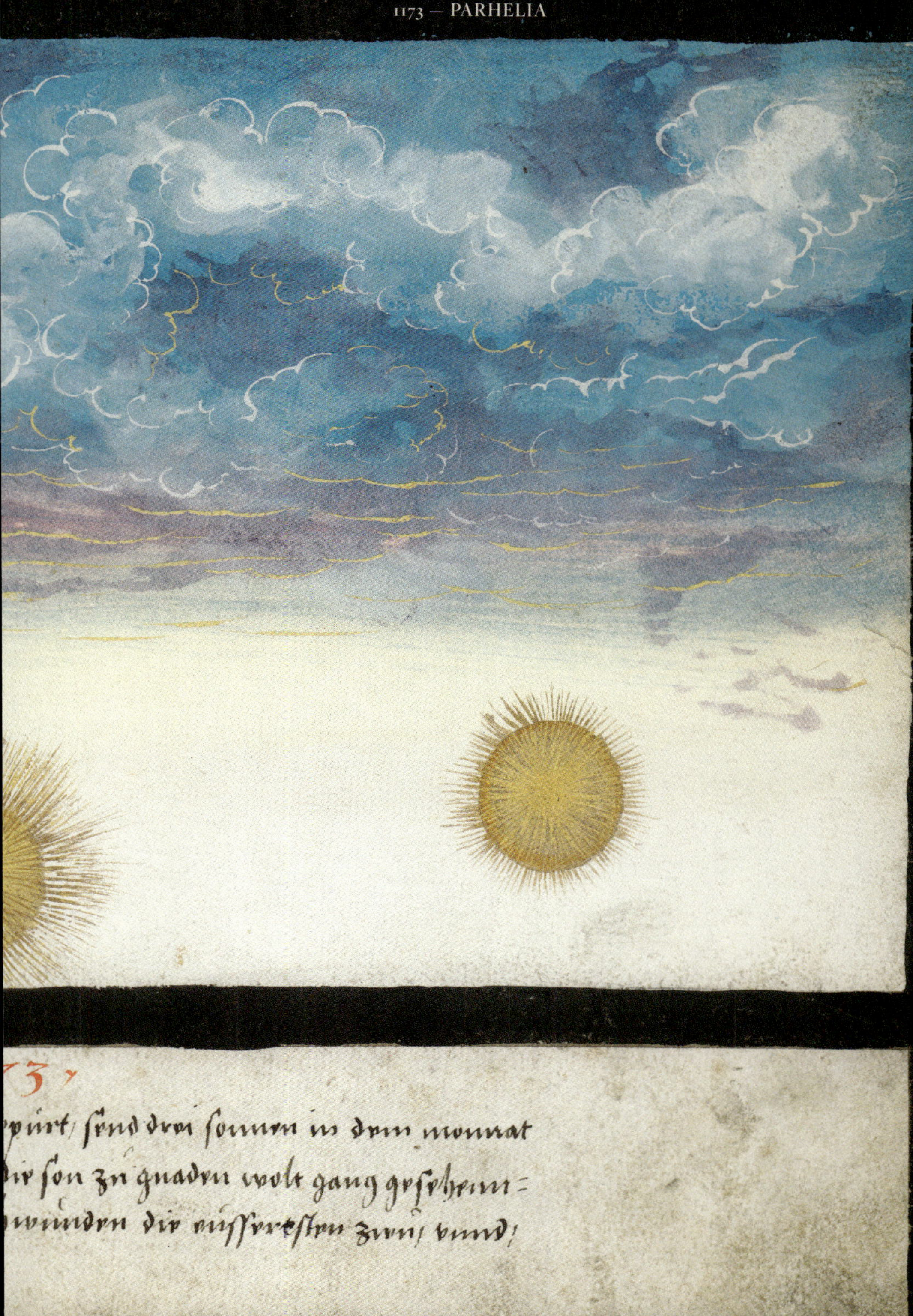
73
spürt, seind drei sonnen in dem monnat
die son zu gnaden wolt gang geschehen=
swunden die ausseresten zwei, vnnd,

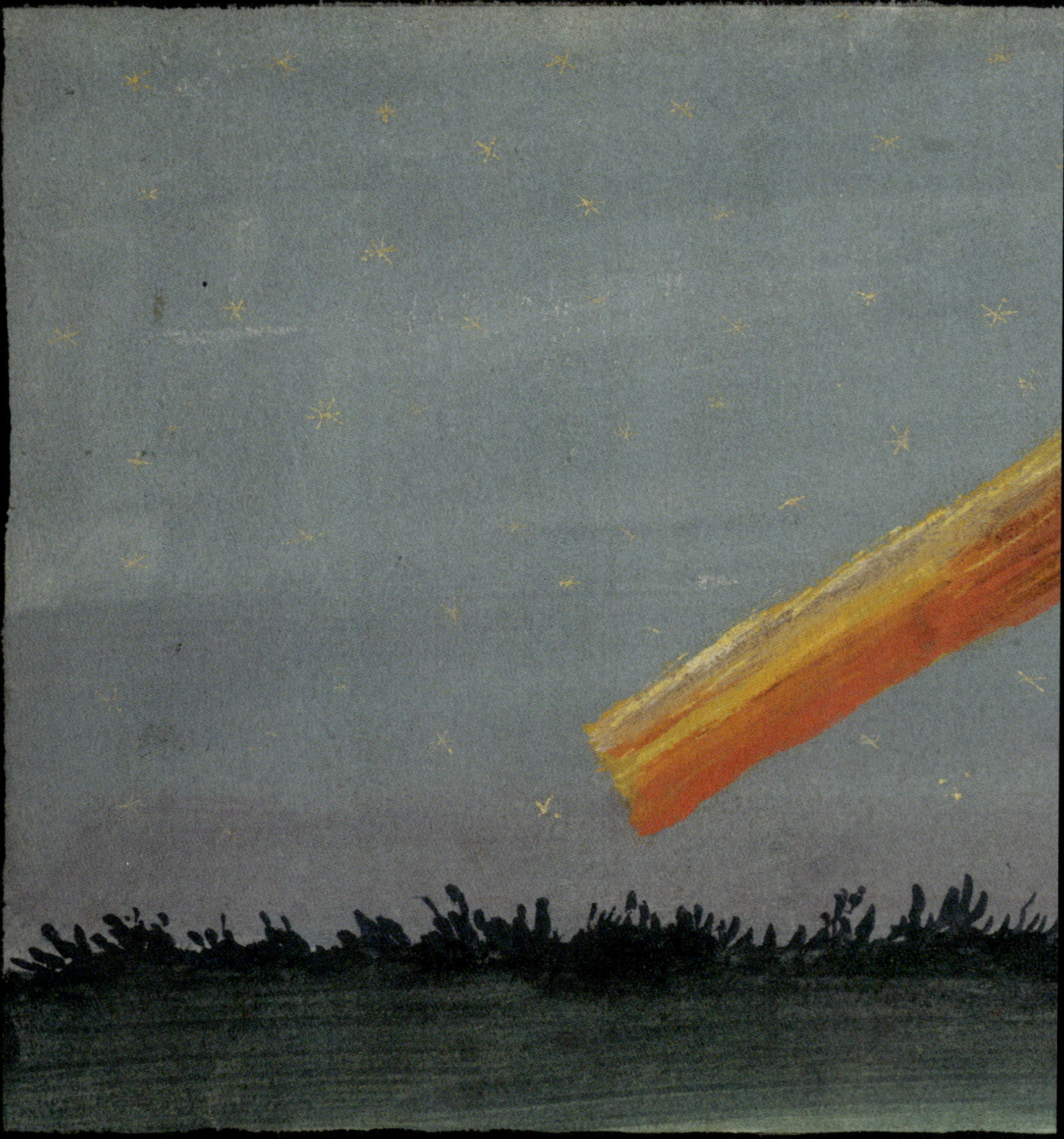

Im m c lxxiii iar nach
gleichsam ainem feürig
steigent an allen orten

·1173

ti gepürt / ward ein grosser glantz gesehen
lcken / in die hoch des firmaments auf
n welschen landen

FOL. 44

1162 — Snow covers Milan
Mailand von Schnee bedeckt | Milan recouverte de neige

In the year A.D. 1162, snow fell twelve times in succession upon Milan, so that the people fell into despair and no one was able to go and see anyone else. And the snow covered some of the houses and trees etc.

Im 1162. Jahr nach der Geburt Christi fiel um Mailand zwölfmal nacheinander Schnee, sodass die Leute verzagten und niemand zu dem anderen kommen konnte. Und der Schnee bedeckte etliche Häuser und Bäume etc.

En l'an 1162 après J.-C., il neigea douze fois d'affilée près de Milan, si bien que les gens sombrèrent dans le désespoir et qu'ils ne purent se rendre les uns chez les autres. Et la neige recouvrit des maisons et des arbres, etc.

FOL. 45

1173 — Parhelia | Nebensonnen | Parhélies

In the year A.D. 1173, three suns were seen in the west in the month of September, when the sun was about to set. And after two hours the outer two disappeared and the other one set after that.

Im 1173. Jahr n. Chr. sind im Monat September im Westen, als die Sonne untergehen wollte, drei Sonnen gesehen worden. Und nach zwei Stunden verschwanden die äußersten beiden, und die andere ging danach unter.

En l'an 1173 après J.-C., trois soleils apparurent à l'ouest au mois de septembre, lorsque le soleil allait se coucher. Et au bout de deux heures, les deux soleils les plus éloignés disparurent et l'autre se coucha ensuite.

FOL. 46

1173 — Fiery shaft | Feuriger Balken | Bille enflammée

In the year A.D. 1173, a great brightness was seen, like a fiery shaft of light climbing up into the height of the firmament, in all parts of Italy.

Im 1173. Jahr n. Chr. wurde ein großer Glanz gesehen, einem feurigen Balken gleich, in die Höhe des Firmaments aufsteigend, an allen Orten in Italien.

En l'an 1173 après J.-C., on vit une vive lueur, semblable à une bille enflammée s'élevant dans les hauteurs du firmament en tous lieux de l'Italie.

FOL. 47

1173 — Flood
Überschwemmung | Inondation

In the year A.D. 1173, there were earthquakes and many wondrous things appeared almost everywhere this year, so that the city of Antioch [...] was destroyed. Because of this the sea flooded in the [...] went back again at [...] were bigger than goose eggs.

Im 1173. Jahr n. Chr. sind Erdbeben und viele wundersam gestaltete Dinge in diesem Jahr fast überall erschienen und gewesen, sodass die Stadt [...] Antiochia [...] zerstört wurde. So überschwemmte das Meer in [...] der [...] wieder zurückging bei [...] größer als Gänseeier waren.

En l'an 1173 après J.-C., il y eut des tremblements de terre et bien des choses prodigieuses se produisirent presque partout cette année-là, à tel point que la ville d'Antioche [...] fut détruite. Et c'est pour cela que la mer s'engouffra dans le [...] revint à [...] furent plus gros que des œufs d'oie.

FOL. 48

1173 — Eclipse | Sonnenfinsternis | Éclipse

In the year A.D. 1173, a great darkness came over the sun and a star appeared nearby, which was in the south. It could be seen clearly throughout Italy.

Im 1173. Jahr n. Chr. erschien eine große Finsternis an der Sonne und dabei ein Stern, der stand im Süden. Der ist in Italien gut gesehen worden.

En l'an 1173 après J.-C., le soleil fut entièrement obscurci et une étoile apparut près de lui, qui se tenait au sud. Elle était très visible dans toute l'Italie.

FOL. 49

1174 — Three moons | Drei Monde | Trois lunes

In the year A.D. 1174, three moons appeared in the German lands with the sign of a cross through their middle, separate and entirely over them, so that the moons were shining behind it.

Im 1174. Jahr n. Chr. erschienen in den deutschen Ländern drei Monde und in der Mitte ein Kreuzzeichen, frei und ganz darüber, sodass die Monde dahinter leuchteten.

En l'an 1174 après J.-C., trois lunes apparurent dans les territoires allemands, avec le signe d'une croix en leur milieu, séparément et les recouvrant toutes, de sorte que les lunes brillaient derrière le signe.

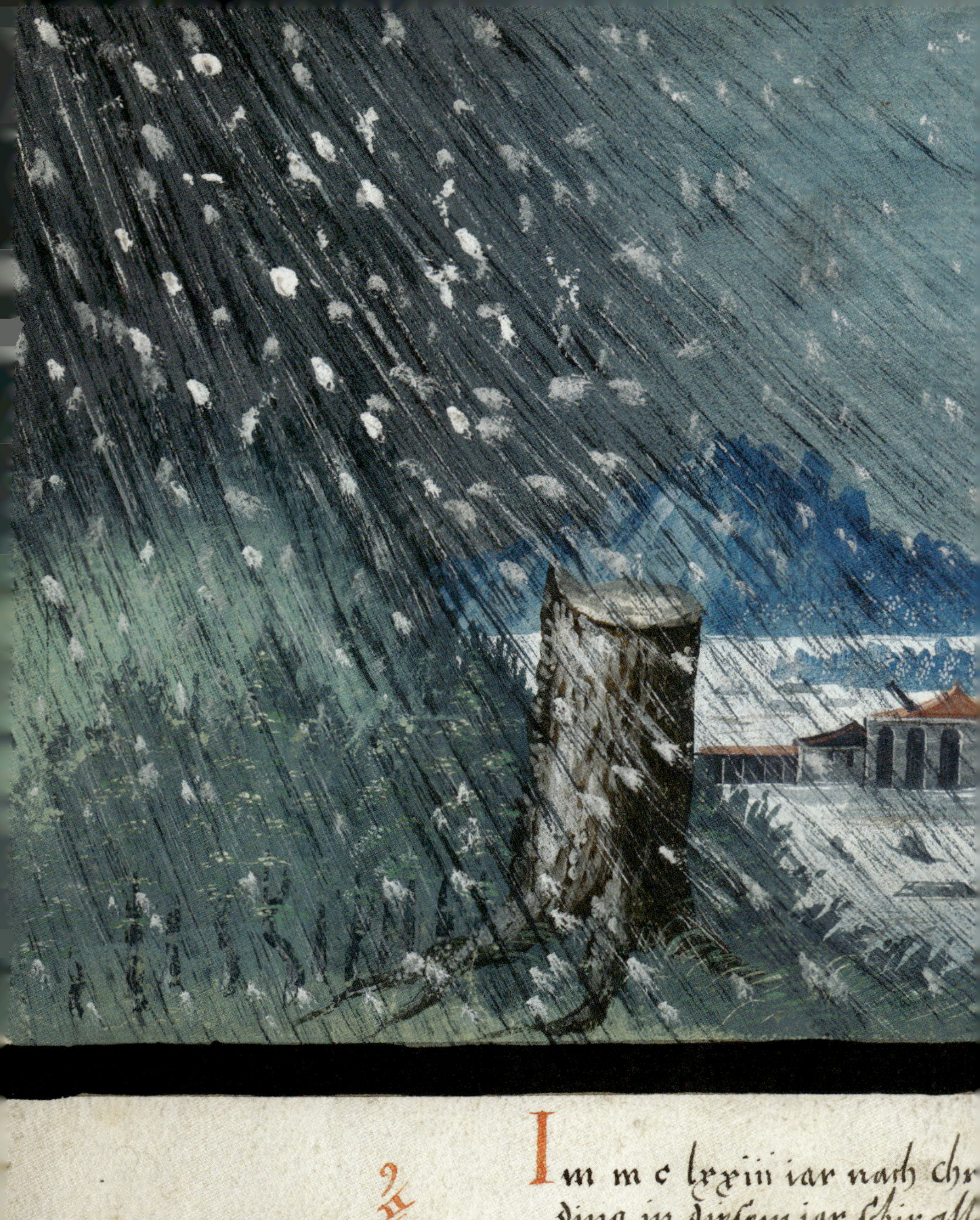

Im m c lxxiii iar nach chr
ding in dirsem iar schir all
tiochia t
der
fu

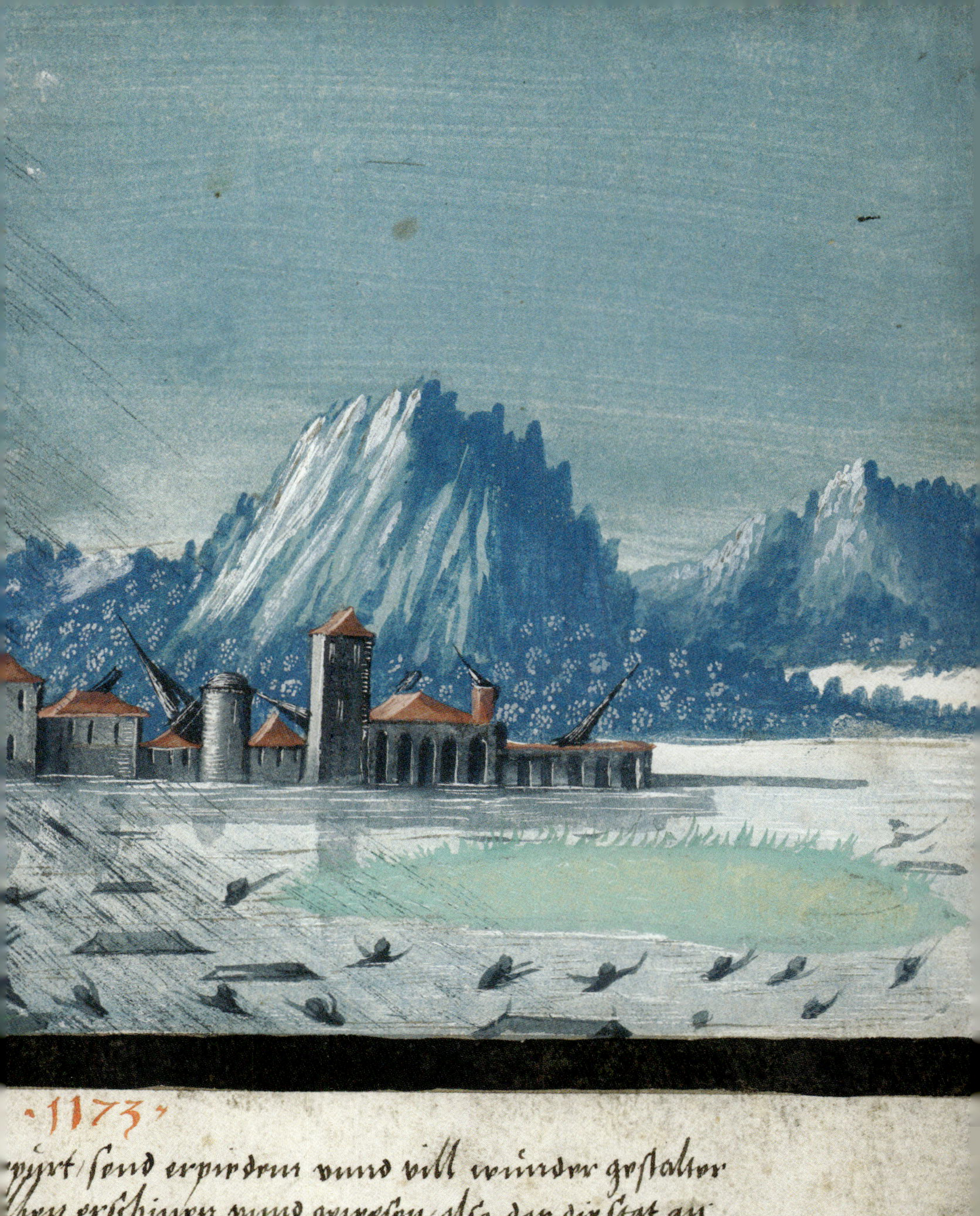

·1173·

gypt / seind erpidem vnnd vill wunder gestalter
lben erschinen vnnd gewesen / also das die stat an
oil ein fiellen so er drencket das mer in
und wider hinder sich ging bey
groser den gans ayer warn

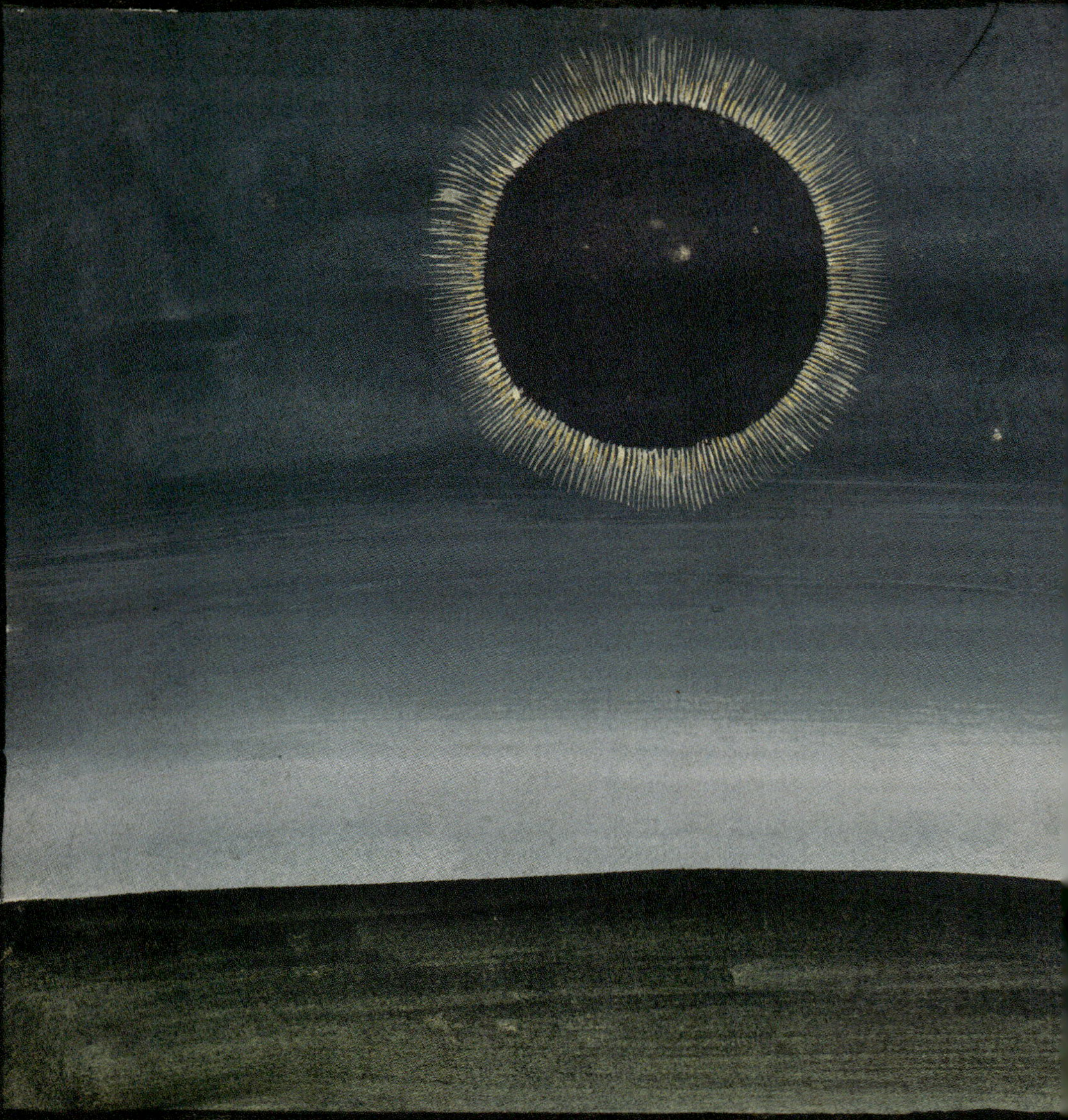

Im m c lxxiii iar
an der sonnwend d
in welsch land fast

1173 ·

[…]n christi gepurt erschin ein grose finsternus
[…]ein stern, der stundt gegen mittag, der ist
[…]hen worden

Im m c lxxiiii iar nach chri
dreij mon vnnd in der mit ei
das die mon dar hinter leu

ůirt/ er schinen in deůtzsch landen
ß zaichen frey folig darůber/
:

Im · D · c · lxxxiiii nach der gepurt christi · er sch
regen · sturm wind vnnd donner schlag · das gle
alls wolt es die stat rom gar ver dilgen vnnd s
plitzen am himel dir sir sahen

commet drei monnat / darnach volget ein solches groses
vor nie erhort was worden vnnd stelt sich das clament
raüsam vill fichs vnnd die menschen sturben von den

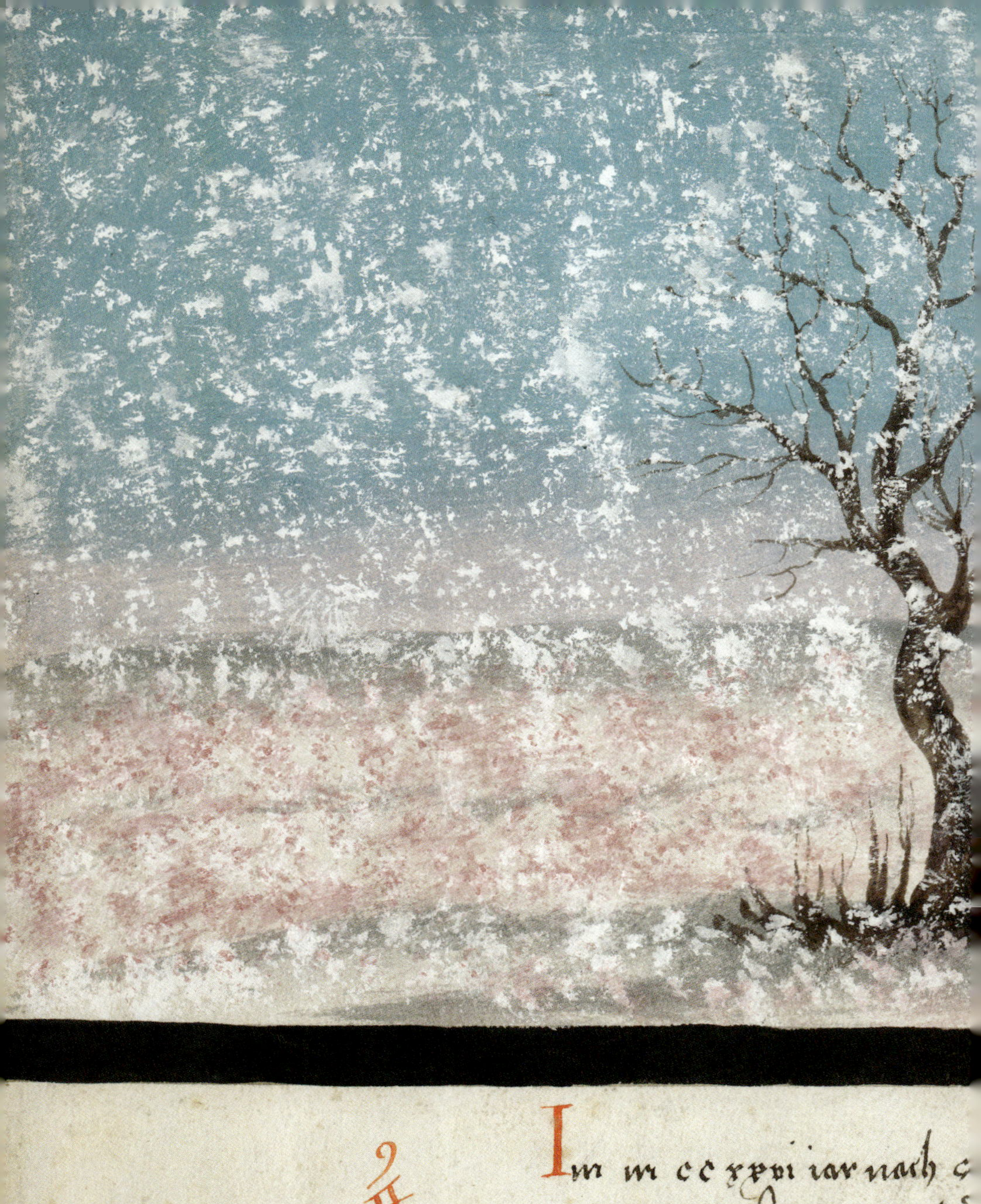

Im m cc xxvi iar nach c
steyer marckt / der von stu
zu sehen ward ·

ZG ·

[illegible] gepurt · fiell ein schnee in der

[illegible] plut ward · vnnd gar greulich

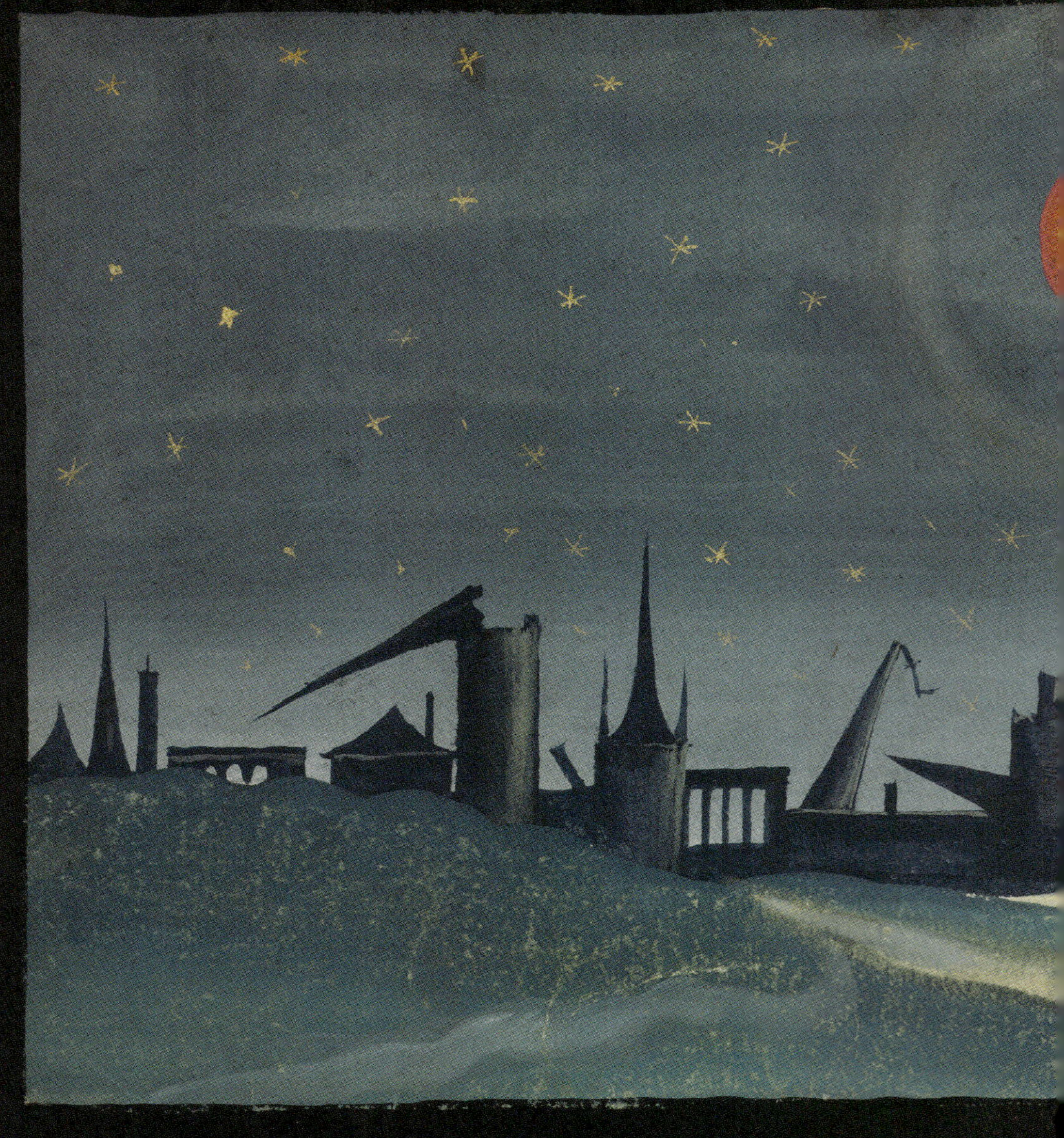

Im m c c xxviii iar nach christi gepurt besch
zuni bei hellem tag nach neun vhr das es
werend bei siben stunden zu der zeit hets a
pergen bey funff tausent menschen vergin
den meer flüssen schier gar ver senckt

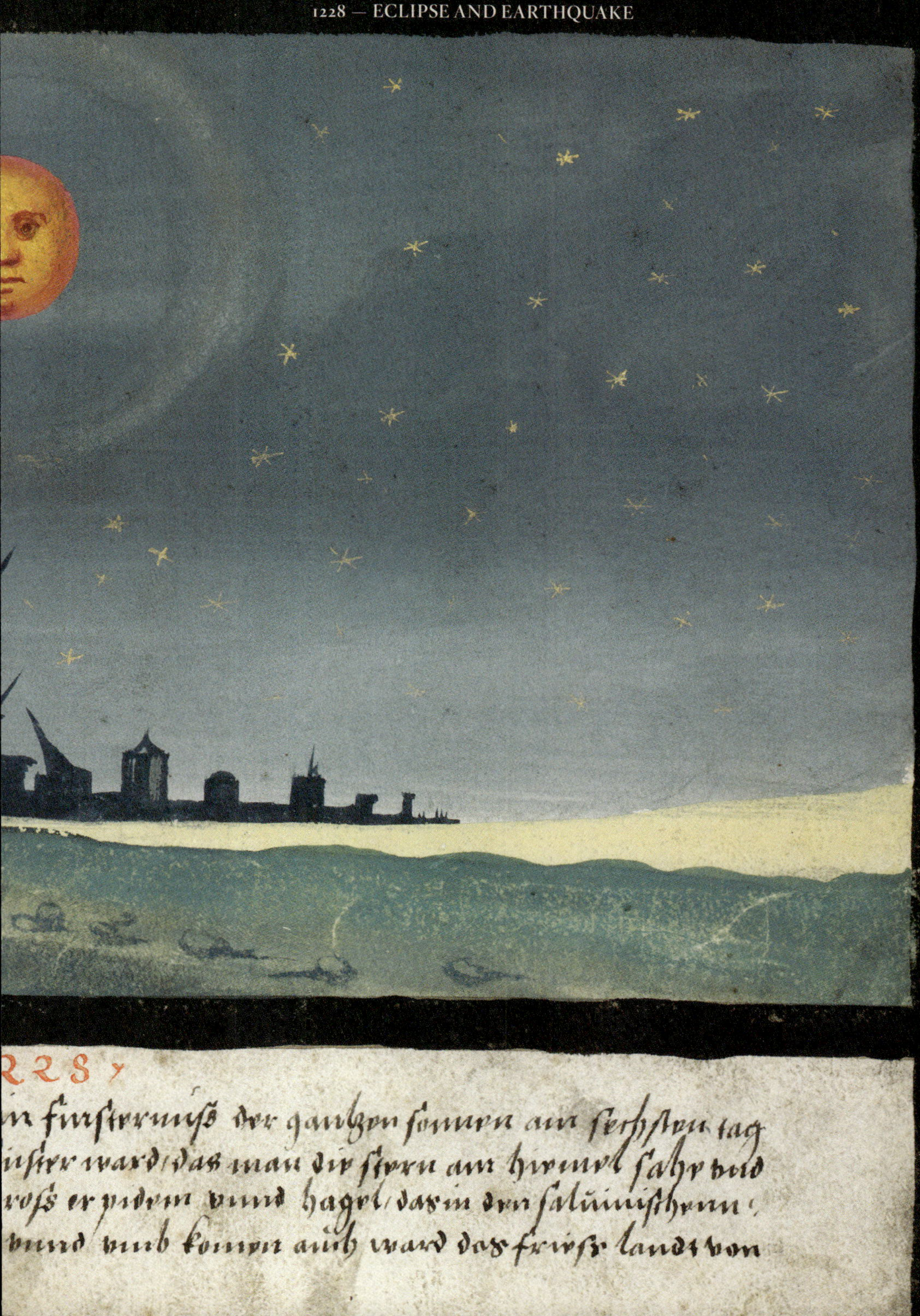
228.
n finsternuss der gantzen sonnen am sechsten tag
nster ward/ das man die stern am himel sahe und
ross erpidem vnnd hagel/ darin den saluunischenn
vnnd vmb komen auch ward das friesz landt von

FOL. 50

1184 [in fact: 684] — Comet | Komet | Comète

In the year A.D. 684, a comet appeared for three months. This was followed by such heavy rain, storms, wind and thunder as had never been heard before. And this element acted as if it wanted to destroy the city of Rome completely, and a great many livestock died in terrible ways. And people died from the lightning in the sky they saw.

Im 684. Jahr nach der Geburt Christi erschien ein Komet drei Monate lang. Danach folgten ein solch großer Regen, Sturm, Wind und Donnerschlag, wie es vorher nie gehört worden war. Und das Element verhielt sich, als wollte es die Stadt Rom völlig vertilgen, und viel Vieh starb auf grausame Weise. Und die Menschen starben durch die Blitze am Himmel, die sie sahen.

En l'an 684 après J.-C., une comète apparut pendant trois mois. S'ensuivirent pluies, tempêtes, vent et tonnerre tels qu'on n'en avait jamais entendu. Et cet élément faisait comme s'il voulait détruire entièrement la ville de Rome, et un très grand nombre de bestiaux périrent de façon terrible. Et les gens moururent des éclairs qu'ils avaient vus dans le ciel.

FOL. 51

1226 — Blood snow in Styria
Blutschnee in der Steiermark | Neige ensanglantée en Styrie

In the year A.D. 1226, snow fell in Styria which straight away turned to blood and was really terrible to behold.

Im 1226. Jahr n. Chr. fiel Schnee in der Steiermark, der sofort zu Blut wurde und ganz grausig anzusehen war.

En l'an 1226 après J.-C., la neige tomba en Styrie et se transforma immédiatement en sang, ce qui était vraiment horrible à voir.

FOL. 52

1228 — Eclipse and earthquake
Sonnenfinsternis und Erdbeben | Éclipse et tremblement de terre

In the year A.D. 1228, the whole of the sun turned dark on the sixth day of June, at the ninth hour during broad daylight, and it became so dark that the stars could be seen in the sky, and it lasted about seven hours. At this time there was also a great earthquake and hailstorm, with the result that some five thousand people died and perished in the Salluvian mountains. As well as this, Frisia was almost completely submerged by high tides from the sea.

Im 1228. Jahr n. Chr. ereignete sich eine Finsternis der ganzen Sonne am sechsten Tag des Juni, bei hellem Tag um die neunte Stunde, dass es so finster wurde, dass man die Sterne am Himmel sah, und dauerte etwa sieben Stunden. Zu der Zeit gab es auch ein großes Erdbeben und Hagel, sodass in den salluvinischen Bergen [Seealpen] etwa fünftausend Menschen starben und umkamen. Auch wurde das Friesland von den Meeresströmen beinahe völlig versenkt.

En l'an 1228 après J.-C., le soleil devint entièrement noir le sixième jour de juin, à la neuvième heure en plein jour, et l'obscurité fut telle qu'on pouvait voir les étoiles dans le ciel, et cela dura sept heures environ. À ce moment, il y eut aussi un grand tremblement de terre et un gros orage de grêle, de sorte qu'environ cinq mille personnes moururent et périrent dans les montagnes salluviennes. De plus, la Frise fut aussi presque complètement submergée par les grandes marées.

FOL. 54

1229 — Blood snow | Blutschnee | Neige ensanglantée

In the year A.D. 1229, snow fell around St Martin's Day and was turned into blood at once and was everywhere recognised as being blood.

Im 1229. Jahr n. Chr., um den Martinstag, fiel Schnee und wurde sogleich in Blut verwandelt und wurde überall als Blut erkannt.

En l'an 1229 après J.-C., aux alentours de la Saint-Martin, la neige tomba et se changea aussitôt en sang et partout on la prit pour du sang.

FOL. 55

1230 — Flood in Frisia
Überschwemmung in Friesland | Inondation en frise

In the year A.D. 1230, an overflowing or flooding of the sea nearly drowned and engulfed the whole of Frisia, so that up to a hundred thousand people drowned and sank in this inundation.

Im 1230. Jahr n. Chr. hat ein Überlaufen oder eine Überschwemmung des Meeres beinahe das ganze Friesland ertränkt und versenkt, so dass in dieser Überflutung bis zu hundert tausend Menschen ertrunken und untergegangen sind.

En l'an 1230 après J.-C., un débordement ou une inondation des eaux de la mer submergea et engloutit toute la Frise, à tel point que jusqu'à cent mille personnes se noyèrent et furent englouties dans cette inondation.

FOL. 56

1234 — Freezing winter | Eisiger Winter | Hiver glacial

In the year A.D. 1234, there was such a terrible frost that people could drive with loaded carts from Venice to Cremona upon the mighty river Po. Also, the wine froze in the barrels so that it had to be thawed through with fire. This was followed by a great famine and death and any people on the ground froze to death and died.

Im 1234. Jahr n. Chr. gab es eine solch grausame Kälte, dass man von Venedig bis nach Cremona auf dem mächtigen Fluss Po mit beladenen Wagen fuhr. Auch gefror der Wein in den Fässern, dass man ihn mit Feuer auftauen musste. Danach folgten ein großes Sterben und Hunger, sodass die Leute am Boden erfroren und starben.

En l'an 1234 après J.-C., eut lieu une vague de froid si terrible que les gens pouvaient rouler avec des carrioles chargées de Venise à Crémone sur le puissant fleuve Pô. Aussi, le vin gela dans les barriques et il fallut le dégeler avec du feu. S'ensuivirent une grande famine et la mort et beaucoup de gens tombèrent à terre gelés et périrent.

13

Im m cc xxix iar nach christi g
vnnd ward als pald in pluett
pluett ver kehrt

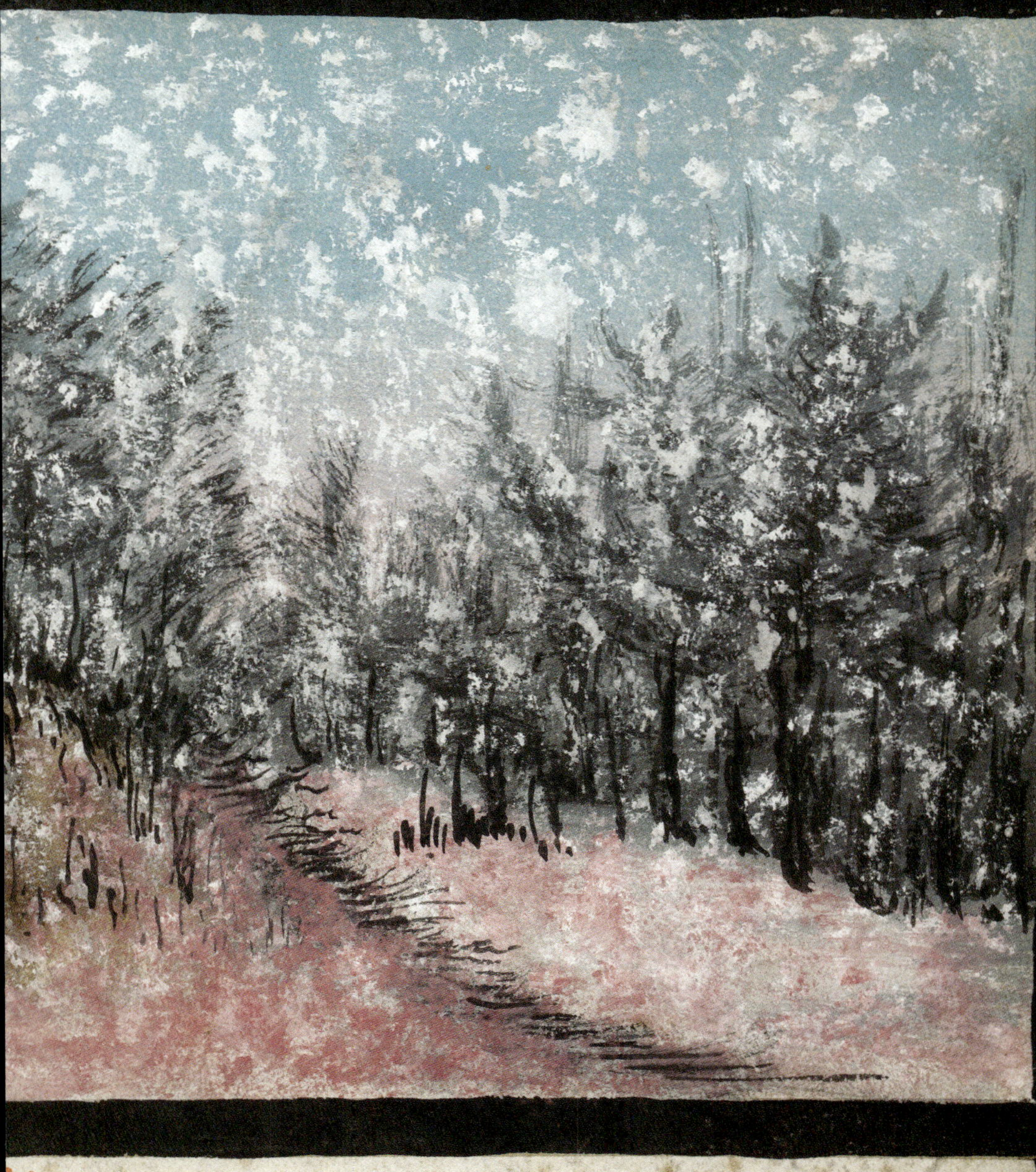

rt / vnnd marthin fill ein schnee
ert / vnnd war vber all füre

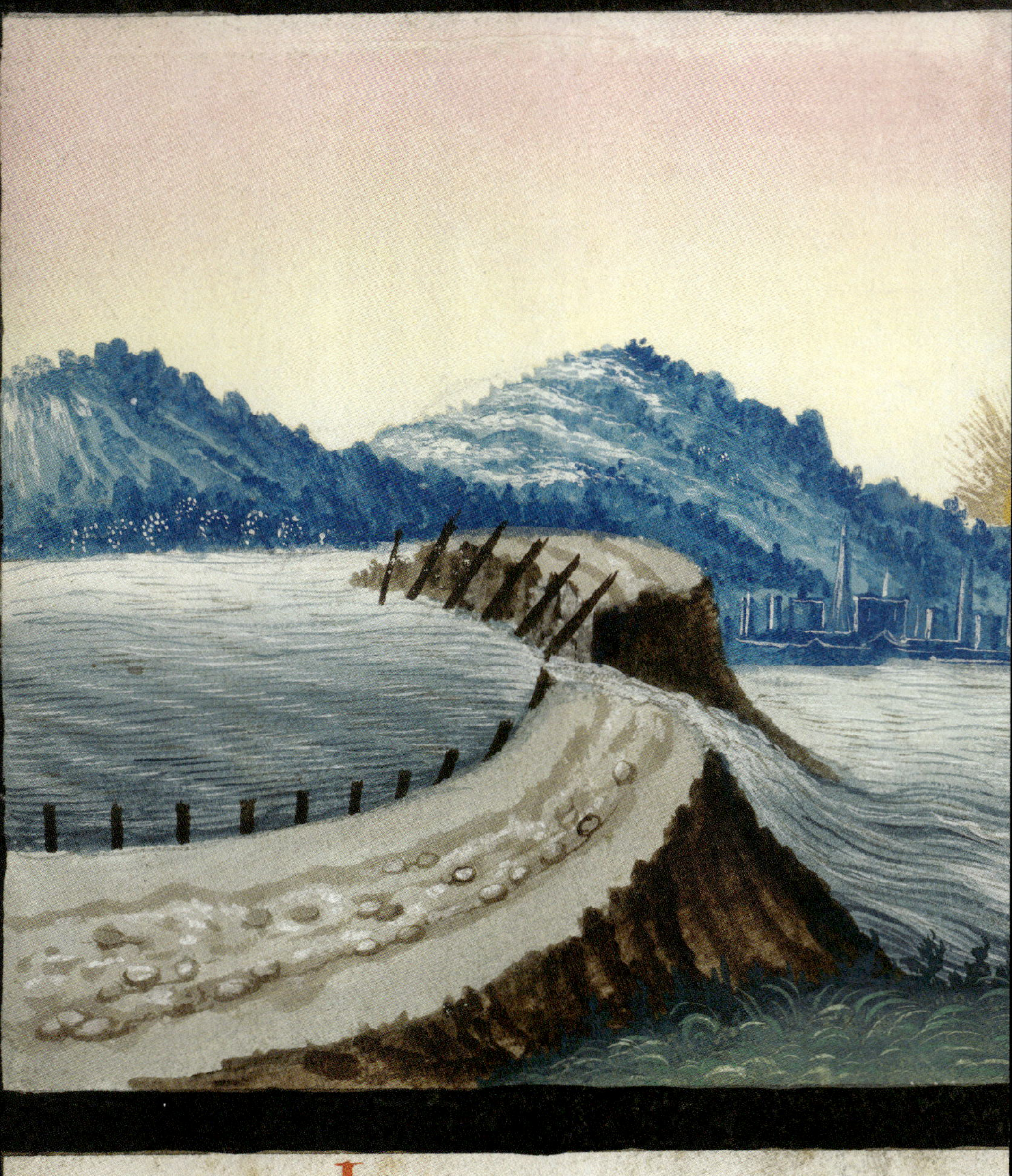

Im m c c x x x iar nach cristi gepurt
schier das gantz frieß land erdrenckt v
in hundert tausent menschen ersof

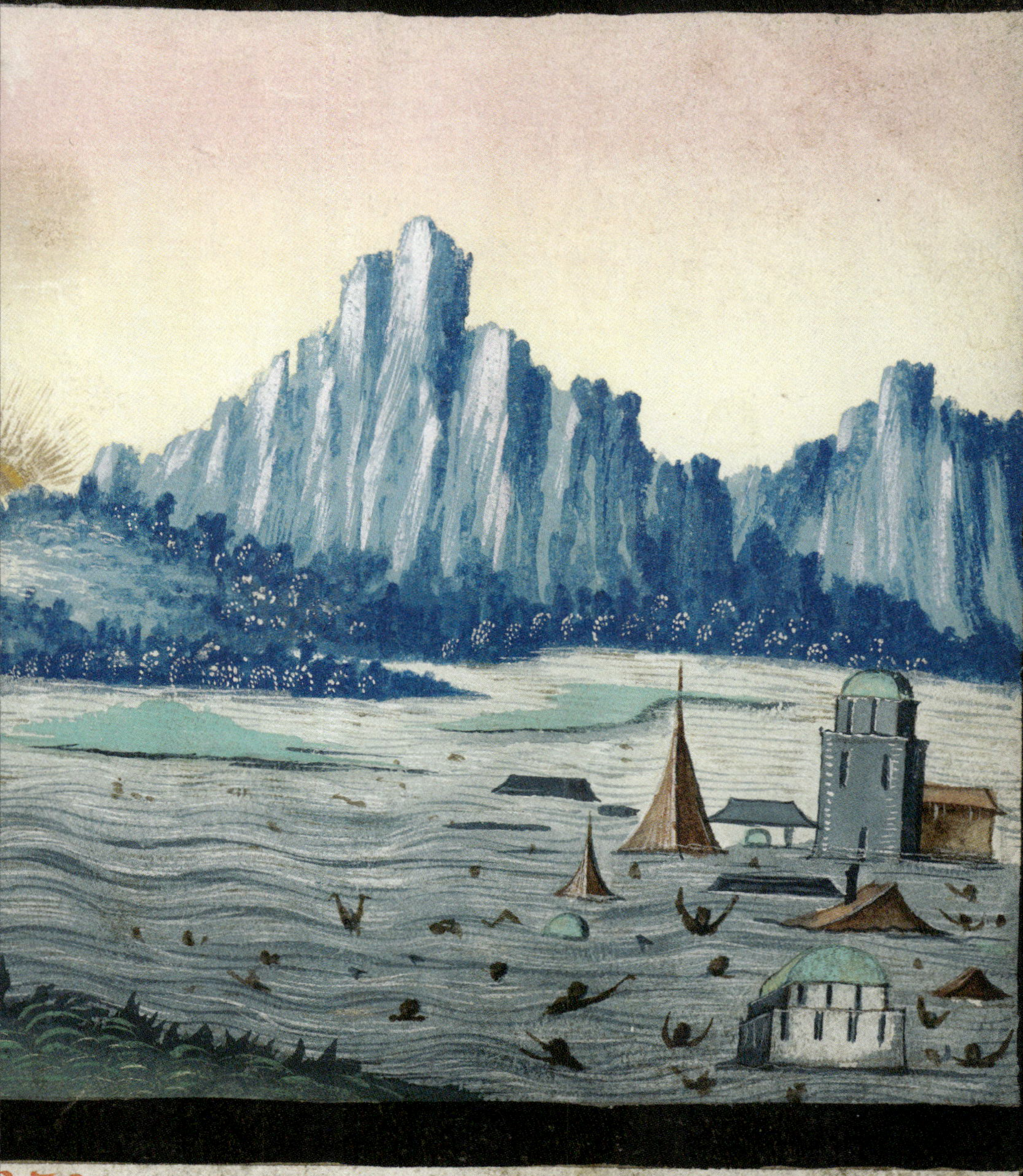

230.

ein auss lauff oder vber schwal des meers
ver senckt/ das in dieser sundt fluss biss
vnnd kinder gangen sind

Im m c c x x x iiii iar nach christi g
von venedig pis gen Croman/ au
en fiur/ er frur auch der wein i
en/ dar nach folget ain groser ster
frurren vnnd sterben

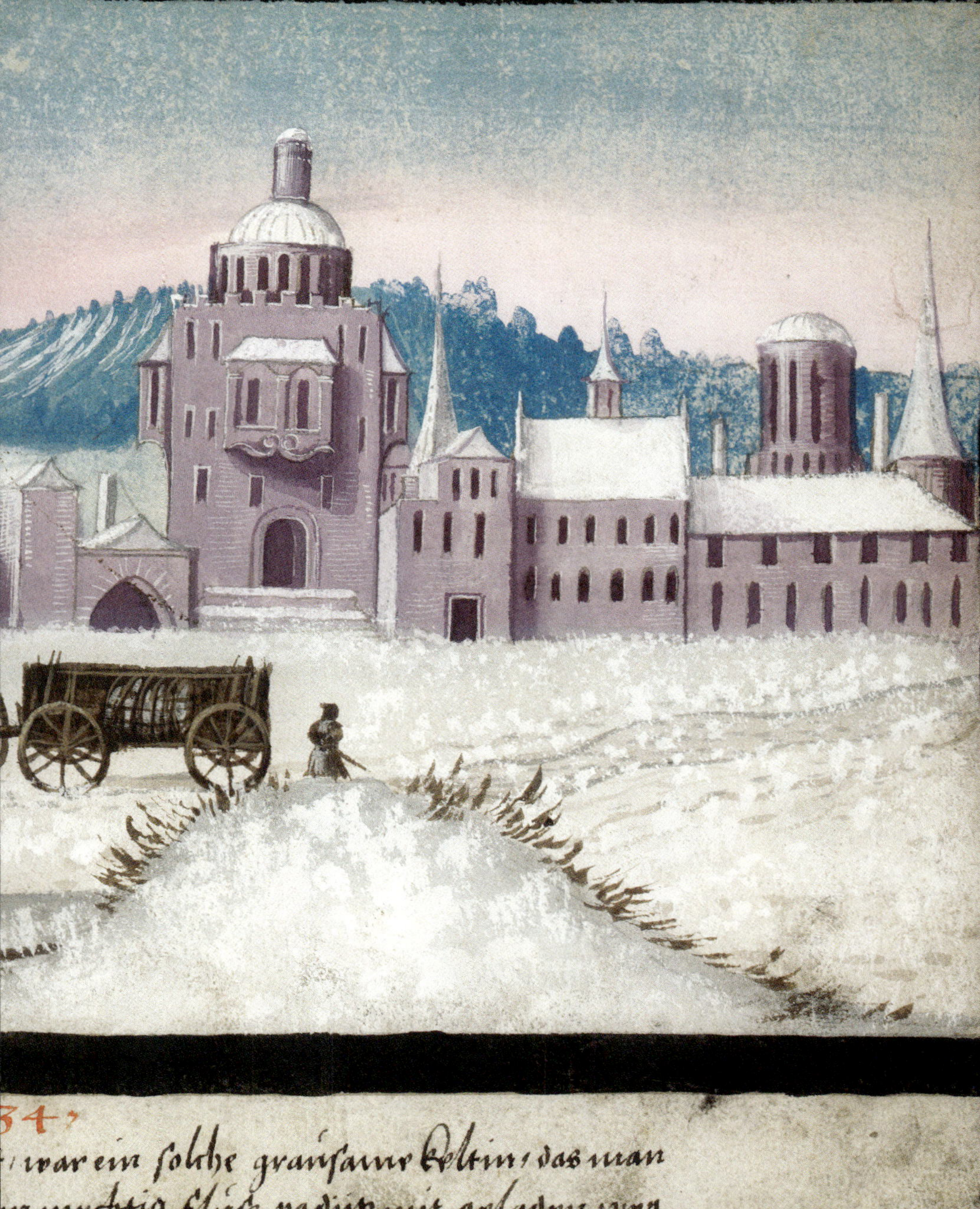

34.

war ein solche grausame keltin, das man

n mechtig fluss paden mit geladen weg

Sern. das mann mit fewr [?] muost auf lem [?]

vnd hunger das die leůt in poden er

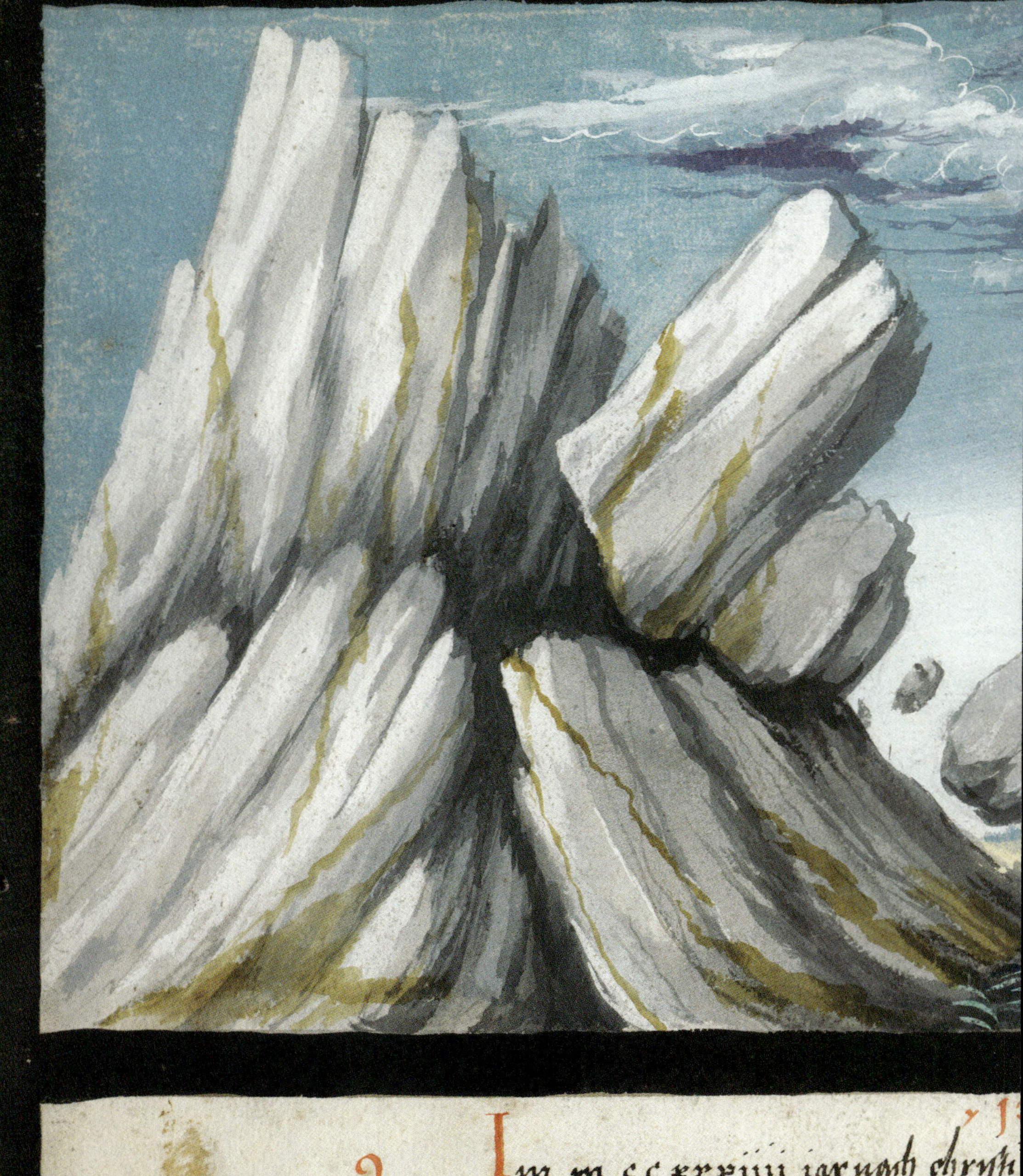

Im m cc xxxiiii iar nach christi
vnnd verdorbet bei funff taus
dan er fiel vber dir ander ber
dorben.

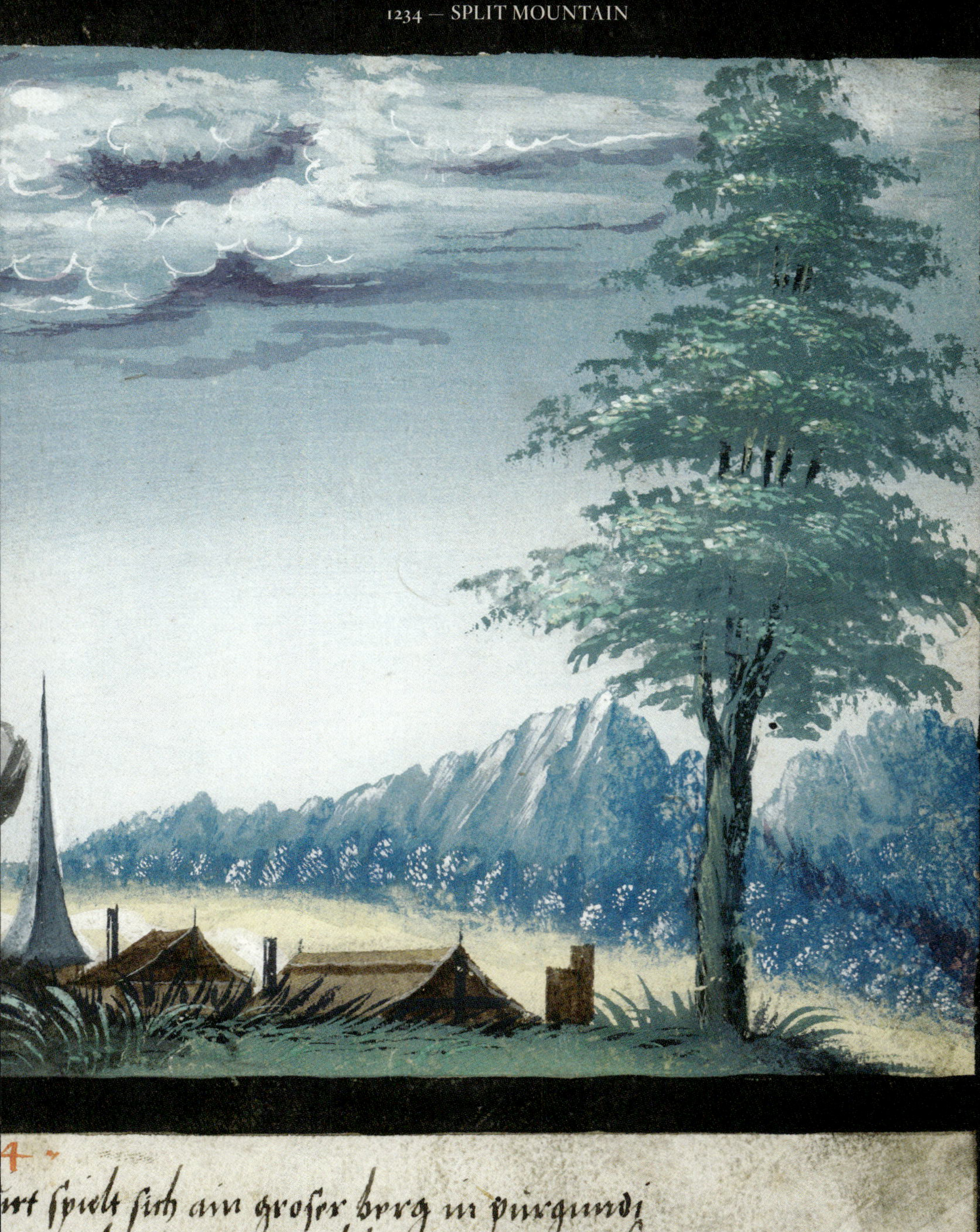

4 ·
rt spielt sich ain groser berg in purgundi
neyschen dir er erschlug unnd erstickt
die thall dar mit sich unnd leutt ver

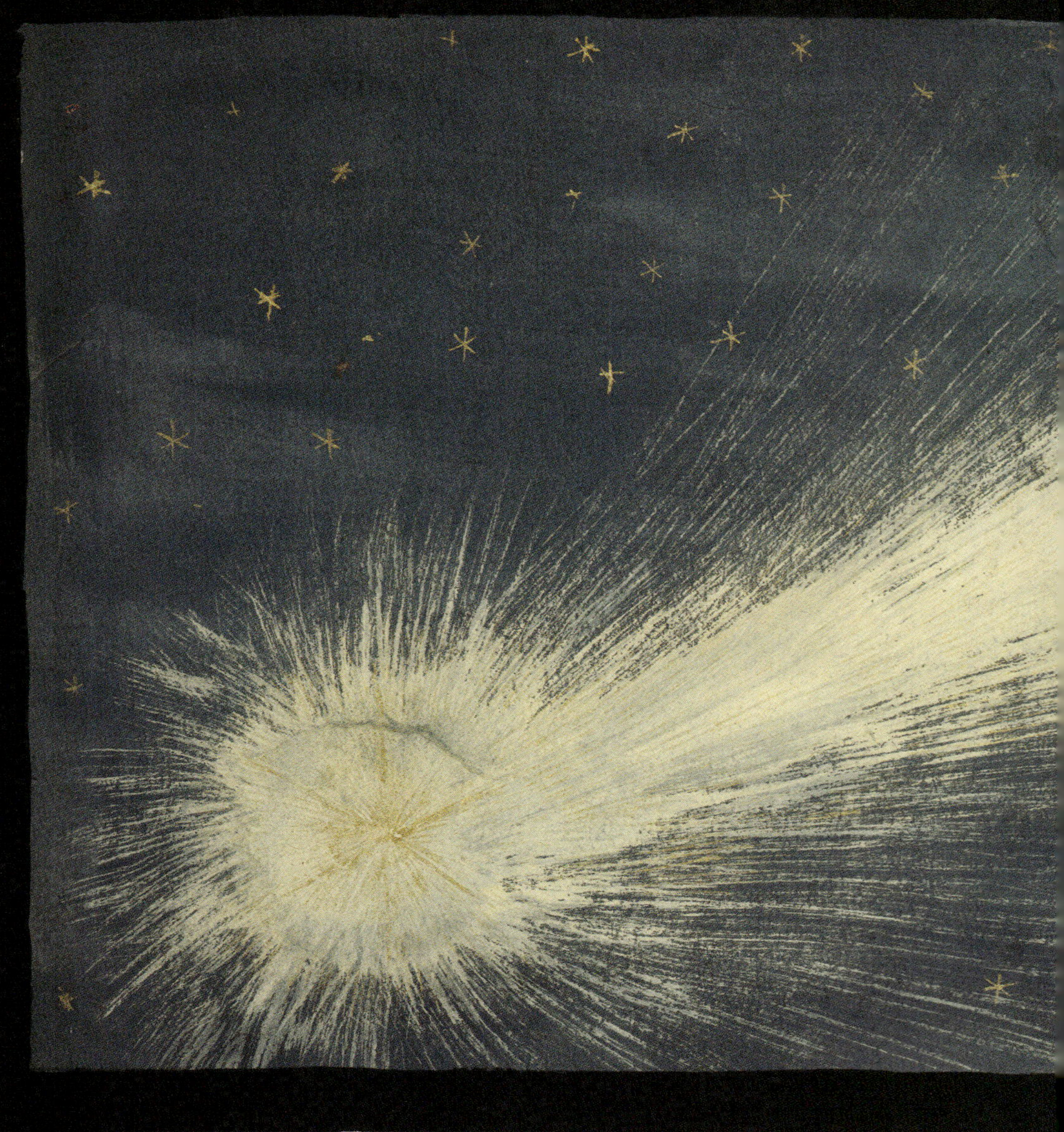

Im m cc lxxxiii iar nach ch
bei drei monaten / von auff gang
stramen / gegen dem nieder gan
ant er wirderumb.

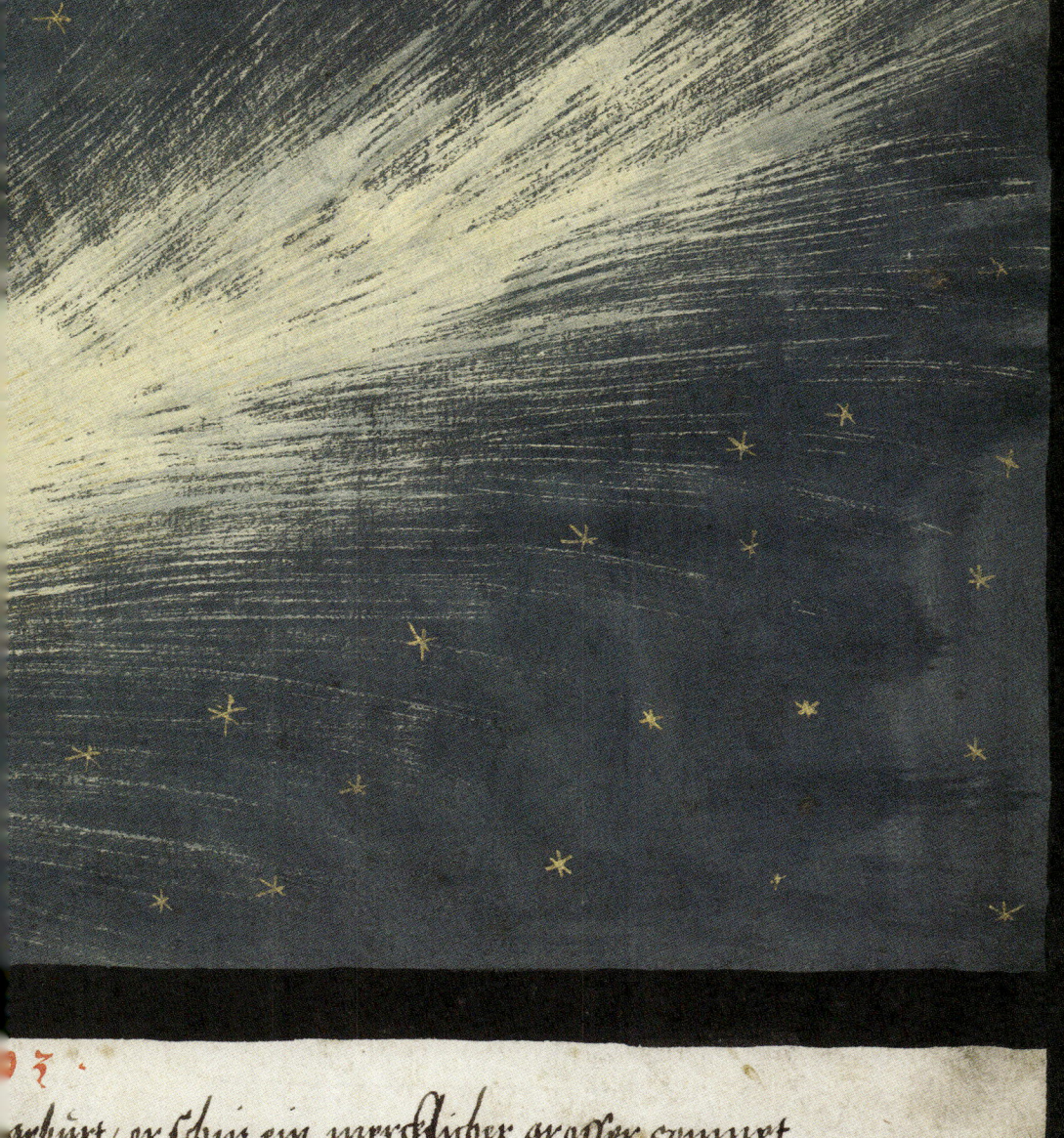

gebürt / er schin ein mercklicher grosser commet
zum mitels des himels steigent vnnd seine
und wie der pabst vrbanus starb verschw

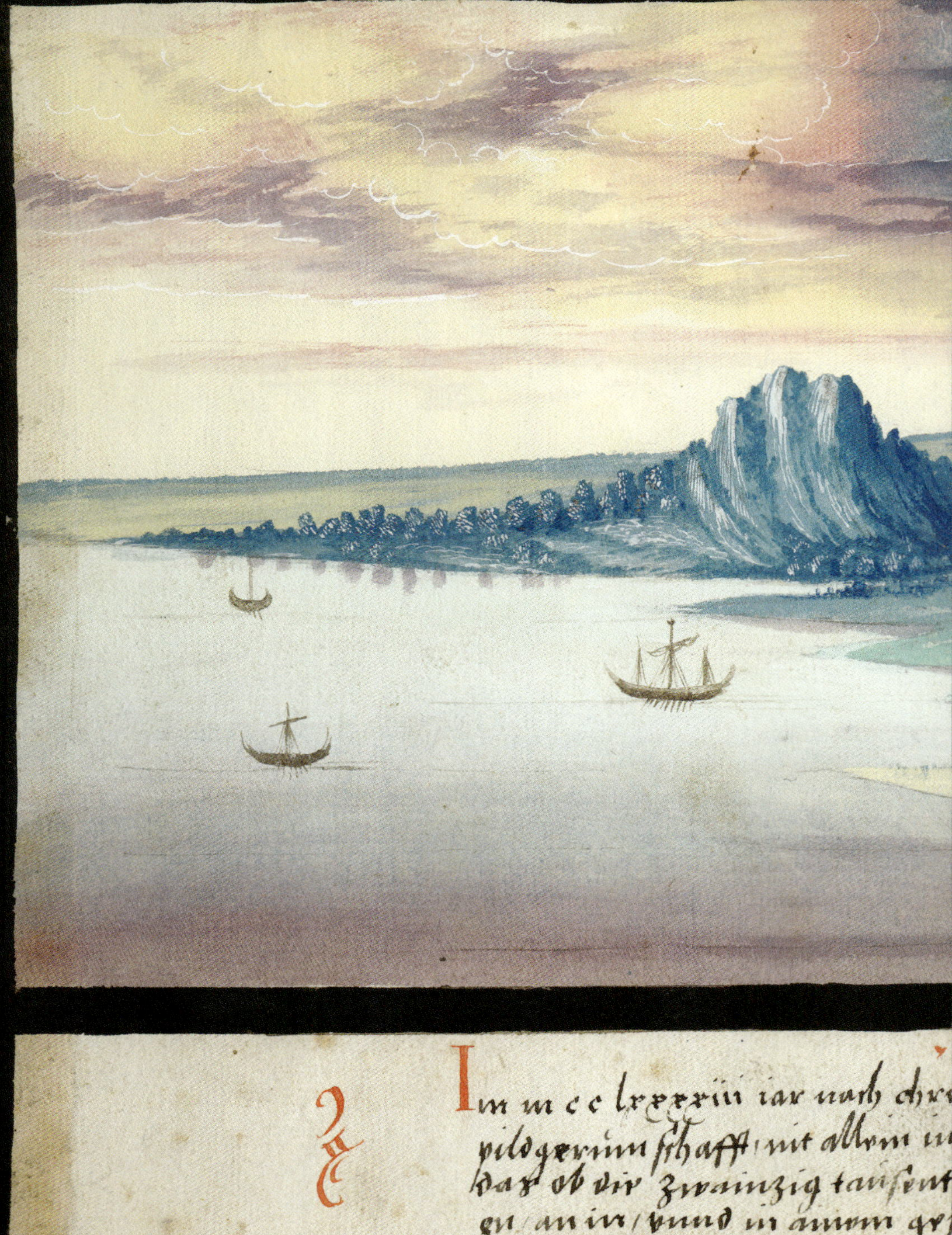

Im m c c lxxxxiii iar nach chr
pildgerinn schafft: nit allein in
das ob dir zwainzig tausent
en/ an im/ vnnd in ainem ge
porten des meers zugen, wir

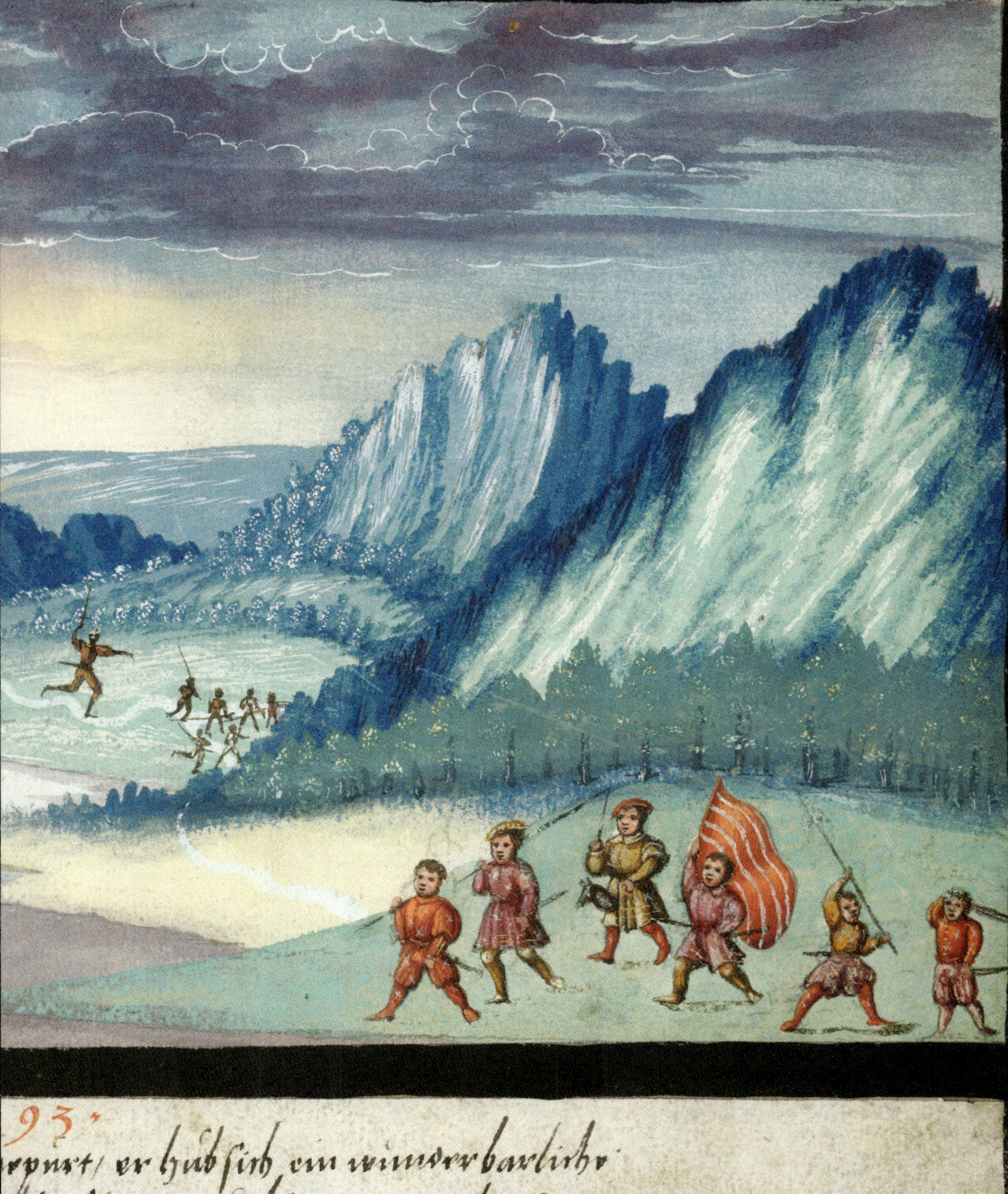

93.

epurt/ er hub sich ein wunderbarliche
ylia sůnder auch in andern landen/
ndern war bezaichnet mit creůtz
st verfůrt/ das sie schar weiß an die
n den ge regenspurg ist gelauffen

FOL. 57

1234 — Split mountain
Gespaltener Berg | Montagne fendue

In the year A.D. 1234, a large mountain in Burgundy split asunder and killed some five thousand people by knocking them down and smothering them. After this it toppled over the other mountains and into the valleys, whereby livestock and more people died.

Im 1234. Jahr n. Chr. spaltete sich ein großer Berg in Burgund und tötete etwa fünftausend Menschen, die er erschlug und erstickte. Danach stürzte er über die anderen Berge in die Täler, wodurch Vieh und Leute starben.

En l'an 1234 après J.-C., une grande montagne de Bourgogne se fendit et fit environ cinq mille victimes en les renversant et les étouffant. Ensuite, elle s'effondra sur les autres montagnes et dégringola dans les vallées par-dessus, ce qui fit périr le bétail et d'autres gens encore.

FOL. 58

1293 — Comet | Komet | Comète

In the year A.D. 1293, a notably large comet appeared for three months, rising in the east and climbing to the middle of the sky, with its rays in the west. And when Pope Urban died, it disappeared again.

Im 1293. Jahr n. Chr. erschien ein beachtlicher, großer Komet während drei Monaten, von Osten bis zur Mitte des Himmels steigend, und seine Strahlen im Westen. Und als der Papst Urban starb, verschwand er wieder.

En l'an 1293 après J.-C., une comète remarquablement grosse apparut pendant trois mois, se levant à l'est et montant jusqu'au midi du ciel, en portant ses rayons jusqu'à l'ouest. Et lorsque mourut le pape Urbain, elle disparut de nouveau.

FOL. 59

1293 — Children's pilgrimage | Kinderwallfahrt | Pèlerinage d'enfants

In the year A.D. 1293, a wondrous pilgrimage commenced – not only in Italy, but also in other countries – with more than twenty thousand children being marked with crosses and led astray through trickery, so that they went in droves to the ports of the sea, just as one might have walked to Regensburg in those days.

Im 1293. Jahr n. Chr. begann eine wundersame Pilgerschaft – nicht allein in Italien, sondern auch in anderen Ländern –, sodass mehr als zwanzigtausend Kinder mit Kreuzen gezeichnet waren und von einer Täuschung verführt wurden, sodass sie scharenweise an die Häfen des Meeres zogen, so wie man damals nach Regensburg gelaufen ist.

En l'an 1293 après J.-C., débuta un pèlerinage extraordinaire – non seulement en Italie, mais aussi dans d'autres pays –, au cours duquel plus de vingt mille enfants furent marqués du signe de la croix et détournés de leur chemin par la ruse, et des foules d'enfants allèrent dans les ports de la mer, tout comme on se serait rendu à Ratisbonne à ce moment-là.

FOL. 60

1298 [in fact: 798] — Miracle of little crosses and ash
Kreuzwunder und Asche | Miracle des petites croix et de cendre

In the year A.D. 798, small crosses appeared on people's clothing and in Italy ash fell from the sky upon the earth, which took the lives of many people – really terrible to see.

Im 798. Jahr nach der Geburt Christi erschienen kleine Kreuze an der Kleidung der Menschen und in Italien fiel Asche vom Himmel auf die Erde, was viele Leute umbrachte – ganz grausam anzusehen.

En l'an 798 après J.-C., de petites croix apparurent sur les vêtements des gens, et en Italie, de la cendre tomba du ciel sur la terre et tua beaucoup de personnes – très horrible à voir.

FOL. 61

1300 — Comet | Komet | Comète

In the year A.D. 1300, a fearful comet appeared in the sky. And this year, on St Andrew's Day, the ground was shaken by an earthquake so that many buildings collapsed. At this time, the first jubilee year was established by Pope Boniface VIII.

Im 1300. Jahr n. Chr. erschien ein furchtbarer Komet am Himmel. Und in diesem Jahr, am Sankt-Andreas-Tag, wurde das Erdreich durch ein Erdbeben erschüttert, sodass viele Gebäude zerstört wurden. Zu der Zeit wurde das erste Jubeljahr von Papst Bonifatius VIII. eingeführt.

En l'an 1300 après J.-C., une comète effrayante apparut dans le ciel. Et en cette année-là, le jour de la Saint-André, le sol fut ébranlé par un tremblement de terre qui fit s'écrouler de nombreuses constructions. C'est à cette époque que le premier jubilé fut décrété par le pape Boniface VIII.

FOL. 62

1304 — Three moons and comet
Drei Monde und Komet | Trois lunes et comète

In the year A.D. 1304, three moons and a comet appeared – seen around midnight for three months – in the German lands and in Italy, just as it is painted here.

Im 1304. Jahr nach Christi Geburt erschienen drei Monde und ein Komet – drei Monate lang gegen Mitternacht gesehen – in deutschen Ländern und Italien, wie dann hier gemalt ist.

En l'an 1304 après J.-C., trois lunes et une comète apparurent – observées vers minuit pendant trois mois – en terres allemandes et en Italie, comme dans cette peinture.

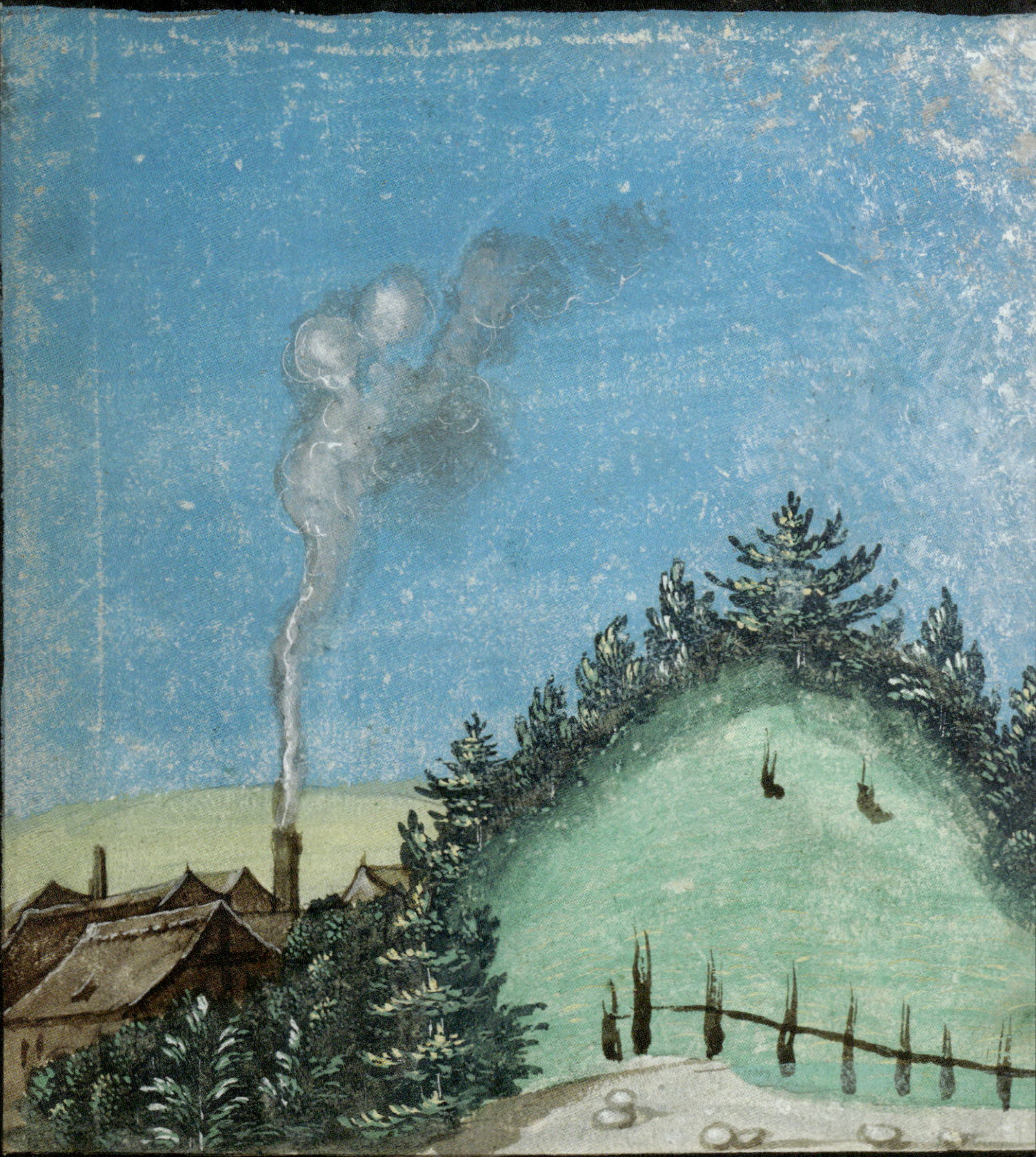

Im Dcclxxxviii iar nach de
menschen klaidung / vnnd fi
dir erden / das vil volcks vmb

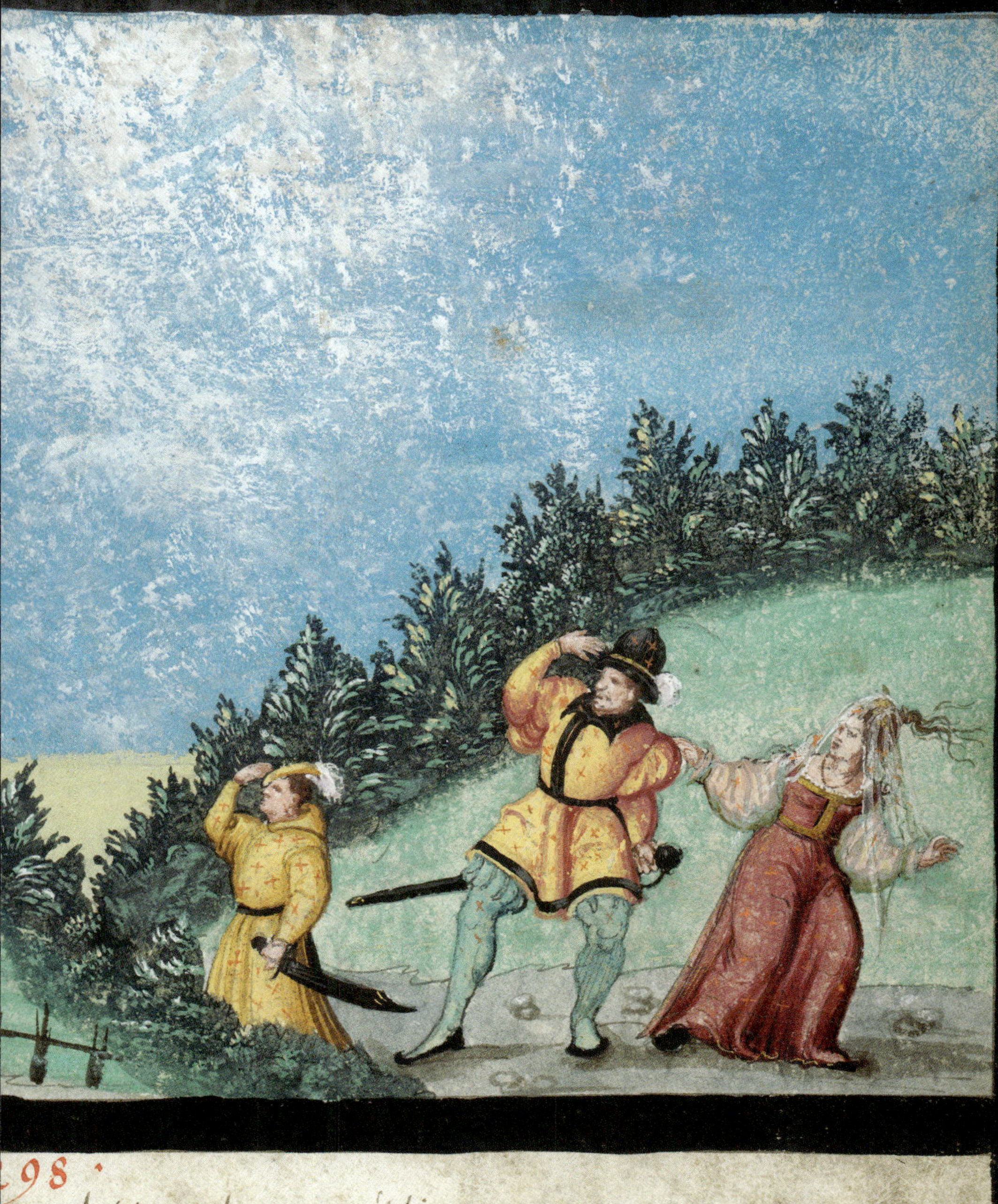

98.

ůrt christi erschinen creützlin an der

welschland· aschen vom himel auff

t gar grausam zů sehen·

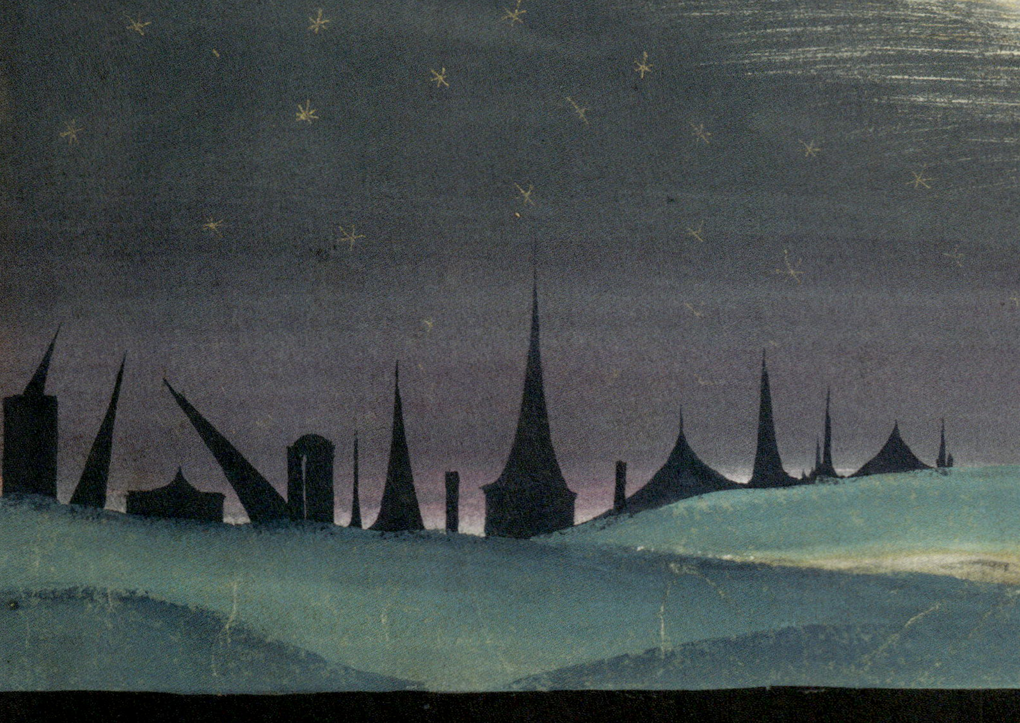

Im m ccc iar nach christi gepu
himel, vnnd in dirsem iar du
rich, durch erdbidem, das vil
erst iubel iar vom pabst bo

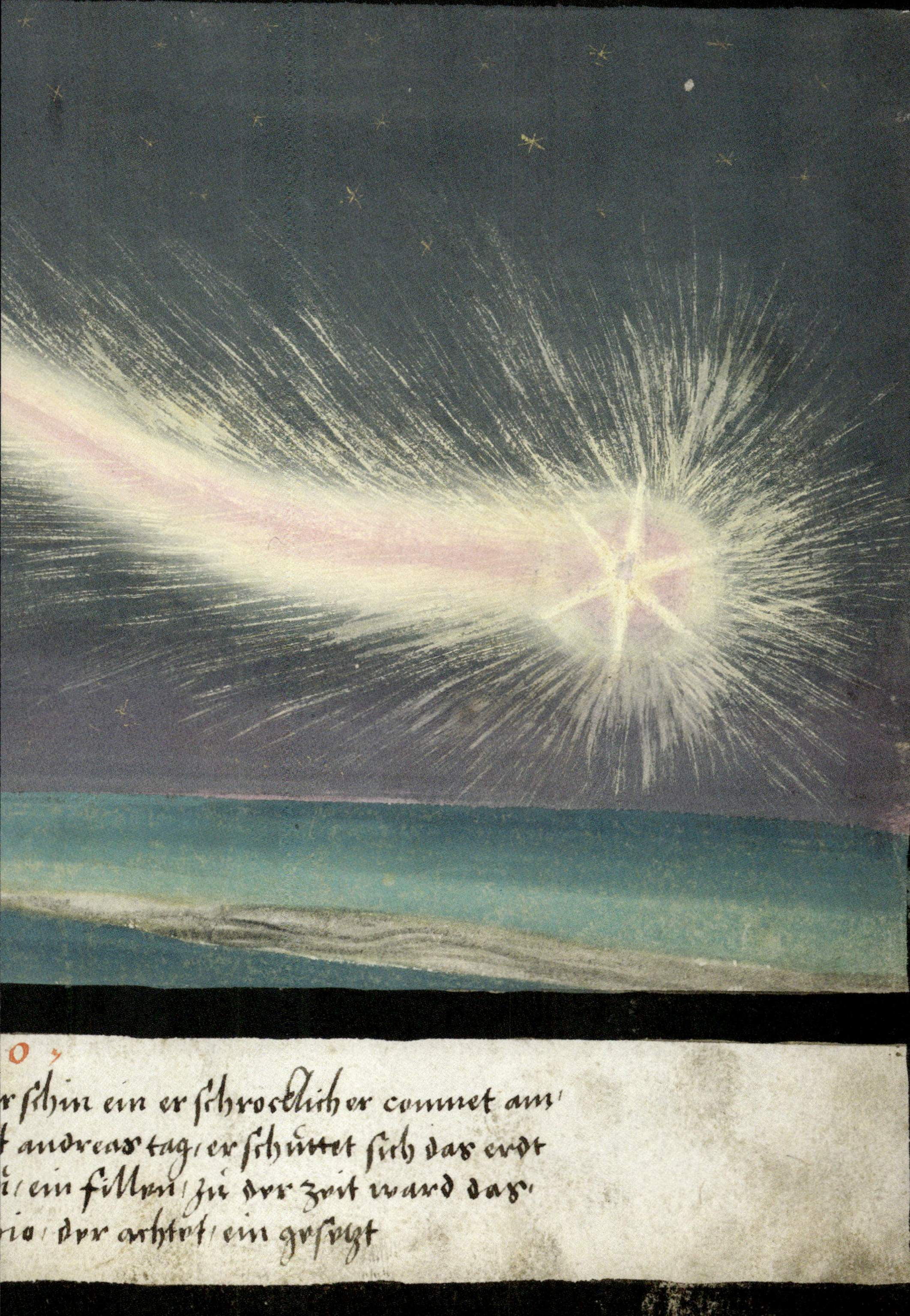
07
r schin ein erschrockhlicher commet am
t andreas tag / erschuttet sich das erdt
ü / ein fillen / zu der zeit ward das
rio / der achtet / ein gesetzt

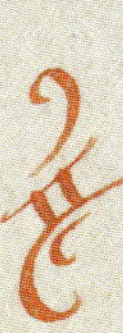

Im m c c c iiii iar nach chri
vnnd ein commet drei mon
sehen · in deutzschen vnnd w
gemalt ist

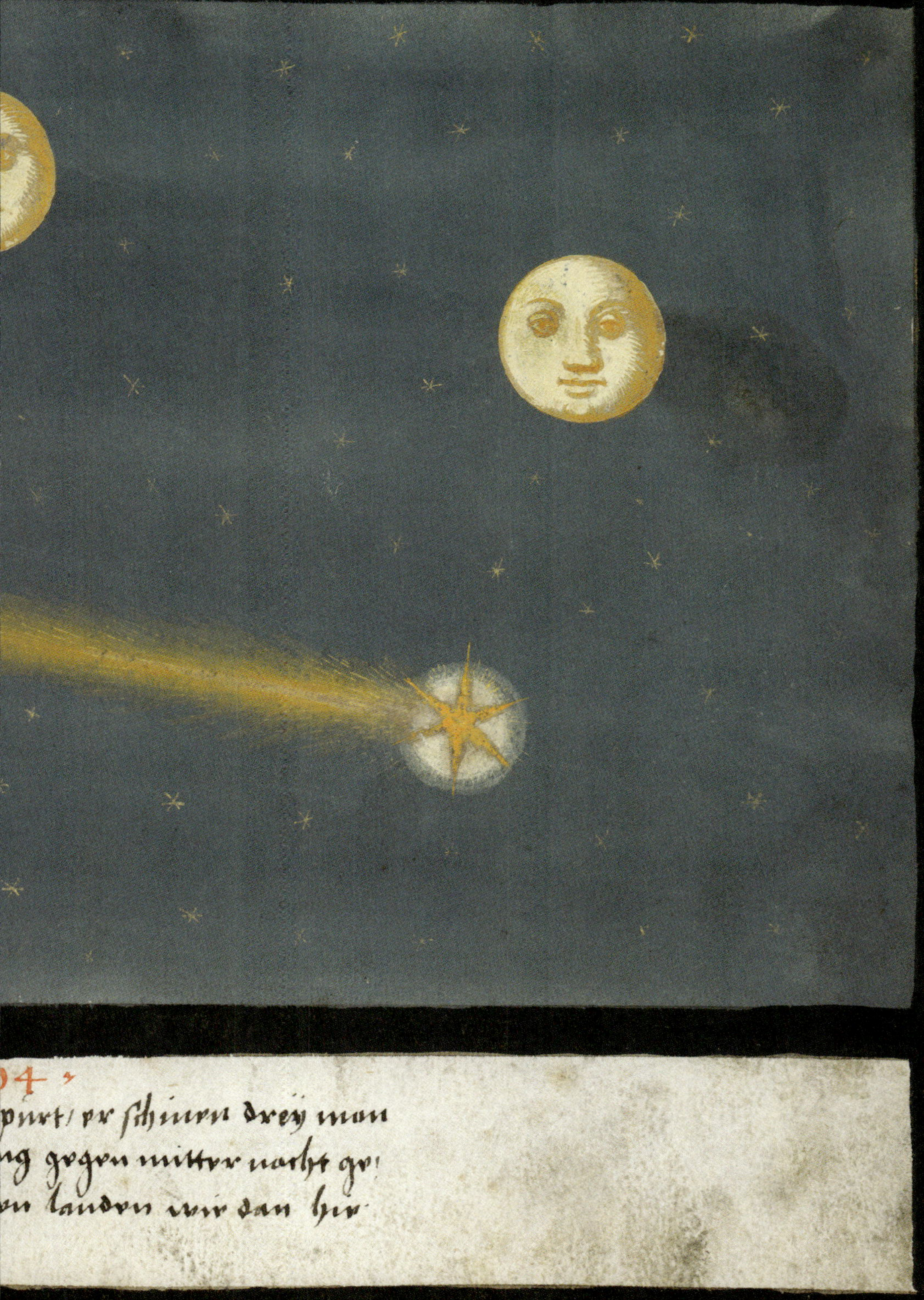
04.
purt/ er schinen drey mon
ng gegen mitter nacht ge:
en landen wir dan hir

, 13

II Im Dcccxxxii iar nach der gepurt christi / se
vnnd in den selbigen hagelstainen / warn wu
im welschlannden ein erdbidem das die

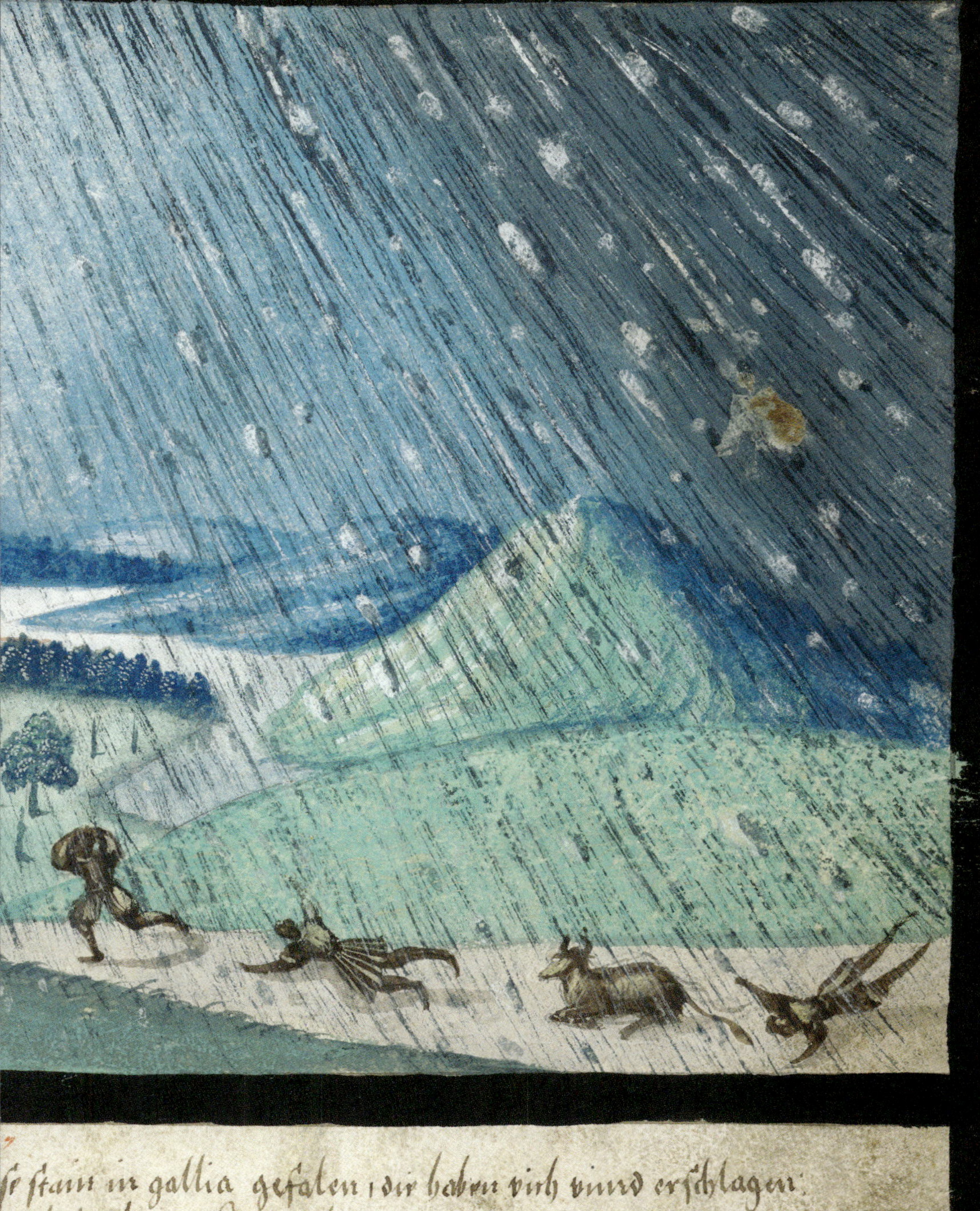

se stain in gallia gefalen, die haben vich vnnd erschlagen:
arliche hortte kurner lenglet gefunden vnnd geschach
vnnd berg ein fiellen, wie hie gemalt ist er

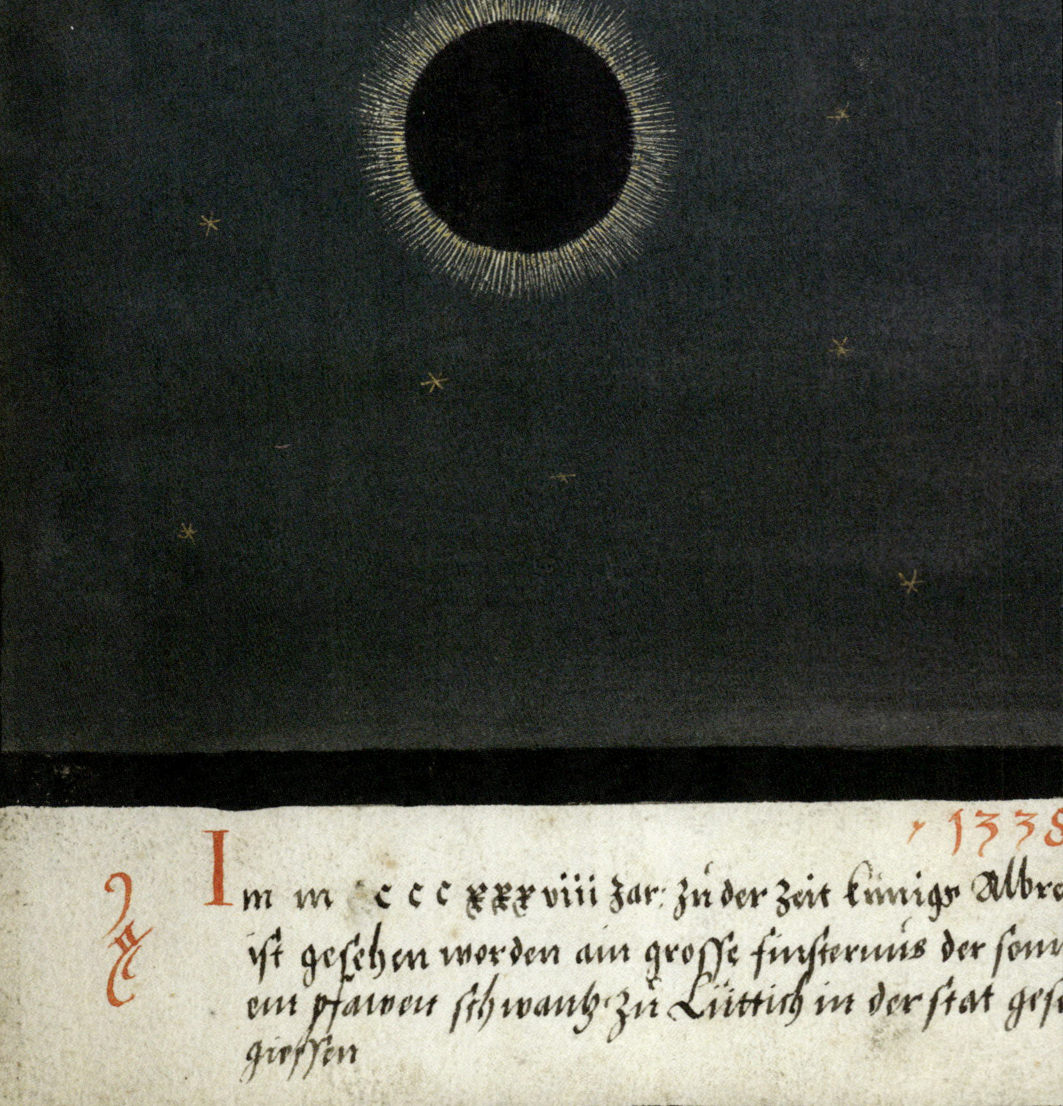
1338
Im m ccc xxxviii Jar: zu der zeit kunigs Albre
ist gesehen worden ain grosse finsternus der son
ein pfawen schwantz zu Lüttich in der stat ges
giessen

zog zu osterreich: Kaiser Sigmundus: Dochterman
dem tag: vnnd auch ain grossen Commeten mit ein:
vorden: darnach gefolget ist ain grosser blut vorr:

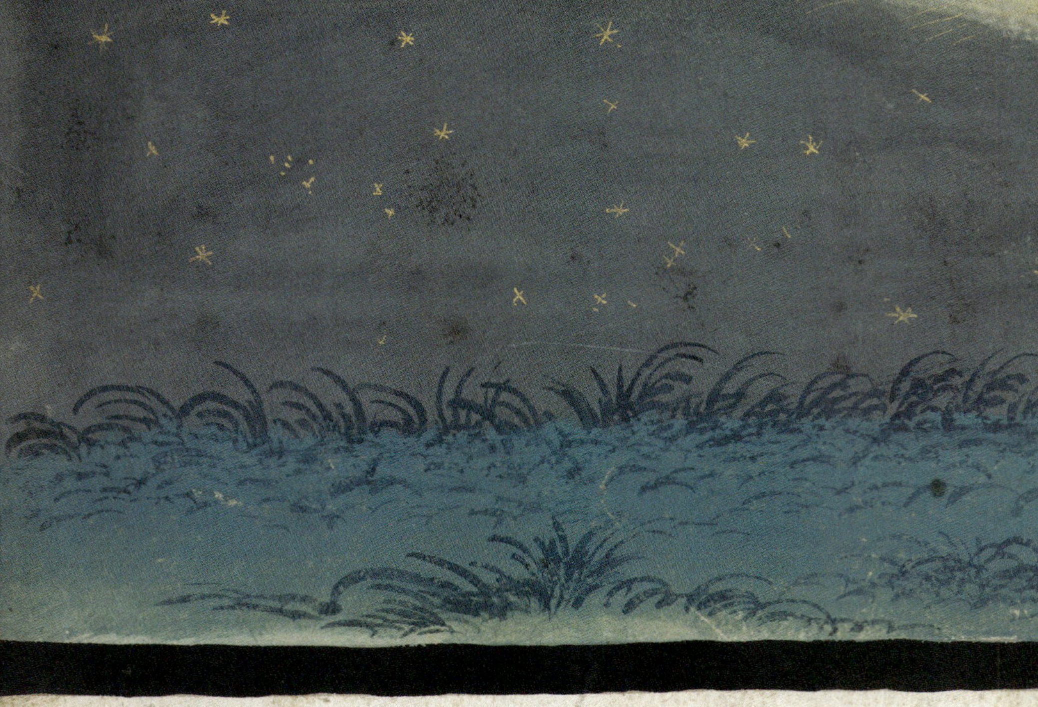

Im m ccc xxxvii i
commet in ittalia zw
lůdwig der viert ai

347.

h christi gepürt erschin ein

onnat. darnach starb kaiser.

t auß bayrn.

FOL. 63

1332 [in fact: 832] — Hail and earthquake in Gaul
Hagel und Erdbeben in Gallien | Grêle et tremblement de terre en Gaule

In the year A.D. 832, large stones fell in Gaul. They killed livestock and [...]. And in these very hailstones were found wonderful, hard grains, somewhat oblong in shape. And an earthquake struck in Italy so that towns and mountains collapsed, as is painted here etc.

Im 832. Jahr nach der Geburt Christi sind große Steine in Gallien herabgefallen. Die haben Vieh [...] erschlagen. Und in eben diesen Hagelsteinen wurden wunderbare, harte Körner in länglicher Form gefunden. Und es ereignete sich in Italien ein Erdbeben, sodass die Städte und Berge zerstört wurden, wie hier gemalt ist etc.

En l'an 832 après J.-C., de grosses pierres s'abattirent en Gaule, touchèrent et tuèrent le bétail [...]. Et dans ces mêmes grêlons, on trouva des grains extraordinaires, durs, un peu oblongs de forme. Et un tremblement de terre se produisit en Italie, qui fit s'effondrer des villes et des montagnes, comme dans cette peinture, etc.

FOL. 64

1338 [in fact: 1438] — Eclipse and comet at Liège
Sonnenfinsternis und Komet in Lüttich | Éclipse et comète à Liège

In the year 1438, in the time of King Albrecht, Duke of Austria and son-in-law of Emperor Sigismund, a great darkening of the sun was seen in the daytime. And also a great comet with a tail was seen in the city of Liège. This was followed by great bloodshed.

Im 1438. Jahr, zu der Zeit König Albrechts, Herzog zu Österreich, Kaiser Sigismunds Schwiegersohn, ist tagsüber eine große Finsternis der Sonne gesehen worden. Und auch ein großer Komet mit einem Schweif ist in Lüttich in der Stadt gesehen worden. Danach folgte ein großes Blutvergießen.

En l'an 1438 après J.-C., au temps du roi Albrecht, duc d'Autriche et gendre de l'empereur Sigismond, une grande obscurité masquant le soleil fut observée en plein jour. Et une grande comète dotée d'une queue fut aussi observée dans la ville de Liège. S'ensuivit un grand bain de sang.

FOL. 65

1347 — Comet in Italy | Komet in Italien | Comète en Italie

In the year A.D. 1347, a comet appeared in Italy for two months. After this, Emperor Louis IV, a Bavarian monarch, died.

Im 1347. Jahr nach Christi Geburt erschien ein Komet in Italien zwei Monate lang. Danach starb Kaiser Ludwig IV., ein Herrscher aus Bayern.

En l'an 1347 après J.-C., une comète apparut en Italie pendant deux mois. Par la suite, l'empereur Louis IV, monarque de Bavière, mourut.

FOL. 66

1348 — Worms and vermin

Würmer und Ungeziefer | Vers et vermines

In 1348, in the first year of the reign of Emperor Charles IV, a great vapour moved densely and hideously in the clouds so that the earth was darkened. At that moment, a great number of worms and vermin fell upon the earth in the East, so that many people died from the stench and hardly ten were left alive out of a thousand.

1348, im ersten Jahr Kaiser Karls IV., bewegte sich ein großer Dunst scheußlich dicht in den Wolken, dass die Erde verfinstert wurde. In dem Moment fiel eine große Anzahl Gewürm und Ungeziefer im Orient auf die Erde, dass von dem Gestank danach viele Leute starben und von tausend kaum zehn übrig blieben.

En 1348, dans la première année du règne de l'empereur Charles IV, une vapeur d'une épaisseur abominable s'introduisit dans les nuages et plongea la terre dans l'obscurité. À ce moment, un nombre considérable de vers et de vermines s'abattit sur la terre dans l'Orient et beaucoup de gens périrent dans cette pestilence et à peine dix personnes sur mille survécurent.

FOL. 67

1351 — Comet and fiery shaft

Komet und feuriger Balken | Comète et bille enflammée

In the year A.D. 1351, in the month of December, a comet was seen in the sky around midnight. Afterwards heavy winds sprang up and a fiery shaft was seen to fall from the sky, which then presaged great disagreement between the pope and the emperor.

Im 1351. Jahr nach Christi Geburt, im Monat Dezember, wurde gegen Mitternacht ein Komet am Himmel gesehen. Danach kamen starke Winde auf und man sah einen feurigen Balken vom Himmel fallen, was dann große Uneinigkeit zwischen dem Papst und dem Kaiser angezeigt hat.

En l'an 1351 après J.-C., au mois de décembre, une comète fut observée dans le ciel vers minuit. Par la suite, des vents puissants se levèrent et on vit une bille enflammée tomber du ciel, ce qui augura une grande discorde entre le pape et l'empereur.

FOL. 68

1357 — Earthquake in Spain

Erdbeben in Spanien | Tremblement de terre en Espagne

In the year A.D. 1357, an earthquake in Spain struck with such force that many buildings and cities were laid low and many people perished.

Im 1357. Jahr nach Christi Geburt ist in Spanien ein solches Erdbeben gewesen, dass viele Gebäude und Städte zerstört wurden und viele Leute umkamen.

En l'an 1357 après J.-C., en Espagne un tremblement de terre fut si puissant qu'un grand nombre de constructions et de villes furent rasées et que bien des gens périrent.

Im m ccc xxxxviii im ersten iar Caro
dampf scheützlich dick in dem gewil
fill ein grosse zu zal gewürm vnnd v
dem gestanck darnach vill volcks star

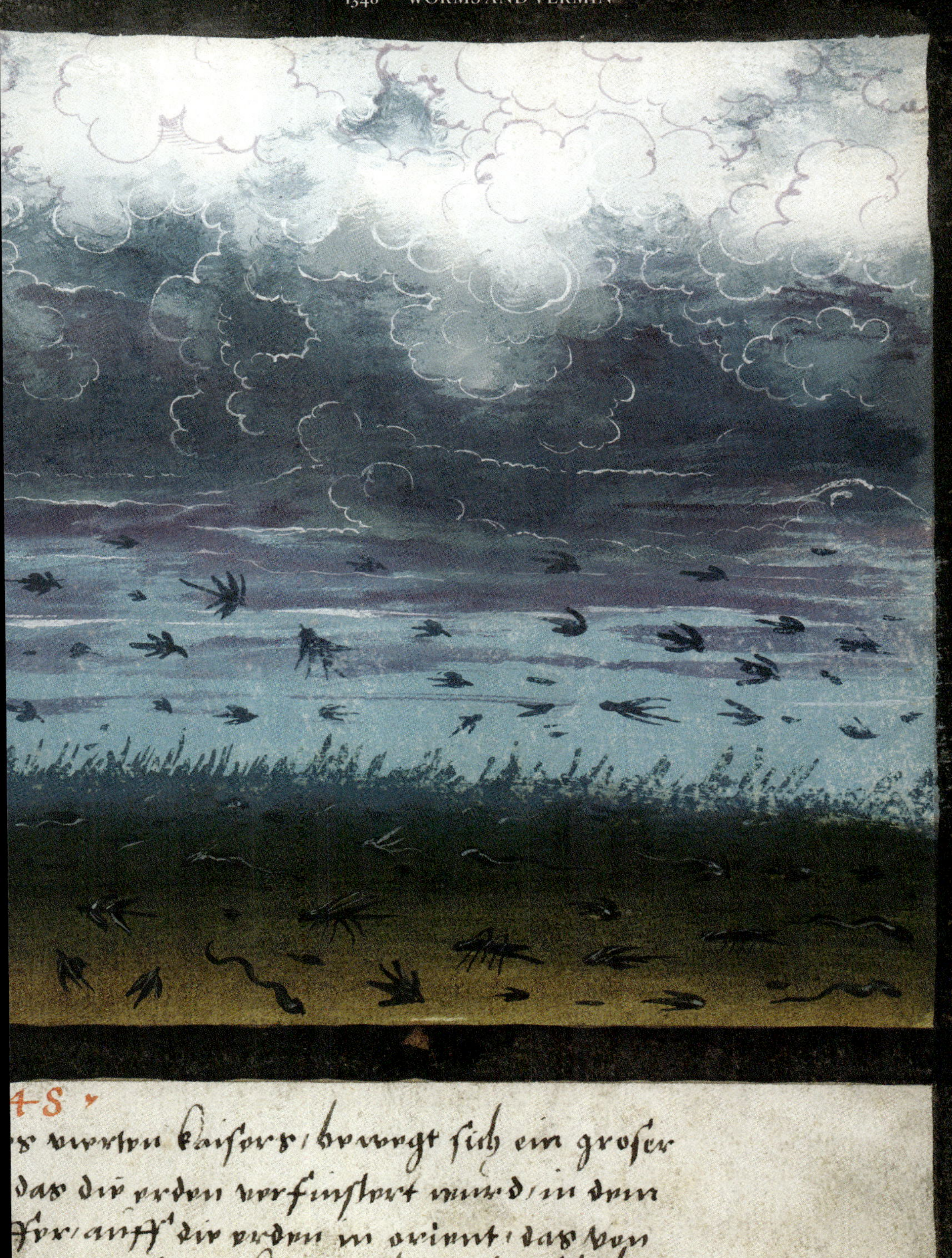

45

r vierten kaisers / bewegt sich ein groser
das die erden verfinstert wurd / in dem
sser / auff die erden in orient / das von
r von tausent kaum zehen vber bliben

Im m c c c l i iar nach christi ge
mitter nacht ein commet an dem
man sahe ain feurigen palcken
zwischen dem babst vnnd keis

in dem monat decembris/ ward gegen
el gesehen/ darnach kamen gros windt vnd
himel fallen/ das/ dan gros vnainigkait :
n ge zaigt hatt

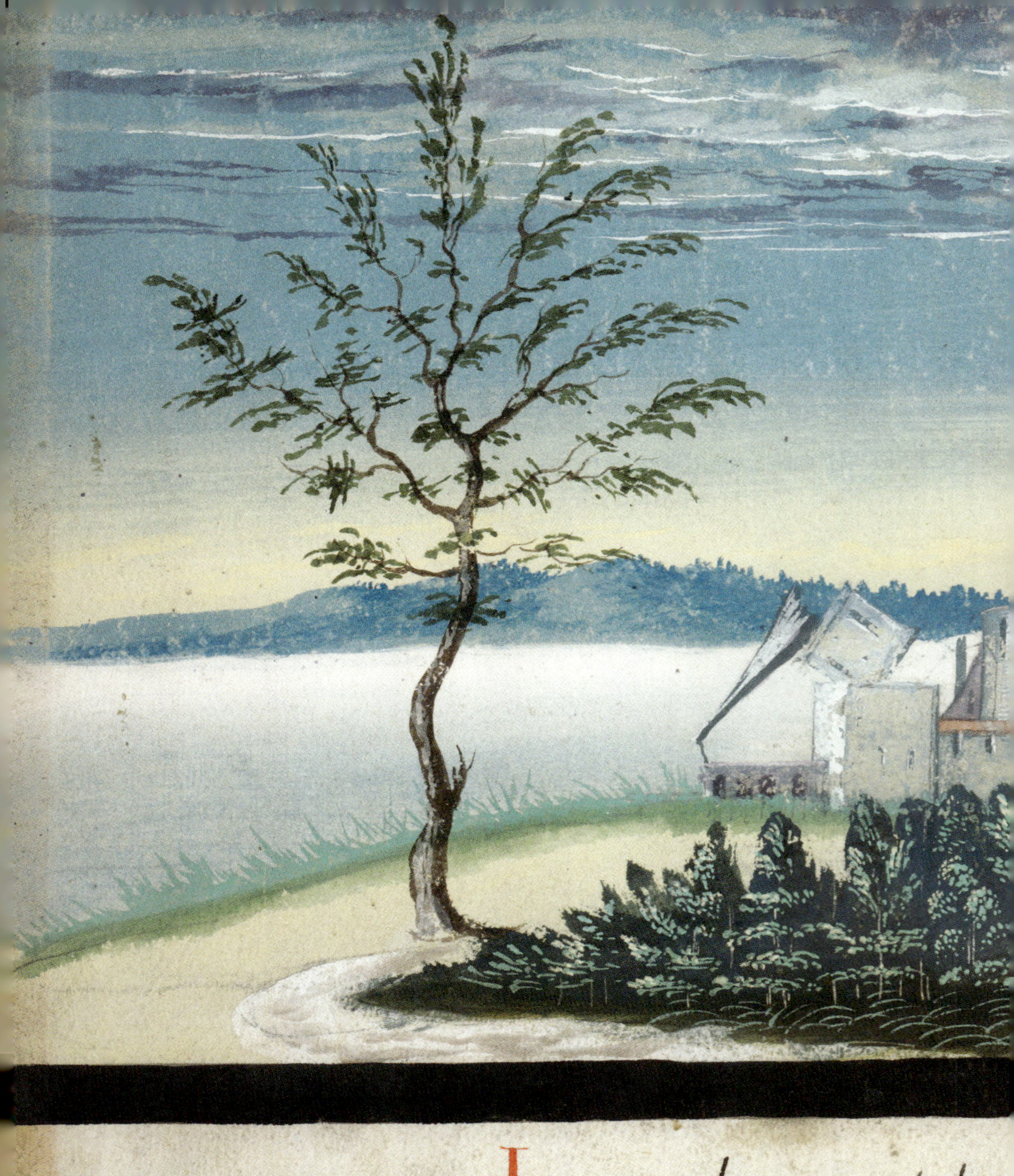

Im m ccc l vii iar nach chri
erbitrein gerissen, das fill g
leütt vmb kamen

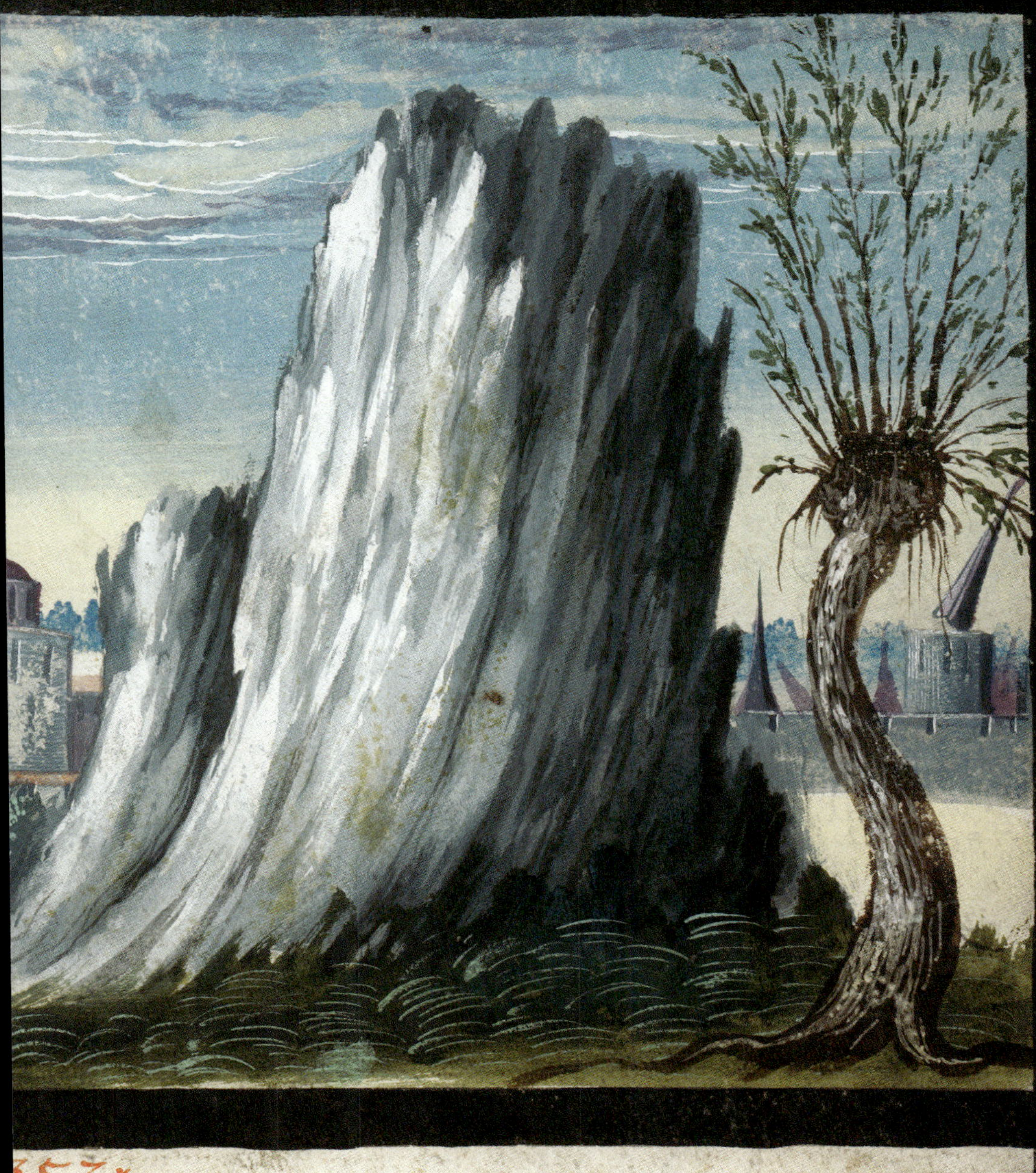

357.

epurt ist zu hispannien ein solcher
vnnd stet nider fillen vnnd vil

Im m ccc lx iar nach chr
finsternus der sonnen, d
vnnd gar finster, zu der

360 ·
rpürt, ward ein solche grose
r dri hellen tag nacht war
starb der pabst inocentius

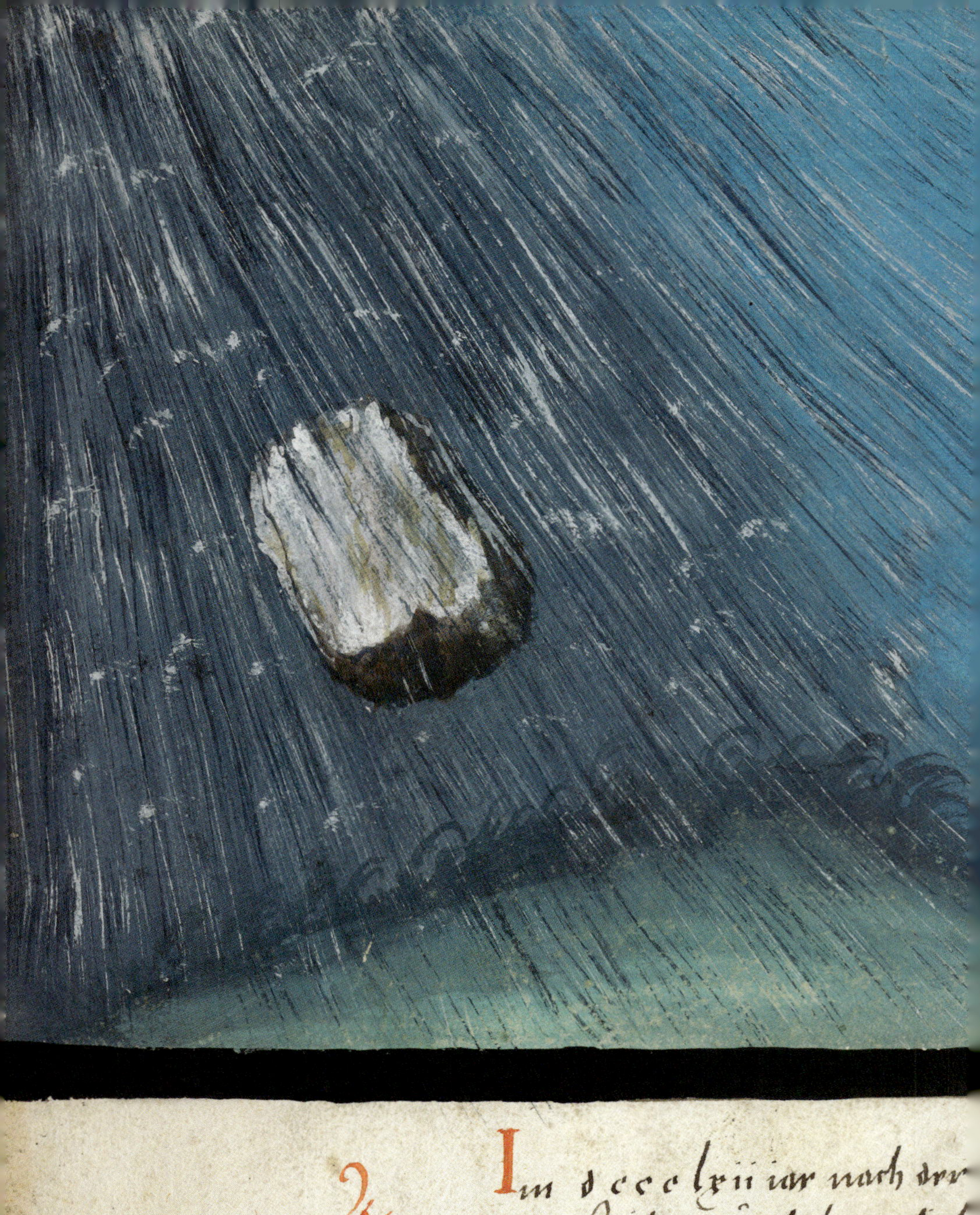

Im dccclxii iar nach der
des kaisers aus sachsen fiel
vom himel in grosem wind
er schinen blut farbe kreuzlei

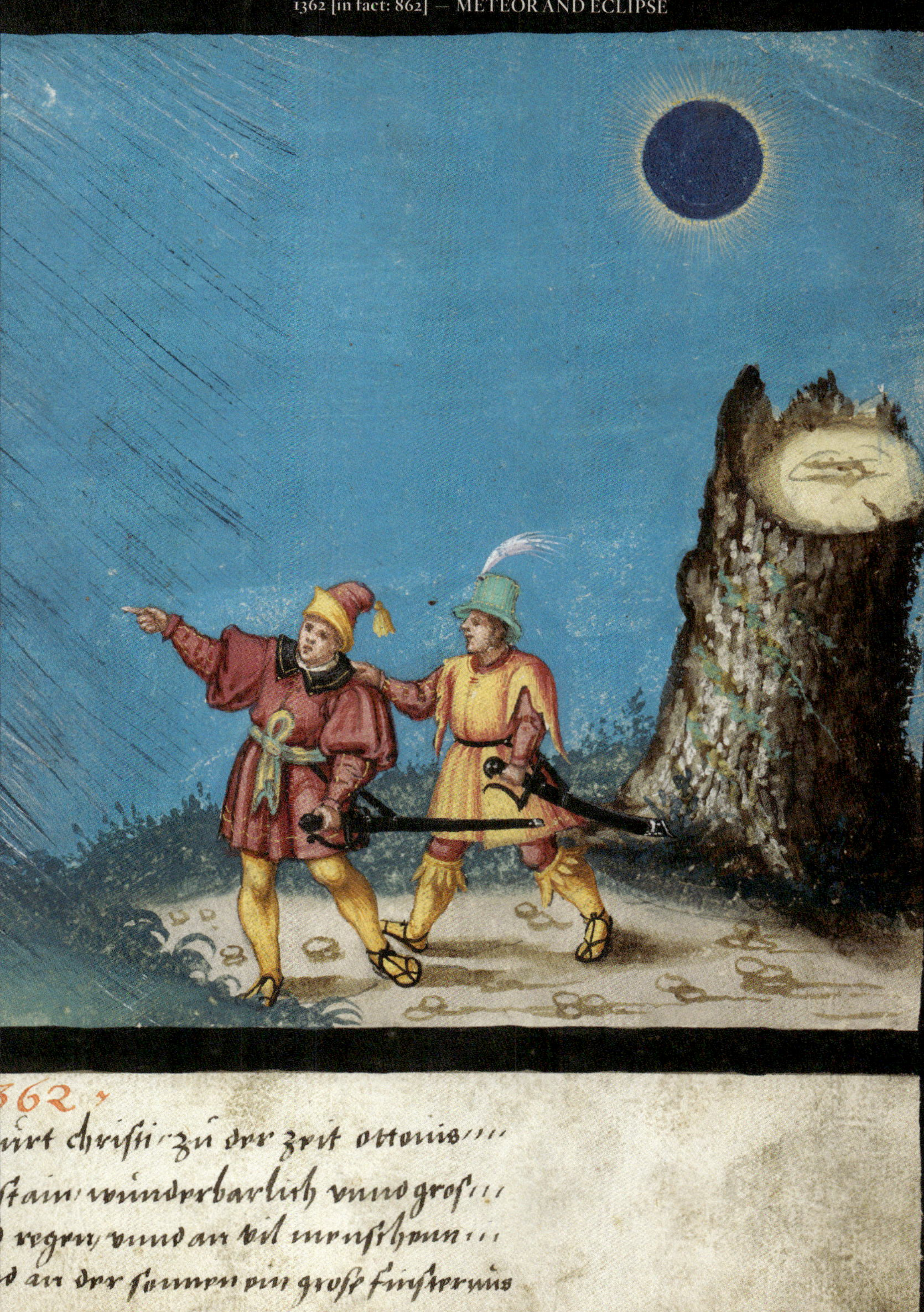
362 .
urt christi zu der zeit ottonis
stain wunderbarlich vnnd gros
regen vnnd an vil menschenn
d an der sonnen ein grose finsternus

Im d c c c lxiiii iar w
stadt/ drei tag vnnd w

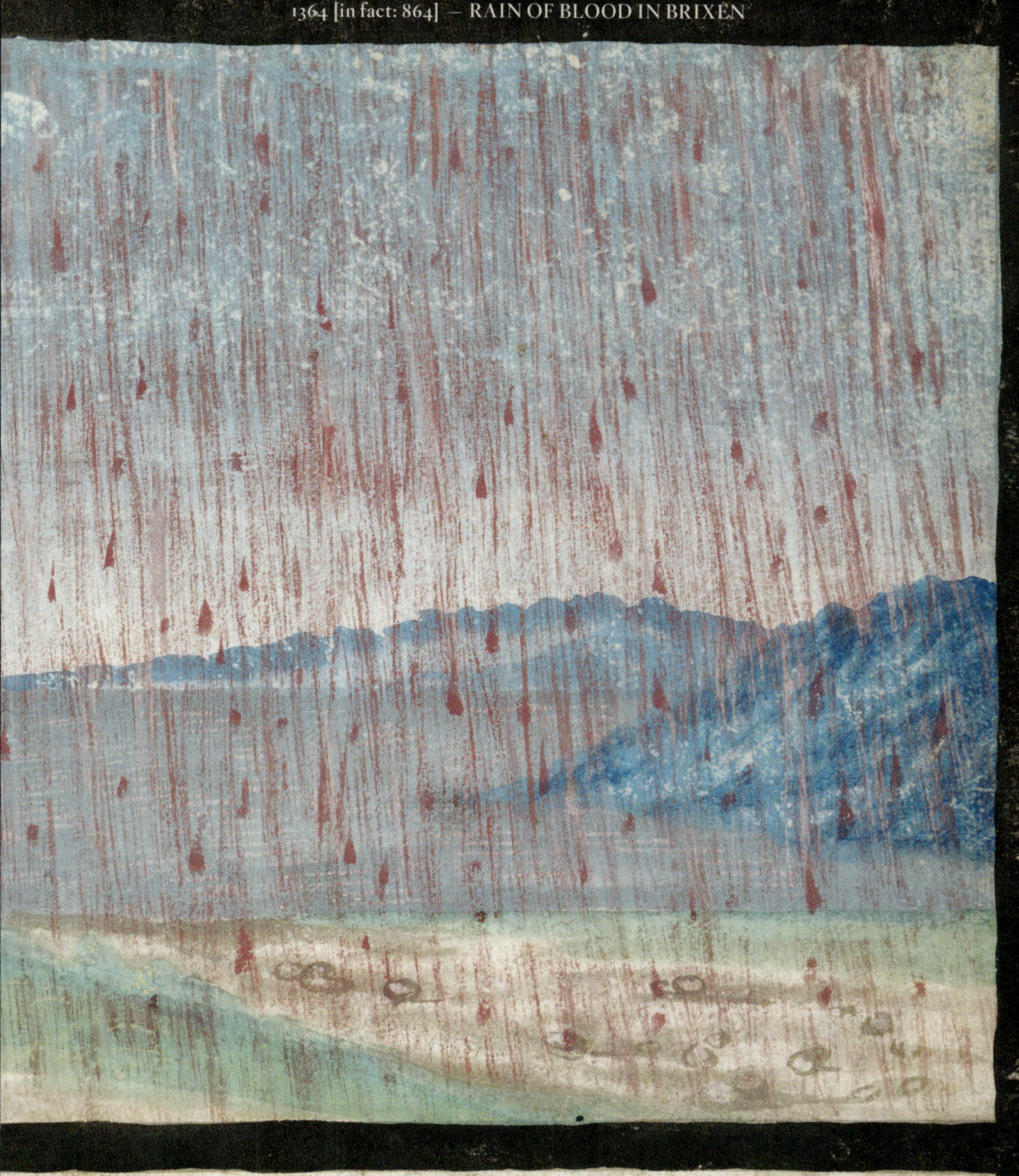

·1364·

christi gepürt/hat es bei der brixanischen

t blut gerengnet wie hir gemalt ist

FOL. 69

1360 — Eclipse
Sonnenfinsternis | Éclipse

In the year A.D. 1360, there was such a great darkening of the sun that in the full light of daytime it was night and completely dark. At this time, Pope Innocent died.

Im 1360. Jahr nach Christi Geburt ereignete sich eine solch große Finsternis der Sonne, dass es am helllichten Tag Nacht war und völlig finster. Zu der Zeit starb der Papst Innozenz.

En l'an 1360 après J.-C., le soleil fut tellement plongé dans l'obscurité qu'en pleine lumière du jour, il faisait nuit et complètement noir. C'est à cette époque que mourut le pape Innocent.

FOL. 70

1362 [in fact: 862] — Meteor and eclipse
Meteorit und Sonnenfinsternis | Météorite et éclipse

In the year A.D. 862, in the time of Otto [912–973], Duke of Saxony, a stone – large and wonderful – fell from the sky during heavy wind and rain. And upon many people, small blood-red crosses appeared and there was a great darkness upon the sun.

Im 862. Jahr nach der Geburt Christi, zu der Zeit Ottos [912–973], Herzog von Sachsen, fiel ein Stein – wunderbar und groß – in starkem Wind und Regen vom Himmel. Und an vielen Menschen erschienen kleine blutfarbene Kreuze und an der Sonne eine große Finsternis.

En l'an 862 après J.-C., au temps d'Otto [912–973], duc de Saxe, une pierre – grande et extraordinaire – tomba du ciel par une pluie et un vent forts. Et, sur beaucoup de gens, apparurent de petites croix rouge sang et une grande obscurité masqua le soleil.

FOL. 71

1364 [in fact: 864] — Rain of blood in Brixen
Blutregen in Brixen | Pluie de sang à Brixen

In the year A.D. 864, it rained blood near the city of Brixen for three days and nights, as is painted here.

Im 864. Jahr nach Christi Geburt hat es bei Brixen drei Tage und Nächte Blut geregnet, wie hier gemalt ist.

En l'an 864 après J.-C., il plut du sang près de la ville de Brixen pendant trois jours et trois nuits, comme le montre cette peinture.

FOL. 72

1364 [in fact: 864] — Plague of locusts in Gaul
Heuschreckenplage in Gallien | Invasion de locustes en Gaule

In the year A.D. 864, countless locusts with wings and two teeth – harder than a stone – flew about everywhere in Gaul and covered the ground like snow and afterwards flew into the sea all at once and drowned there. Afterwards the sea washed this vermin ashore and it caused a great stench so that many people died.

Im 864. Jahr nach Christi Geburt sind zahllose Heuschrecken mit Flügeln und zwei Zähnen – härter als ein Stein – in Gallien umhergeflogen und haben den Boden bedeckt wie der Schnee und sind danach auf einmal in das Meer geflogen und darin ertrunken. Danach hat sie das Meer an die Küste geworfen, und das Ungeziefer machte einen großen Gestank, sodass viele Leute starben.

En l'an 864 après J.-C., d'innombrables locustes ayant des ailes et deux dents – plus dures que la pierre – envahirent le ciel de Gaule et recouvrirent le sol comme de la neige et par la suite s'envolèrent pour plonger dans la mer toutes à la fois et s'y noyer. Ensuite la mer rejeta cette vermine sur le rivage et celle-ci émit une grande pestilence qui fit mourir beaucoup de gens.

FOL. 73

1383 — Cloudburst and flood
Wolkenbruch und Überschwemmung | Averse diluvienne et inondation

In the year A.D. 1383, on St James's Day, a cloudburst broke over the imperial city [according to Franck 1531: Giengen an der Brenz] so that everyone thought they were going to die. Then the water carried off the houses and swept away the buildings. In the year before there was no wind in Germany and the grain was really cheap.

Im 1383. Jahr nach Christi Geburt, am Sankt-Jakobstag, da ging ein Wolkenbruch in der Reichsstadt nieder [laut Franck 1531: Giengen an der Brenz], dass jedermann zu sterben glaubte. Denn das Wasser nahm die Häuser mit sich und riss die Gebäude fort. In dem Jahr davor gab es keinen Wind in Deutschland, und das Korn war ganz billig.

En l'an 1383 après J.-C., le jour de la Saint-Jacques, une forte averse s'abattit sur la ville impériale [Giengen an der Brenz, selon Franck 1531] et chacun crut qu'il allait mourir. Puis les eaux emportèrent les maisons et balayèrent les constructions. L'année précédente, il n'y avait pas eu de vent en Allemagne et le grain était fort bon marché.

Im d ccc lxiiii iar nach christi gep
zwairn, zenen, herter dan ein st
wir der schne darnach vners ma
darnach hats das wrer an das g
grosen gestanckt das vill volcks

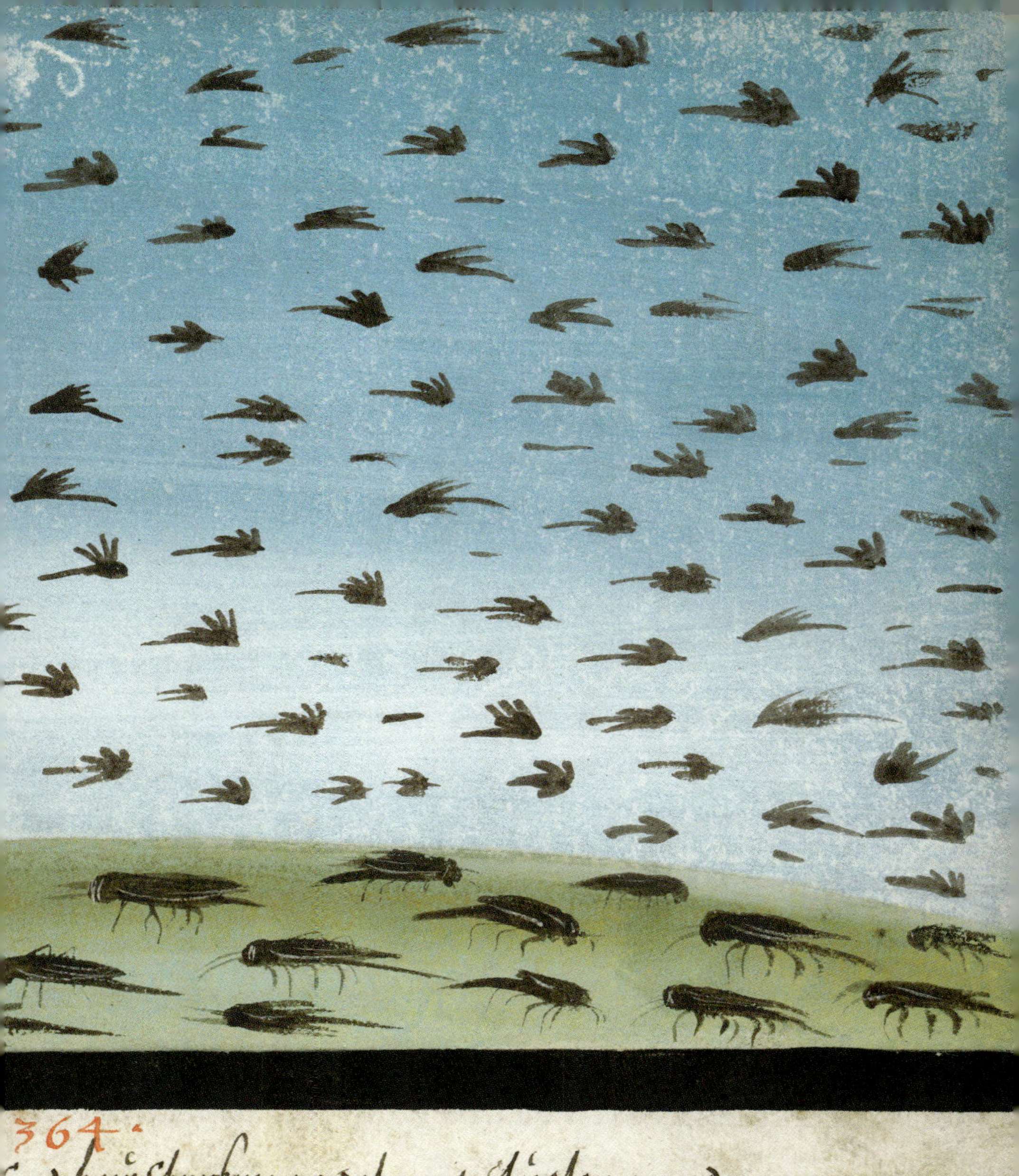

364.

end hew schrecken · an zal · mit fluglen vnnd
in gallia geflogen vnd das erdrich bedeckt ·
das merr geflogen vnd dar in erdrincken
t geworffen : vnd das vnzifer machet ain
b

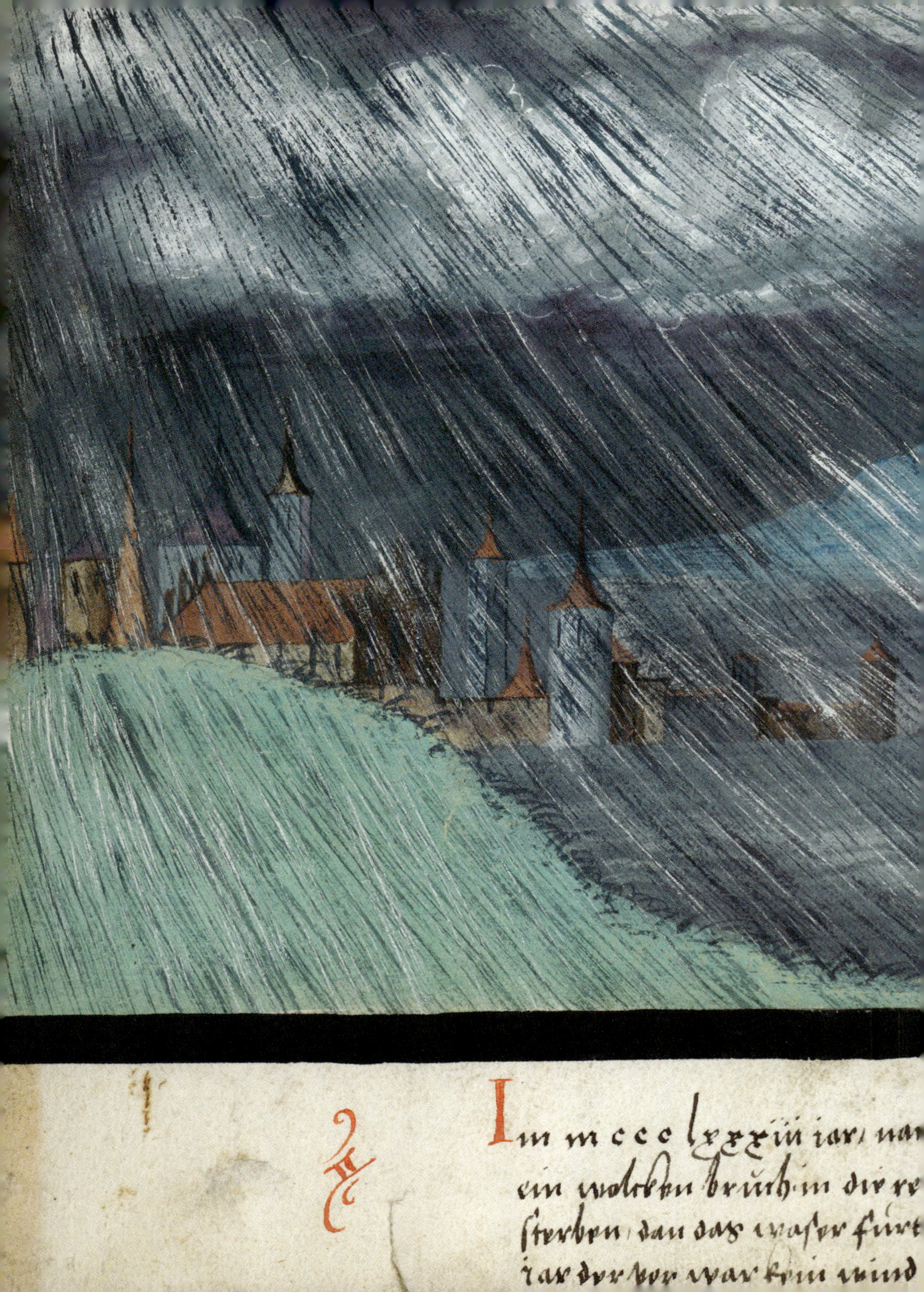
Im mccclxxxiiii iar, nam
ein wolcken bruch in dir re
sterben, dan das wasser fuirt
iar der vor war kein wind

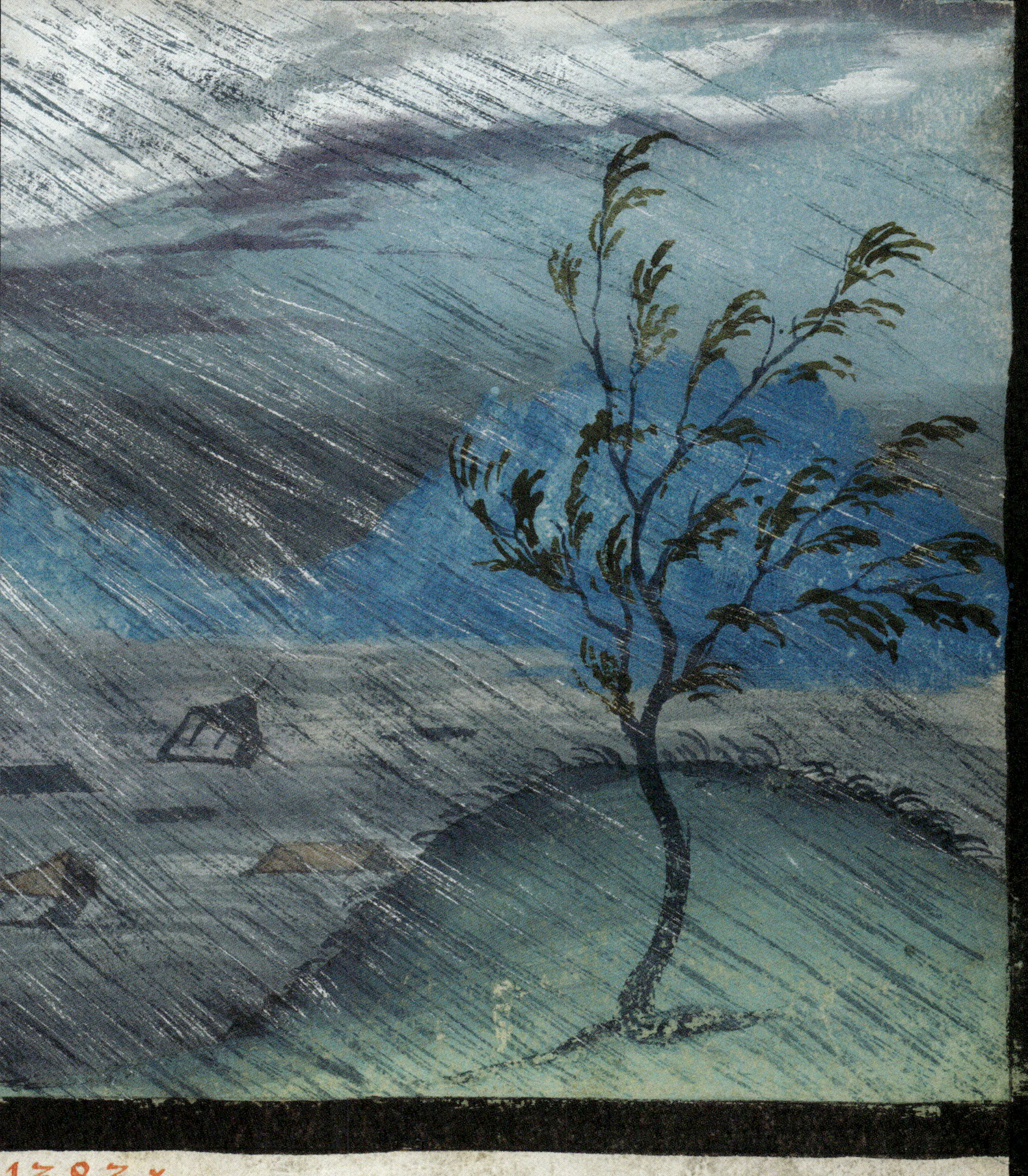

1383.

risti gepurt an sant iacobs tag da kam
at gewegen. das sich yederman versach zu
heuser hin weg vnd riss die gepeü in dem
eutschland vnd war das korn gar wolfail

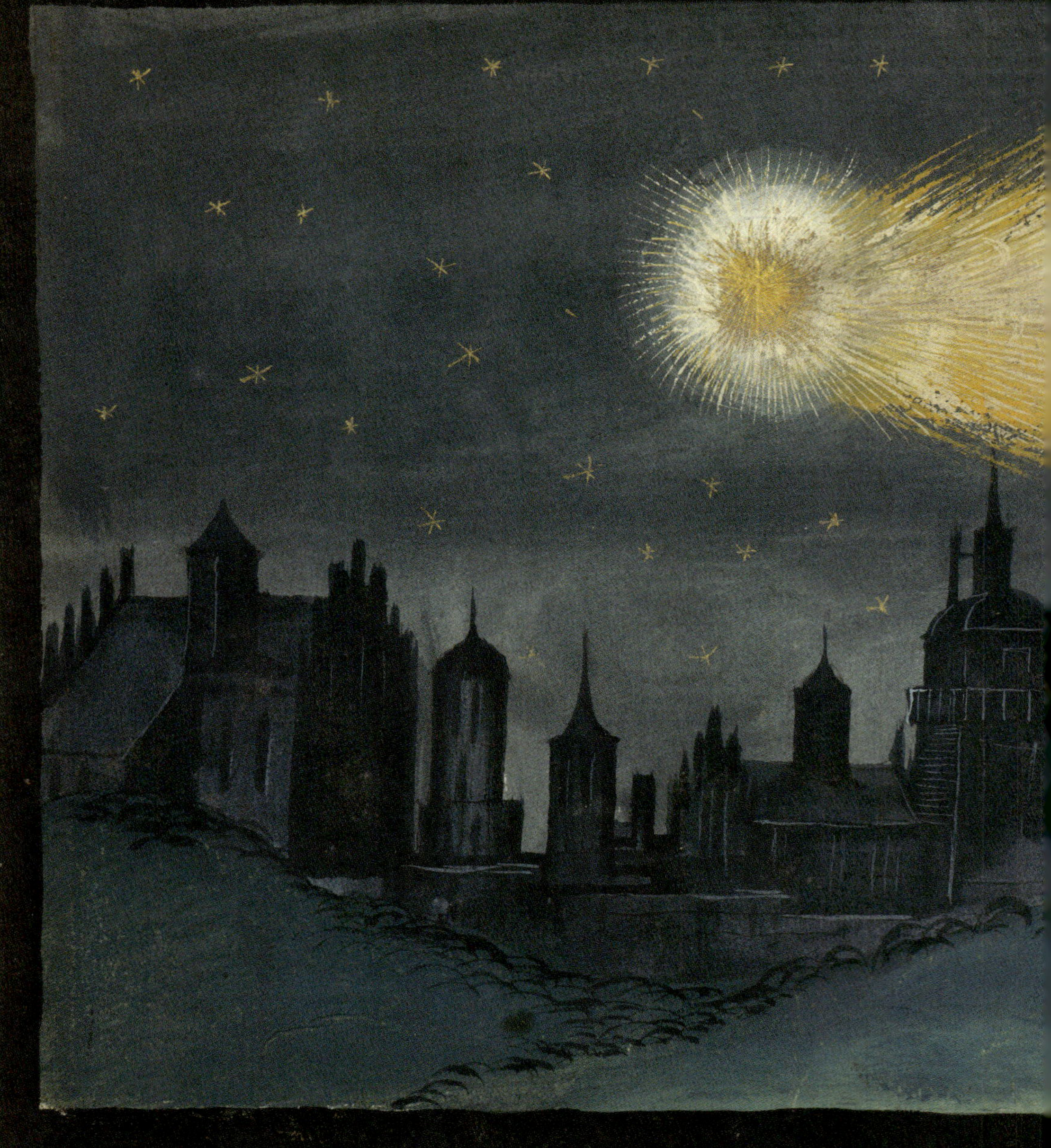

Im m cccc i iar nach chri
mit einem pfawen schwa
folget ein groser merckl

-01

purt: er schin ein grosser commet
n hirmet/ im tüschland/ darnach;
: pestilentz im schwaben land : :

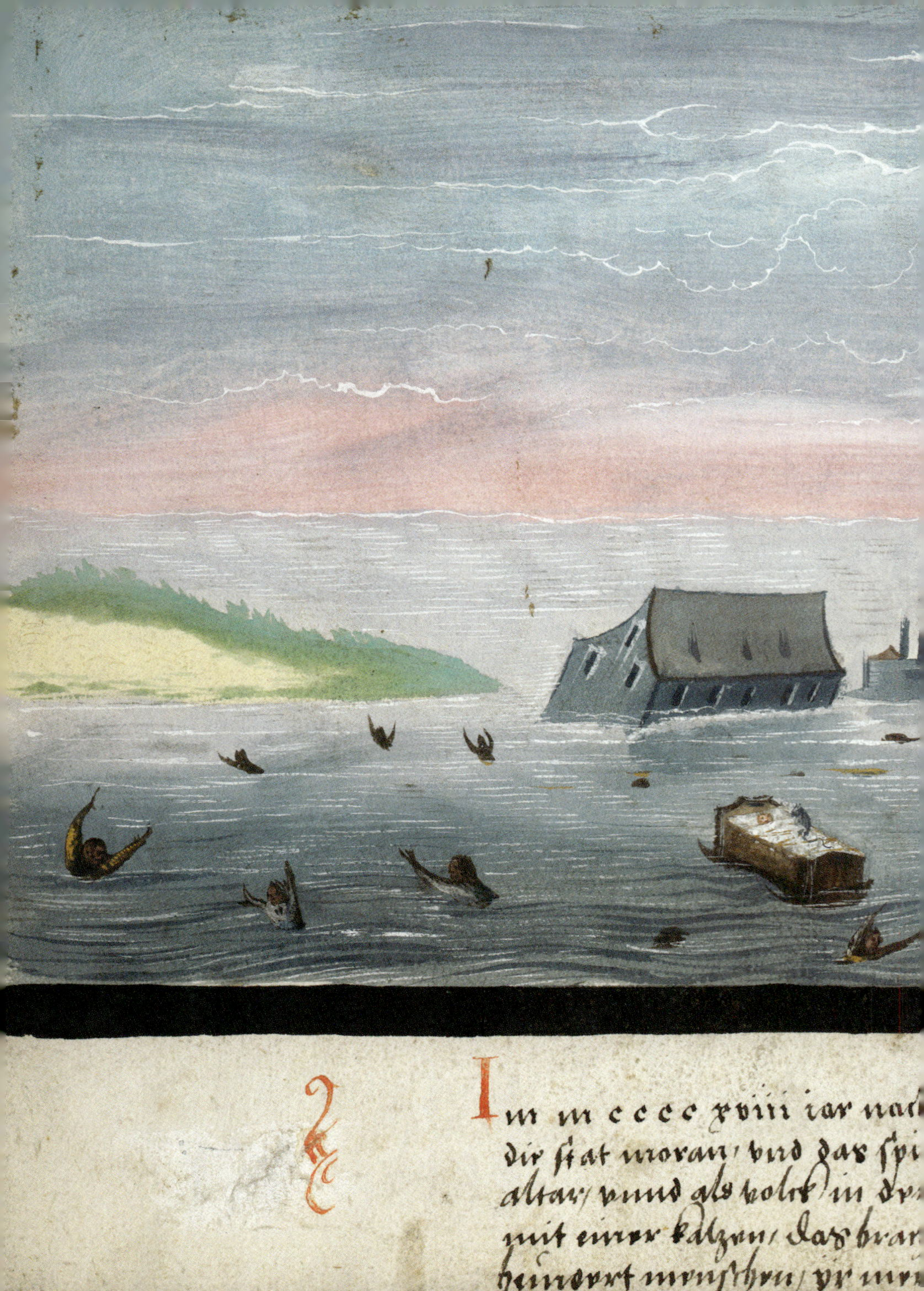
Im m cccc xviii iar nac
dir ſtat moran, vnd das ſpi
altar, vnnd als volck in dr
mit einer katzen, das bran
hundert menſchen, yr mri

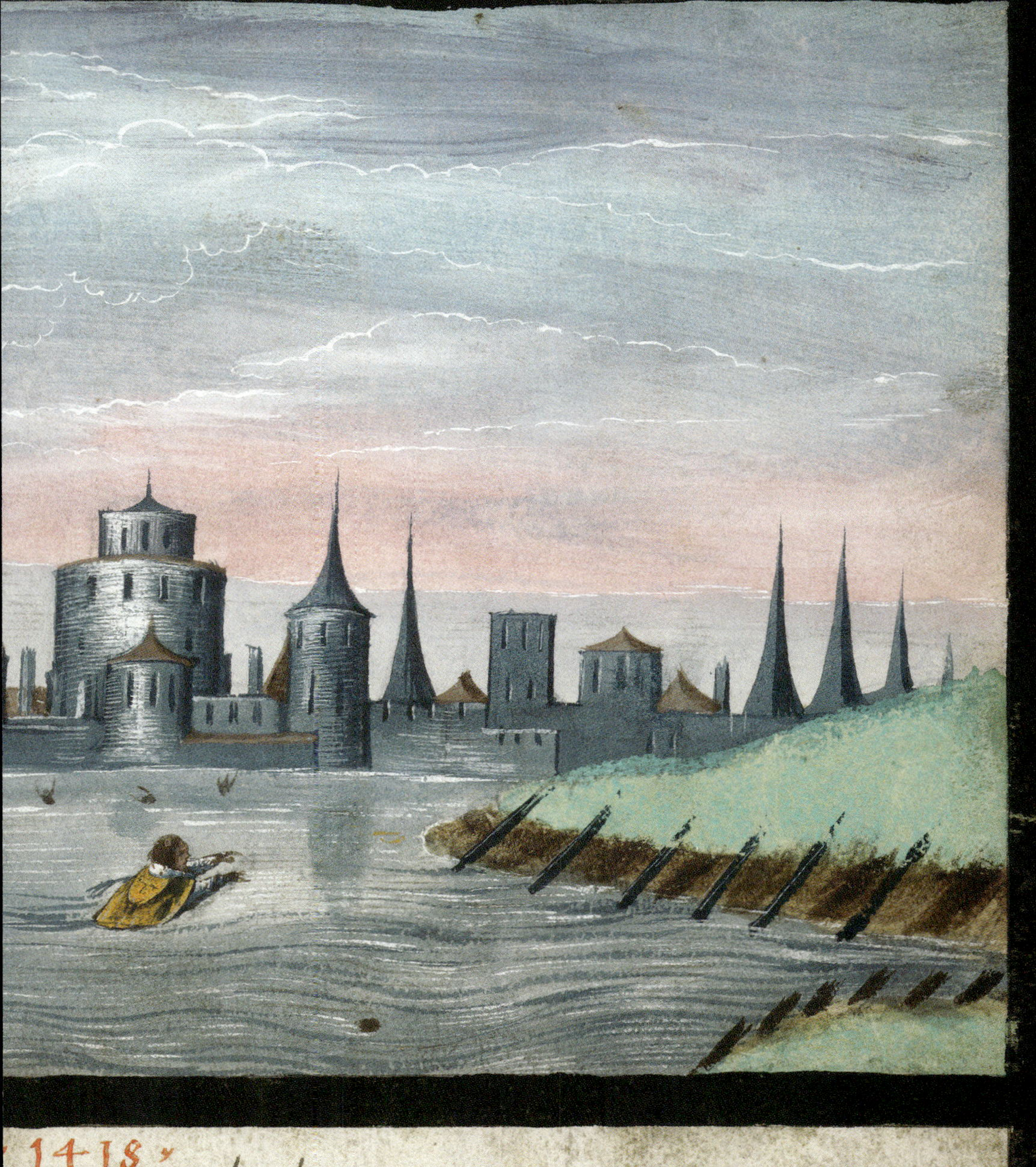

1418

risti gepurt / brach der see bey moran ab vnnd er riss
ar vor / mit sampt der kirchen / den pfaffen ob dem
chen / vnd ein kindt schwam daher in ainer wiegen
an zu polen dar von / sunst ver dorben bei vier
weniger / etc

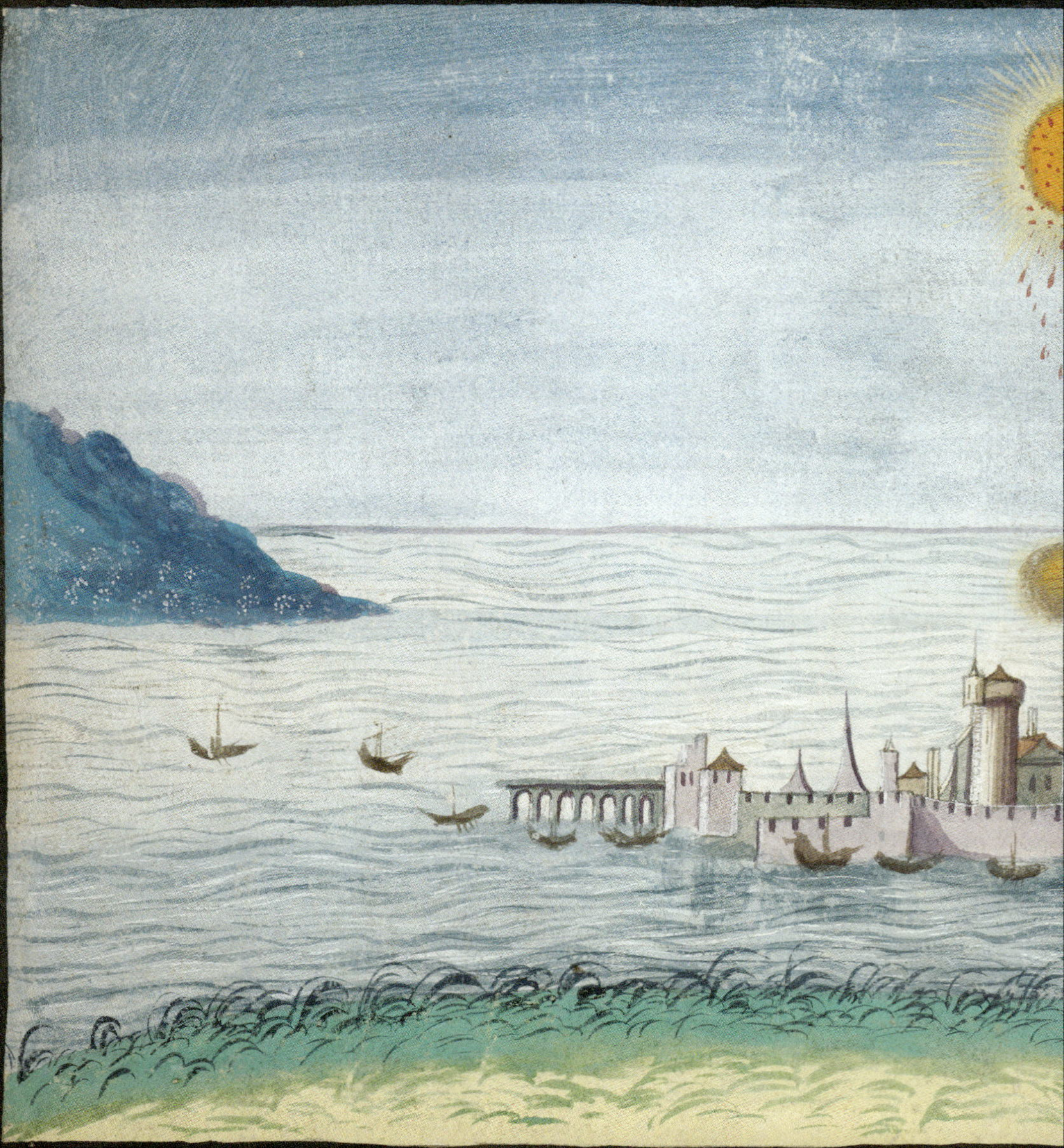

Im d c c c c xxxviii iar·
sonnen· als blutt schwitzet
vnnd anders wo der gesch

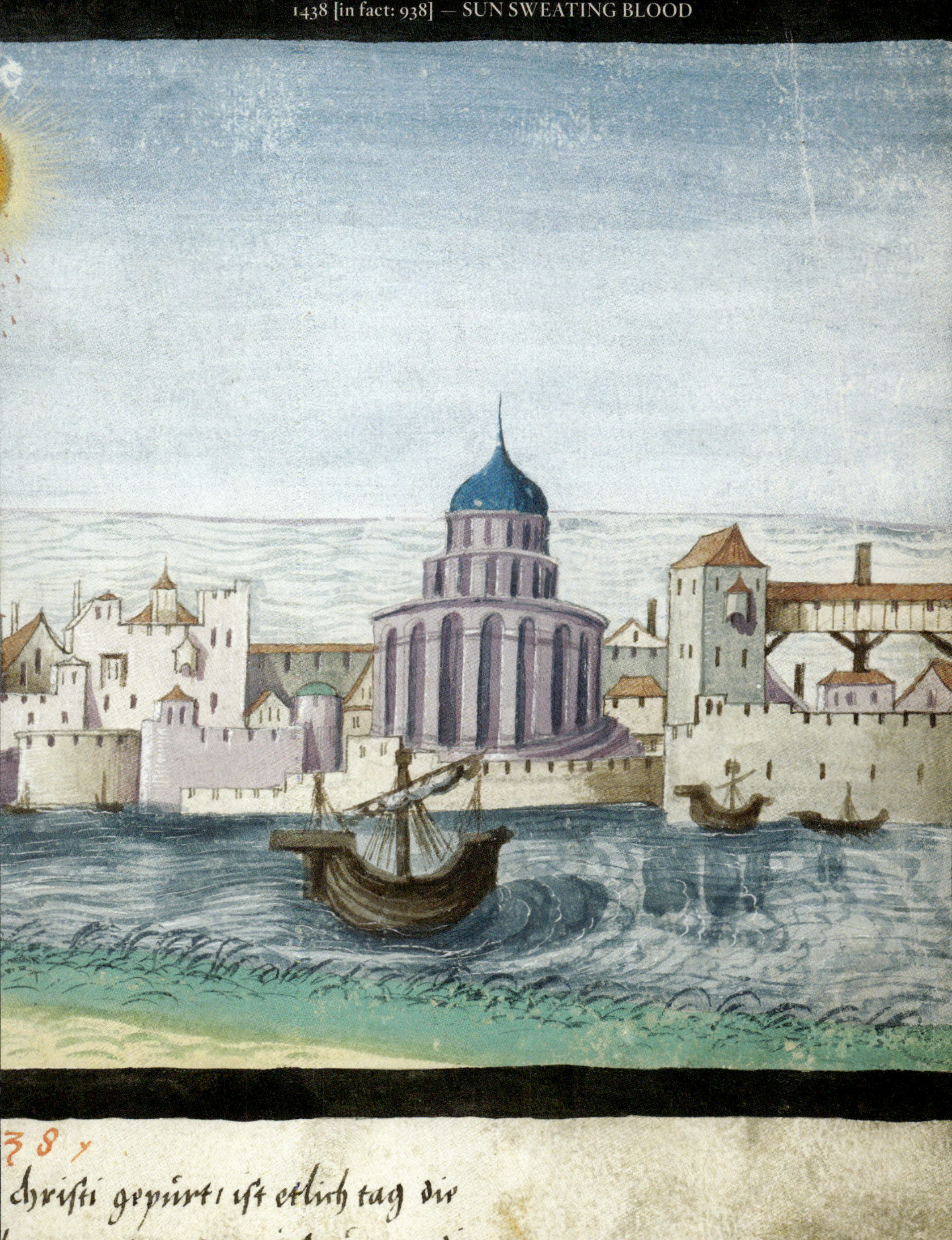
38
christi gepurt, ist etlich tag dir
hen worden, dar auf zu venedig
gefolgt hat

FOL. 74

1401 — Comet | Komet | Comète

In the year A.D. 1401, a large comet with a peacock tail appeared in the sky over Germany. This was followed by a most severe plague in Swabia.

Im 1401. Jahr nach Christi Geburt erschien ein großer Komet mit einem Pfauenschweif am Himmel in Deutschland. Danach folgte eine große, schlimme Seuche im Schwabenland.

En l'an 1401 après J.-C., une grande comète dotée d'une queue de paon apparut dans le ciel d'Allemagne. S'ensuivit une très grave peste en Souabe.

FOL. 75

1418 — Flood near Meran
Überschwemmung bei Meran | Inondation près de Merano

In the year A.D. 1418, the lake near Merano overflowed its shores and swept away the city of Merano and the hospital on its near side, along with the church, the priest at the altar and all the people in the church. And a child was floating off in a cradle along with a cat. It was rescued in Bozen. Apart from this, some four hundred people died – probably more rather than fewer etc.

Im 1418. Jahr nach Christi Geburt trat der See bei Meran über die Ufer, und er riss die Stadt Meran fort und das Spital davor mitsamt der Kirche, dem Priester an dem Altar und allen Leuten in der Kirche. Und ein Kind schwamm daher in einer Wiege mit einer Katze. Das rettete man in Bozen. Sonst starben etwa vierhundert Menschen – eher mehr von ihnen als weniger etc.

En l'an 1418 après J.-C., le lac situé près de Merano déborda et balaya la ville de Merano et l'hôpital qui se trouvait tout près, ainsi que l'église, le prêtre à l'autel et tous les fidèles de l'église. Et un enfant flottait dans un berceau avec un chat. Il fut sauvé à Bozen. En outre, environ quatre cents personnes périrent, sinon plus, etc.

FOL. 76

1438 [in fact: 938] — Sun sweating blood
Blut schwitzende Sonne | Le soleil sue du sang

In the year A.D. 938, the sun was seen to be sweating blood for several days. This was followed by sudden deaths in Venice and other places.

Im 938. Jahr nach Christi Geburt ist etliche Tage die Sonne Blut schwitzend gesehen worden. Darauf ist zu Venedig und anderswo der jähe Tod gefolgt.

En l'an 938 après J.-C., on vit le soleil suer du sang pendant plusieurs jours. S'ensuivirent des morts soudaines à Venise et ailleurs.

FOL. 77

1448 — Eclipse | Sonnenfinsternis | Éclipse

In the year 1448, on the first day of September, at the sixth hour before midday, a darkening of the sun – just as painted here – was seen. This was followed by great outbreaks of war and bloodshed, murder, looting and tyranny in England, France, Spain and Flanders, Apulia in Italy and Germany. Great misfortune also befell the Greeks at the hands of the Turks.

Im 1448. Jahr, am ersten Tag des Septembers, in der sechsten Stunde vor Mittag Uhr, ist eine Finsternis der Sonne – wie dann hier gemalt – gesehen worden. Danach sind großer Krieg und Blutvergießen, Mord, Raub und Tyrannei in England, Frankreich, Spanien und Flandern, Apulien in Italien und Deutsch land gefolgt. Auch geschah den Griechen durch die Türken großer Schaden.

En l'an 1448, le premier jour de septembre, à la sixième heure avant midi, on observa une grande obscurité noyer le soleil, comme dans cette peinture. S'ensuivirent de grandes guerres avec bain de sang, assassinats, pillage et tyrannie en Angleterre, en France, en Espagne, en Flandre, en Apulie (en Italie) et en Allemagne. De grands malheurs s'abattirent aussi sur les Grecs de la main des Turcs.

FOL. 78

1448 — Hail in Augsburg | Hagel in Augsburg | Grêle à Augsbourg

In the year 1448, on the fifth of September, on St Matthew's Day, two similar hailstorms fell on Augsburg within half a quarter of an hour of each other. In the first there were stones resembling a lot [c. 120 g] hen's or goose eggs, that in fact weighed half a pound. The other hailstorm passed by a quarter of a mile away. And in the same year, wine and grain were cheap – one bottle of Alsace for 5 pfennigs or 4, a bottle of Neckar wine for 2 or 3 pfennigs, one tub of hulled grain for 20 groschen, the spelty grain for 13 gro[schen], oats for 9 groschen.

Im 1448. Jahr, am fünften September, am Sankt-Matthäus-Tag, gingen zwei gleichartige Hagel eine halbe Viertelstunde nacheinander über Augsburg nieder. Im ersten waren Steine von etwa acht Lot [ca. 120 g] wie Hühnereier und Gänseeier, die halbpfündig waren. Der andere Hagel ist eine Viertelmeile davon entfernt vorübergezogen. Und in demselben Jahr sind Wein und Korn billig gewesen – ein Maß Elsässer für 5 Pfennig und für 4, ein Maß Neckar für 2 und 3 Pfennig, ein Schaff entspelztes Getreide für 20 Groschen, das spelzige Getreide für 13 Gro[schen], den Hafer für 9 Groschen.

En l'an 1448, le cinquième jour de septembre, jour de la Saint-Matthieu, deux orages de grêle identiques s'abattirent sur Augsbourg à un demi-quart d'heure d'intervalle. Dans le premier, les grêlons étaient gros de huit lots (env. 120 g) comme des œufs de poule ou d'oie, c'est-à-dire une demi-livre. L'autre orage passa à un quart de mille de là. Et, la même année, le vin et le grain étaient bon marché : une bouteille d'Alsace pour 5 pfennigs ou 4, une bouteille de Neckar pour 2 ou 3 pfennigs, un tonneau de grain mondé pour 20 groschen, le grain proprement dit pour 13 gro[schen], l'avoine pour 9 groschen.

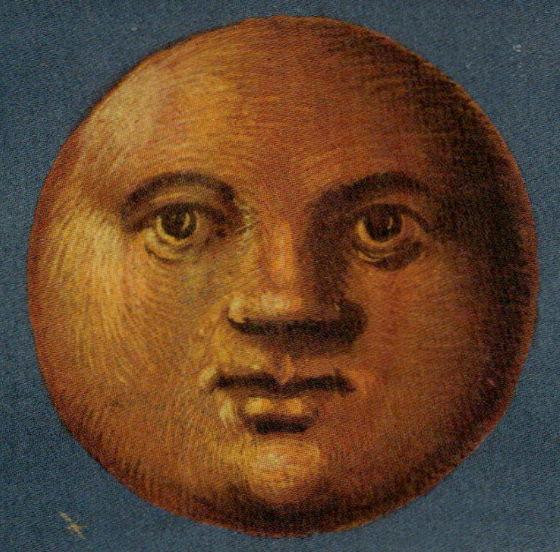

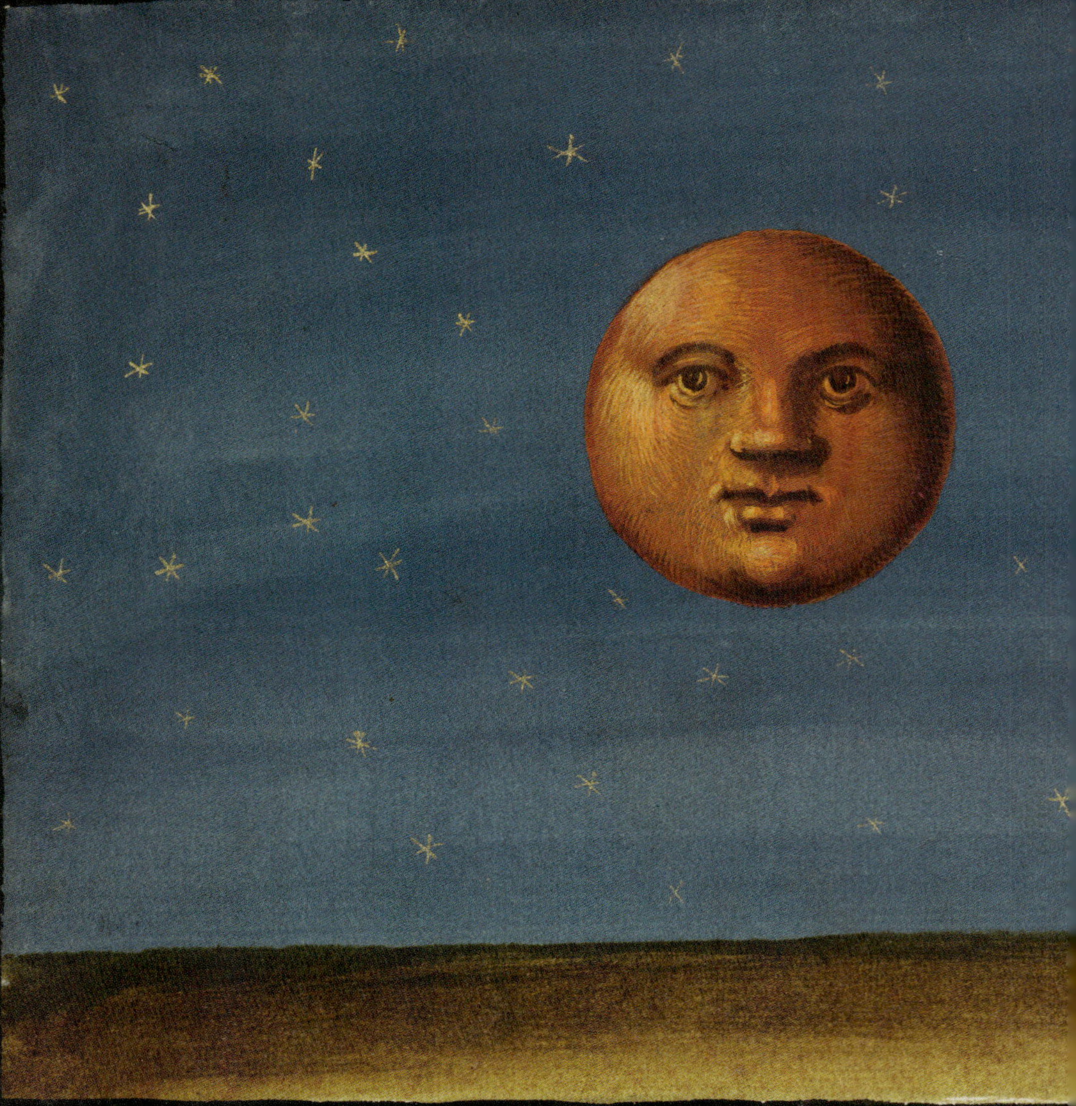

144

Im mcccc xxxxviii Jar am ersten tag Septem
der sonnen wie dan hie gemolt/ geschehen wor
ver giessen zu engelland franckreich spannien
dar inert rab vnnd Thirannei/ auch beschach de

or mittag vnnd sechs vhr ist ein finsternus
ar nach ist gefolget grosser krieg vnnd blut
d flandern appollo Jttalia vnnd teutzsland
iehen vom turcken grosser schaden ……

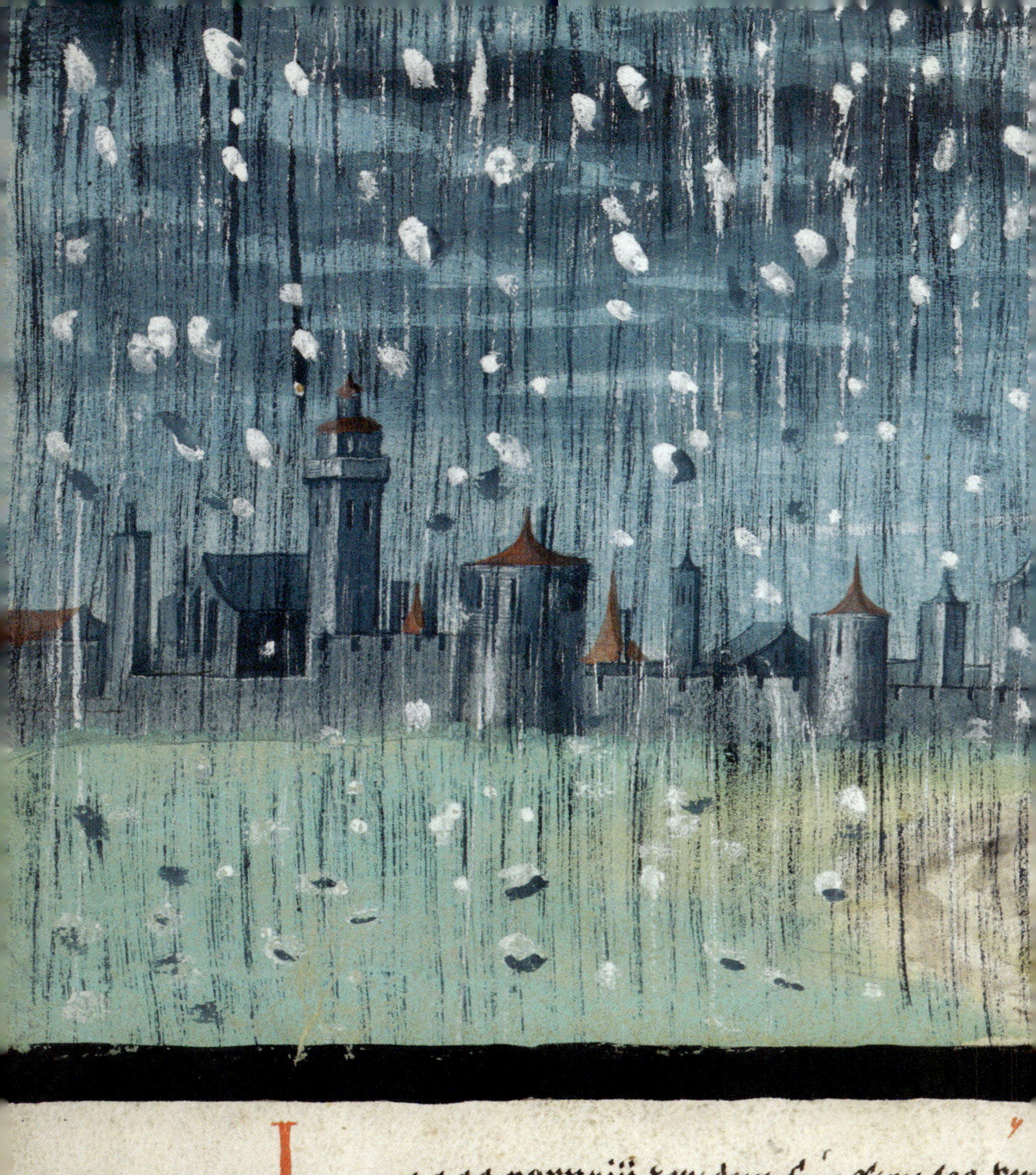

Im m c c c c xxxx viii Jar: dem fünfften tag Sep
augspurg ein halbe viertel stund nach einem
wie die gans air die halb pfündig gewesen sin
vom: vnnd in dem selbigen Jar ist wein vnnd k
vmb iiii ain mas necker wein vmb ii vnd iii pfen
den haber vmb ix groschen

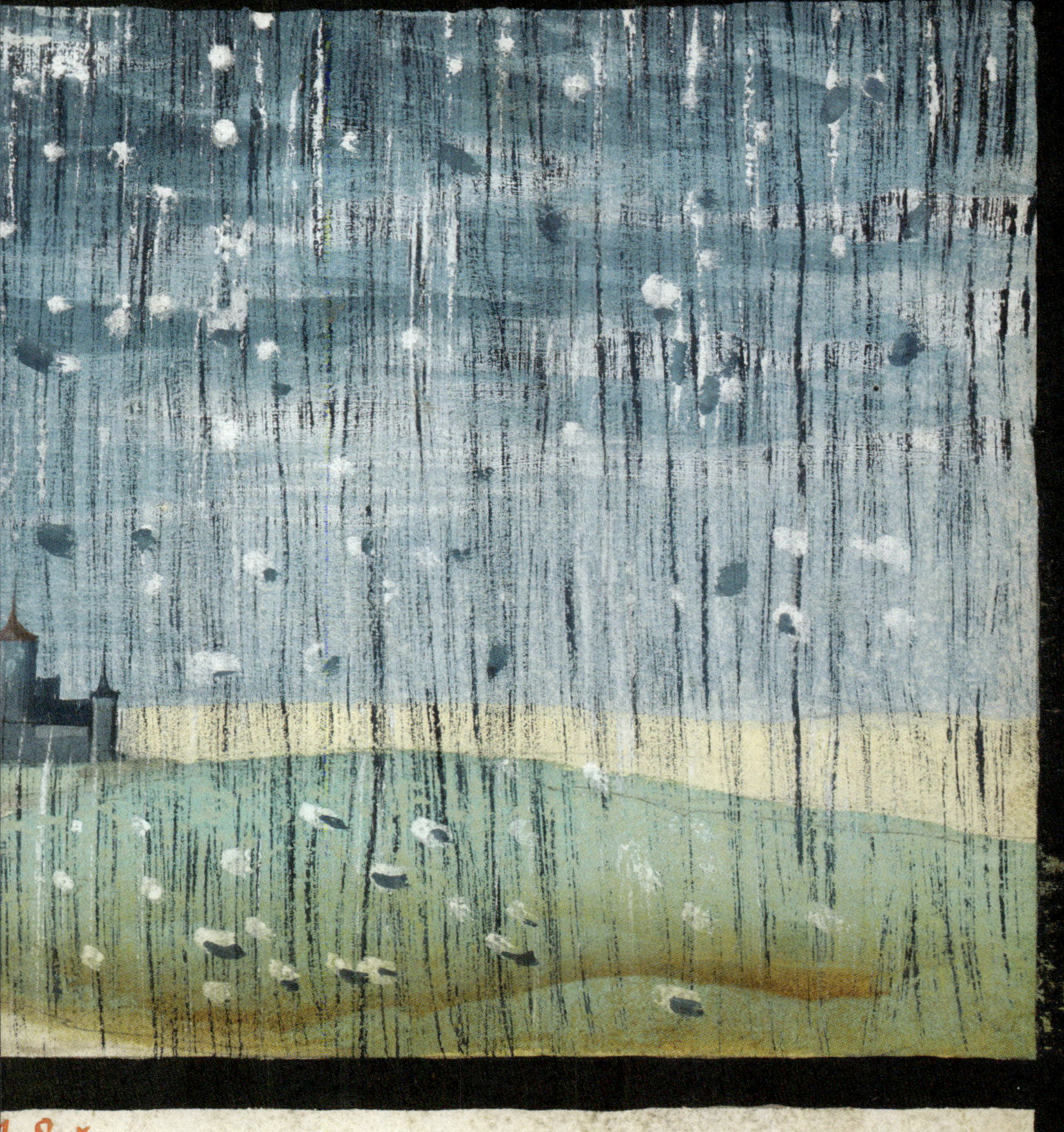

48 ·

er an sanct matheus tag giengen zwen gleich hagel über
s im ersten stain bey acht lotten wie die henne air / unnd
nder hagel ist für über gangen / ein fiertel meil dar
wollfail gewessen / ein maß elsesser umb v pfennig unnd
ain schaff kern umb xx groschen das korn umb xiii gro:

Im m cccclvi zar in
vnnd vber ain iar noch
das in teutzsland gesch

1456

monnet Juni erschin ein commet
rosserer der gar erschrocken lich sahe
worden: wie hie gemalt ist

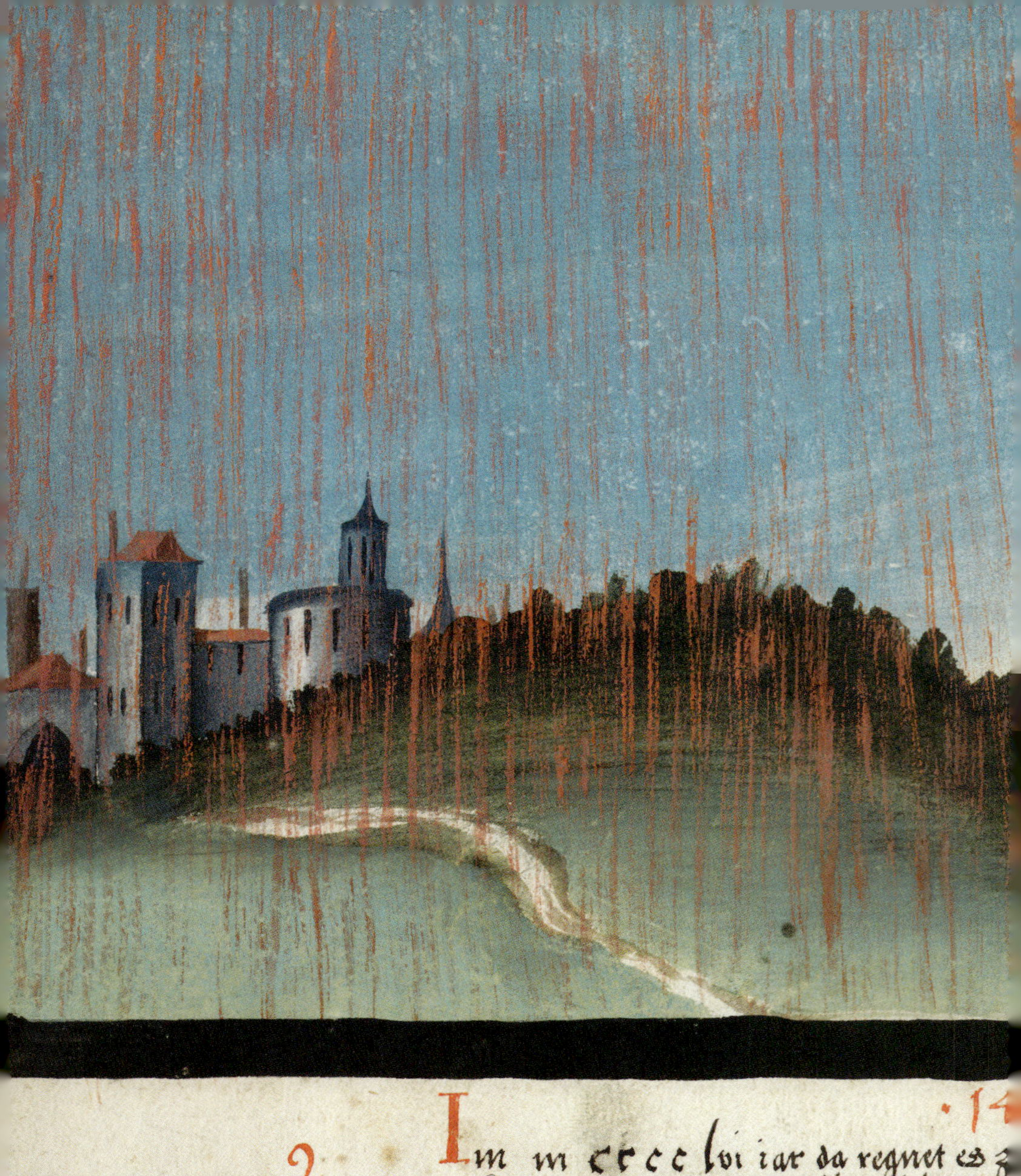

·14

Im m cccc lvi iar da regnet es z
Liguria regnet es flaisch welchs dan
hie gemalet ist·

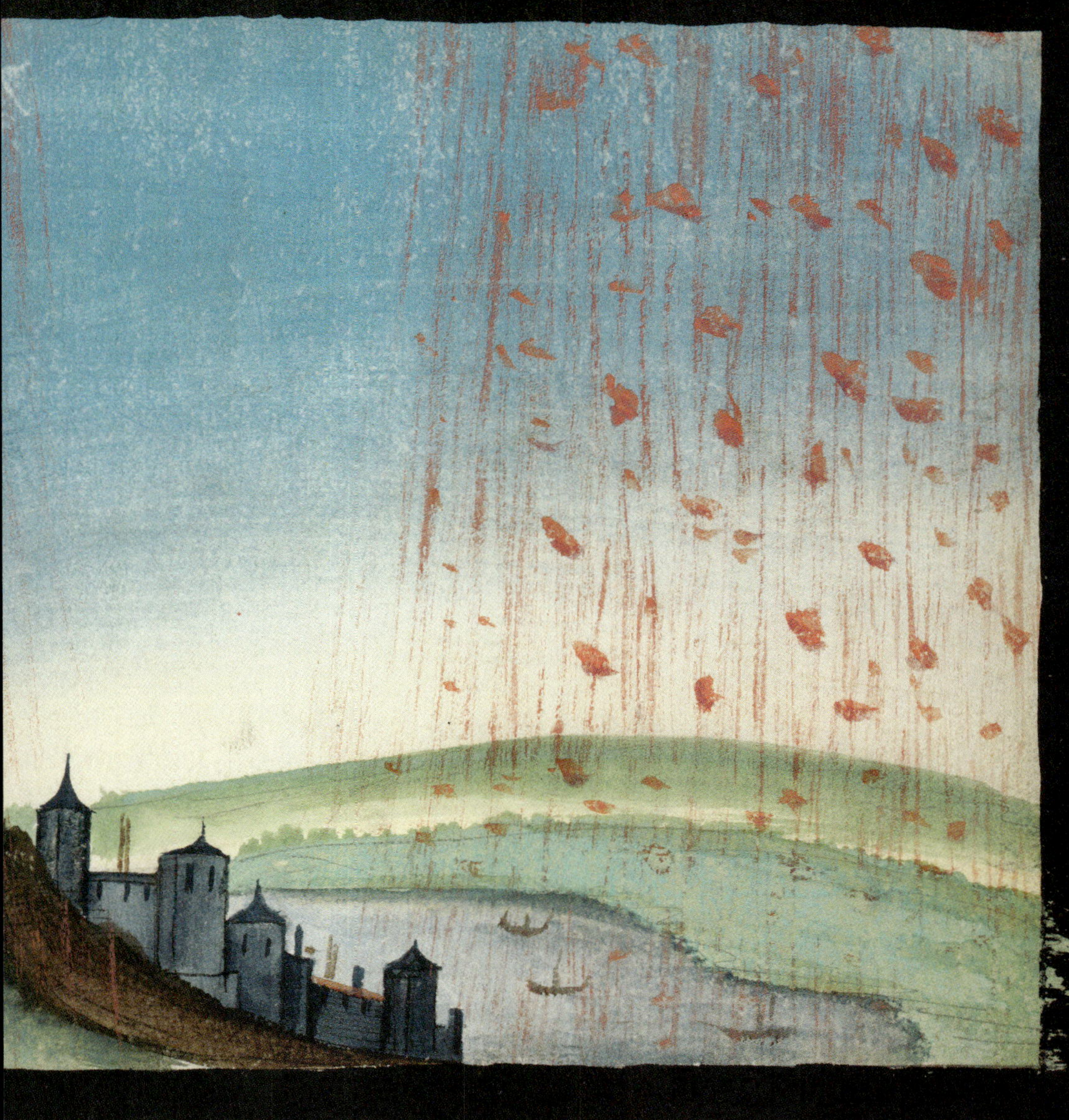

6 ×

n recht plůt vnnd in dem lannd

derbarlich gewessen ist wir dan

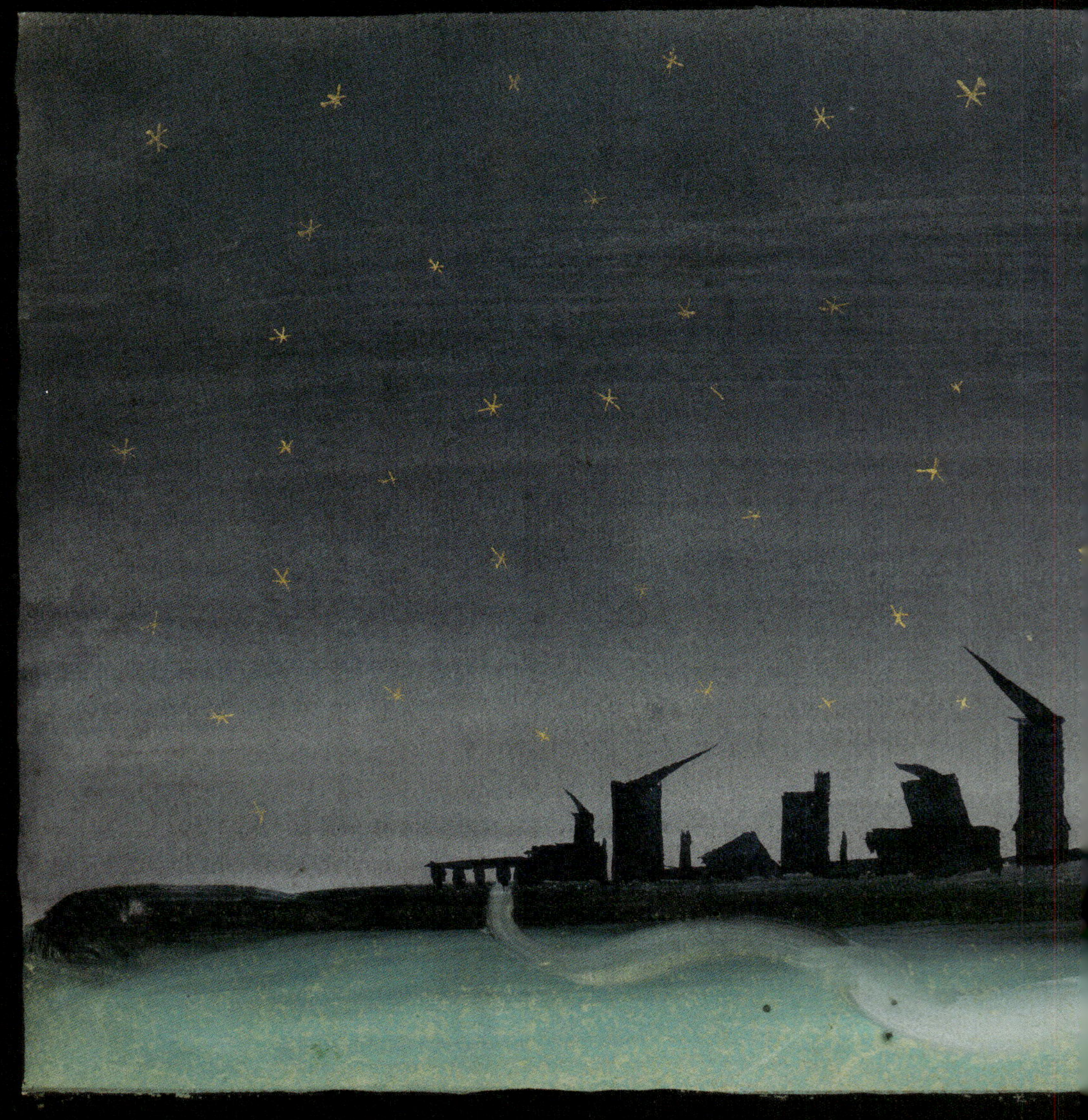

Im m c c c c lvi Jar den sechsten
hatt es solch grausam erbiden geh
ander steten, der gleichen bei men
fallen sind viel kirchen, unnd g
verfallen unnd verderben unn

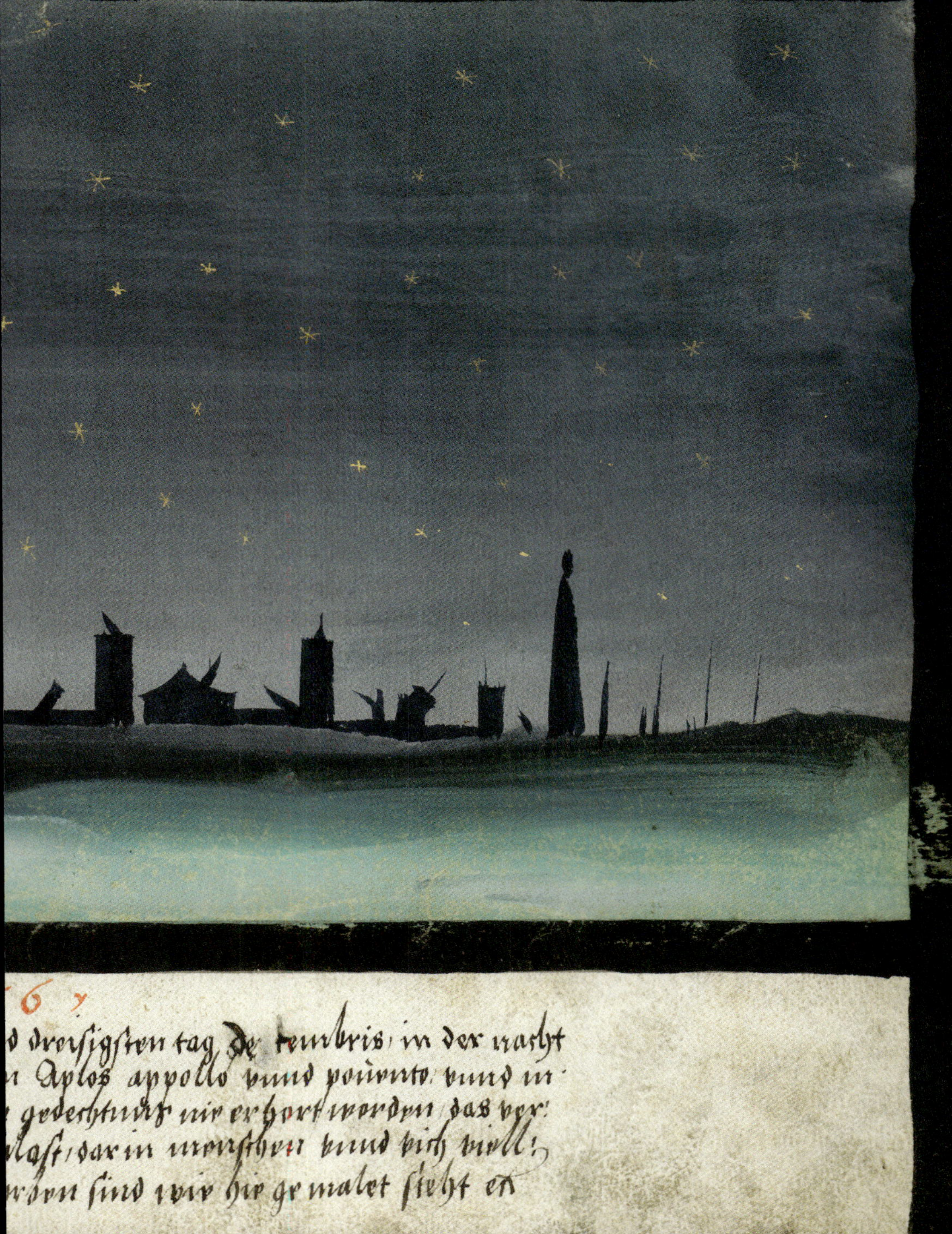

67

d dreissigsten tag decembris in der nacht
n Aplos appollo vnnd porvnto vnnd in
gedechtnus nie erhort worden das ver:
slast dar in menschen vnnd vich viell:
rden sind wie hie ge malet steht en

FOL. 79

1456 — Comets in Germany
Kometen in Deutschland | Comètes en Allemagne

In the year 1456, in the month of June, a comet appeared and within a year of that a yet bigger one, which looked really terrible, and was seen in Germany, just as it is painted here.

Im 1456. Jahr, im Monat Juni, erschien ein Komet und während eines Jahres noch ein größerer, der ganz schrecklich aussah, was in Deutschland gesehen worden ist, wie hier gemalt ist.

En l'an 1456, au mois de juin, une comète apparut et, pendant cette année-là, il y en eut une autre encore plus grosse, qui avait l'air vraiment terrible et qui fut observée en Allemagne, comme dans cette peinture.

FOL. 81

1456 — Rain of blood and of flesh
Blut- und Fleischregen | Pluie de sang et de viande

In the year 1456 it rained real blood in Rome and in the region of Liguria it rained flesh, which at that time was wondrous, even as it is painted here.

Im 1456. Jahr regnete es zu Rom wahrhaft Blut, und in dem Land Ligurien regnete es Fleisch, welches damals wundersam gewesen ist, wie dann hier gemalt ist.

En l'an 1456, il plut du vrai sang à Rome et dans la région de Ligure il plut de la viande, ce qui était extraordinaire à l'époque, même dans cette peinture.

FOL. 82

1456 — Earthquake | Erdbeben | Tremblement de terre

In the year 1456, on the sixth and on the thirtieth of December, there was such a terrible earthquake during the night in Naples, Apulia and Benevent and in other cities. The like had never been experienced within living memory, to the extent that many churches and great palaces collapsed, in which many people and large numbers of livestock met their deaths, perished and died, just as painted here etc.

Im 1456. Jahr, am sechsten und am dreißigsten Dezember, gab es in der Nacht ein solch grausames Erdbeben in Neapel, Apulien und Benevent und in anderen Städten. Dergleichen ist seit Menschengedenken nie gehört worden: dass viele Kirchen eingefallen sind und große Paläste, worin viele Menschen und viel Vieh zu Tode gekommen, zugrunde gegangen und gestorben sind, wie hier gemalt ist etc.

En l'an 1456, le sixième jour et le trentième jour de décembre, il y eut un terrible tremblement de terre pendant la nuit à Naples, en Apulie et à Bénévent, et dans d'autres villes. Jamais de mémoire d'homme on n'avait vécu des choses telles que nombre d'églises et de palais somptueux s'étaient effondrés, à l'intérieur desquels beaucoup de gens et de bestiaux trouvèrent la mort, périrent et trépassèrent, comme dans cette peinture, etc.

FOL. 83

1462 [in fact: 962] — Comet
Komet | Comète

In the year A.D. 962, a great and wonderful comet appeared in the sky in Italy. This was followed by a great famine, so that many people perished and were found dead in alleys.

Im 962. Jahr nach der Geburt Christi erschien in Italien ein wunderbarer, großer Komet am Himmel. Danach folgte eine große Hungersnot, sodass viele Leute starben und tot in der Gasse gefunden wurden.

En l'an 962 après J.-C., une grande et merveilleuse comète apparut dans le ciel en Italie. S'ensuivit une grande famine dans laquelle beaucoup de gens périrent et furent trouvés morts dans les rues.

FOL. 84

1478 — Miracle of brother Claus (Niklaus von Flüe)
Wunder von Bruder Claus (Niklaus von Flüe)
Miracle de frère Claus (Niklaus von Flüe)

In the year 1478 Brother Claus lived in a wilderness near Lucerne, beside the Flüeli at Unterwalden, near a little chapel, without physical sustenance for twenty years. But a priest, who read the mass, did eat, however. The Brother was buried though in Haslau.

Im 1478. Jahr hat Bruder Claus in einer wilden Einöde nahe bei Luzern, am Flüeli in Unterwalden, bei einer kleinen Kapelle, zwanzig Jahre ohne leibliche Nahrung gelebt. Und ein Priester, der die Messe gelesen hat, der hat aber gegessen. Der Bruder liegt aber zu Haslau begraben.

En l'an 1478, frère Claus vécut sur une terre en friche près de Lucerne, près du Flüeli à Unterwalden, près d'une petite chapelle, sans subsistance pendant vingt ans. Mais un prêtre, qui disait la messe, mangeait en revanche. Toutefois, le frère est enterré à Haslau.

FOL. 85

1482 [in fact: A.D. 79] — Eruption of Mount Vesuvius
Vesuvausbruch | Éruption du mont Vésuve

In the year 1482 the high mountain, rich in oil and wine, of Vesuvius in Campania – situated four thousand paces from the city of Naples – burst open at its summit or peak and threw up such a fire that cities and villages and all the trees burned up. Also a poet, called Pliny the Elder, wanted to see the fire but the fire consumed him too.

Im 1482. Jahr ist der hohe öl- und weinreiche Berg Vesuv in Kampanien – viertausend Schritt von der Stadt Neapel gelegen – im Gipfel oder in der Spitze aufgerissen und hat ein solches Feuer heraufgeschleudert, dass Städte und Dörfer und alle Bäume verbrannt sind. Auch wollte ein Dichter, Plinius der Ältere genannt, das Feuer sehen und das Feuer verschlang auch ihn.

En l'an 1482, la grande montagne, riche en huile et en vin, du Vésuve en Campanie – situé à quatre mille pas de la ville de Naples – se fendit par le sommet ou le pic et fit jaillir tellement de feu que les villes et les villages et tous les arbres brûlèrent. Aussi, un poète, nommé Pline l'Ancien, voulut voir le feu, mais le feu le consuma, lui aussi.

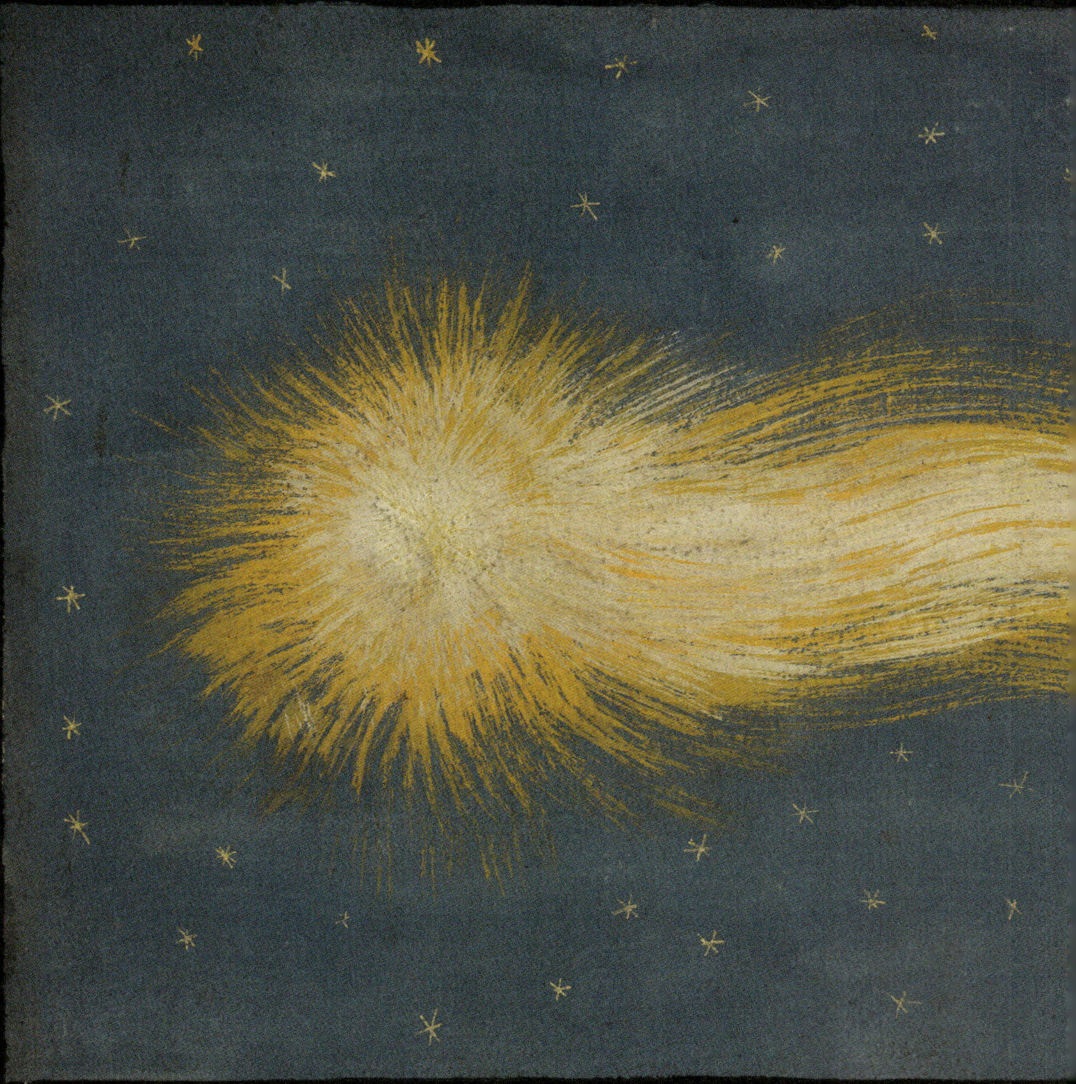

Im d cccc lxii iar nach de
ein wunderbarlicher gros
ain groser hunger, das b
gefunden ward:

62.

ůrt christi, in welsch land erschin
ůrt an dem himel, dar nach folget
olcks, starb, also todt auff der gassen

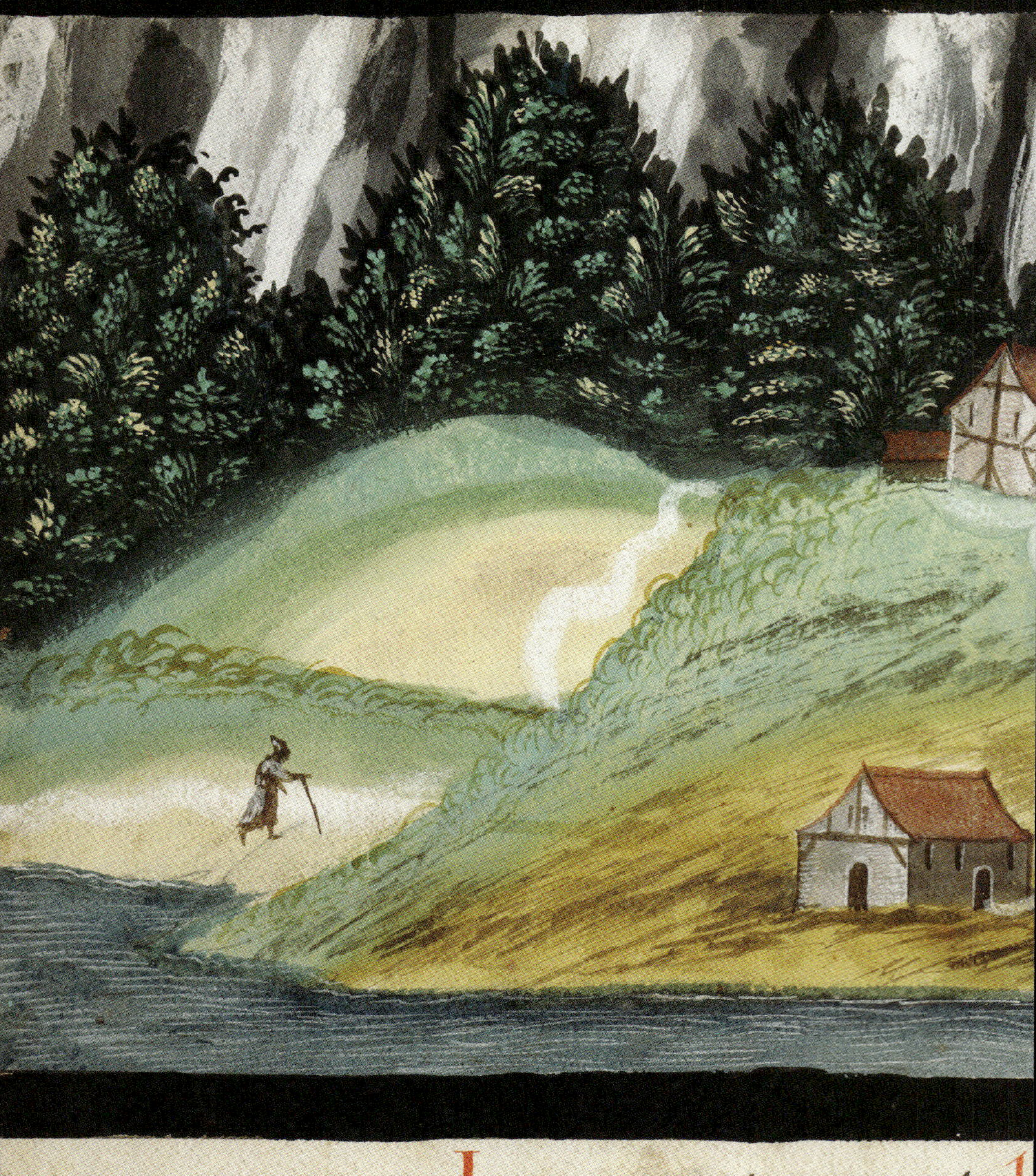

Im m c c c c lxxviii Jar hat g
ain ödden nahent bey lutzer
zwainzig iar bey ainem lebe
der hat aber gessen der pru

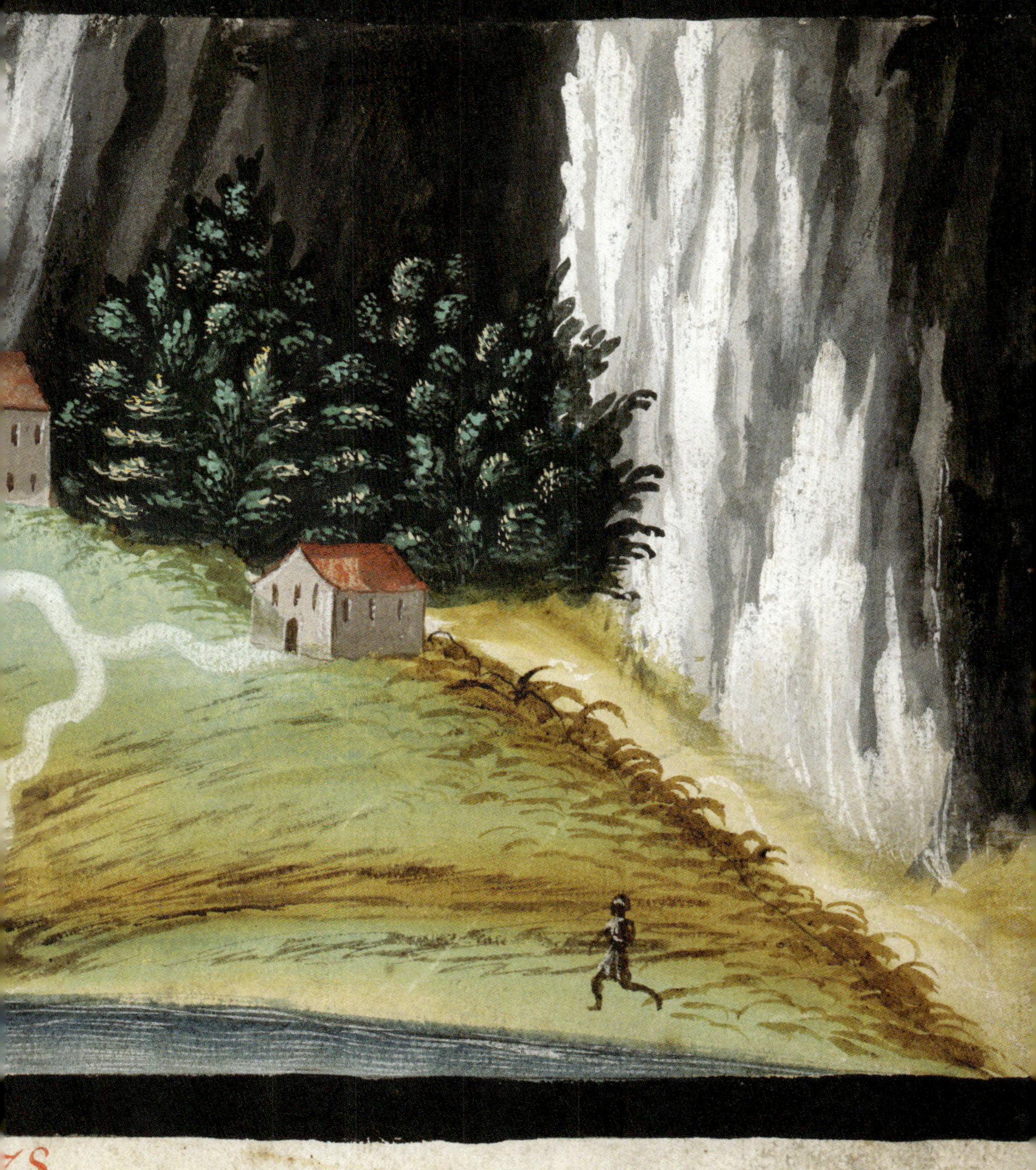

78
rt průder Claus preising in ainer wilden
r flů in vnder walden an leibliche speiß
vnnd ain priester der meß hat gelesen
ligt aber zů hasslaw begraben

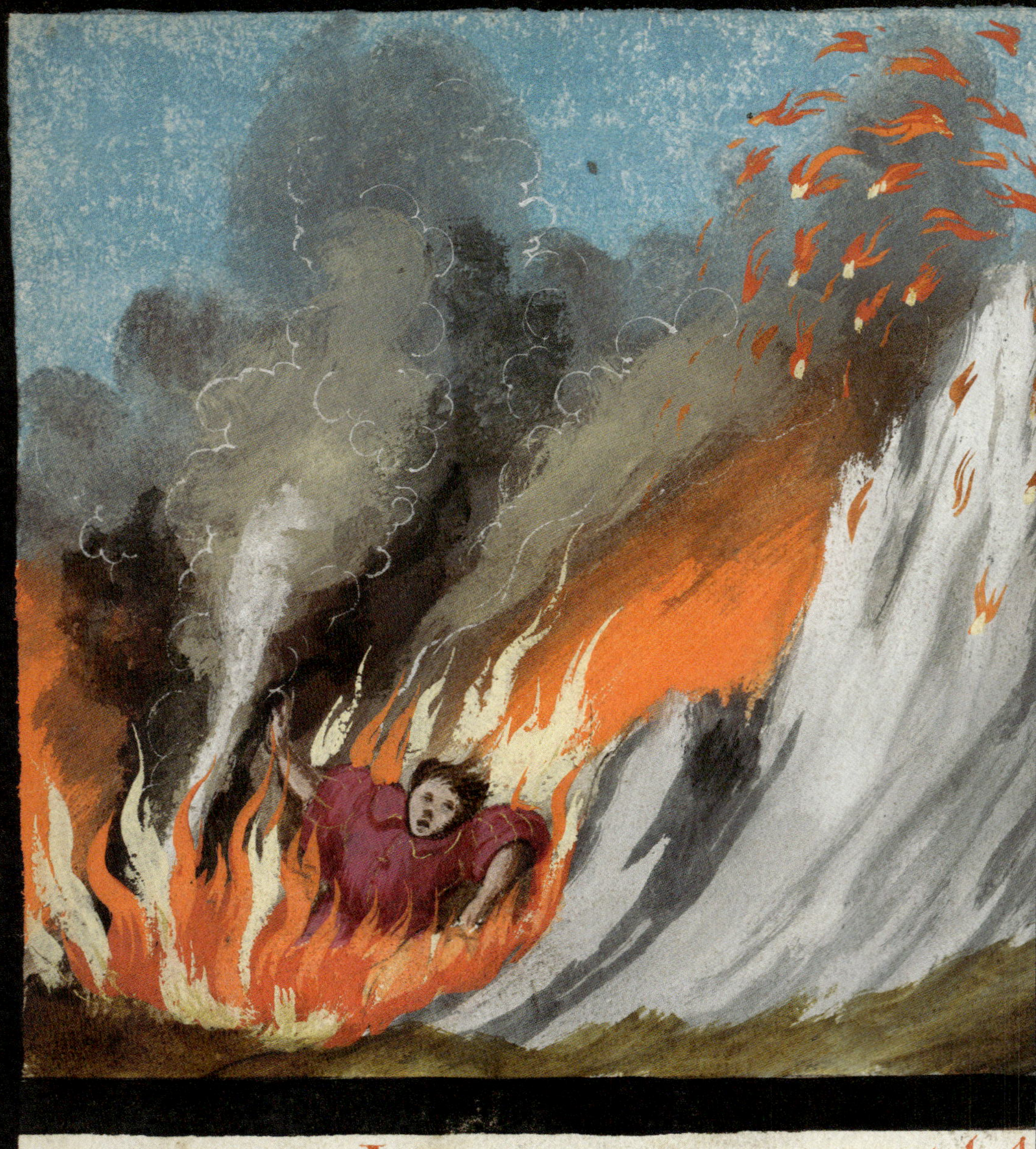

·14

Im m cccc lxxxii iar/ ist der hoch o

vier tausent schrit von der stat urapo

aus solches feuer/ heraus geworffen da

brunnen auch wolt ein priest plinu

vnnd verschlickt in das feuer auch

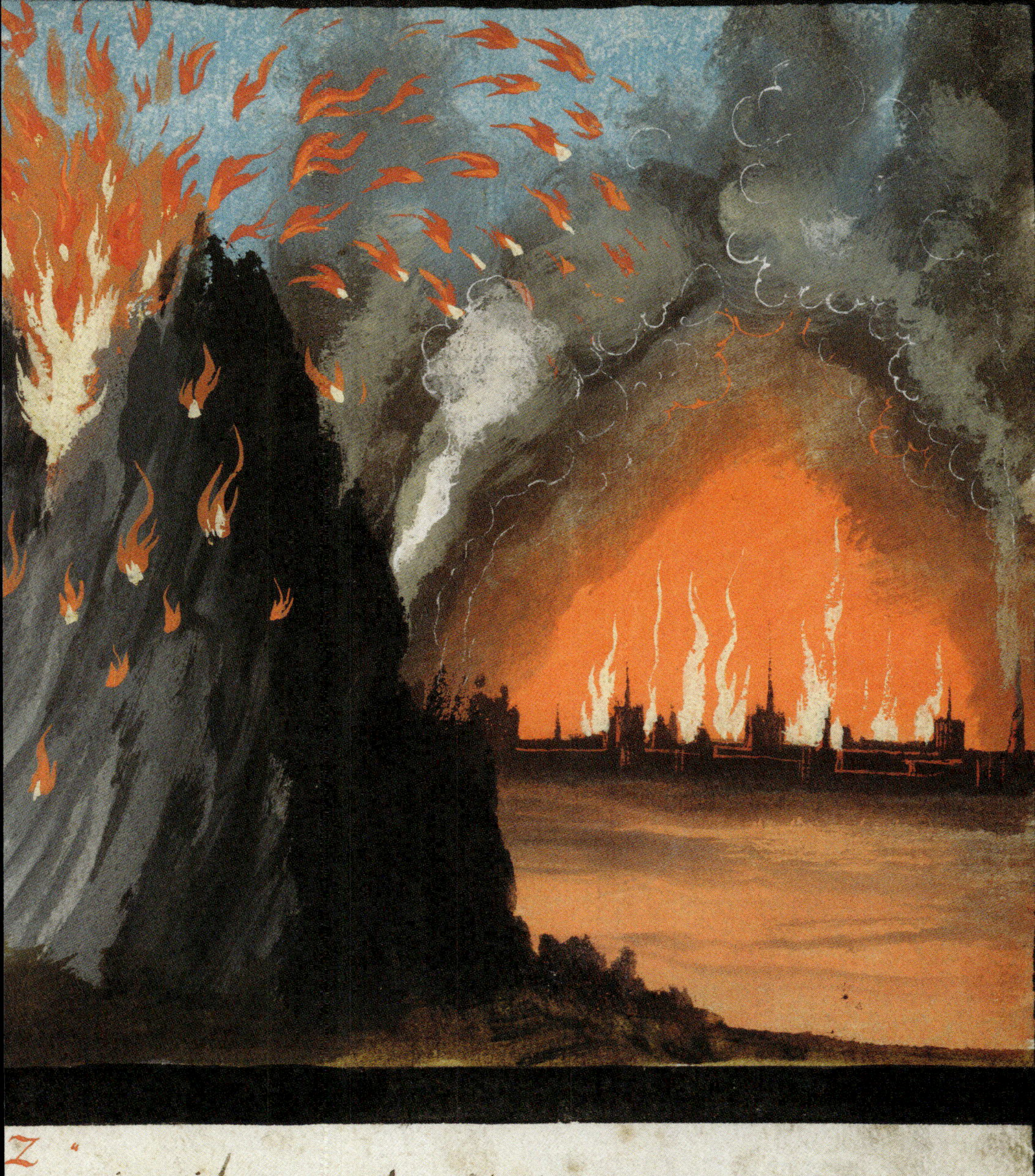

Z

nd wein reich perg vestiuuius in Campania
rlegen im gipffel oder spitz auff gerisen und
stett vnnd dorffer vnnd al perin send ver-
r ander grenant wolt das feuer sehen:

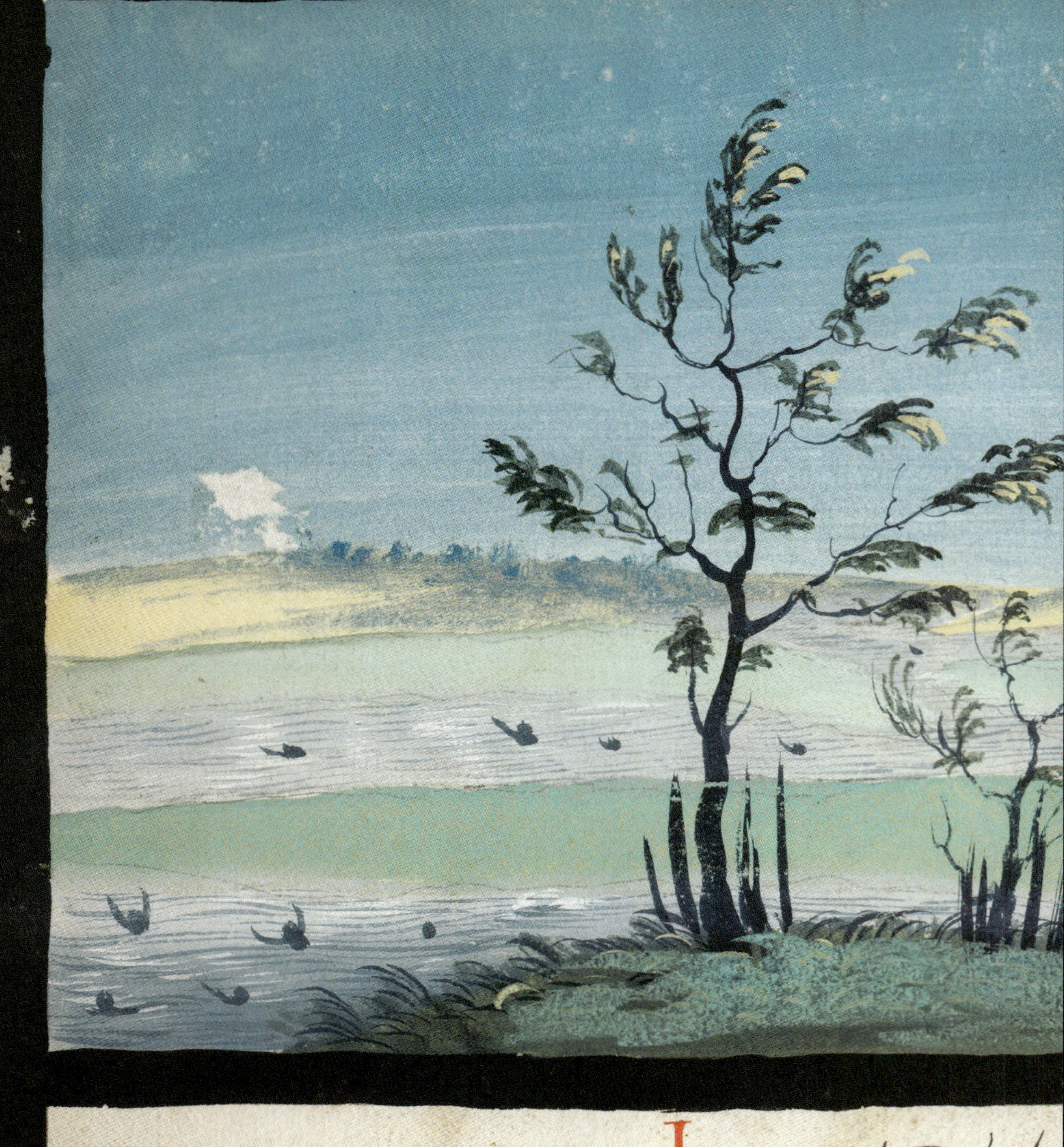

Im m cccc lxxx Jar li
vnnd der Rein also auß
vich ertruncken / dar von

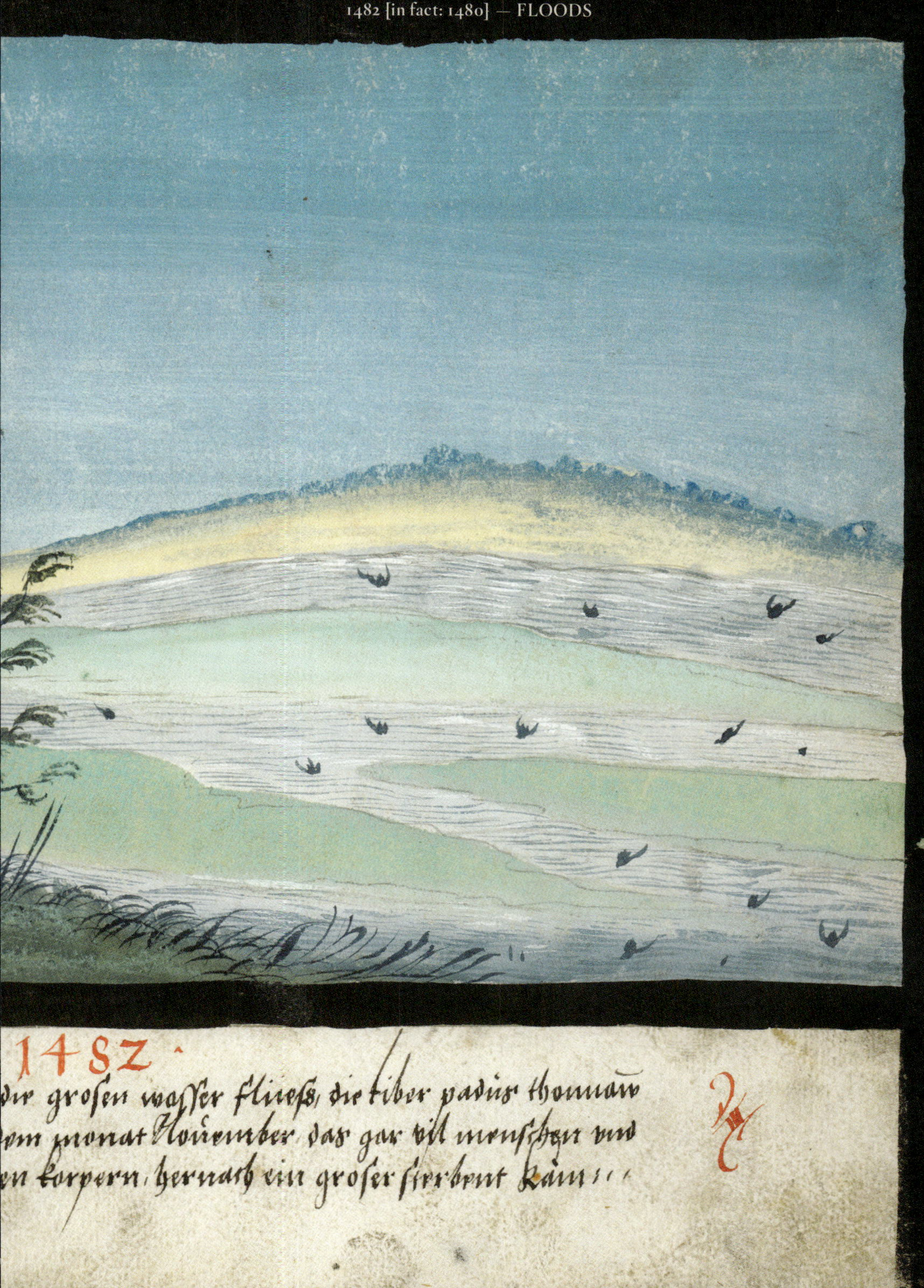
1482
dir grosen wasser fliess, die tiber padus thonaw
dem monat Nouember das gar vil menschen vnd
en korpern. hernach ein groser sterbent kam

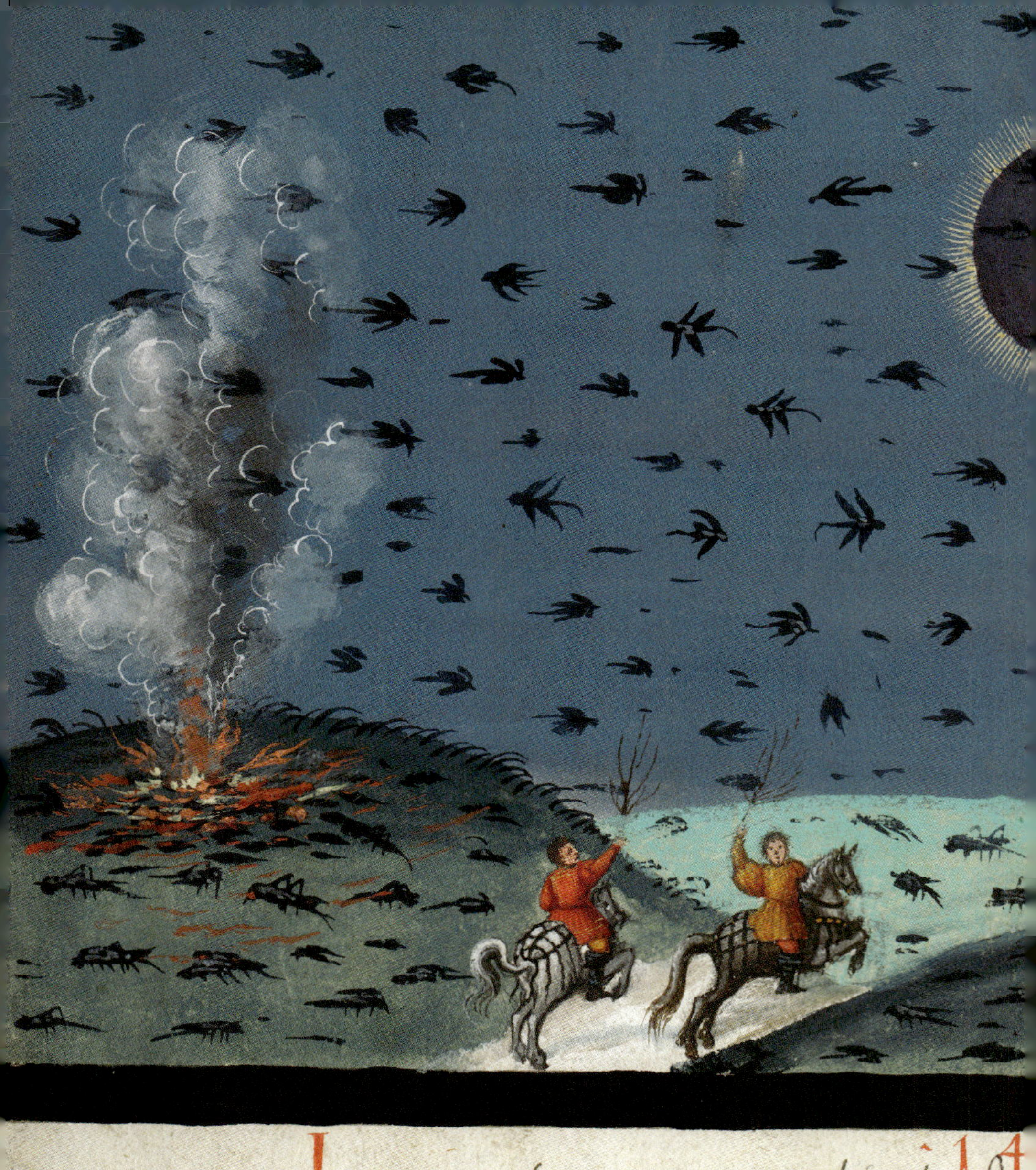

14

Im m cccclxxxiii Jar sind die hew schrecken
brügen ver wüst / vnnd wo es margraff ludwi
satt in Lamparttia verderpt / dies sie todten ve
sterinng gesehen worden an der sonnen / vnnd e
zwantzig tausent menschen gestorben vnnd zu

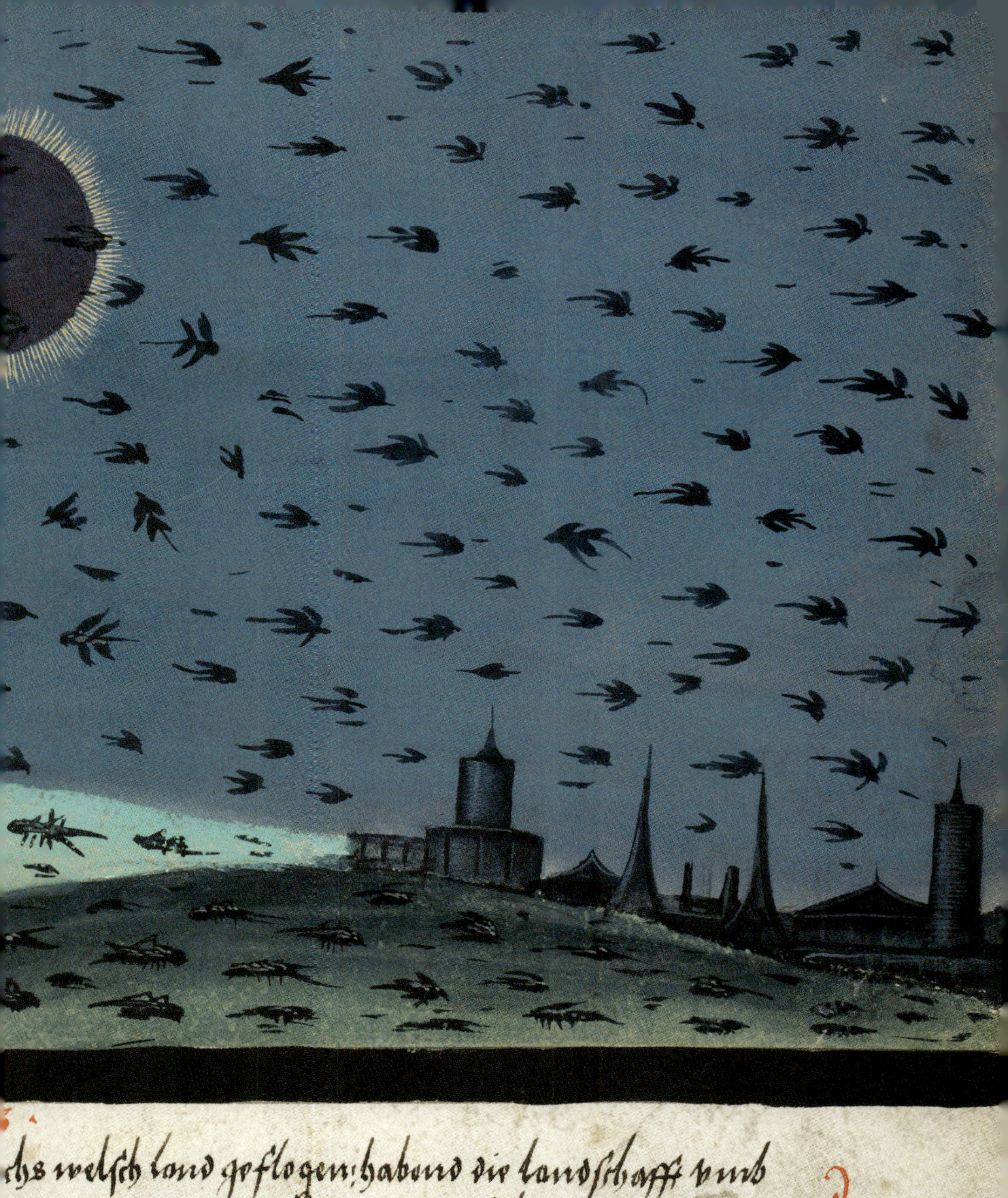

chs welsch land geflogen: habend die landtschafft vnnd
mantūa nit vor kumen wer: so hetten si die gantz
unen vnnd hin wegk geiagē dem nach ist ein fur
ach ist grosser sterbent komen das zu priren ob die
dig bey dreisig tausent gestorben sind ....

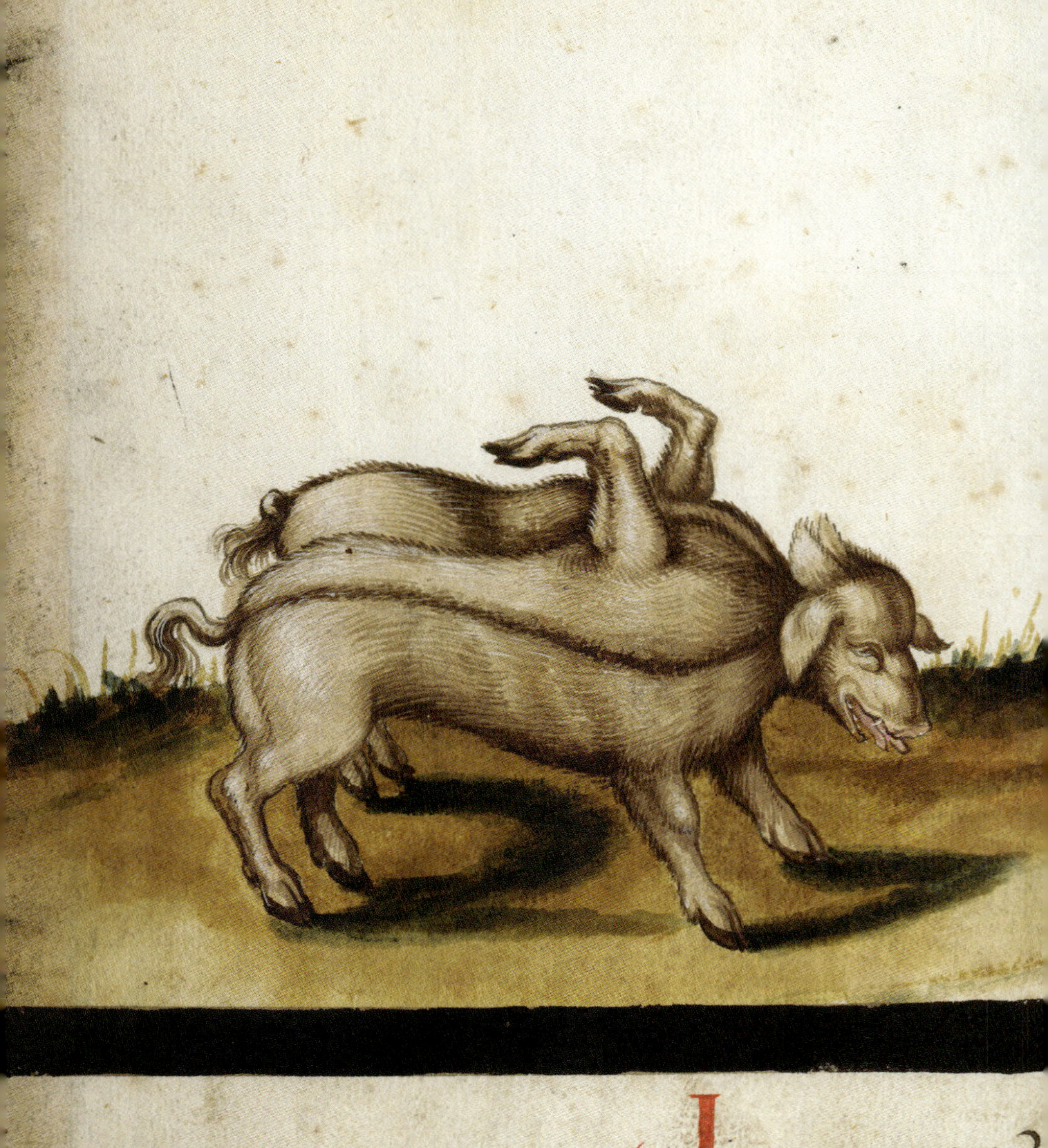

Im M cccc l
die zwaÿ schwein
schweinß wůette

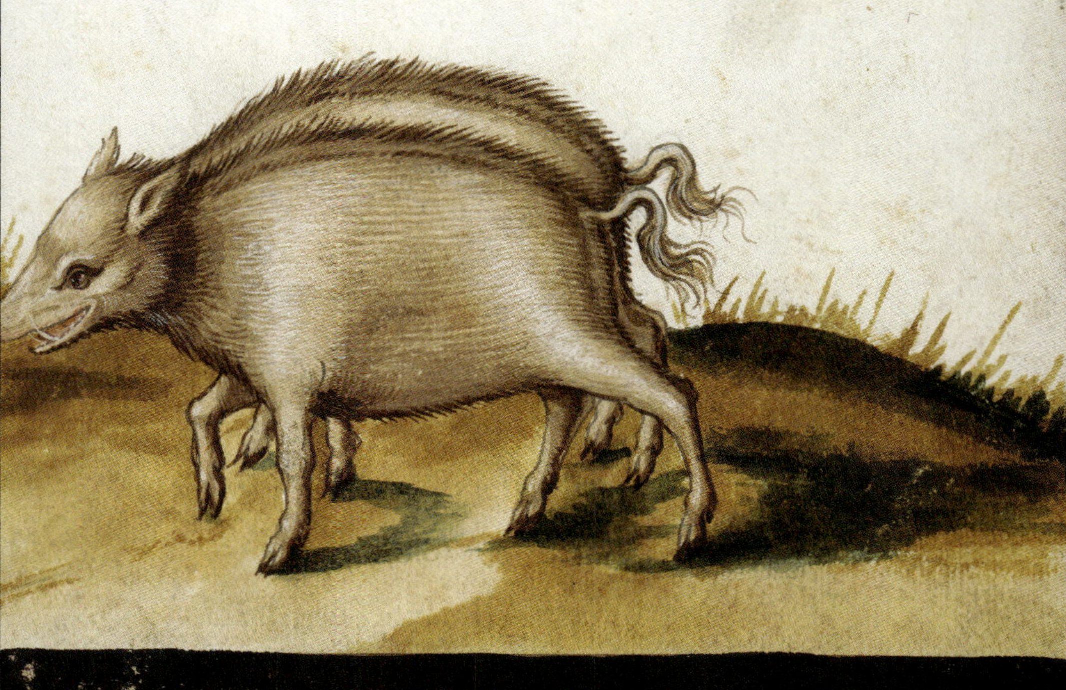

1495

xcv iar auf den monat zuni send
n rein strom gefallen von zweyen
ir hie ver zaichnet und gemalet

FOL. 86

1482 [in fact: 1480] — Floods | Überschwemmungen | Inondations

In the year 1480 the great rivers Tiber, Po, Danube and Rhine burst their banks in the month of November so much so that a great many people and livestock drowned and a great pestilence broke out afterwards because of the dead bodies.

Im 1480. Jahr traten die großen Flüsse Tiber, Po, Donau und der Rhein im Monat November so über die Ufer, dass sehr viele Menschen und Vieh ertranken und durch die toten Körper danach eine große Seuche ausbrach.

En l'an 1480, les grands fleuves Tibre, Pô, Danube et Rhin entrèrent en une telle crue au mois de novembre qu'un très grand nombre de personnes et d'animaux d'élevage se noyèrent et qu'une formidable pestilence se propagea à cause des cadavres.

FOL. 87

1483 — Plague of locusts | Heuschreckenplage | Locustes

In the year 1483 locusts swarmed in Italy, laid waste to the district around Brixen, and if Margrave Louis of Mantua had not prevented it they would have destroyed all the crops in Lombardy. He had them killed, burned or chased away. Afterwards, a darkening of the sun was seen and then came a great dying, so that more than twenty thousand people died in Brixen and around thirty thousand died in Venice.

Im 1483. Jahr sind die Heuschrecken durch Italien geflogen, haben die Landschaft um Brixen verwüstet und wenn Markgraf Ludwig von Mantua dem nicht zuvorgekommen wäre, dann hätten sie die ganze Saat in der Lombardei zunichte gemacht. Er ließ sie töten, verbrennen und fortjagen. Anschließend ist eine Finsternis der Sonne gesehen worden, und danach ist ein großes Sterben gekommen, so dass zu Brixen mehr als zwanzigtausend Menschen gestorben und zu Venedig etwa dreißigtausend gestorben sind.

En l'an 1483, les locustes envahirent l'Italie, dévastèrent la région de Brixen et, si le margrave Louis de Mantoue n'était pas intervenu, elles auraient détruit toutes les récoltes de Lombardie. Il les fit tuer, brûler ou chasser. Par la suite, on vit le soleil s'assombrir et la mort s'ensuivit par laquelle plus de vingt mille personnes périrent à Brixen et environ trente mille à Venise.

FOL. 88

1495 — Two sows and their pigs
Zwei Sauen und ihre Ferkel | Deux truies et leurs porcelets

In the year 1495, in the month of June, the two pigs were born of two sows near the Rhine, as recorded and painted here.

Im 1495. Jahr im Monat Juni sind die zwei Schweine am Rhein-strom geboren worden von zwei Mutterschweinen, wie hier verzeichnet und gemalt.

En l'an 1495, au mois de juin, deux porcs naquirent de deux truies près du Rhin, comme on le voit consigné et peint ici.

FOL. 90

1496 — Tiber monster | Tibermonster | Monstre du Tibre

In A.D. 1496, in the month of January, at the time the Tiber burst its banks high and wide near Rome: what wondrous creature appeared, found dead where the raging and the might of the Tiber's waters had subsided, and was in this shape and form, as it is painted there.

1496 nach Christi Geburt, im Monat Januar, zu der Zeit, als der Tiber hoch und weit bei Rom über die Ufer getreten ist: welch Wundertier zeigte sich tot aufgefunden dort, wo das Wüten und die Kraft des Wassers des Tiber nachgelassen hatte, und ist in dieser Gestalt und Form gewesen, wie es da gemalt ist.

En 1496 après J.-C., au mois de janvier, à l'époque où le Tibre entra dans une forte et vaste crue près de Rome : quelle créature extraordinaire apparut, trouvée morte, une fois que la colère et la puissance des eaux du Tibre s'étaient assagies, sous cette forme et cette allure, comme le montre cette peinture.

FOL. 91

1503 — Miracle of the crosses | Kreuzwunder | Miracle des petites croix

In the year 1503 small crosses in various colours fell upon the shirts of many people. And in the same year, three popes were elected in Rome within six weeks.

Im 1503. Jahr fielen Kreuzchen in mancher lei Farben auf die Hemden vieler Menschen. Und in demselben Jahr wurden in Rom in sechs Wochen drei Päpste gewählt.

En l'an 1503, de petites croix tombèrent en diverses couleurs sur les chemises de beaucoup de gens. Et, la même année, trois papes furent élus à Rome en six semaines.

FOL. 92

1506 — Comet | Komet | Comète

In the year 1506, a comet appeared for several nights and turned its tail towards Spain. In this year, a lot of fruit grew and was completely destroyed by caterpillars or rats. This was followed eight and nine years later, in this country and in Italy, by an earthquake, so great and violent that in Constantinople a great many buildings were knocked down and people perished.

Im 1506. Jahr erschien etliche Nächte ein Komet und wandte den Schweif Richtung Spanien. In diesem Jahr wuchsen viele Früchte und wurden von den Raupen oder Ratten völlig zunichte gemacht. Danach folgte im achten und neunten Jahr hierzulande und in Italien ein so gewaltiges und großes Erdbeben, dass zu Konstantinopel sehr viele Gebäude und Leute zugrunde gingen.

En l'an 1506, une comète apparut pendant plusieurs nuits et tourna sa queue vers l'Espagne. En cette année, beaucoup de fruits poussèrent et furent entièrement détruits par des chenilles ou des rats. S'ensuivit un tremblement de terre la huitième et la neuvième années dans ce pays et en Italie qui fut si puissant et si violent qu'à Constantinople, un très grand nombre de constructions s'écroulèrent et que des gens moururent.

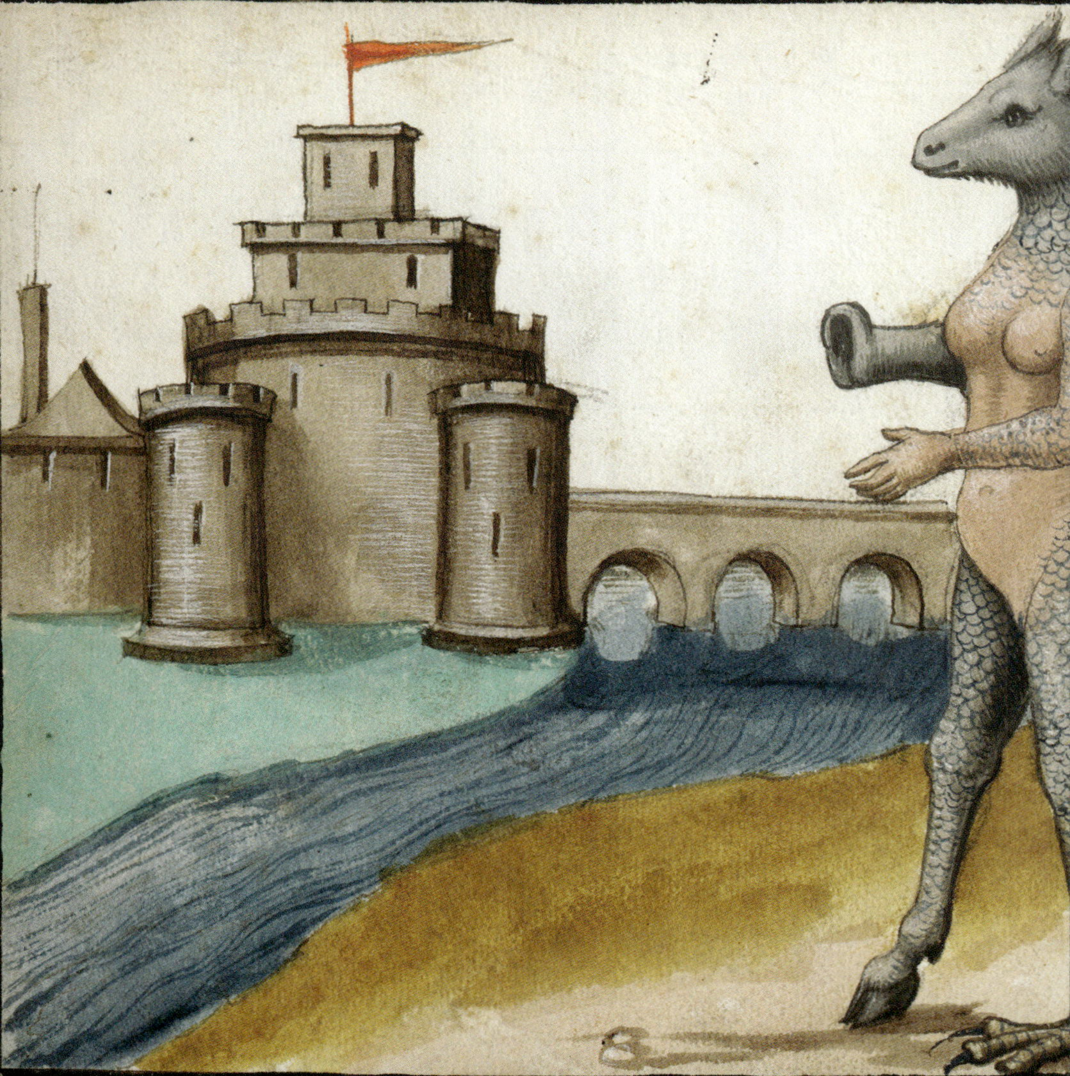

·14

Als man zalt nach Christi Gepürt M c c c c lxxxxvi v
gelauffen ist/ wolches wunder werk erscheint todt gefun
vnnd ist in dieser gestalt vnnd form gewessen wie es da g

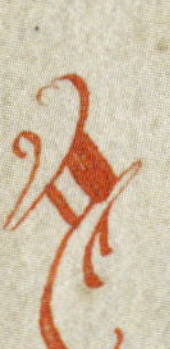

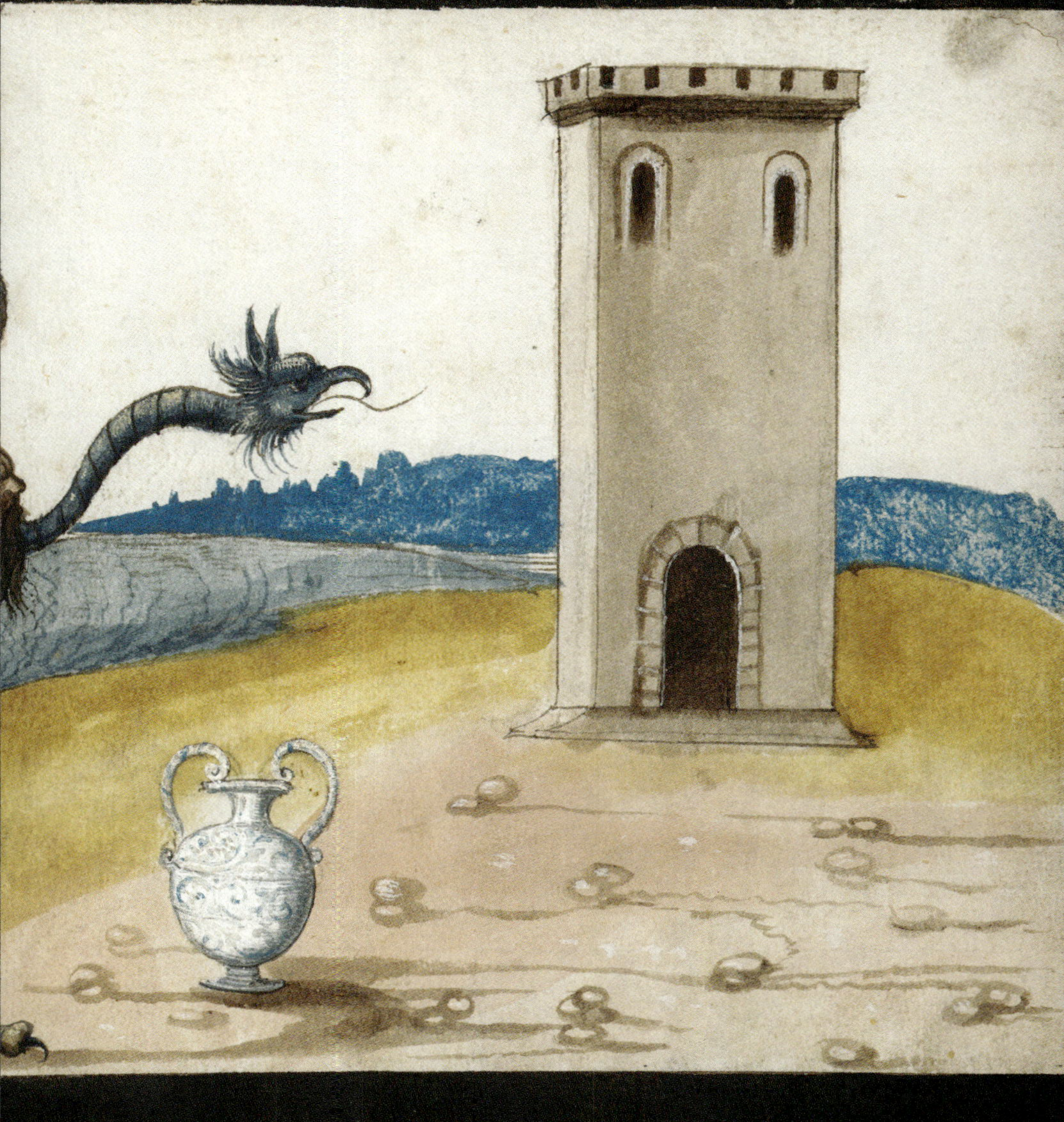

6

n Monat Fenner zů der zeit als die tiber hoch vnnd weit zů rom aůſs
zeſein da die wůtung vnnd die ſterck des waſſers der Tiber gefallen was
t iſt

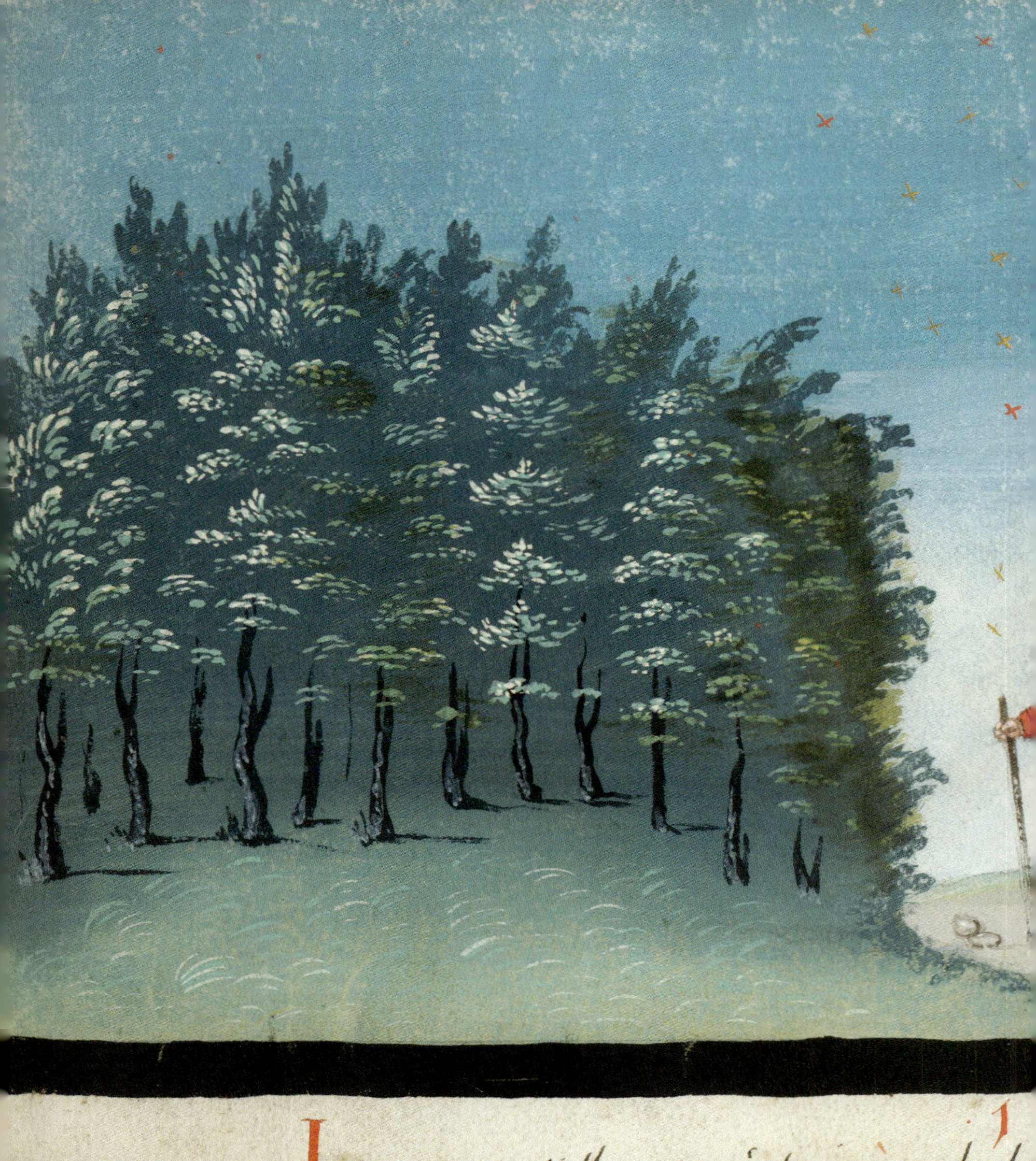

Im m ɔ iiij Jar fiellen die creutzlin in mancherla
dem selbigen iar: würden zu Rom in sechs w

3.

en auf virller menschen hemmeder vnnd im
drey bebst erwelt

A

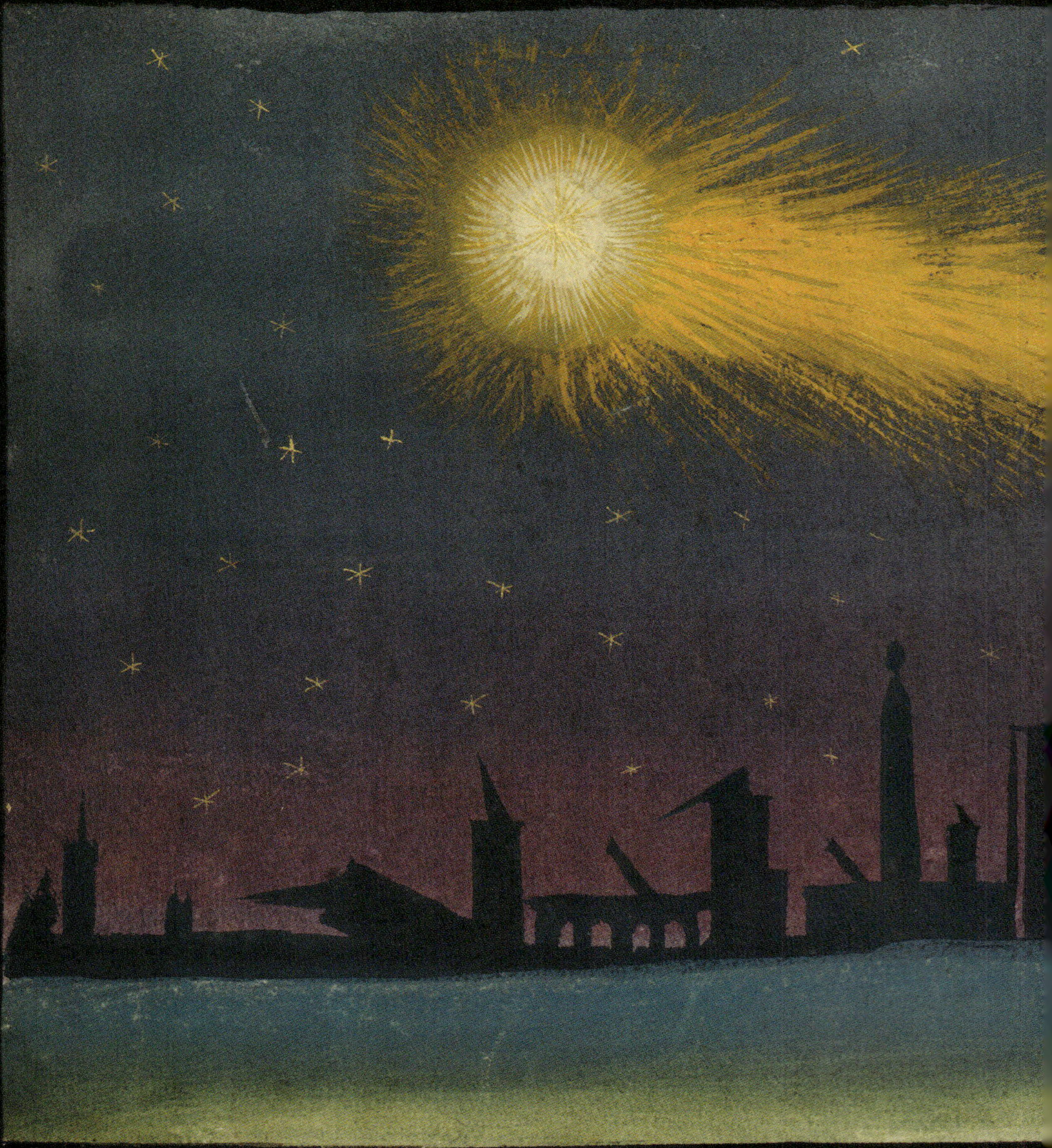

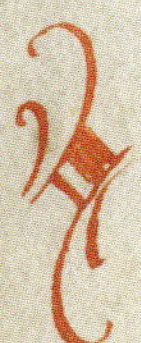

·15

Im m D vi Jar er schin etlich necht ein Commet ke
vil frucht / vnnd wurd von den raupen oder valze
hie zu lannd vnnd in welsch land ein so gewalt
gebew vnnd leut verfiellen

n schwantz gegen hispannien in diesem iar wüchsen
ver derpt darnach folget im acht vnnd neünnten iarr:
vnd grosse erbidem das zu Canstantinopel gar vill

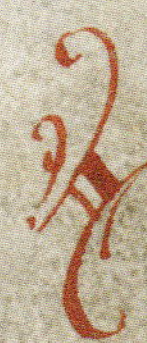

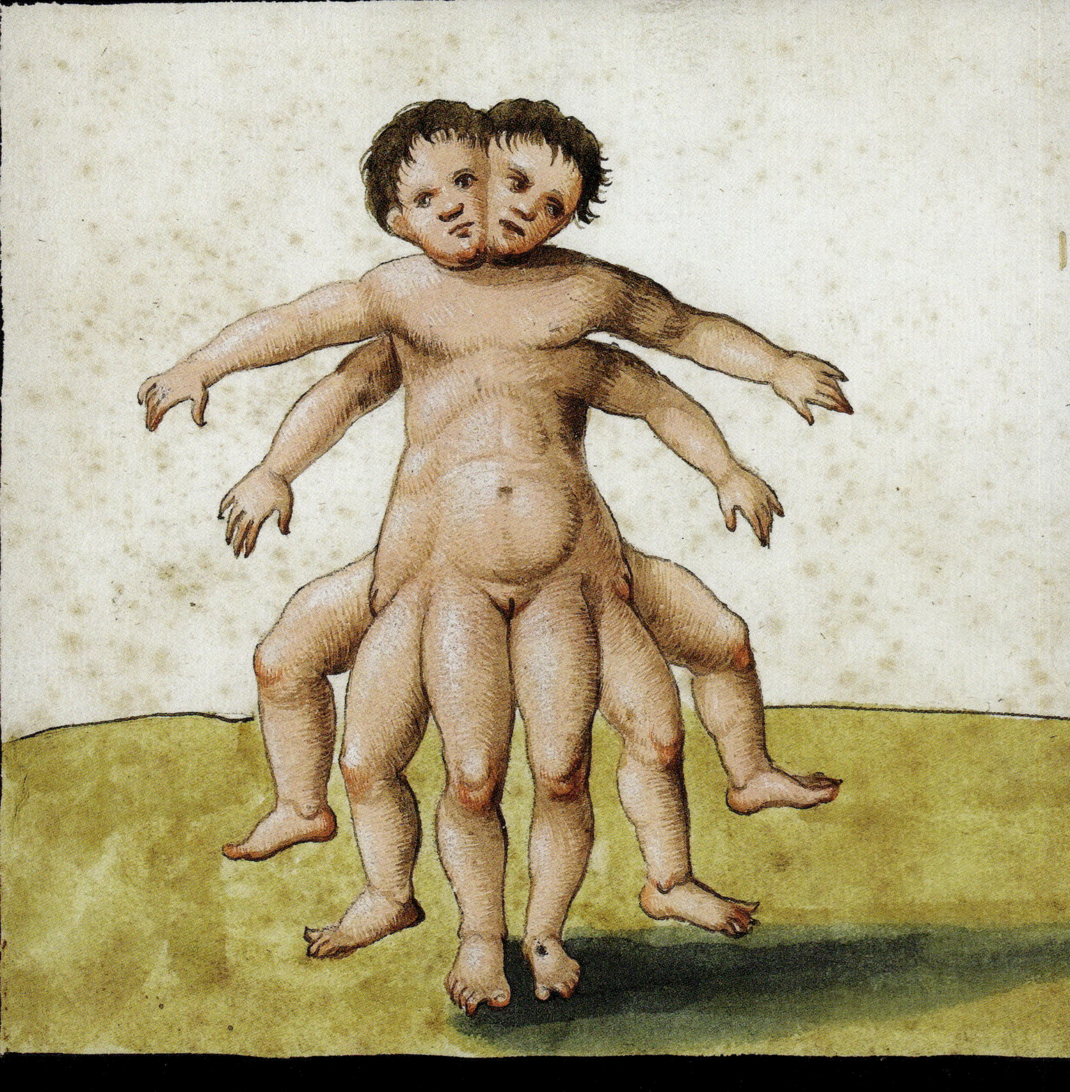

15

Alls man zalt nach Christi gebürt M D xiii Jar in dem Jenner ist v
begraben/ vnnd von Anthoni Raydthabt der zeit der Greffin
nen tüchlen gebunden/ vnnd aigentlich mit allem fleiss b
Burgkmair maller fleysigklich angeben das zu verzaichn

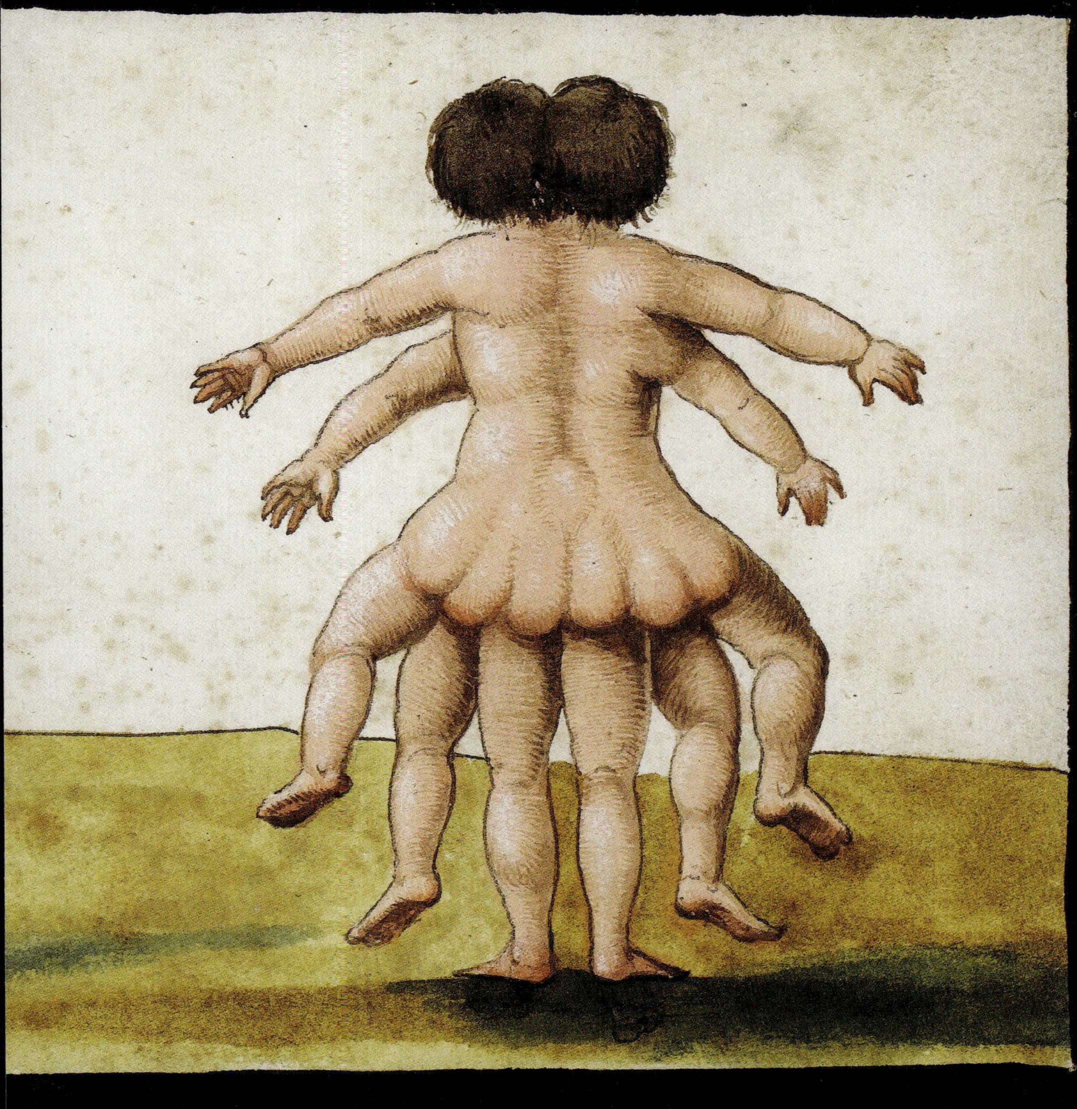

ier metzerin zu pleyburg geboren worden todt von mütter leyb kumen vnnd
aderon pfleger daselbst in vier stunden wieder auff graben vnd güsser sei
in bey wesen eines priesters daselbst vnnd Nachmals hansen
e ob stet

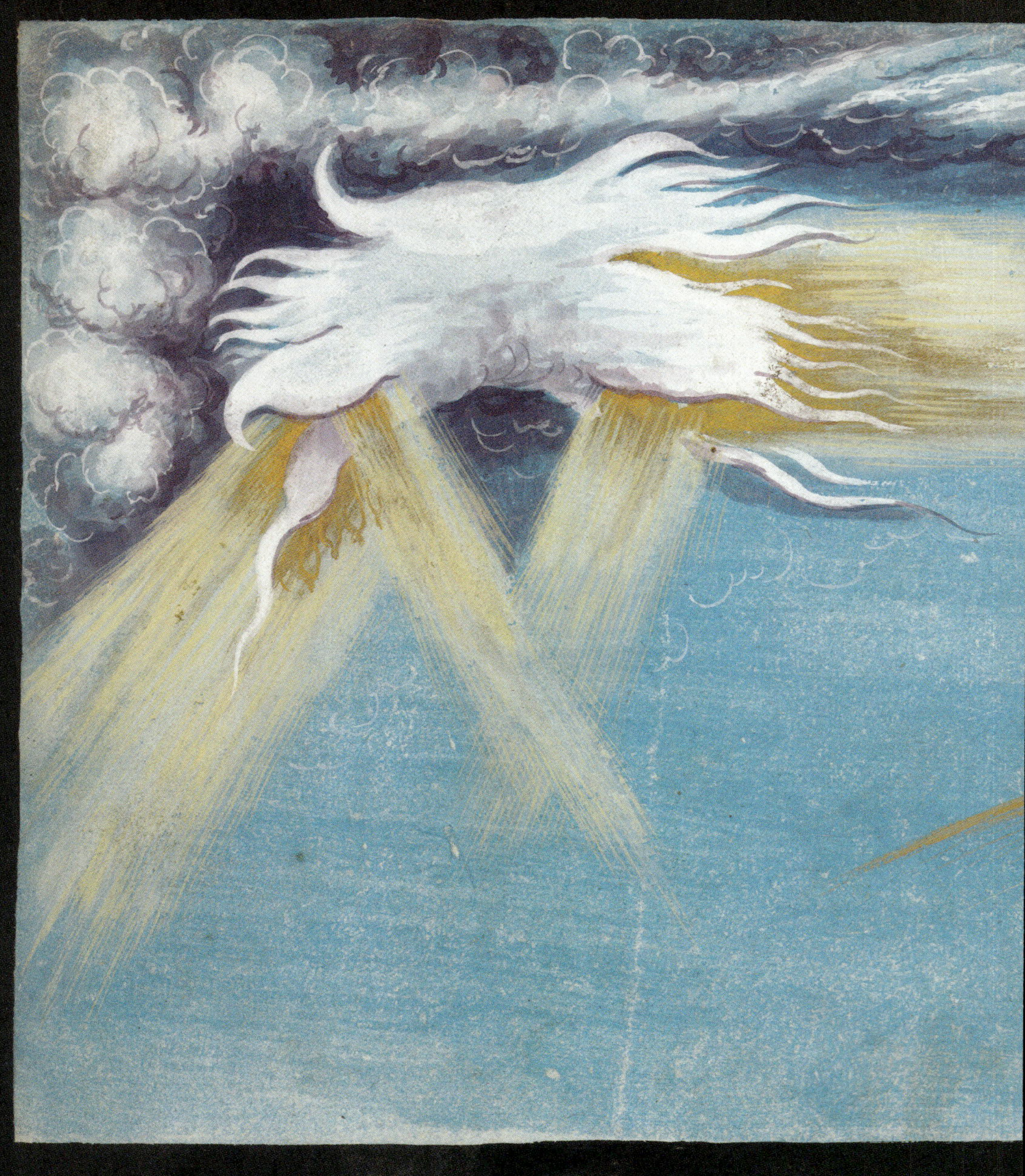

1513

Im m d xiii Jar ist diser gesicht ain vierthail
einer meil von aldenburg bey hellem tag umb
xii vhr gesehen worden

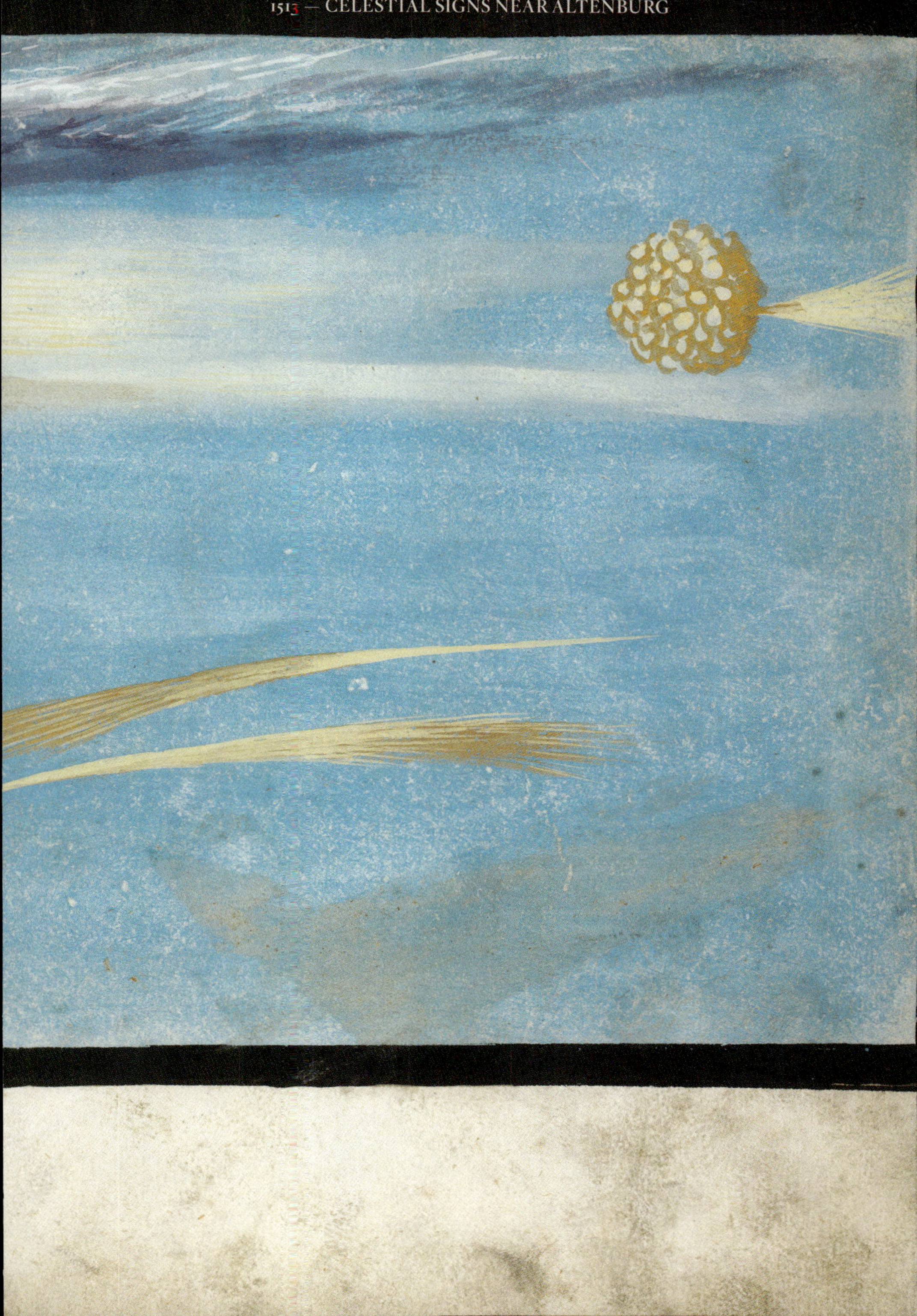

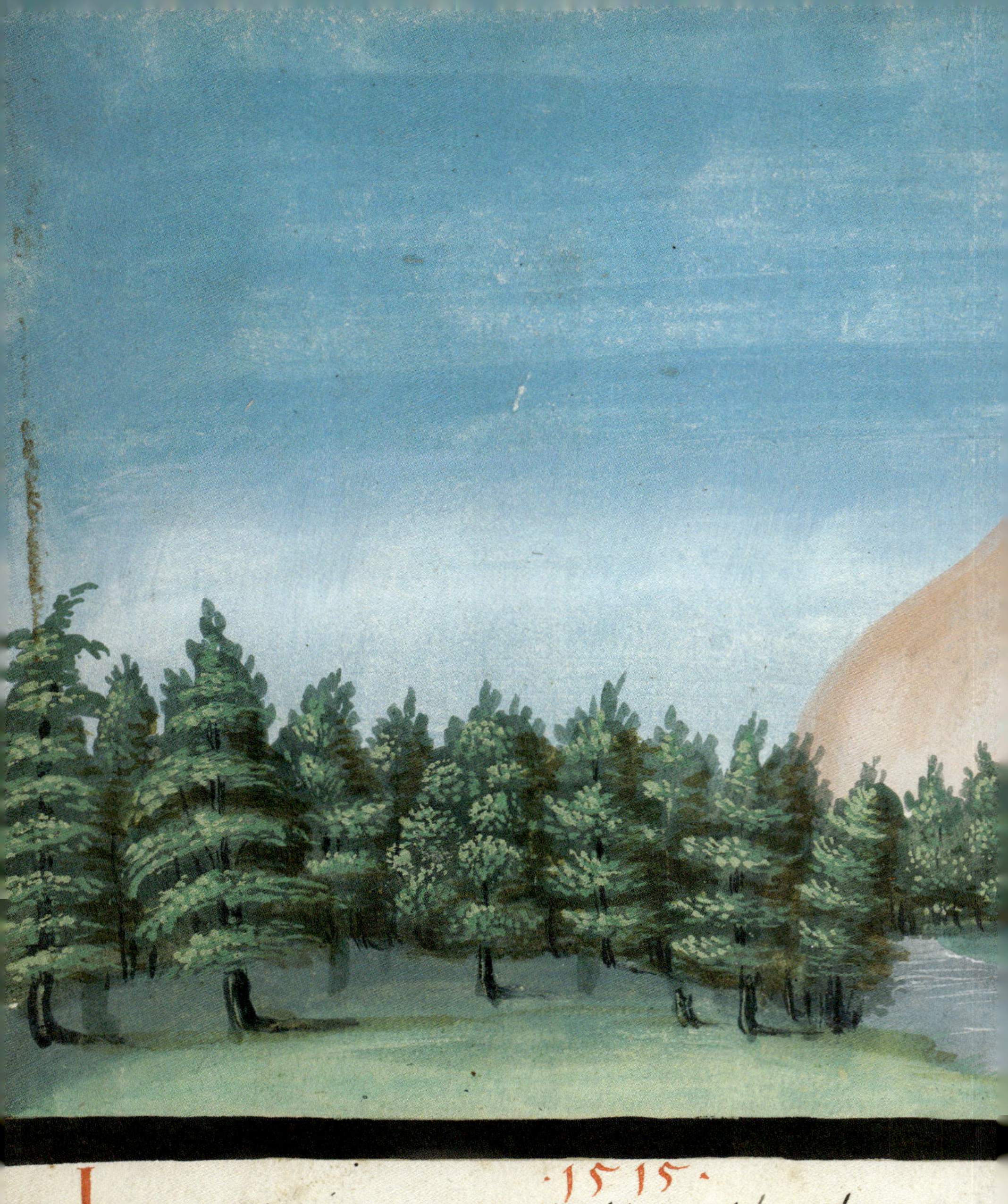

·1515·

Im m D xv Jar im monnat mayen ist dis gesicht gesehen worden / zu perlin / vnnd sol es der Chürfürst margraff : Joachim von Brandenburg selbs auch gesehen haben

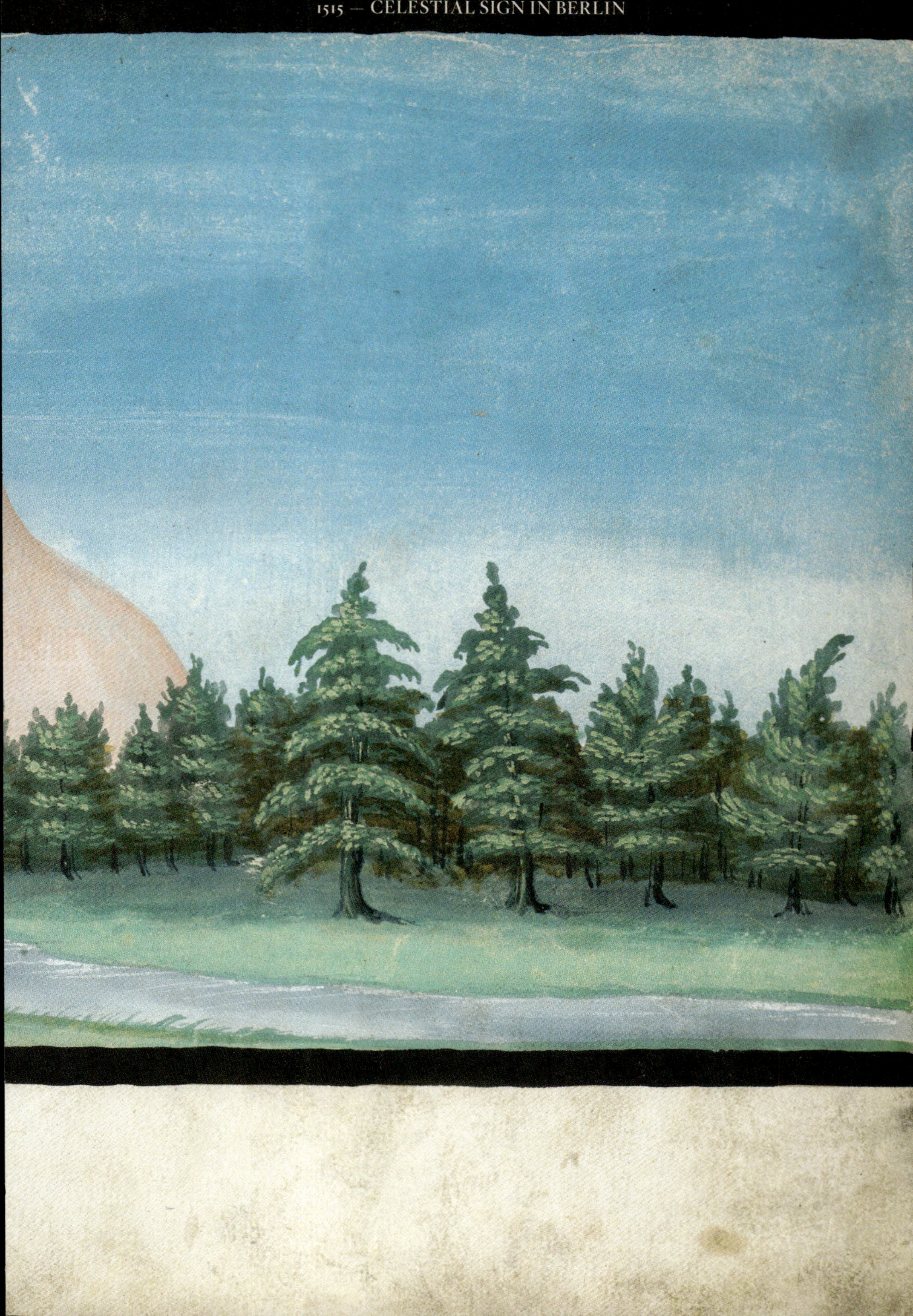

FOL. 93

1513 — Monstrous birth

Missgeburt | Naissance des enfants difformes

In the year A.D. 1513, in January, it was told that this was born to a Metzerin in Bleiburg, issuing dead from its mother's womb then to be buried, and four hours later dug up again by Anton Raidhaupt himself, at that time the Countess of Lodron's steward, unwrapped from its shroud and examined very carefully in the presence of a priest. Afterwards the painter Hans Burgkmair was commissioned to record it in detail, as it appears above.

Im Jahr 1513 n. Chr., im Januar, ist dies von einer Metzerin in Bleiburg geboren worden, tot aus dem Mutterleib gekommen und begraben und von Anton Raidhaupt selbst, zu dieser Zeit Verwalter der Gräfin von Lodron, in vier Stunden wieder ausgegraben, aus seinem Tuch herausgenommen und sehr genau mit aller Sorgfalt im Beisein eines Priesters beschaut. Später ist dem Maler Hans Burgkmair aufgetragen worden, es mit Sorgfalt darzustellen, wie es oben steht.

Au mois de janvier de l'an de grâce 1513, une Metzerin a accouché à Bleiburg d'un enfant mort-né et depuis enterré. Exhumé par Anton Raidhaupt en personne, à cette époque régisseur de la comtesse de Lodron, quatre heures plus tard, extrait de son linceul et examiné très attentivement en présence d'un prêtre. Plus tard, le peintre Hans Burgkmair a été chargé de le représenter scrupuleusement comme il est ci-dessus.

FOL. 94

1513 — Celestial signs near Altenburg

Himmelszeichen bei Altenburg | Signes célestes près d'Altenburg

In the year 1513 this manifestation was seen a quarter of a mile from Altenburg in broad daylight at noon.

Im 1513. Jahr ist diese Erscheinung eine Viertelmeile von Altenburg entfernt am helllichten Tag um 12 Uhr gesehen worden.

En l'an 1513, ce phénomène fut observé à un quart de mille d'Altenburg en plein jour à midi.

FOL. 95

1515 — Celestial sign in Berlin

Himmelszeichen in Berlin | Signe céleste à Berlin

In the year 1515, in the month of May, this manifestation was seen in Berlin and the Prince-Elector Margrave Joachim of Brandenburg is said to have seen it himself as well.

Im 1515. Jahr, im Monat Mai, ist diese Erscheinung in Berlin gesehen worden, und der Kurfürst Markgraf Joachim von Brandenburg soll es selbst auch gesehen haben.

En l'an 1515, au mois de mai, ce phénomène fut observé à Berlin et on dit que le prince-électeur margrave Joachim de Brandebourg l'observa, lui aussi.

FOL. 97

1516 — Two anomalous horses

Zwei wundersame Pferde | Deux chevaux anormaux

In the country of the Romans, a mare gave birth to a hare instead of a young foal.

In the year 1516, an extremely small horse was born in Weißreußen, all white like a lamb, and was presented to Emperor Maximilian, of glorious remembrance.

Im Land der Römer hat ein Mutterpferd einen Hasen zur Welt gebracht anstatt eines jungen Fohlens.

Im 1516. Jahr ist ein solches Rösslein in Weißreußen geboren, ganz weiß wie ein Lamm, und ist Kaiser Maximilian als ruhmvolles Andenken geschenkt worden.

Au pays des Romains, une jument mit bas un lièvre au lieu d'un poulain.

En l'an 1516, un tout petit cheval naquit à Weißreußen, blanc comme un agneau, et fut offert à l'empereur Maximilien de glorieuse mémoire.

FOL. 98

1518 — Shape-changing star

Seine Form verändernder Stern | Étoile changeante

In the year 1518 this star with such a diversely changing shape was seen on St Andrew's Eve, November 29, in Weimar over the grove – called "Klein-Weylucht".

Im 1518. Jahr ist dieser Stern mit solcher, mannigfaltig veränderter Gestalt am Sankt-Andreas-Abend, dem 29. November, zu Weimar über dem Wäldchen – „Klein-Weylucht" genannt – gesehen worden.

En l'an 1518, cette étoile fut observée sous toutes ces diverses formes le soir de la Saint-André, 29 novembre, à Weimar au-dessus du bosquet appelé « Klein-Weylucht ».

FOL. 99

1519 — Parhelia | Nebensonnen | Parhélies

Seen in the year 1519, on the 11th of January, the day before the demise of Emp[eror] Ma[ximilian], of glorious remembrance.

Im 1519. Jahr, am 11. Januar, dem Tag vor Kai[ser] Ma[ximilians] Hinscheiden gesehen worden, zu seinem ruhmvollen Gedenken.

Observé en l'an 1519, le 11e jour de janvier, la veille du trépas de l'emp[ereur] Ma[ximilien], de glorieuse mémoire.

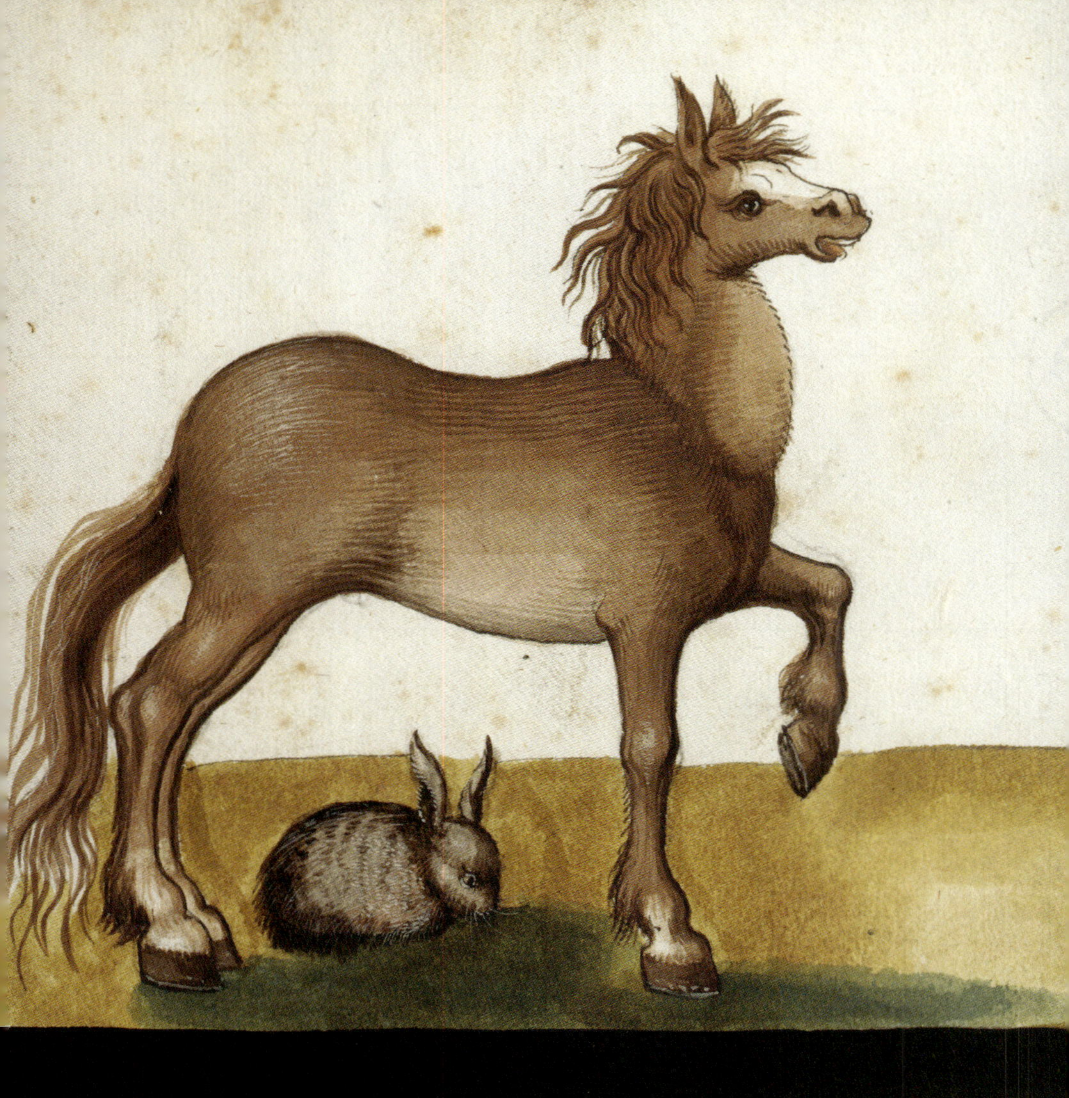

·1516·

In der romer land hatt ein mutter pferd ein hasen bracht/ an stat einer iungen fülx

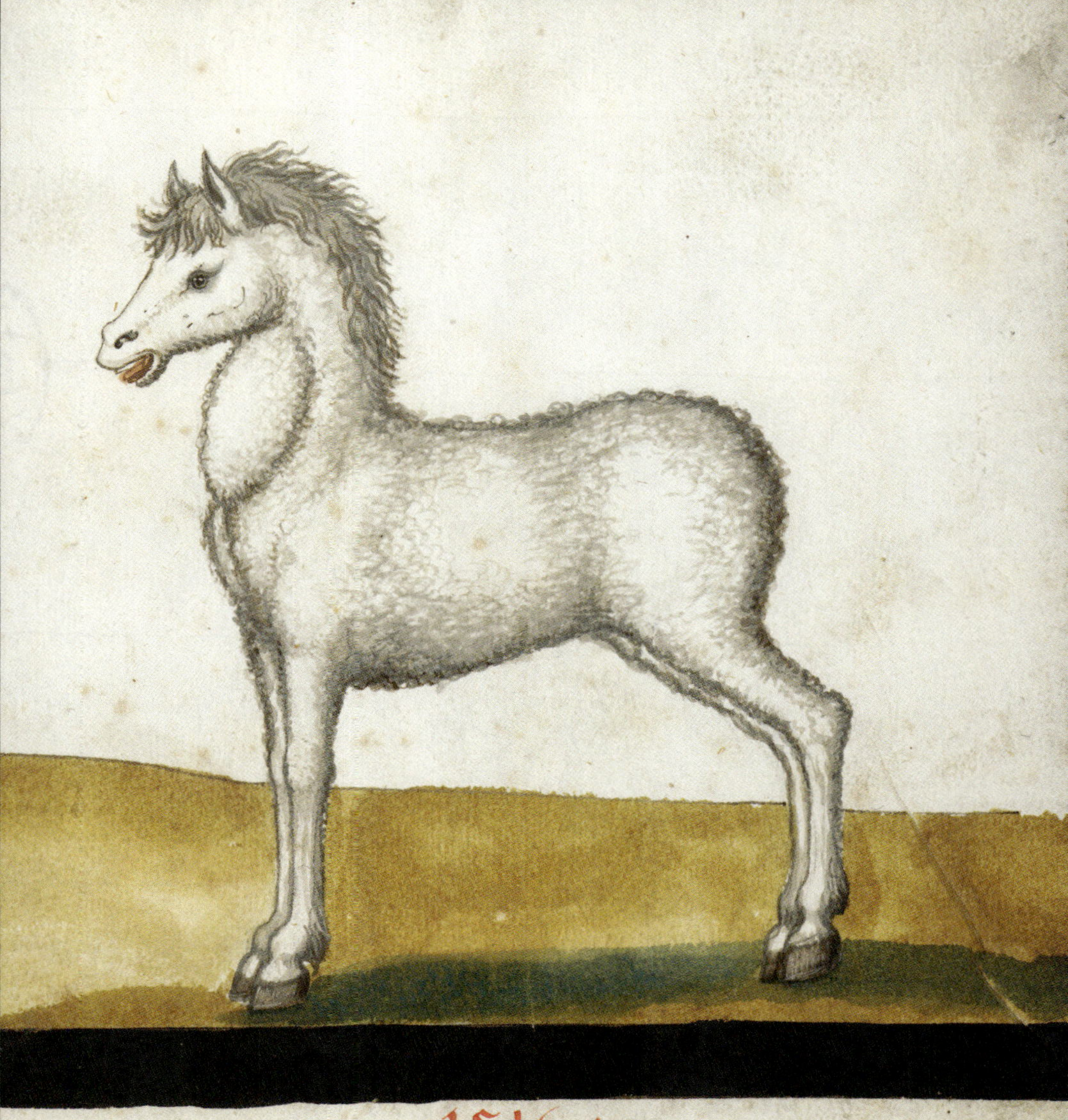

·1516·

Im m d xvi iar, ist ain solchs rosslein in weiss reusen
gefallen, gantz weiss wie ein lamb, vnnd ist kaiser
maximilian hoch loblicher gedechtnus geschenckt
wordenn

·1518·

Im M D xviii Jar ist dieser stern mit sollicher manigfeltiger
verenderung an Sanct andreas abent den xxix tag Novembr
is/ zu wein mar vber dem holzlain genant das klain weylin
gesehen worden

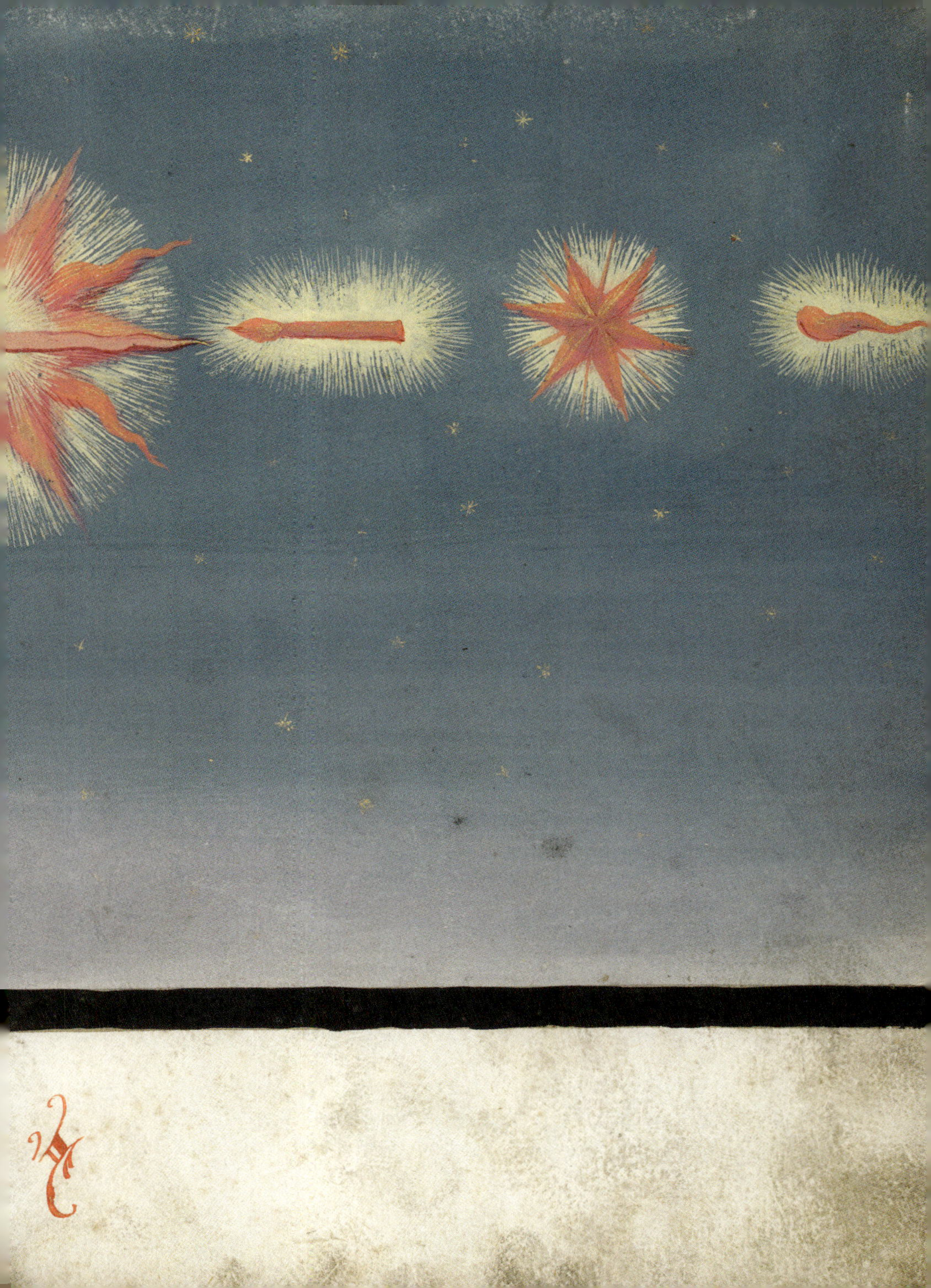

1519

Im m d x ix Jar den xi tag Jannari den nechsten tag
vor kay. Mayt hoch loblicher gedechtnus absterben gese-
henn worden

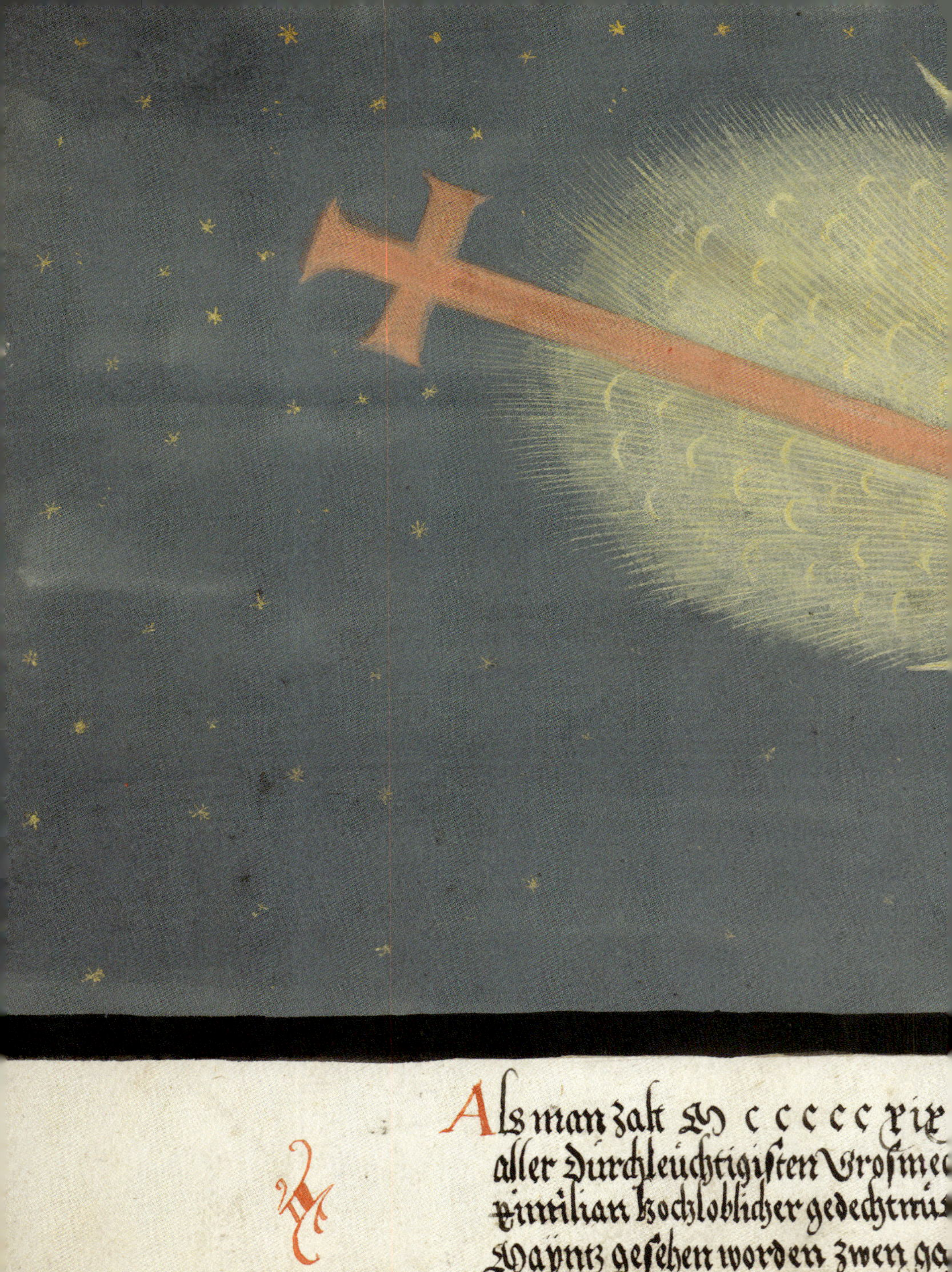
Als man zalt M c c c c c xix
aller Durchleuchtigisten Grosmec
ximilian hochloblicher gedechtnus
Mayntz gesehen worden zwen ga
herauff an den Rhein vnd das kreu

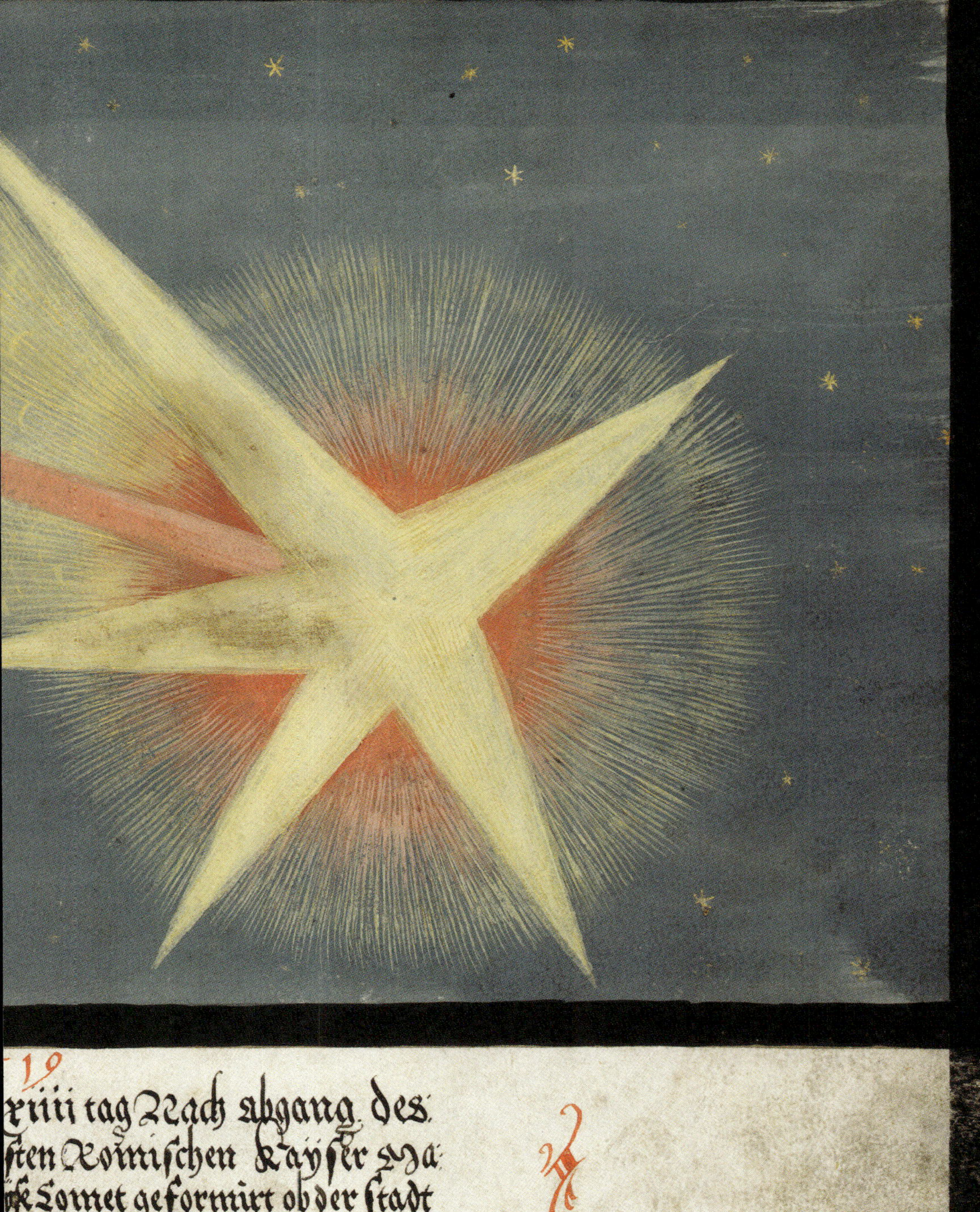

19
xxiiii tag Nach abgang des:
ſten Romiſchen Kayſer Ma:
ſe Comet geformirt ob der ſtadt
ag der geſtalt das ſich der ſtern
nab wertz geſtelt hat:

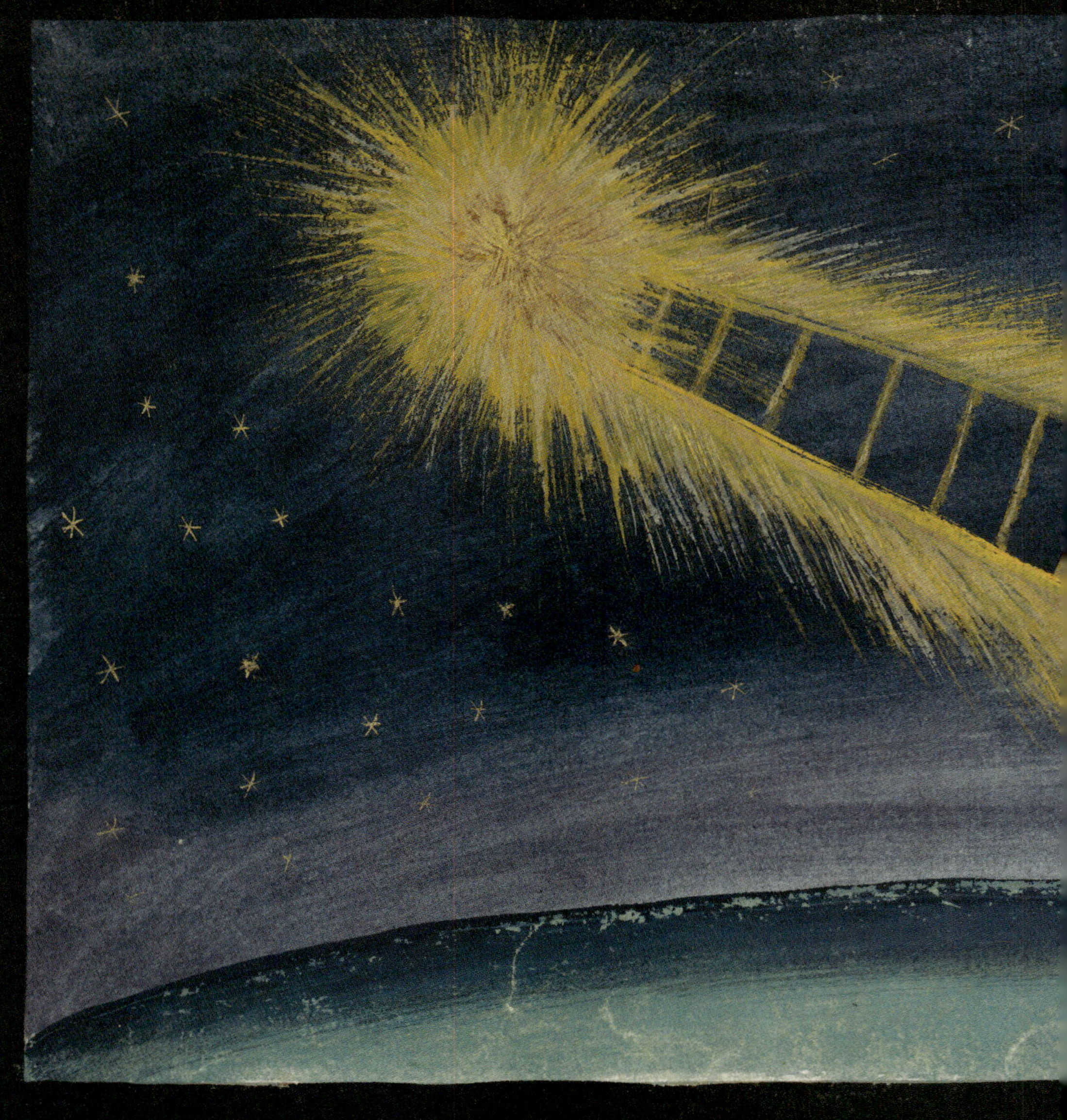

Als man zalt Nach Christi vnsers ha
vmb die zeit seiner geburt in mitter
der krosnitz ob Strasburg in kerer

·1519·

ichers M C C C C C X I X iar

t ist diser bezaichenter Comet an:

sehen worden

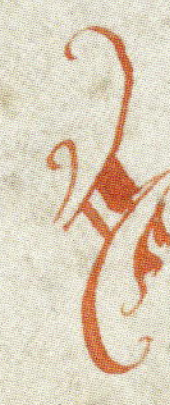

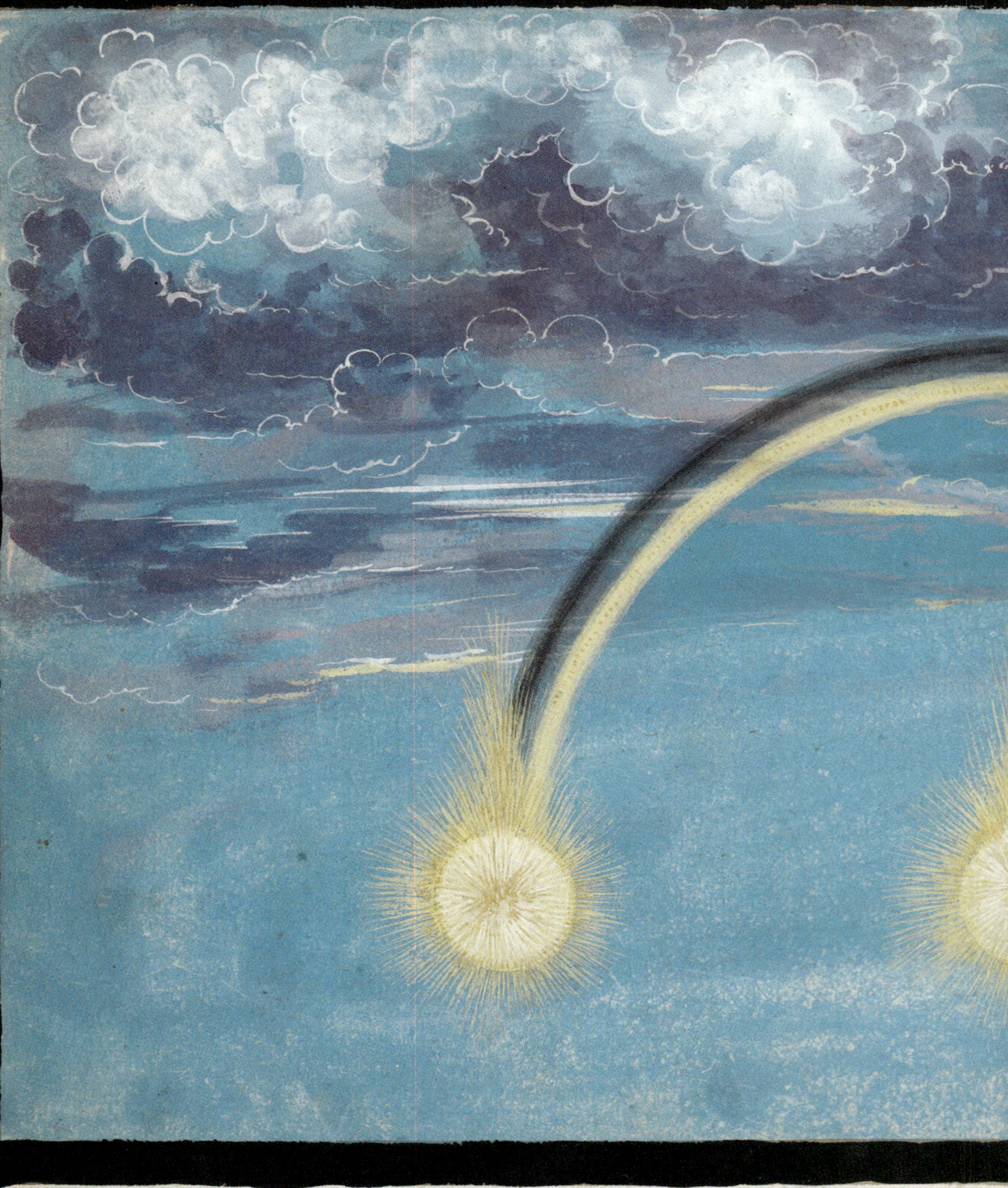

1520

Im m d xx am funfften tag des monats Januari Frůe do
die Son auff ist gangen: hat man zů wien die drey Sonnē
gesehen die da genent werden paraphoß

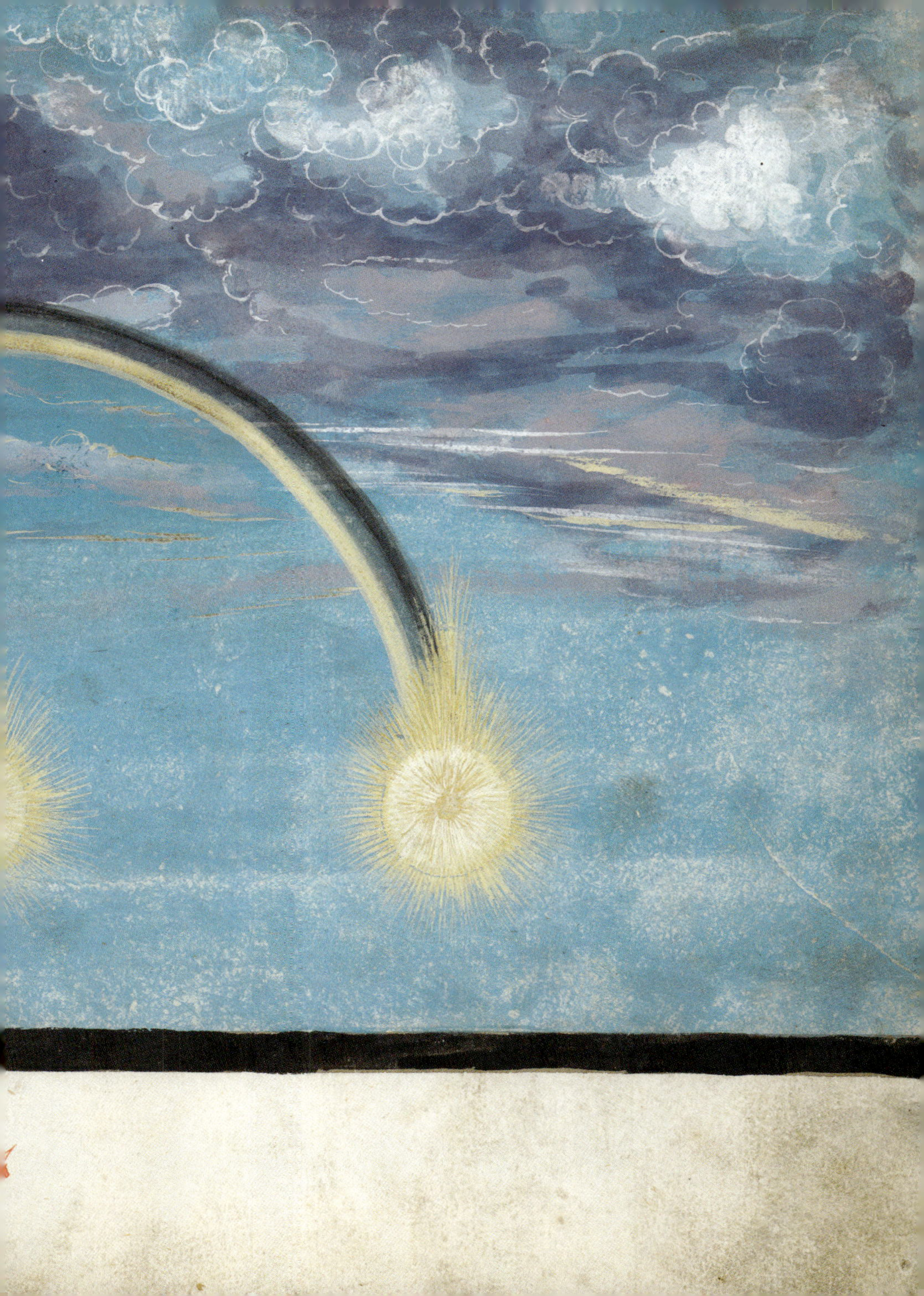

FOL. 100

1519 — Comet at Mainz

Komet in Mainz | Comète à Mayence

In the year 1519, on the 14th day after the death of His Serene Highness, the mighty Roman Emperor Maximilian – of glorious remembrance – this comet was seen over the city of Mainz for two whole days, so positioned in relation to the Rhine that the star pointed upstream and the cross downstream.

Im Jahr 1519, am 14. Tag nach dem Tod des allerdurchlauchtigsten, großmächtigsten Römischen Kaisers Maximilian – ruhmvollen Andenkens –, ist dieser so geformte Komet über der Stadt Mainz zwei ganze Tage gesehen worden, dergestalt, dass sich der Stern rheinaufwärts und das Kreuz abwärts gestellt hat.

En l'an 1519, le 14e jour suivant la mort de son altesse sérénissime, le puissant empereur romain Maximilien – de glorieuse mémoire –, la comète représentée ici fut observée au-dessus de la ville de Mayence pendant deux jours entiers, de telle sorte que l'étoile s'était orientée vers l'amont du Rhin et la croix vers l'aval.

FOL. 101

1519 — Comet | Komet | Comète

In the year 1519 after Christ, our Saviour, around the time of his birth, the comet drawn here was seen in the middle of the night near Kraßnitz turned towards Strasbourg.

Im Jahr 1519 nach Christus, unserem Heiland, um die Zeit seiner Geburt, ist mitten in der Nacht dieser gezeichnete Komet bei Kraßnitz in Richtung Straßburg gewandt gesehen worden.

En l'an 1519 après le Christ, notre Sauveur, à l'époque de sa naissance, la comète ici dessinée fut observée au milieu de la nuit près de Kraßnitz, tournée vers Strasbourg.

FOL. 102

1520 — Parhelia over Vienna

Nebensonnen über Wien | Parhélies dans le ciel de Vienne

In 1520, on the fifth day of the month of January, the three suns were seen in Vienna in the morning at sunrise, and these are known as "Paraphog".

1520, am fünften Tag des Monats Januar, hat man früh, als die Sonne aufgegangen ist, zu Wien die drei Sonnen gesehen, die da „Paraphog" genannt werden.

En 1520, le cinquième jour du mois de janvier, ces trois soleils furent observés à Vienne le matin quand le soleil se levait et on les qualifia de « Paraphog ».

FOL. 103

1520 — Halo and torch over Vienna

Halo und Fackel über Wien | Halo et torche dans le ciel de Vienne

In the year 1520, on the fourth of January, this sign was seen in Vienna for three hours until five after midday. It is called "Halo" and is like the moon.

Afterwards, after midnight, at one o'clock or a little later, this sign was seen.

Im 1520. Jahr, am vierten Januar, ist zu Wien drei Stunden lang bis um fünf nach Mittag dieses Zeichen gesehen worden. Es wird Halo genannt und ist dem Mond gleich.

Anschließend, nach Mitternacht, um ein Uhr oder ein wenig danach, hat man dieses Zeichen gesehen.

En l'an 1520, le quatrième jour de janvier, ce signe fut observé à Vienne pendant trois heures jusqu'à cinq heures après midi. On l'appelle « Halo » et il est semblable à la lune.

Par la suite, après minuit, à une heure ou un peu plus tard, ce signe fut observé.

FOL. 104

1520 — Lunar halo over Vienna

Mondhalo über Wien | Halo lunaire dans le ciel de Vienne

In the year 1520, on the 6th day of the month of January, at around eight o'clock in the evening, in the city of Vienna the sign was seen, around the glow of the moon.

Im 1520. Jahr, am 6. Tag des Monats Januar, hat man um acht Uhr nach Mittag, am Abend, in der Stadt Wien das Zeichen um den Mondschein herum gesehen.

En l'an 1520, le sixième jour du mois de janvier, ce signe fut observé dans la ville de Vienne autour du clair de lune à huit heures après midi le soir.

FOL. 106

1520 — Parhelia over Vienna

Nebensonnen über Wien | Parhélies dans le ciel de Vienne

In the year 1520, on the seventh day of the month of January, three suns, which are called "Parahelios", were seen in Vienna in Austria from sunrise until ten or a little later.

Im 1520. Jahr, am siebten Tag des Monats Januar, hat man vom Aufgang der Sonne bis um zehn oder ein wenig später drei Sonnen, welche „Parahelios" genannt werden, zu Wien in Österreich gesehen.

En l'an 1520, le septième jour du mois de janvier, trois soleils, appelés « Parahelios », furent observés à Vienne en Autriche à partir du lever du soleil jusqu'à dix heures ou un peu plus tard.

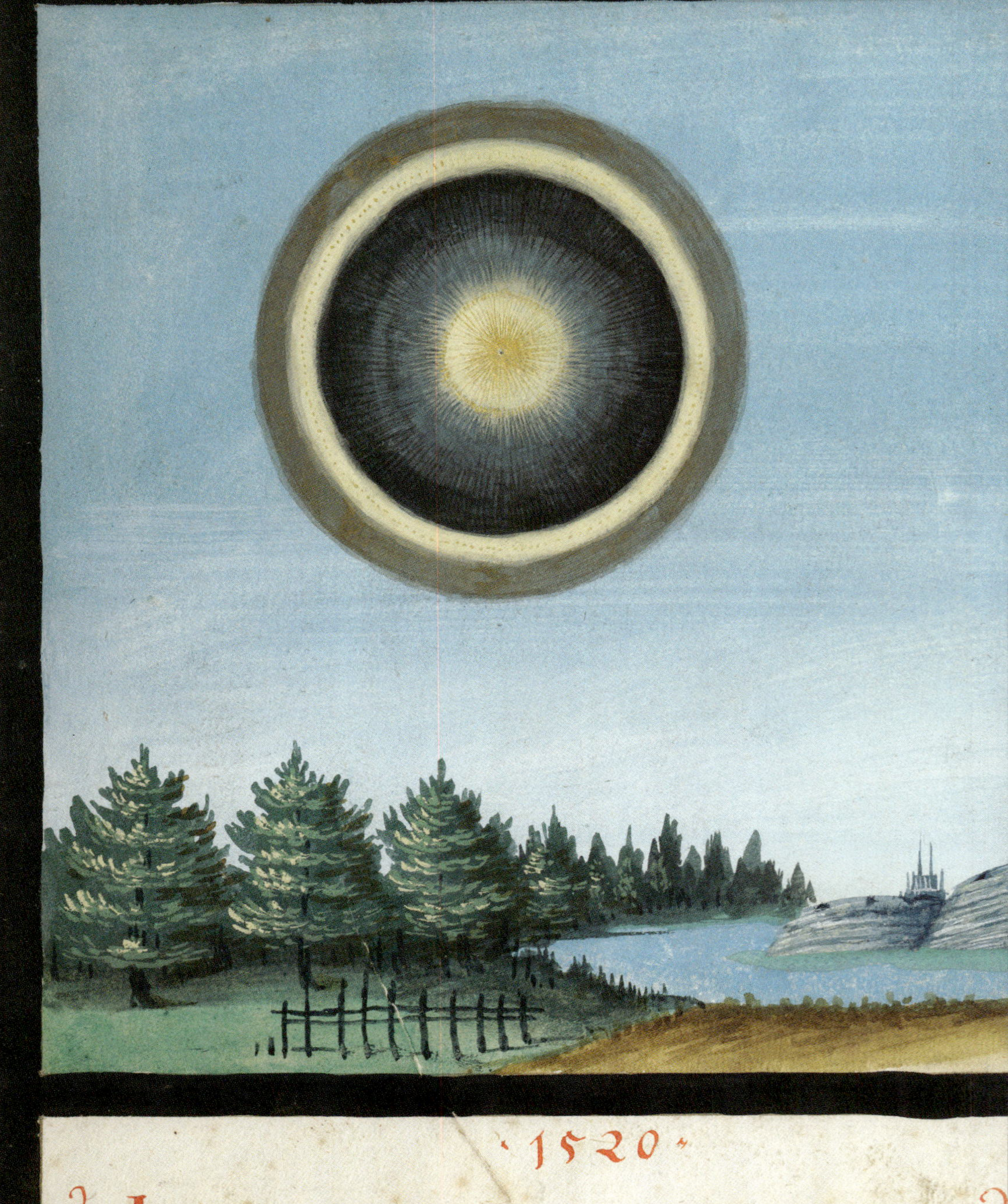

·1520·

Im m D xx Jar den vierten tag Januari drey stund bis auff funffe nach mittag zu wien ist dieses zaichen ge sehen worden / ist genent halo ist gleich dem mon:

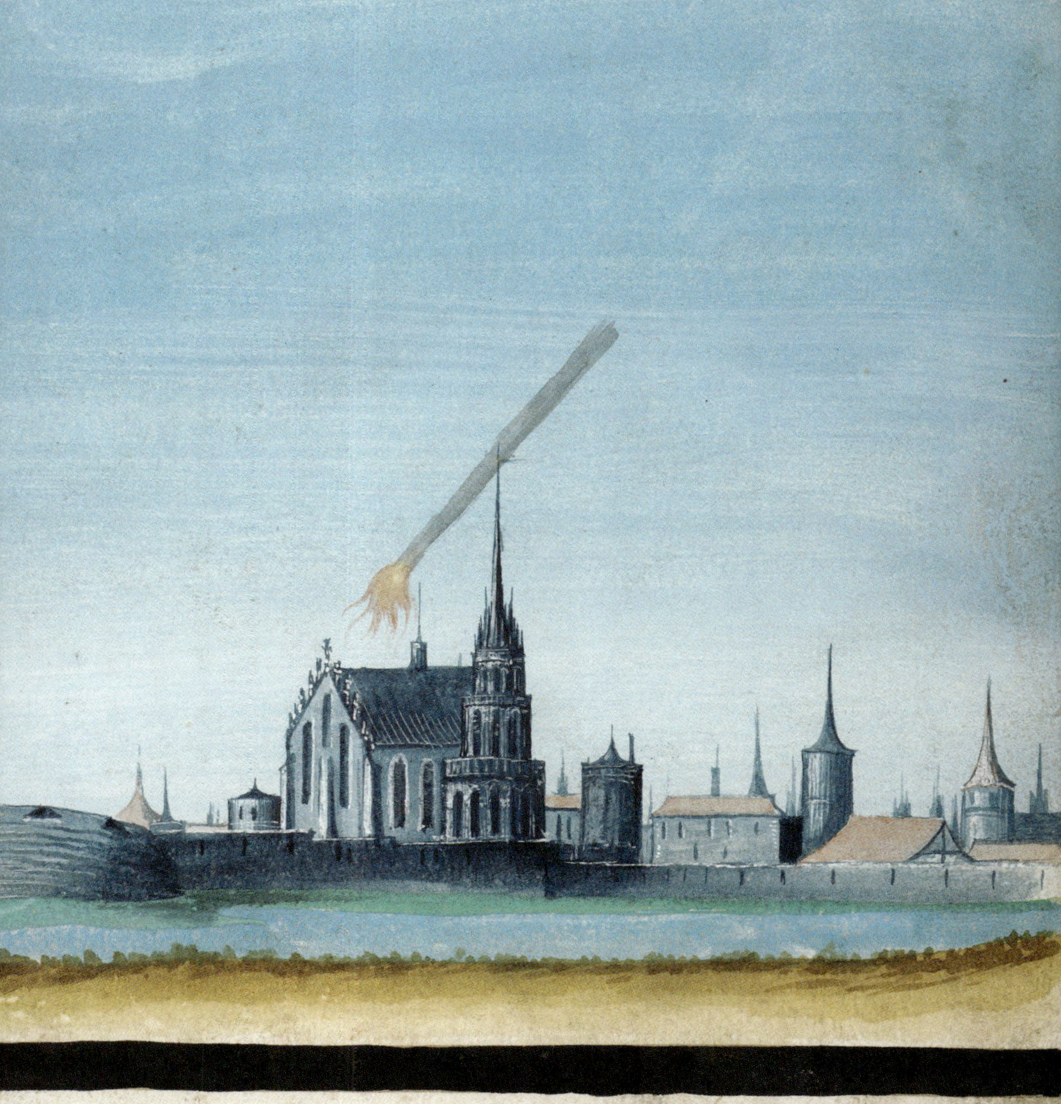

1520

Dem nach/nach mitter nacht vmb ein vrh oder ein wenig dar nach/hat man dieses zaichen gesehen

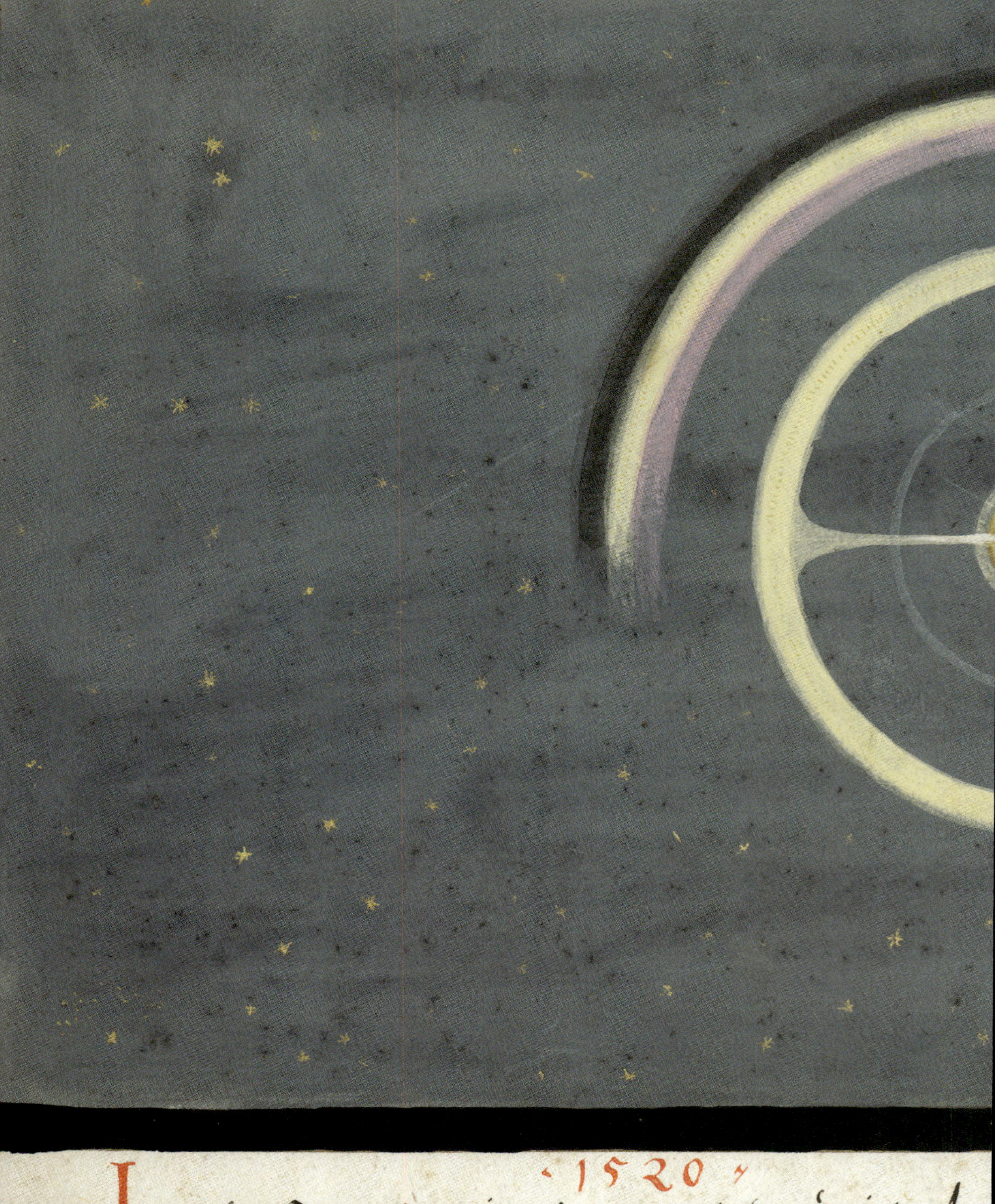

·1520·

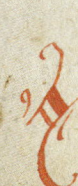

Im m d xx Jar an dem vi tag des monnats Januari vmb acht vr noch mittag in der nacht in der statt wien hatt man das zeichen vmb den mon schein gesehen·

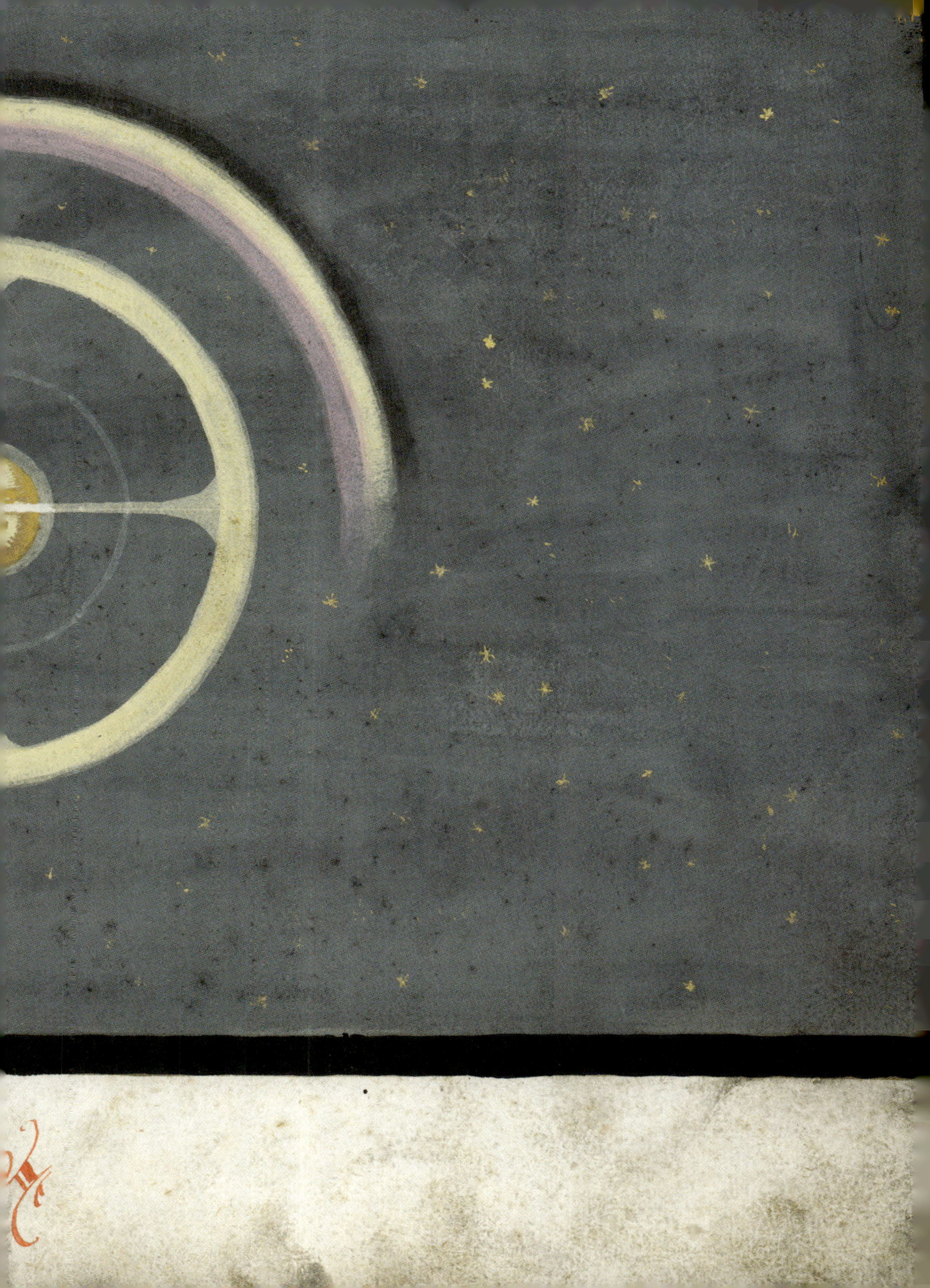

·1520·

Im m d xx Jar den siebenden tag des monats Januari
von auffgang der Sonnen: pis auff zehene oder ein wen
ig mer hat man gesehen drey sonnen welche genent werdē
Parahelios zu wien in osterreich

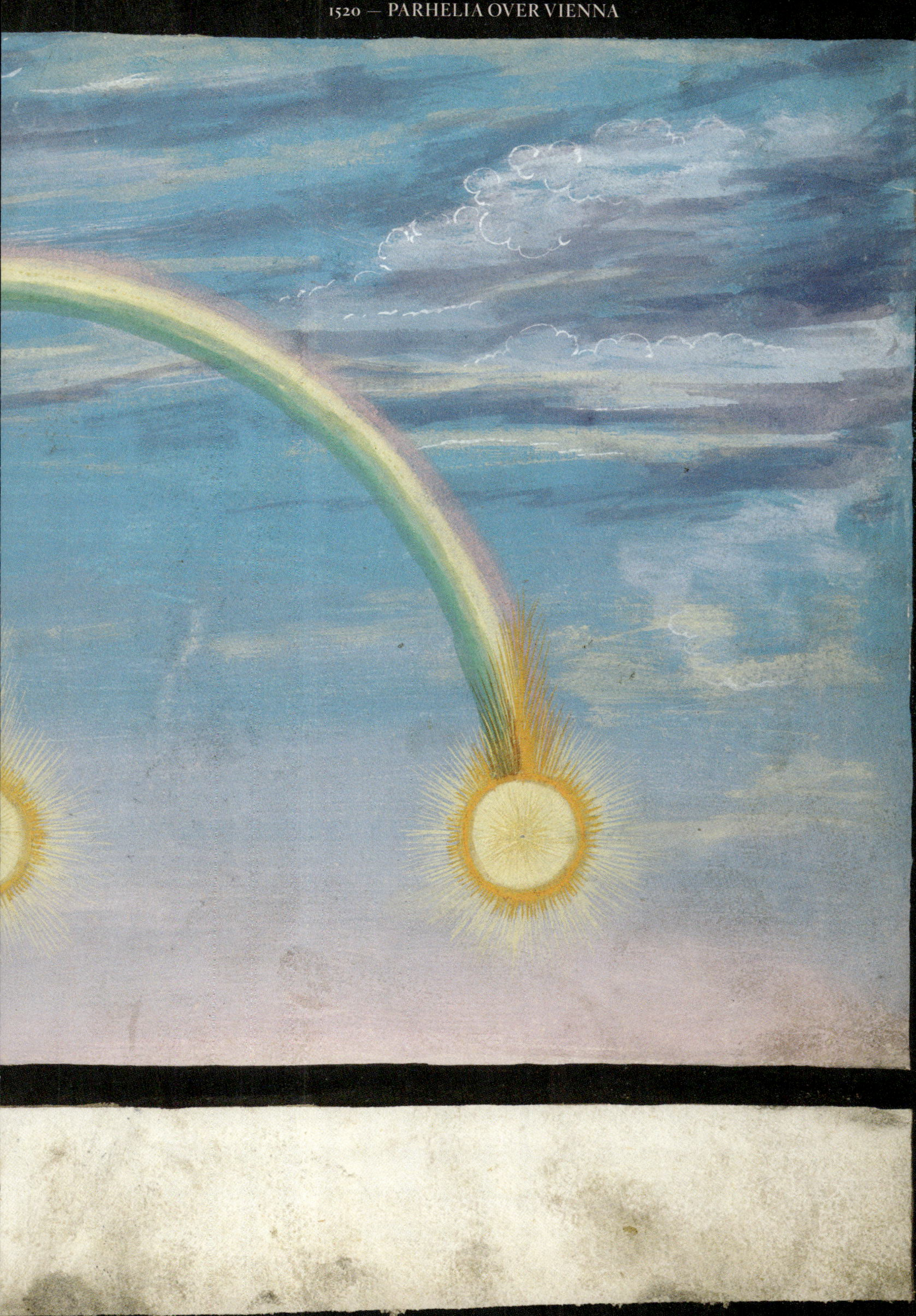

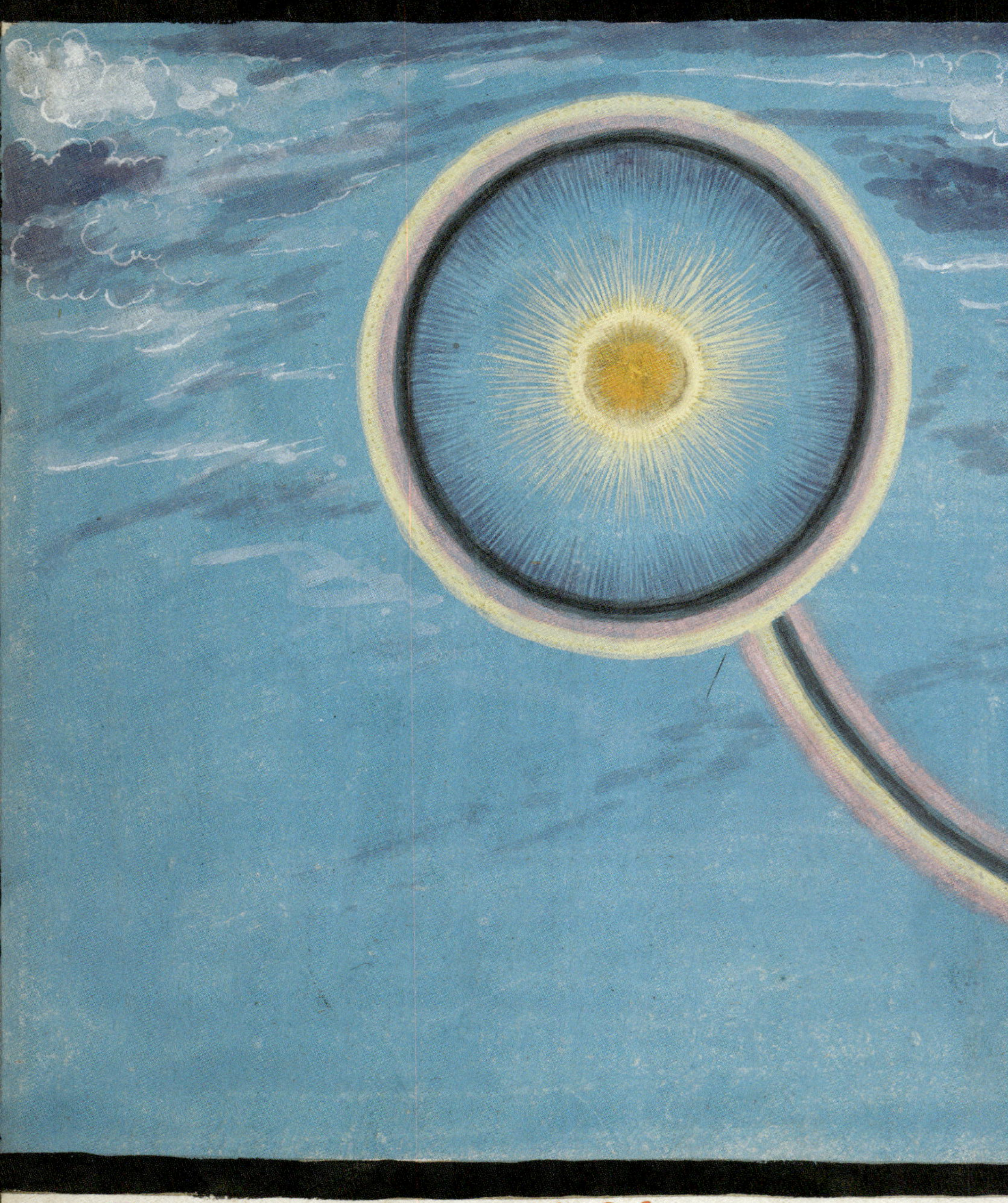

·1520·

Im M D XX Jar den vi tag des monnats Jannuari vmb drey vr nach mittag ist gesehen worden: zu wien vmb die Sonnen dis zaichen das do genent wirt hallo maximus:

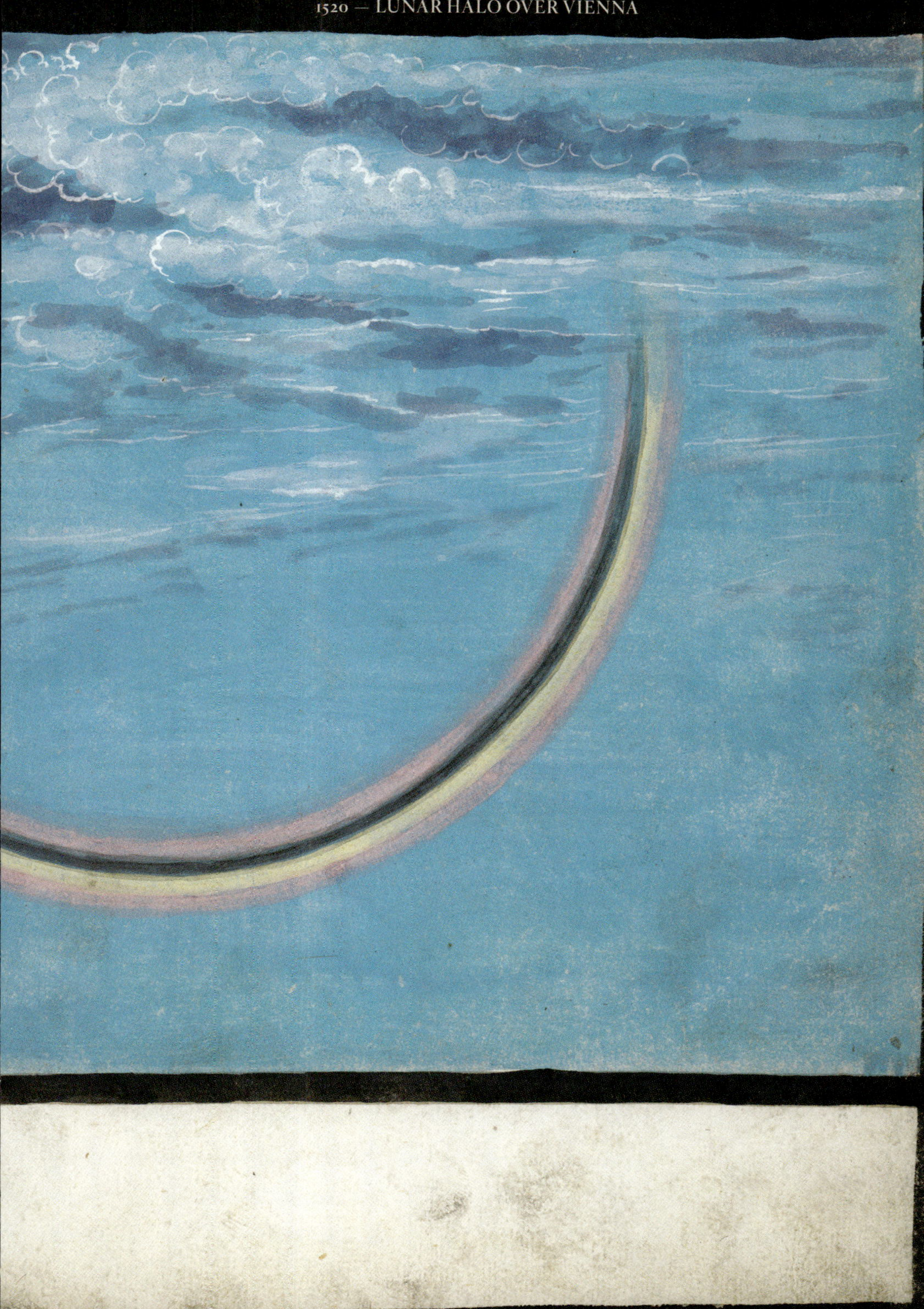

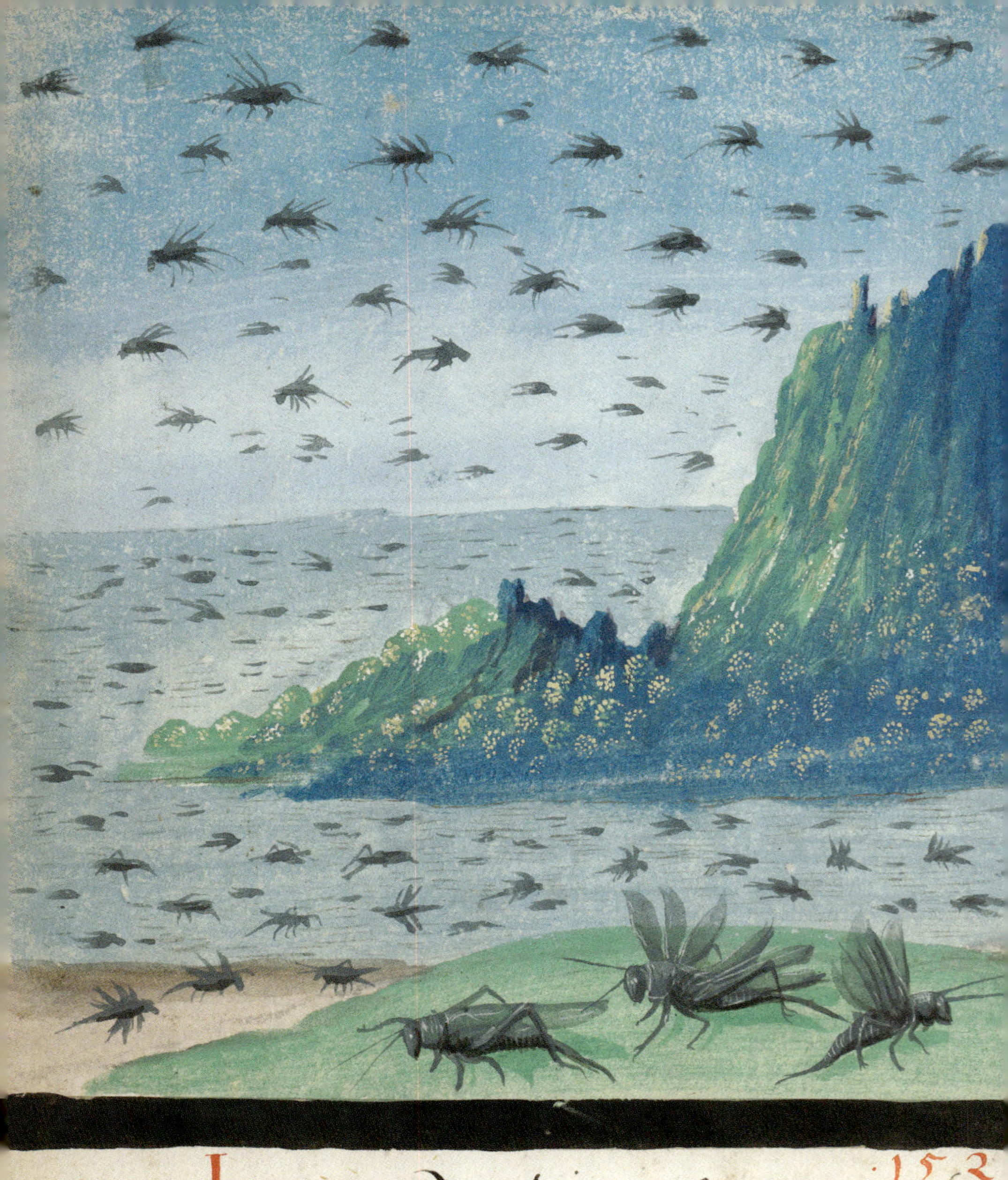

152

Im m d xxvii Jar hat ein graußsamer wind auß de
reich polen geworffen, die dan grossen schaden den me
grau vnnd goldfarb wie hie gemalt steet · -

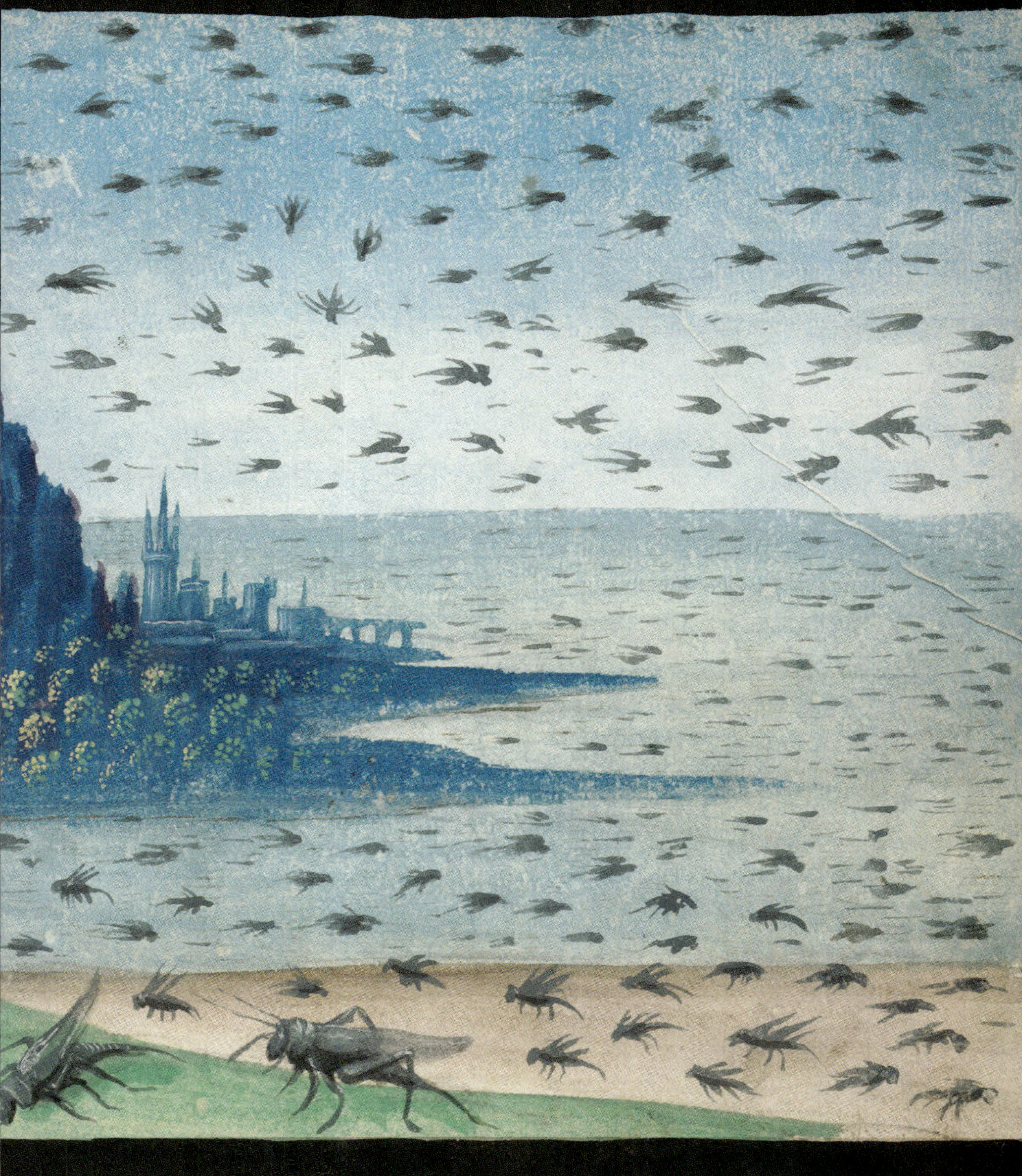

rckei groſ ſcharen der heuw ſchrecken in das küng
n vnnd vich zu gefügt haben / die heuw ſchrecken ſind

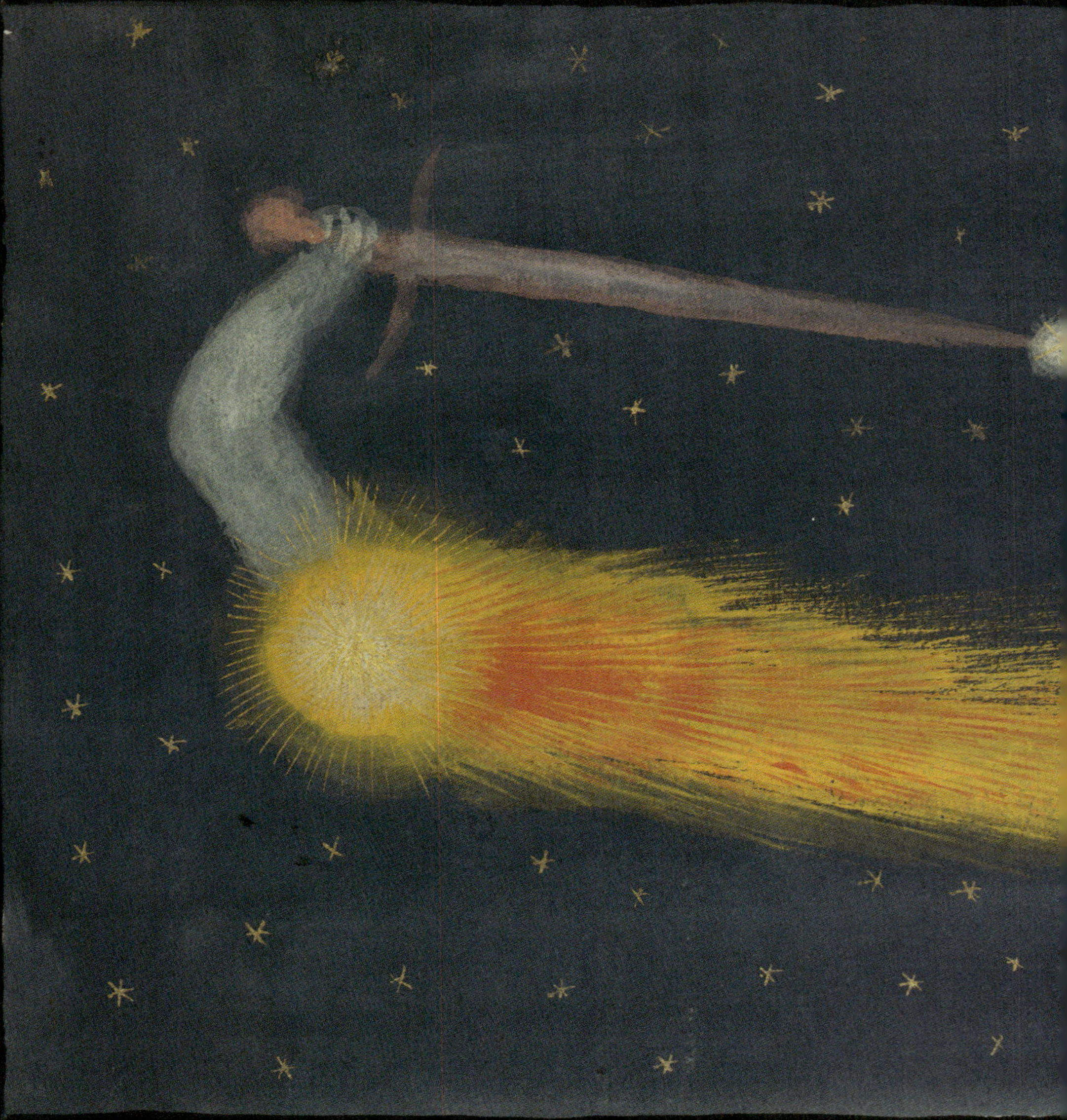

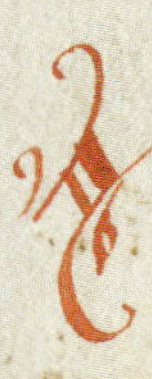

Im m d xxvii Jar den ailfften tag octobris zu mor · 15
worden / fünff viertel stund lang / darnach wurde
farb gleich geel rott / voren das haubt gleich einem
welt / darein schlagen unnd an der schwerts spitz
wolken farber strom der lennger was dan d

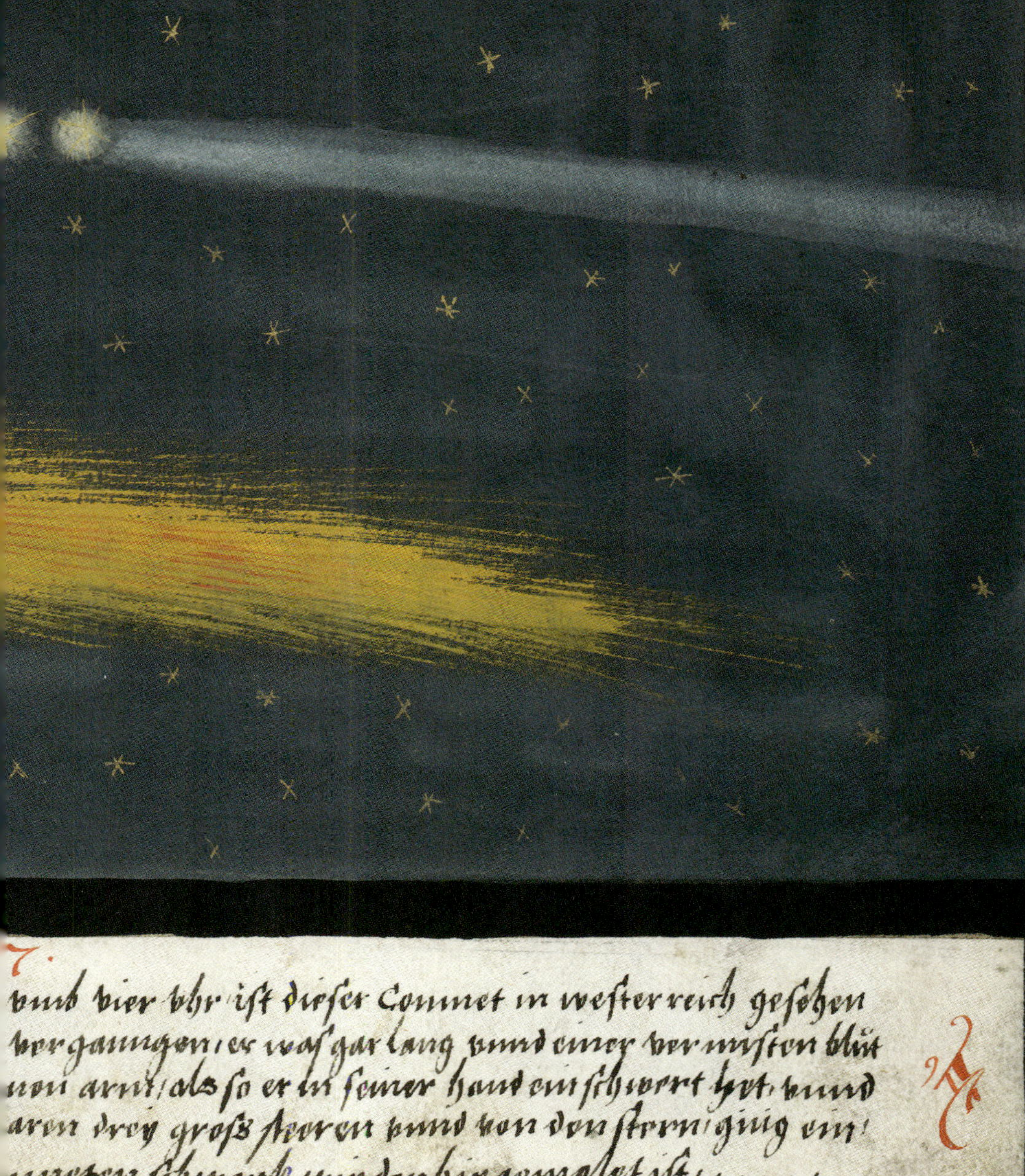
7.
vnnd vier vhr ist dieser Commet in westerreich gesehen
vergangen, er was gar lang vnnd einer ver misten blüt
von arm, als so er in seiner hant ein schwert het, vnnd
aren drey gross steren vnnd von den stern ging ein
vnnten schwantz wie dan hir gemalet ist

FOL. 107

1520 — Lunar halo over Vienna | Mondhalo über Wien | Halo lunaire dans le ciel de Vienne

In the year 1520, on the 6th day of the month of January, this sign around the sun, which is called "Halo Maximus", was seen in Vienna at three o'clock in the afternoon.

Im 1520. Jahr, am 6. Tag des Monats Januar, ist um drei Uhr nach Mittag zu Wien dieses Zeichen um die Sonne gesehen worden, das da „Halo Maximus" genannt wird.

En l'an 1520, le sixième jour du mois de janvier, ce signe entourant le soleil, appelé « Halo Maximus », fut observé à Vienne à trois heures après midi.

FOL. 109

1527 — Plague of locusts in Poland
Heuschreckenplage in Polen | Invasion de locustes en Pologne

In the year 1527 a terrible wind from Turkey carried great hordes of locusts into the kingdom of Poland, which then caused great harm to the people and livestock. The locusts were grey and gold colour, just as is painted here.

Im 1527. Jahr hat ein grausamer Wind aus der Türkei große Scharen von Heuschrecken in das Königreich Polen getragen, die dann den Menschen und dem Vieh großen Schaden zugefügt haben. Die Heuschrecken sind grau und goldfarben gewesen, wie hier gemalt ist.

En l'an 1527, un vent terrible venu de Turquie précipita des hordes de locustes dans le royaume de Pologne, ce qui causa de grands maux aux gens et au bétail. Les locustes étaient grises et dorées, comme dans cette peinture.

FOL. 110

1527 — Comet | Komet | Comète

In the year 1527, on the eleventh of October, at four o'clock in the morning, this comet was seen in Westrich for five quarters of an hour and then it disappeared again. It was extremely long and yellowish-red, like a diluted blood in colour. At the front the head was like a bent arm, as if it had a sword in its hand and was poised to start striking with it. And at the point of the sword there were three big stars and from the stars there issued a cloud-coloured stream, which was longer than the comet's tail, just as it is painted here.

Im 1527. Jahr, am elften Oktober, morgens um vier Uhr, ist dieser Komet in der Region Westrich fünf Viertelstunden lang gesehen worden und danach wieder verschwunden. Er war ganz lang und gelbrot, einer vermischten Blutfarbe gleich. Voran das Haupt gleich einem gebogenen Arm, als ob er in seiner Hand ein Schwert hätte und dreinschlagen wollte. Und an der Spitze des Schwerts waren drei große Sterne, und von den Sternen ging ein wolkenfarbener Strom aus, der länger war als der Kometenschweif, wie dann hier gemalt ist.

En l'an 1527, le onzième jour d'octobre, à quatre heures du matin, cette comète fut observée dans le Westrich pendant cinq quarts d'heure, puis disparut. Elle était très longue et jaune orangé, couleur de sang dilué. À l'avant, la tête ressemblait à un bras replié, comme s'il portait une épée à la main et s'apprêtait à frapper. Et à la pointe de l'épée, il y avait trois étoiles et des étoiles jaillissait un courant couleur de nuage, plus long que la queue de la comète, comme dans cette peinture.

FOL. 111

1527 — Comet | Komet | Comète

In the year 1527 several streaks like long spears were seen next to the comet, with several faces and small swords in amongst them, all intermingled in a pale red colour. Between them could be seen several large flames that blazed very brightly and with a fiery light. And the faces, with hair and beards the colour of grey clouds, were seen here and there to be flickering through each other as if they were lying in water that was flowing in rivulets of blood, and as if everything was mixing up together, which looked so terrifying that many who saw it died.

Im Jahr 1527 sind neben dem Kometen viele Streifen wie lange Spieße gesehen worden, dazwischen viele Gesichter und kleine Schwerter vermischt in blassroter Farbe. Zwischen diesen sah man viele große Flammen, die ganz hell und feurig leuchteten. Und die Gesichter – hier und da, mit Haaren und Bärten von einer Farbe wie graue Wolken – sah man durcheinanderflimmern, als lägen sie in fließendem Wasser aus Blutstreifen und als ob alles durcheinanderstrebte, was schreckenerregend ausgesehen hat, sodass viele, die es gesehen haben, gestorben sind.

En l'an 1527 ont été observées à côté de la comète de nombreuses bandes ressemblant à de longs épieux, entre elles de nombreux visages et de petites épées mélangés, de couleur rouge pâle. On voyait entre ceux-ci beaucoup de grandes flammes qui brillaient de manière très claire et ardente. Et on voyait les visages – ici et là avec des chevelures et des barbes d'une couleur évoquant les nuages gris – scintiller en désordre, comme s'ils étaient dans de l'eau courante avec des filets de sang, et comme si tout se brouillait, ce qui avait un aspect terrifiant, si bien que nombre de gens qui l'ont vu en sont morts.

FOL. 112

1527 — Parhelia over Kaufbeuren
Nebensonnen über Kaufbeuren | Parhélies dans le ciel de Kaufbeuren

In the year 1527, on the seventeenth of February, three suns were seen in Kaufbeuren enclosed within two rainbows in the sky, adjacent to the mountains. And the two outer suns were red on the sides facing the sun in the middle and yellow on the sides facing the rainbow. And a white streak went through the middle and the shining of the inner rainbow was so yellow that no one could see into it because of its brightness.

Im 1527. Jahr, am siebzehnten Februar, sind zu Kaufbeuren drei Sonnen in zwei Regenbogen eingeschlossen am Himmel, an das Gebirge angrenzend, gesehen worden. Und die zwei äußeren Sonnen sind zur mittleren Sonne hin rot und zum Regenbogen hin gelb gewesen. Und ein weißer Streifen ist in der Mitte dort hindurchgegangen und der innere Regenbogen ist so gelb in seinem Schein gewesen, dass man nicht hineinsehen konnte wegen der Helligkeit.

En l'an 1527, le dix-septième jour de février, trois soleils furent observés à Kaufbeuren, encerclés par deux arcs-en-ciel dans le ciel, adjacents aux montagnes. Et les deux soleils extérieurs étaient rouges du côté du soleil du milieu et jaunes du côté de l'arc-en-ciel. Et une bande blanche les traversait par le milieu et l'arc-en-ciel intérieur était d'un éclat si jaune que personne ne pouvait le regarder directement tant il brillait.

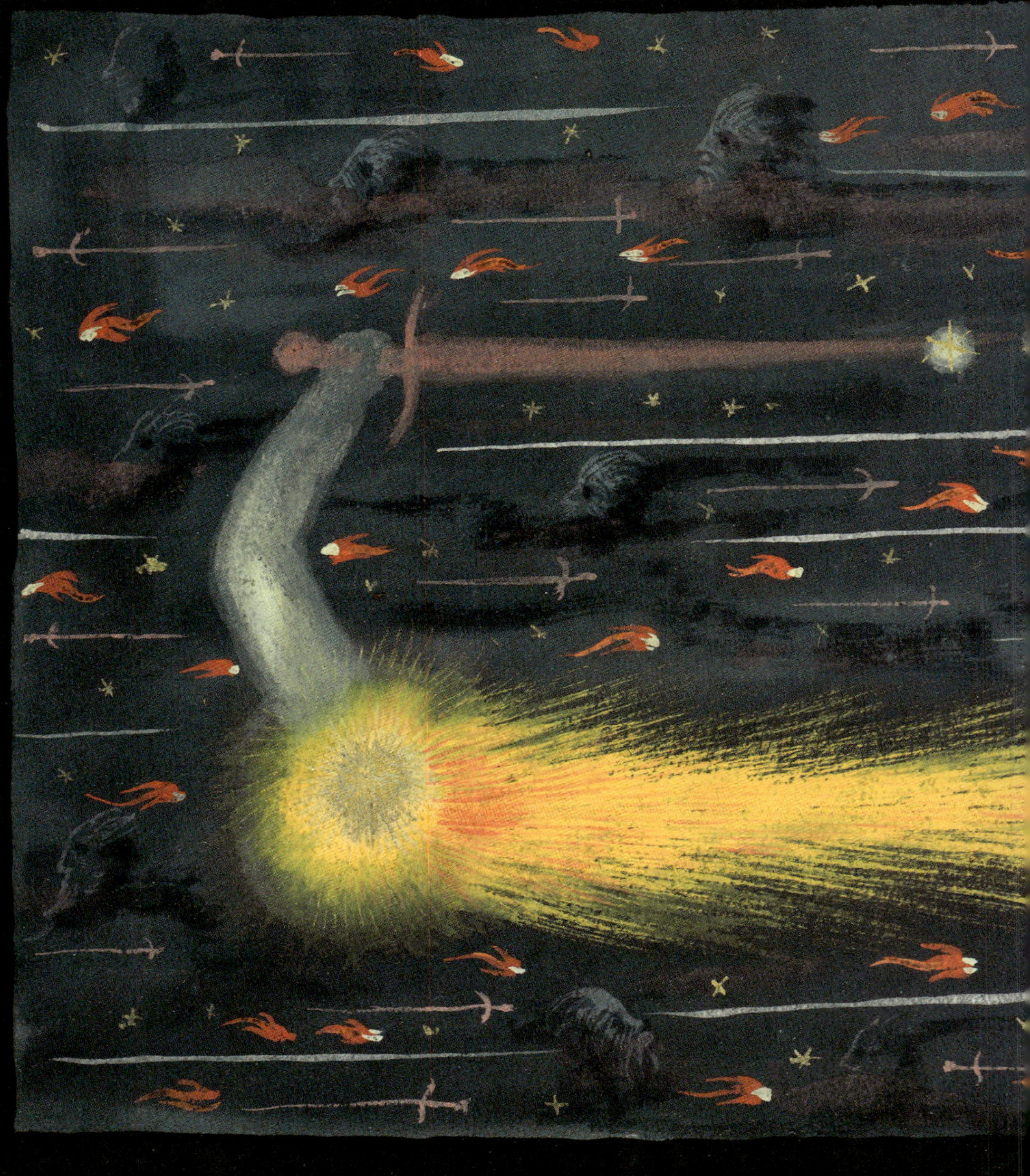

Im m d xxvii Jar ist neben den Connetten gesehe
vnnd klainer schwerter vermischt als sich ainer b
die gantz hell vnnd feurig schinen vnnd die an
er grawen wolcken farb als legen sie im blut st
ob er als durch ein ander arbeitet das grausam

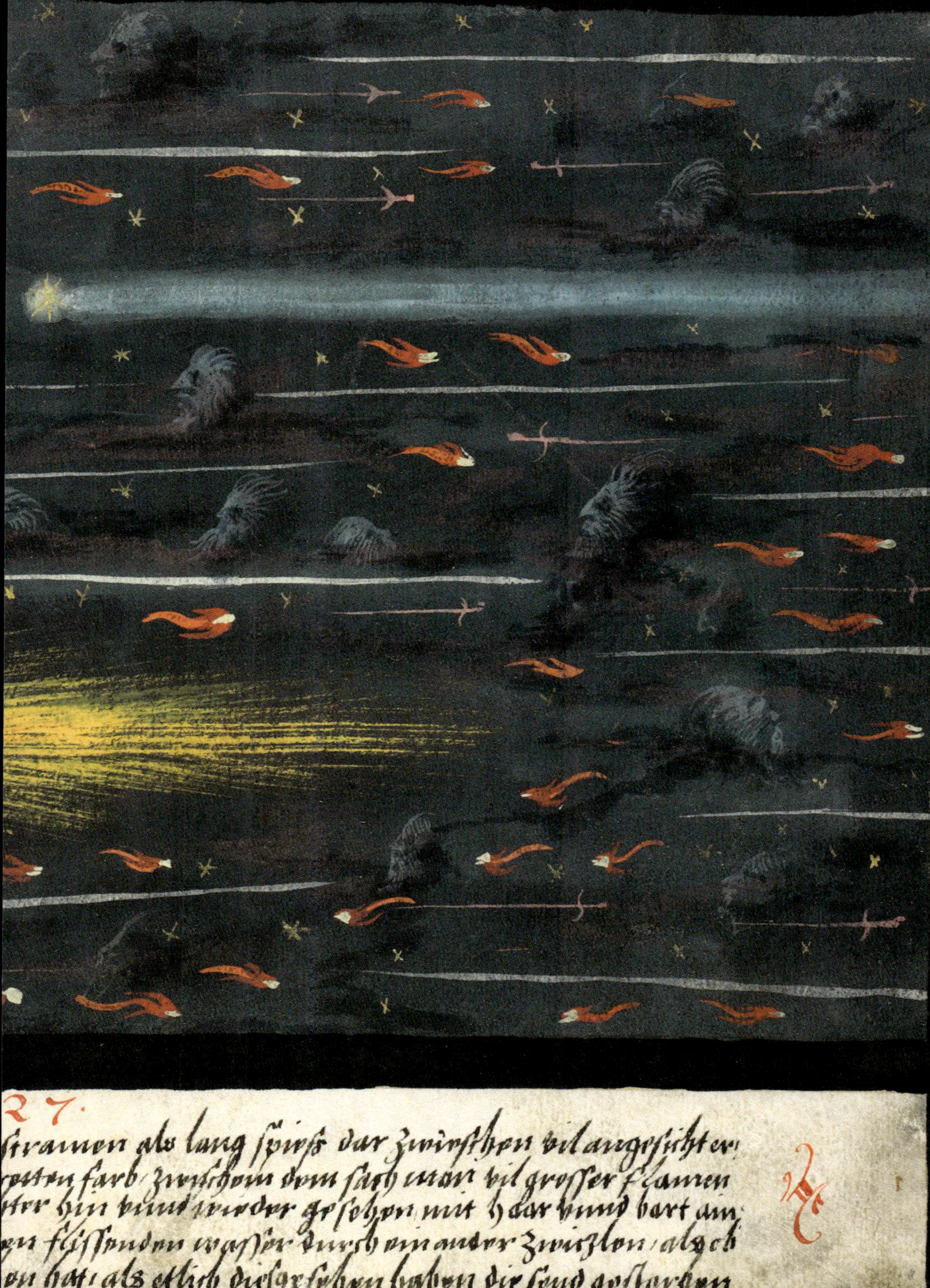
27.
strainen als lang spiess dar zwischen vil angesichter:
speten farb zwischen dem sach man vil grosser flamen
ter hin vnnd wider gesehen mit haar vnnd bart an
en flissenden wasser durch ein ander zwischen: als ge
en hat: als etlich die gesehen haben die seind gestorben

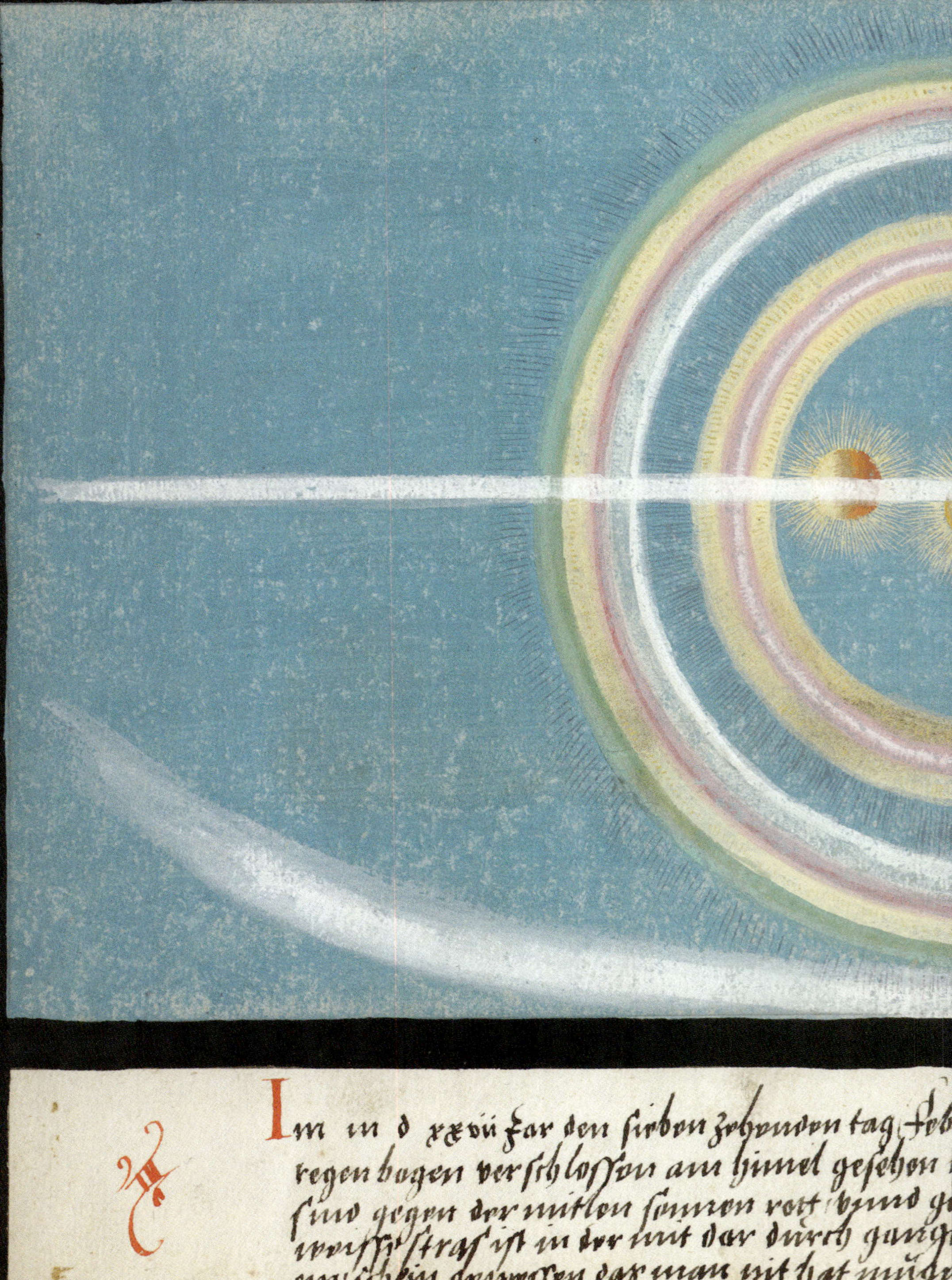

Im m d xxvii Jar den sibenzehenden tag Feb
regen bogen verschlossen am himel gesehen
sind gegen der mitlen sunnen rott / bund g
weisse strass ist in der mit dar durch gang
ein schein gewessen das man nit hat müg

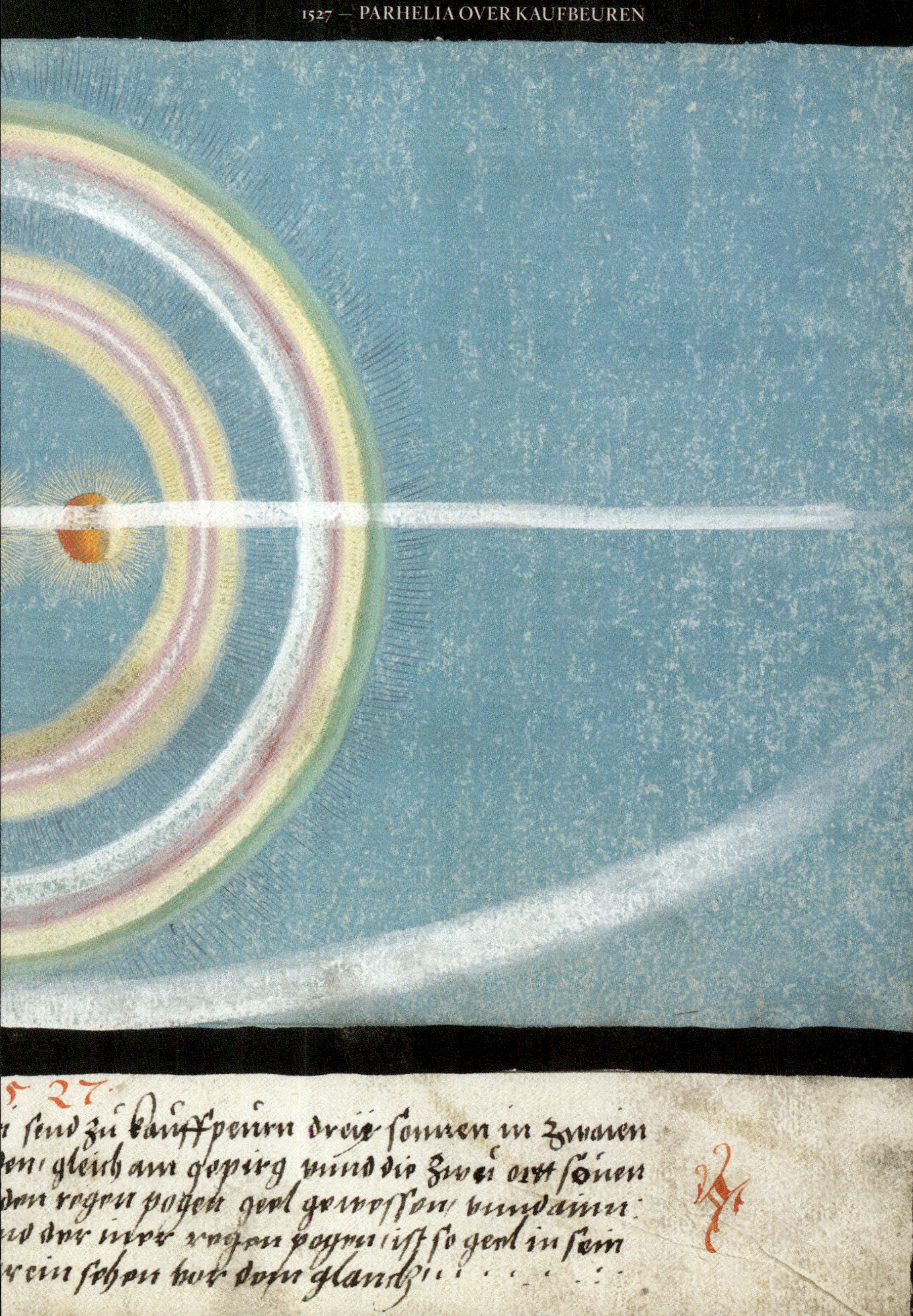
527.
send zu kauffpeurn dreÿ sonnen in zwaien
den gleich am gepirg vnnd die zwei ort sonen
den regen pogen gel gewessen vnnd ainer
der inner regen pogen ist so gel in sein
ein schen vor dem glantz

Im m D xxviii iar/ auff den sechzehen
zwolff vr/ nach mittag/ ist die gestalt
zu augspurg gesehen worden/ vnd hat

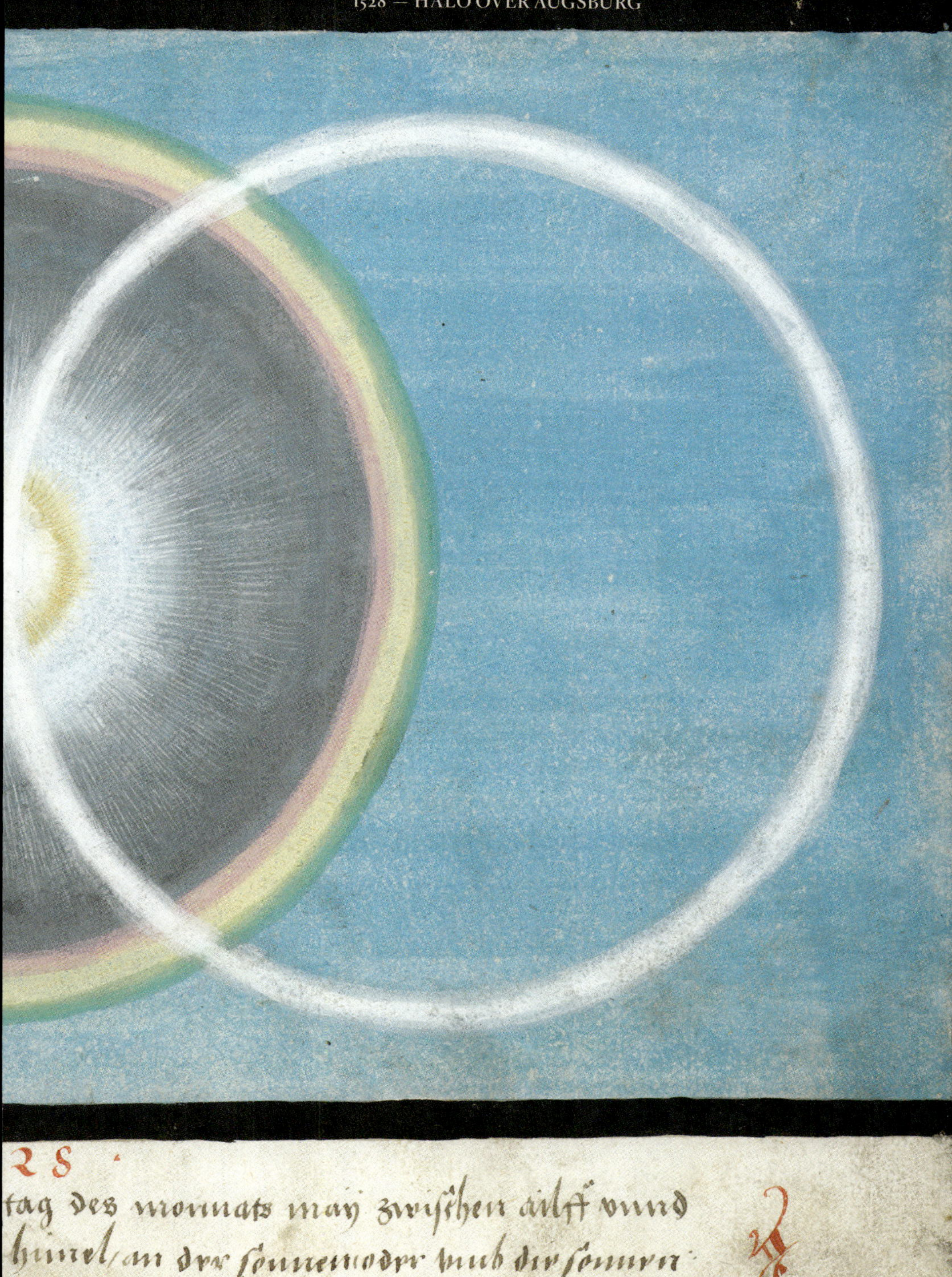
28
tag des monnats may zwischen ailff vnnd
himel, an der sonnen oder vmb die sonnen
bei anderhalb stund gewert oder lenger

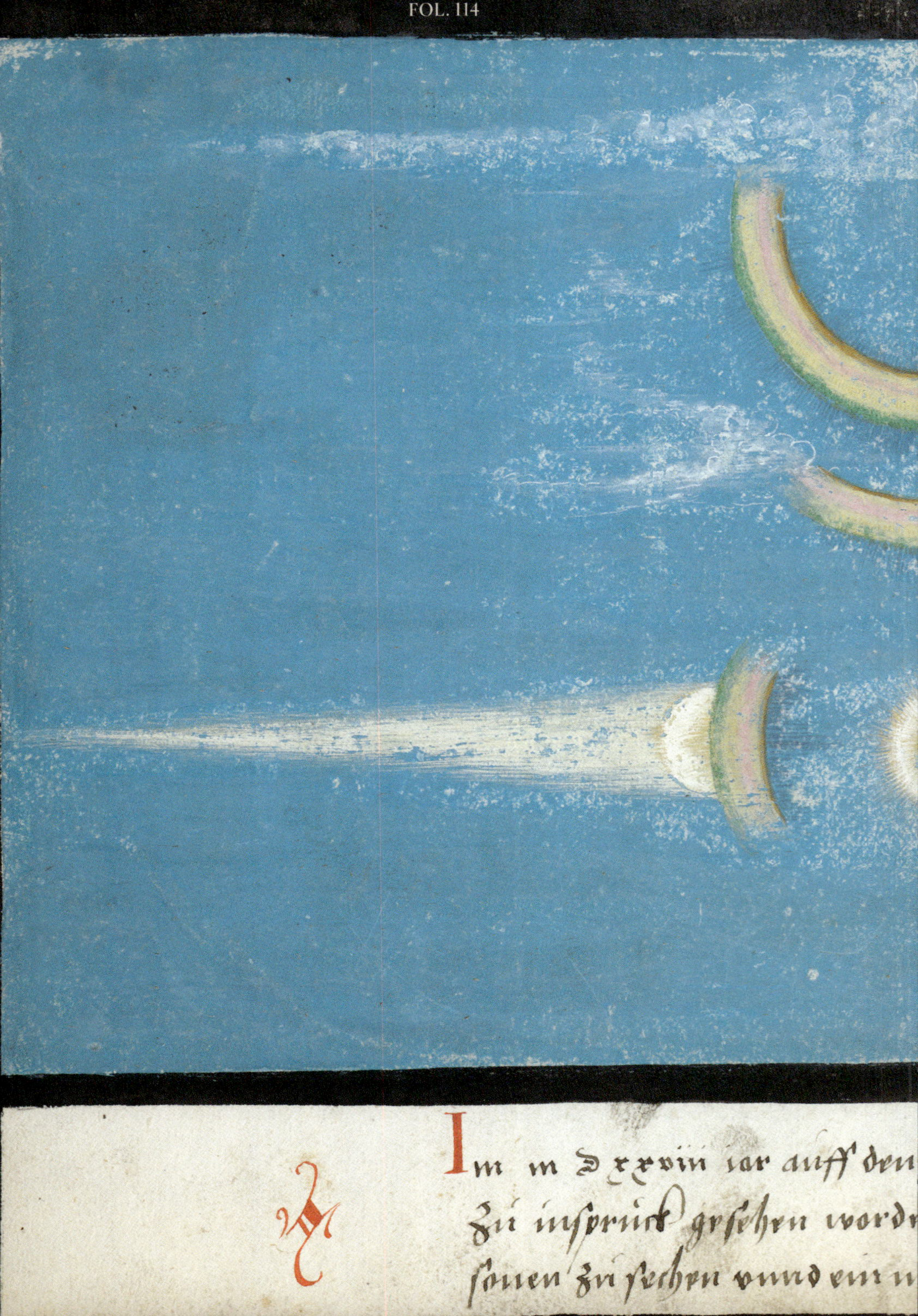
Im m D xxviii iar auff den
zu insprück gesehen word
sonen zu sechen vnnd ein n

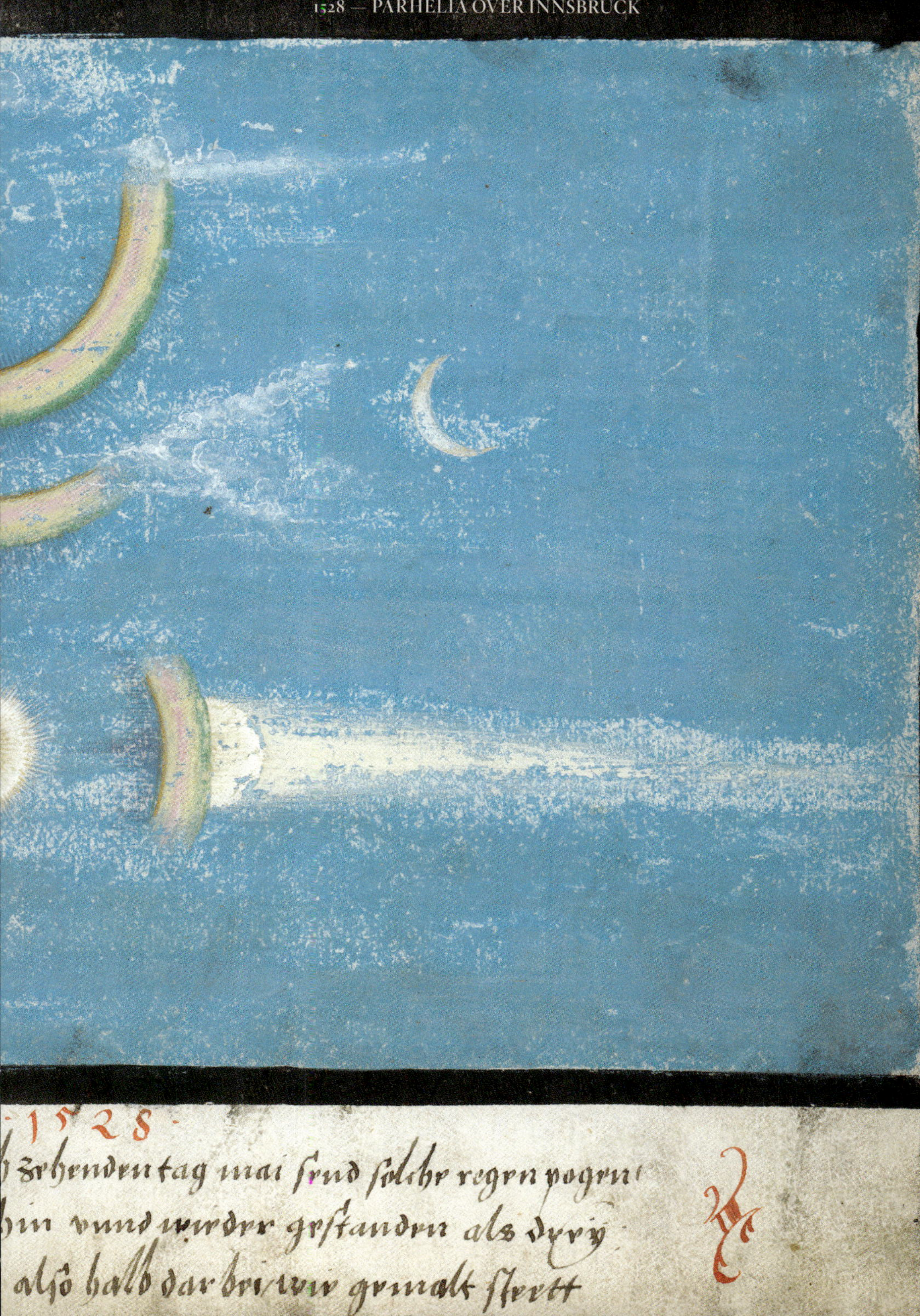
1528
zehenden tag mai sind solche regen pogen
hin vnnd wider gestanden als drey
also halb dar bei wir gemalt stett

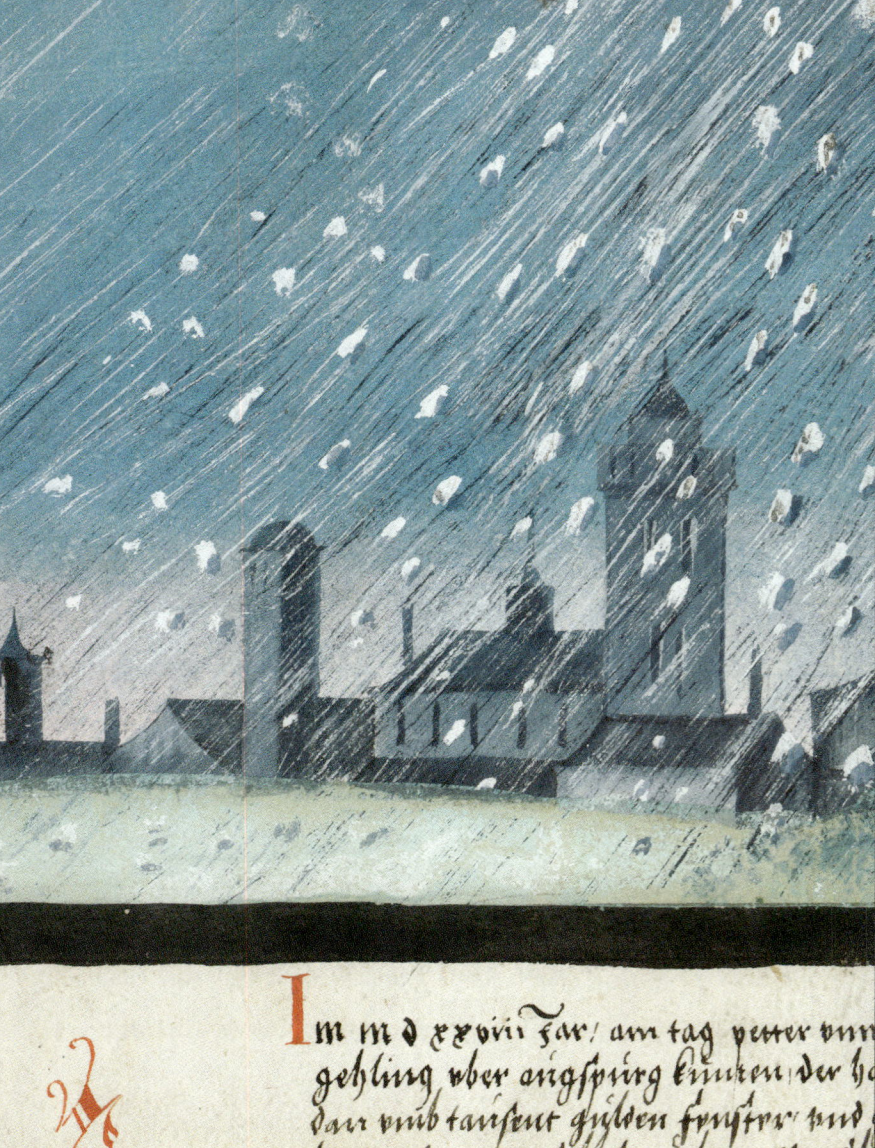

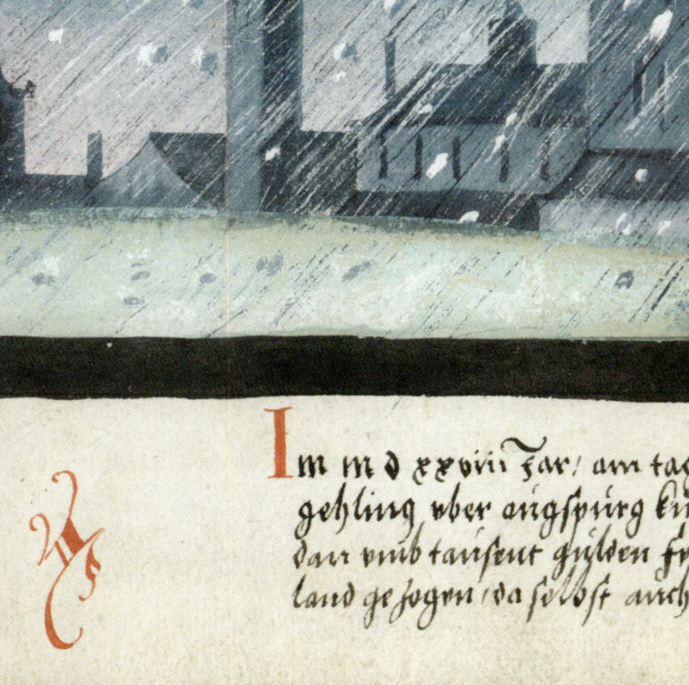

Im m d xxviii Jar / am tag petter
gehling vber augspurg kumen / der
dan vmb tausent gulden fenster vnd
land ge sogen / da selbst auch grossen

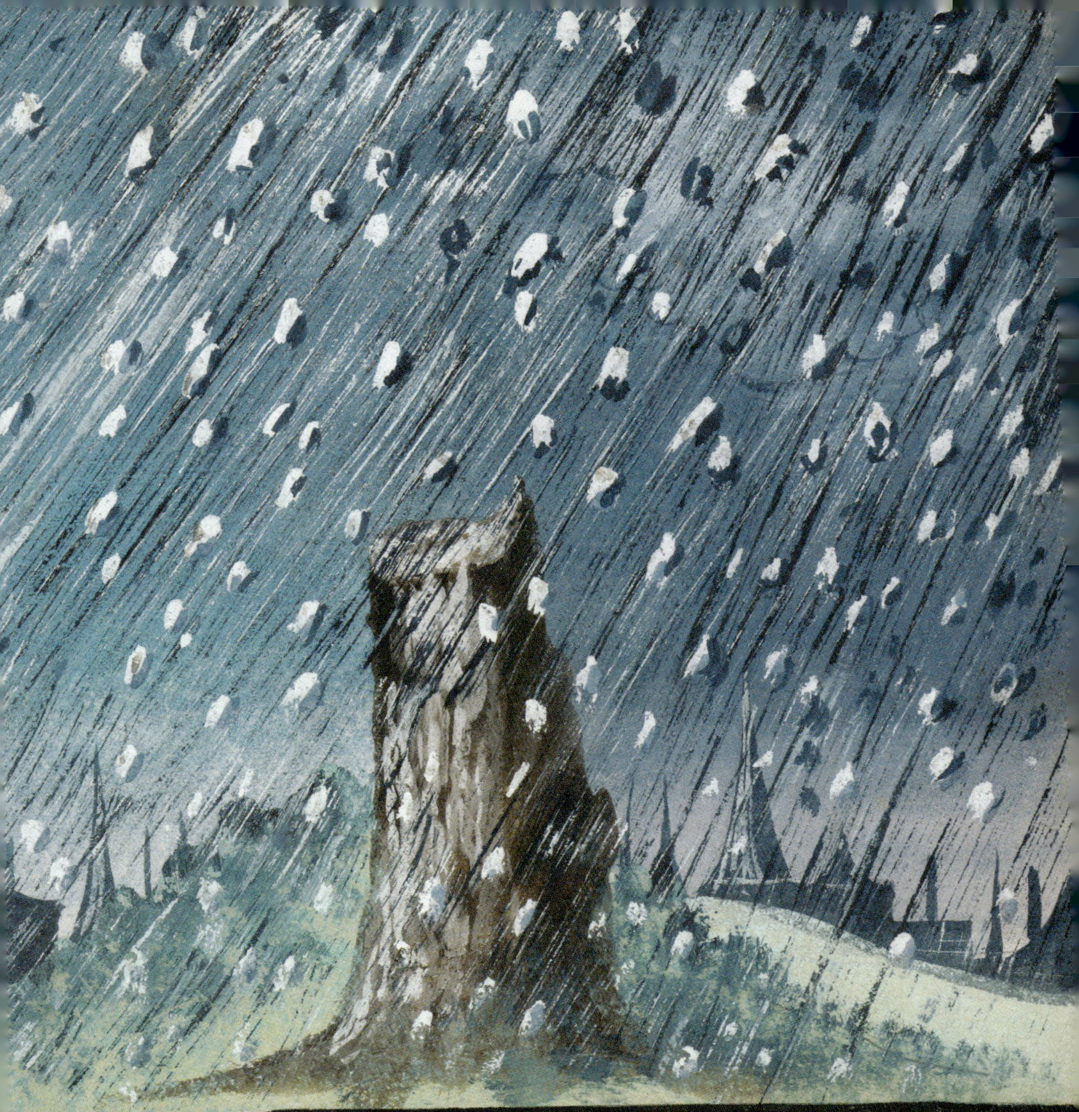

528.

ule; vmb vesper zeit ist so ein groser hagel
n viertel stund gewert vnnd hat vire
r erschlagen, vnnd ist auch vber das peir
ain korn vnnd andern früchtte gethā

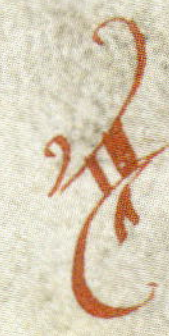

FOL. 113

1528 — Halo over Augsburg

Halo über Augsburg | Halo dans le ciel d'Augsbourg

In the year 1528, on the sixteenth day of the month of May, between the eleventh and twelfth hour after midday, this formation was seen in the sky in Augsburg on the sun or around the sun and stayed for about one and a half hours or longer.

Im 1528. Jahr, auf den sechzehnten Tag des Monats Mai, ist zwischen der elften und zwölften Stunde nach Mittag, dieses Gebilde zu Augsburg am Himmel an der Sonne oder um die Sonne gesehen worden und ist fast anderthalb Stunden oder länger geblieben.

En l'an 1528, le seizième jour de mai, entre la onzième et la douzième heure après midi, cette formation fut observée dans le ciel à Augsbourg sur le soleil ou autour du soleil et y resta pendant environ une heure et demie ou plus longtemps.

FOL. 114

1528 — Parhelia over Innsbruck

Nebensonnen über Innsbruck | Parhélies dans le ciel d'Innsbruck

In the year 1528, on the sixteenth day of the month of May, such rainbows were seen in Innsbruck – appearing here and there, while at the same time three suns were to be seen – and a moon as a half beside them, as is painted here.

Im 1528. Jahr, sind auf den sechzehnten Tag des Monats Mai solche Regenbogen zu Innsbruck gesehen worden – hier und dort auftauchend, ebenso waren drei Sonnen zu sehen – und ein Mond so halb daneben, wie hier gemalt ist.

En l'an 1528, le seizième jour du mois de mai, ces arcs-en-ciel furent observés à Innsbruck – apparaissant ici et là, en même temps que trois soleils – ainsi qu'une moitié de lune près d'eux, comme le montre cette peinture.

FOL. 115

1528 — Hail in Augsburg

Hagel in Augsburg | Grêle à Augsbourg

In the year 1528, on the Feast of Saints Peter and Paul, a hailstorm so great came upon Augsburg suddenly around late afternoon. It lasted a quarter of an hour and shattered more than a thousand guilders' worth of windows and glass and also passed over Bavaria, and there too caused great damage to the grain and fruit as well.

Im 1528. Jahr, an Peter und Paul, ist um die Vesperzeit so ein großer Hagel plötzlich über Augsburg gekommen. Der hat eine Viertelstunde gedauert und hat für mehr als tausend Gulden Fenster und Glas zerschlagen und ist auch über Bayern gezogen, hat daselbst auch großen Schaden am Korn und anderen Früchten angerichtet.

En l'an 1528, le jour de la Saint-Pierre et Paul, un très fort orage de grêle s'abattit soudain sur Augsbourg vers la fin de l'après-midi. Il dura un quart d'heure et brisa pour plus de mille florins de fenêtres et de verre et traversa aussi la Bavière, où il causa aussi de grands dommages au grain et aux fruits.

FOL. 116

1529 — Flood

Überschwemmung | Inondation

In the year 1529 there was such an awful lot of water in the Rhine that in the villages it carried off houses with people and livestock. And a child in a cradle was caught near Heidelberg, having floated for six miles. And it did not meet with any harm.

Im 1529. Jahr ist so schrecklich viel Wasser im Rheinstrom gewesen, dass er in Dörfern Häuser mit Leuten und Vieh fortgerissen hat. Und ein Kind ist bei Heidelberg in einer Wiege aufgefangen worden, das sechs Meilen geschwommen ist. Und ihm ist kein Leid widerfahren.

En l'an 1529, le fleuve Rhin grossit si terriblement que dans les villages il emporta des maisons avec leurs habitants et le bétail. Et un enfant dans un berceau fut recueilli près de Heidelberg, après avoir parcouru six milles sur l'eau. Et il n'avait subi aucune souffrance.

FOL. 117

1529, 1532 — Two-headed calf and a stillborn calf

Doppelköpfiges Kalb und ein tot geborenes

Veau à deux têtes et veau mort-né

In the year 1529, on the fourteenth day of the month of January, this calf was born in Langweid near Augsburg, but came out dead from the mother. And I, Hans Burgkmair, painter, bought the skin for half a guilder from a parchment-maker, who had bought it for only six kreuzer.

In the year 1532, a calf such as this was born in a village near Donauwörth, just as is painted and recorded here etc.

Anno 1529, am vierzehnten Tag des Monats Januar, ist dieses Kalb bei Augsburg in Langweid geboren, aber tot aus der Mutter herausgekommen. Und ich, Hans Burgkmair, Maler, habe die Haut für einen halben Gulden von einem Pergamentmacher gekauft, der sie für nur sechs Kreuzer gekauft hat.

Im 1532. Jahr ist ein solches Kalb geboren, bei Donauwörth in einem Dorf, wie hier gemalt und verzeichnet ist etc.

En l'an 1529, le quatorzième jour du mois de janvier, ce veau naquit à Langweid près d'Augsbourg, mais sa mère le mit bas mort. Et moi, Hans Burgkmair, peintre, en achetai la peau pour un demi-florin à un parcheminier, qui ne l'avait achetée que six kreuzers.

En l'an 1532, un veau de cette sorte naquit près de Donauwörth dans un village, comme on le voit consigné et peint ici, etc.

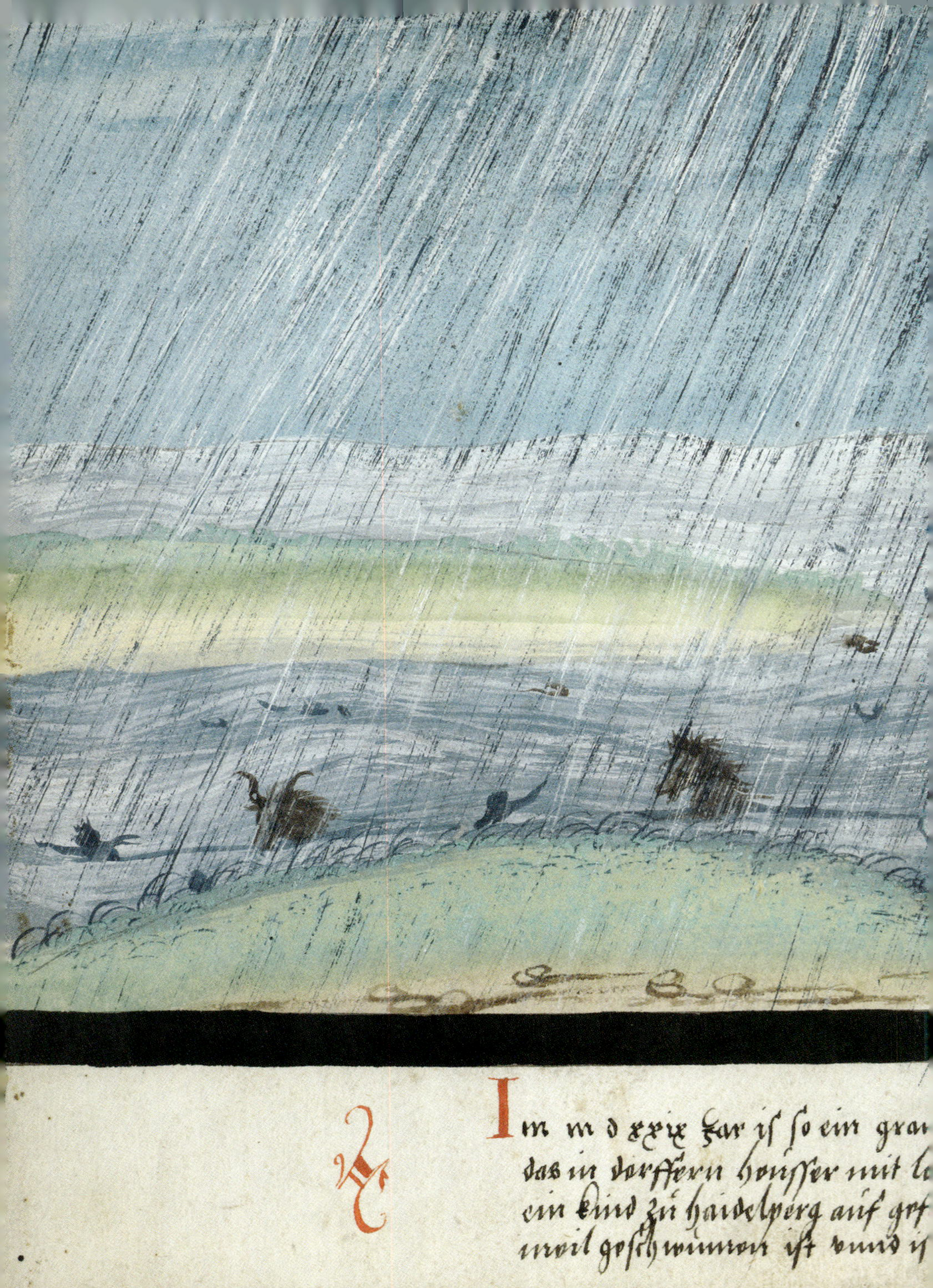

Im m d xxix Jar is so ein grau
das in dorffern heusser mit l
ein kind zu haidelperg auf gr
weil geschwummen ist vnnd i

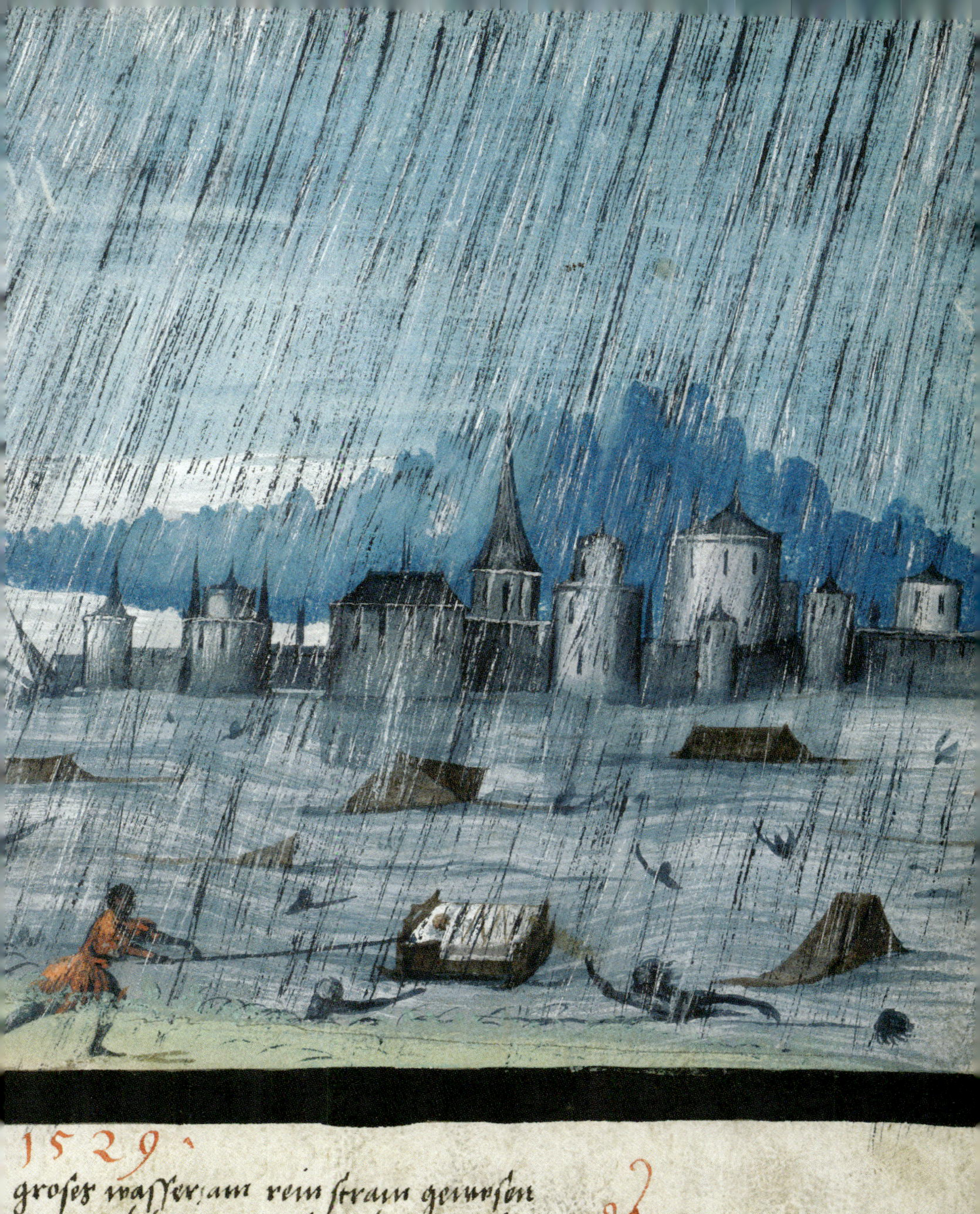

1529 ·

groser wasser · am rein strain gewesen
und vich hin weg gefurt hat · vnnd ist
y worden · in einer wiegen · das selbs
kain laid wider faren · · · · · · · ·

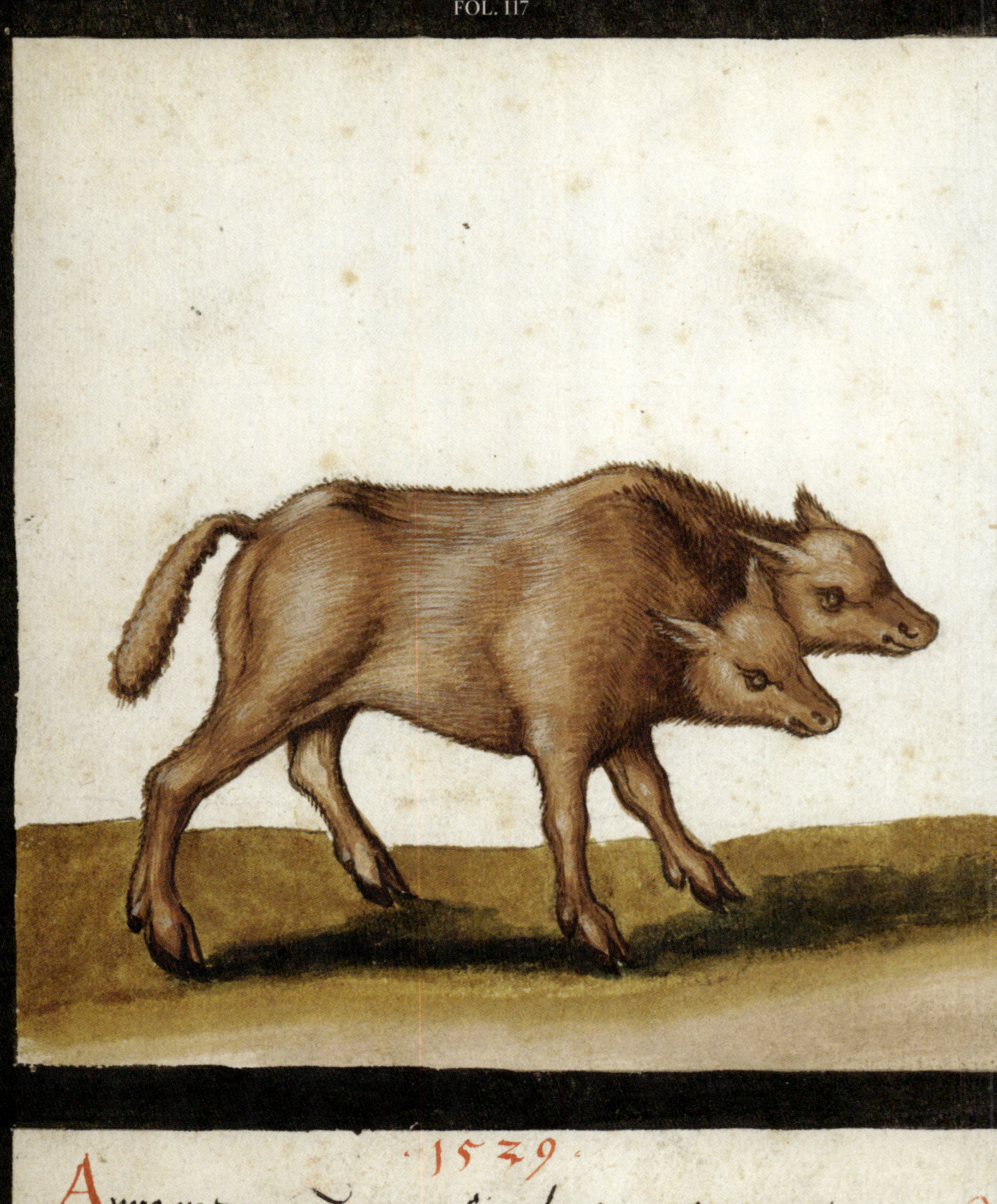

·1529·

Anno m d xxix Jar den fierzehenden tag des monats
Jenuari ist dis kalb bey Augspurg zu lanndtwaid gefallen
aber thot von der mutter kumen/ vnnd ich hanns bur-
ckmair maler hab die haut vmb ein halben gulden
kaufft/ von einem burmeister/ der sie nur vmb vi
kreitzer kaufft hat

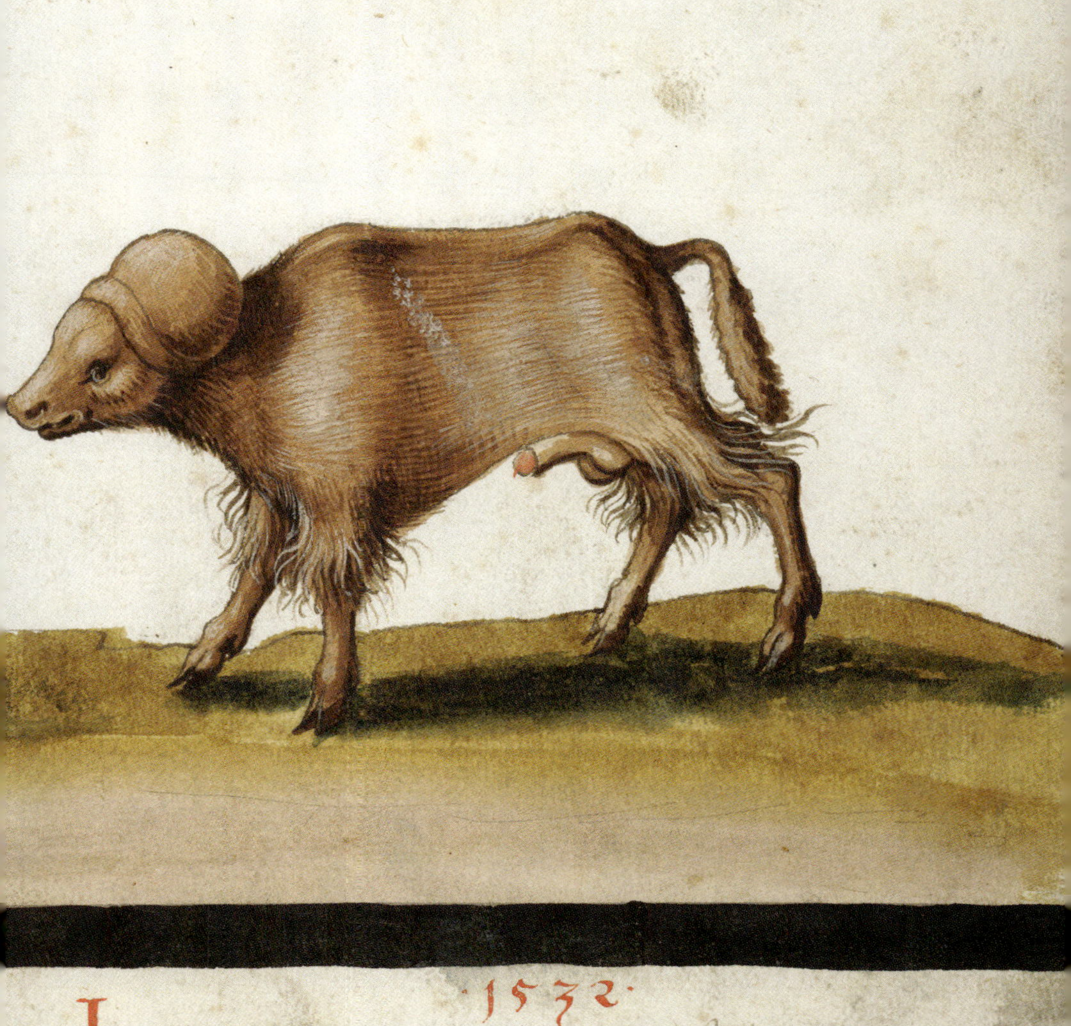

·1532·

Im m d xxxii iar ist ain solches kalb gefallen bey thomma werd in einem dorff wie hie gemalt· vnnd ver zaichnet etc

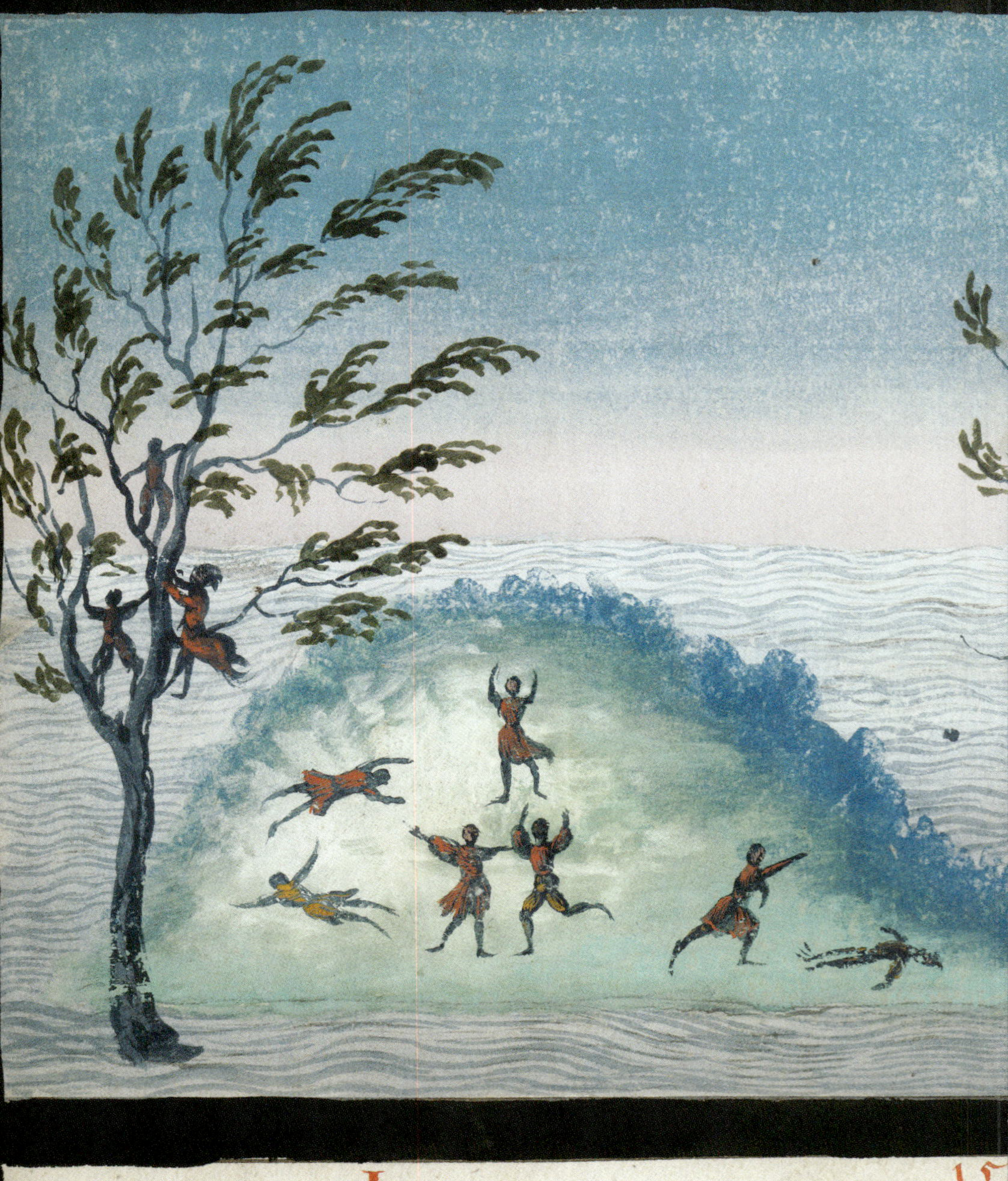

15

Im m d xxx zar den funfften tag noue
selannd das die stadt flising, da die gewalt
vnnd die gannßen landtschafft gar erdren
auff die perg, vnnd mussten hungers sterb
ist warheit, dan ich das von schreiben ka

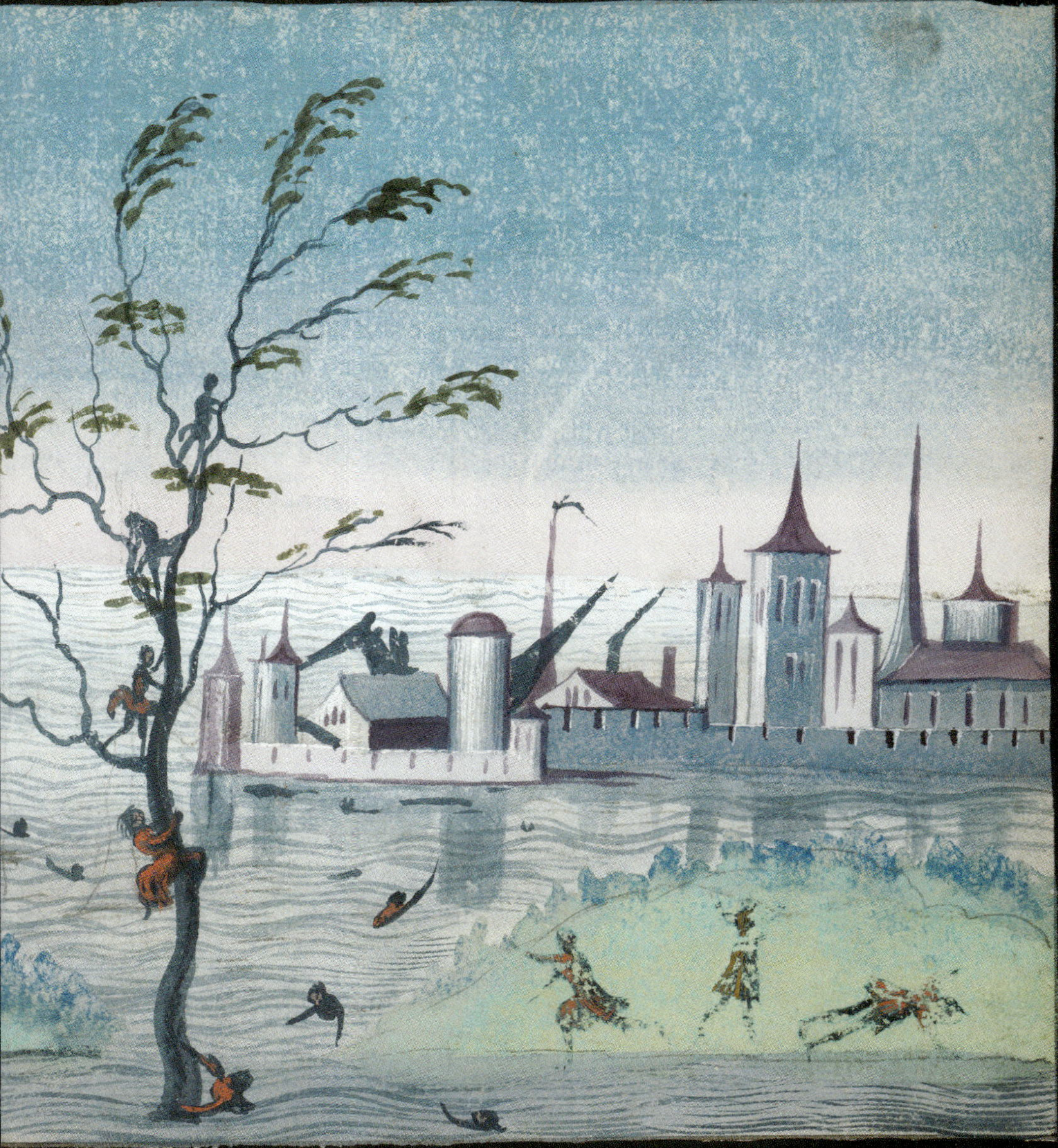

ir, wass so groser wint in flanderen unnd
schiff an künigen, mer dan halb hin riss.
auch flach vil folckes auf die paum e
ar auff, das es grausamer geschehen

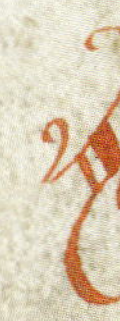

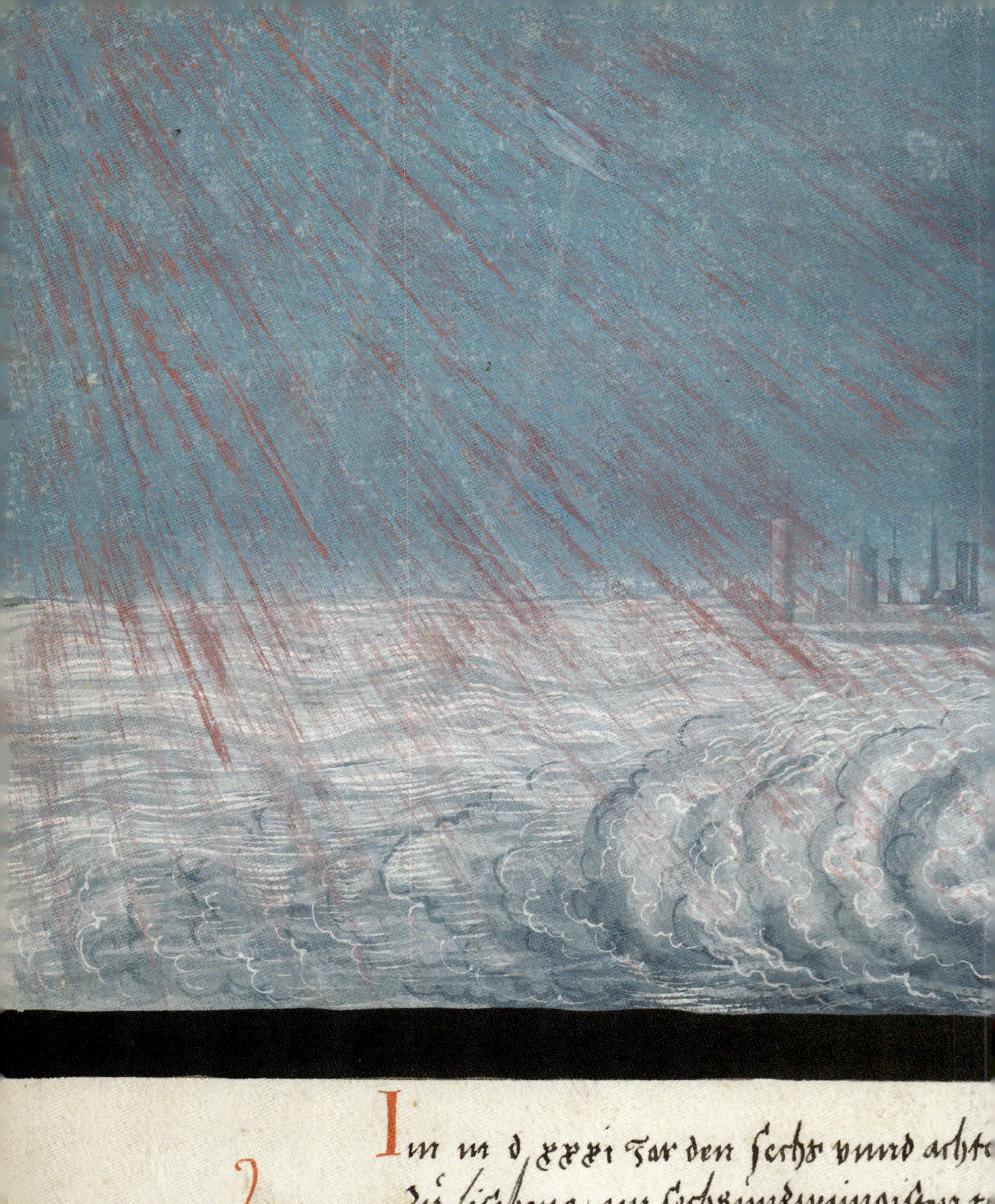

Im m d xxxi Jar den sechs vnnd achte
zu lisabona am sechsvnndzwaintzigisten ta
rige zaichen gesehen worden, vnd am
auch am himel gesehen worden, dar
zwai hundert heuser ein gefallen seind.

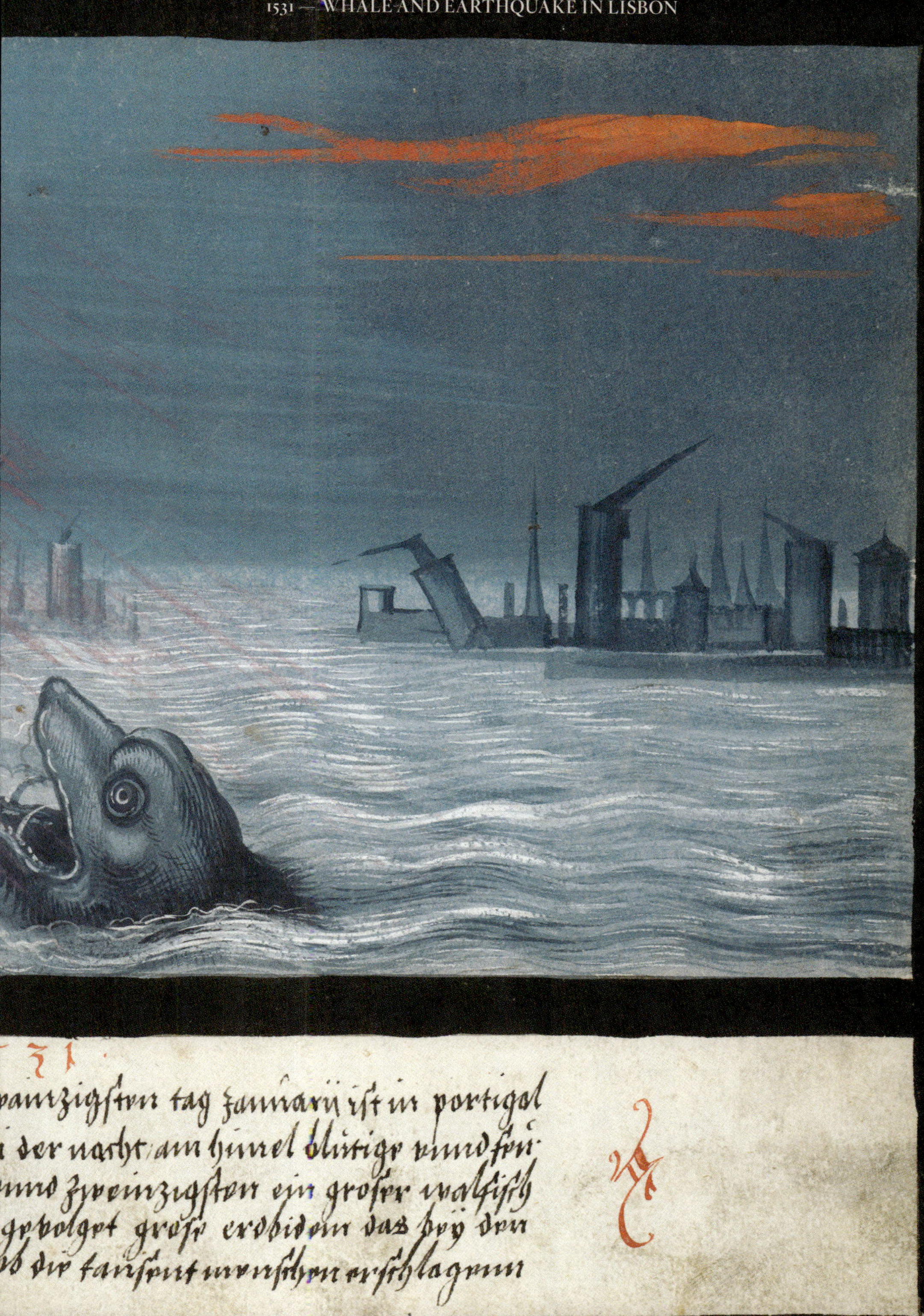
31
vantzigsten tag Jannarij ist in portigal
n der nacht am himel blutiger vnnd feu
vnnd zweinzigsten ein groser walfisch
gevolget gross erdbidem das bey den
s dir tausent menschen erschlagenn

FOL. 118

1530 — Flood in Vlissingen

Überschwemmung in Vlissingen | Inondation à Vlissingen

In the year 1530, on the fifth of November, there was such a great storm in Flanders and Zeeland that more than half the city of Vlissingen, where the huge ships arrive, was carried away and the entire district was completely submerged. Also, many people fled up into the trees and mountains and there could not help but die of hunger, which was more terrible to behold than I can write about, etc.

Im 1530. Jahr, am fünften November, gab es einen so großen Sturm in Flandern und Zeeland, dass es mehr als die Hälfte der Stadt Vlissingen, wo die gewaltigen Schiffe ankommen, fortriss und die ganze Landschaft völlig überschwemmte. Auch flohen viele Leute auf die Bäume und die Berge und mussten daraufhin an Hunger sterben, dass es grausamer anzusehen war, als ich davon schreiben kann etc.

En l'an 1530, le cinq novembre, une tempête balaya la Flandre et la Zélande et fut si forte qu'elle emporta plus de la moitié de la ville de Vlissingen, où arrivent les grands navires, et que toute la région fut complètement submergée. Aussi, beaucoup de gens se réfugièrent dans les arbres et sur les montagnes et ne purent qu'y mourir de faim, ce qui fut plus horrible à voir que ce que je peux en écrire, etc.

FOL. 119

1531 — Whale and earthquake in Lisbon

Wal und Erdbeben in Lissabon | Baleine et tremblement de terre à Lisbonne

In the year 1531, on the twenty-sixth and the twenty-eighth of January, bloody and fiery signs were seen at night in the sky in Lisbon in Portugal on the twenty-sixth day and then on the twenty-eighth a great whale was seen in the sky. This was followed by great earthquakes, so that about two hundred houses collapsed and more than a thousand people were killed.

Im 1531. Jahr, am sechs- und achtundzwanzigsten Januar, sind in Portugal zu Lissabon am sechsundzwanzigsten Tag nachts am Himmel blutige und feurige Zeichen gesehen worden und ist am achtundzwanzigsten zudem ein großer Walfisch am Himmel gesehen worden. Darauf folgten große Erdbeben, sodass etwa zweihundert Häuser eingefallen sind und mehr als tausend Menschen erschlagen wurden.

En l'an 1531, le vingt-six et le vingt-huit janvier, des signes ensanglantés et enflammés furent observés la nuit dans le ciel à Lisbonne au Portugal le vingt-sixième jour, puis le vingt-huitième jour une grande baleine fut observée dans le ciel. S'ensuivirent de grands tremblements de terre qui firent s'écrouler environ deux cents maisons et plus de mille personnes furent tuées.

FOL. 120

1531 — Comet over Strasbourg

Komet über Straßburg | Comète dans le ciel de Strasbourg

In the year 1531, on St Bartholomew's Day, a comet was seen for some time in the sky every night in Strasbourg and in other places, just as is painted here.

Im 1531. Jahr, an Sankt Batholomäus, ist zu Straßburg und anderswo eine Zeit lang ein Komet jede Nacht am Himmel gesehen worden, wie hier gemalt ist.

En l'an 1531, à la Saint-Barthélemy, une comète fut observée pendant un certain temps dans le ciel chaque nuit à Strasbourg et ailleurs, comme dans cette peinture.

FOL. 121

1531 — Four comets | Vier Kometen | Quatre comètes

In the year 1531 four comets appeared in the sky opposite one another, such that they could be seen in certain places in the Netherlands, just as they are painted.

Im 1531. Jahr haben vier Kometen einander gegenüber am Himmel gestanden, dass man sie in den Niederlanden an manchen Orten gesehen hat, wie sie gemalt sind.

En l'an 1531, quatre comètes se tinrent dans le ciel face à face, de telle sorte qu'elles furent observées en certains lieux des Pays-Bas, comme le représente cette peinture.

FOL. 122

1531 — Comet | Komet | Comète

In the year 1531 a comet was seen in the Netherlands which showered fiery flames like a blacksmith making sparks from iron – quite fearsome to see, just as is painted here.

Im 1531. Jahr ist ein Komet in den Niederlanden gesehen worden, der Feuerflammen versprengt hat, wie ein Schmied Eisenfunken wirft – ganz furchtbar anzusehen, wie hier gemalt ist.

En l'an 1531, une comète fut observée aux Pays-Bas, qui émettait de vives flammes comme un forgeron fait des étincelles, vision vraiment effrayante, comme le montre cette peinture.

FOL. 123

1531 — Monster captured near Salzburg

Monster bei Salzburg gefangen genommen | Monstre capturé près de Salzbourg

In the year 1531 a wondrous creature, which was all grey and hairy, with the head of a bearded man and four feet with sharp claws, was caught by the bishop's huntsmen in the forest of Salzburg. It was taken to the court, but it would neither eat nor drink and suffered quite horribly.

Im 1531. Jahr ist zu Salzburg von den Jägern des Bischofs im Wald ein wundersames Tier gefangen worden, das ganz grau und haarig gewesen ist, mit einem bärtigen Menschenkopf, mit vier Füßen und scharfen Klauen. Das hat man an den Hof gebracht, aber es wollte weder essen noch trinken und litt ganz grausam.

En l'an 1531, une créature extraordinaire, qui était toute grise et poilue, avec une tête d'homme à barbe et quatre pieds aux griffes acérées, fut capturée par les chasseurs de l'évêque dans la forêt de Salzbourg. Elle fut conduite à la cour, mais refusa de manger ou de boire et dépérit de manière atroce.

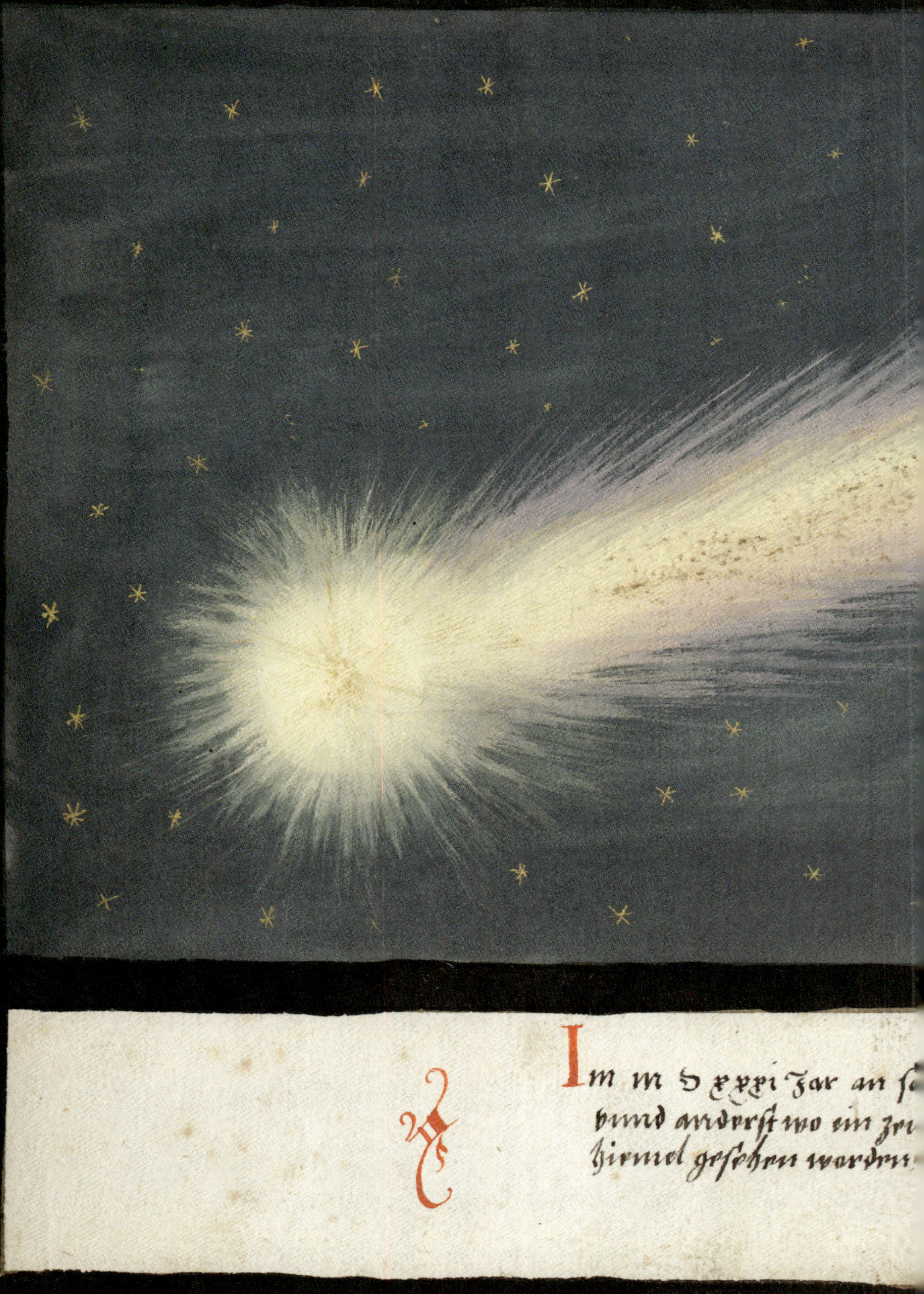

Im m D xxxi Jar an s
vnnd anderst wo ein ze
himel gesehen worden

31
artolmei ist zu strassburg:
z ein comet alls nachtam
hie gemalt ist . . . .

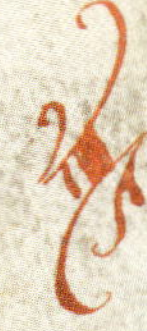

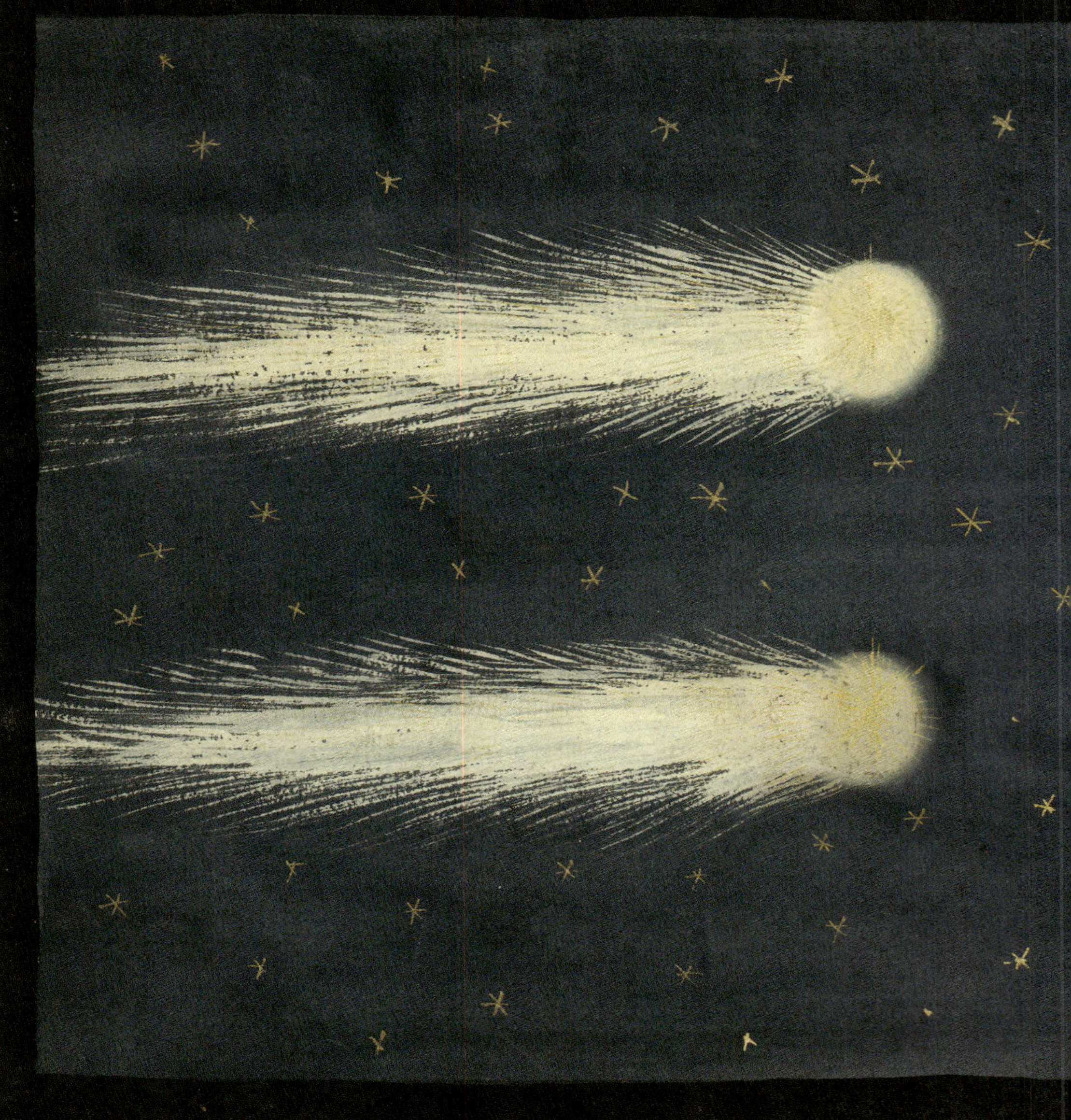

Im m d xxxi Jar se
am himmel gestan-
urhen artten gesch

1531

uier commeten gegen ein andern
as mans im niederlandt an ma:
at wie sie gemalet sind……

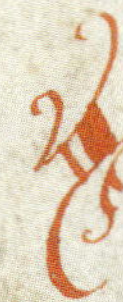

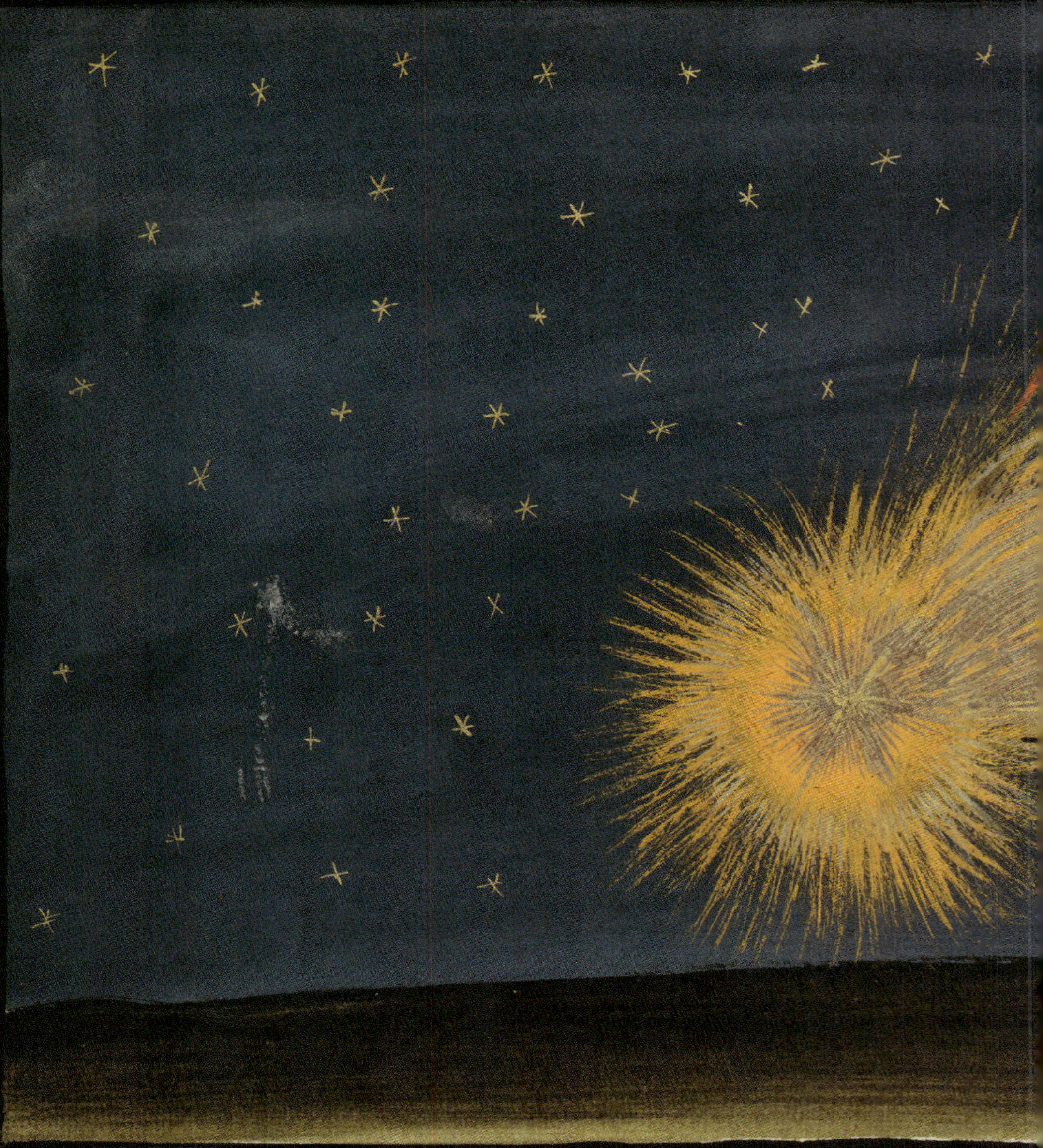

Im m d xxxi Jar ist e
der feüwer flame
flamen von wirfft
malt ist:

·1531·

mmet im niederlant gesehen worden
im ge sprengt wie ein schnit erst
er schrecklich gesehen wie hie ge

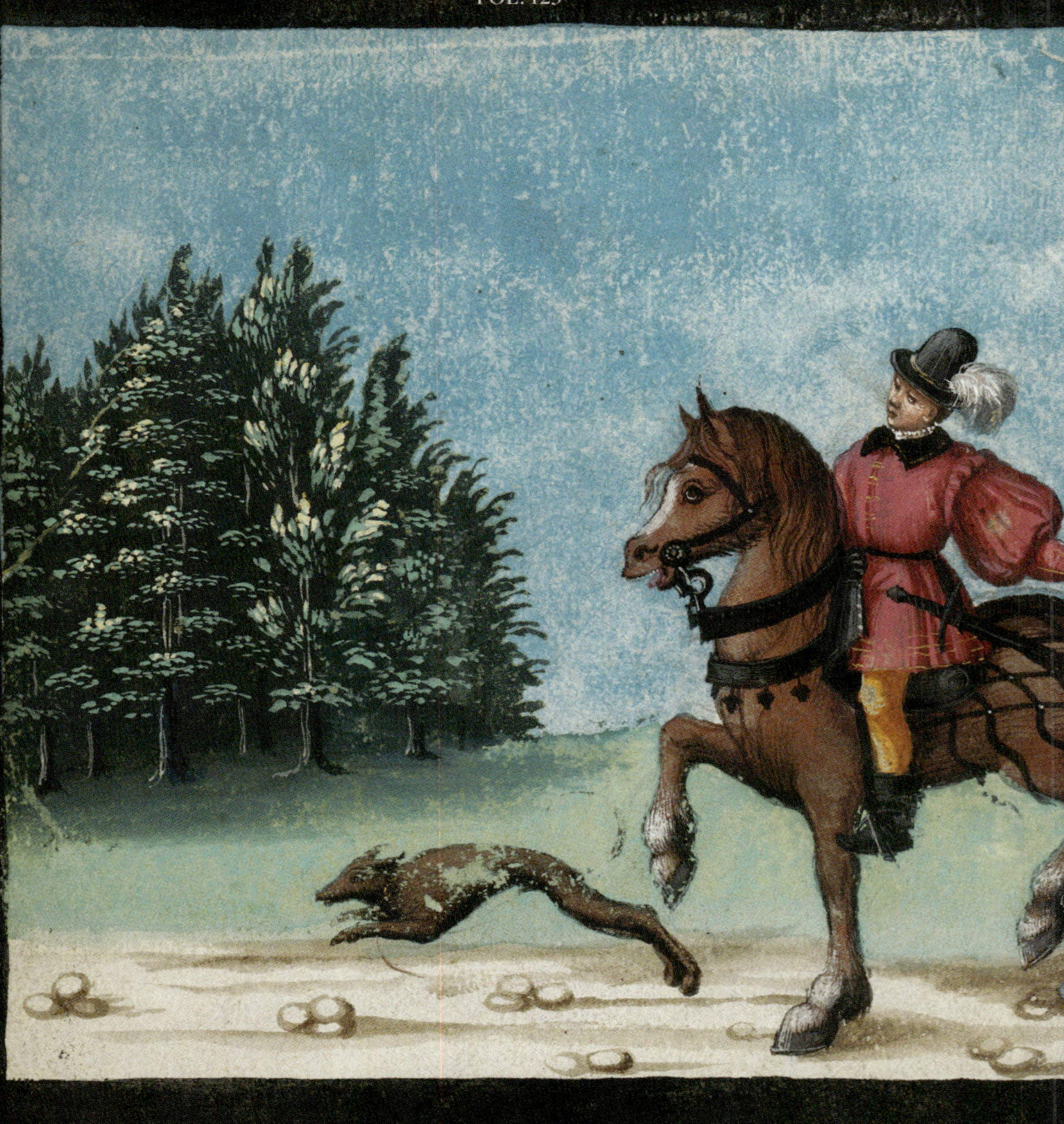

Im m d xxxi Jar ist zu Salzb
thier gefangen werden in dem
einem bartigen menschen k
ge hof bracht aber es hat wed
grausam

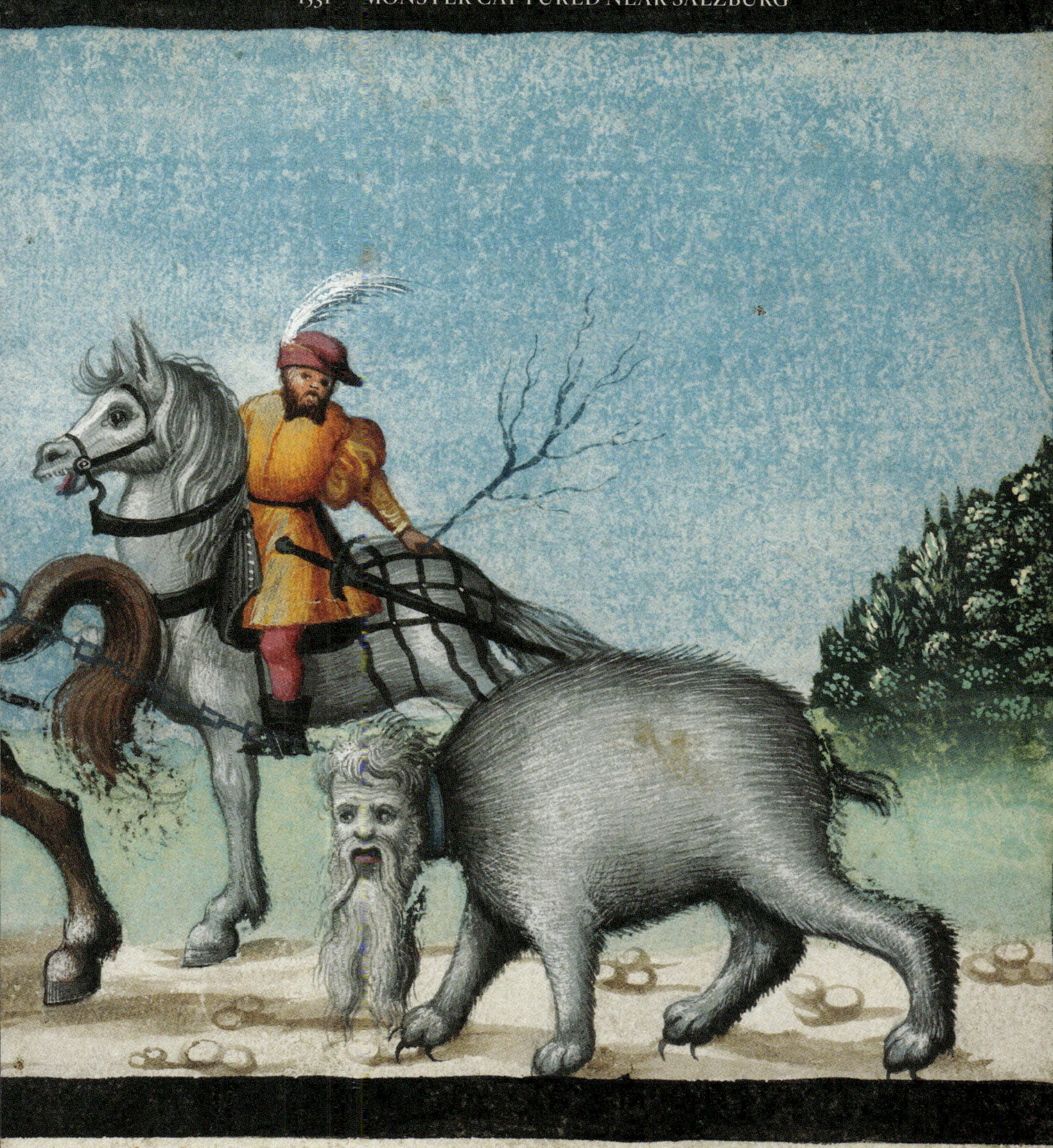

·1531·

von der bischoffs waid leutten ain wunderbarlich
z, das gantz graw vnnd hagrig gewesen ist, mitt
mit vier fuessen vnd scharpffen clawen das hat
sen nach trincken wollen vnnd sich gantz

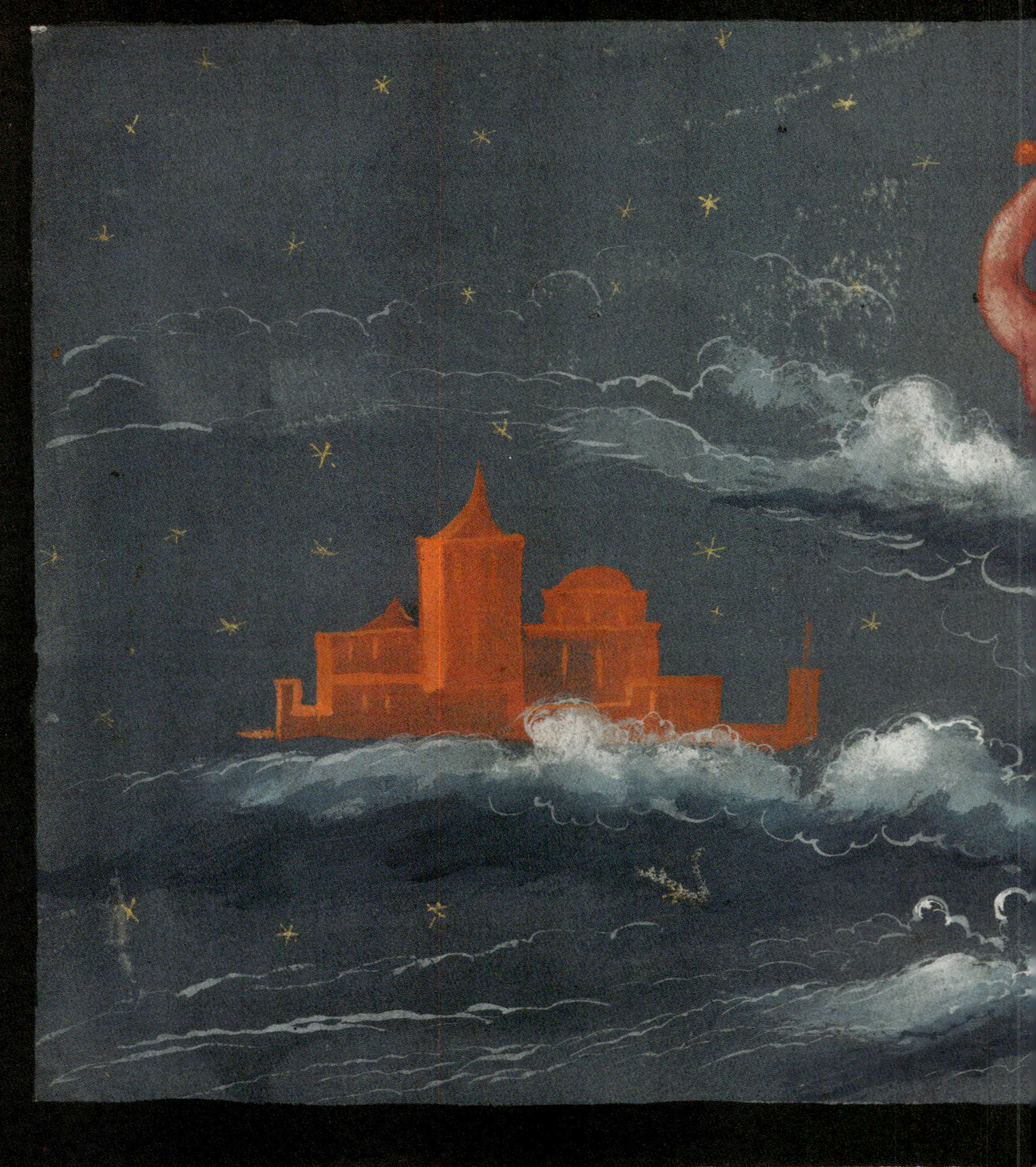

Im m d xxxi jar: ist xurb
bkrist bild vnnd ein schwer
ein feuwriger schloss vnn
gemal stcht er

1531

burg vnnd andern gegenten ein blutig
iner hand gesehen worden, auch
gegen ein raisigen zeug wie hie

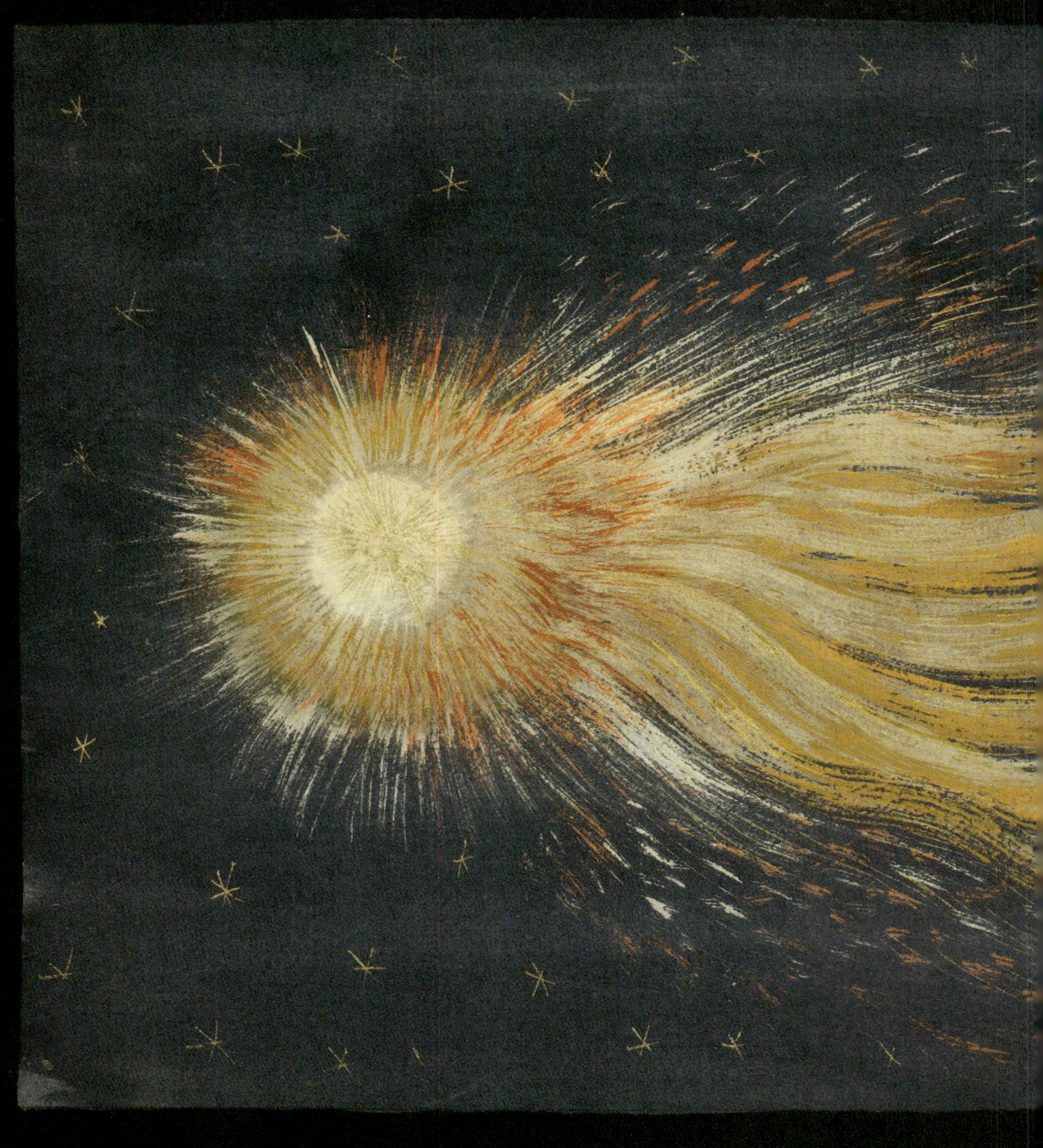

Von dem Cometen oder pfawen schwantz / so i
sich zů erst erzaigt vnnd darnach vil nächt ob
hen ist worden Nach der gepurt Christi

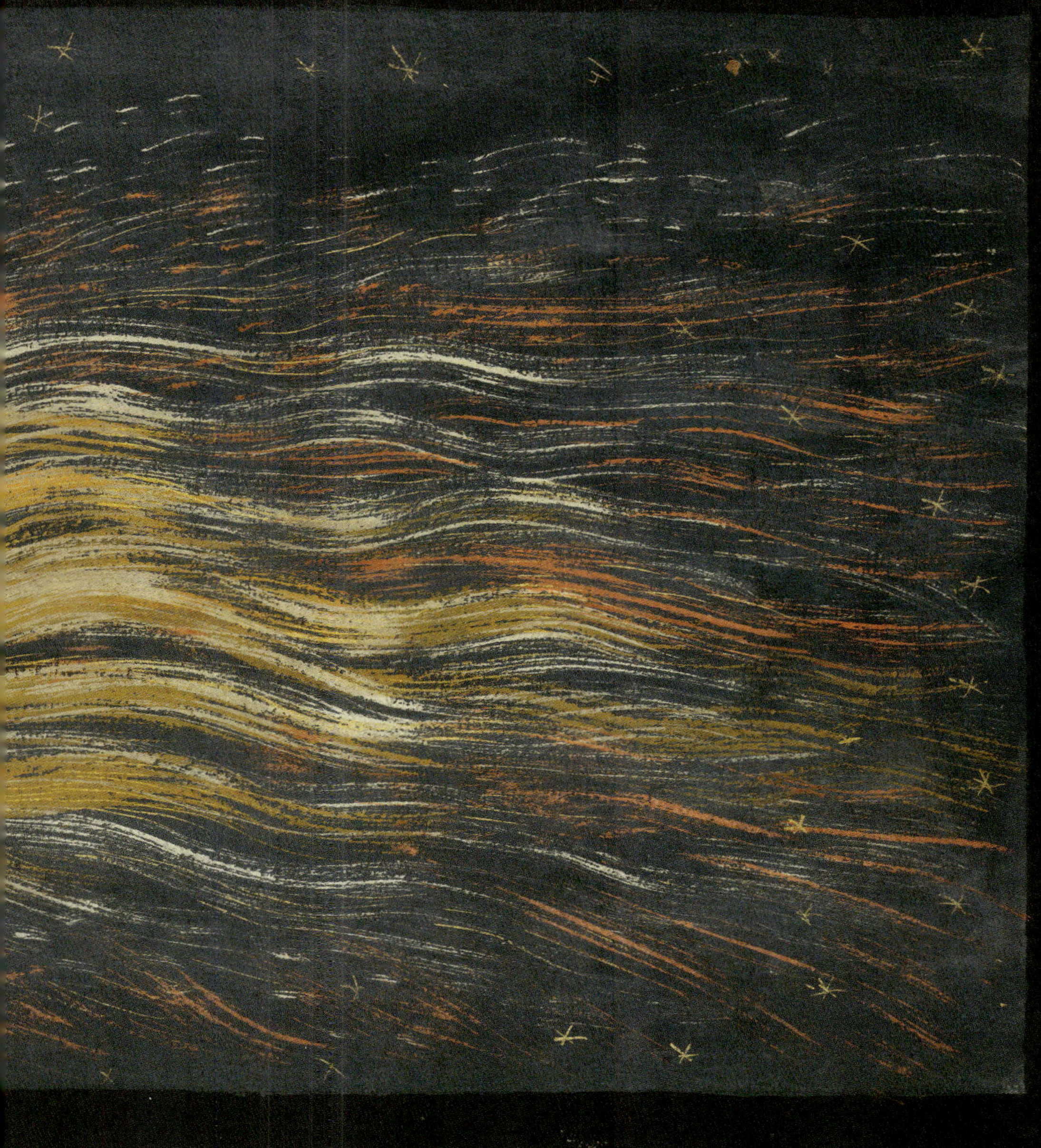

hem hochteutschen lād vmb den x tag des Augsten
rais. spies lang anderhalb schůch brait am hiemel gese:
x x x i jar

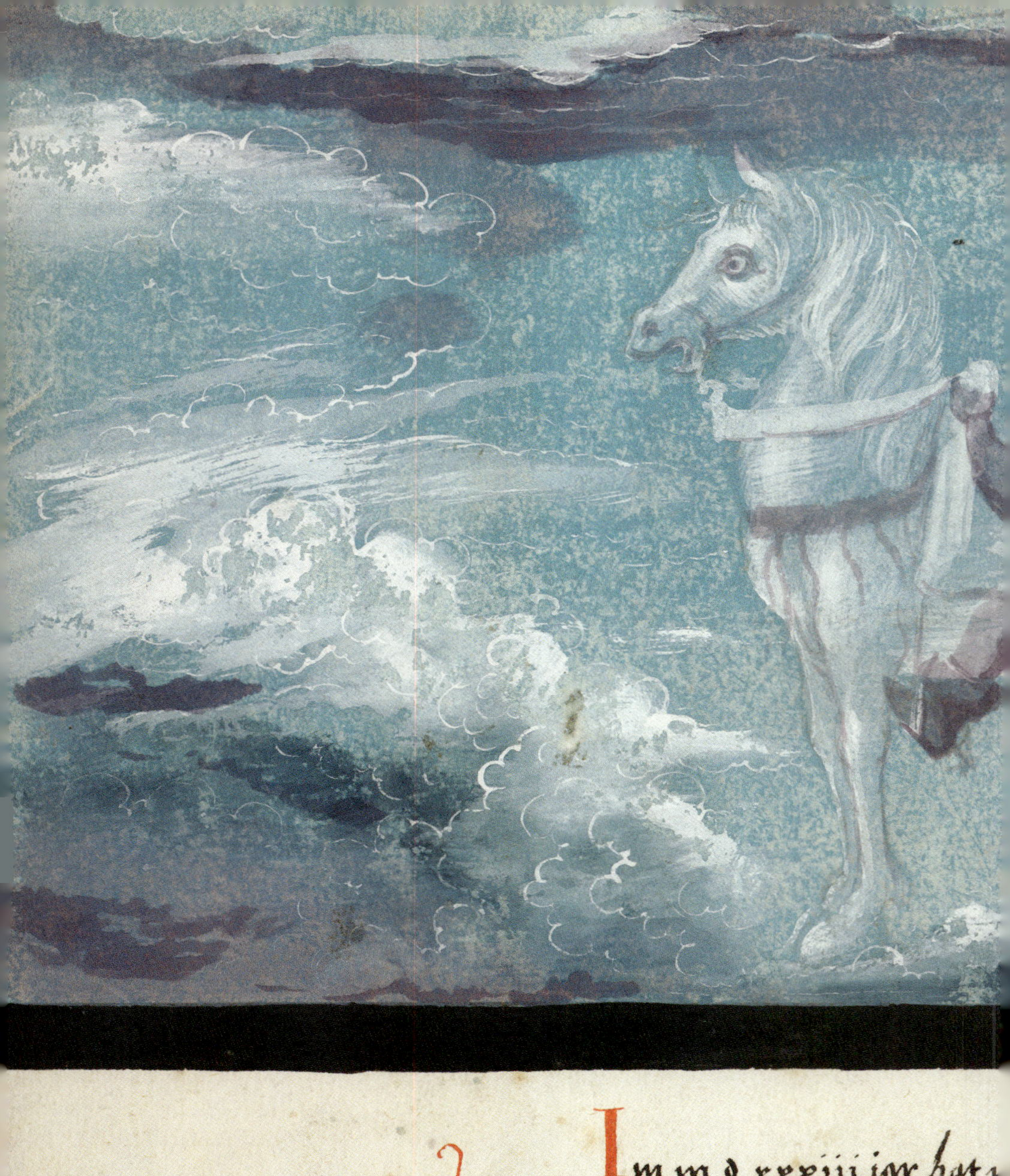

Im m d xxxiii iar hat
lüfften gesehen wund
wie dan hir gemal ist

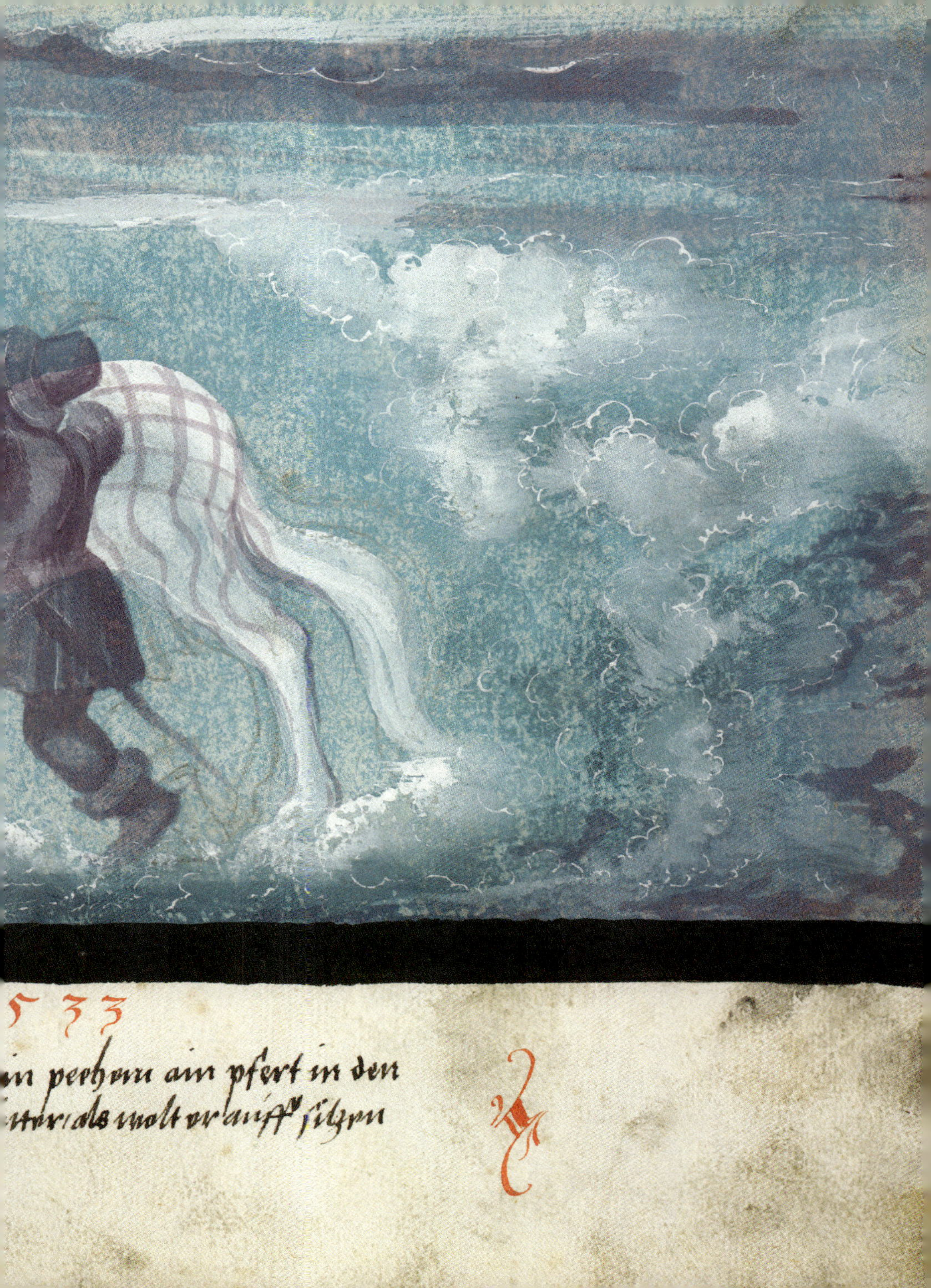
533
in perhem ain pfert in den
itter/ als wolt er auff sitzen

FOL. 124

1531 — Celestial swordsman, castle and army over Strasbourg
Himmlischer Schwertkämpfer, Himmelsburg und Kriegsheer über Straßburg
Homme à l'épée, château et armée dans le ciel de Strasbourg

In the year 1531 a bloody vision with a sword in its hand was seen near Strasbourg and in other parts, as well as a fiery citadel and opposite that an armed host on horseback, just as is painted here etc.

Im 1531. Jahr ist bei Straßburg und in anderen Gegenden ein blutiges Luftbild mit einem Schwert in seiner Hand gesehen worden, zudem eine feurige Burg und gegenüber ein berittener Heereszug, wie hier gemalt ist etc.

En l'an 1531, une apparition ensanglantée, tenant une épée à la main, fut observée près de Strasbourg et dans d'autres régions, ainsi qu'une citadelle embrasée et face à elle un régiment de cavaliers, comme dans cette peinture, etc.

FOL. 125

1531 — Comet | Komet | Comète

Of the comet or comet's tail, as it first appeared in certain of the High German districts around the 10th day of August and then for many nights – more than a lance in length [c. 5 m], one and a half shoes wide – was seen in the sky, 1531 years after the birth of Christ.

Von dem Kometen oder Kometenschweif, wie er sich in einigen hochdeutschen Ländern um den 10. Tag des Augusts zuerst zeigte und danach viele Nächte – über einen Reisspieß lang [ca. 5 m], anderthalb Schuh breit – am Himmel gesehen worden ist, 1531 Jahre nach der Geburt Christi.

Une comète ou une queue de la comète, telle qu'elle apparut dans certaines régions de la Haute-Allemagne vers le dixième jour d'août et pendant de nombreuses nuits – plus longue qu'une lance [env. 5 m], large d'un soulier et demi – fut observée dans le ciel, 1531 années après la naissance du Christ.

FOL. 126

1533 — Celestial horseman over Bohemia
Himmlischer Reiter über Böhmen | Cavalier céleste dans le ciel de Bohême

In the year 1533 a horse in the air was seen in Bohemia, and a horseman, as if he wanted to mount it, just as is painted here.

Im 1533. Jahr hat man in Böhmen ein Pferd in den Lüften gesehen und einen Reiter, als wollte er aufsitzen, wie dann hier gemalt ist.

En l'an 1533, un cheval fut observé dans les airs en Bohême, ainsi qu'un cavalier, comme s'il voulait monter, comme dans cette peinture.

FOL. 127

1533 — Dragons over Bohemia
Drachen über Böhmen
Dragons dans le ciel de Bohême

In the year 1533, in October, flying dragons were seen in Bohemia and the Vogtland, as well as in the small area of Ascher [Aš, city in Czech Republic], a crest on their heads, a snout like a pig, and with two wings. This then went on for several days, with over four hundred of them, both big and small, flying together, as is painted here.

Im 1533. Jahr, im Oktober, hat man in Böhmen und dem Vogtland, auch im Ascher Ländchen [Aš, Stadt in der Tschechischen Republik] fliegende Drachen gesehen, auf dem Kopf eine Krone, ein Rüssel wie ein Schwein, und auch zwei Flügel. Es dauerte dann etliche Tage an, dass jeden Tag von ihnen mehr als vierhundert miteinander geflogen sind, sowohl große als auch kleine, wie hier gemalt ist.

En l'an 1533, en octobre, des dragons volants furent observés en Bohême et dans le Vogtland, ainsi que dans la petite région d'Ascher [Aš, ville en Tchéquie], une crête sur la tête, un groin comme celui d'un cochon, et avec deux ailes. Cela dura ensuite plusieurs jours, à tel point que plus de quatre cents d'entre eux volèrent en groupe chaque jour, grands et petits, comme dans cette peinture.

FOL. 128

1533 — Comet | Komet | Comète

In the year 1533, on the twenty-seventh of July, at two o'clock after midnight, a terrible comet appeared and was also seen for many days after this, which the astronomers interpreted when unrest later broke out in Germany etc.

Im 1533. Jahr, am siebenundzwanzigsten Juli, um zwei Uhr nach Mitternacht, ist ein grausamer Komet erschienen und auch viele Tage danach gesehen worden, den die Astronomen gedeutet haben, als sich danach ein Aufruhr in Deutschland ereignet hat etc.

En l'an 1533, le vingt-sept juillet, à deux heures après minuit, une terrible comète apparut et fut aussi observée pendant de nombreux jours par la suite, ce que les astronomes interprétèrent quand l'agitation régna ensuite en Allemagne, etc.

FOL. 129

1533 — Dragons | Drachen | Dragons

1533 years after the birth of Christ, on the Friday after St Ursula, the 24th day, such wondrous dragons were seen in the air for nigh on two hours around 10 o'clock at night in several places near Hilpoltstein and at the Hoffleins House there.

1533 Jahre nach Christi Geburt, am Freitag nach Ursula, dem 24. Tag, in der Nacht um 10 Uhr, sind an manchen Orten bei Hilpoltstein und dort am Hoffleinshaus solche wundersamen Drachen wohl etwa 2 Stunden in der Luft gesehen worden.

1533 années après la naissance du Christ, le vendredi qui suivit la Sainte-Ursule, le vingt-quatrième jour, des dragons extraordinaires furent observés dans les airs pendant près de deux heures vers dix heures du soir en plusieurs lieux près de Hilpoltstein et là, à la Maison Hofflein.

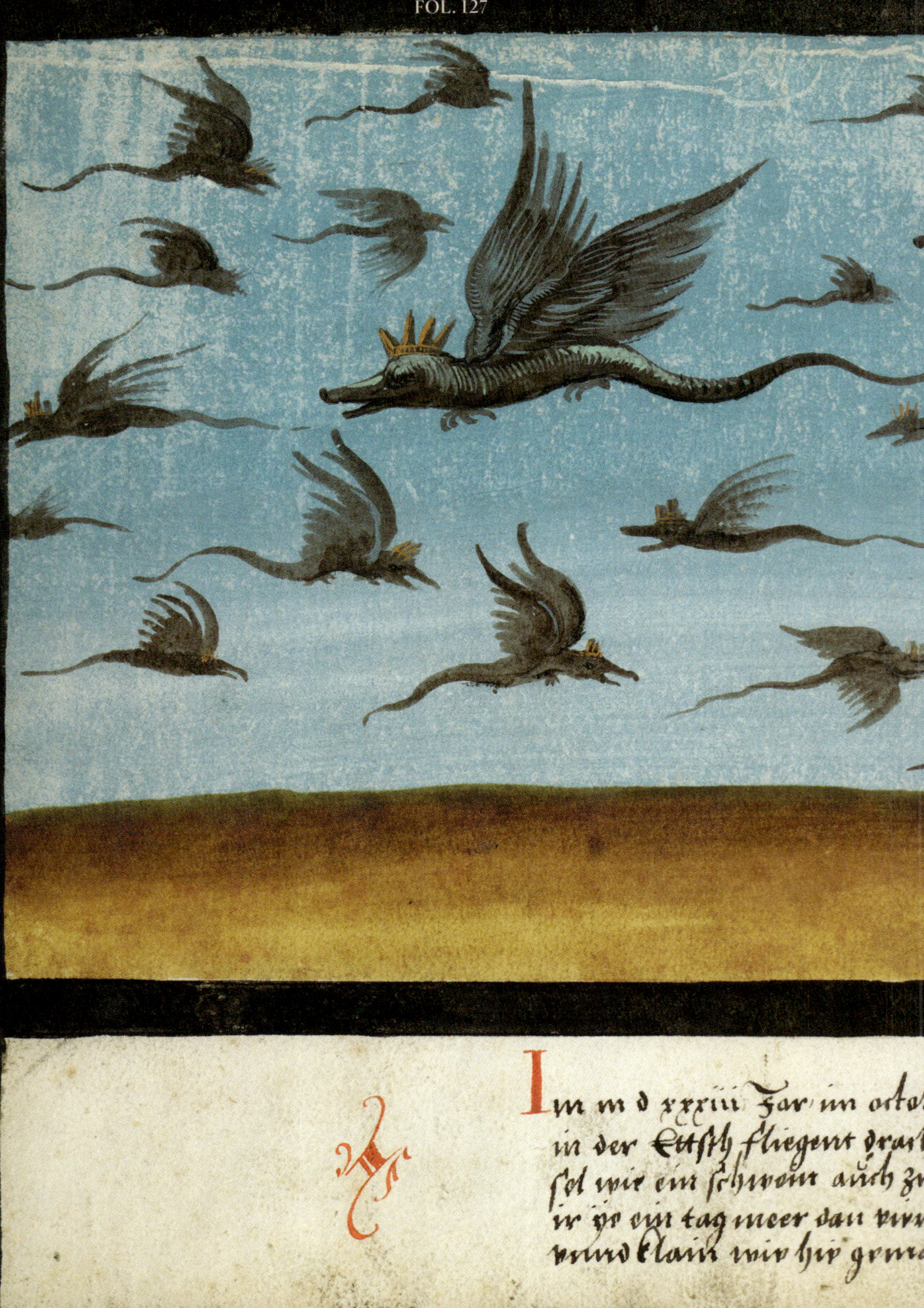
Im m d xxxiii Jar im
in der Ettsch fliegent
sol wie ein schwein auch
ir ye ein tag meer dan
vnnd klain wie hie

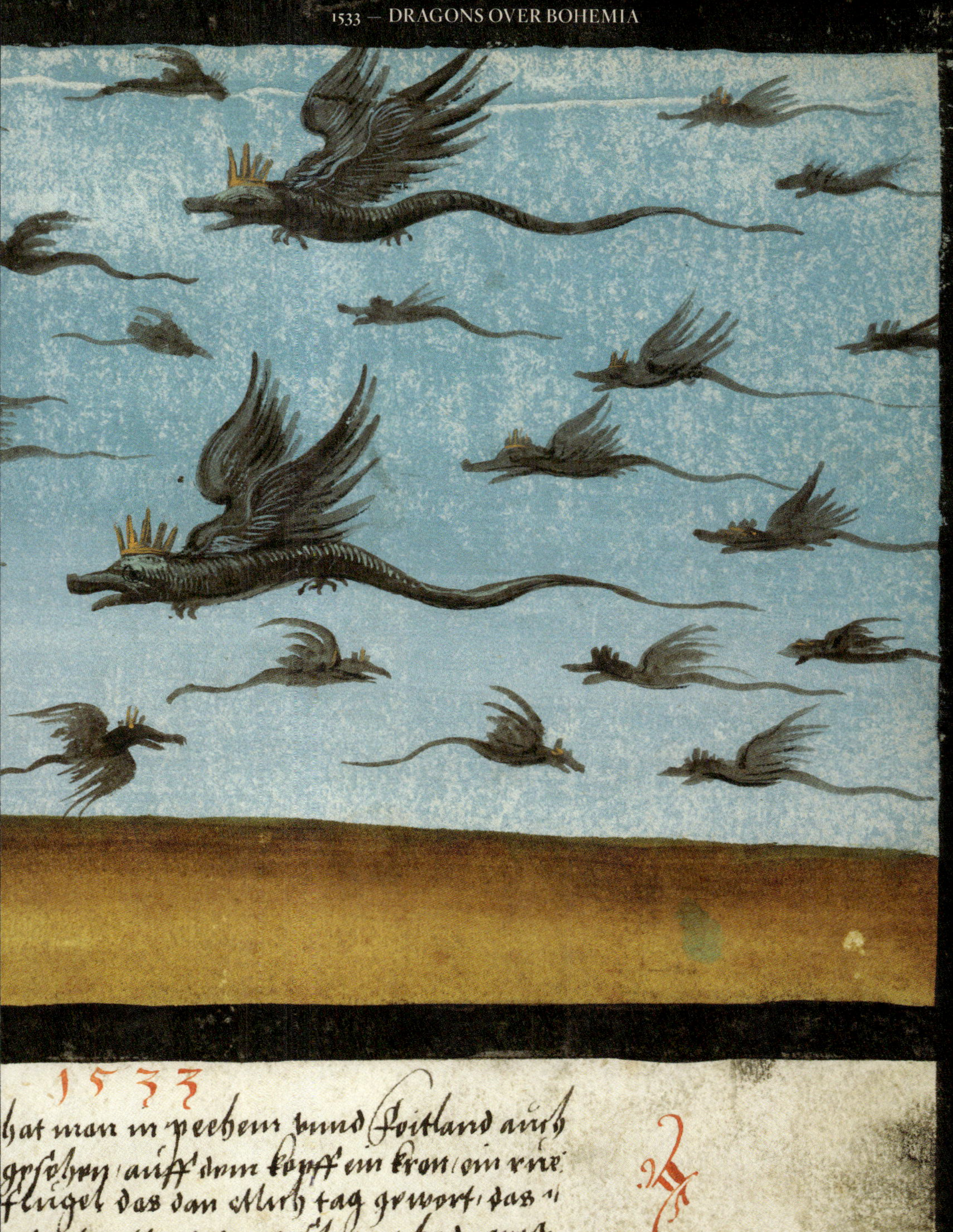
1533
hat man in peehem vnnd Foitland auch
gesehen auff dem kopff ein kron ein yde
flugel das dan etlich tag gewert das
undert mit ainder geflogen bede groß
lehet

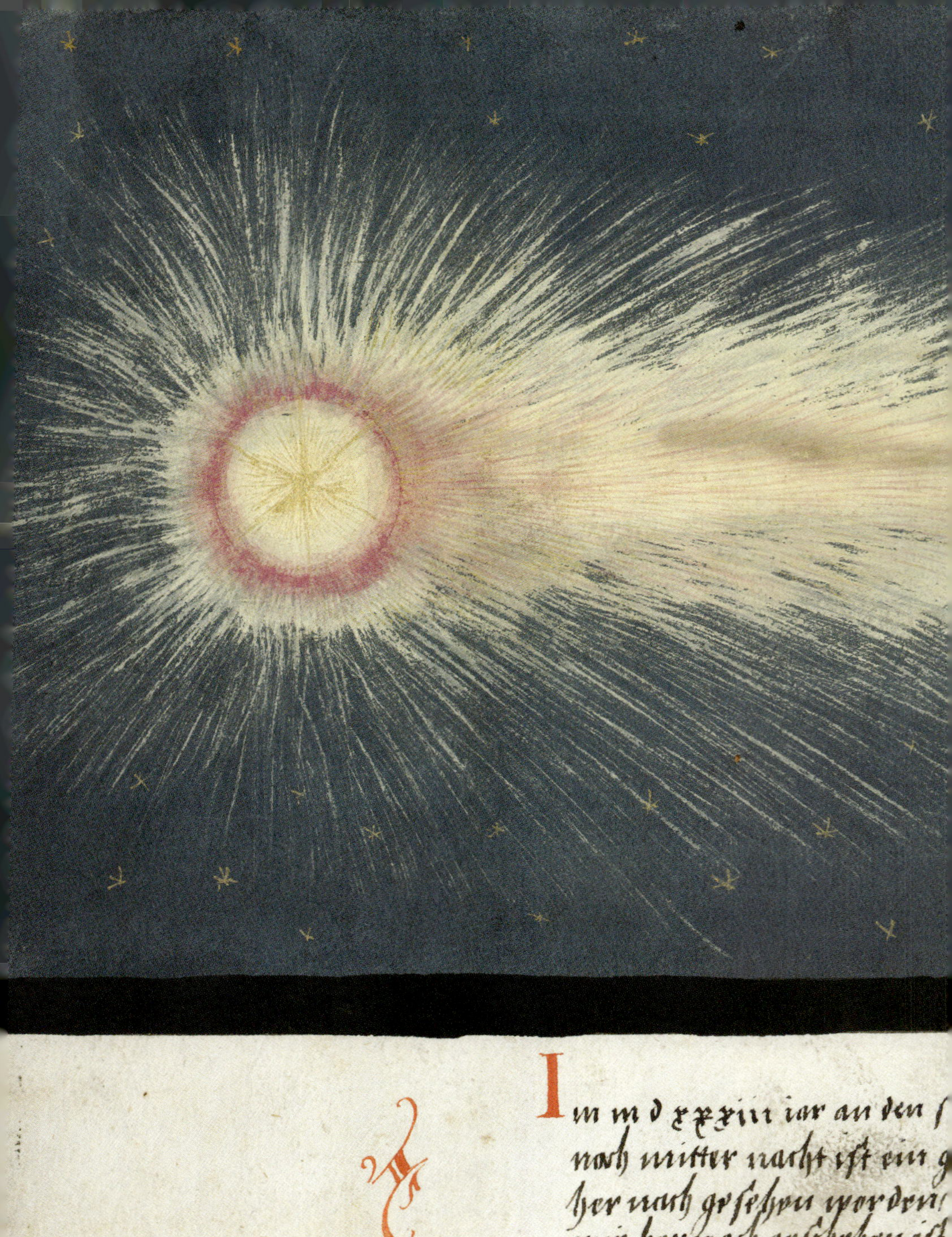

Im m d xxxiii iar an den ſ
nach mitter nacht ist ein g
her nach gesehen worden,
wir her nach geschehen ist.

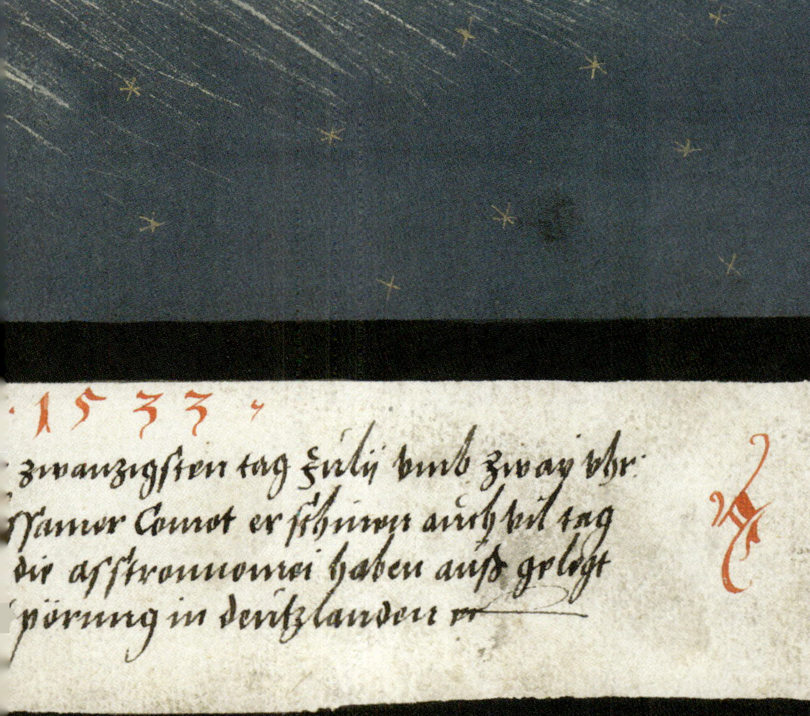
·1533·
zwanzigsten tag Julij vnnd zway vhr
ssamer Comet er schinen auch vil tag
die asstronnomei haben auss gelegt
pörung in deutzlanden

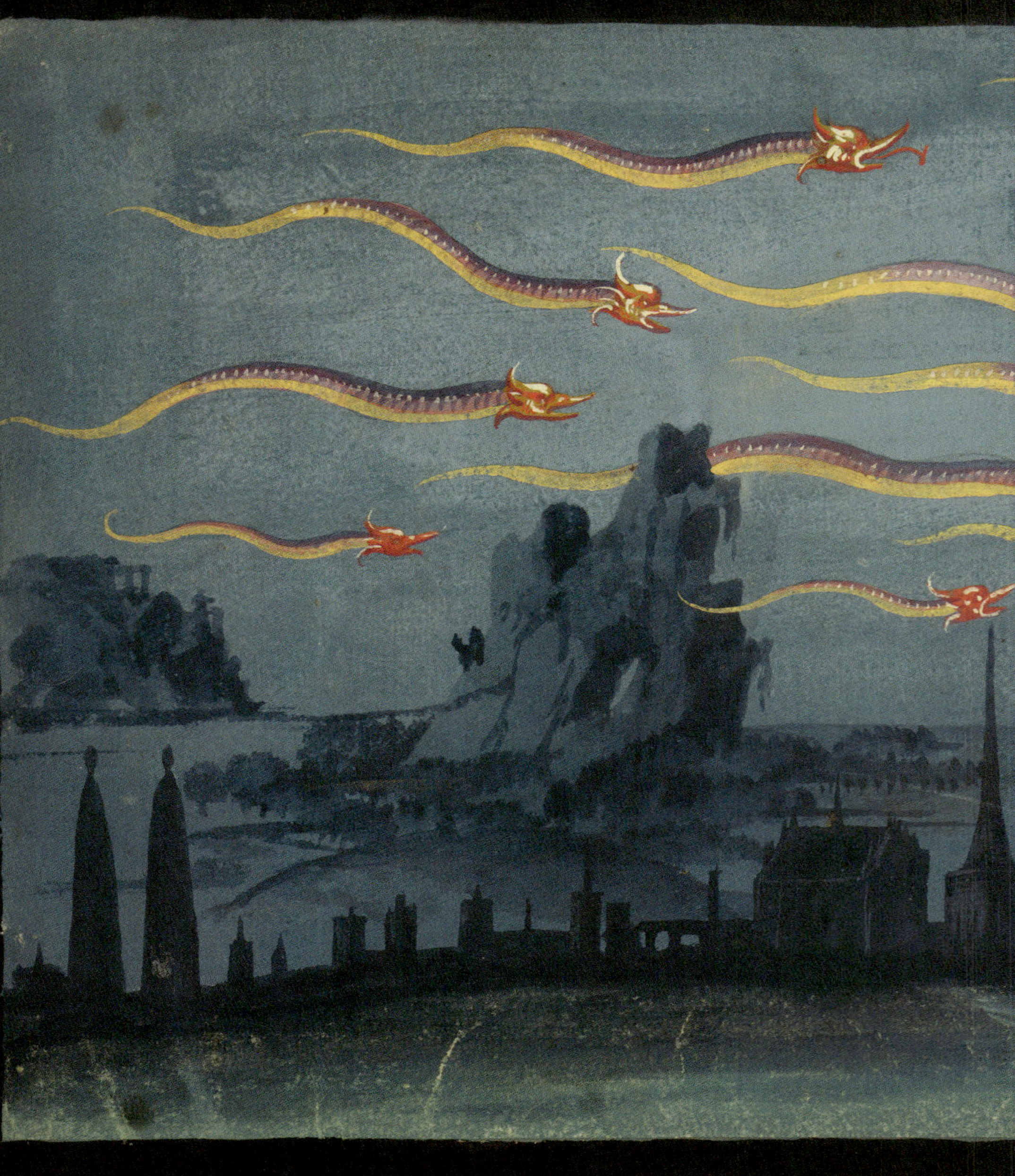

Nach Cristÿ gepurt 1533 Jar am Freytag nach
an manchen Ortten zw Hilbaltstain Vn
barlichen drachen In Lüfften gesehen worden

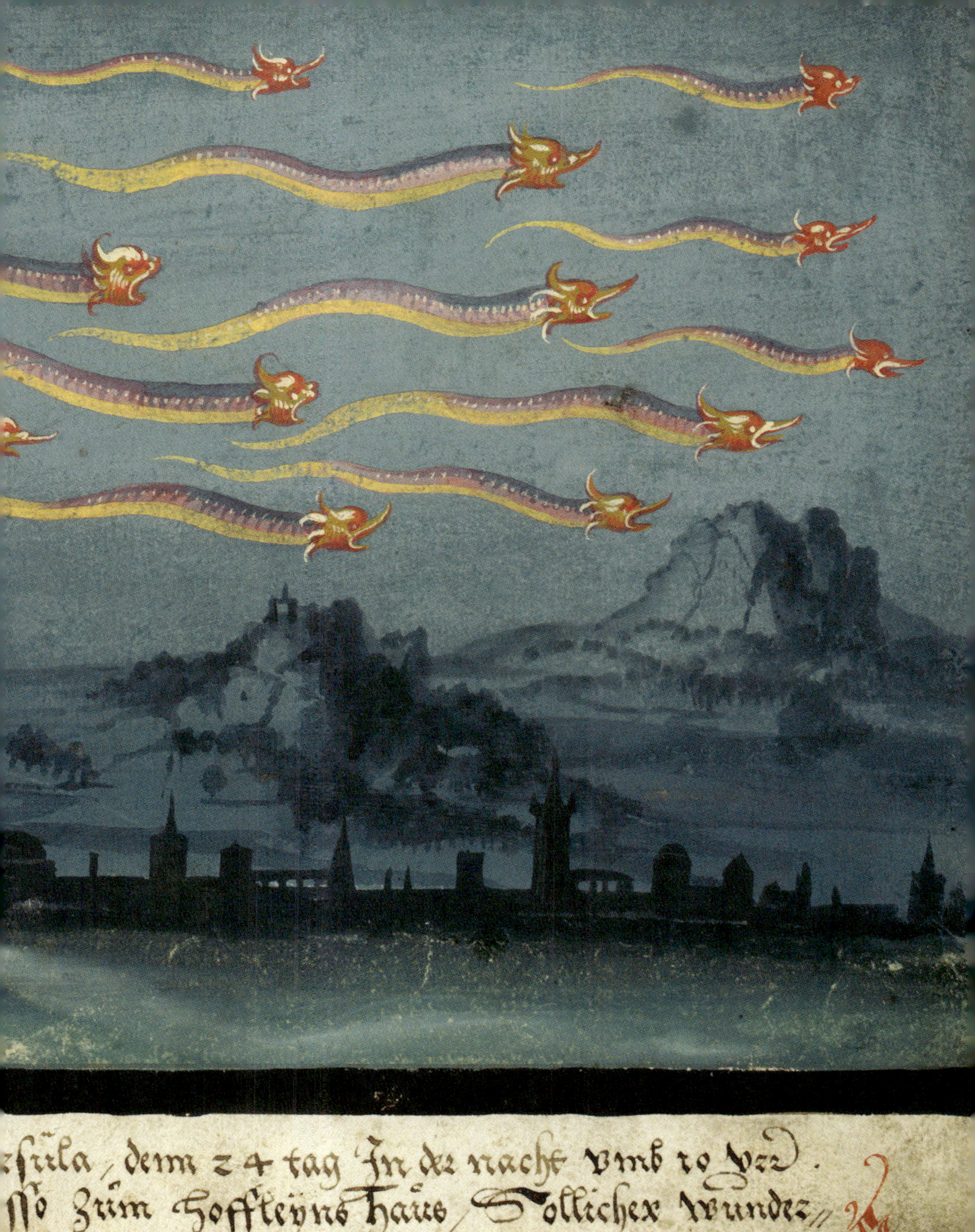

rsüla, dem 24 tag In der nacht vmb 10 vrr.
sso zum Hoffleyns haus, Sollicher wunder //
ee bey . 2 . Stünden
33.

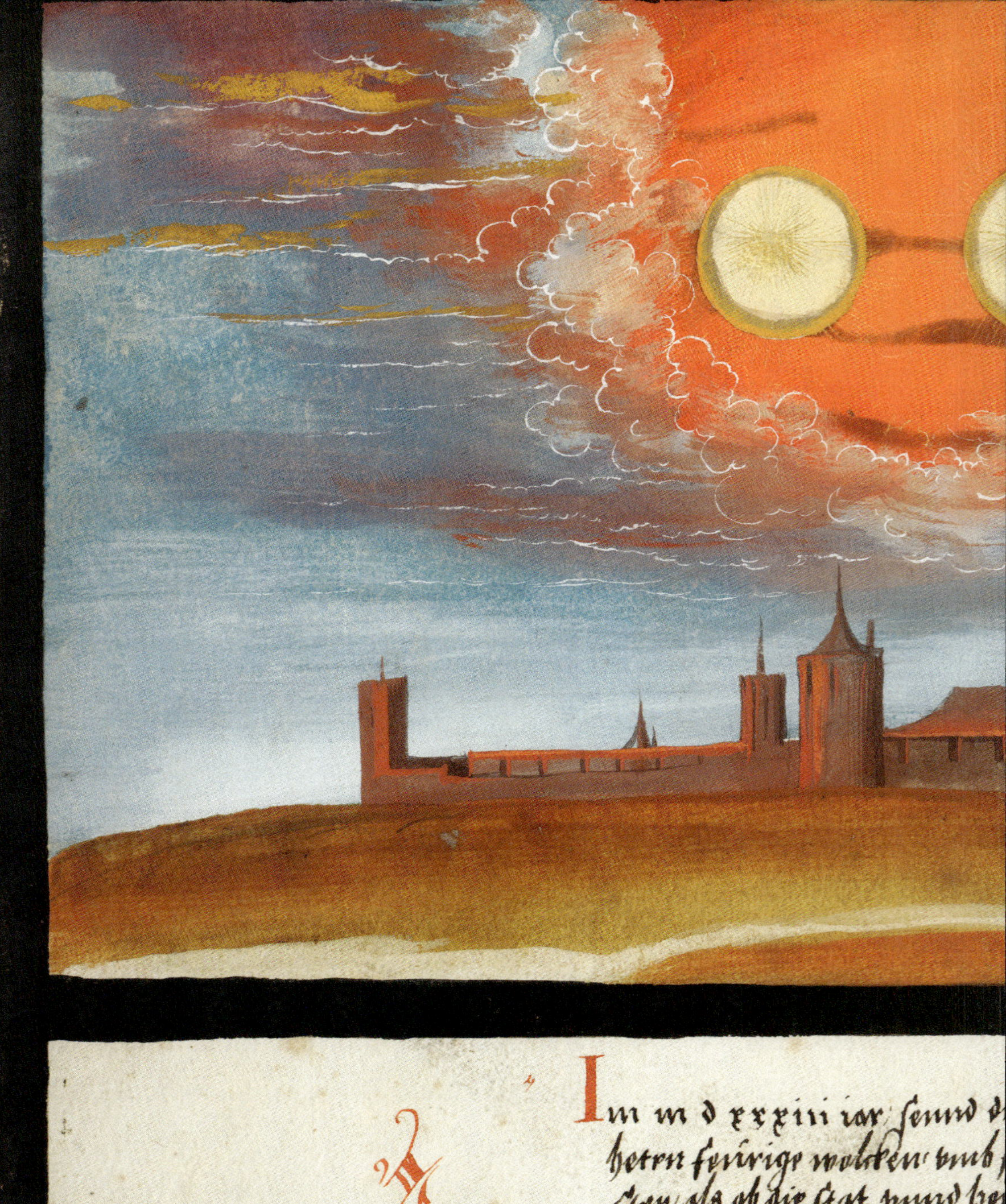
Im m d xxxiiii iar/ seind
hetrn feürige wolken/ vnnd
ster/ als ob dir stat vnnd

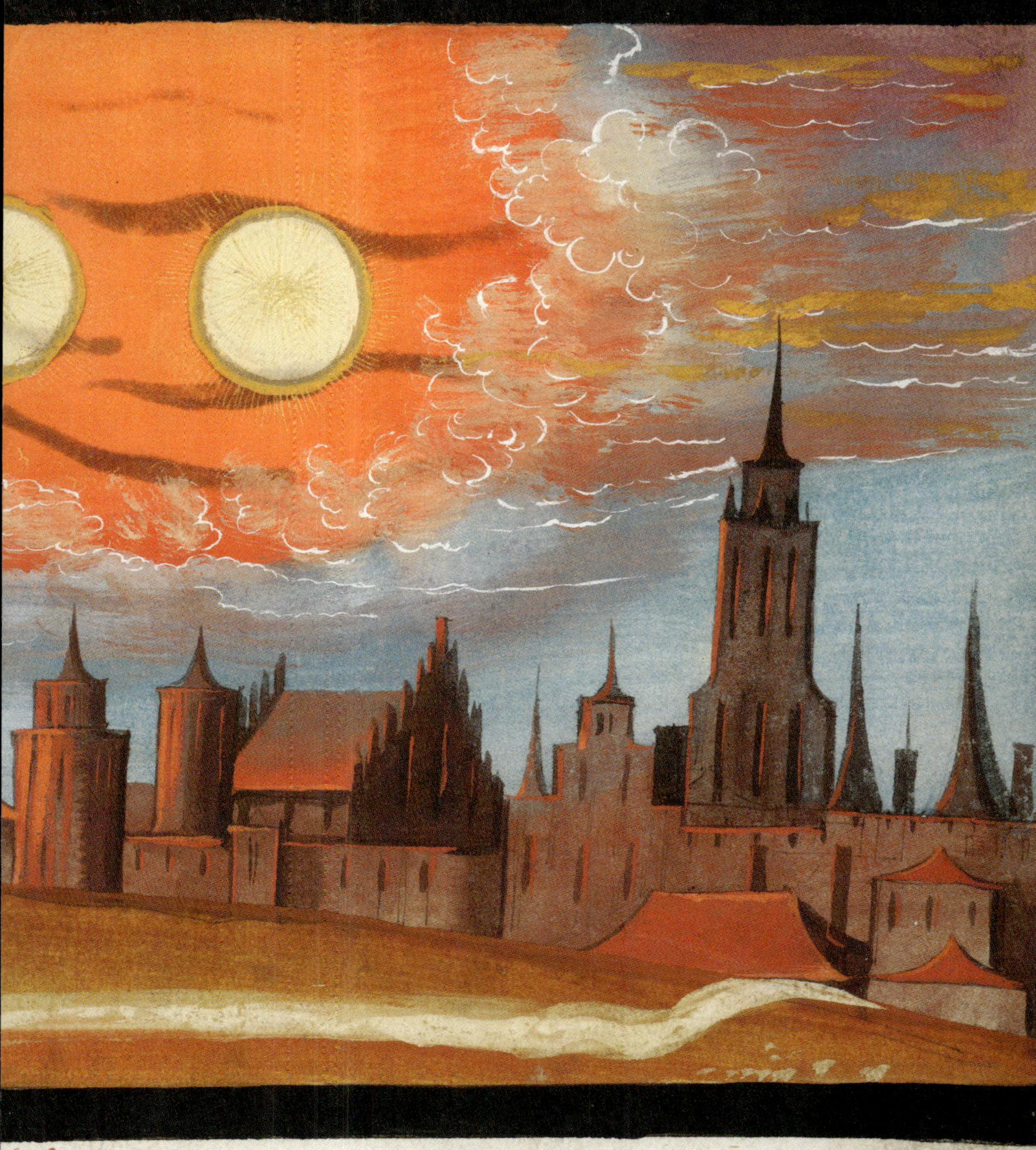

1533
sonnen in gleichem schein als ob sie
vnnd stunden vber der stat mun:
brennend/ wie hie gemalt ·

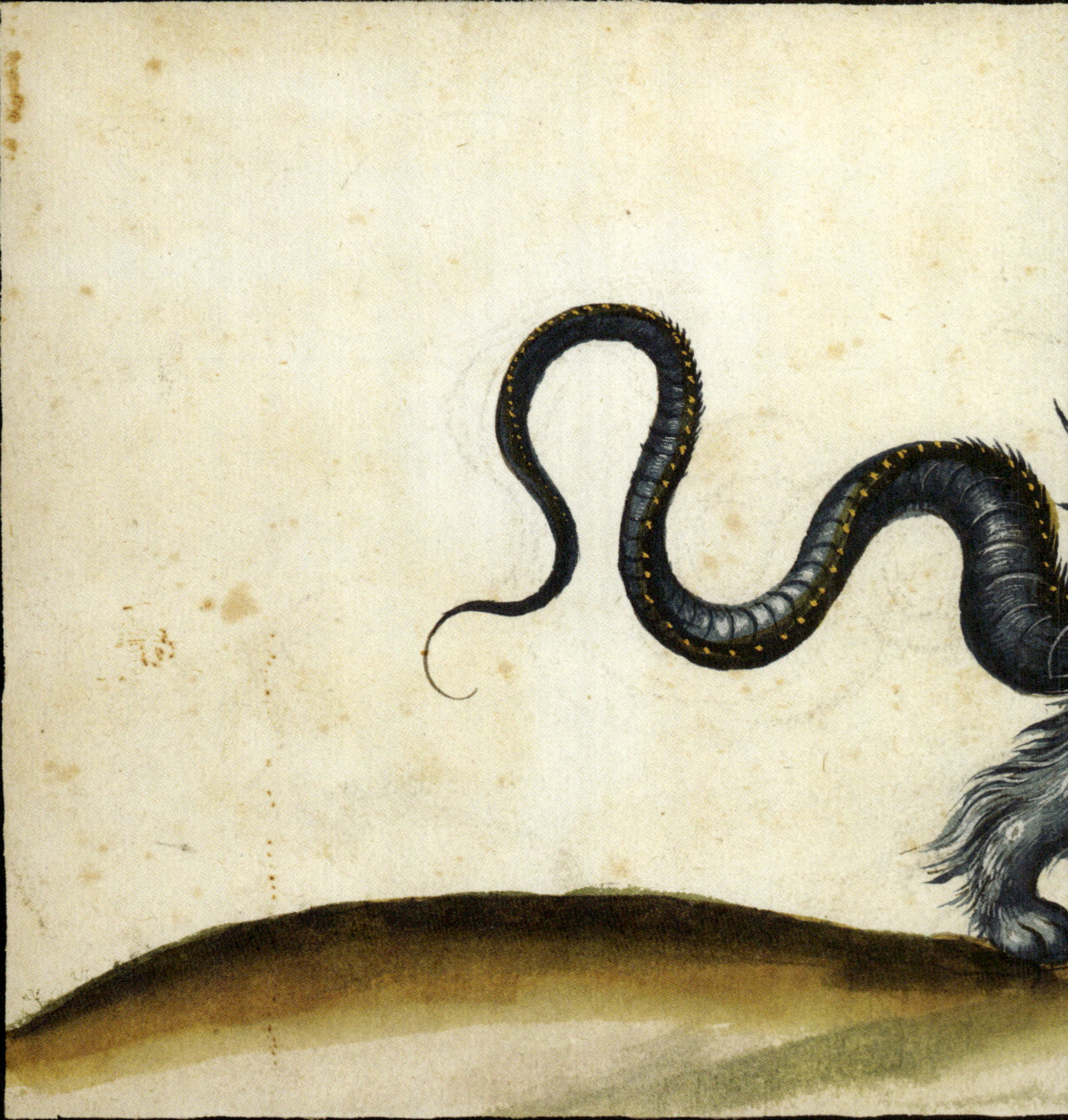

Im m d xxxiiii Jar hat m
meer wonnen gefanngen,
ist gestalt wir hir gemal

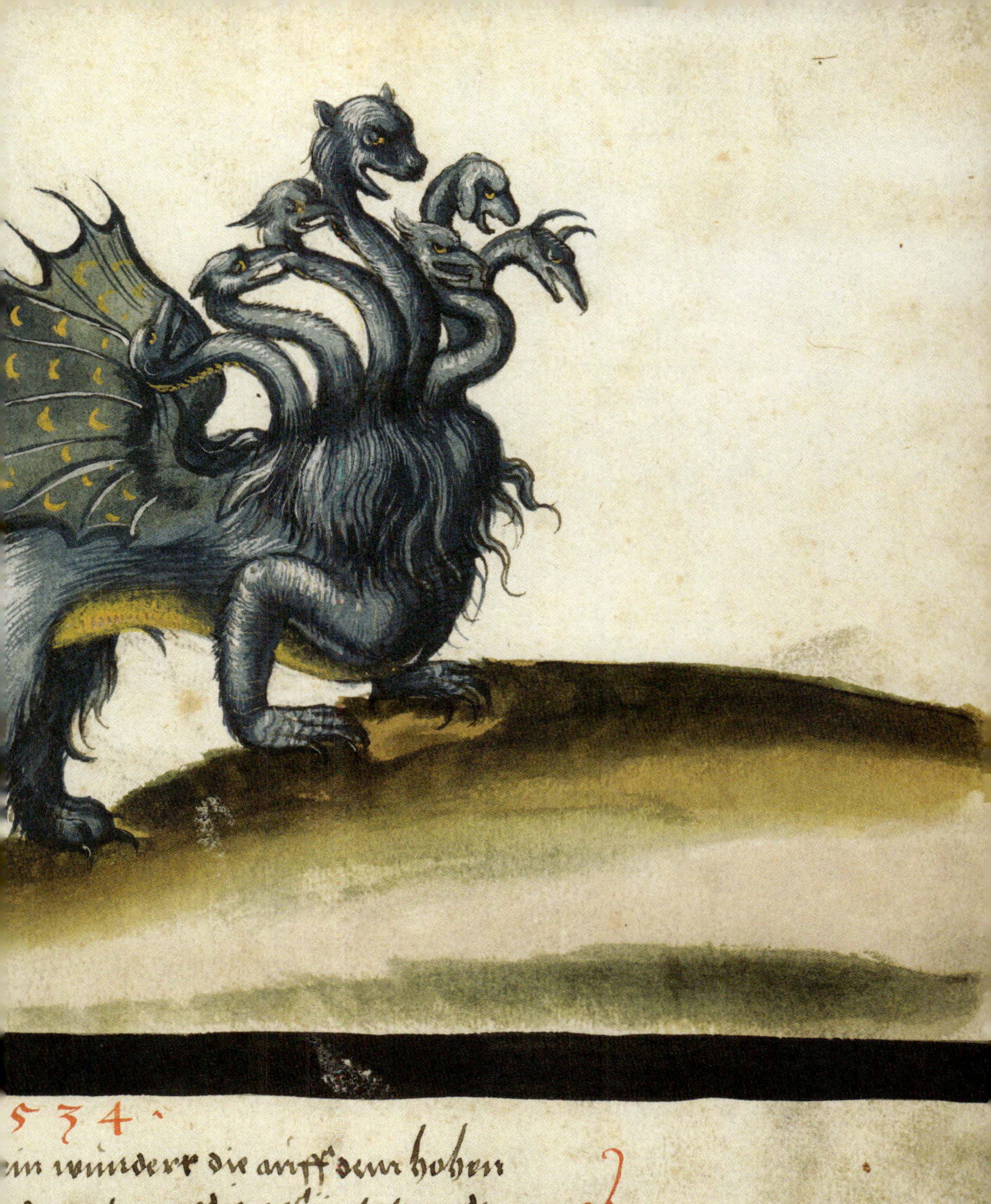

534.

in wundert die auff dem hohen
id gen venedig gefürt / vnnd
ht

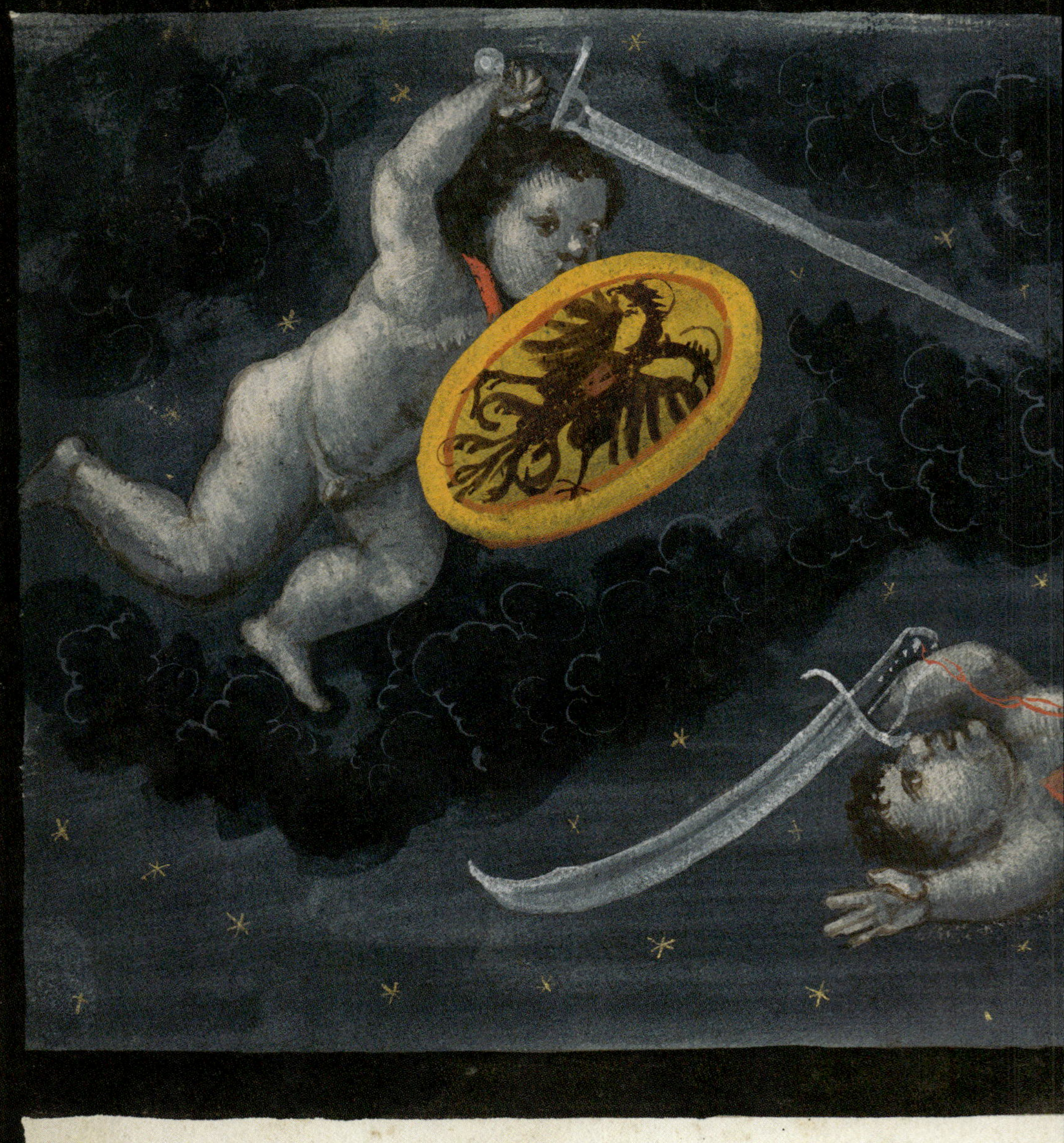

7 Im m d xxxvi iar hat docter
ain solchs wunder am himm
wie er dan die stundt hat wol
mel hat er die gesicht gesehen

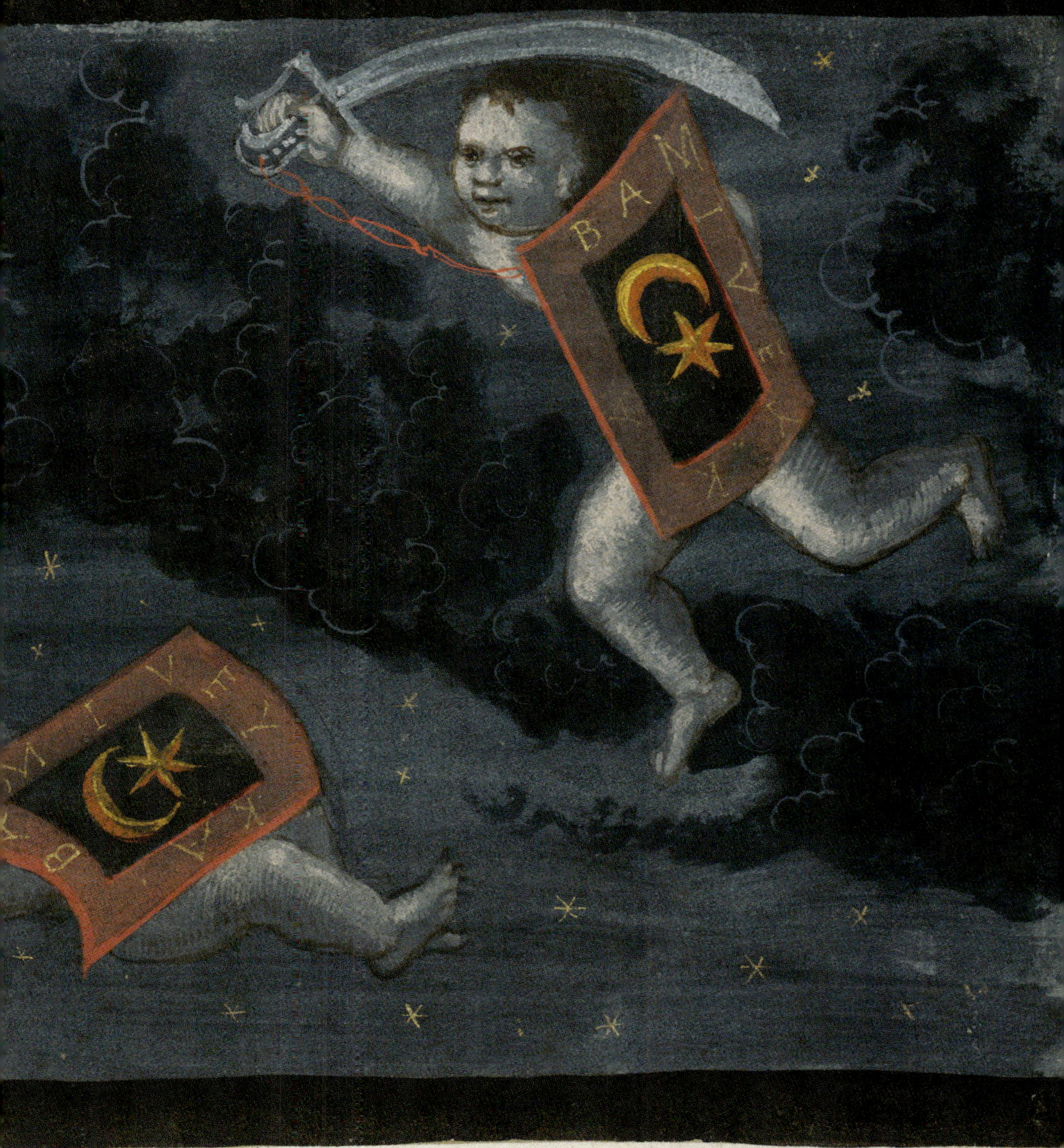

1536.

nnes dolzbürger/ zu medina in hispania:
sehen an der siebenten nacht des hornungs
erfaren nach seiner kunst der astronomi
r hie verzaichnet und gemalt ist.

FOL. 131

1533 — Parhelia over Münster
Nebensonnen über Münster | Parhélies dans le ciel de Münster

In the year 1533 three suns shone at the same time, as if they had fiery clouds around them, and they stayed over the city of Münster, as if the city and its houses were burning, as painted here.

Im 1533. Jahr schienen drei Sonnen gleichzeitig, als ob sie feurige Wolken um sich hätten, und standen über der Stadt Münster, als ob die Stadt und die Häuser brannten, wie hier gemalt.

En l'an 1533, trois soleils brillèrent simultanément, comme s'ils étaient entourés de nuages enflammés, et ils restèrent au-dessus de la ville de Münster, comme si la ville et ses maisons étaient embrasées, comme le montre cette peinture.

FOL. 133

1534 — Sea creature | Meeresgeschöpf | Créature marine

In the year 1534 one of the wonderful creatures which live in the open sea was caught and taken to Venice, and it looks just as it is painted here.

Im 1534. Jahr hat man eines der wunderbaren Wesen, die im offenen Meer leben, gefangen und nach Venedig gebracht, und es sieht aus, wie hier gemalt ist.

En l'an 1534, une des créatures merveilleuses qui vivent en pleine mer fut capturée et emportée à Venise, et elle ressemble à cette peinture.

FOL. 134

1536 — Celestial battle of three children
Himmelsschlacht dreier Kinder | Combat céleste de trois enfants

In the year 1536 Doctor Johannes Doltzburger saw such a wonder in the sky in Medina in Spain. It was on the seventh night of February, when preparing to calculate the time through his art of astronomy, that he saw the apparition, just as it is recorded and painted here.

Im 1536. Jahr hat Doktor Johannes Doltzburger zu Medina in Spanien ein solches Wunder am Himmel gesehen. Als er in der siebenten Nacht des Februars anhand seiner Kunst der Astronomie die Zeit in Erfahrung bringen wollte, hat er die Erscheinung gesehen, wie hier verzeichnet und gemalt ist.

En l'an 1536, le docteur Johannes Doltzburger observa ce prodige dans le ciel de Medina en Espagne. C'est la septième nuit de février, alors qu'il allait calculer l'heure par son art de l'astronomie, qu'il observa l'apparition, comme on le voit consigné et peint ici.

FOL. 135

1537 — Explosion in Heidelberg

Explosion in Heidelberg | Explosion à Heidelberg

Furthermore, on St Mark's Day in this 37th year at 4 o'clock after midday, a thunderstorm broke out in Heidelberg – violent, wild and blustering – with great, awful and terrible peals of thunder. And with the third peal of thunder it struck the old castle, which is called Old Heidelberg. In that place there was more than 200 tons of gunpowder, which sparked because of the lightning-strike and the [...].

Ferner ist am Sankt-Markus-Tag in diesem 37. Jahr um 4 Uhr nach Mittag zu Heidelberg ein Gewitter ausgebrochen – gewaltig, wild und stürmisch – mit großen, schrecklichen, grausamen Donnerschlägen. Und mit dem dritten Donnerschlag hat es in das alte Schloss, das man Alt-Heidelberg nennt, eingeschlagen. An dem Ort waren mehr als 200 Tonnen Pulver, welche sich durch den Blitzschlag entzündet und das [...].

De plus, le jour de la Saint-Marc en cette 37e année à quatre heures après midi, un orage éclata à Heidelberg – violent, furieux et tumultueux – avec des coups de tonnerre puissants, affreux et terribles. Et au troisième coup de tonnerre, il frappa le vieux château, que l'on appelle le Vieux Heidelberg. En ce lieu se trouvaient 200 tonnes de poudre, qui prirent feu à cause de la foudre et le [...].

FOL. 136

1538 — Parhelia near Schönefeld

Nebensonnen bei Schönefeld | Parhélies près de Schönefeld

In the year 1538 such a manifestation was seen around the sun near Schönefeld, and moreover, three suns were seen at once, but also the curious rings stayed in the sky brightly for about four hours.

Im 1538. Jahr ist bei Schönefeld eine solche Erscheinung an der Sonne gesehen worden, dass man zudem je drei Sonnen gesehen hat, aber auch die seltsamen Ringe standen etwa vier Stunden lang hell am Himmel.

En l'an 1538, ce phénomène fut observé autour du soleil près de Schönefeld et, de plus, trois soleils furent observés en même temps, mais aussi les étranges cercles brillèrent sans bouger dans le ciel pendant environ quatre heures.

FOL. 137

1538 — Plague of flies and thunderstorm

Fliegenplage und Gewitter | Mouches et orage

In the year 1538 flies as big as gnats were seen in the Castel Sant'Angelo in Rome, so that the pope had to flee them. And whoever they bit, died. A storm broke out at the same time too and fire fell from the sky.

Im 1538. Jahr sind in Rom in der Engelsburg Fliegen so groß wie Schnaken gesehen worden, dass der Papst vor ihnen fliehen musste. Und wen sie gestochen haben, der ist gestorben. Auch ereignete sich ein Unwetter zu der Zeit, dass das Feuer vom Himmel fiel.

En l'an 1538, des mouches grosses comme des moucherons furent observées au château Sant'Angelo à Rome, à tel point que le pape dut fuir. Et ceux qu'elles piquaient mouraient. Un orage eut lieu au même moment, à tel point que le feu s'abattit du ciel.

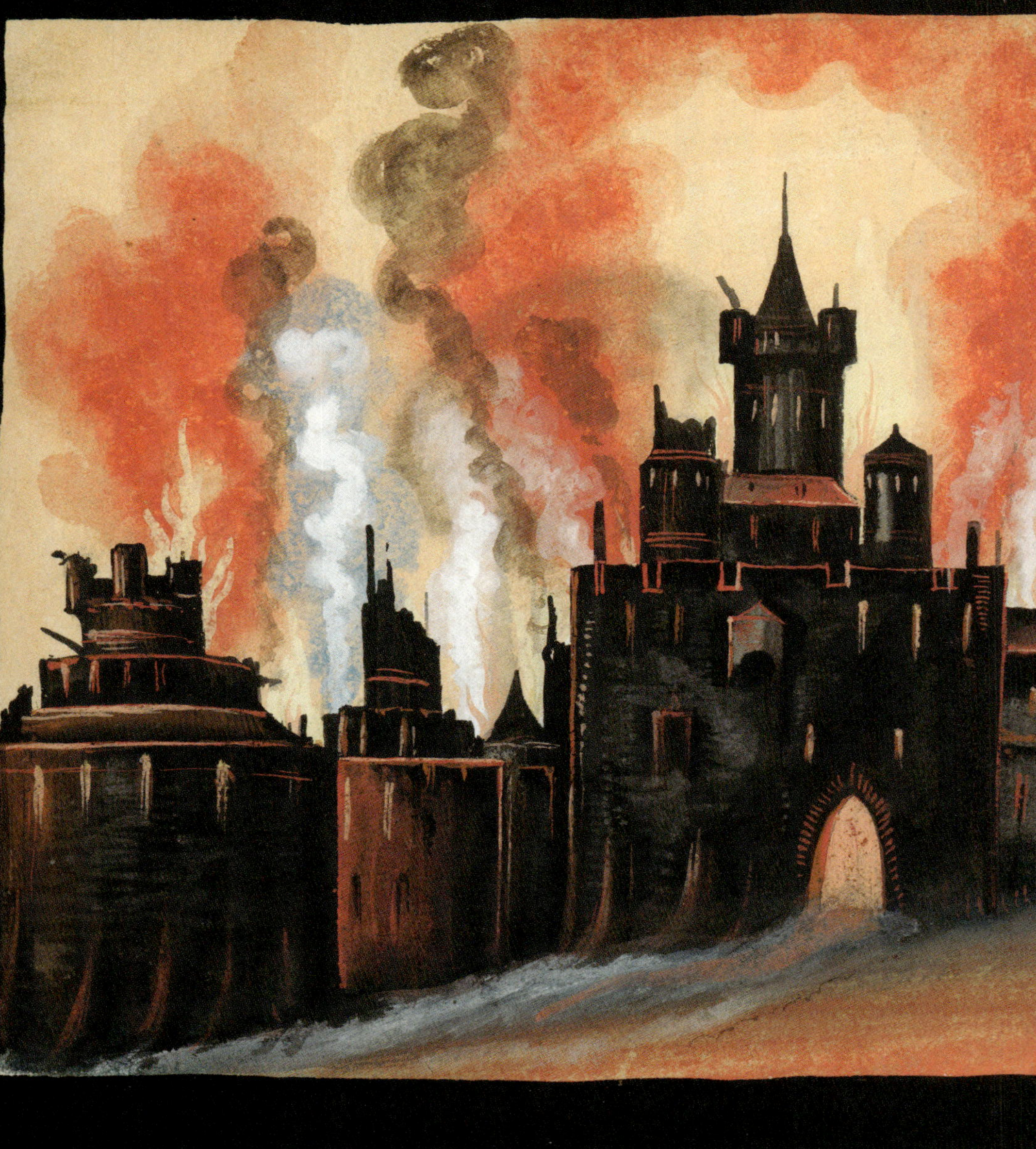

Item auf sannct marxtag/ in dirsem
ain wetter angebrochen/ fast wild vnnd
schlegen/ vnd hat in dem dritten doner sch
on dem ort mer dan ii hundert thunen pulf

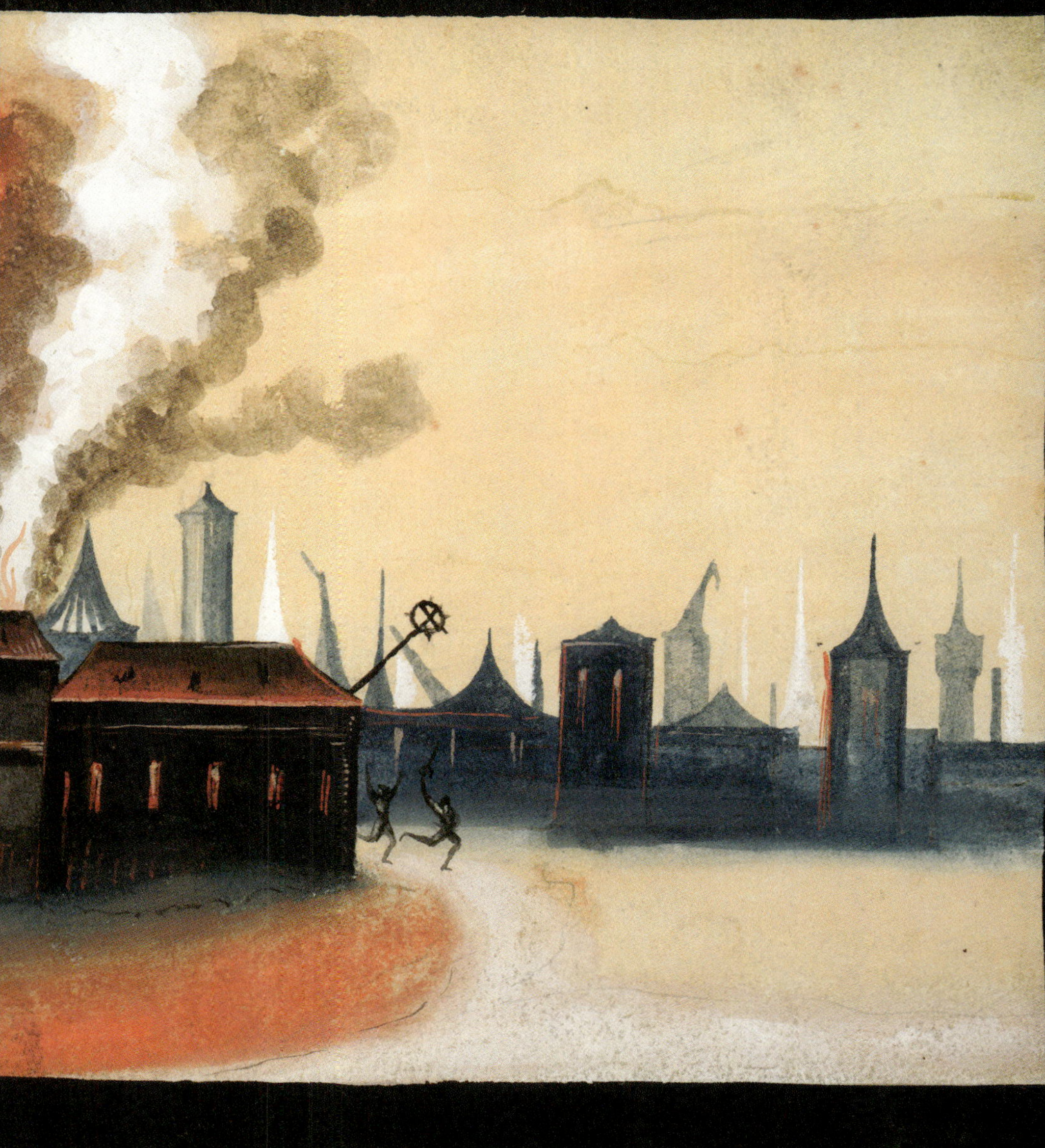

537.
ii iar/ vnnd iiii vr nach mittag ist zů Hadelberg
stům/ mit grossen erschrecklichen grausamen doner
n das alt Schloß/ das man alt heidelberg nent geschlagen
wesen/ welch sich vom donerschlag an gezunt/ vnd das

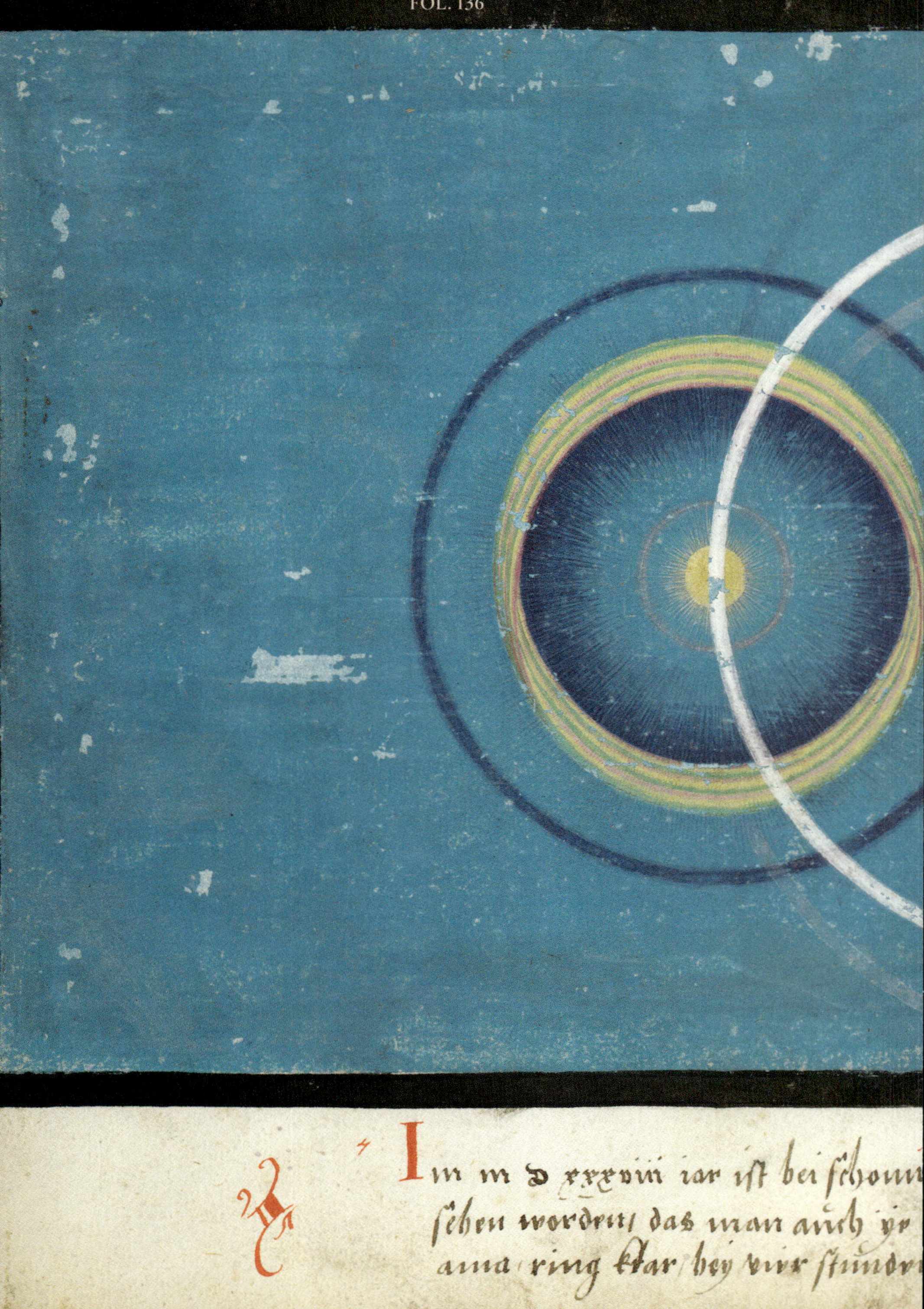
Im m d xxxviii iar ist bei schoun
sehen worden, das man auch ir
ainn ring klar bey vier stunde

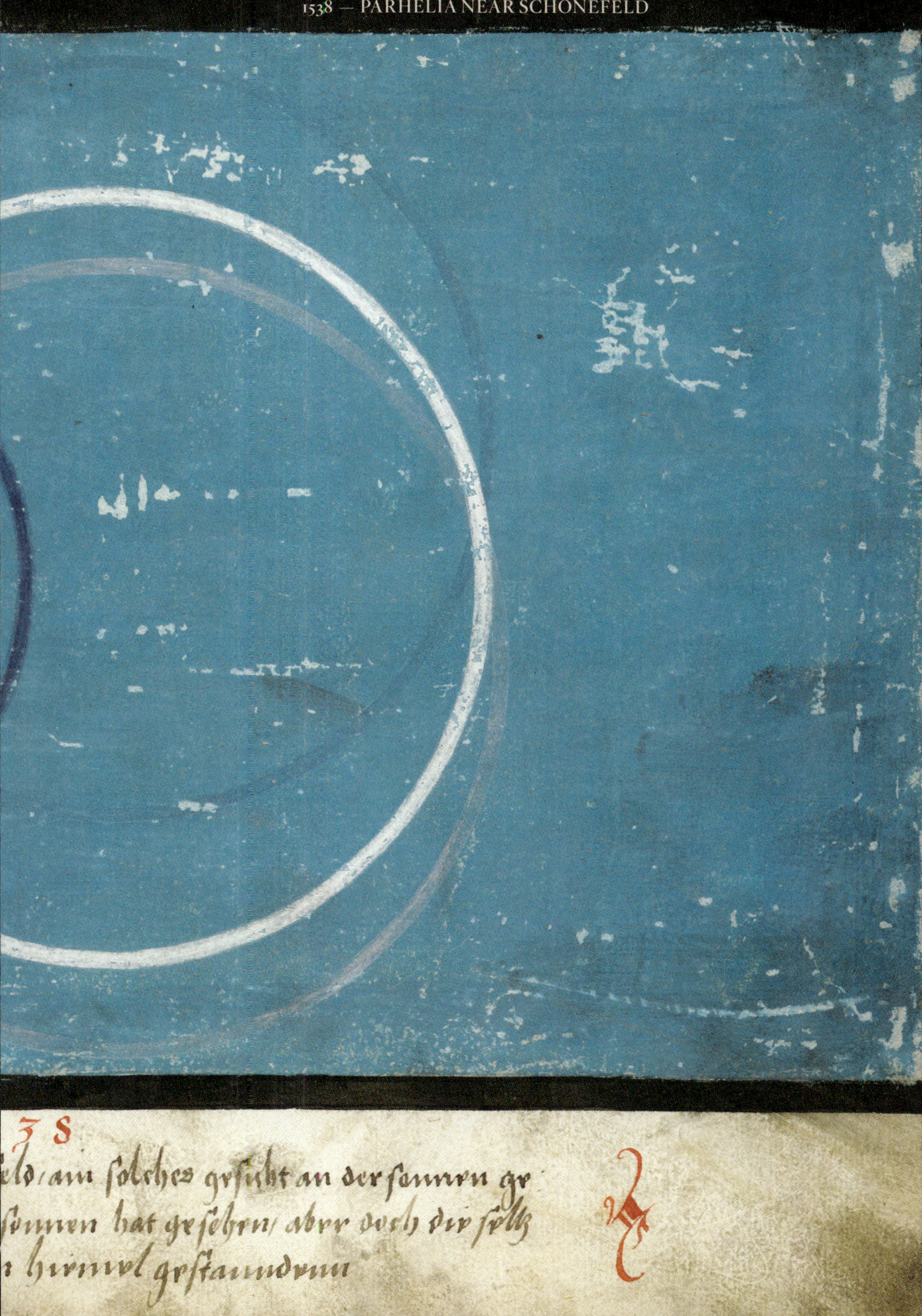
38
ain solches gesicht an der sonnen ge
sonnen hat gesehen/ aber doch dir selb
himmel gestanndenn

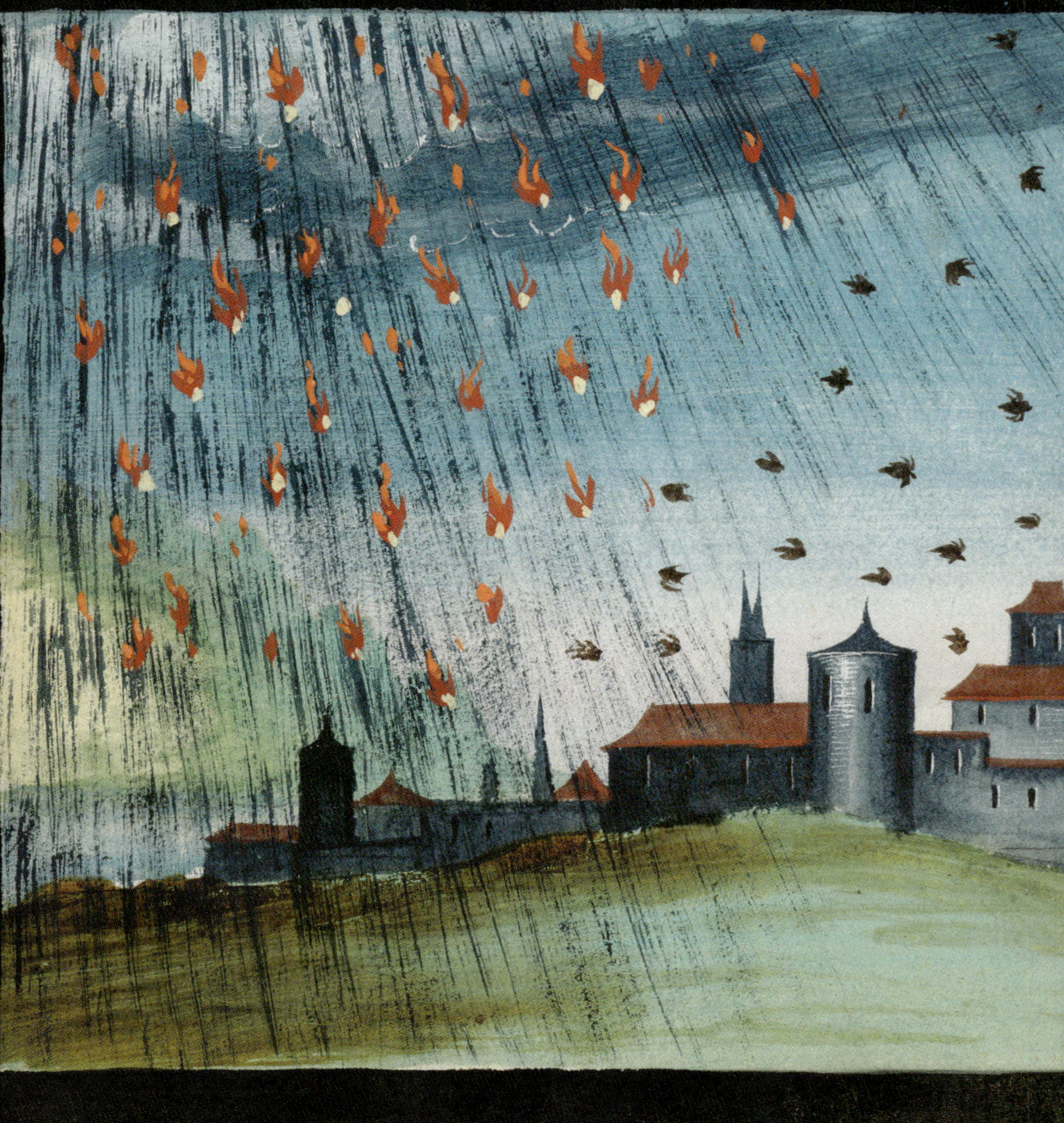

Im m Dxxxviii iar/ da s
wie die schnacken gsehen
vnnd wen sie gstochen h
zu der zeit/ das das feürr

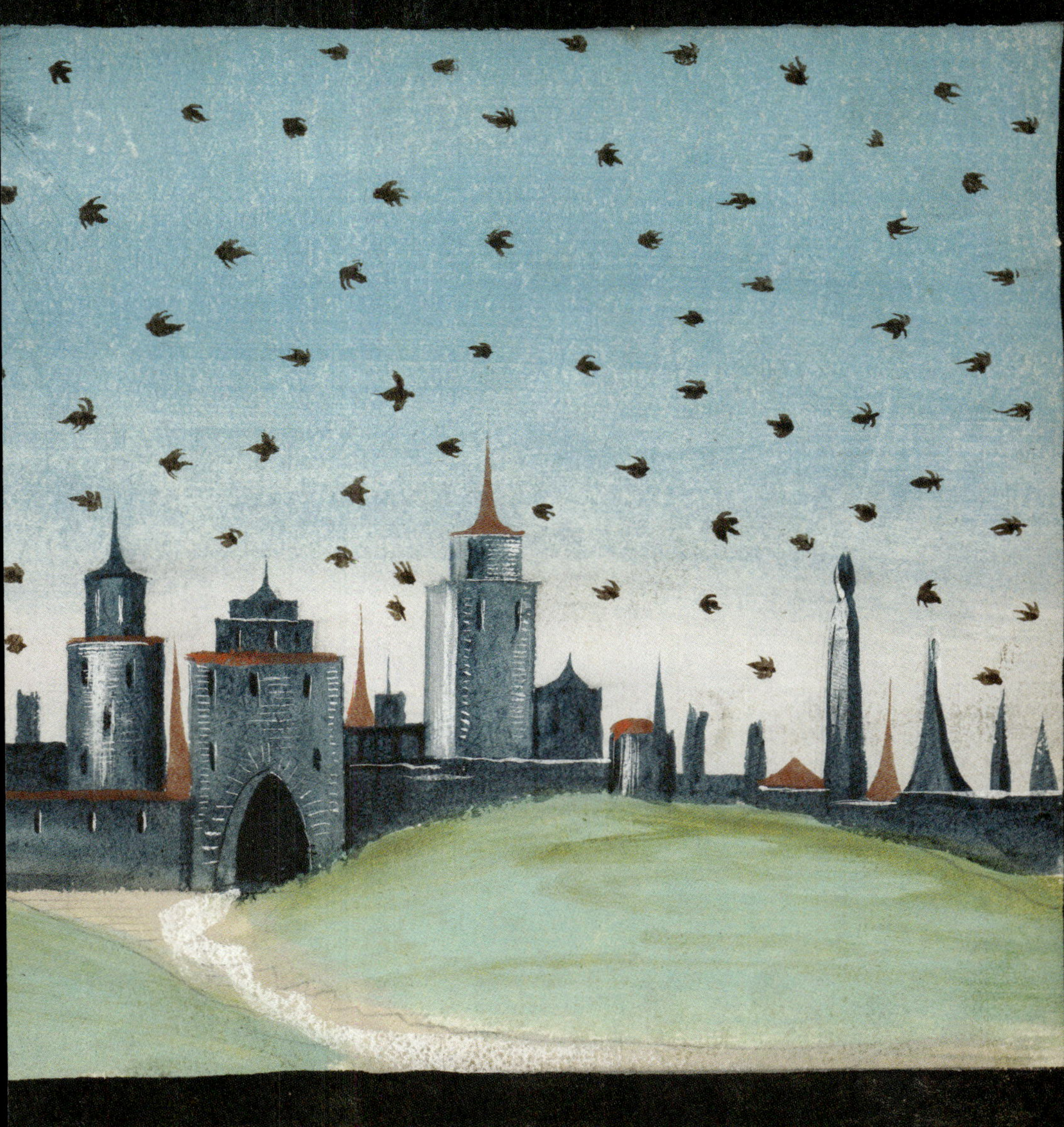

·1538·

zu rom in der engelburg groß fliegen

en/ das sie der pabst hat müssen fliehen:

d der ist gestorben/ auch ward ein wetter

r himmel fiell

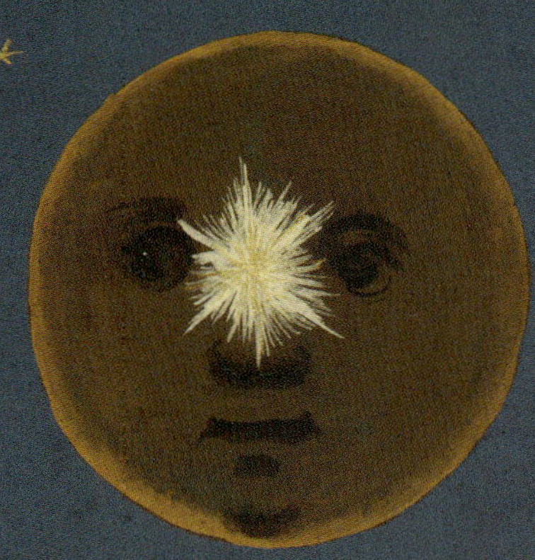

Im m D xxxx iar/ ist zu würt
Zaichen/ gesehen worden/ an
bey nacht/ der mon finster/ vn
Zwainzigsten tag novemb

·1540·

uff einem reichstag seltzam wunder

sechs un zwaintzigsten Novemb[er]

n stern darin / vnnd am sieben

an solche zaichen gesehen an stern

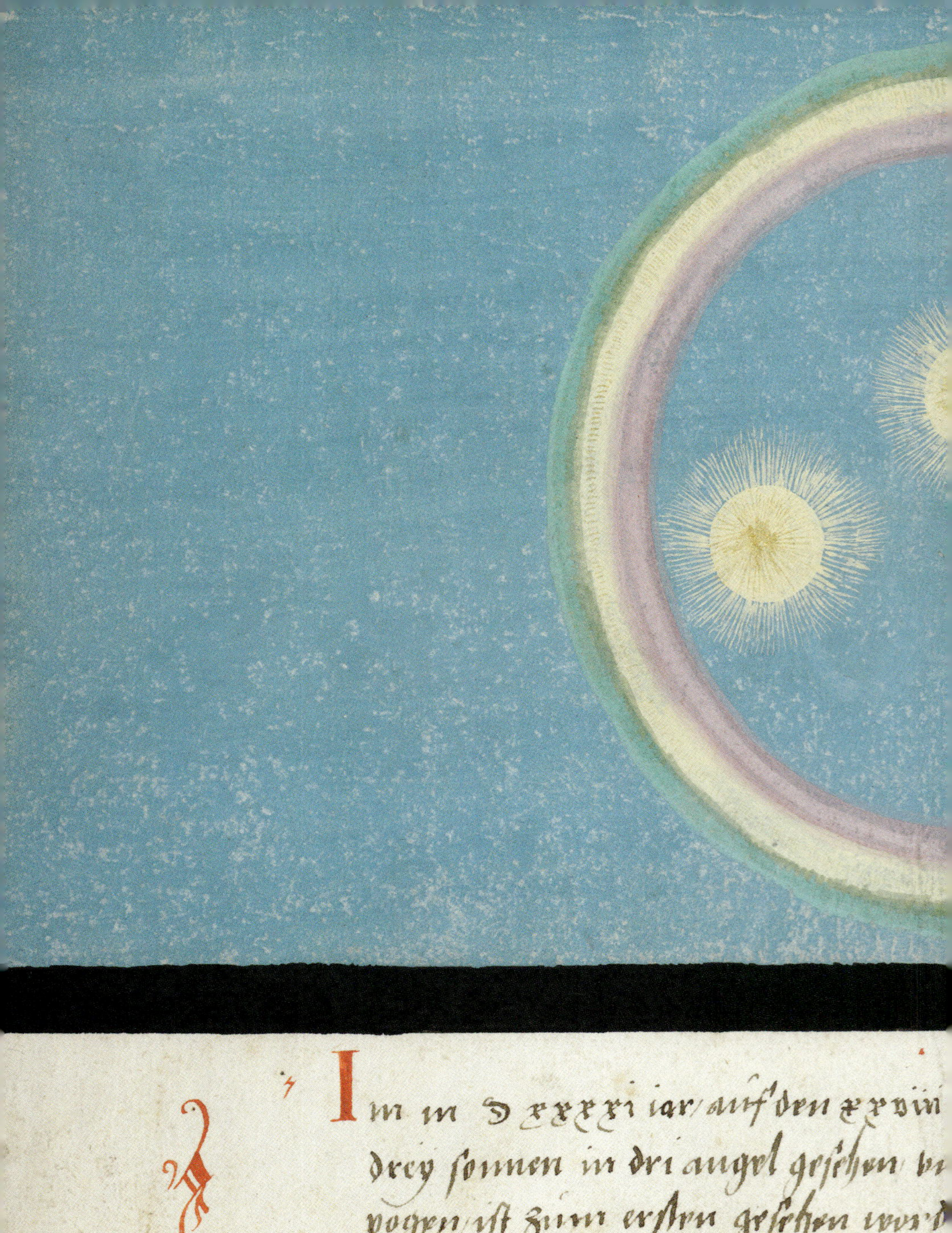

Im m D xxxxi iar/ auf den xxviii
drey sonnen in dri augel gesehen w
pogen ist zum ersten gesehen word
sonnen/ mit sampt dem regenpoge

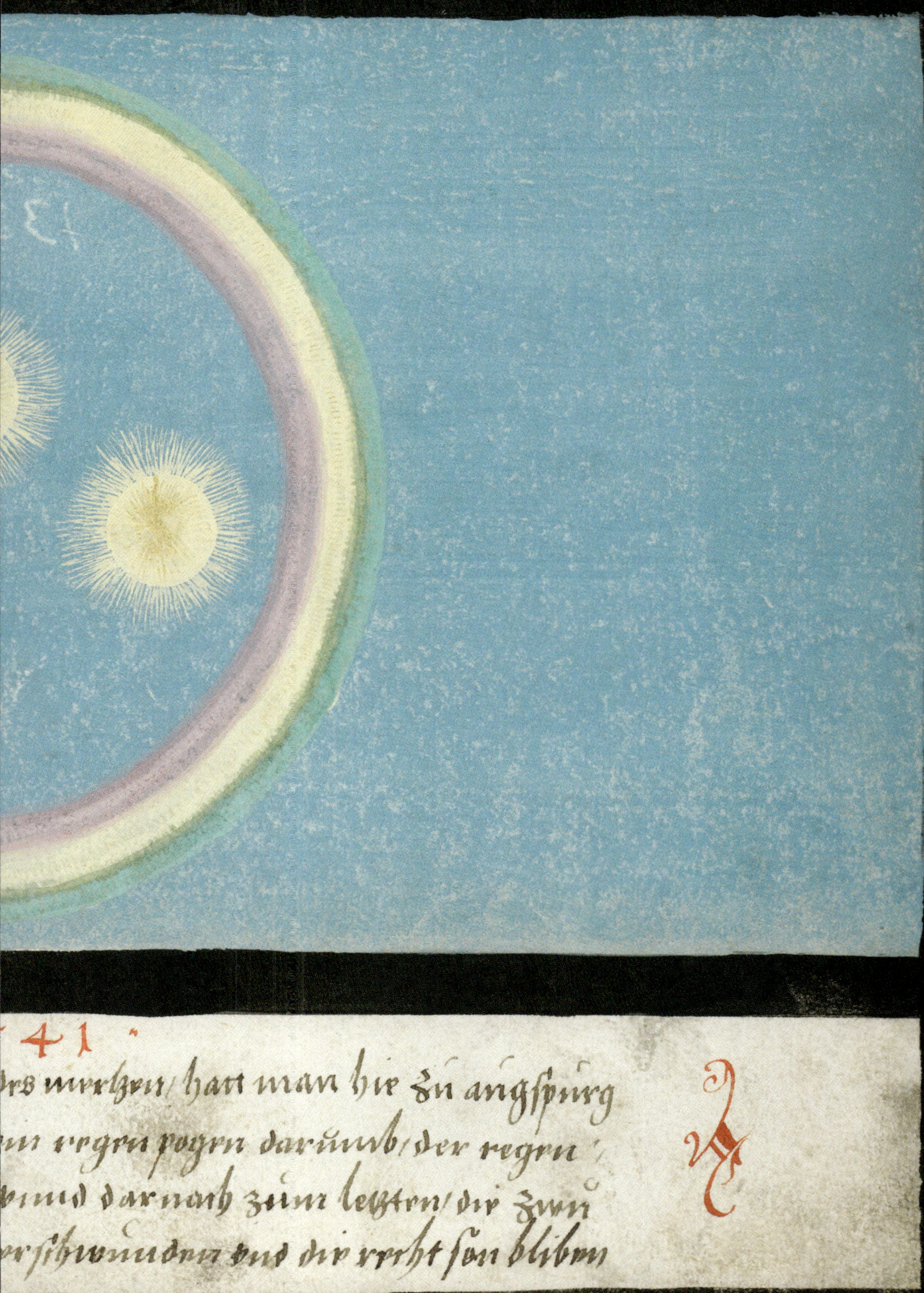
41
des mertzen/ hatt man hie zu augspurg
en regen pogen darumb/ der regen
und darnach zum letsten/ die zwen
erschwunden vnd die recht sun bliben

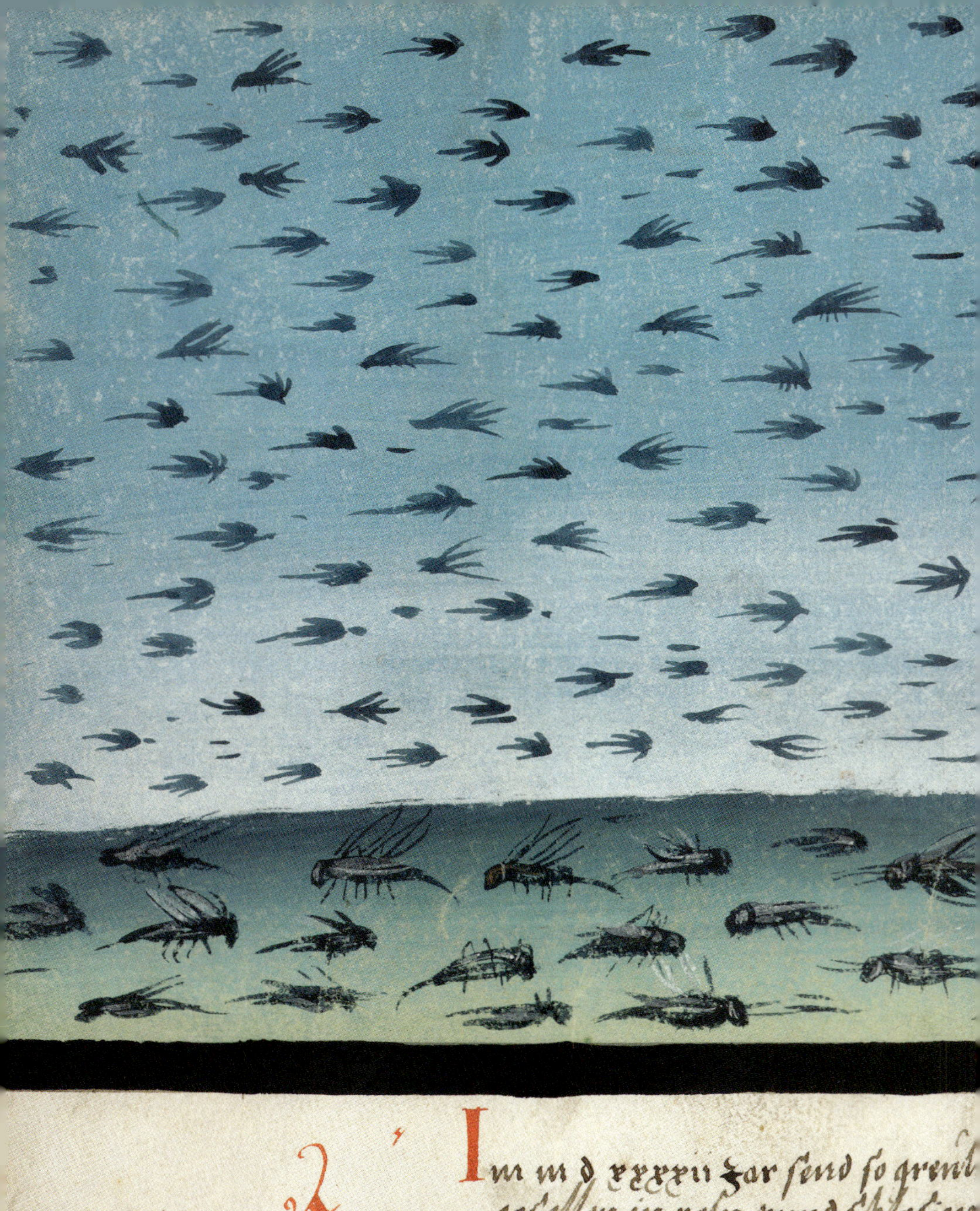

Im m d xxxxii Jar seind so grew
gefallen in poln vnnd schlesien
hin nach von wegen des gestan
gewyssen wir hie gewalt ist e

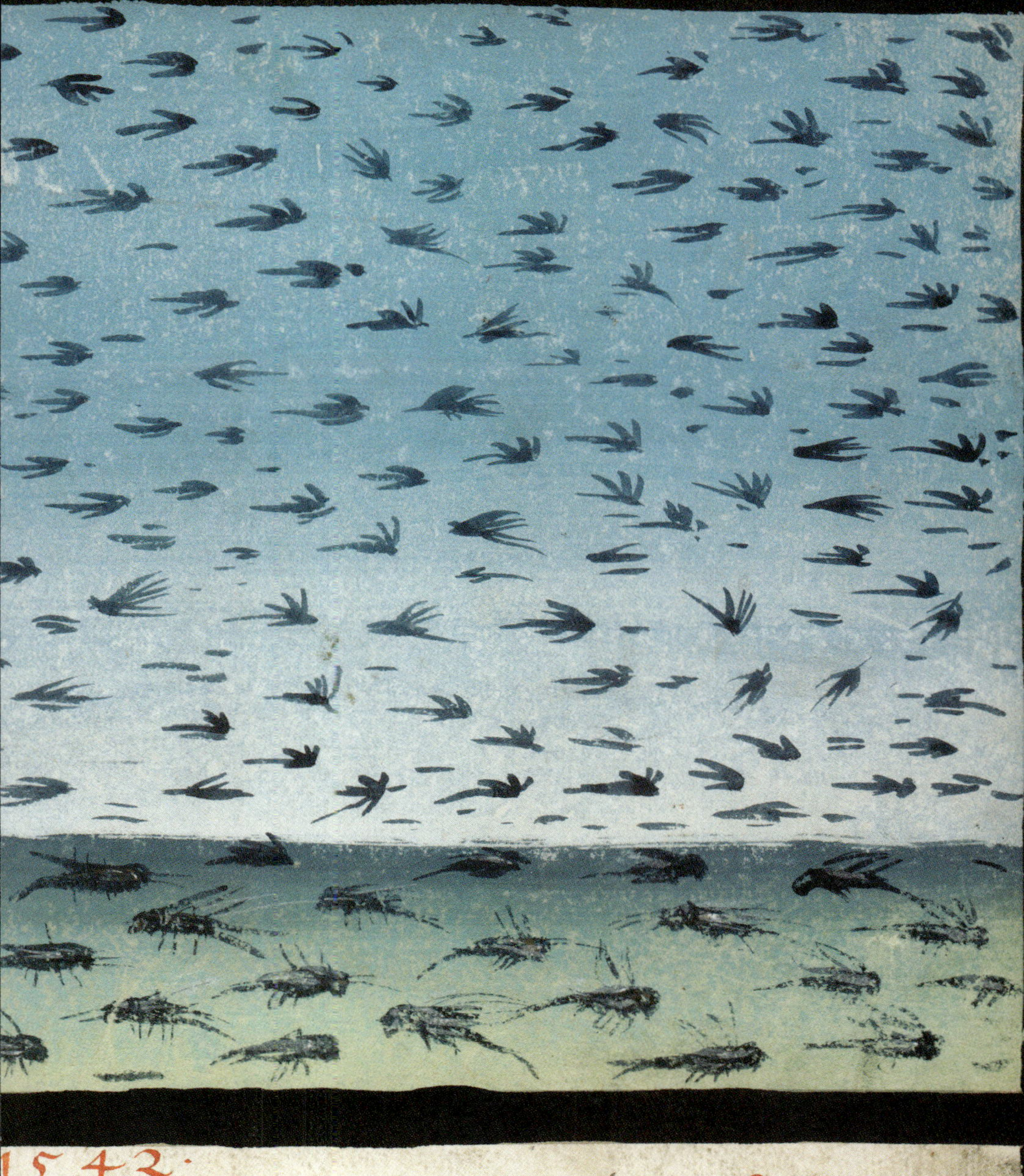

1542.
n schrecken im September vnnd october
h zu marlend vnnd dieterichs pern das
ar vill volcks starb vnnd sind gestalt

FOL. 138

1540 — Wondrous moon and stars over Worms
Wundersamer Mond und Sterne über Worms
Lune et étoiles merveilleuses dans le ciel de Worms

In the year 1540, strange miraculous signs were seen at a Reichstag in Worms. On the twenty-sixth of November, the moon was dark at night and inside it was a star. And on the twenty-seventh of November signs such as these were seen on the stars.

Im 1540. Jahr sind in Worms auf einem Reichstag seltsame Wunderzeichen gesehen worden. Am sechsundzwanzigsten November bei Nacht war der Mond finster und in ihm war ein Stern. Und am siebenundzwanzigsten November hat man solche Zeichen an den Sternen gesehen.

En l'an 1540, d'étranges signes miraculeux furent observés à un Reichstag de Worms. Le vingt-six novembre, la nuit, la lune était noire et elle contenait une étoile. Et le vingt-sept novembre des signes comme ceux-ci furent observés sur les étoiles.

FOL. 139

1541 — Parhelia over Augsburg
Nebensonnen über Augsburg | Parhélies dans le ciel d'Augsbourg

In the year 1541, on the 28th day of March, three suns in a triangle with a rainbow around them were seen here in Augsburg. The rainbow was seen first and then last, two of the suns disappeared along with the rainbow and the sun on the right remained.

Im 1541. Jahr, am 28. Tag des März, hat man hier zu Augsburg drei Sonnen im Dreieck und einen Regenbogen um sie herum gesehen. Der Regenbogen ist als Erstes und danach als Letztes gesehen worden, die zwei Sonnen sind mitsamt dem Regenbogen verschwunden und die rechte Sonne ist geblieben.

En l'an 1541, le vingt-huit mars, trois soleils en triangle, entourés d'un arc-en-ciel, furent observés ici à Augsbourg. L'arc-en-ciel fut observé en premier puis en dernier, deux soleils disparurent avec l'arc-en-ciel et le soleil de droite resta visible.

FOL. 141

1542 — Plague of locusts | Heuschreckenplage | Invasion de locustes

In the year 1542, such loathsome locusts invaded Poland and Silesia, as well as Milan and Theodoric's Verona, in September and October, that afterwards a great many people died on account of the stench. And they looked just as it is painted here etc.

Im 1542. Jahr sind so grauenerregende Heuschrecken im September und Oktober in Polen und Schlesien, auch in Mailand und Dietrichs Verona eingefallen, dass danach wegen des Gestanks sehr viele Leute starben. Und diese sahen so aus, wie hier gemalt ist etc.

En l'an 1542, ces répugnantes locustes envahirent la Pologne et la Silésie, ainsi que Milan et la Vérone de Théodoric en septembre et en octobre, ce qui causa la mort d'un très grand nombre de personnes en raison de la pestilence. Et elles avaient l'allure que l'on voit sur cette peinture, etc.

FOL. 142

1542 — Comet | Komet | Comète

In the year 1542, on St Rupert's Day, the twenty-seventh of September, a comet was seen in the sky not far from the moon for many days, just as is painted here.

Im 1542. Jahr, am Tag Ruperti, dem siebenundzwanzigsten September, ist ein Komet nicht weit vom Mond viele Tage am Himmel gesehen worden, wie hier gemalt ist.

En 1542, le jour de la Saint-Rupert, le vingt-sept septembre, une comète fut observée dans le ciel non loin de la lune pendant plusieurs jours, comme dans cette peinture.

FOL. 144

1542 — Celestial fire over Augsburg
Himmelsfeuer über Augsburg | Incendie céleste dans le ciel d'Augsbourg

In the year 1542 a fire in the sky was seen here in Augsburg, burning like a great brazier in the clouds at midnight, which many trustworthy people saw for a long time.

Im 1542. Jahr ist hier zu Augsburg ein Feuer am Himmel gesehen worden, das wie eine große Feuerpfanne in den Wolken um 12 Uhr in der Nacht brannte, was viele glaubwürdige Leute eine lange Zeit gesehen haben.

En l'an 1542, un incendie dans le ciel fut observé ici à Augsbourg, brûlant comme un grand brasier dans les nuages à minuit, vu par beaucoup de gens dignes de foi pendant longtemps.

FOL. 145

1543 — Wondrous hen and wondrous fish
Wundersames Huhn und wundersamer Fisch | Poule et poisson merveilleux

In the year 1543, a four-legged chick hatched out in Dillingen and then suddenly died. But it was nonetheless carefully painted from life by the bishop's painter.

In the year 1543, such a wonder fish was caught in the Danish Sea as is painted and recorded here. And it was brought back alive to the city of Copenhagen.

Im 1543. Jahr ist in Dillingen ein solches vierfüßiges Hennlein ausgeschlüpft und danach plötzlich gestorben – aber dennoch sorgfältig abgemalt durch den Maler des Bischofs daselbst.

Im 1543. Jahr hat man einen solchen Wunderfisch im dänischen Meer gefangen, wie dann hier gemalt und verzeichnet ist. Und er ist so lebendig in die Stadt Kopenhagen gebracht worden.

En l'an 1543, cette petite poule quadrupède avait éclos à Dillingen, puis mourut soudainement, mais fut tout de même soigneusement représentée par le peintre de l'évêque.

En 1543, ce poisson merveilleux fut pêché dans la mer du Danemark comme on le voit consigné et peint ici. Et il fut aussi rapporté vivant dans la ville de Copenhague.

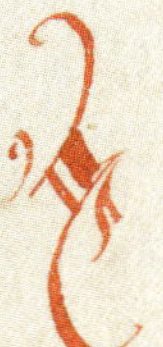

4 Im m d xxxiij Jar am
Septembris ist ein Com
gesehen worden bilta

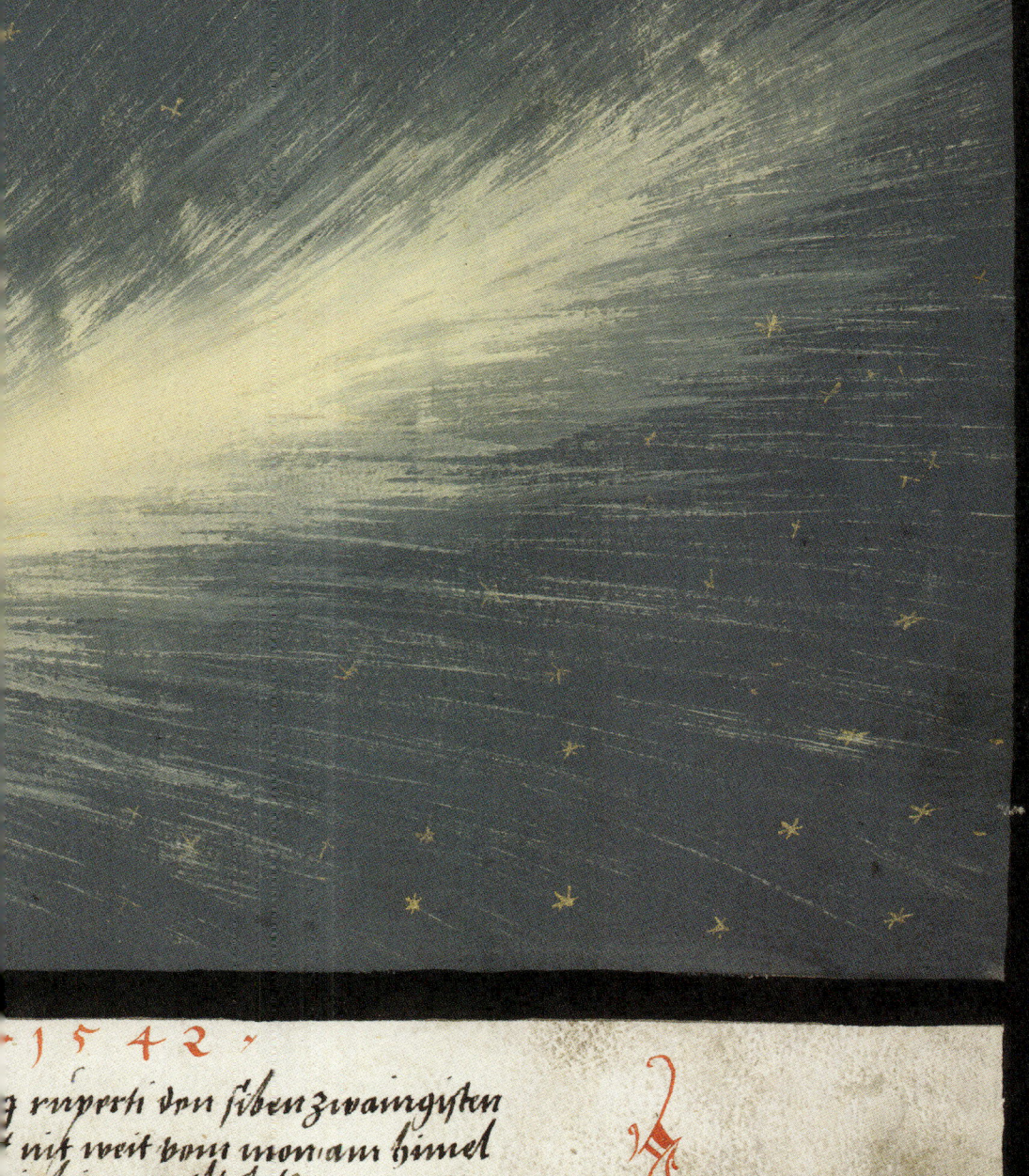

1542
ruperti den sibenzwaingisten
nit weit vom mon am himel
hir gemalt stet

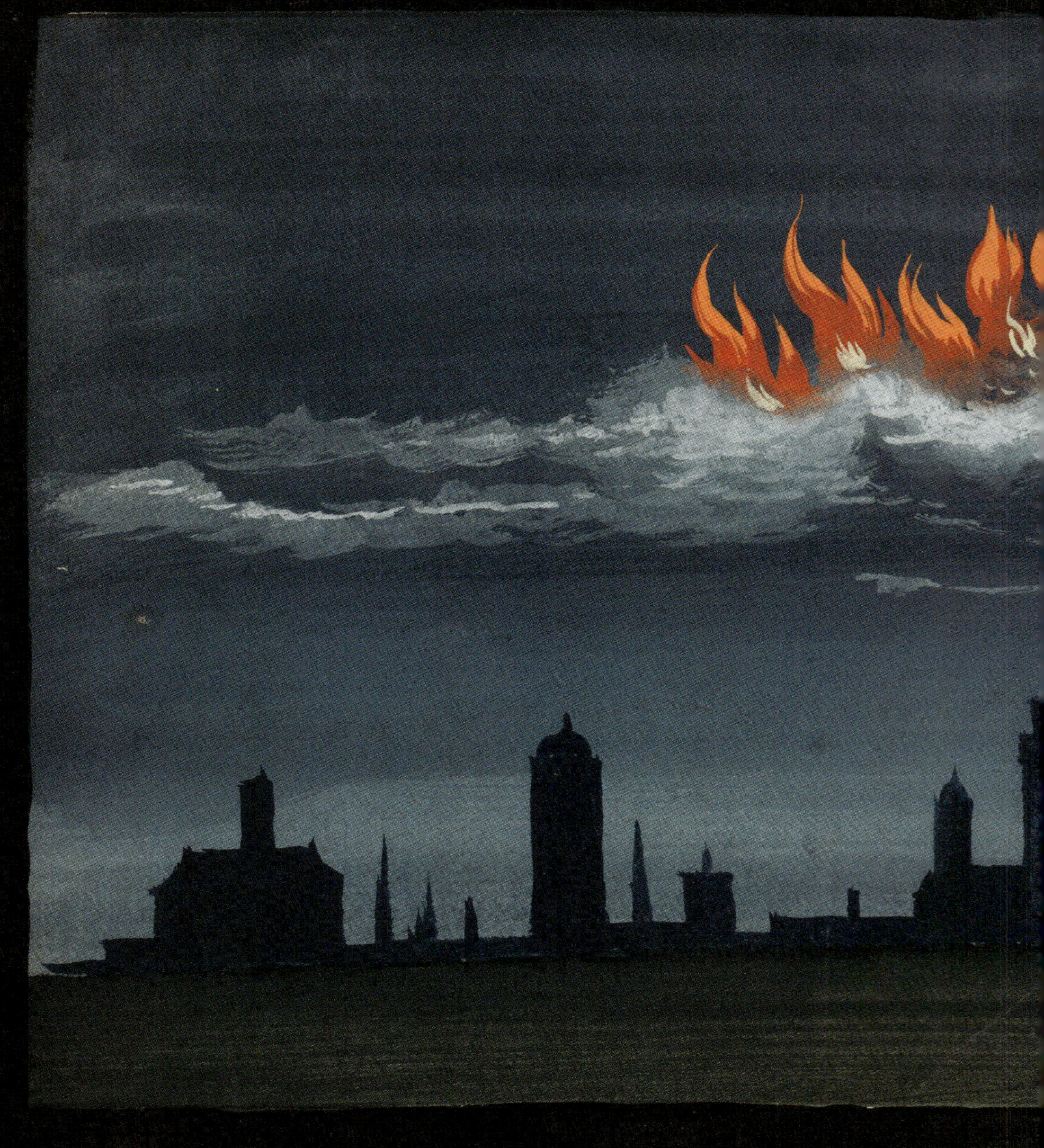

Im m D xxxxii iar ist gesche
am himel, wie ein gros feu
xii vr in der nacht das vil gla
zeit

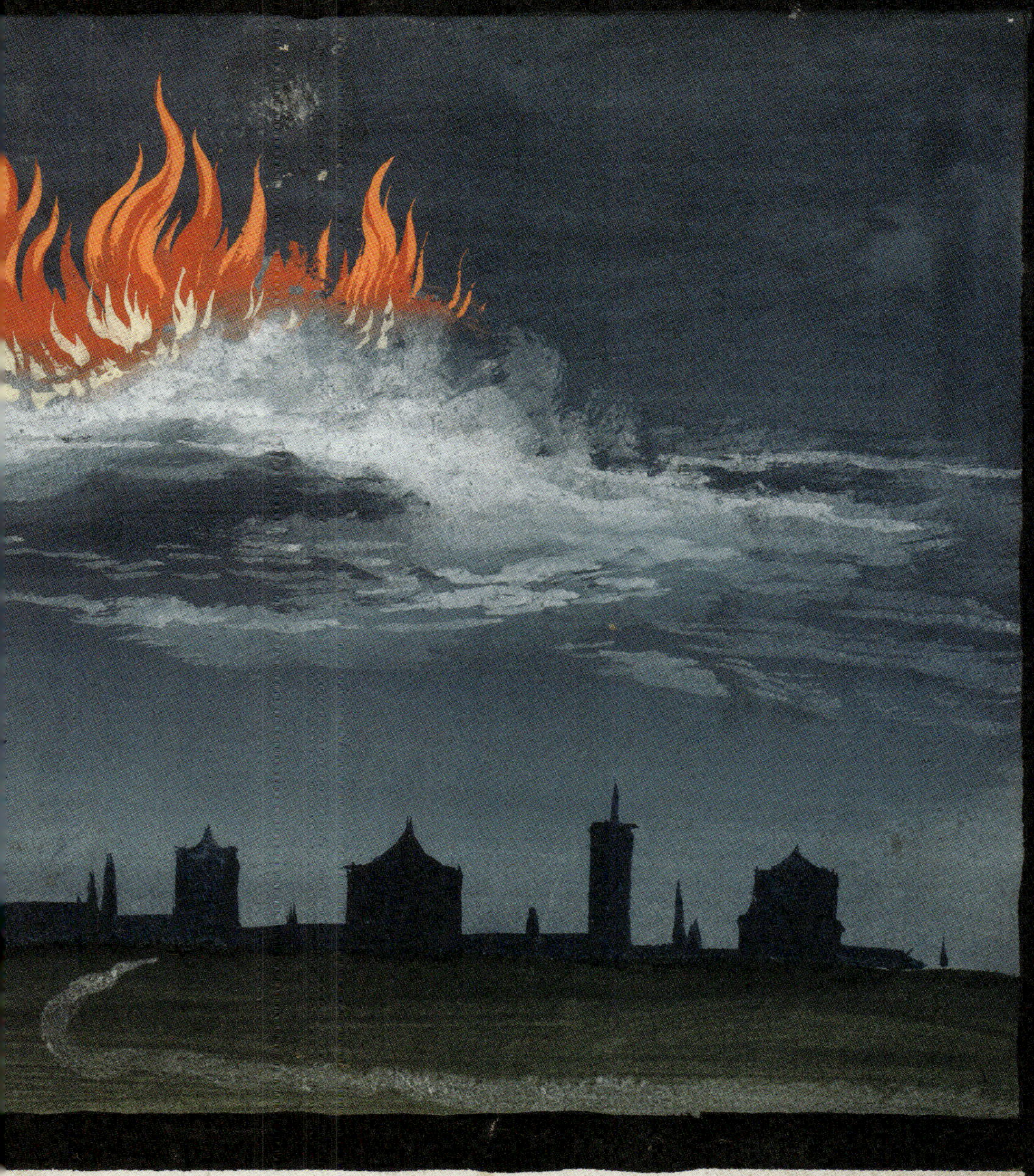

542.
worden/ hie zů augspurg ein feuer/
flammen/ prinnet/ in grewlich vnnd
hafftig leüt hand gesehen ain lange

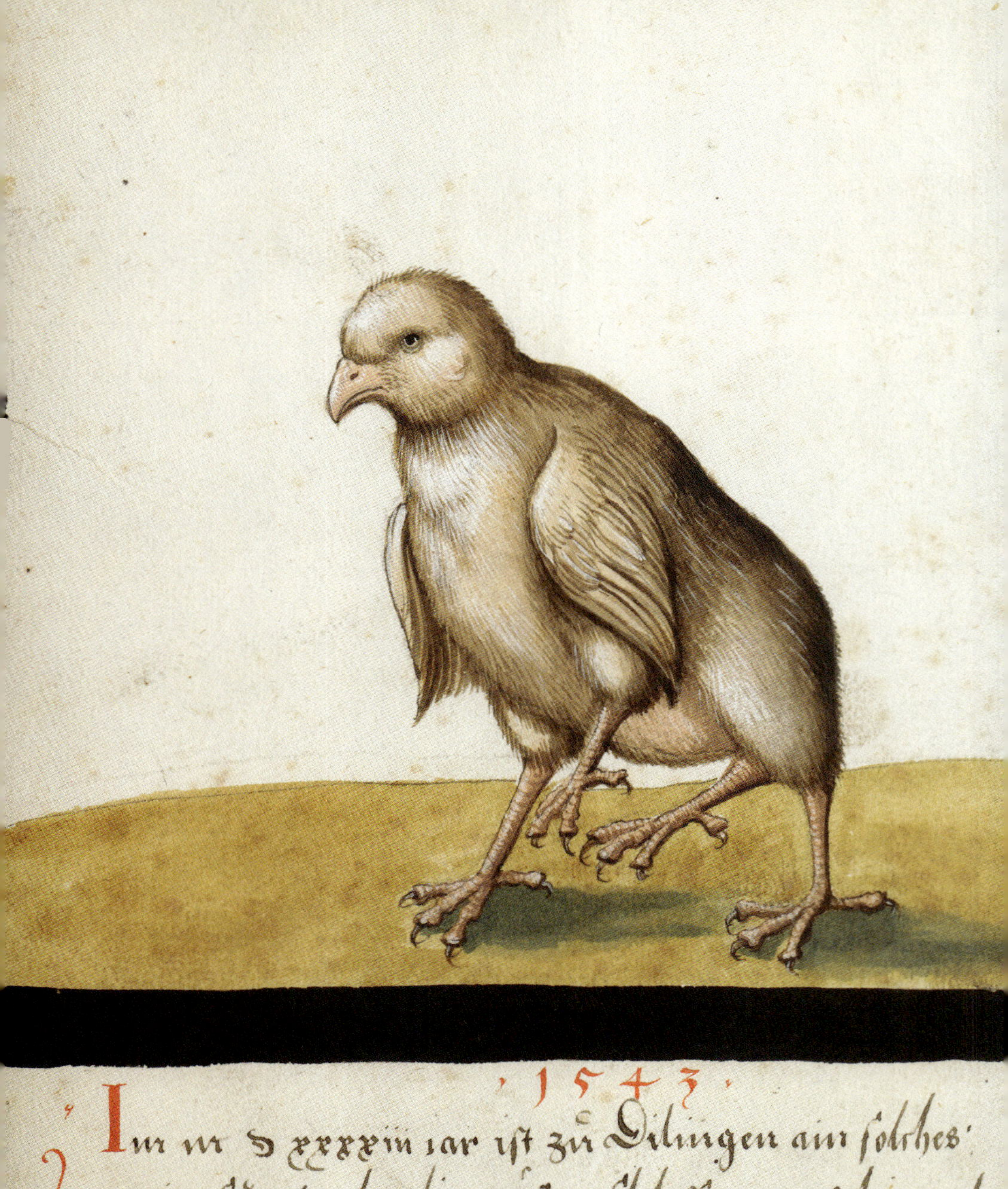

·1543·

Im m D xxxxiii iar ist zů Dilingen ain solches vier füeßigs heŭrlin aŭß geschloffen/ vnnd hinnach gehling gestorben/ aber doch fleisig abgemalt durch des bischoffs maler daselbst.

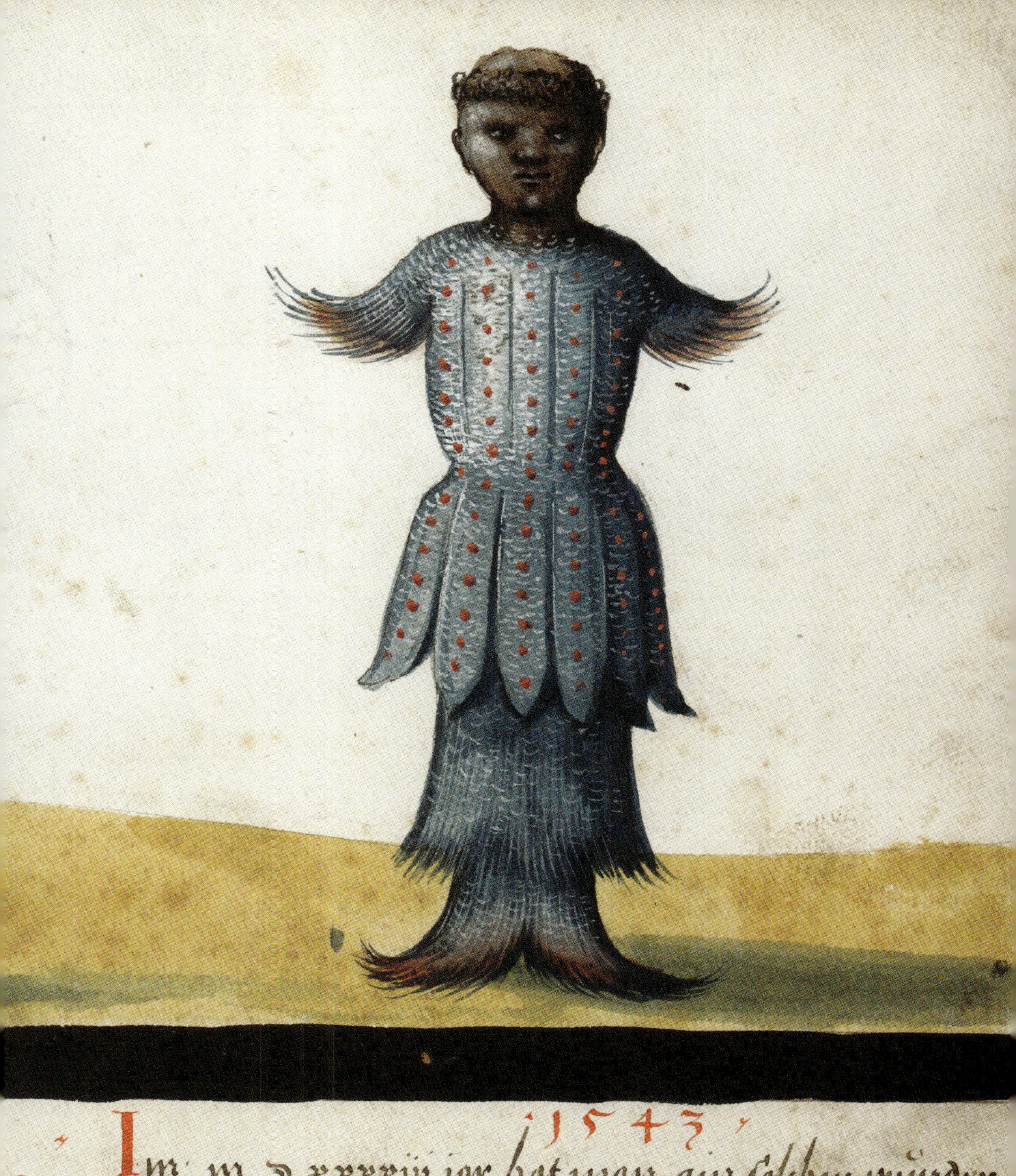

.1543.

Im: m D xxxxiii iar hat man ain solchen wůnder fisch in den denmarckischen see gefangen wie dan hie gemalt vnnd ver zaichnet ist / vnnd in die stat Köpenhagen also lebendig bracht worden.

·15

Im M D xxxiii iar auf den vierten
pforzhaim vnnd in dem dorff zeffen
gesehen, dar van vil feuer flamen f

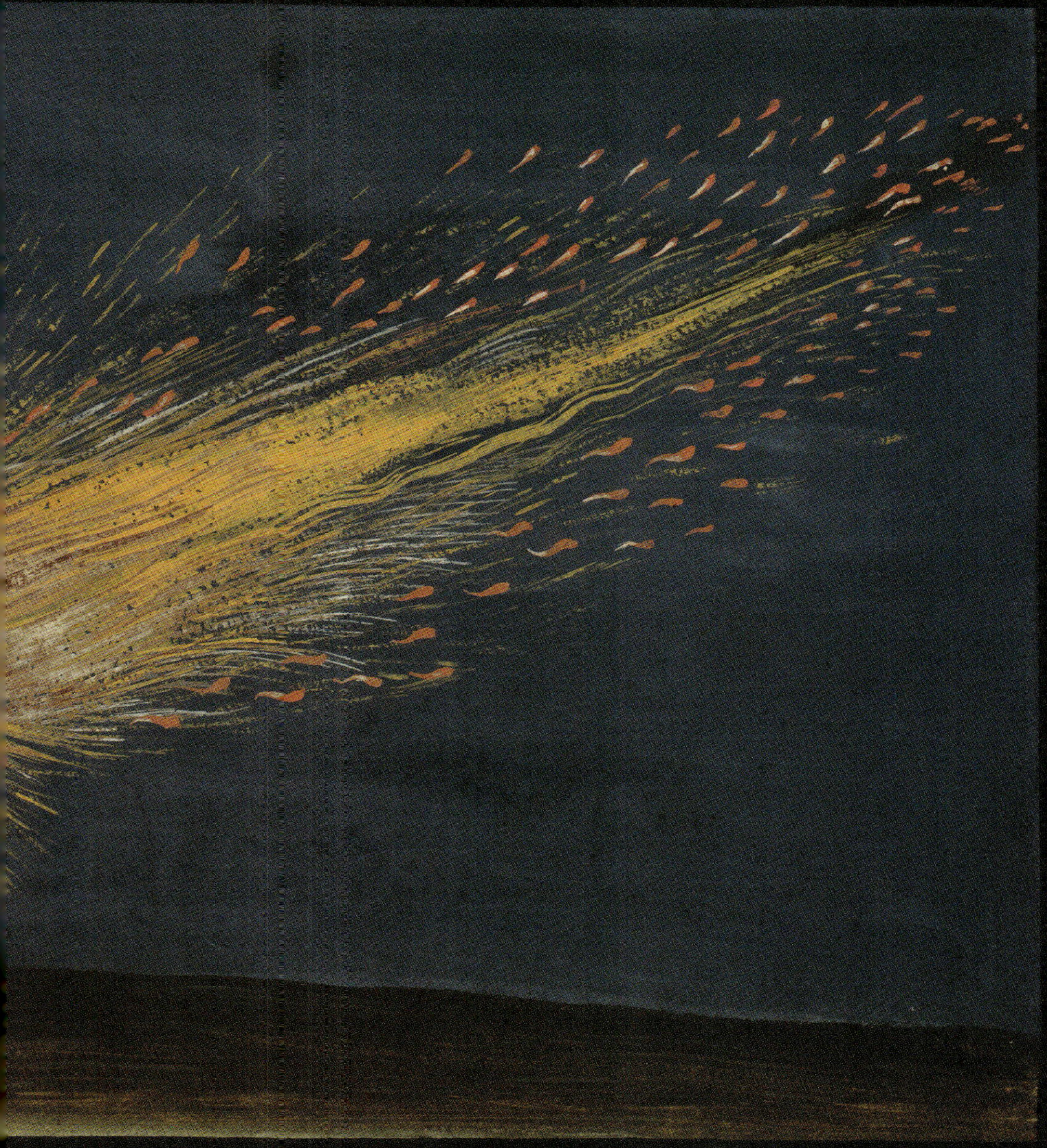

g der monat maij hat man am himel zu
ůsen genant ain grausamen commetenn
gefalen dar aus dan seltzam ding gefolgett

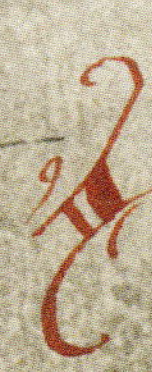

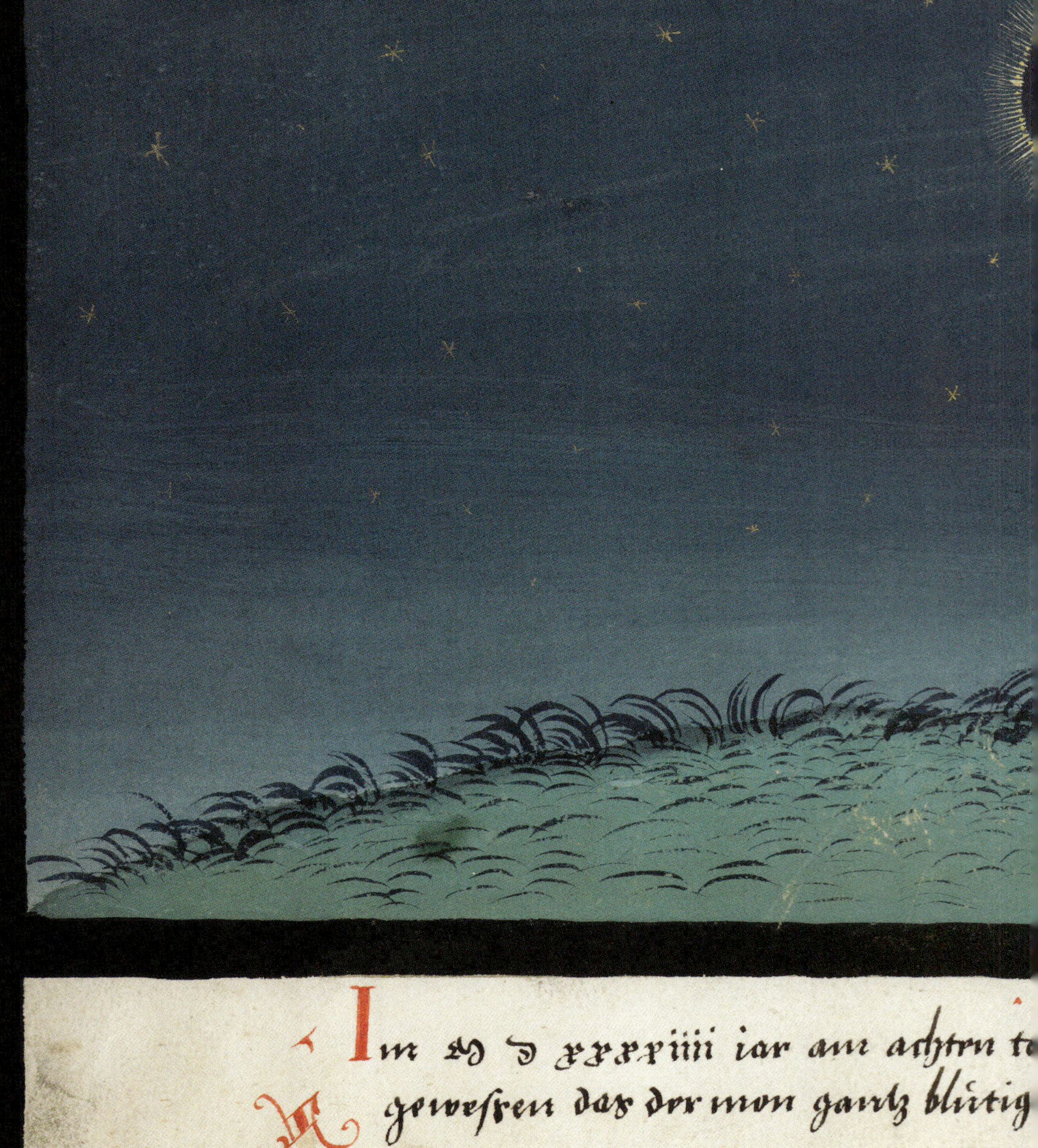
Im M D xxxxiiii iar am achten
gewesen das der mon gantz blütig

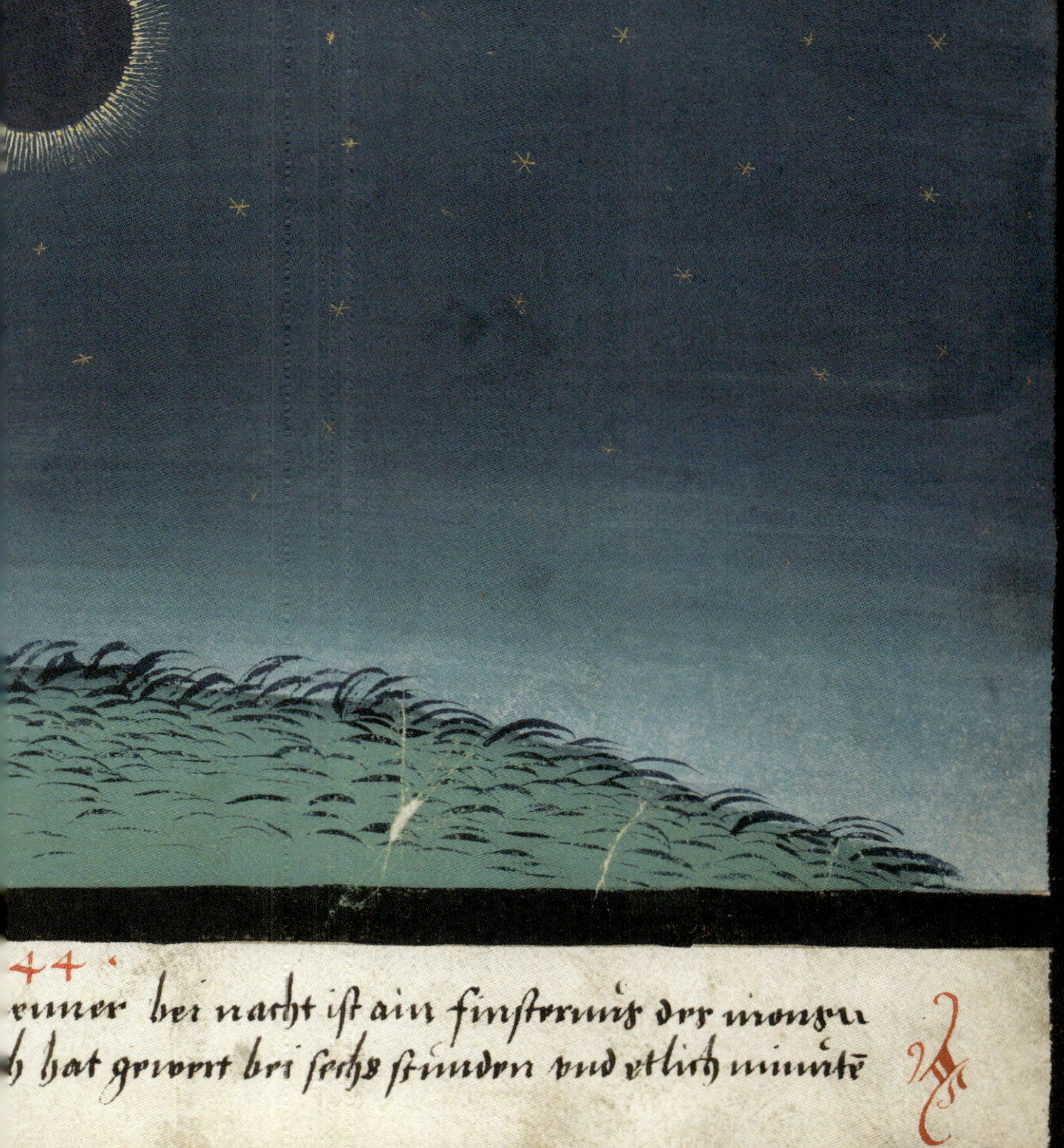
44 ·
enner bei nacht ist ain finsternus der monen
h hat gewert bei sechs stunden vnd etlich minutẽ

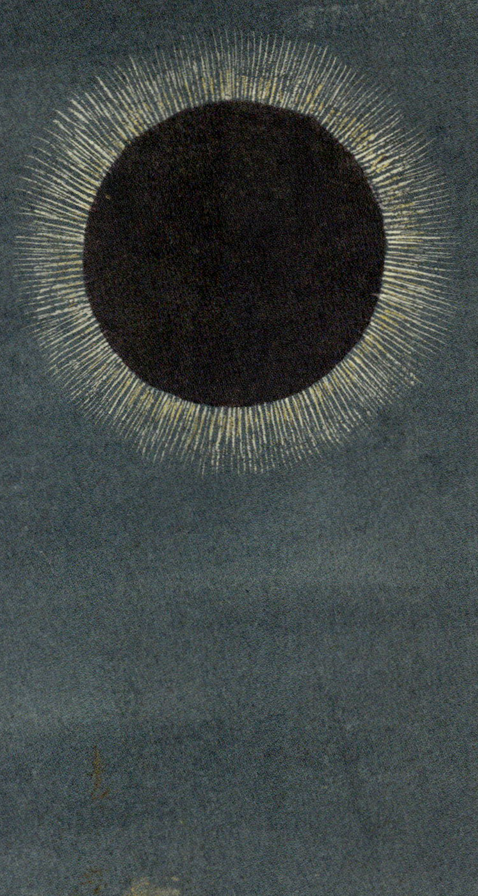

Im m. D xxxxiiii iar auff d
der sonnen zu augspurg vn
worden zu morgen vmb a
biss aulff vr das er so finster
kunden sehen vnd gegen d

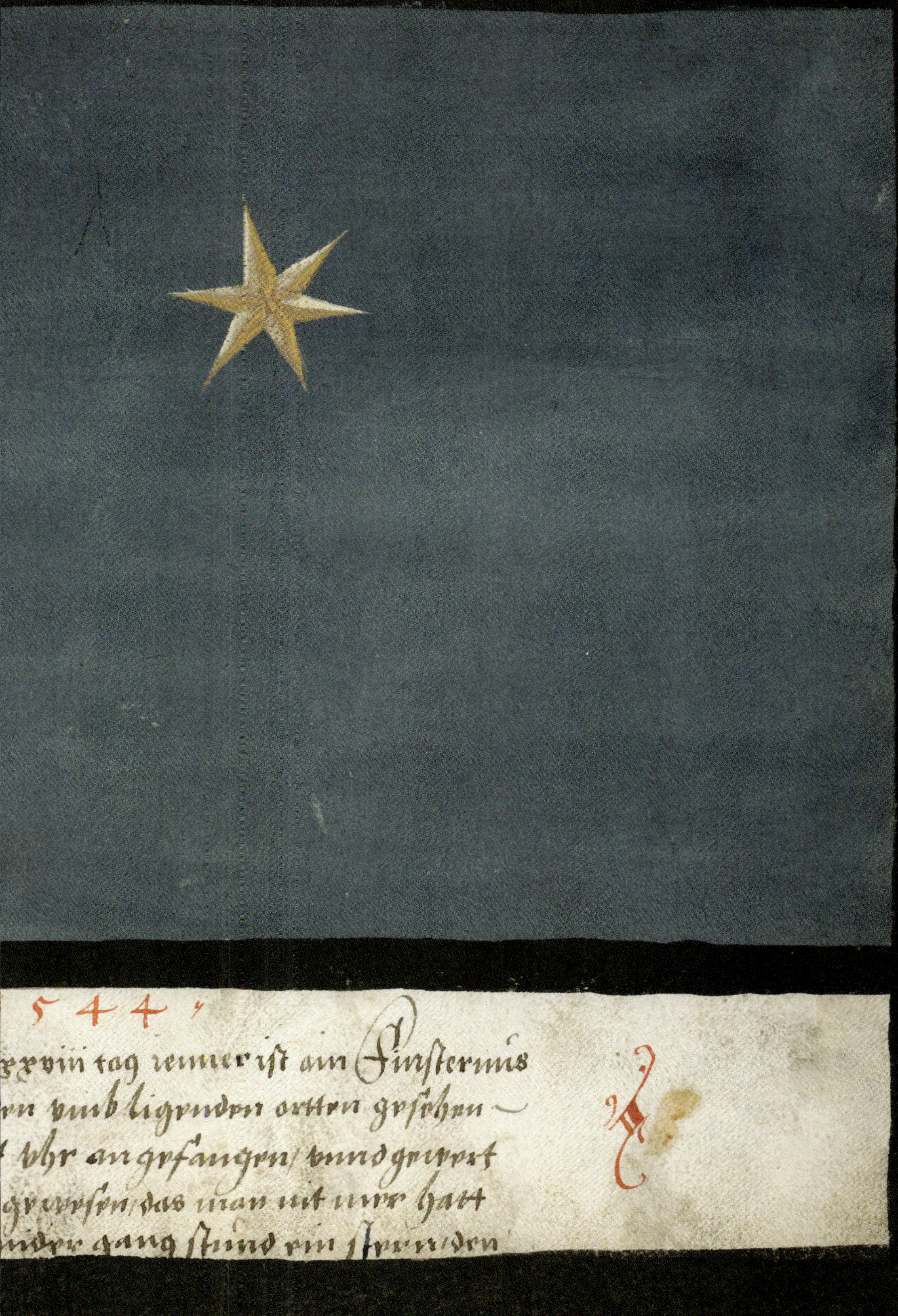

1544

xxviii tag Jenner ist ain Finsternus

rn vnnd ligenden ortten gesehen

uhr angefangen / vnnd geweret

gewesen / das man nit mer hatt

under gang stund ein stern / den

FOL. 146

1543 — Comet over Pforzheim and Zaisenhausen
Komet über Pforzheim und Zaisenhausen
Comète dans le ciel de Pforzheim et Zaisenhausen

In the year 1543, on the fourth day of the month of May, a terrible comet was seen in the sky over Pforzheim and in the village called Zaisenhausen, with many fiery flames falling from it. And after this there followed some strange things.

Im 1543. Jahr hat man auf den vierten Tag des Monats Mai am Himmel zu Pforzheim und in dem Dorf names Zaisenhausen einen grausamen Kometen gesehen, von dem viele Feuerflammen herabgefallen sind, worauf dann seltsame Dinge folgten.

En l'an 1543, le quatrième jour du mois de mai, une terrible comète fut observée dans le ciel à Pforzheim et dans le village appelé Zaisenhausen, d'où tombèrent de nombreuses flammes de feu, à la suite de quoi eurent lieu d'étranges phénomènes.

FOL. 147

1544 — Lunar eclipse | Mondfinsternis | Éclipse de lune

In the year 1544, on the eighth of January, there was a darkening of the moon at night, so that the moon looked all bloody, and this lasted some six hours and several minutes.

Im 1544. Jahr, am achten Januar, ist bei Nacht eine Finsternis des Mondes gewesen, sodass der Mond ganz blutig aussah, und hat etwa sechs Stunden und einige Minuten gedauert.

En l'an 1544, le huitième jour de janvier, la lune fut obscurcie la nuit, de sorte que la lune semblait ensanglantée, et cela dura environ six heures et plusieurs minutes.

FOL. 149

1544 — Eclipse and star over Augsburg
Sonnenfinsternis und Stern über Augsburg
Éclipse et étoile dans le ciel d'Augsbourg

In the year 1544, on the 28th of January, a darkening of the sun was seen in Augsburg and surrounding parts, which started in the morning at eight o'clock and lasted until eleven o'clock, and it was so dark that nothing could be seen any more and in the west there was a star, which [...].

Im 1544. Jahr, am 28. Januar, ist eine Finsternis der Sonne in Augsburg und den umliegenden Orten gesehen worden, die morgens um acht Uhr angefangen und bis elf Uhr gedauert hat, dass es so finster gewesen ist, dass man nichts mehr sehen konnte, und im Westen stand ein Stern, den [...].

En l'an 1544, le vingt-huit janvier, le soleil fut plongé dans l'obscurité à Augsbourg et dans les environs, à partir du matin à huit heures et jusqu'à onze heures, et il fit si noir que l'on ne pouvait plus rien voir du tout et à l'ouest se tenait une étoile.

FOL. 150

1545 — Celestial battle over Poland
Himmelsschlacht über Polen | Bataille céleste dans le ciel de Pologne

In the year 1545, on the twenty-ninth day of March, on Palm Sunday, a terrible, ghastly vision was seen in the kingdom of Poland. At eight o'clock in the morning, a great peal of thunder struck. After this, three red crosses were seen in the east, in the middle of which was a man in armour with a fiery sword. A great band of warriors came towards him on horseback and on foot and fought with him until one o'clock in the afternoon. But he defeated them and retained his place between the three crosses. Then a dragon appeared and devoured the man.

Im 1545. Jahr, am neunundzwanzigsten Tag des März, am Palmsonntag, ist eine grausame, schreckliche Erscheinung in dem Königreich Polen gesehen worden. Morgens um acht Uhr hat sich ein großer Donnerschlag ereignet. Nach diesem hat man im Osten drei rote Kreuze gesehen, in der Mitte einen Mann in Rüstung mit einem feurigen Schwert. Dem ist eine große Kriegerschar zu Pferd und zu Fuß entgegengekommen und hat mit ihm gekämpft bis um ein Uhr nach Mittag. Doch hat er sie besiegt und den Platz zwischen den drei Kreuzen für sich allein behalten. Da ist ein Drache erschienen und hat den Mann verschlungen.

En l'an 1545, le vingt-neuvième jour de mars, le dimanche des Rameaux, un phénomène terrible et atroce fut observé dans le royaume de Pologne. À huit heures du matin, un grand coup de tonnerre se produisit. Ensuite, on vit à l'est trois croix rouges et au milieu un homme en armure portant une épée enflammée. Une grande troupe de guerriers vint vers lui à cheval et à pied et se battit contre lui jusqu'à une heure après midi. Mais il les vainquit et conserva sa place entre les trois croix. Puis, un dragon apparut et dévora l'homme.

FOL. 151

1545 — Angel on rainbows | Engel auf Regenbogen | Ange sur arcs-en-ciel

And on the previously mentioned day, there came a terrible darkness, such that the sky was completely black, so that people could not see one another at all. The darkness lasted until the next day – that is the thirtieth of March – until nine o'clock in the morning. Then the day came back and three beautiful rainbows were seen, on which was seated a beautiful angel. He was seen for about one and a half hours. After that he disappeared again and fine weather then followed.

Und an dem zuvor genannten Tag, da ist eine grausame Finsternis gekommen, dass der Himmel ganz schwarz gewesen ist, sodass man einander nicht sehen konnte. Die Finsternis hat bis zum nächsten Tag gedauert – das ist der dreißigste März –, bis um neun Uhr vor Mittag. Dann ist der Tag zurückgekommen und drei schöne Regenbogen wurden gesehen, auf denen ein schöner Engel saß. Den hat man wohl anderthalb Stunden gesehen. Danach ist er wieder verschwunden, und dann ist schönes Wetter gefolgt.

Et le même jour que précédemment, une terrible obscurité plongea le ciel dans un noir total, si bien que les gens ne pouvaient plus du tout se voir. Cette obscurité dura jusqu'au lendemain – le trente mars –, jusqu'à neuf heures avant midi. Puis, la lumière du jour revint et on vit trois magnifiques arcs-en-ciel sur lesquels un ange était assis. Il fut visible pendant environ une heure et demie. Ensuite, il disparut et le beau temps s'ensuivit.

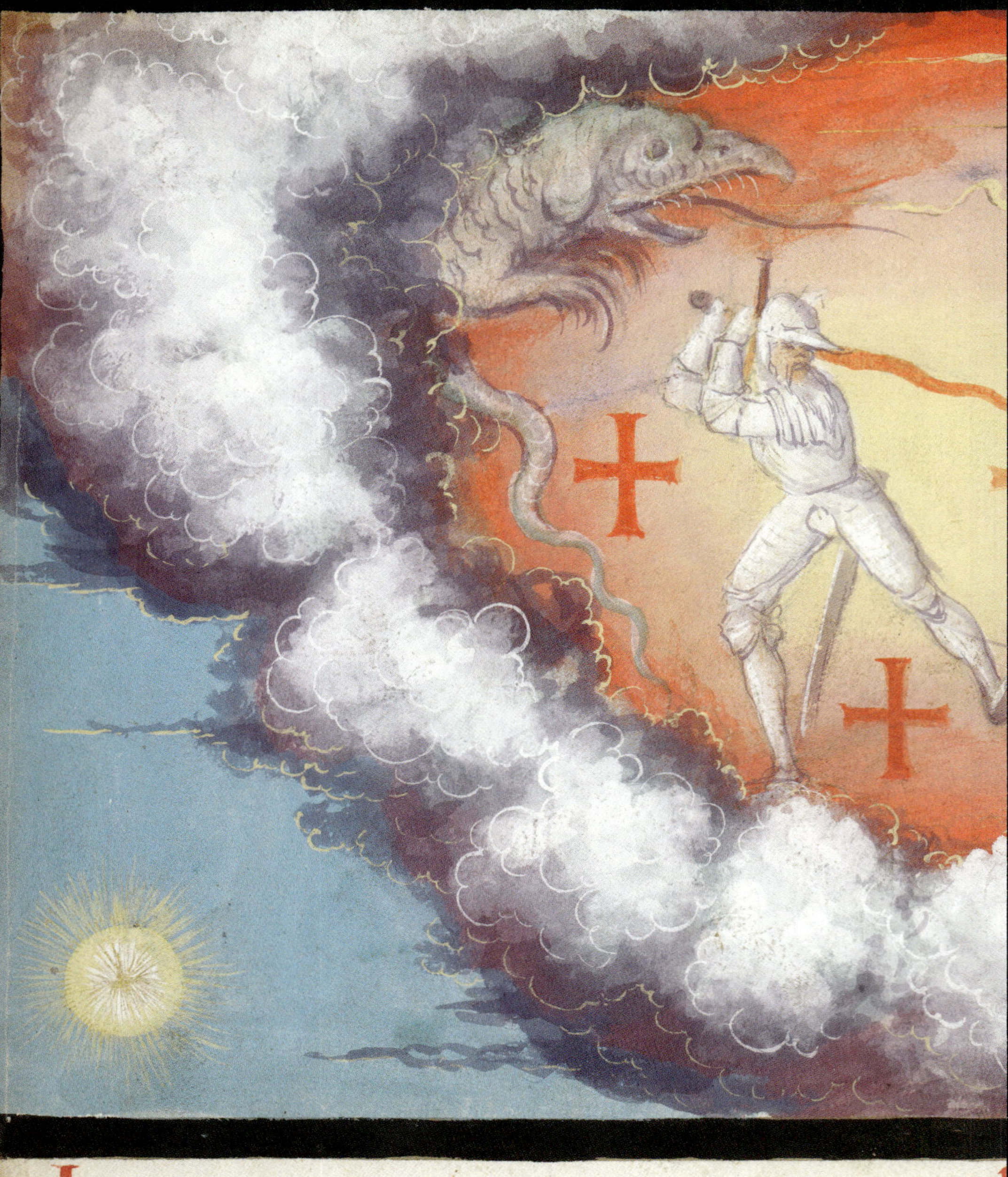

Im m d xxxxv iar den neün vnnzwaintzigisten tag de
gesicht in dem künigreich polen gesehen worden, de
Men, nach disem hat man gesehen gegen auf gang d
man, mit einem feürigen schwert dem ist ein g
im gestriten biss vmb ain. vr nach mitag doch hat
er allein behalten da ist ein trach erschinen vn

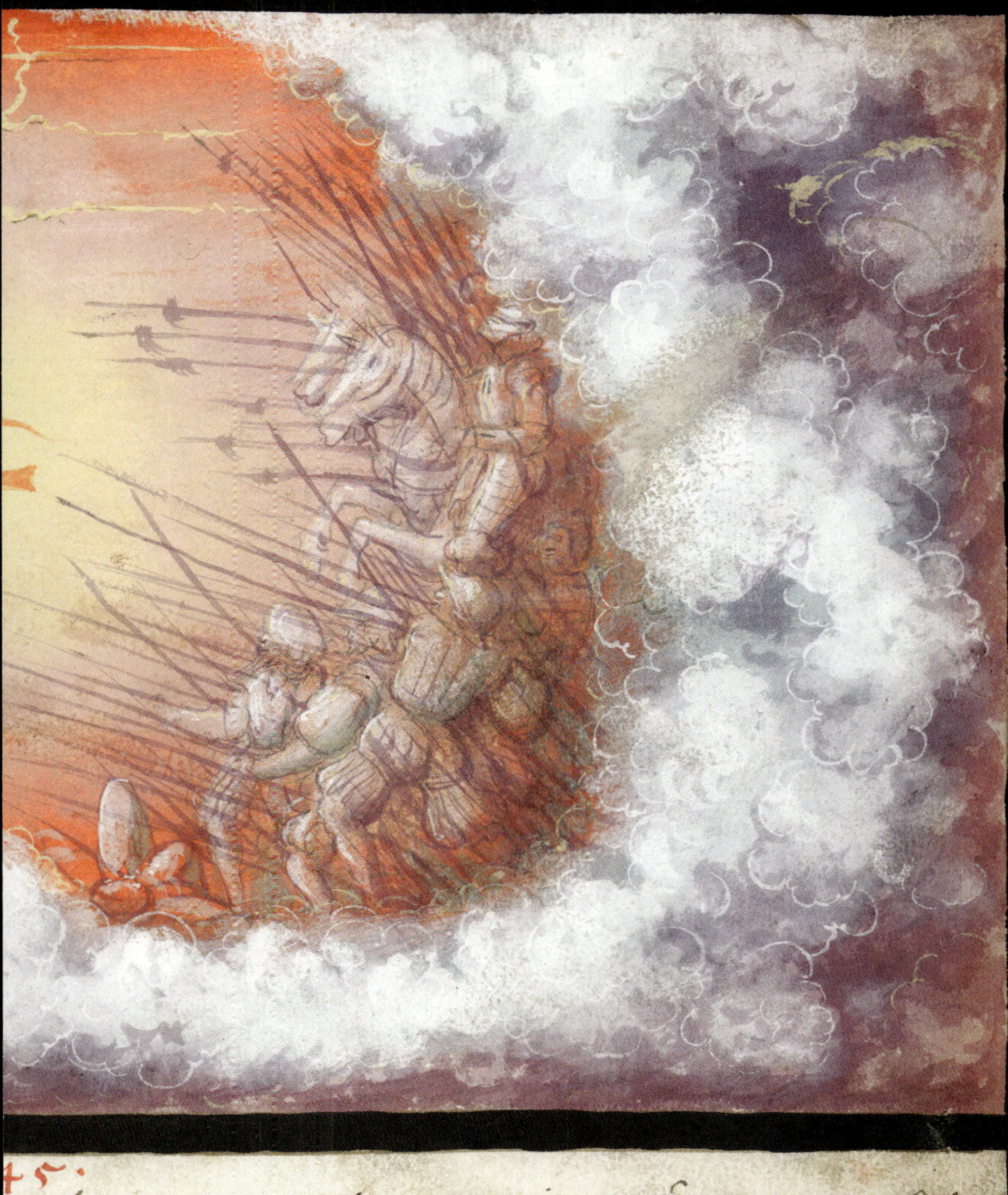

45.
rrtzehen an dem palm tag ist ein grausam erschrocklich
orgens umb acht uhr ist ein groser donner schlag geschehen
eimen drey rotter creutz in der mit ein geharnischten
r hauf zu ross und fus ent gegen kumen und mit
s uber wunden und den platz zwischen den drey creutz
en man ver schlungen

15.4

Vnnd an dem vorgemelten tag, da ist ein grausa
gewesen das man ein ander nit sehen hat kündn
M das ist der dreissigist des mertzen, bis vmb neu
drey schöner regenpogen gesehen worden, auff de
anderthalb stund gesehen, darnach ist er wider v

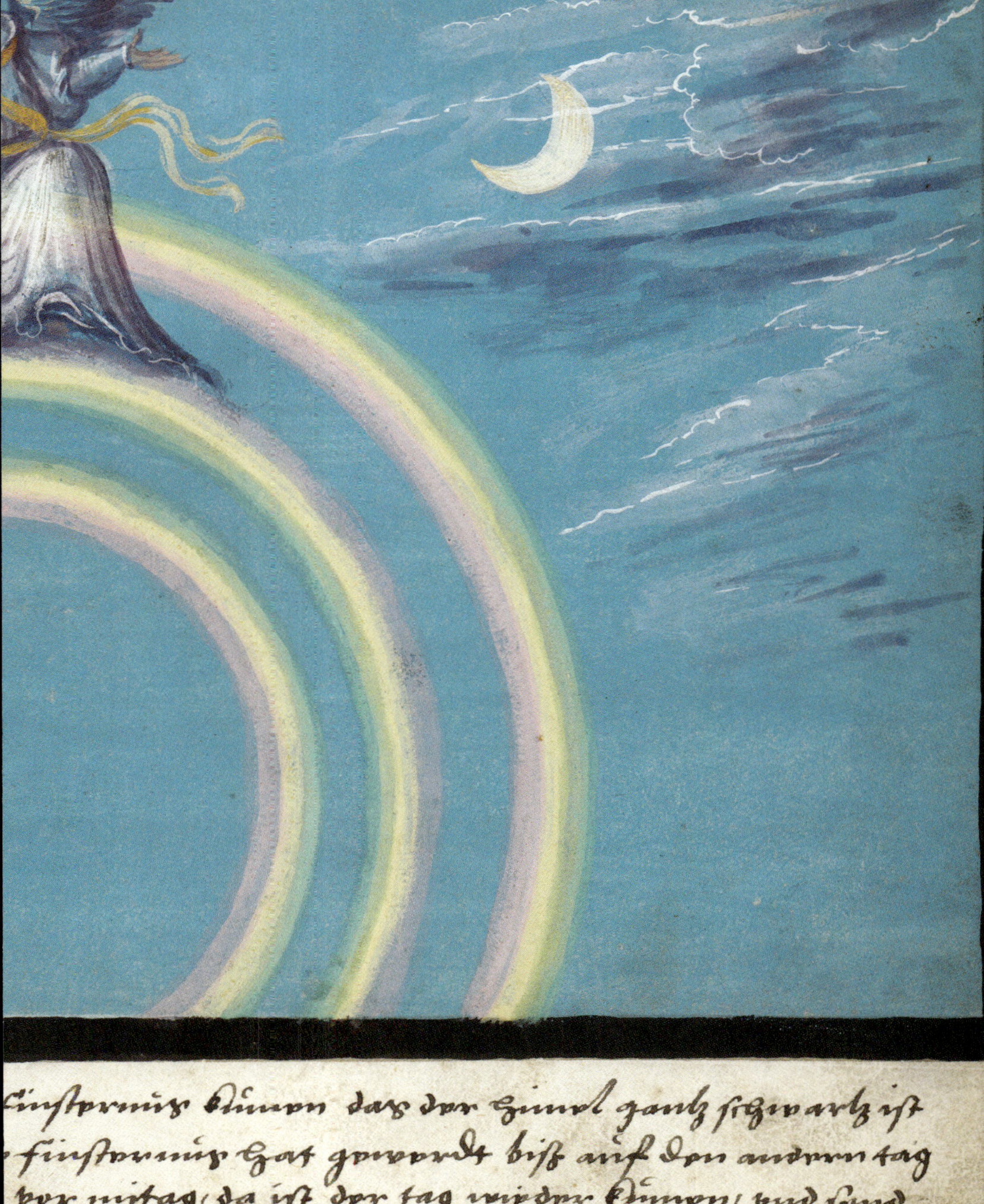
finsternus kumen das der himel gantz schwartz ist
finsternus hat gewerdt biß auf den andern tag
vor mitag, da ist der tag wider kumen, und send
in schonner engel gesessen ist, den hat man wol
gefunden, und darnach schon wetter grunet

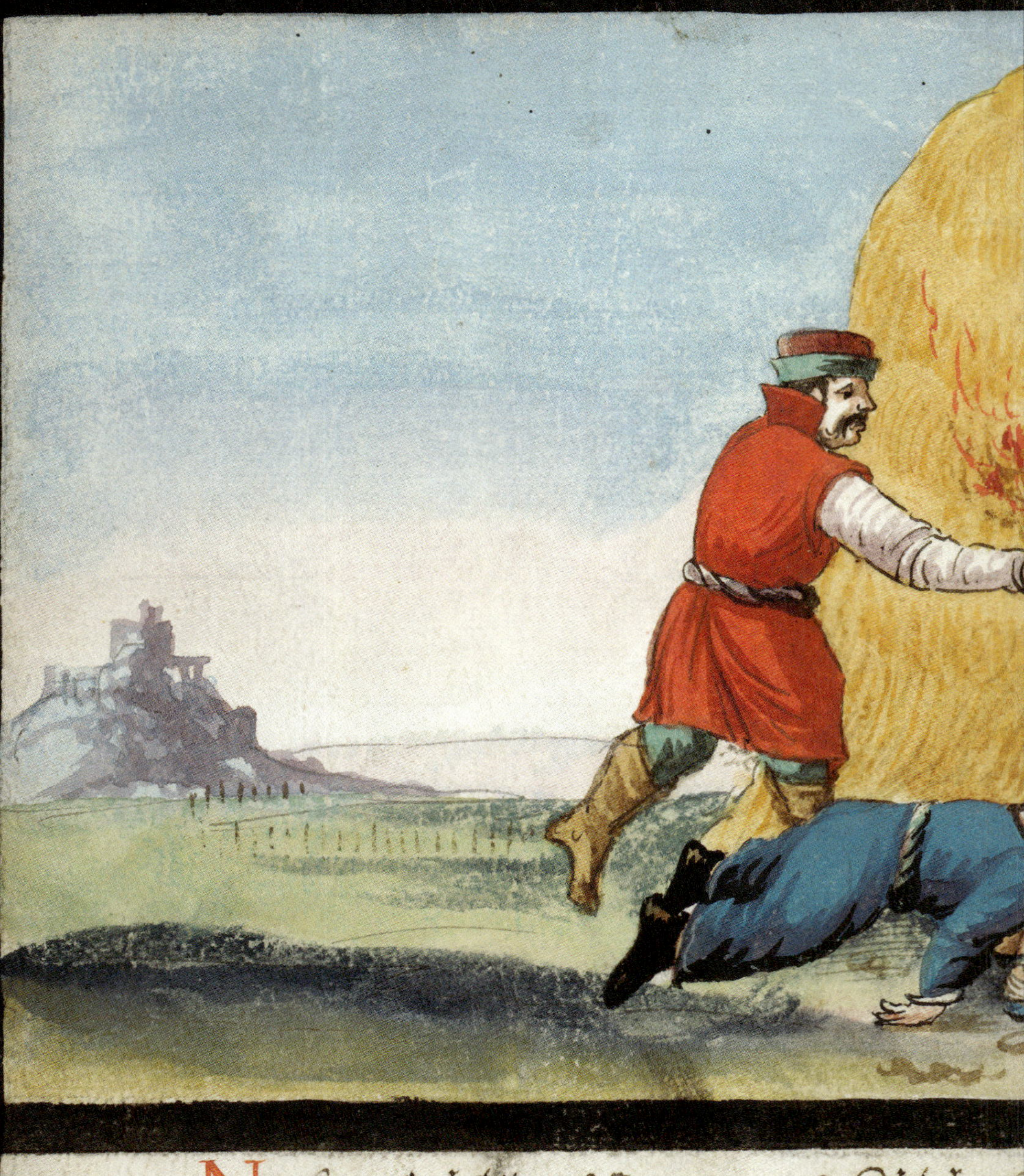

Nach Cristy gebürt 1545 Jar ist im
hiffer vom Nattern vnnd Edexen/ Fr
daruon gestorben sind/ vnd hand gressen

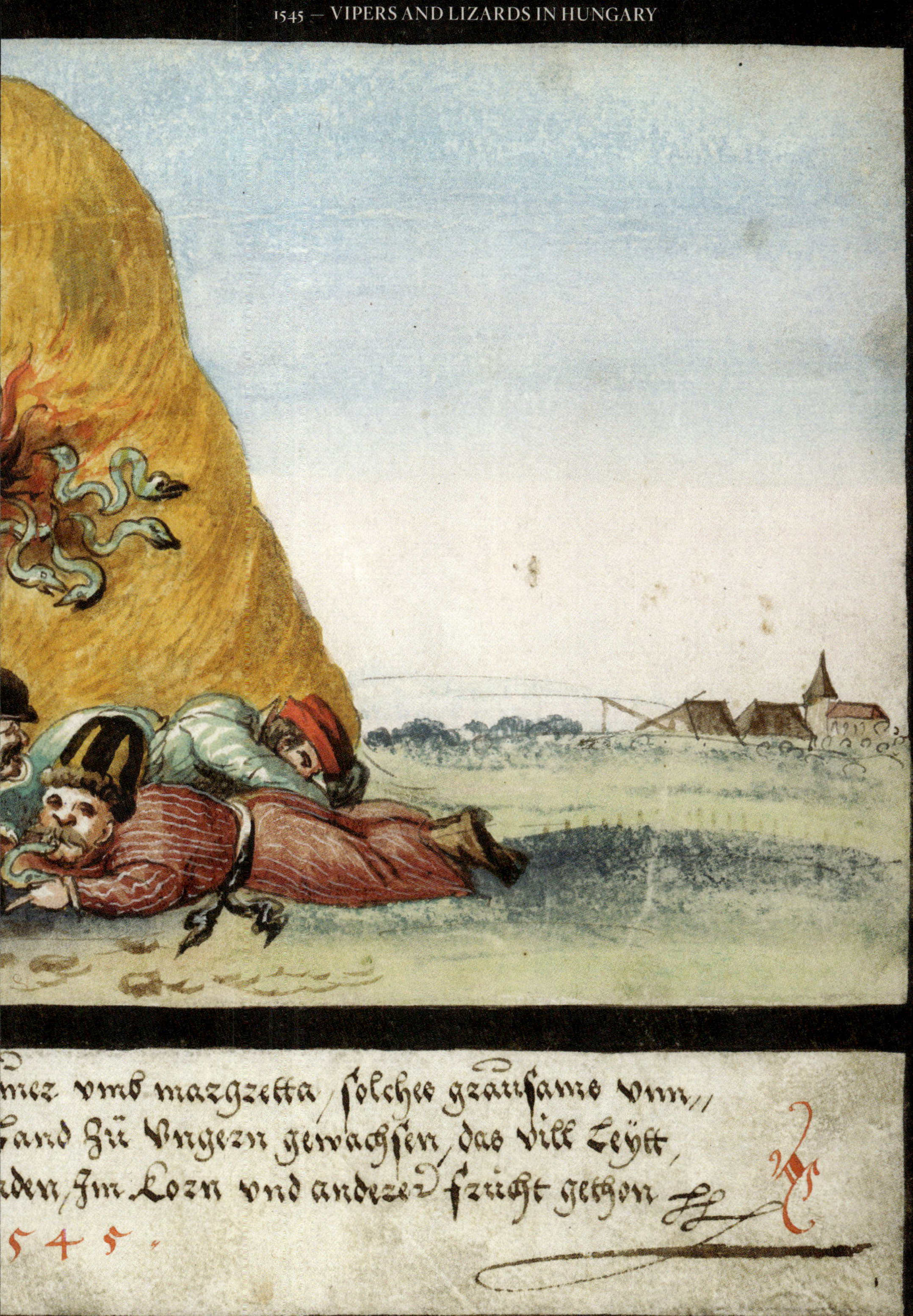
mer vmb margretta, solches grausame vnn,,
Land zu Vngern gewachsen, das vill Leytt
den, Im Korn vnd anderer frucht gethon
545.

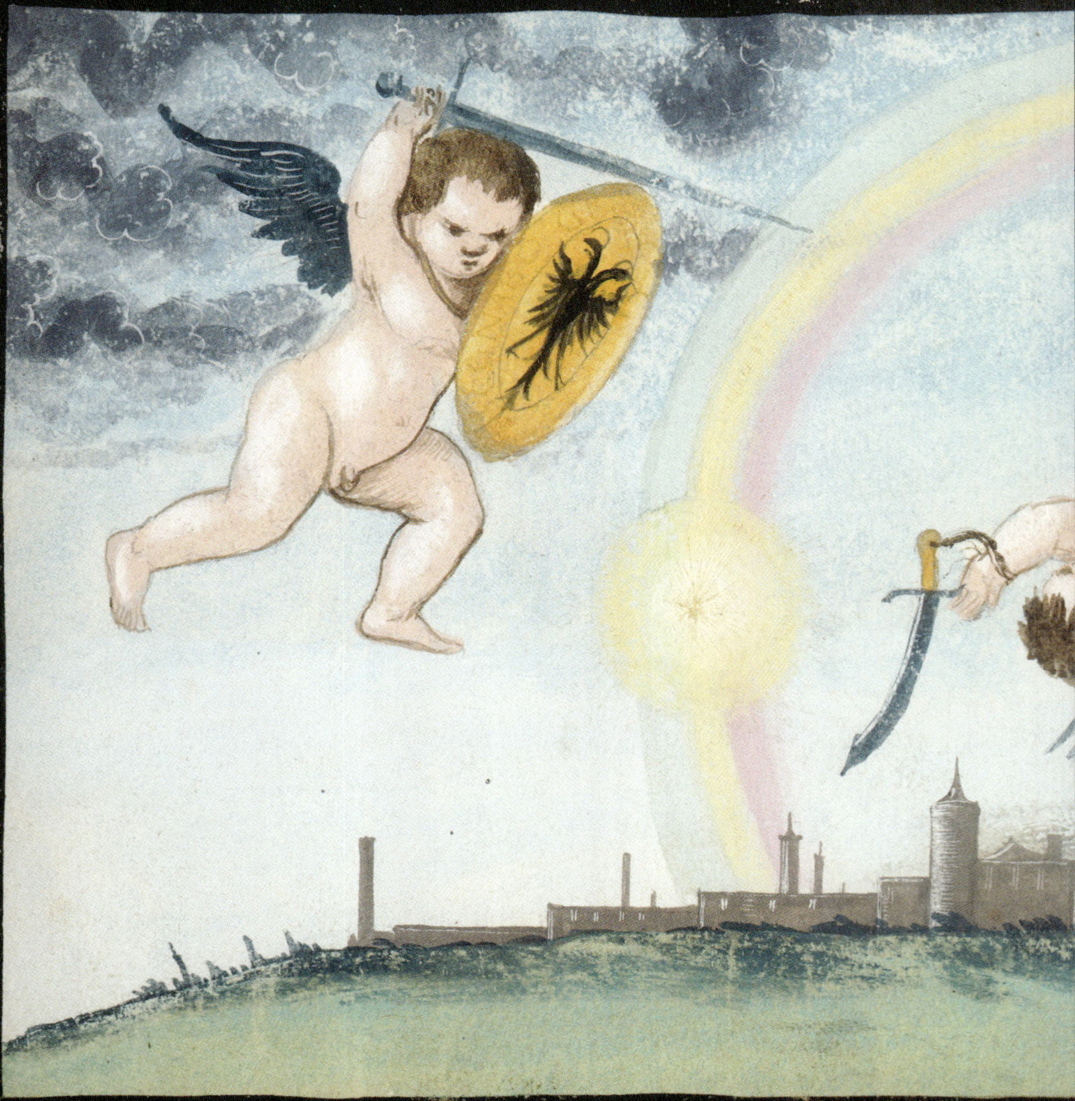

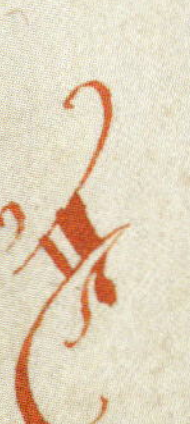

Anno M D xxxxvi den xxvi Februari umb viiii v
von einem Ersamen bürger in der stat kascha g
bürgern mer gesehen: vnnd in druck zubring
geben wie das sie ob der stat ofen in lüfften obgmelts ta

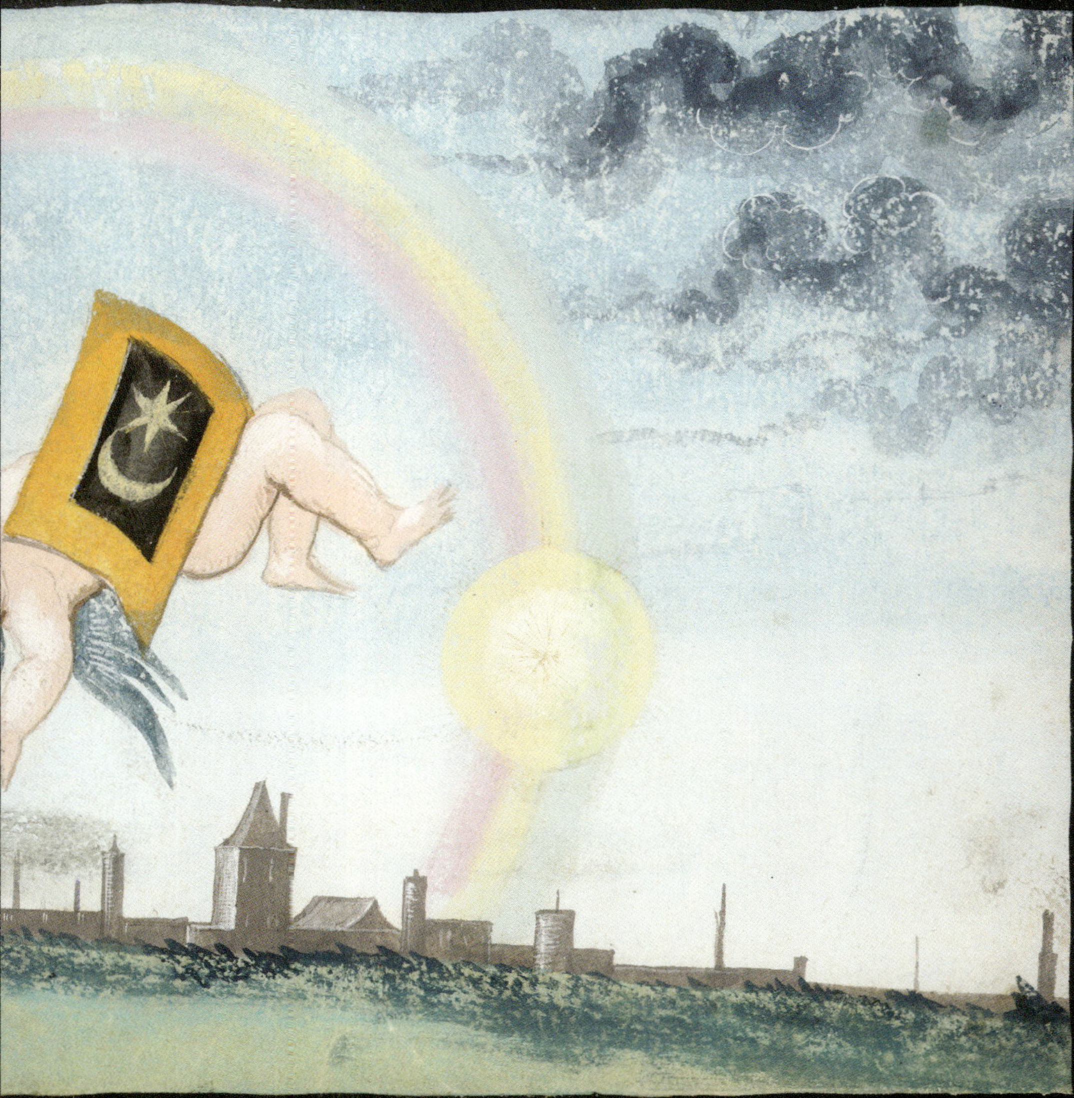

546,

r mittag ist dises wunderbar vnd seltzam gesicht
att gelegen im land zu vngern sampt andern erbarn
r nstlich begert vnd des dise warhafftige anzeigen
nnd stunden gesehen haben

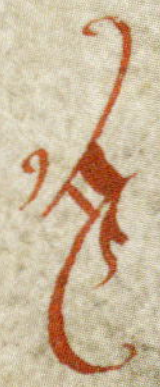

FOL. 153

1545 — Vipers and lizards in Hungary
Nattern und Eidechsen in Ungarn | Vipères et lézards en Hongrie

1545 years after the birth of Christ, in the summer around St Margaret's day, such terrible vermin in the form of vipers and lizards appeared in the land of Hungary that many people died as a result. And they did great harm to the grain and various fruit.

1545 Jahre nach Christi Geburt ist im Sommer, um Margaretha, solches grausame Ungeziefer von Nattern und Eidechsen im Land zu Ungarn zum Vorschein gekommen, dass viele Leute dadurch gestorben sind. Und sie haben großen Schaden am Korn und an anderer Frucht angerichtet.

1545 années après la naissance du Christ, en été vers la Sainte-Marguerite, d'horribles vermines en forme de vipères et de lézards apparurent dans le pays de Hongrie, qui firent mourir beaucoup de gens. Et elles causèrent beaucoup de dommages au grain et à divers fruits.

FOL. 154

1546 — Celestial battle of two children
Himmelsschlacht zweier Kinder | Combat céleste de deux enfants

In the year 1546, on February 26, at 8 o'clock in the morning, this wonderful and strange vision was seen by an honourable inhabitant of the city called Kaschau – situated in the land of Hungary – and by other reputable inhabitants who earnestly requested it to be put into print. And the information they provided about it was truthful concerning how they saw over the city what is painted above, up in the air for days and hours.

Anno 1546, am 26. Februar, um 8 Uhr vor Mittag, ist diese wunderbare und seltsame Erscheinung von einem ehrenhaften Einwohner in der Kaschau genannten Stadt – im Land zu Ungarn gelegen – und anderen ehrbaren Einwohnern gesehen und in Druck zu bringen ernsthaft begehrt worden. Und darüber geben sie wahrheitsgemäße Meldung, wie sie über der Stadt in der Luft oben Gemaltes Tage und Stunden gesehen haben.

En l'an 1546, le vingt-six février, à huit heures avant midi, cette apparition prodigieuse et étrange fut observée par un habitant honorable de la ville appelée Kaschau – située dans le pays de Hongrie – et par d'autres habitants de bonne réputation qui demandèrent ardemment à ce que cela fût imprimé. Et ce qu'ils rapportèrent était véridique quant à ce qu'ils virent au-dessus de la ville, et qui est peint ci-dessus, dans les airs pendant des jours et des heures.

FOL. 155

1546 — Explosion in Mechelen | Explosion in Mechelen | Explosion à Malines

In the year 1546, in the month of August, the fire from the sky fell upon or struck a tower or building in Mechelen in the Netherlands, in which there was more than four hundred tons of gunpowder. And exactly half the city burned down, which is also a special sign from God.

Im 1546. Jahr, in dem Monat August, ist zu Mechelen in den Niederlanden das Feuer vom Himmel in einen Turm oder ein Gebäude gefallen oder eingeschlagen, worin mehr als vierhundert Tonnen Pulver gewesen sind. Und ganz genau die halbe Stadt ist abgebrannt, was dann auch ein besonderes Zeichen von Gott ist.

En l'an 1546, au mois d'août, le feu du ciel tomba ou s'abattit sur une tour ou un bâtiment à Malines aux Pays-Bas, où se trouvaient plus de quatre cents tonnes de poudre. Et exactement la moitié de la ville fut détruite par le feu, ce qui est aussi un signe particulier envoyé par Dieu.

FOL. 156

1546 — Stars | Sterne | Étoiles

In the year 1546, at the beginning of December, two mighty stars were seen here in the sky a large distance from each other – the smaller one towards the west and the bigger one following it. The smaller star was three times as big as any other star in the sky, but the bigger one was about eight times as big. It was burning like a torch in the sky. And day after day they moved further apart from each other, but the bigger one climbed higher up than the other.

Im 1546. Jahr, am Anfang des Dezembers, sind zwei gewaltige Sterne hier am Himmel einen großen Schritt voneinander entfernt gesehen worden, der kleinere Richtung Westen und der größere folgte ihm nach. Der kleinere Stern ist dreimal so groß gewesen wie sonst ein anderer Stern am Himmel, aber der größere wohl achtmal so groß. Der brannte wie eine Fackel am Himmel. Und von Tag zu Tag gingen sie weiter auseinander, aber der größere stieg hinauf in die Höhe über den anderen.

En l'an 1546, au début de décembre, deux puissantes étoiles furent observées ici dans le ciel, très éloignées l'une de l'autre, la plus petite vers l'ouest, la plus grosse étant dans la même zone. La plus petite étoile était trois fois plus grosse que n'importe quelle autre étoile du ciel, mais la plus grosse était environ huit fois plus grosse. Elle brûlait comme une torche dans le ciel. Et jour après jour elles s'éloignèrent l'une de l'autre, mais la plus grosse s'éleva au-dessus de l'autre.

FOL. 157

1547 — Celestial battle, lions over Glarus
Himmelsschlacht, Löwen über Glarus | Combat céleste, lions dans le ciel de Glarus

1547 years after the birth of Christ, on July 22, such an occurrence was seen in a clear sky in the country of Glarus, which then endured well into the night.

1547 Jahre nach Christi Geburt, am 22. Juli, ist ein solches Ereignis am hellen Himmel im Land Glarus gesehen worden, das dann noch ganz bis in die Nacht angedauert hat.

1547 années après la naissance du Christ, le 22 juillet, cet événement fut observé dans un ciel clair dans le pays de Glarus, et il dura jusque tard dans la nuit.

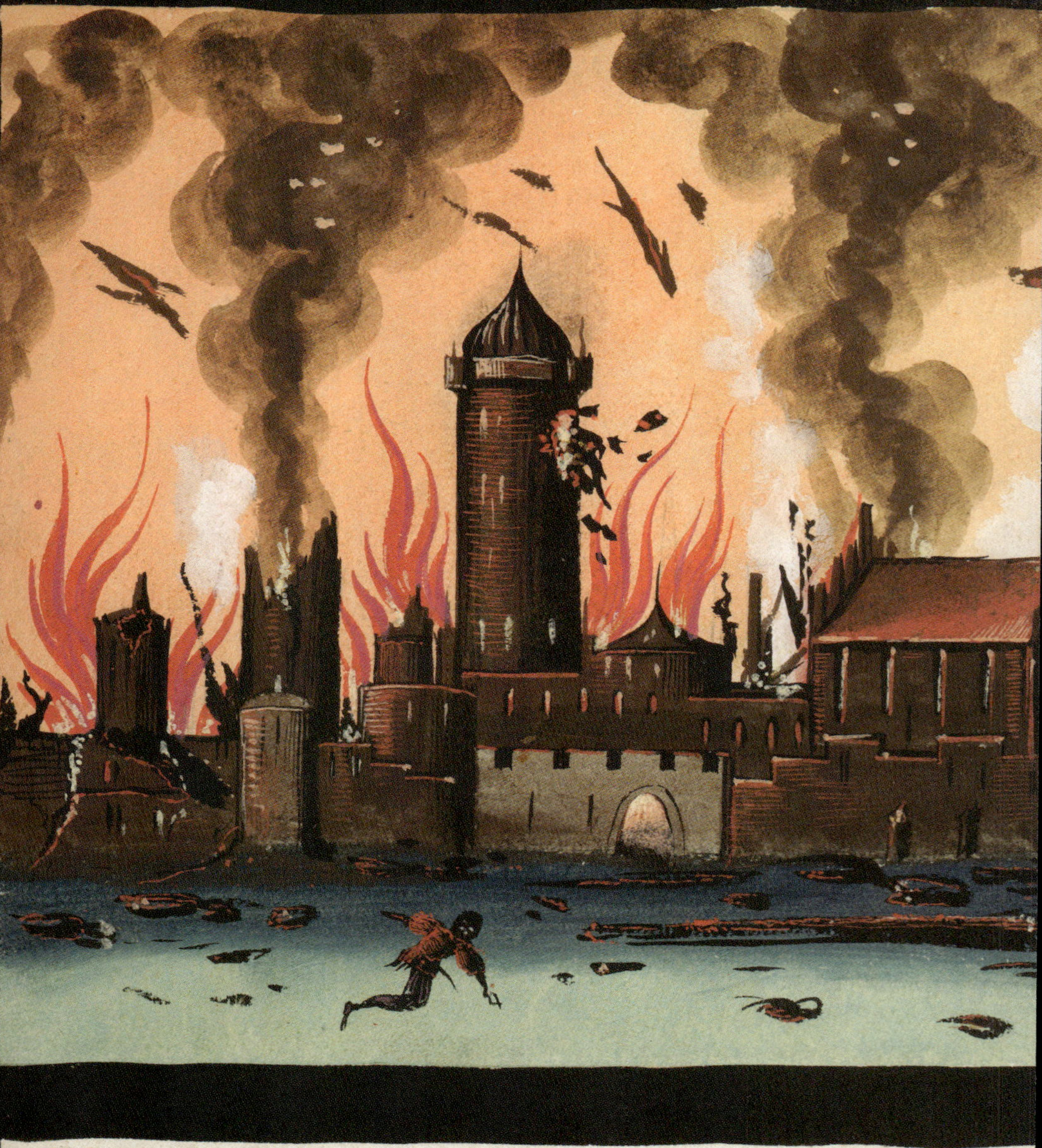

Im M D xxxxvi iar in dem m
feürr von Hiemel in ain thürn
vier hündert thünnen pülfers, ist
brannt das dan auch ein son

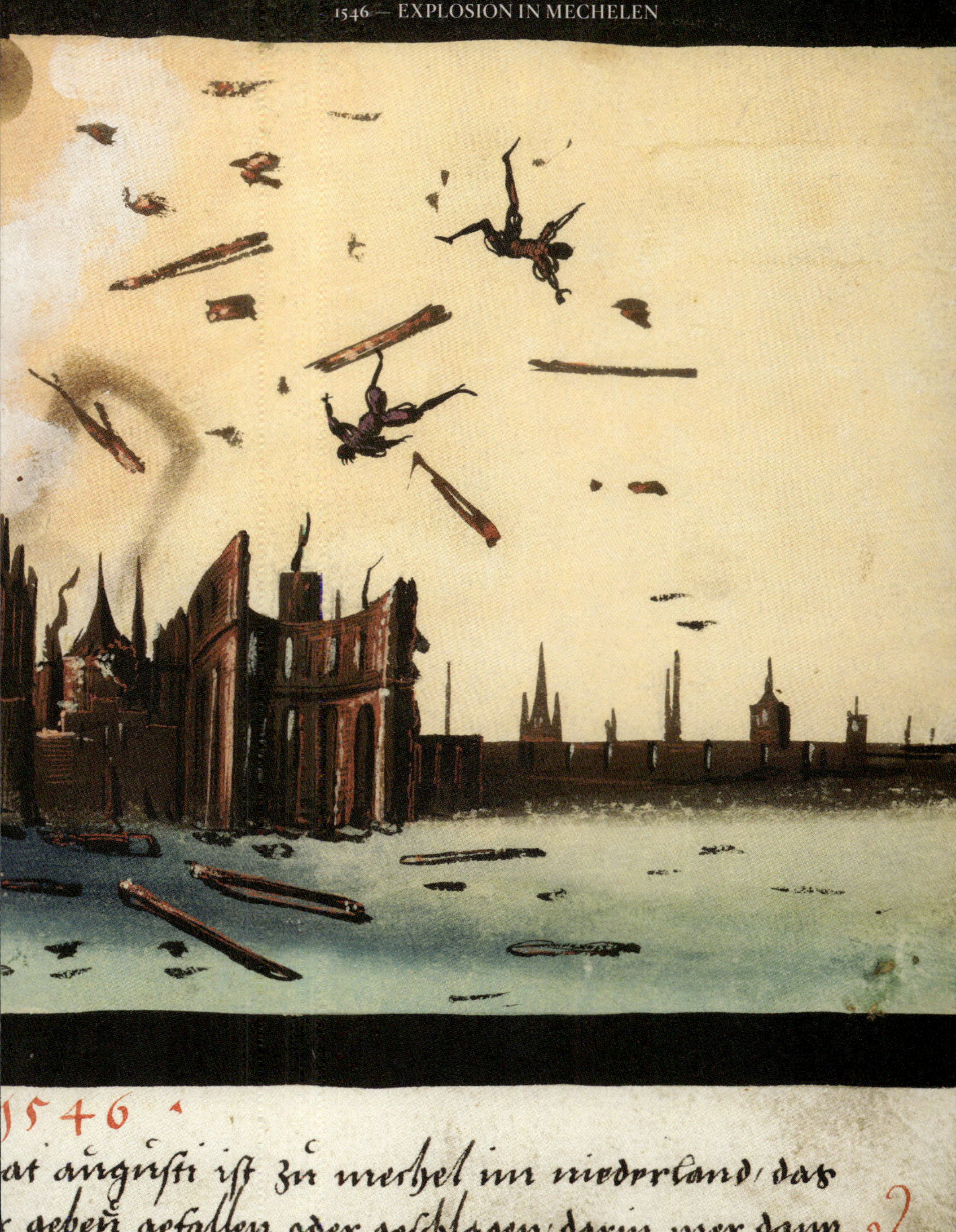

1546 .

at augusti ist zu mechel im niederland das
r geben gefallen oder geschlagen darin mer dann
rssen unnd gar gnau die halb stad ist ab ge:
lich zaichen von gott ist

15

Im M D xxxxvi iar im anfang der Christm
worden/ ain grosen schrit von ain ander/ der kl
nach/ der klainer stern ist drei mal so groß ge
groser wol acht mal so groß der bran wie ein f
sie weiter von ain ander/ aber groser stig über

als ſend zwen gewaltig ſtern hie am himel geſehen
r gegen dem nider gang / vnnd der groſſer ging im
en als ſunſt ain anderer ſtern am himel / aber der
l am himel / vnd ein tag nach dem andern gingen
in die hoch über den andern /

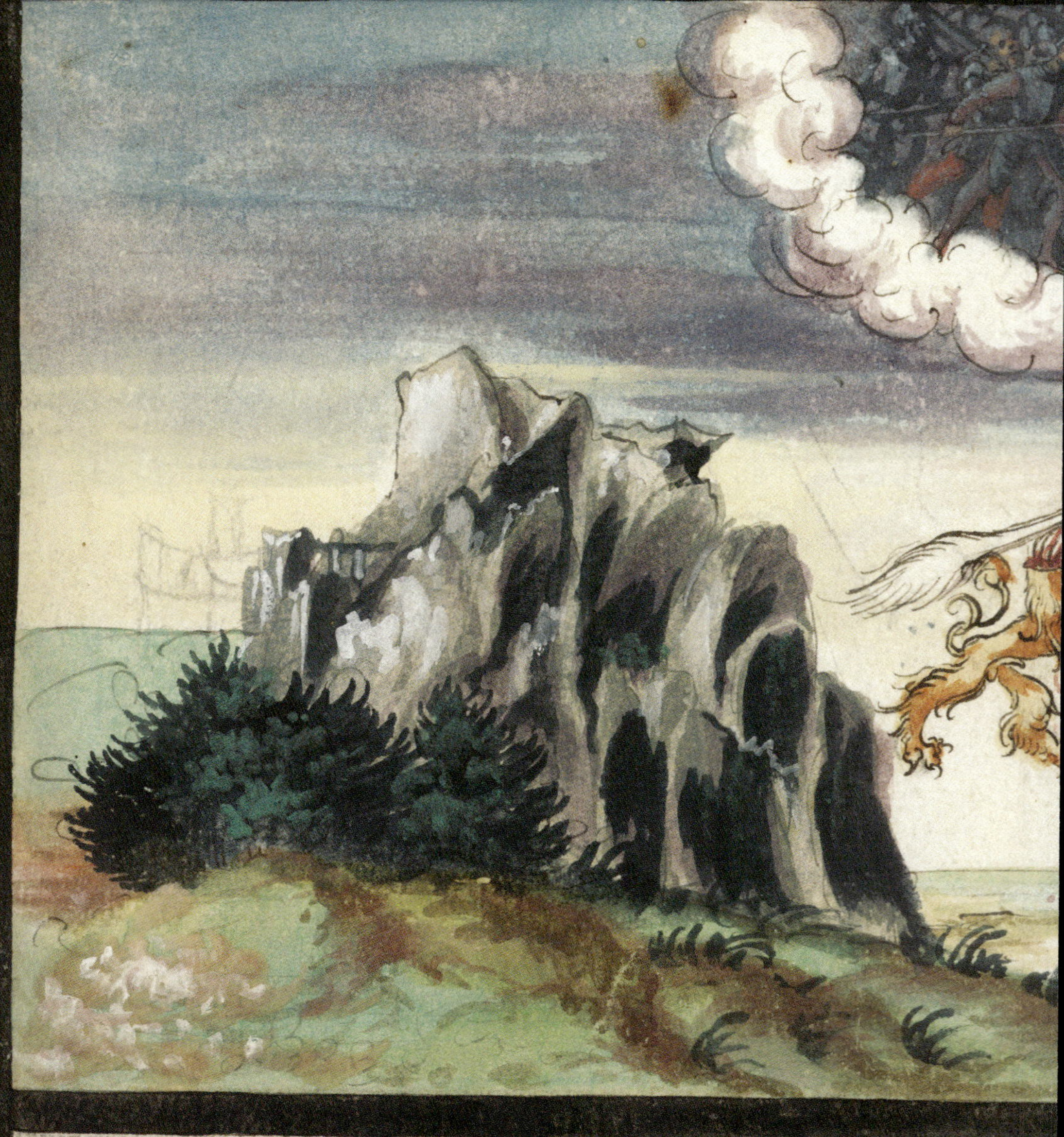

Nach Christy geburt 1547 Jar denn
helln Himell gesehen worden, Im Lan
· 99. Nacht gewe
·154

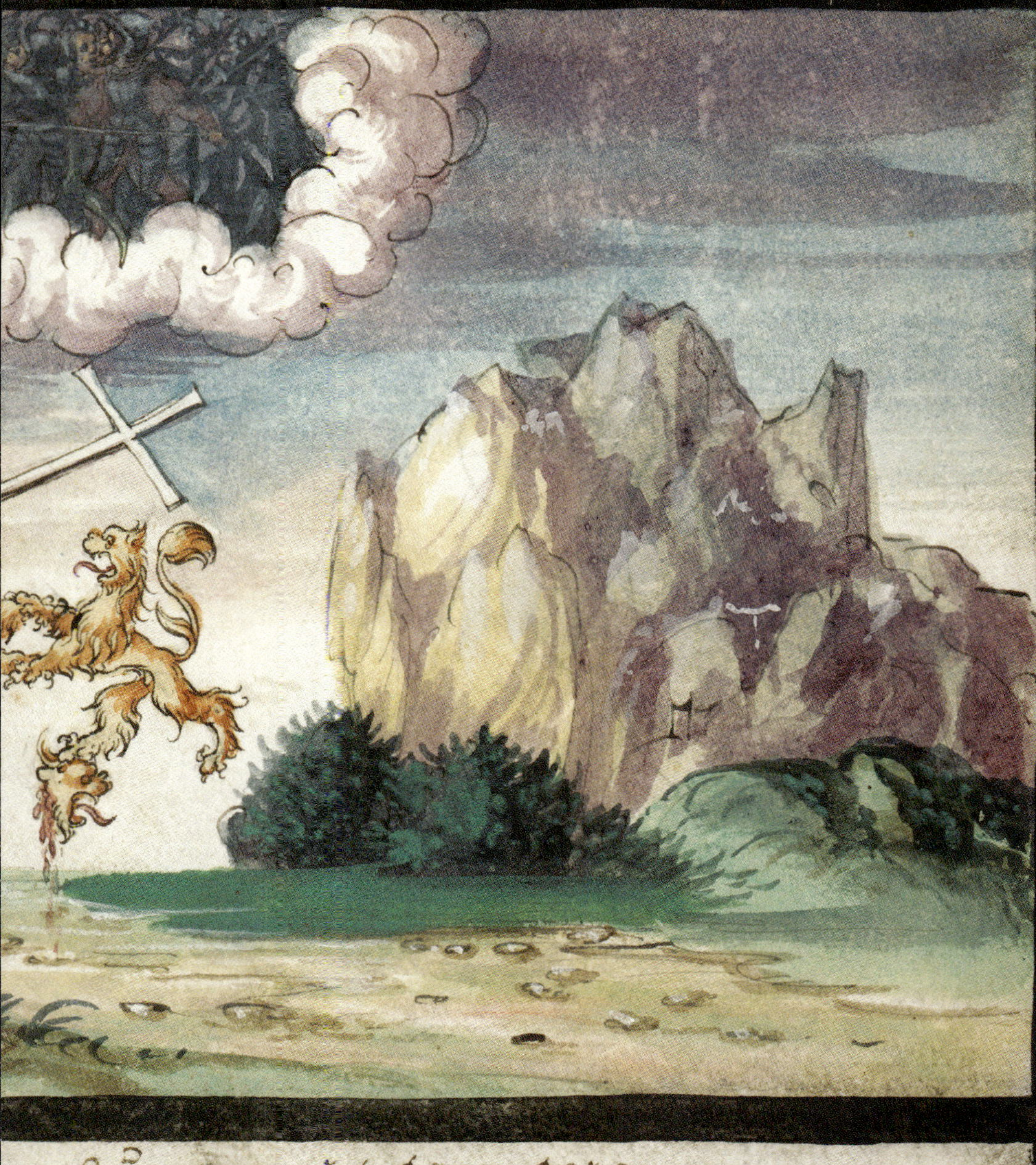

ag Heüwmonat, ist solche geschicht am
ozÿß, das daim gaz nach, biß in die
hatt

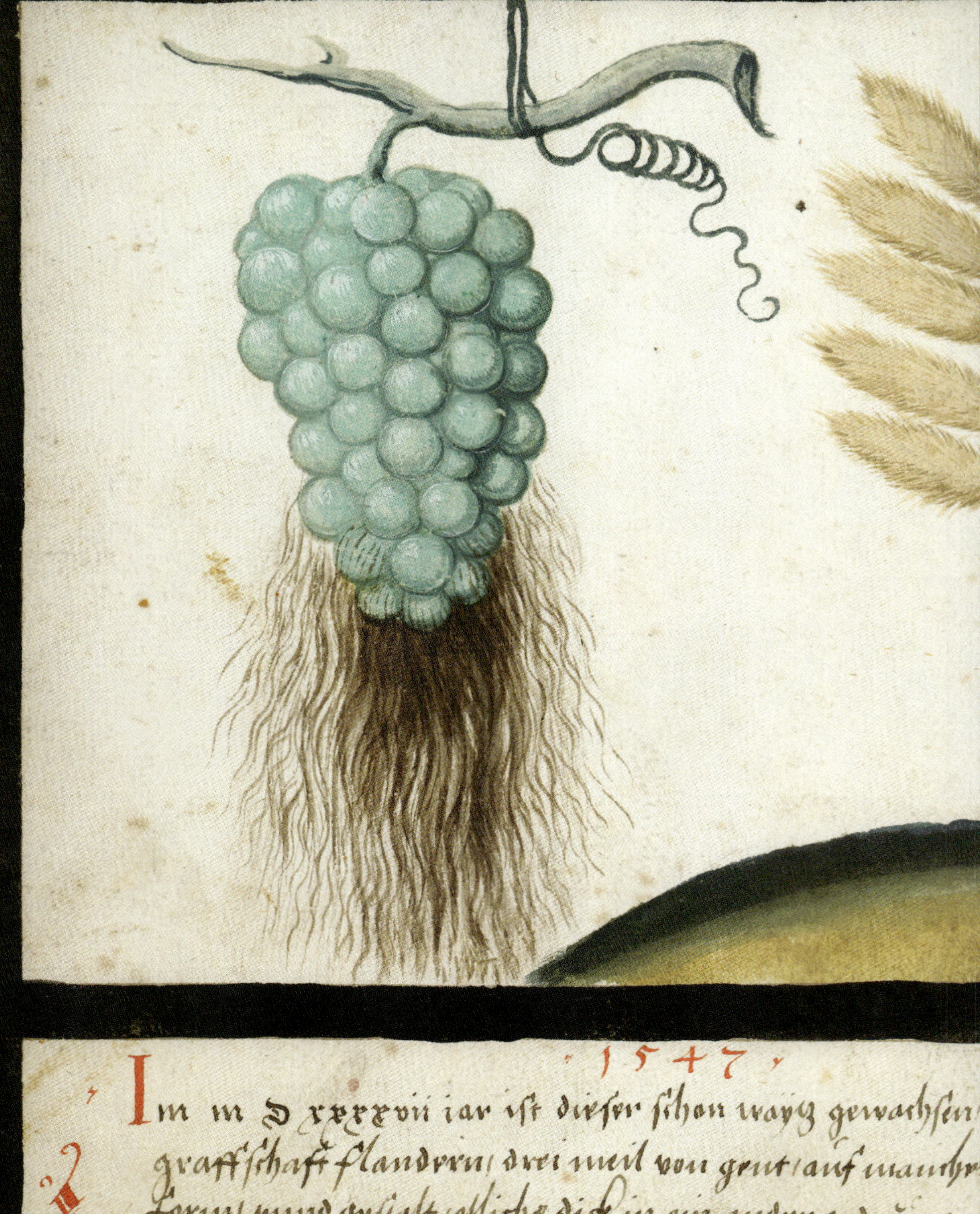

·1547·

Im m D xxxxvii iar ist dieser schon waytz gewachsen
graffschaft flandern, drei meil von gent, auf manchr
form, unnd gestalt, etliche dick in ein ander gedrungen
ch mit zerthailten ehern, als mit vier acht zwelff b
fürff zehen ehern auf einem halm, wir hir gemal

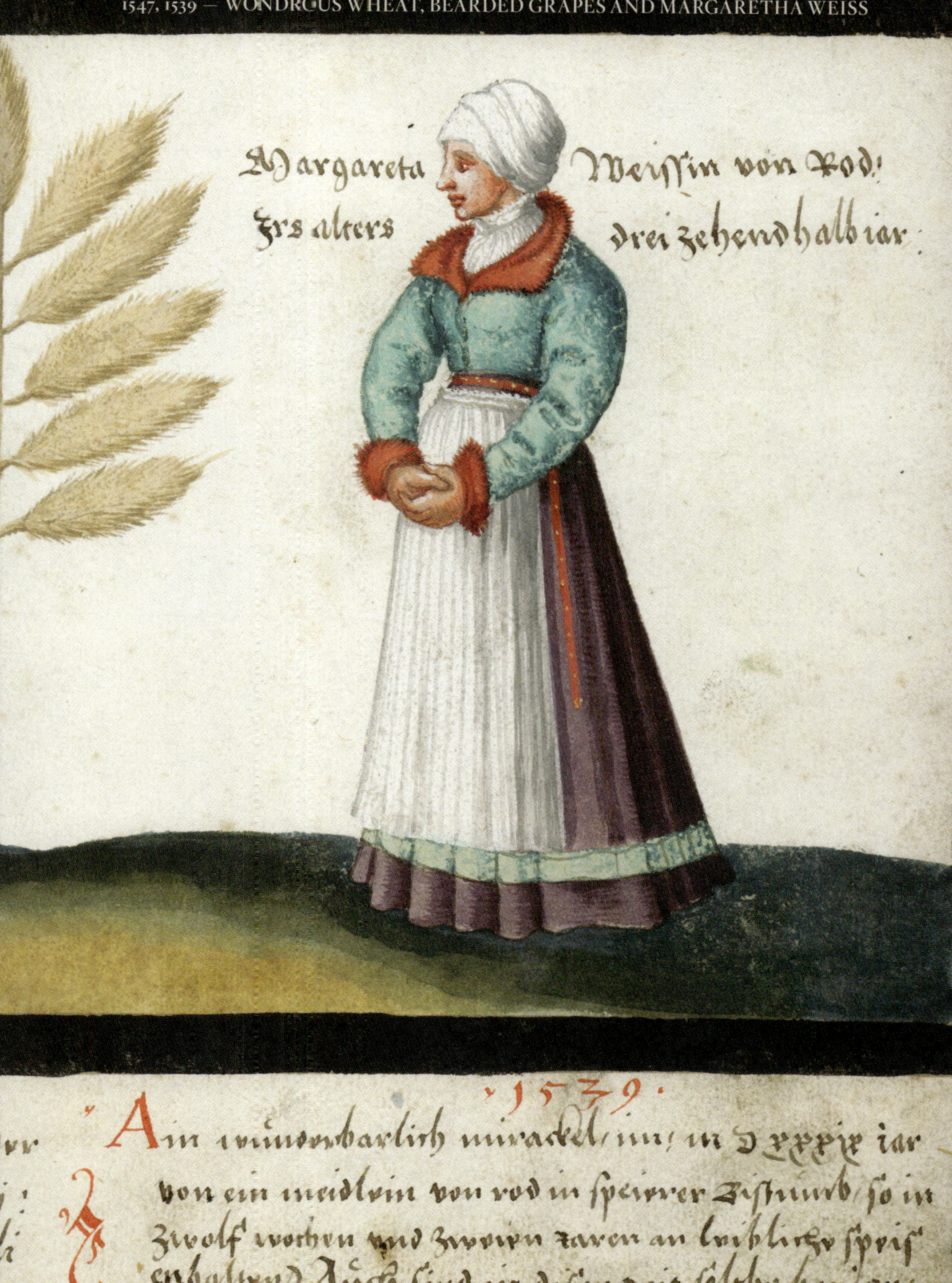
Margareta Weissin von Rod:
Irs alters dreizehendhalb iar.
1539.
Ain wunderbarlich miracke, im, in XXXIX iar
von ein meidlein von rod in speirrer Bistumb, so in
zwolf wochen und zweien iaren an leiblicher speis
enhaltend. Auch sind in diser zeit solche harige
trauben am necker und rein gewaxen. wie vornen

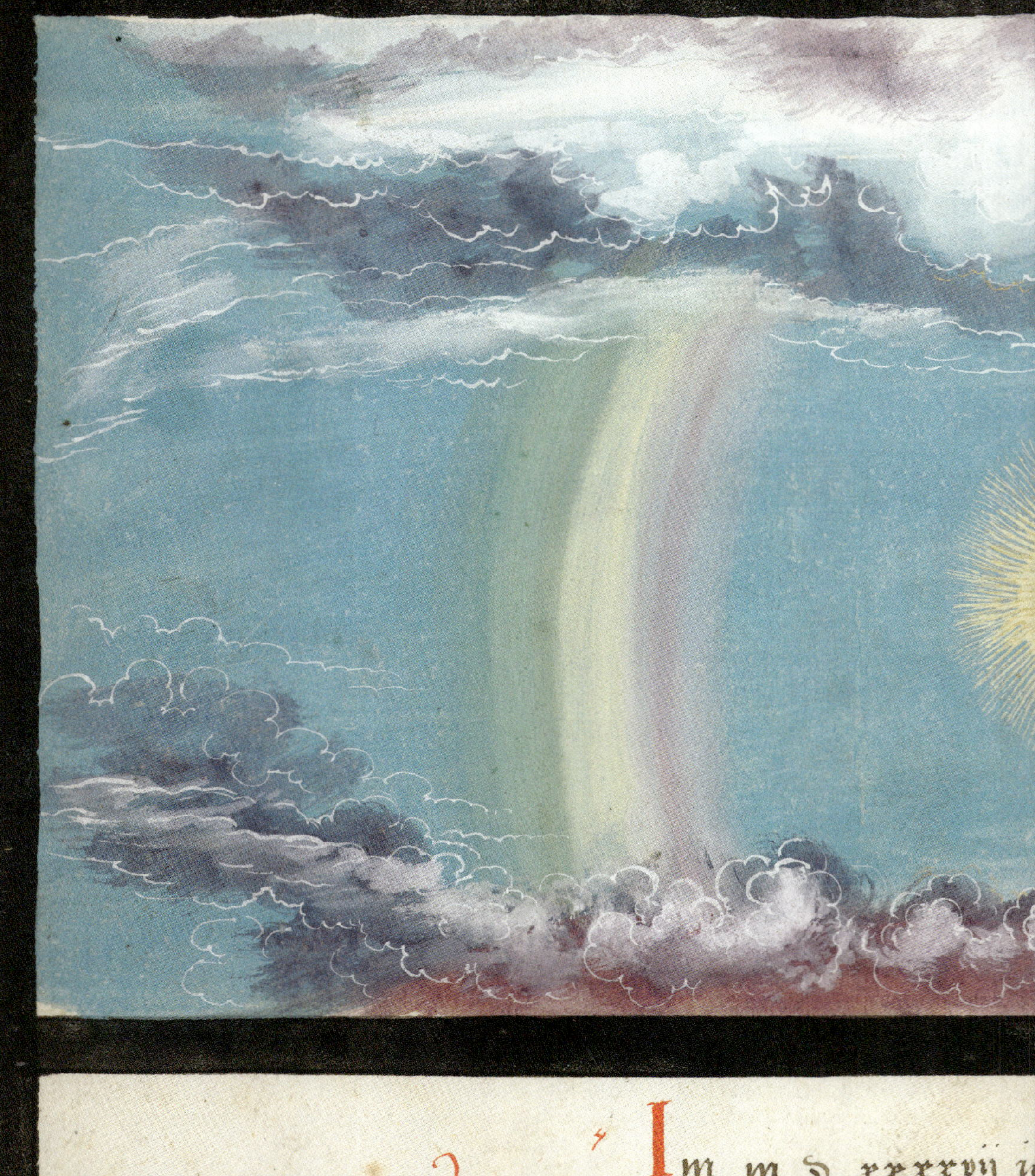

Im m d xxxxvii i
hat man hir zu ang
dir sonnen auss dem
hen ein lange zeit

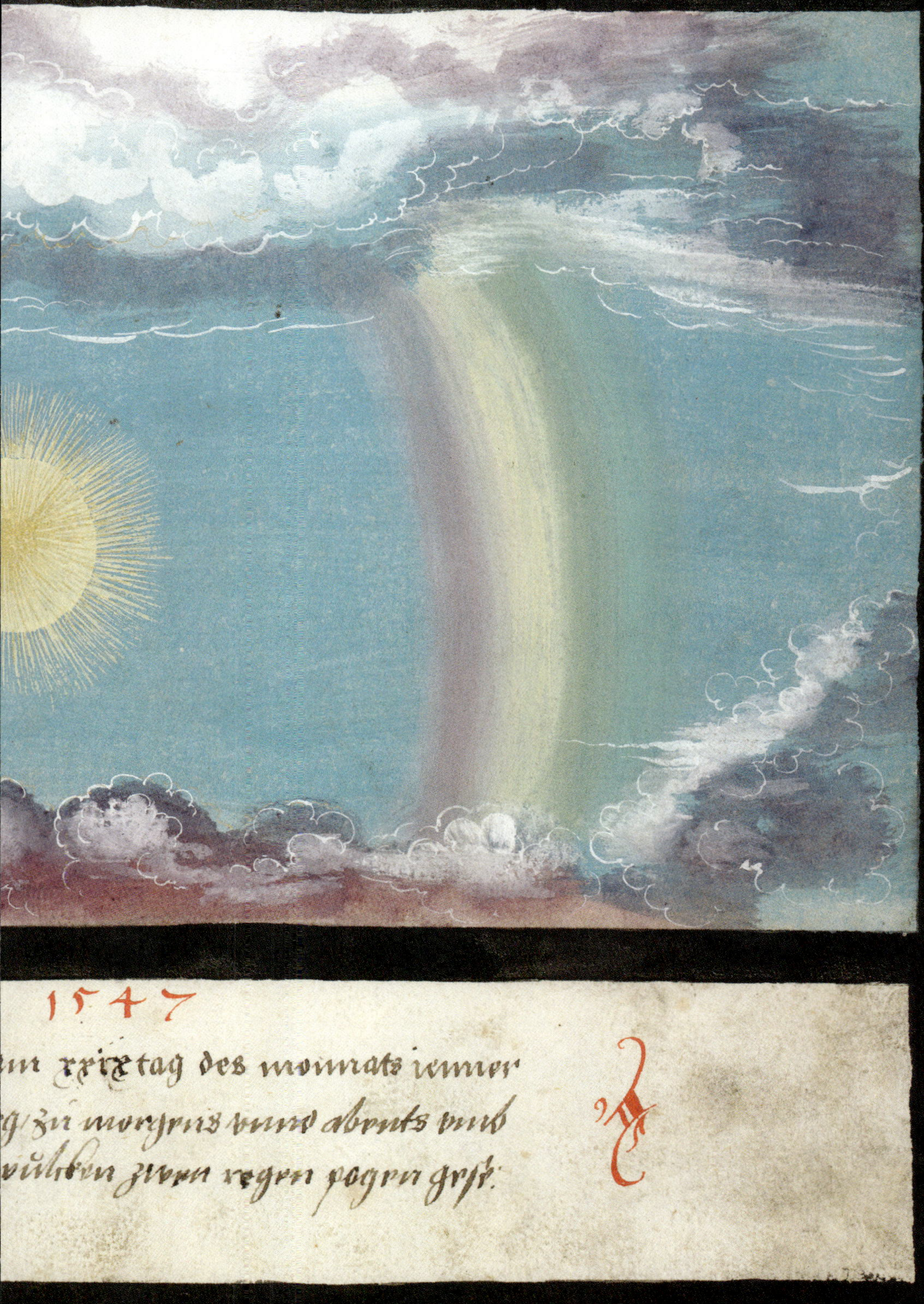

1547

am xxix tag des monats ienner
g zu morgens vnnd abents vnd
wülken zwen regen pogen gsͤt.

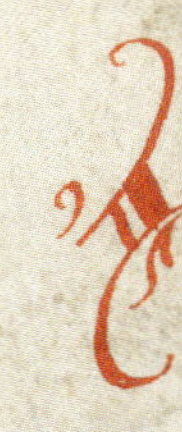

FOL. 158

1547, 1539 — Wondrous wheat, bearded grapes and Margaretha Weiß
Wunderweizen, bärtige Trauben und Margaretha Weiß
Blé merveilleux, raisin poilu et Margaretha Weiß

In the year 1547 this lovely wheat grew in the county of Flanders, three miles from Ghent, in various shapes and forms – some pressed closely together, some with divided ears, as well as with four, eight, twelve, up to fifteen ears on one stalk, just as is painted here.

A wonderful miracle in the year 1539, concerning a young girl from Roth in the Diocese of Speyer, who refrained from taking any physical sustenance for two years and twelve weeks. At this time too such hairy grapes grew beside the Neckar and the Rhine, as above. – Margaretha Weiß von Roth, thirteen and a half years old

Im 1547. Jahr ist dieser schöne Weizen in der Grafschaft Flandern, drei Meilen von Gent, in mancherlei Form und Gestalt gewachsen – mancher dicht aneinander gedrungen, mancher mit zerteilten Ähren, sowie mit vier, acht, zwölf, bis zu fünfzehn Ähren auf einem Halm, wie hier gemalt ist.

Ein wunderbares Mirakel im 1539. Jahr von einem jungen Mädchen aus Roth im Speyerer Bistum, das sich zwei Jahre und zwölf Wochen leiblicher Nahrung enthalten hat. Auch sind in dieser Zeit solche haarigen Trauben am Neckar und Rhein gewachsen wie oben. – Margaretha Weiß von Roth, dreizehneinhalb Jahre alt

En l'an 1547, ce beau blé poussa dans le comté de Flandre, à trois milles de Gand, sous différentes formes : certains serrés les uns contre les autres, d'autres aux épis séparés, ainsi qu'avec quatre, huit, douze et jusqu'à quinze épis sur une seule tige, comme dans cette peinture.

Un merveilleux miracle en l'an 1539, à propos d'une jeune fille de Roth dans le diocèse de Speyer, qui s'abstint de se nourrir pendant deux ans et douze semaines. Au même moment ce raisin poilu poussa sur les rives du Neckar et du Rhin comme ci-dessus. – Margaretha Weiß von Roth, treize ans et demi

FOL. 159

1547 — Halo over Augsburg
Halo über Augsburg | Halo dans le ciel d'Augsbourg

In the year 1547, on the 29th day of the month of January, two rainbows were seen here in Augsburg around the sun and between the clouds, for a long time in the morning and in the evening.

Im 1547. Jahr, am 29. Tag des Monats Januar, hat man hier zu Augsburg morgens und abends um die Sonne herum, zwischen den Wolken, eine lange Zeit zwei Regenbogen gesehen.

En l'an 1547, le vingt-neuvième jour du mois de janvier, deux arcs-en-ciel furent observés ici à Augsbourg autour du soleil et entre les nuages, pendant une longue durée le matin et le soir.

FOL. 160

1549 — Various celestial signs
Verschiedene Himmelszeichen
Signes célestes divers

In A.D. 1549, on the holy eve of Whitsun, many individuals saw such an occurrence at night on a heath between Cologne and Braunschweig near to a farm – which is called "Ahoff" – which then endured for a very long time.

1549 n. Chr., an dem heiligen Pfingstabend, haben viele Personen ein solches Ereignis nachts auf einer Heide zwischen Köln und Braunschweig bei einem Hof – der heißt der „Ahoff" – gesehen, was dann sehr lange angedauert hat.

En 1549 après J.-C. la sainte veille de la Pentecôte, beaucoup de personnes virent cet événement la nuit sur une lande entre Cologne et Braunschweig près d'une ferme – appelée « Ahoff » –, lequel dura ensuite très longtemps.

FOL. 161

1549 — Parhelia near Nördlingen
Nebensonnen bei Nördlingen | Parhélies près de Nördlingen

In A.D. 1549, on Simon' and Jude's Day, such a manifestation was seen in broad daylight near Nördlingen and in other places in the Ries and in Swabia, just as is recorded and painted here.

1549 n. Chr., am Tag Simon und Judas, hat man am helllichten Tag bei Nördlingen und anderswo im Ries und in Schwaben eine solche Erscheinung gesehen, wie sie hier verzeichnet und gemalt ist.

En 1549 après J.-C., le jour de la Saint-Simon et Jude, ce phénomène fut observé en plein jour près de Nördlingen et ailleurs en Ries et en Souabe, comme on le voit consigné et peint ici.

FOL. 163

1549 — Lunar halo over Swabia
Mondhalo über Schwaben | Halo lunaire dans le ciel de Souabe

In A.D. 1549, on October 6, such a manifestation was seen around the moon at night in the Ries and in Swabia on a clear night.

1549 n. Chr., am 6. Oktober, hat man nachts im Ries und Schwabenland am Mond bei heller Nacht solche Erscheinung gesehen.

En 1549 après J.-C., le six octobre, ce phénomène fut observé autour de la lune, de nuit en Ries et en Souabe par une nuit claire.

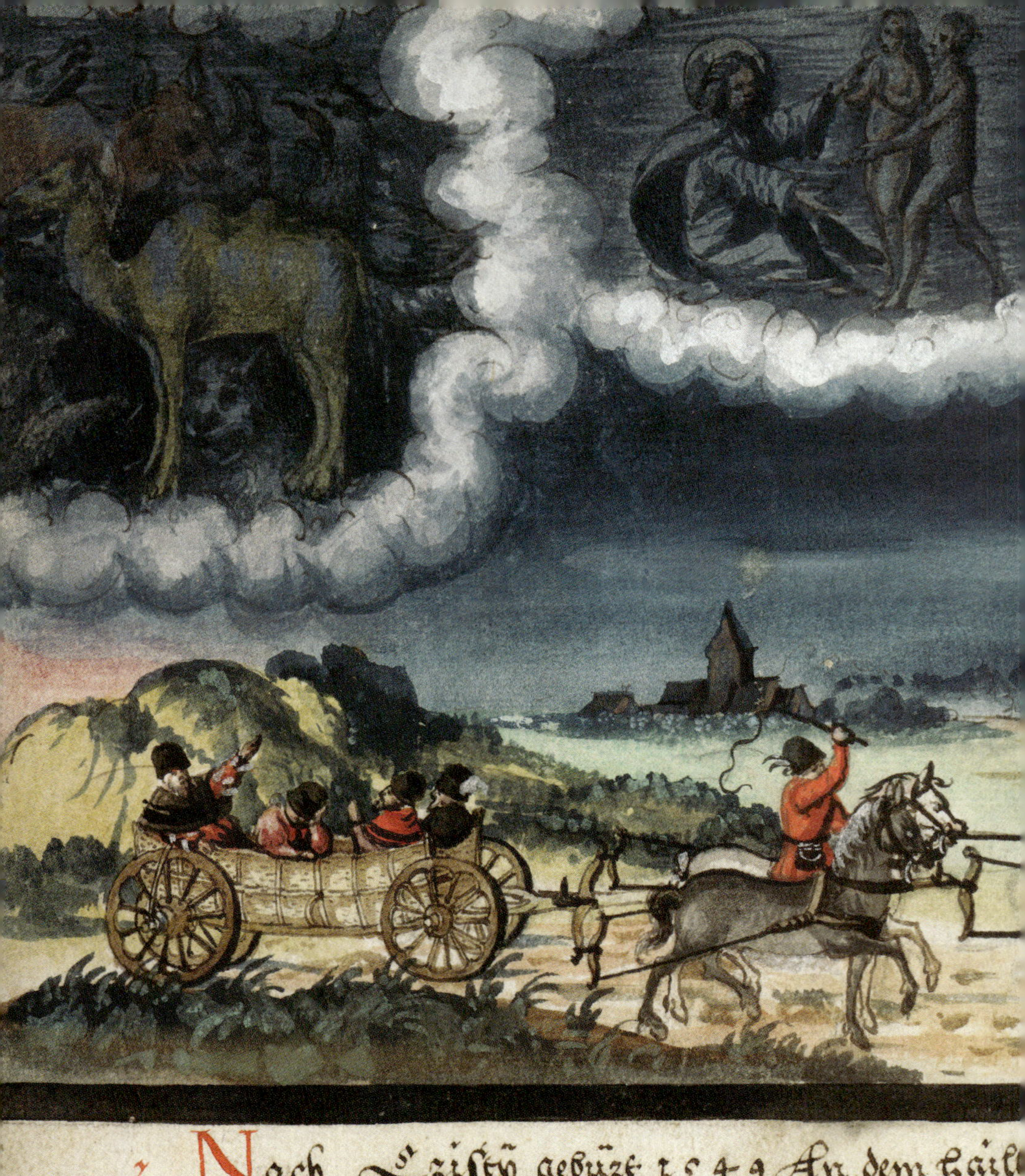

Nach Cristÿ gebůrt 1549 An dem Hail

solche geschicht, beÿ der nacht, Aůff ain

beÿ ainem Hoff der haist der Ahoff gese

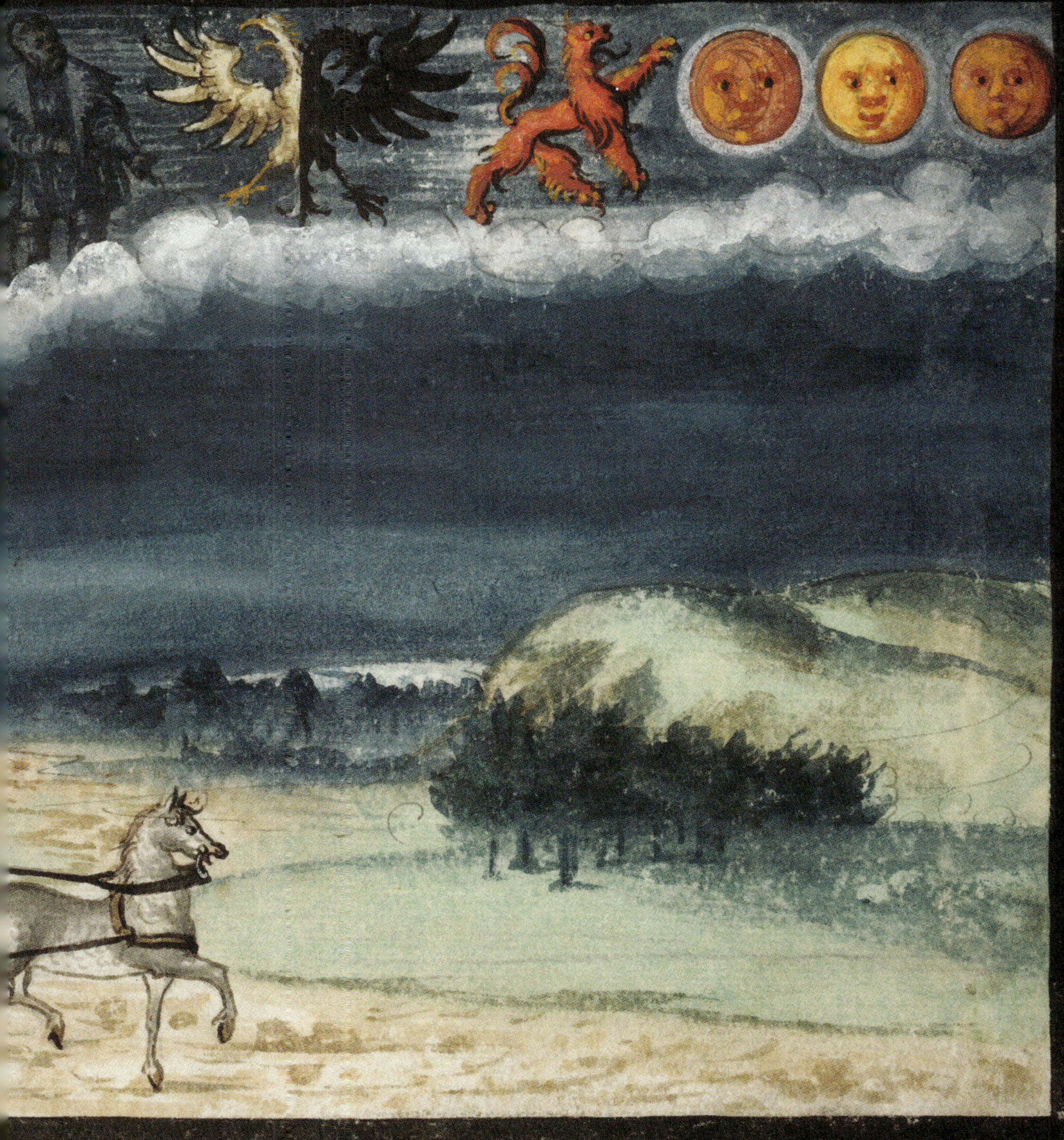

pfingst Abentt / Hannd vill personen ⁊.
Heyden zwischen Cöln vnd braunschweig
das dan gar lang gewert hatt

9

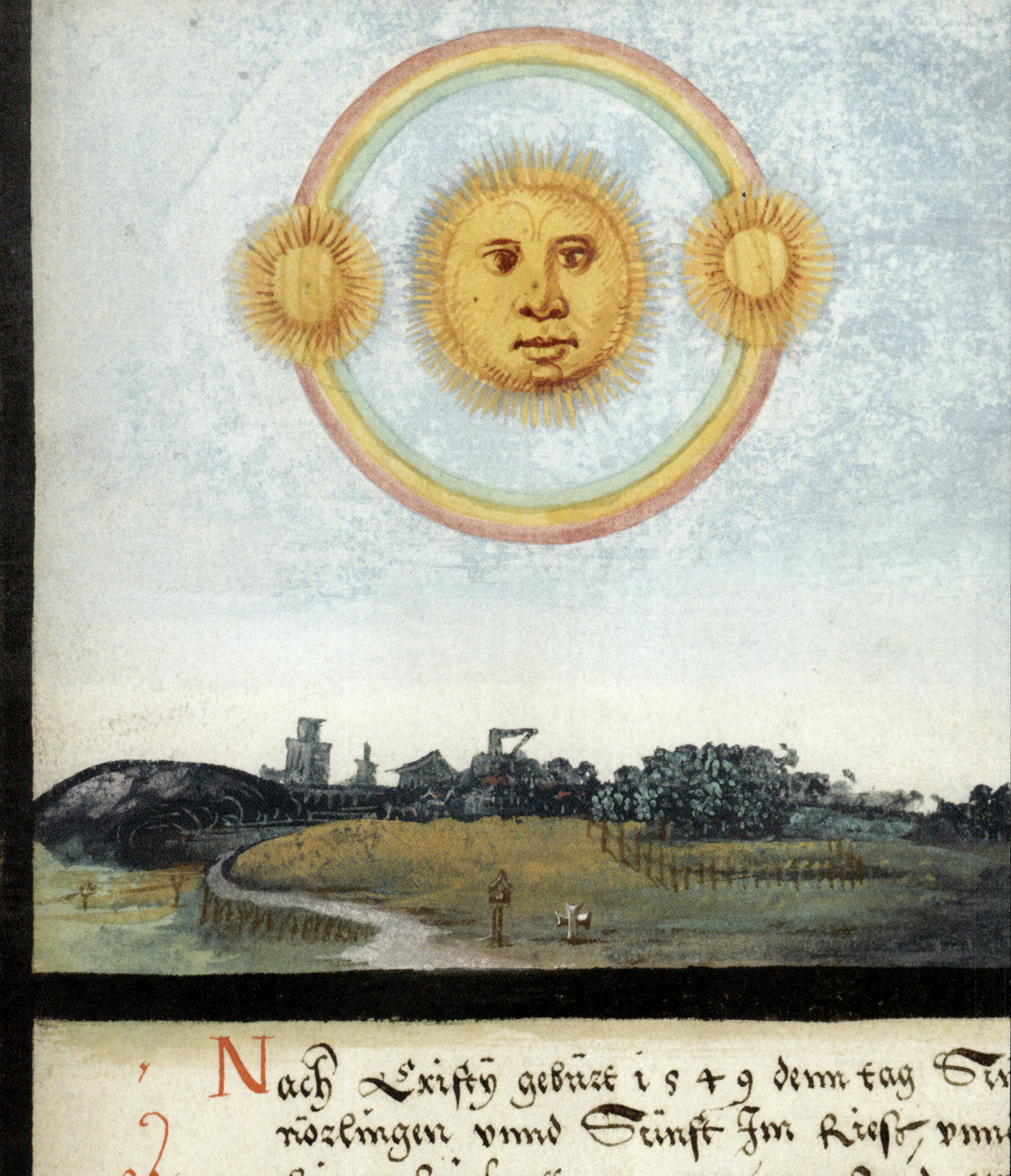

Nach Christy geburt 1549 dem tag Sw
nörlingen vnnd Sunst Im Riess, vnn
hie verzaichnett vnnd, ger

15

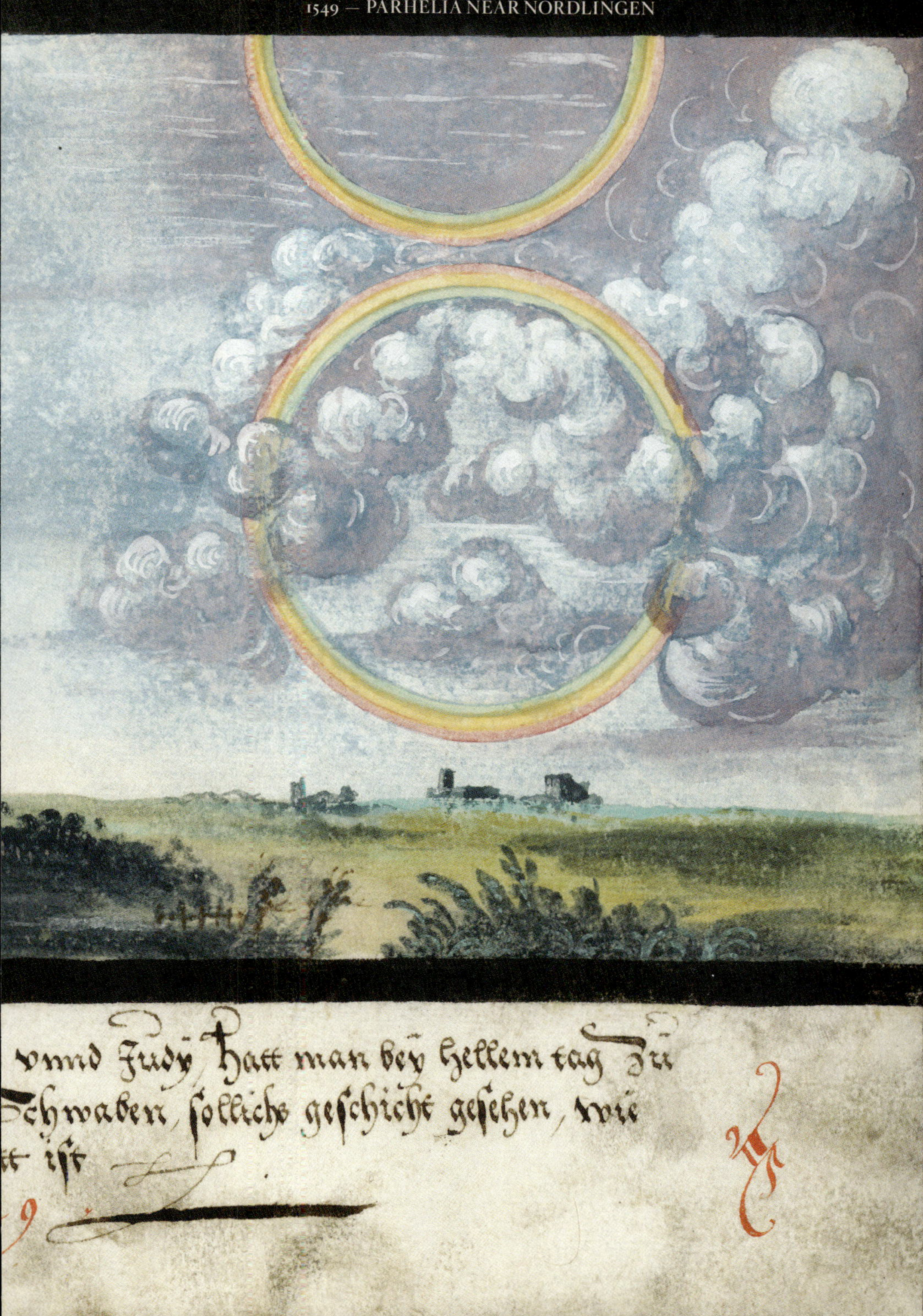
vnnd Judy, Hatt man bey hellem tag zu
Schwaben, sollichs geschicht gesehen, wie
tt ist

Nach Cristy geburt 1549 dem
Ries vnnd Schwaben Land, am

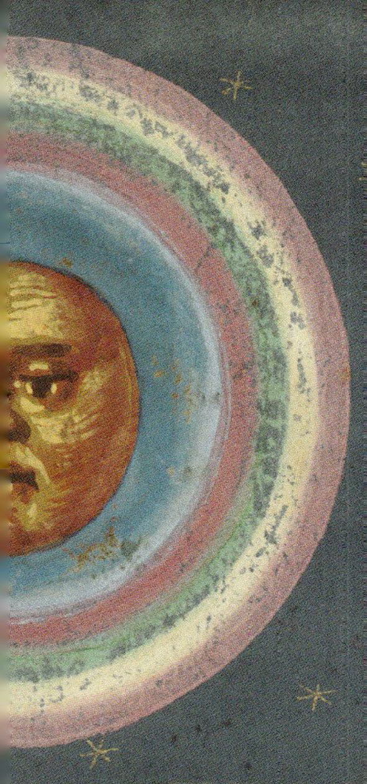

549.
g Octobris Hatt man bey der nacht Im
n bey Heller nacht soliche geschicht gesehen

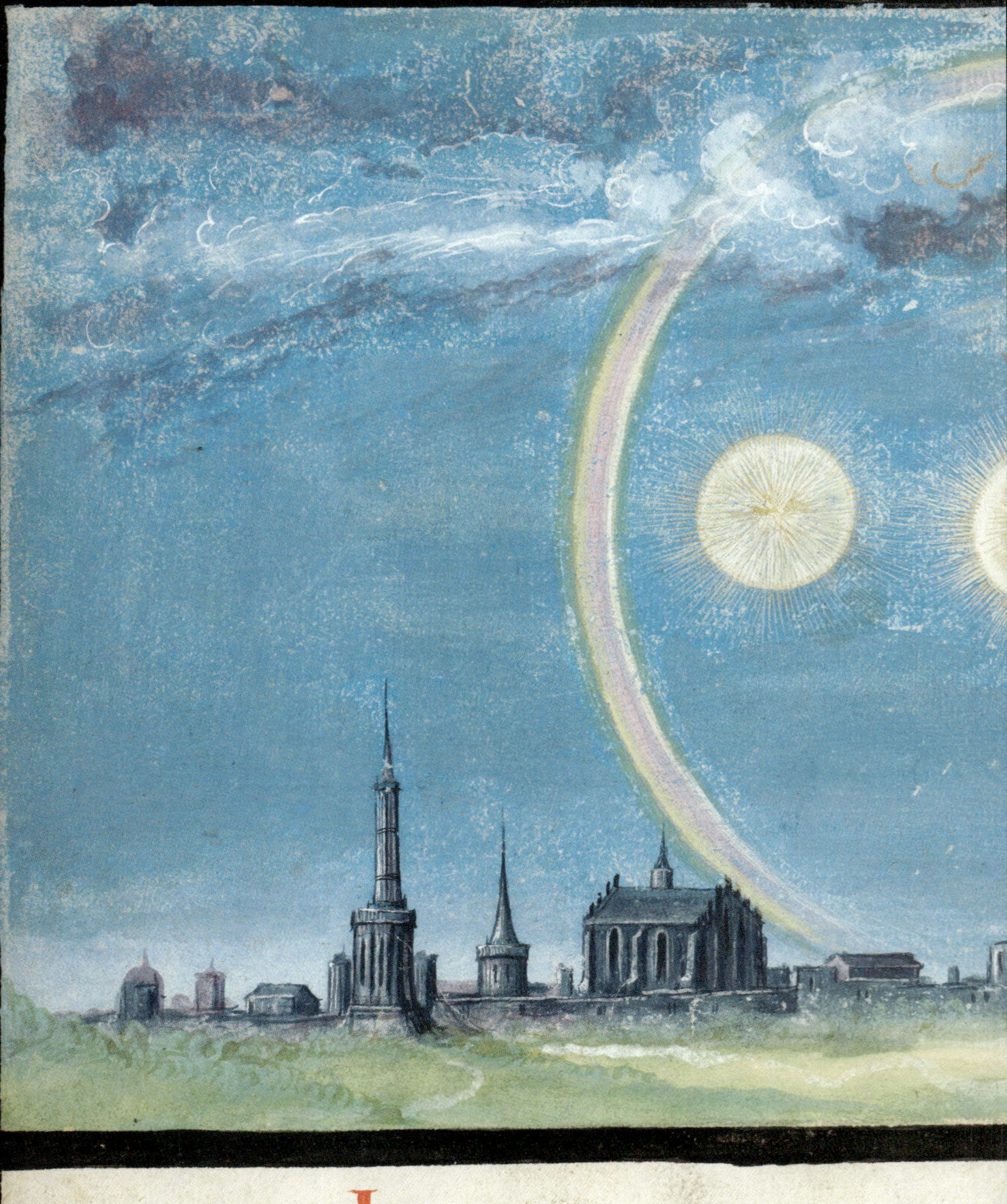

Im M D xxxxviiii iar auf den acht v
hat man dirser gesicht an dem him-
pogen: dir menigklich gesehen hat a

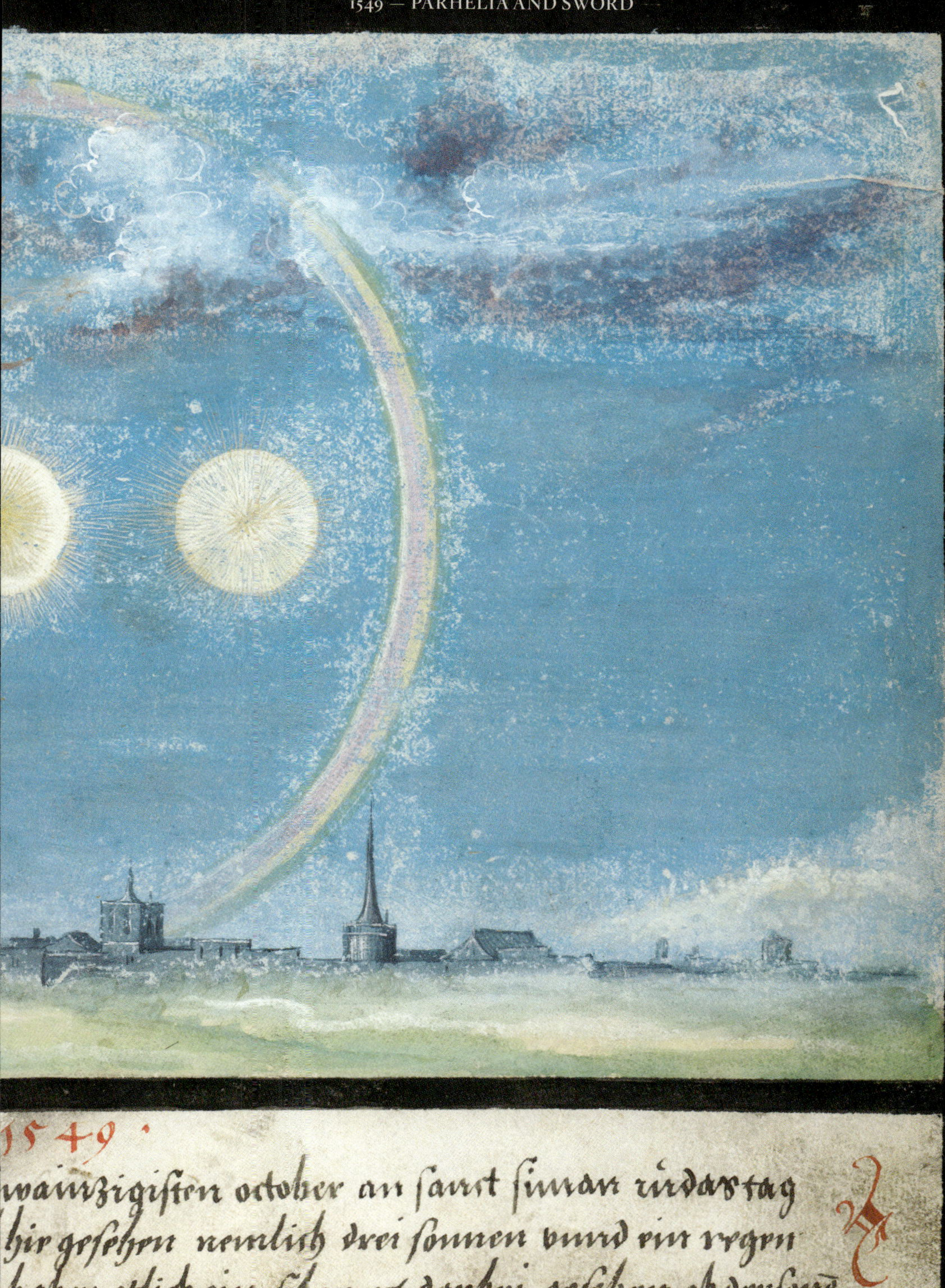
549.
wainzigisten october an sannt simon iudastag
hir gesehen nemlich drei sonnen vnnd ein regen
haben etlich ein schwert darbei gesehen ob der sone

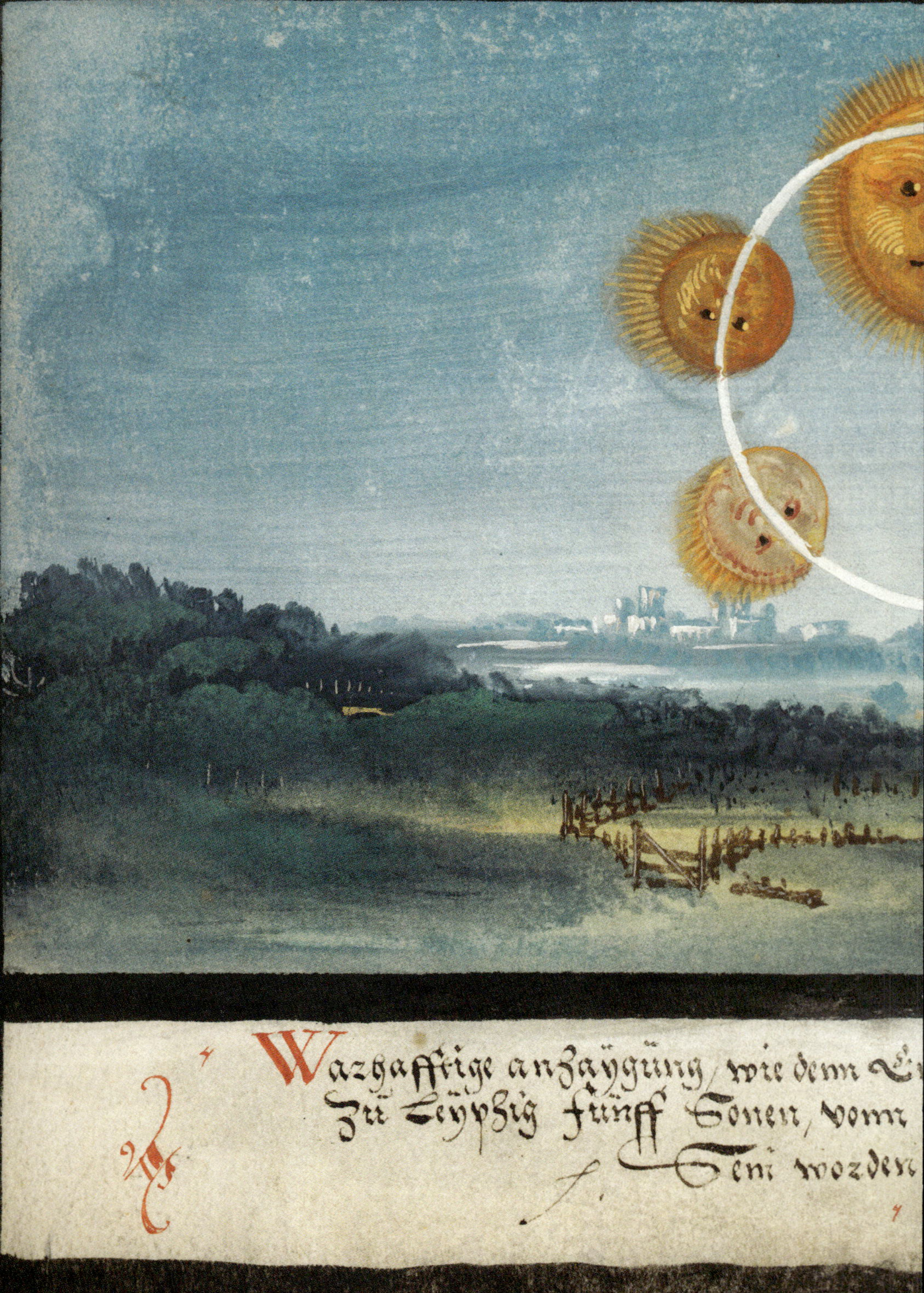
Warhafftige anzaygung / wie dem
Zu Leypzig funff Sonen / vom
Seni worden

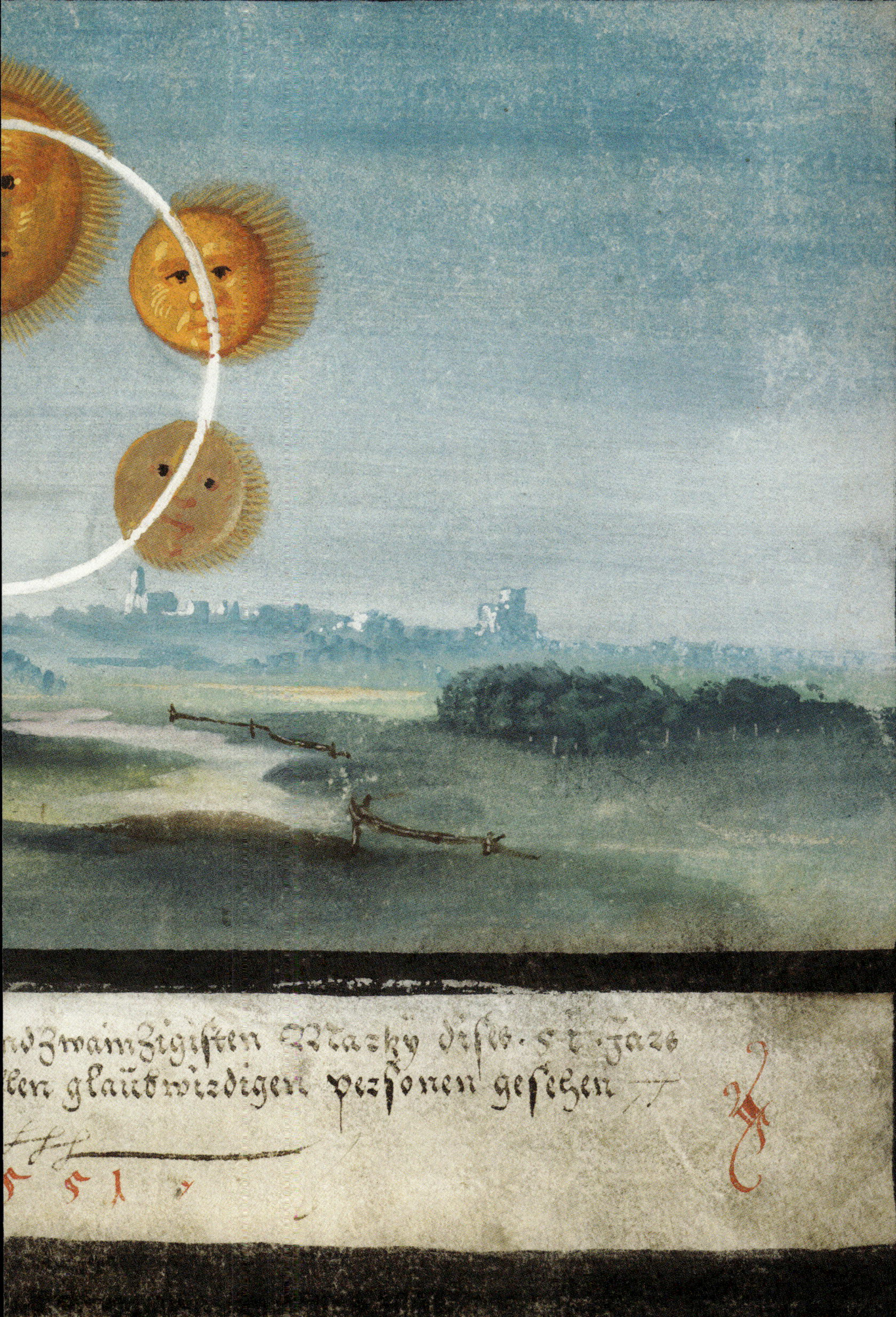
zwainzigisten Marcÿ dises · 5 1 · Jars
glaubwirdigen personen gesehen

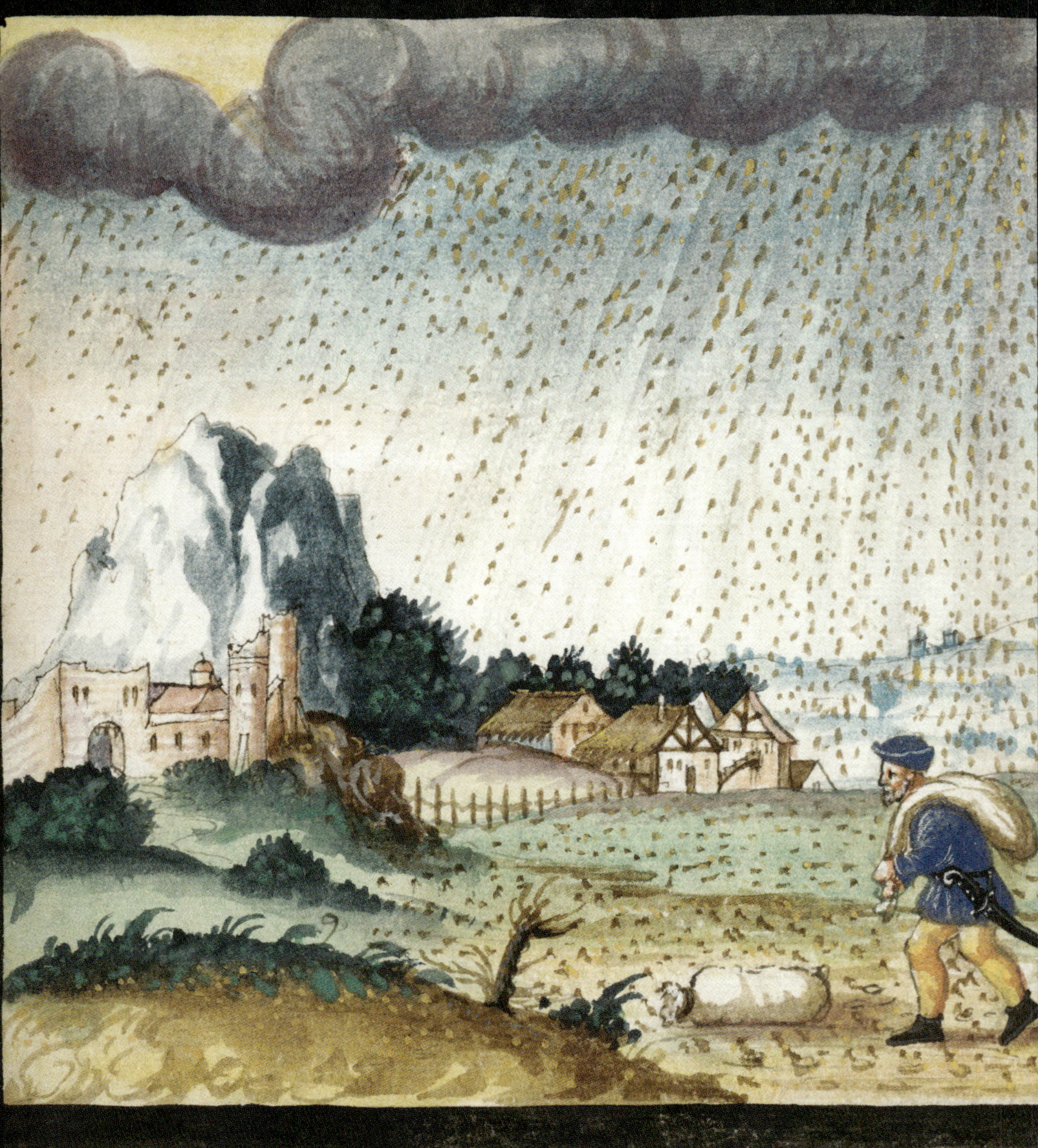

Nach Cristy geburt 1550 Jar Jm 23 tag marcy
haißt Klagenfurtt, Ligt in Kernten, Hatt es be
gezegnett bey. 6. meyll weckh Lang, das darnach
Vnnd Costlich gutt

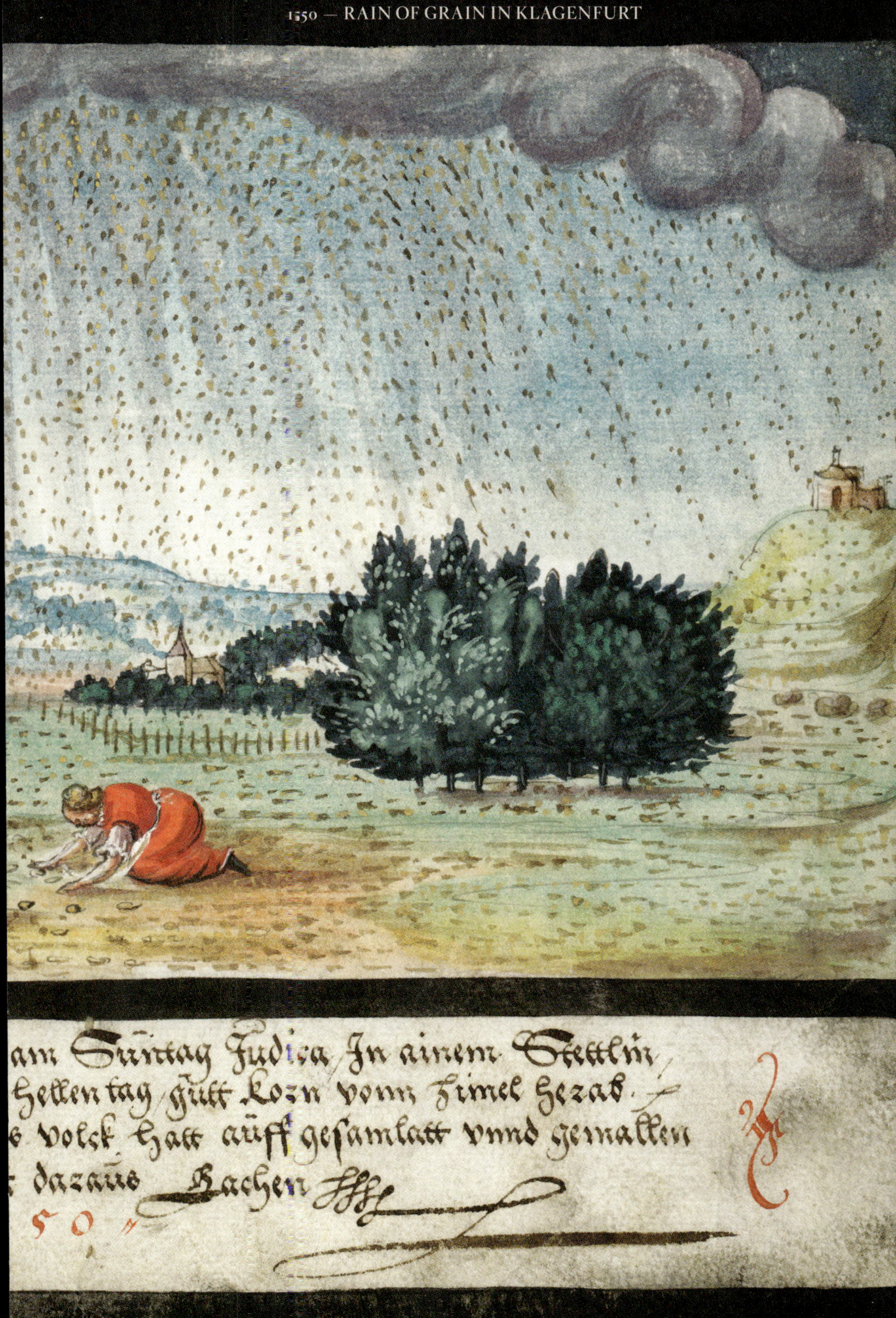
am Suntag Judica In ainem Stettlin
hellen tag gült Korn vom himel herab
s volck hatt auff gesamlatt vnnd gemallen
t daraus Bachen
50

FOL. 164

1549 — Parhelia and sword

Nebensonnen und Schwert | Parhélies et épée

In the year 1549, on the twenty-eighth of October, on St Simon and St Jude's Day, this manifestation was seen here in the sky, namely three suns and a rainbow, which everyone saw. Several people also saw a sword over the sun.

Im 1549. Jahr, am achtundzwanzigsten Oktober, am Sankt-Simon-und-Judas-Tag, hat man diese Erscheinung hier am Himmel gesehen, nämlich drei Sonnen und einen Regenbogen, die jeder gesehen hat. Auch haben etliche ein Schwert dabei gesehen über der Sonne.

En l'an 1549, le vingt-huit octobre, le jour de la Saint-Simon et Jude, ce phénomène fut observé ici dans le ciel, à savoir trois soleils et un arc-en-ciel, que tout le monde vit. Plusieurs personnes virent aussi dans la même zone une épée au-dessus du soleil.

FOL. 165

1551 — Five suns over Leipzig

Fünf Sonnen über Leipzig | Cinq soleils dans le ciel de Leipzig

Truthful report of how, on the twenty-first of March of this 51st year, five suns were seen in Leipzig by many trustworthy persons.

Wahrheitsgemäße Meldung, wie am einundzwanzigsten März dieses 51. Jahres zu Leipzig fünf Sonnen von vielen glaubwürdigen Personen gesehen worden sind.

Relation véridique sur la manière dont, le vingt et un mars de cette 51e année, cinq soleils furent observés à Leipzig par beaucoup de personnes dignes de foi.

FOL. 166

1550 — Rain of grain in Klagenfurt

Kornregen in Klagenfurt | Pluie de grain à Klagenfurt

1550 years after the birth of Christ, on March 23, on the fifth Sunday in Lent, in a little town – called Klagenfurt, in Carinthia – good grain rained down from the sky in broad daylight about 6 miles down the road, which the people gathered up and then milled and from which they baked deliciously good bread.

1550 Jahre nach Christi Geburt, am 23. März, hat es am Sonntag Judica in einem Städtchen in Kärnten – Klagenfurt genannt – am helllichten Tag etwa 6 Meilen entlang des Weges gutes Korn vom Himmel herabgeregnet, das die Leute danach aufgesammelt und gemahlen haben und woraus sie köstlich gutes Brot gebacken haben.

1550 années après la naissance du Christ, le 23 mars, le cinquième dimanche de carême dans une petite ville – appelée Klagenfurt, en Carinthie – une averse de bon grain tomba du ciel en plein jour sur environ 6 milles de distance, que les gens récoltèrent, et moulurent par la suite et avec lequel ils firent un pain délicieux.

FOL. 167

1550 — Spring of blood
Blutquelle | Source de sang

In A.D. 1550, in the month of June, a spring of blood welled up on a meadow between Halle and Merseburg at Meissen so that both nobles and commoners went out of the city in their hundreds and saw such a marvel.

1550 nach Christi Geburt, im Monat Juni, ist eine Quelle mit Blut auf einer Wiese zwischen Halle und Merseburg in Meißen aufgebrochen, dass edle und unedle Personen zu etlichen Hundert aus der Stadt gegangen sind und solches Wunderwerk gesehen haben.

En 1550 après J.-C., au mois de juin, une source de sang jaillit dans une prairie entre Halle et Merseburg en Misnie, si bien que nobles et roturiers sortirent de la ville par centaines et observèrent ce prodige.

FOL. 168

1550 — Malformed pigeon | Missgestaltete Taube | Pigeon difforme

1550 years after the birth of Christ, such a pigeon was found in a village by the name of Rickatshofen, near Lindau, as is painted here, with 4 feet and two sets of hindquarters.

1550 Jahre nach Christi Geburt ist eine solche Taube in einem Dorf namens Rickatshofen, bei Lindau gelegen, gefunden worden, wie hier gemalt ist, mit 4 Füßen und zwei Hinterteilen.

1550 années après la naissance du Christ, ce pigeon fut découvert dans un village appelé Rickatshofen, près de Lindau, comme le montre cette peinture, avec 4 pattes et deux arrière-trains.

FOL. 169

1551 — Parhelia and sword over Swabia
Nebensonnen und Schwert über Schwaben
Parhélies et épée dans le ciel de Souabe

1551 years after the birth of Christ, in the month of March, such an occurrence was seen in Swabia in broad daylight on more than one occasion.

1551 Jahre nach Christi Geburt, im Monat März, hat man solches Ereignis im Schwabenland bei hellem Tag mehr als einmal gesehen.

1551 années après la naissance du Christ, au mois de mars, cet événement fut observé en Souabe en plein jour et plus d'une fois.

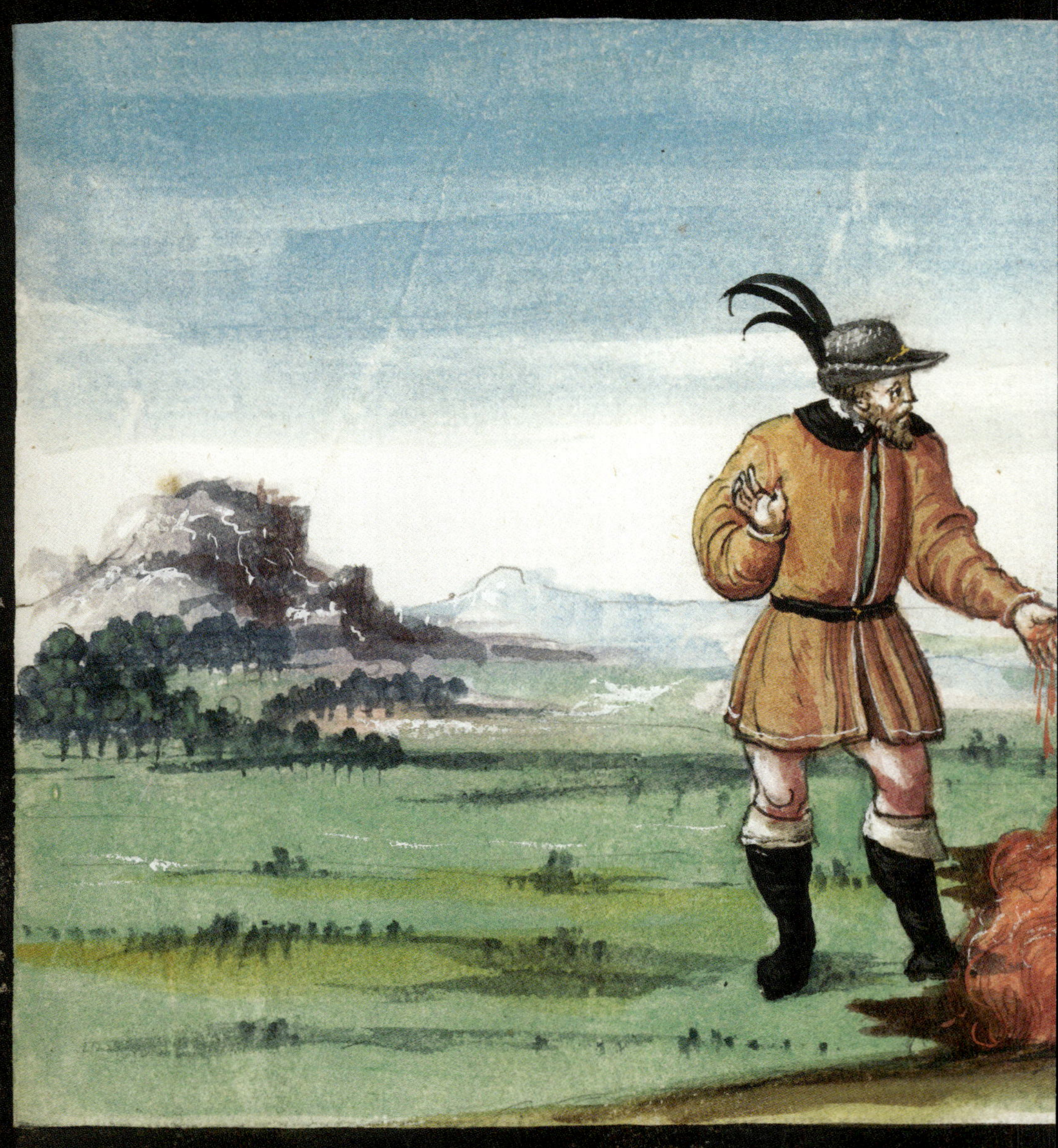

Nach Cristy geburt 1550 Im Monnatt Jun
wissen auff brochen zwichen hall vnd mör
personen edel vnnd vnedell auß der statt ga
15

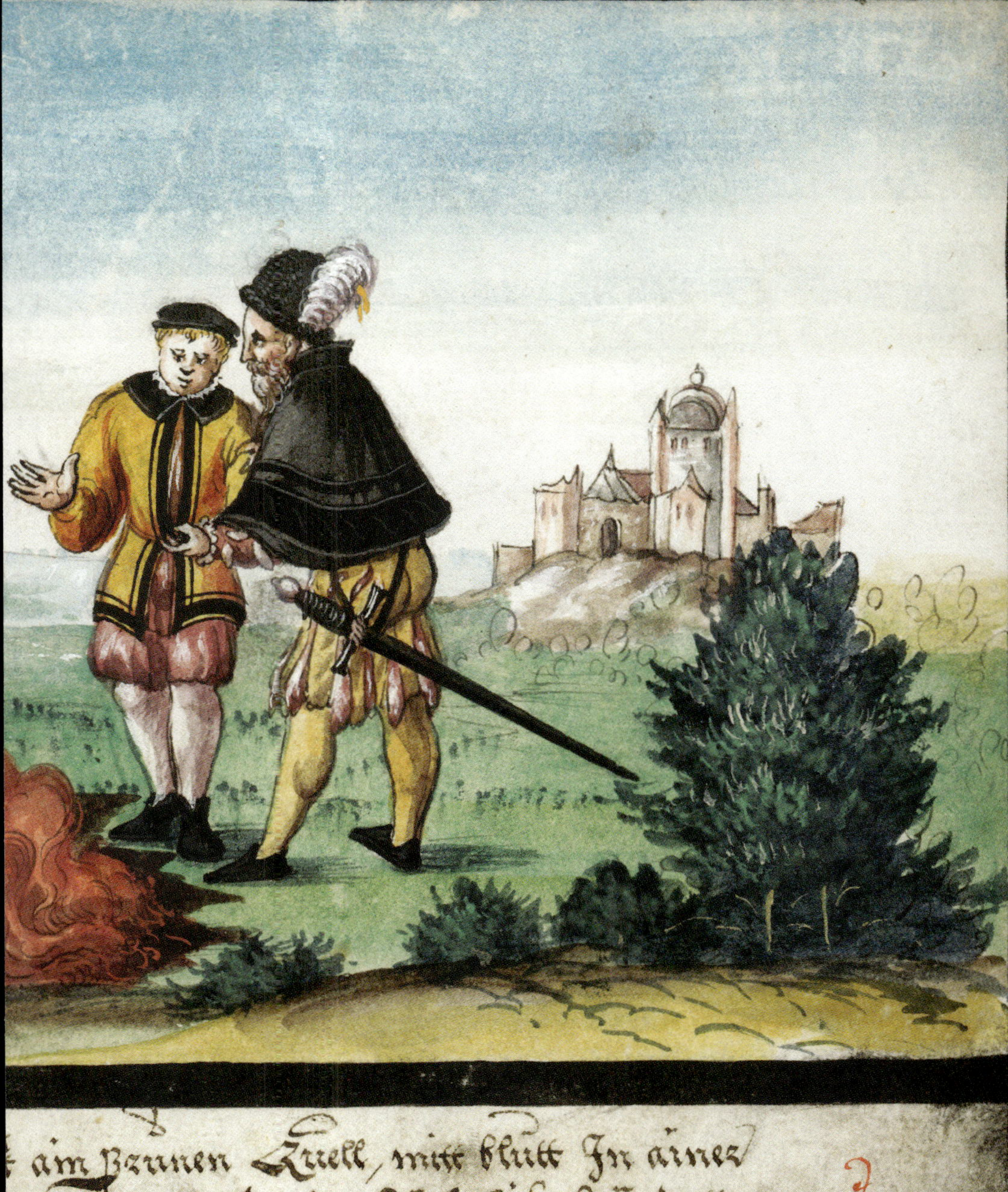
t am Brunen Quell, mitt blutt Jn ainer
zg Jn meyssen, das zu ettlich hundert
n, vnd Solichs wunder werck gesehen

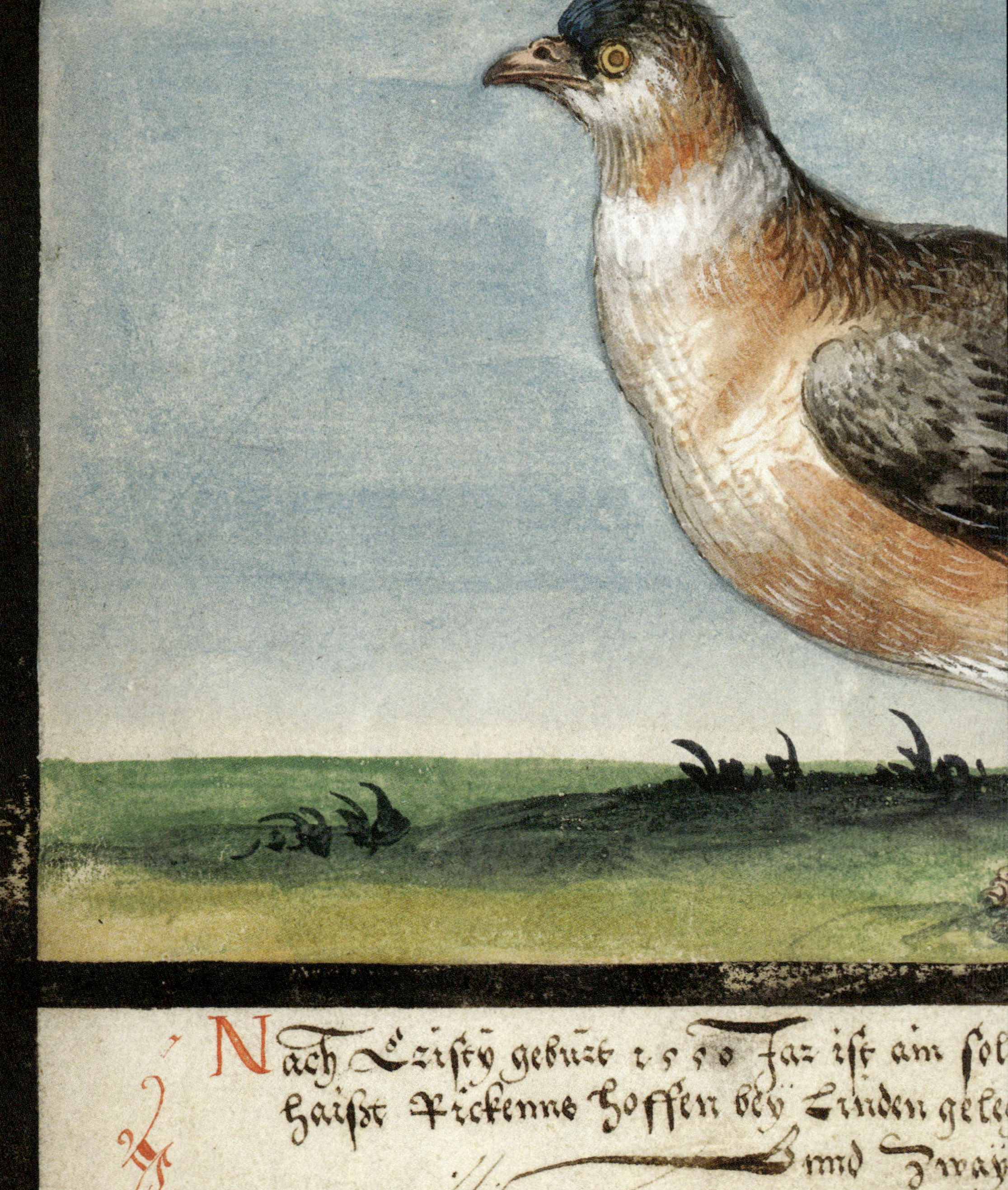
Nach Cristy geburt 1550 Jar ist ain
haist Rickenns Hoffen bey Linden
vnnd

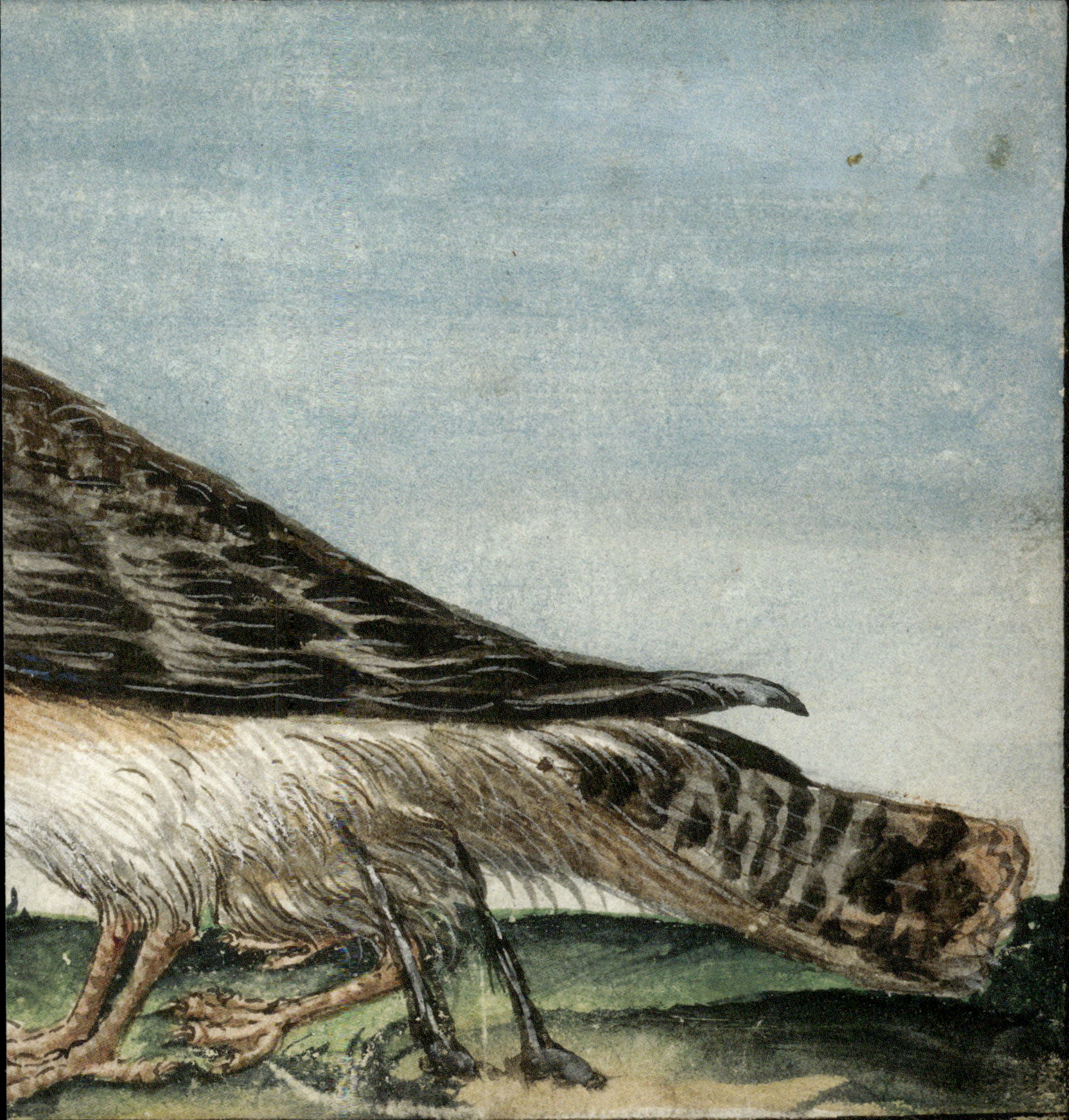

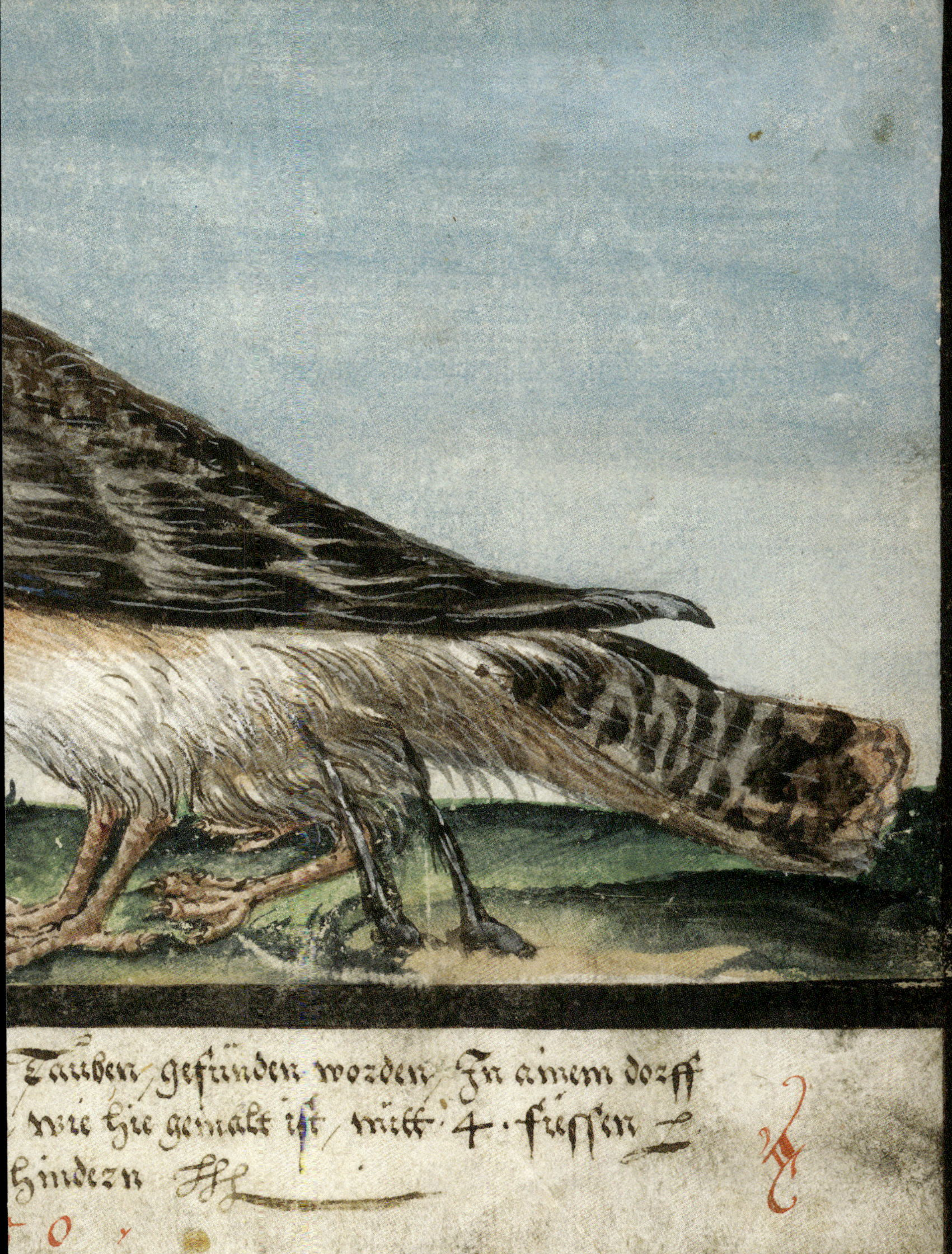

Tauben gefünden worden In ainem dorff
wie hie gemalt ist mitt 4 · fuessen
hindern

0

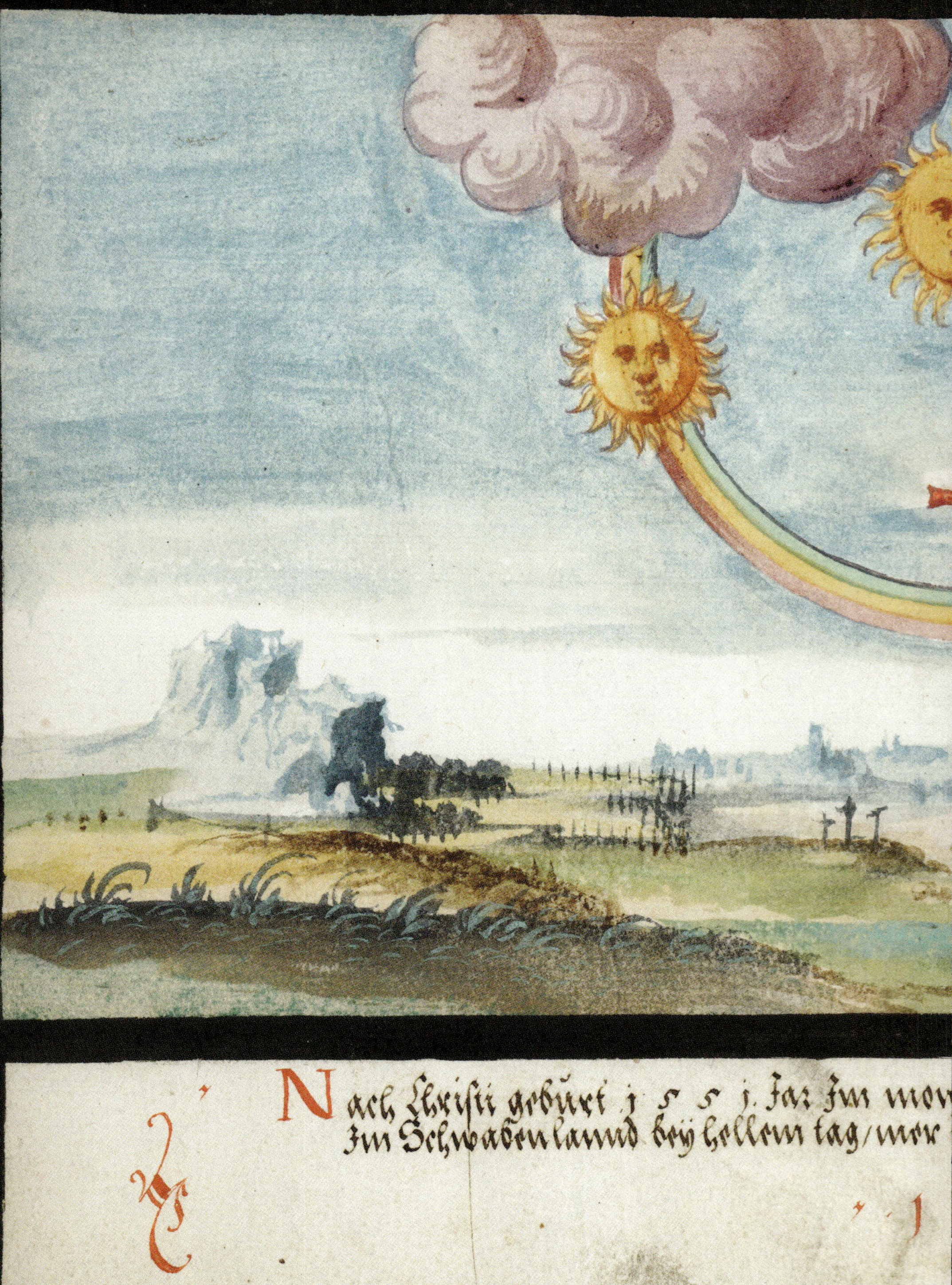

Nach Christi geburt 1 5 5 1. Jar Zum mon
Zu Schwabenlannd bey hellem tag/ wer

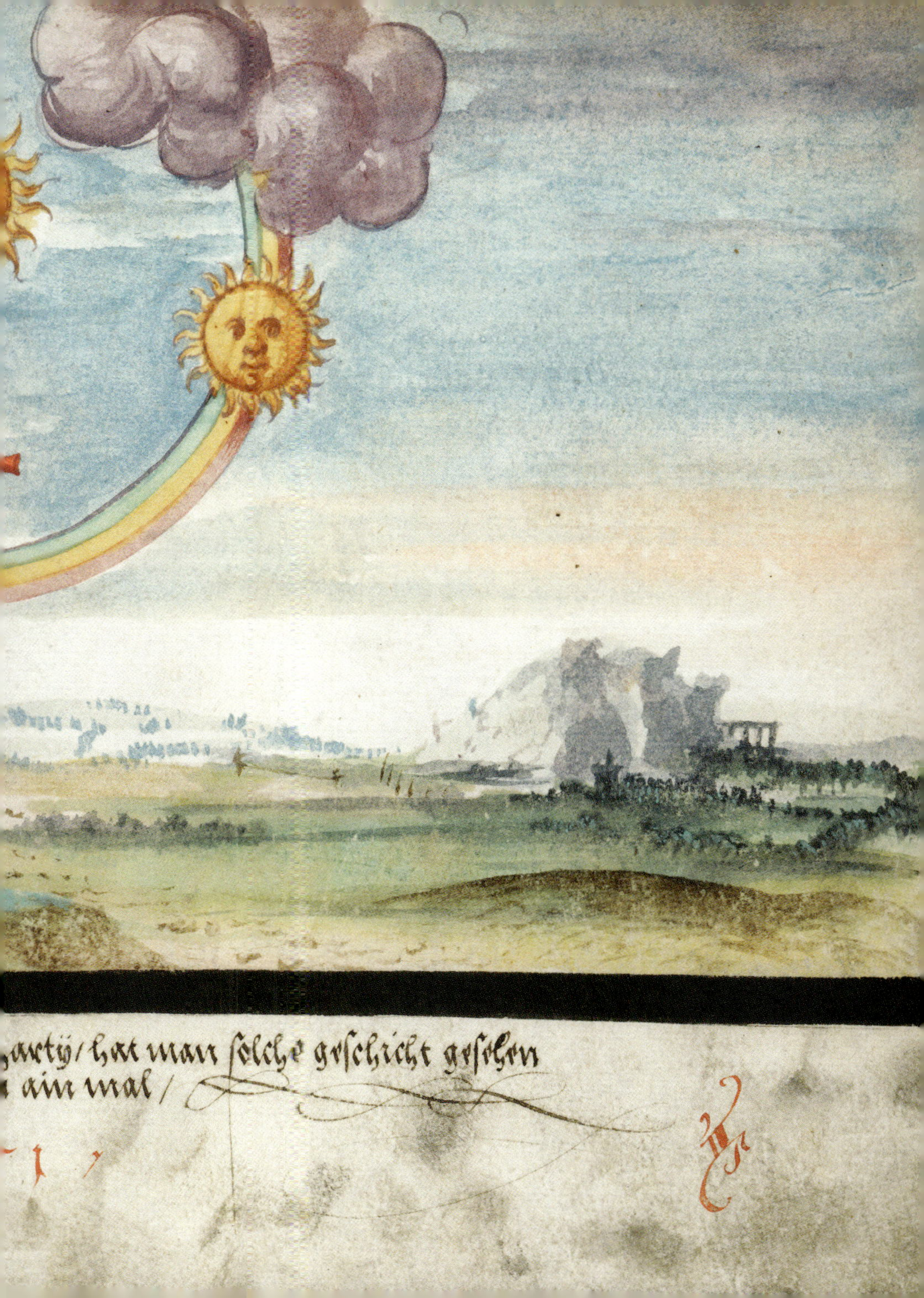
artij/ hat man solche geschicht gesehen
ain mal /

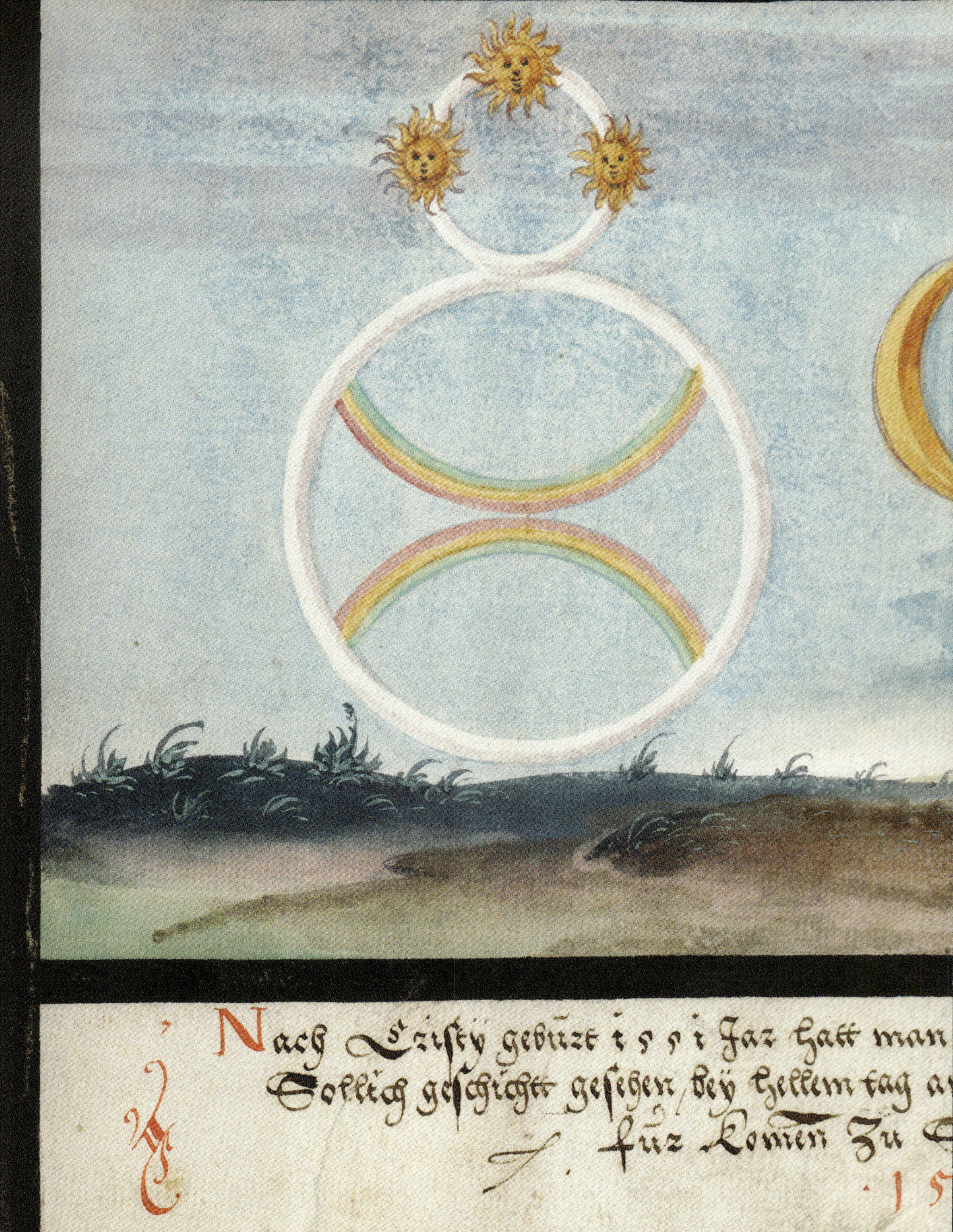
Nach Christÿ geburt 1 5 5 1 Jar hatt man
Sollich geschicht gesehen, beÿ hellem tag
fur komen Zu
15

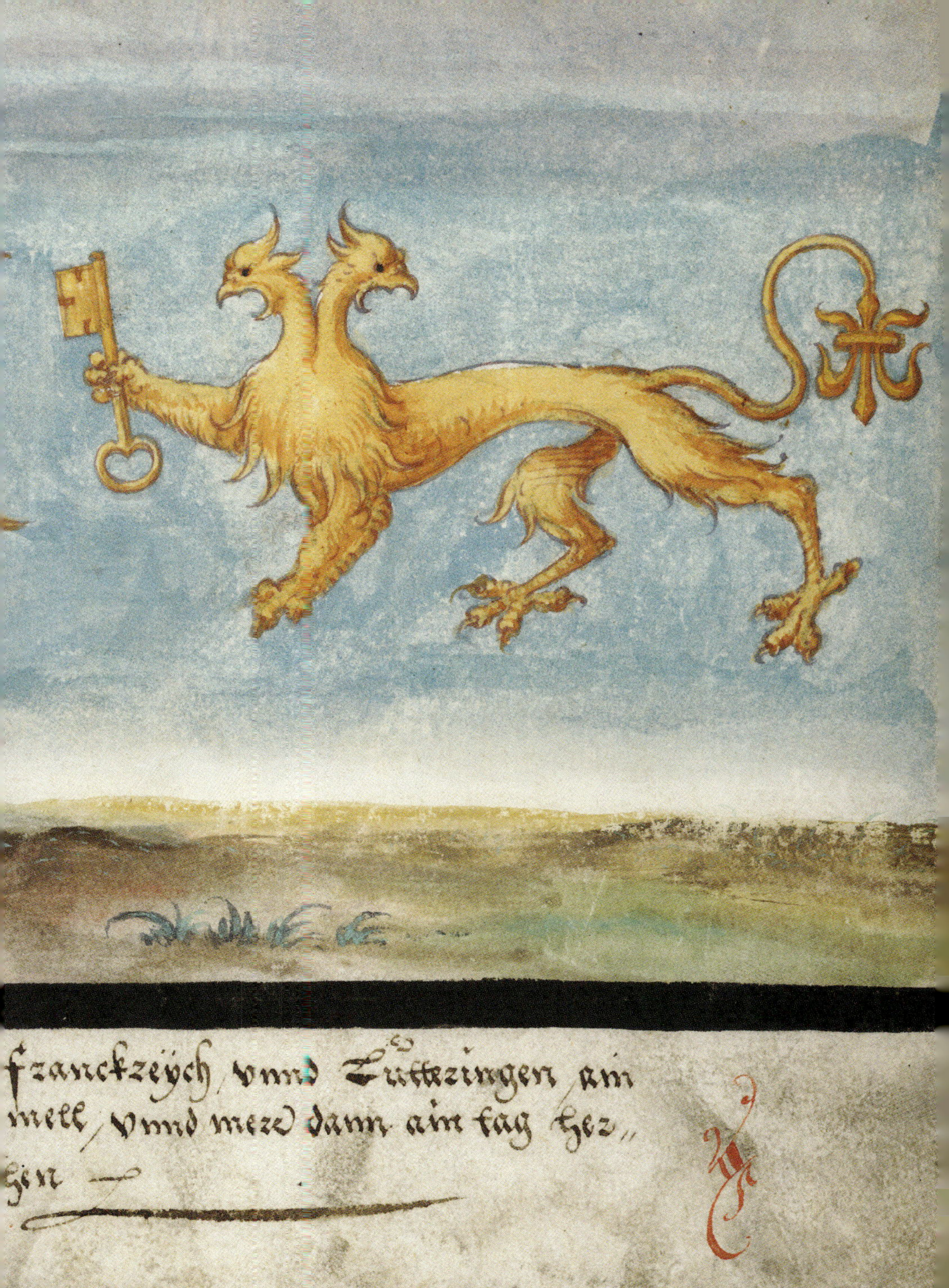
franckreÿch, vnnd Lůttringen ain
mell, vnnd merr dann ain tag her=
hin

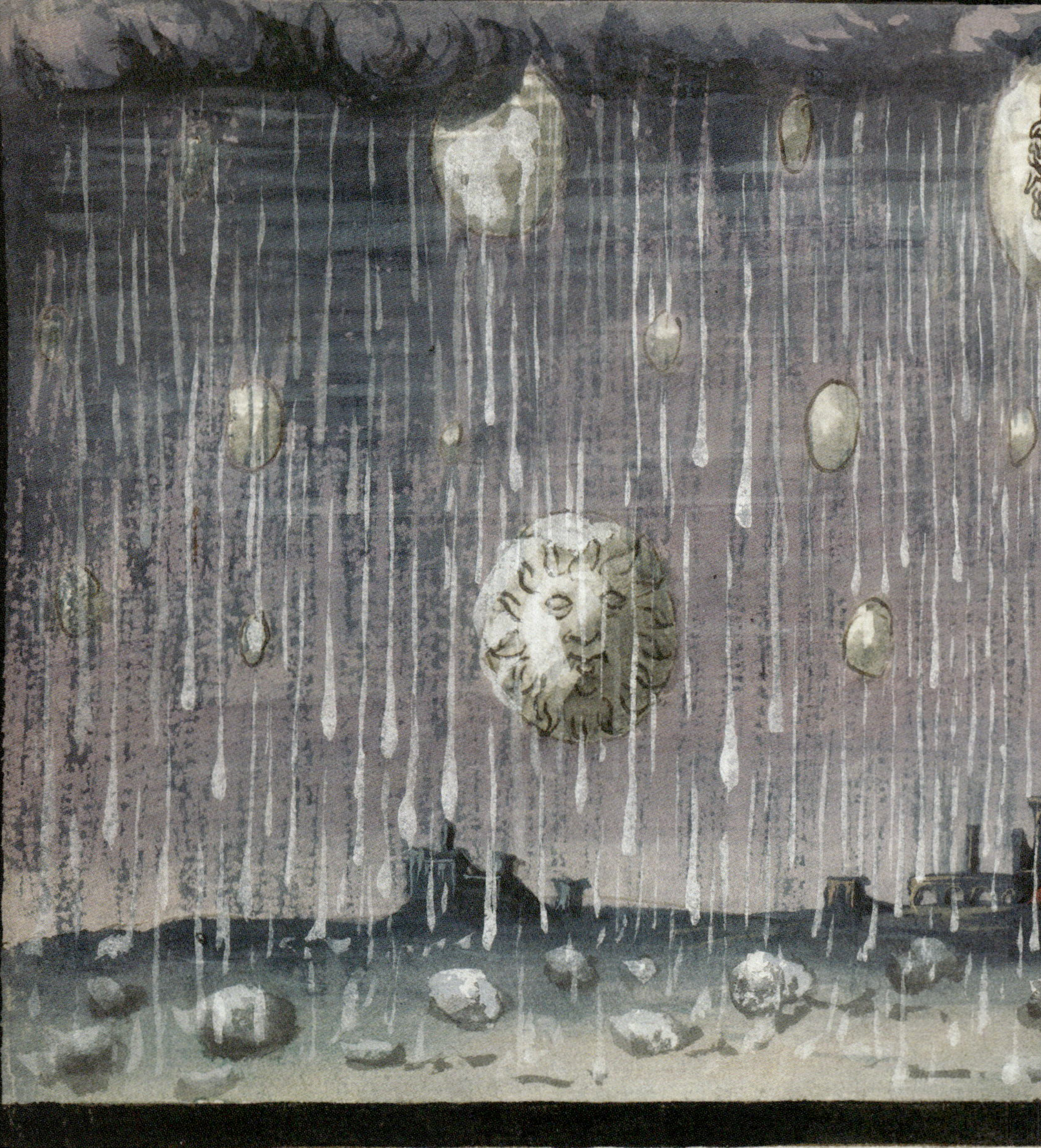

Nach Christi gebürt 1 5 5 2. den 17. tag Maij:
zü Dordrecht zum Hollanndt gefallen / das die
vnnd hat bey einer halben stünndt gewehrt / Dis
Rot / vnnd da sie ergangen sind / haben sie grausa

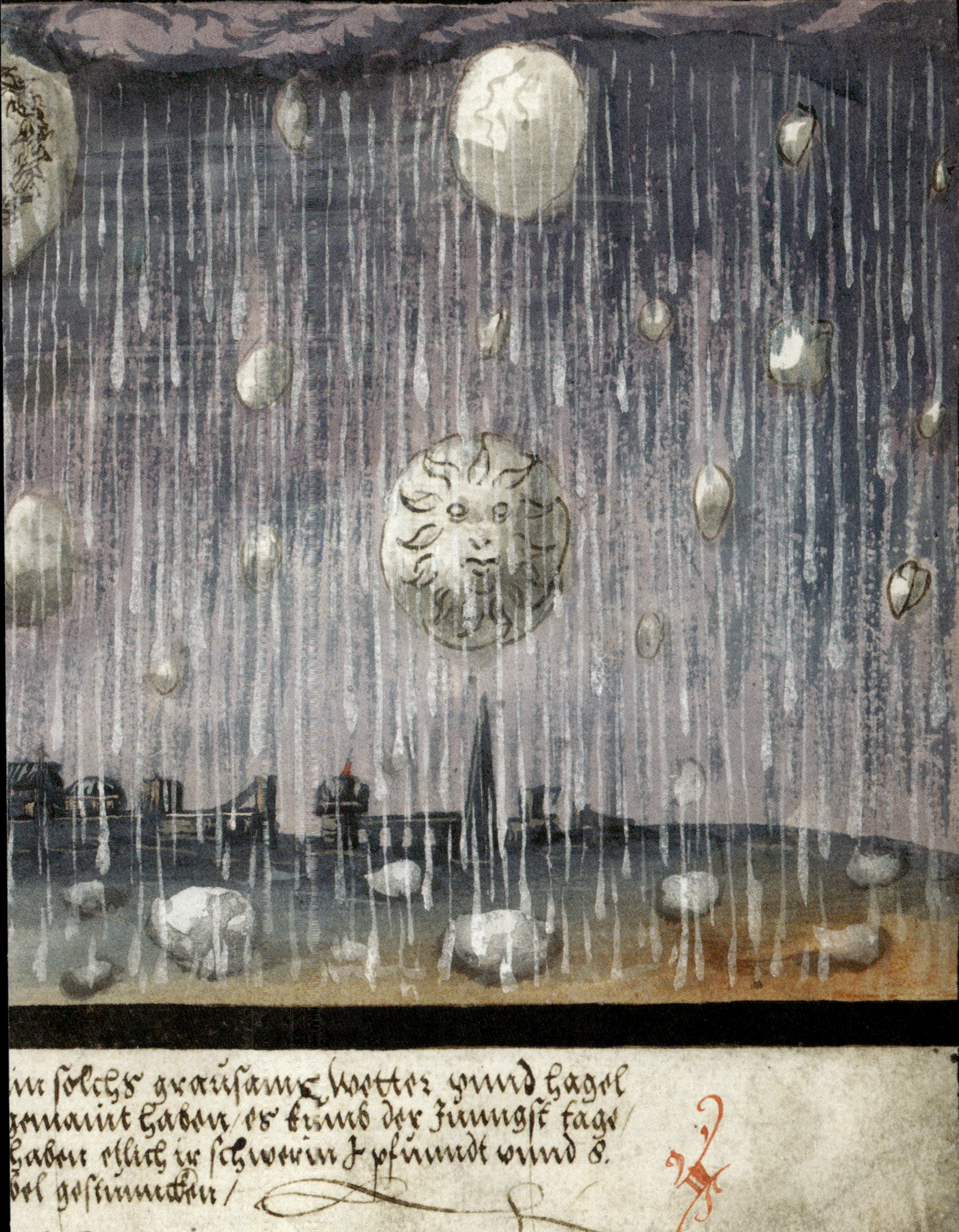

ein solchs grausam wetter vnnd hagel
gemaint haben/ es kume der Jungst tage
haben etlich in schwerin 3 pfundt vnnd 8.
vel gestimmetten/

52

FOL. 170

1551 — Various celestial signs
Verschiedene Himmelszeichen | Signes célestes divers

1551 years after the birth of Christ, such an occurrence was seen in the sky in France and in Lorraine in broad daylight, which came forth and could be seen for more than a day.

1551 Jahre nach Christi Geburt hat man in Frankreich und Lothringen ein solches Ereignis bei hellem Tag am Himmel gesehen, das mehr als einen Tag hervorgekommen und zu sehen gewesen ist.

1551 années après la naissance du Christ, cet événement fut observé dans le ciel en France et en Lorraine en plein jour, qui apparut et fut visible pendant plus d'une journée.

FOL. 171

1552 — Hail in Dordrecht | Hagel in Dordrecht | Grêle à Dordrecht

In A.D. 1552, on May 17, such a terrible storm with hail descended on Dordrecht in Holland, that the people thought the Day of Judgement was coming. And it lasted about half an hour. Several of the stones weighed up to a few pounds and 8 lot. And where they fell, they gave a frightful stench.

1552 n. Chr., am 17. Mai, ist ein solch grausames Unwetter mit Hagel zu Dordrecht in Holland niedergegangen, dass die Leute gedacht haben, es käme der jüngste Tag. Und es hat etwa eine halbe Stunde gedauert. Etliche der Steine haben ihre schweren Pfund und 8 Lot. Und wo sie herabgefallen sind, haben sie grausam übel gestunken.

En 1552 après J.-C., le 17 mai, un terrible orage avec de la grêle s'abattit sur Dordrecht en Hollande, à tel point que les gens crurent venu le jour du Jugement dernier. Et cela dura environ une demi-heure. Plusieurs grêlons pesaient plusieurs livres et 8 lots. Et là où ils tombèrent, ils émirent une affreuse pestilence.

FOL. 172

St John's vision of Christ and the seven candlesticks
Die Vision des Johannes von Christus und den sieben Leuchtern
Vision du Christ et des sept candélabres par saint Jean

Revelation 1:12–18 – 12 Then I turned to see the voice that was speaking to me, and on turning I saw seven golden lampstands, 13 and in the midst of the lampstands one like a son of man, clothed with a long robe and with a golden sash around his chest. 14 The hairs of his head were white, like white wool, like snow. His eyes were like a flame of fire, 15 his feet were like burnished bronze, refined in a furnace, and his voice was like the roar of many waters. 16 In his right hand he held seven stars, from his mouth came a sharp two-edged sword, and his face was like the sun shining in full strength. 17 When I saw him, I fell at his feet as though dead. But he laid his right hand on me, saying, "Fear not, I am the first and the last, 18 and the living one. I died, and behold I am alive forevermore [...]."

Offenbarung 1,12–18 – 12 [...] Und als ich mich umwandte, sah ich sieben goldene Leuchter 13 und mitten unter den Leuchtern einen, der war einem Menschensohn gleich, angetan mit einem langen Gewand und gegürtet um die Brust mit einem goldenen Gürtel. 14 Sein Haupt aber und sein Haar war weiß wie weiße Wolle, wie der Schnee, und seine Augen wie eine Feuerflamme 15 und seine Füße wie Golderz, das im Ofen glüht, und seine Stimme wie großes Wasserrauschen; 16 und er hatte sieben Sterne in seiner rechten Hand, und aus seinem Munde ging ein scharfes, zweischneidiges Schwert[...] 17 Und als ich ihn sah, fiel ich zu seinen Füßen wie tot; und er [...] sprach zu mir: Fürchte dich nicht! Ich bin der Erste und der Letzte 18 und der Lebendige. Ich war tot, und siehe, ich bin lebendig von Ewigkeit zu Ewigkeit [...].

Apocalypse 1:12–18 – 12 [...] Je vis sept candélabres d'or, 13 et, au milieu des candélabres, comme un Fils d'homme revêtu d'une longue robe serrée à la taille par une ceinture en or. 14 Sa tête, avec ses cheveux blancs, est comme de la laine blanche, comme de la neige, ses yeux comme une flamme ardente, 15 ses pieds pareils à de l'airain précieux que l'on aurait purifié au creuset, sa voix comme la voix des grandes eaux. 16 Dans sa main droite il a sept étoiles, et de sa bouche sort une épée acérée, à double tranchant ; et son visage, c'est comme le soleil qui brille dans tout son éclat. 17 À sa vue, je tombai à ses pieds, comme mort ; mais il posa sur moi sa main droite en disant : « Ne crains pas, je suis le Premier et le Dernier, 18 le Vivant ; je fus mort, et me voici vivant pour les siècles des siècles [...]. »

FOL. 173

St John and the Twenty-Four Elders in heaven
Johannes und die vierundzwanzig Ältesten im Himmel
Saint Jean et les vingt-quatre Vieillards au ciel

Revelation 4:2–4 – 2 [...] a throne stood in heaven, with one seated on the throne. 3 And he who sat there had the appearance of jasper and carnelian, and around the throne was a rainbow that had the appearance of an emerald. 4 Around the throne were twenty-four thrones, and seated on the thrones were twenty-four elders, clothed in white garments, with golden crowns on their heads.

Offenbarung 4,2–4 – 2 [...] ein Thron stand im Himmel und auf dem Thron saß einer. 3 Und der da saß, war anzusehen wie der Stein Jaspis und Sarder; und ein Regenbogen war um den Thron, anzusehen wie ein Smaragd. 4 Und um den Thron waren vierundzwanzig Throne und auf den Thronen saßen vierundzwanzig Älteste, mit weißen Kleidern angetan, und hatten auf ihren Häuptern goldene Kronen.

Apocalypse 4:2–4 – 2 [...] un trône était dressé dans le ciel, et, siégeant sur le trône, Quelqu'un... 3 Celui qui siège est comme une vision de jaspe et de cornaline ; un arc-en-ciel autour du trône est comme une vision d'émeraude. 4 Vingt-quatre sièges entourent le trône, sur lesquels sont assis vingt-quatre Vieillards vêtus de blanc, avec des couronnes d'or sur leurs têtes.

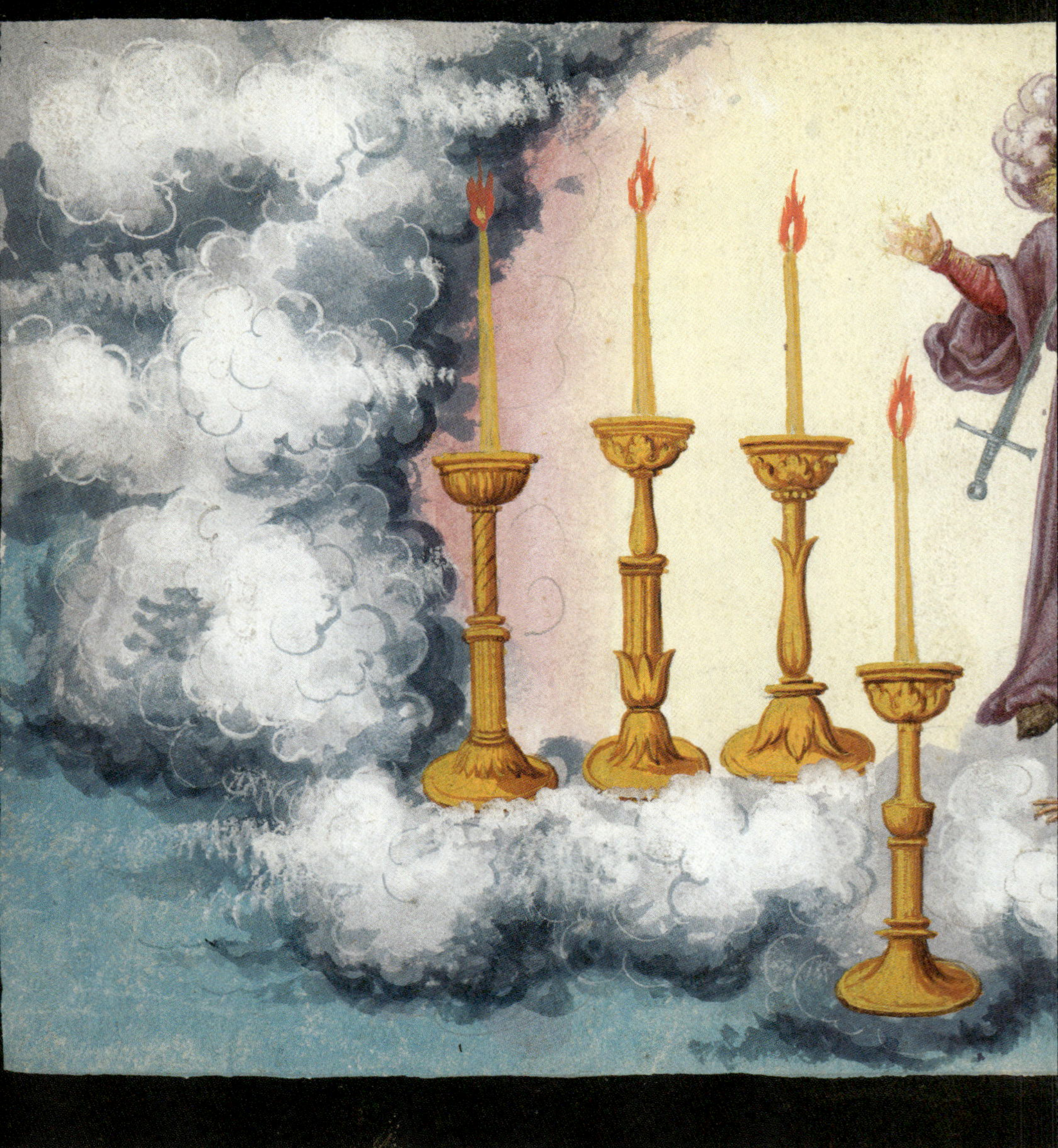

am ij capitel

Vnd ich wand mich vmb zu sehen nach der stim die mit mir redet / vnd als ich mich
der war eins menschen son gleich / der war an gethan mit einem kittel / vnnd
war weys wie woll vnd als der schnee vnd sein augen wie ein fewer fläme
vnd hat siben sterne in seiner rechten hand / vnnd aus seinem munde ging
ich in sahe fil ich zu seinen füssen als ein todter vnd er legt sein hant auff m
tod vnd sie ich bin lebondig von ewigkait zu ewigkait

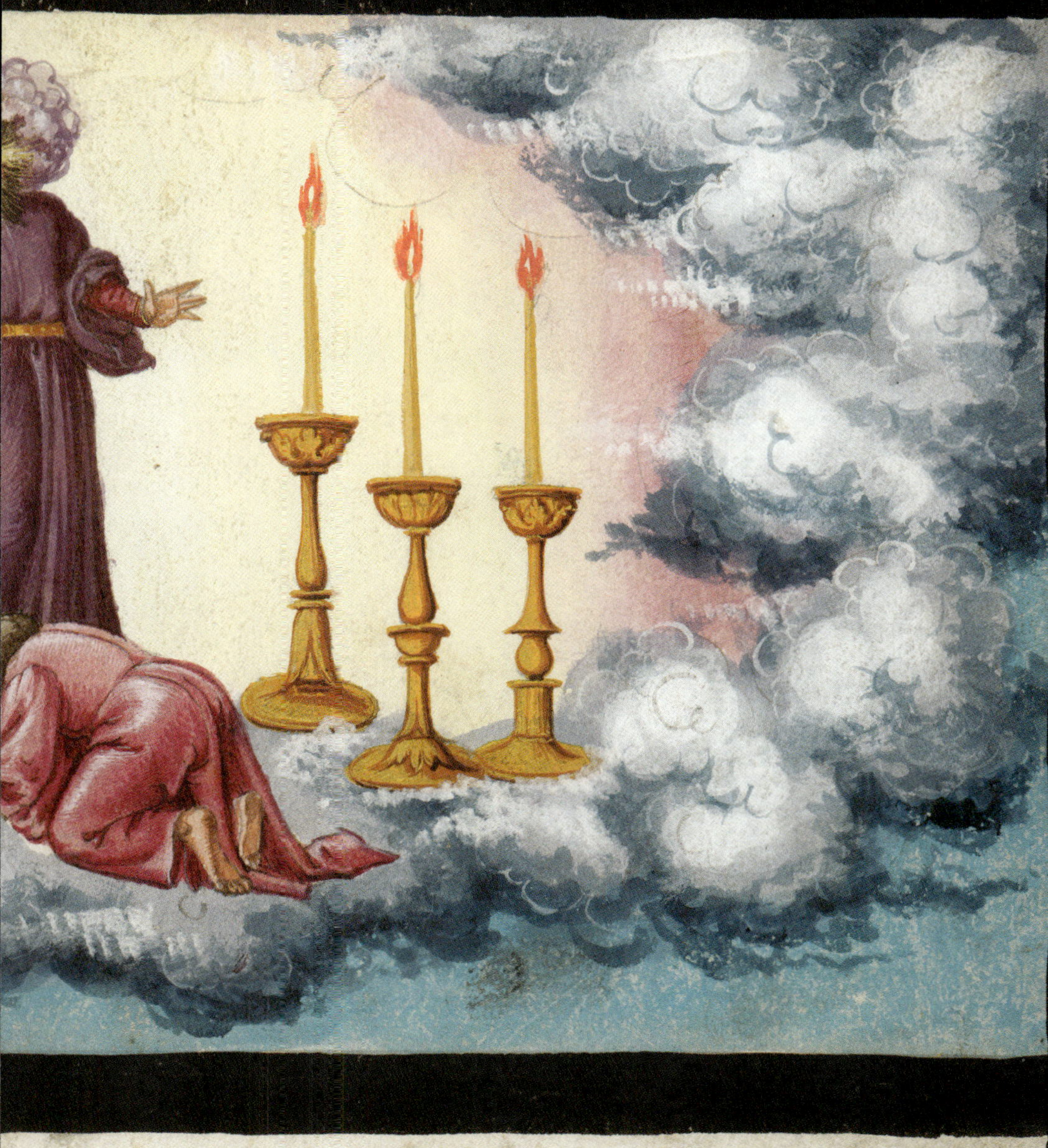

dt/ sahe ich siben gülde leuchter vnd miten vnder den guldenen leuchtern einen n
rtet vmb die brüste mit einem gülden gürtel/ sein haubt aber vnnd sein haar
ine füeß gleich wie ein glüend ertz vnnd sein stim wie groß wasser rauisch
scharpf zweyschneydig schwert vnd sein angesicht leuchtet wie die helle son vnd als
nd sprach förcht dich nit ich bin der erst vnd der letzt vnd der lebendige ich warr

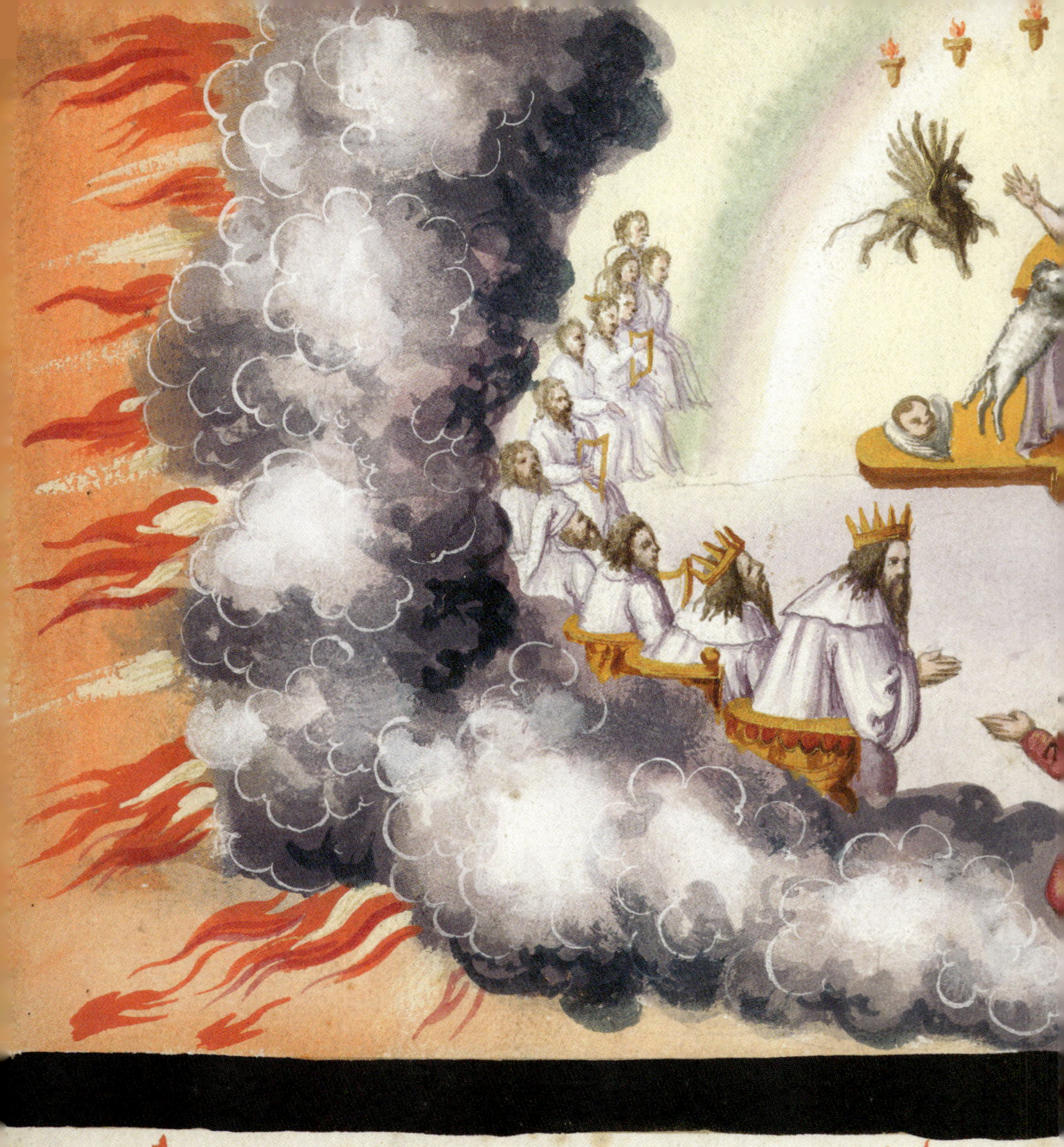

am iiii capitel

a Ain stůl war gesetzt im himmel vnnd auff dem stůl ward einer
vnnd ein regenbogen war vmb den stůl gleich anzůsehen wie
liiij vnnd auff den stůlen sassen vier vnnd zwainzig Eltis
güldene kronnen

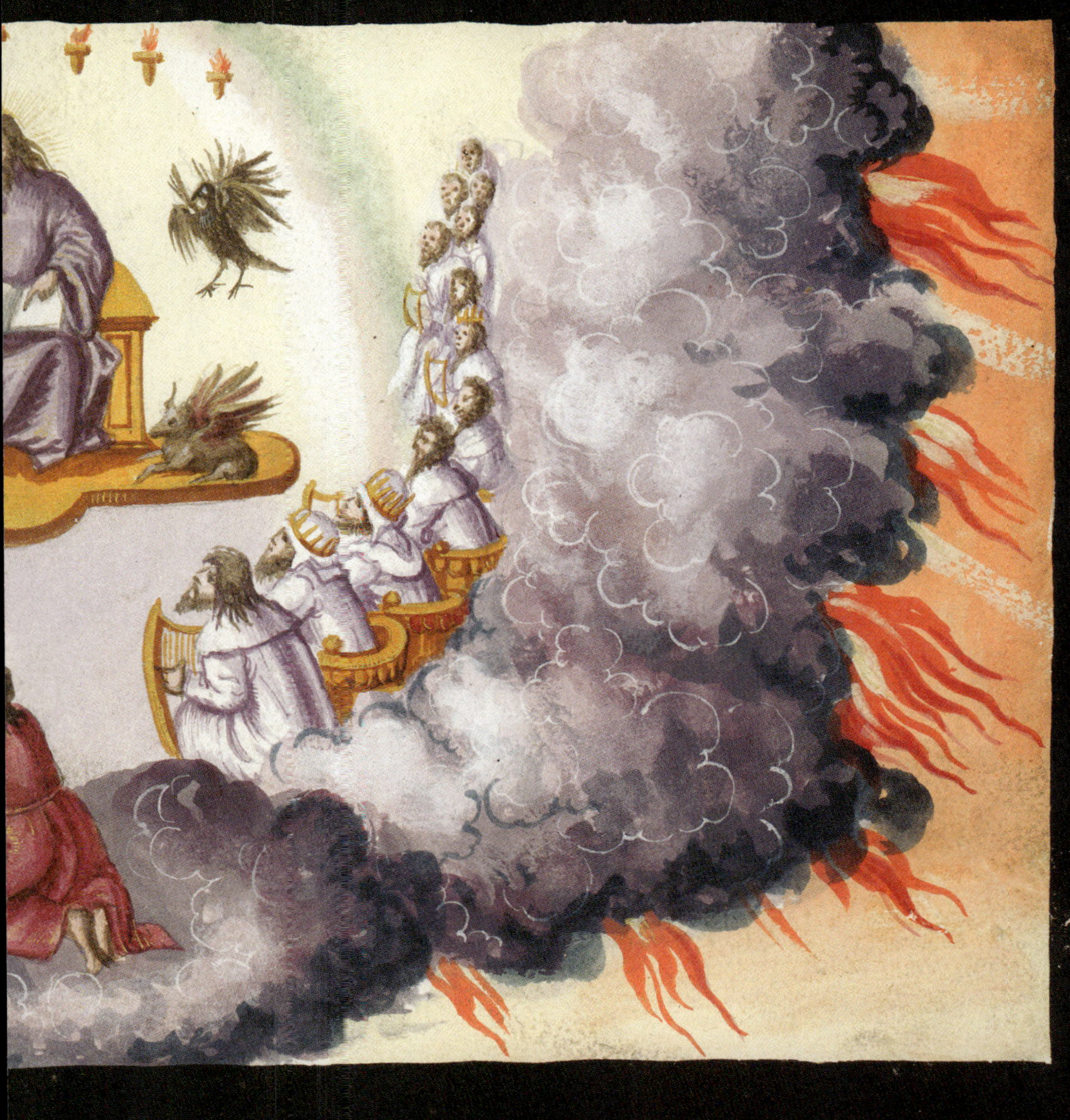

drauff sass war gleich an zusehen wie der stain Jaspis vnnd sardis:
Schmaragd vnnd vmb den stül waren vier vnnd zwainzig stüle
mit weissen klaidern angethan vnnd hatten auff iren haubten

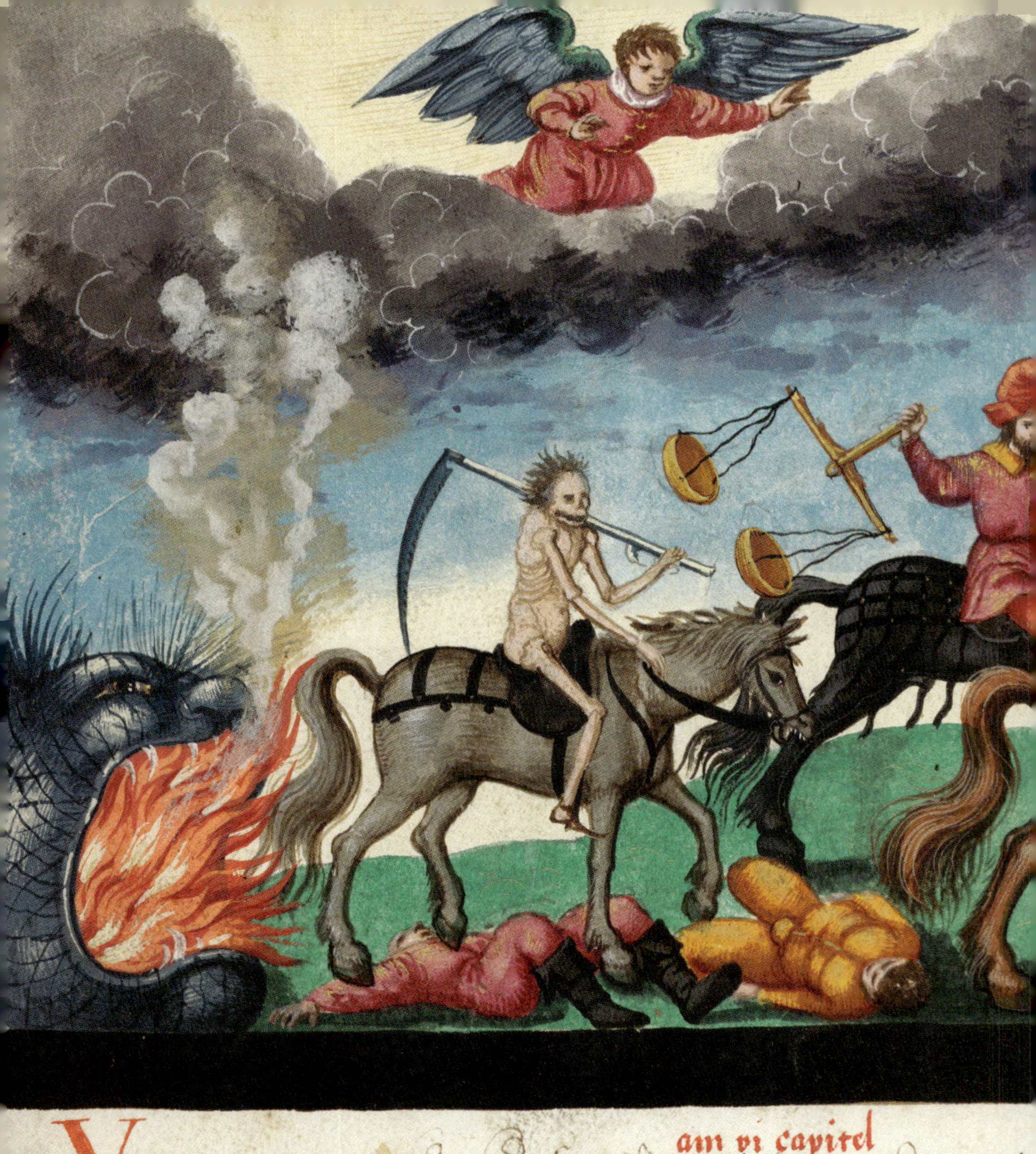

am vi capitel

4 Vnnd da es das dritte siegel auffthet horet ich das drit thier sagen kum vnd si
sass / ward gegeben dem frieden zu nemen von der Erden / vnnd das sie
5 vnnd da es das dritte siegel auffthet horet ich das dritte thier sagen ku
ein wage in seiner hand vnnd ich horet ein stimm mitten vnder den

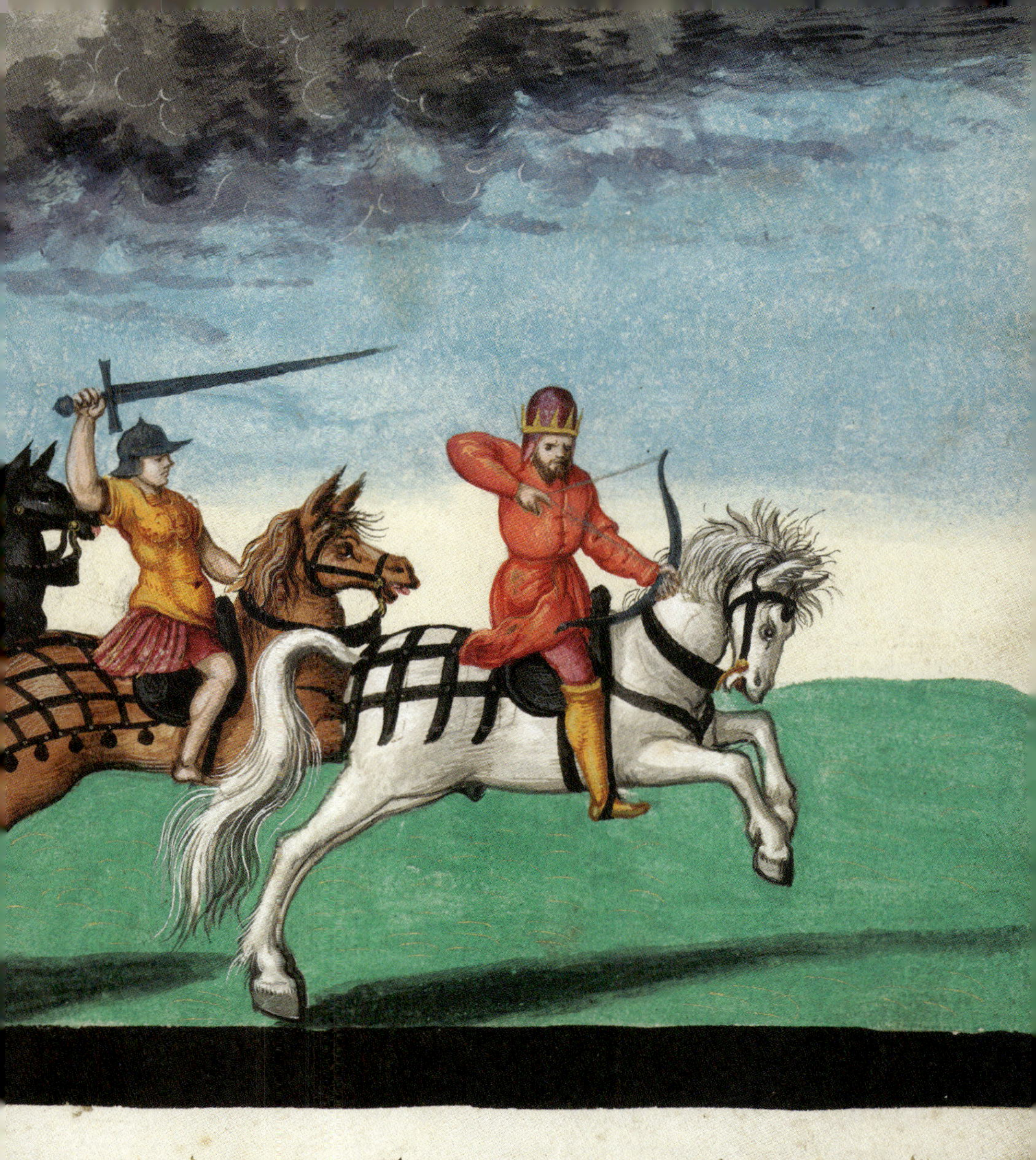

vnnd es ging aus ein ander pfert/ das war radt/ vnnd dem der darauff

vnnder einander er wurgten/ vnnd im ward ein groß schwert gegebenn

vnnd siehe zu vnnd ich sahe ein schwartz pfert vnnd der drauff saß het

thieren/ ein maß weitzen vmb ein pfennig vnnd drey maß gersten vmb

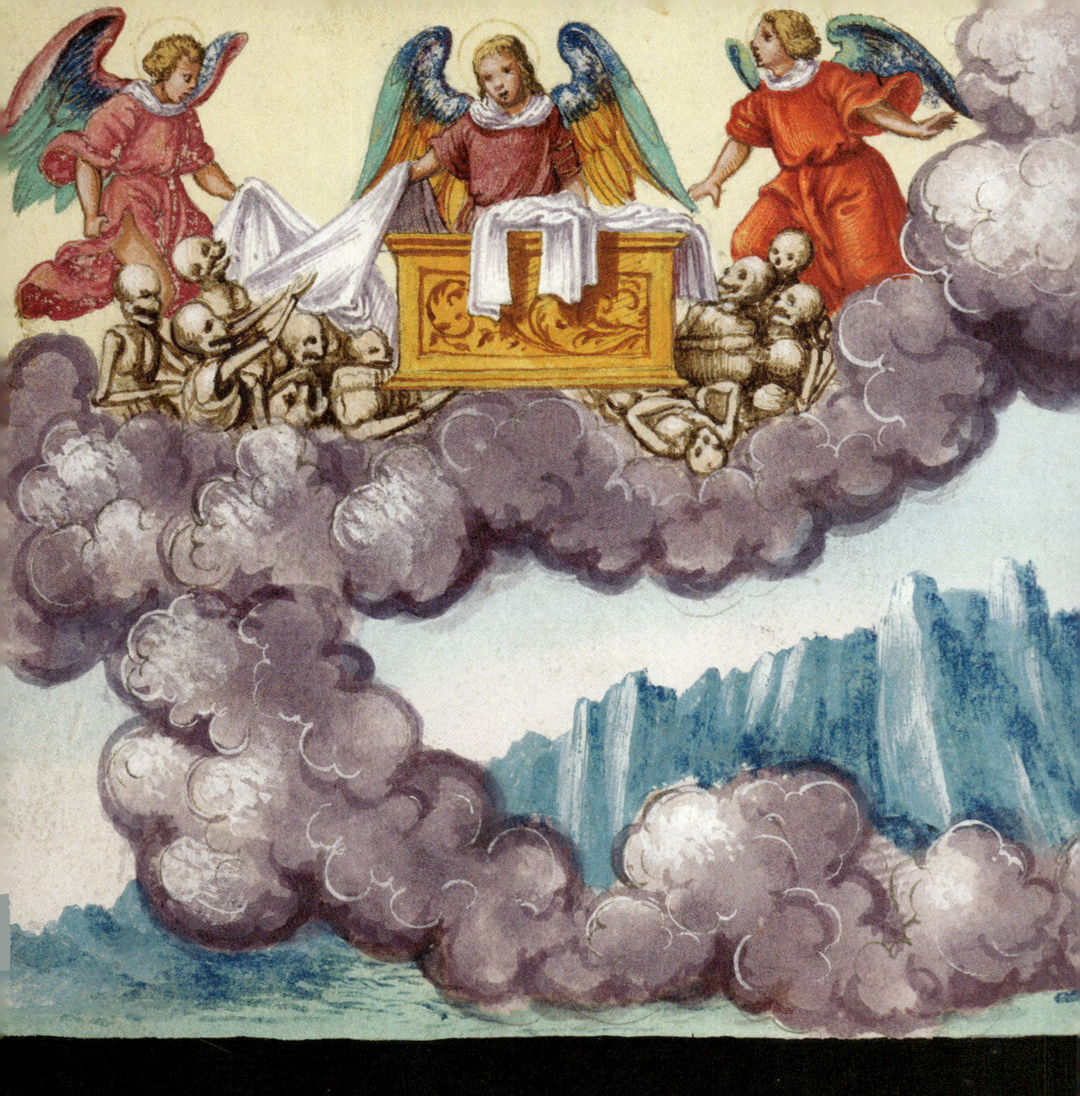

am vi capitel

Vnnd da es das funffter sygel auf thet sahe ich vnder dem altar die seelen de
willen das sie hatten vnnd sie schrien mit lautter stim vnnd sprache
blut an denen die auff erden wonen / vnnd inen wurden gegebe
noch ein kleine zeit bis das erfület wurden ire mit knecht v

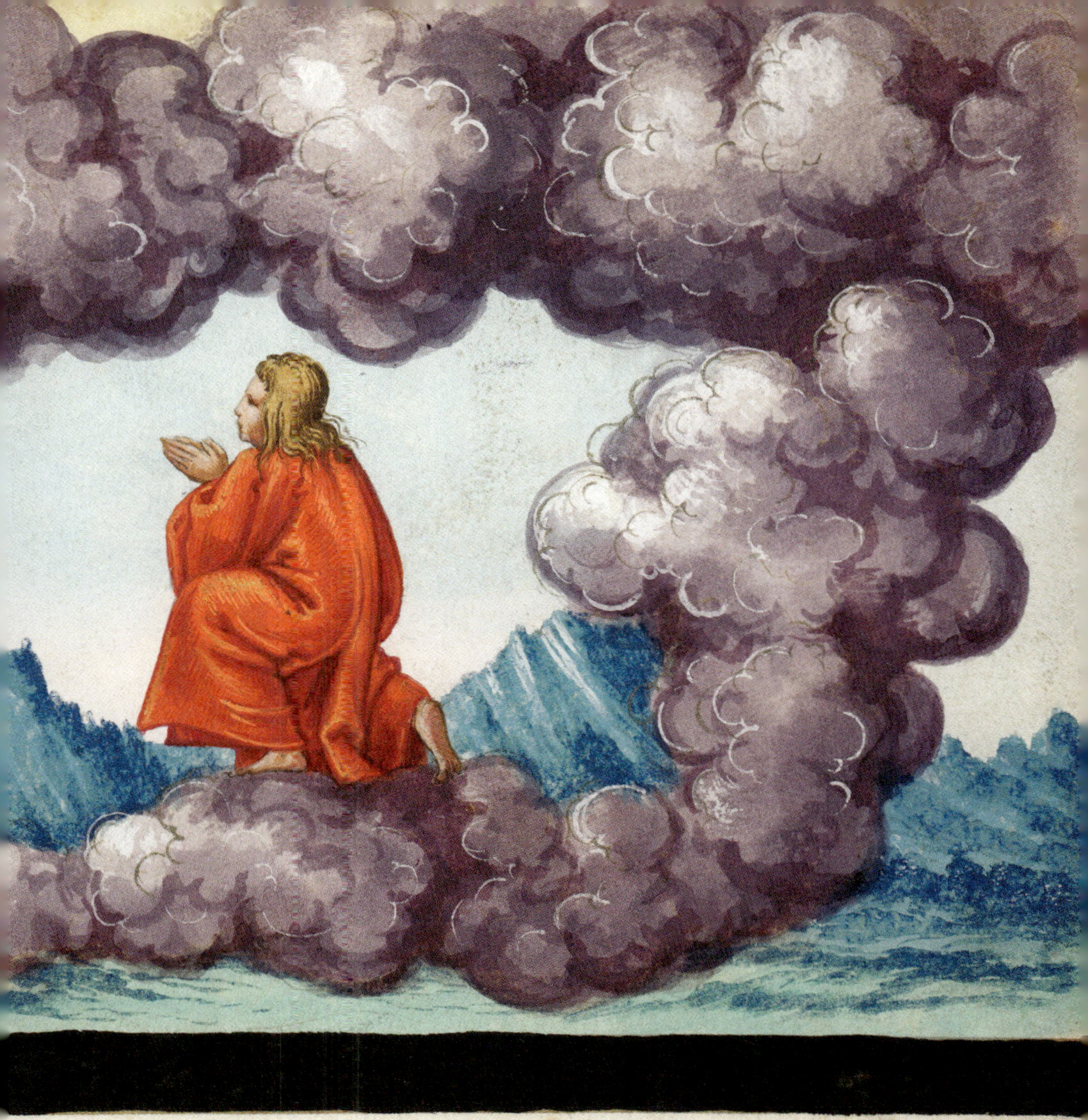

erwürget waren umb des wort Gottes willen unnd umb des zeügnus.
dü heyliger unnd warhafftiger wie lange richtestü unnd rechest nit unser.
nen yeglichem ein weisswadt unnd ward zu in gesagt das sie rügetenn.
brueder die auch sollen noch ertodtet werden gleich wie sie er-

FOL. 174

Four horsemen | Vier Reiter | Quatre cavaliers

Revelation 6:3–6 – 3 When he opened the second seal, I heard the second living creature say,
"Come!" 4 And out came another horse, bright red. Its rider was permitted to take peace from the
earth, so that people should slay one another, and he was given a great sword. 5 When he opened the
third seal, I heard the third living creature say, "Come!" And I looked, and behold, a black horse!
And its rider had a pair of scales in his hand. 6 And I heard what seemed to be a voice in the midst
of the four living creatures, saying, "A quart of wheat for a denarius, and three quarts of barley
for [...]."

Offenbarung 6,3–6 – 3 Und als es das zweite Siegel auftat, hörte ich die zweite Gestalt sagen:
Komm! 4 Und es kam heraus ein zweites Pferd, das war feuerrot. Und dem, der darauf saß, wurde
Macht gegeben, den Frieden von der Erde zu nehmen, dass sie sich untereinander umbrächten, und
ihm wurde ein großes Schwert gegeben. 5 Und als es das dritte Siegel auftat, hörte ich die dritte
Gestalt sagen: Komm! Und ich sah, und siehe, ein schwarzes Pferd. Und der darauf saß, hatte eine
Waage in seiner Hand. 6 Und ich hörte eine Stimme mitten unter den vier Gestalten sagen: Ein
Maß Weizen für einen Silbergroschen und drei Maß Gerste für [...].

Apocalypse 6:3–6 – 3 Lorsqu'il ouvrit le deuxième sceau, j'entendis le deuxième Vivant crier :
« Viens ! » 4 Alors surgit un autre cheval, rouge feu ; celui qui le montait, on lui donna de bannir la
paix hors de la terre, et de faire que l'on s'entr'égorgeât ; on lui donna une grande épée. 5 Lorsqu'il
ouvrit le troisième sceau, j'entendis le troisième Vivant crier : « Viens ! » Et voici qu'apparut à mes
yeux un cheval noir ; celui qui le montait tenait à la main une balance, 6 et j'entendis comme une
voix, du milieu des quatre Vivants, qui disait : « Un litre de blé pour un denier, trois litres d'orge
pour [...]. »

FOL. 175

Opening the fifth seal
Öffnung des fünften Siegels | Ouverture du cinquième sceau

Revelation 6:9–11 – 9 When he opened the fifth seal, I saw under the altar the souls of those who had
been slain for the word of God and for the witness they had borne. 10 They cried out with a loud
voice, "O Sovereign Lord, holy and true, how long before you will judge and avenge our blood on
those who dwell on the earth?" 11 Then they were each given a white robe and told to rest a little
longer, until the number of their fellow servants and their brothers should be complete, who were
to be killed as they themselves had been.

Offenbarung 6,9–11 – 9 Und als es das fünfte Siegel auftat, sah ich unten am Altar die Seelen
derer, die umgebracht worden waren um des Wortes Gottes und um ihres Zeugnisses willen.
10 Und sie schrien mit lauter Stimme: Herr, du Heiliger und Wahrhaftiger, wie lange richtest du
nicht und rächst nicht unser Blut an denen, die auf der Erde wohnen? 11 Und ihnen wurde gegeben
einem jeden ein weißes Gewand, und ihnen wurde gesagt, dass sie ruhen müssten noch eine kleine
Zeit, bis vollzählig dazukämen ihre Mitknechte und Brüder, die auch noch getötet werden sollten
wie sie.

Apocalypse 6:9–11 – 9 Lorsqu'il ouvrit le cinquième sceau, je vis sous l'autel les âmes de ceux qui
furent égorgés pour la Parole de Dieu et le témoignage qu'ils avaient rendu. 10 Ils crièrent d'une
voix puissante : « Jusques à quand, Maître saint et vrai, tarderas-tu à faire justice, à tirer vengeance
de notre sang sur les habitants de la terre ? » 11 Alors on leur donna à chacun une robe blanche en
leur disant de patienter encore un peu, le temps que fussent au complet leurs compagnons de ser-
vice et leurs frères qui doivent être mis à mort comme eux.

FOL. 176

Opening the sixth seal

Öffnung des sechsten Siegels | Ouverture du sixième sceau

Revelation 6:12–14 – 12 When he opened the sixth seal, I looked, and behold, there was a great earthquake, and the sun became black as sackcloth, the full moon became like blood, 13 and the stars of
the sky fell to the earth as the fig tree sheds its winter fruit when shaken by a gale. 14 The sky van-
ished like a scroll that is being rolled up, and every mountain and island was removed from its place.

Offenbarung 6,12–14 – 12 Und ich sah: Als es das sechste Siegel auftat, da geschah ein großes
Erdbeben, und die Sonne wurde finster wie ein schwarzer Sack, und der ganze Mond wurde wie
Blut, 13 und die Sterne des Himmels fielen auf die Erde, wie ein Feigenbaum seine Feigen abwirft,
wenn er von starkem Wind bewegt wird. 14 Und der Himmel wich wie eine Schriftrolle, die zusam-
mengerollt wird, und alle Berge und Inseln wurden wegbewegt von ihrem Ort.

Apocalypse 6:12–14 – 12 Et ma vision se poursuivit. Lorsqu'il ouvrit le sixième sceau, alors il se fit
un violent tremblement de terre, et le soleil devint noir comme une étoffe de crin, et la lune devint
tout entière comme du sang, 13 et les astres du ciel s'abattirent sur la terre comme les figues avortées
que projette un figuier tordu par la tempête, 14 et le ciel disparut comme un livre qu'on roule, et les
monts et les îles s'arrachèrent de leur place.

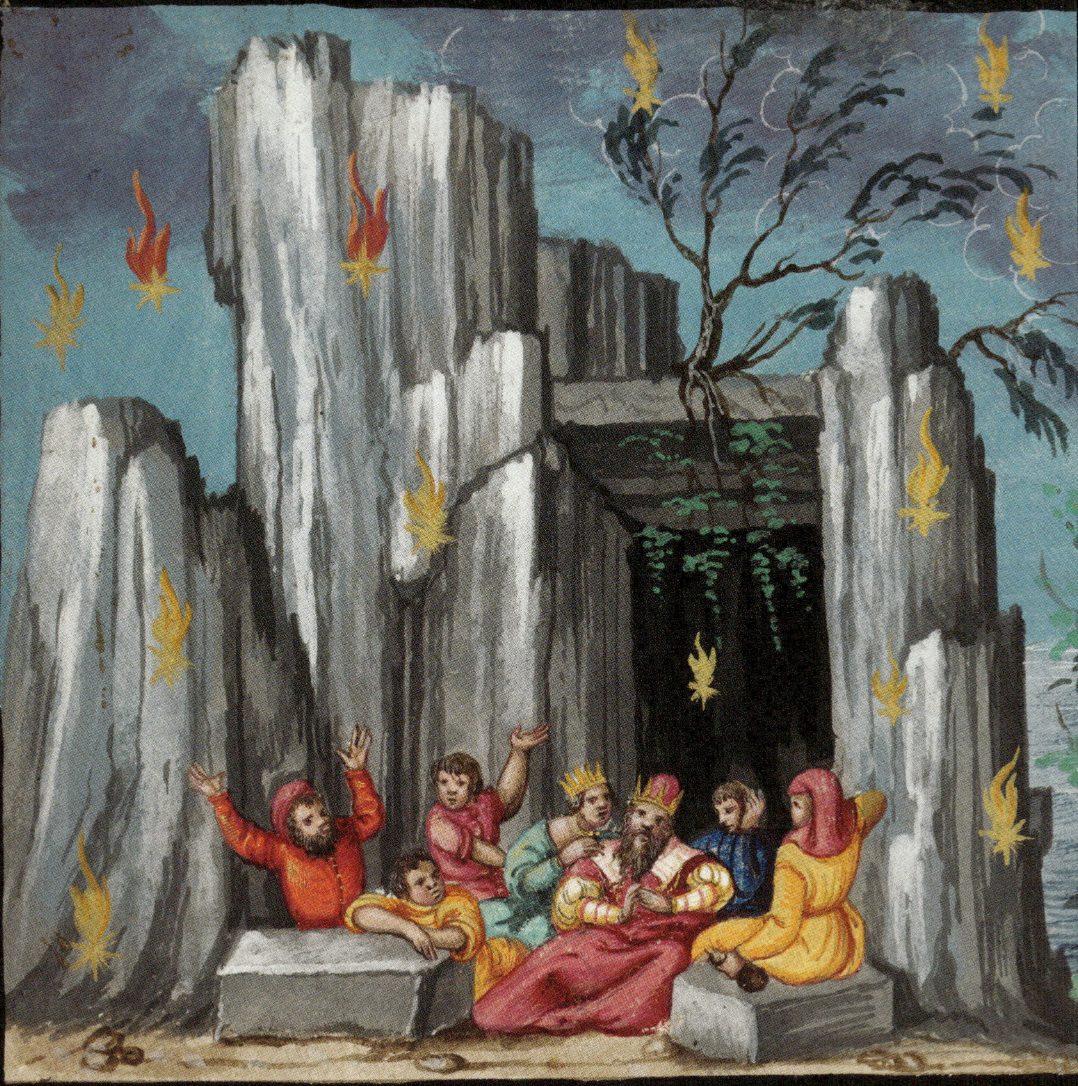

am vi capitel

Vnnd ich sahe das es das sechste siegel auff thet vnnd siehe da war

vnnd der mon ward wie blůt vnnd die stern des hiemels fielen au

dem grosen wind beweget wirt vnnd der hiemel entweich wie e

en orten

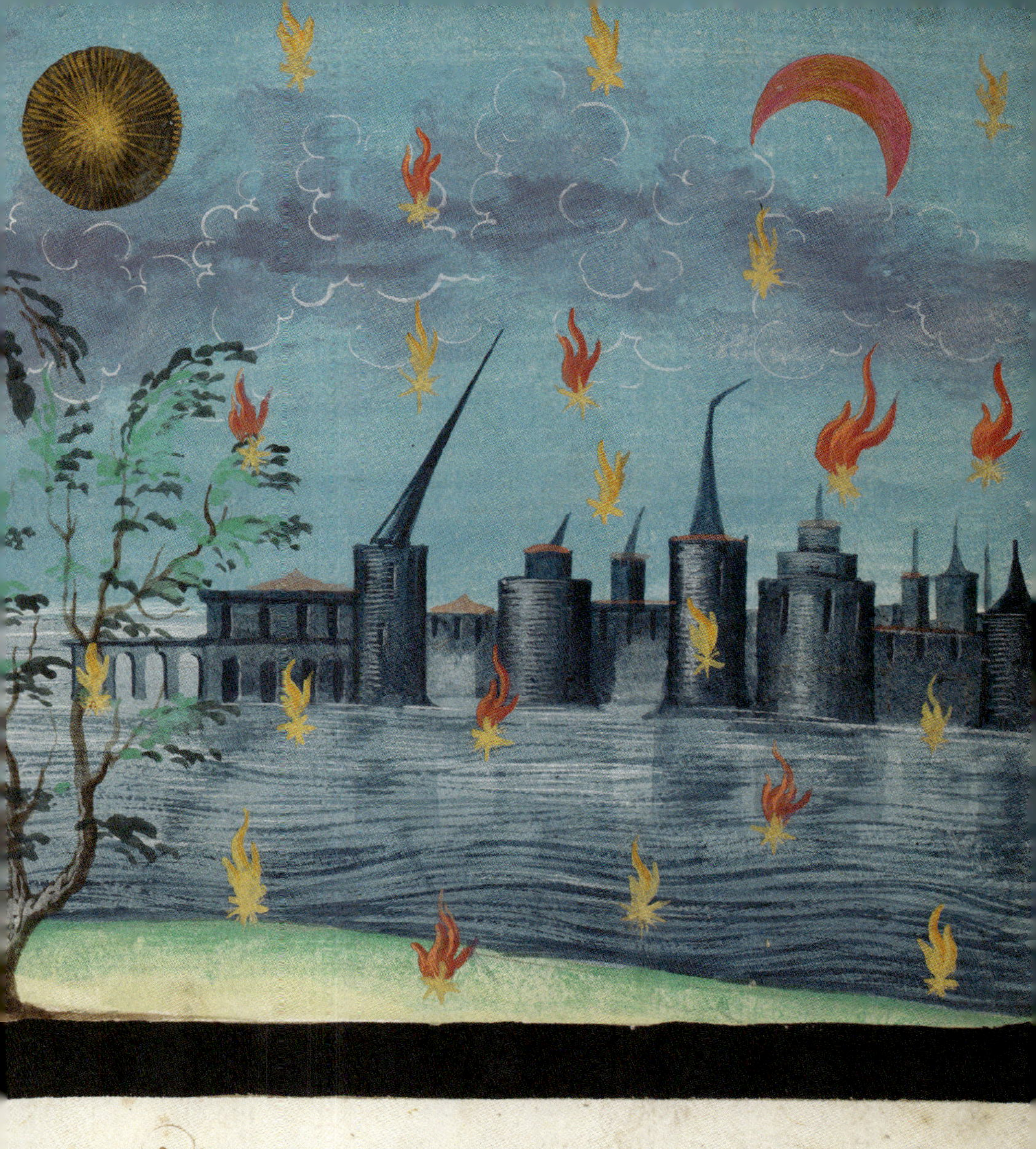

grosses erdbeben vnnd die sonne ward schwartz wie härin sack:
erden/gleich wie ein feigenbaum sein feigen abwirfft wen er von
ngewickelt büch/ vnnd alle berge vnnd insülen würden beweget aus ir:

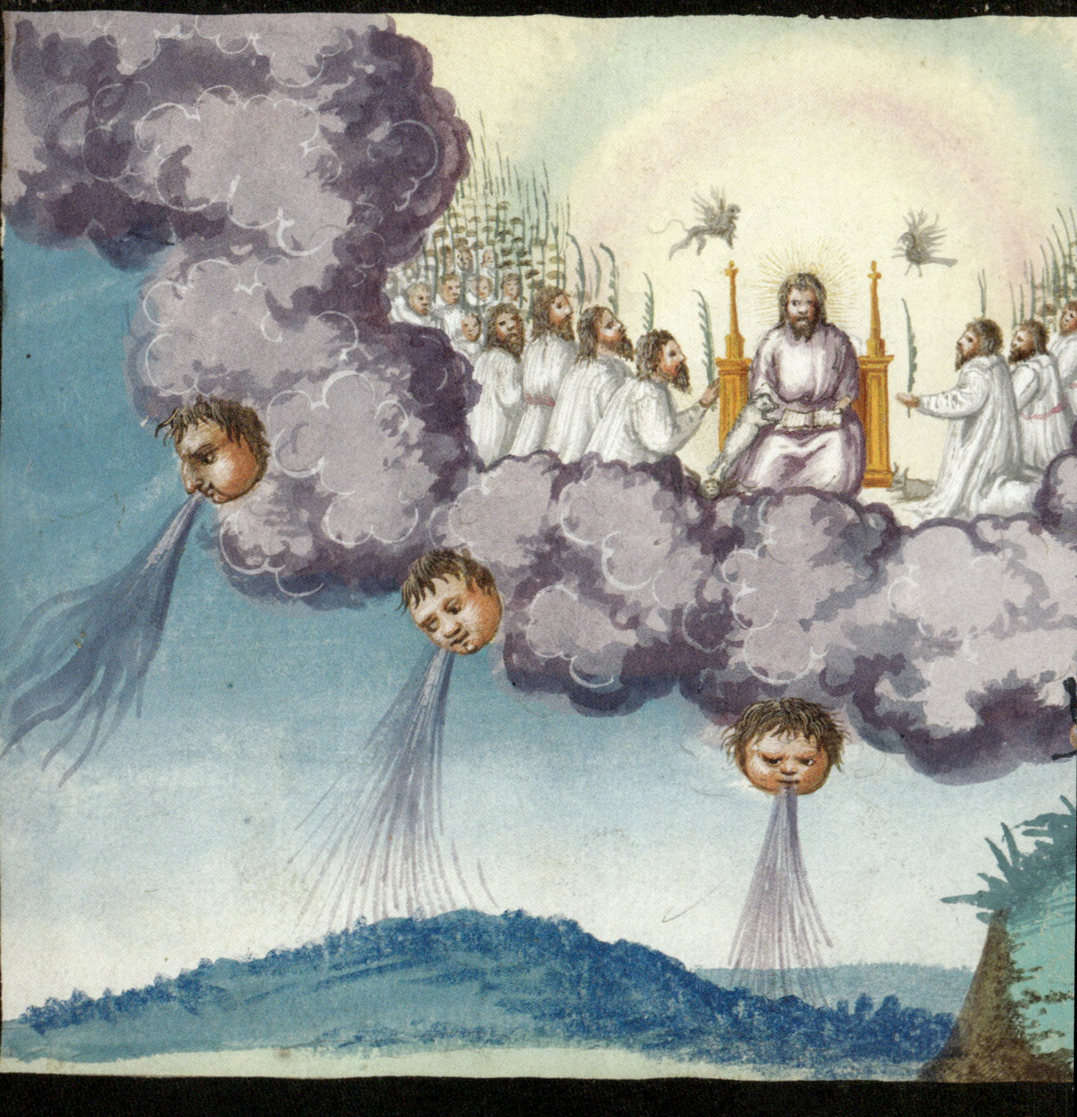

am vii capitel

Vnnd darnach sahe ich vier engel stehen aüff den vier ecken der erden ai
baum vnnd sahe ein andern engel aüff steigen von der sonnen
liij grosser stime zü den vier engeln/ welchen geben ist zü beschedige
das meer noch die beüme bis das wir ver siegeln die knech

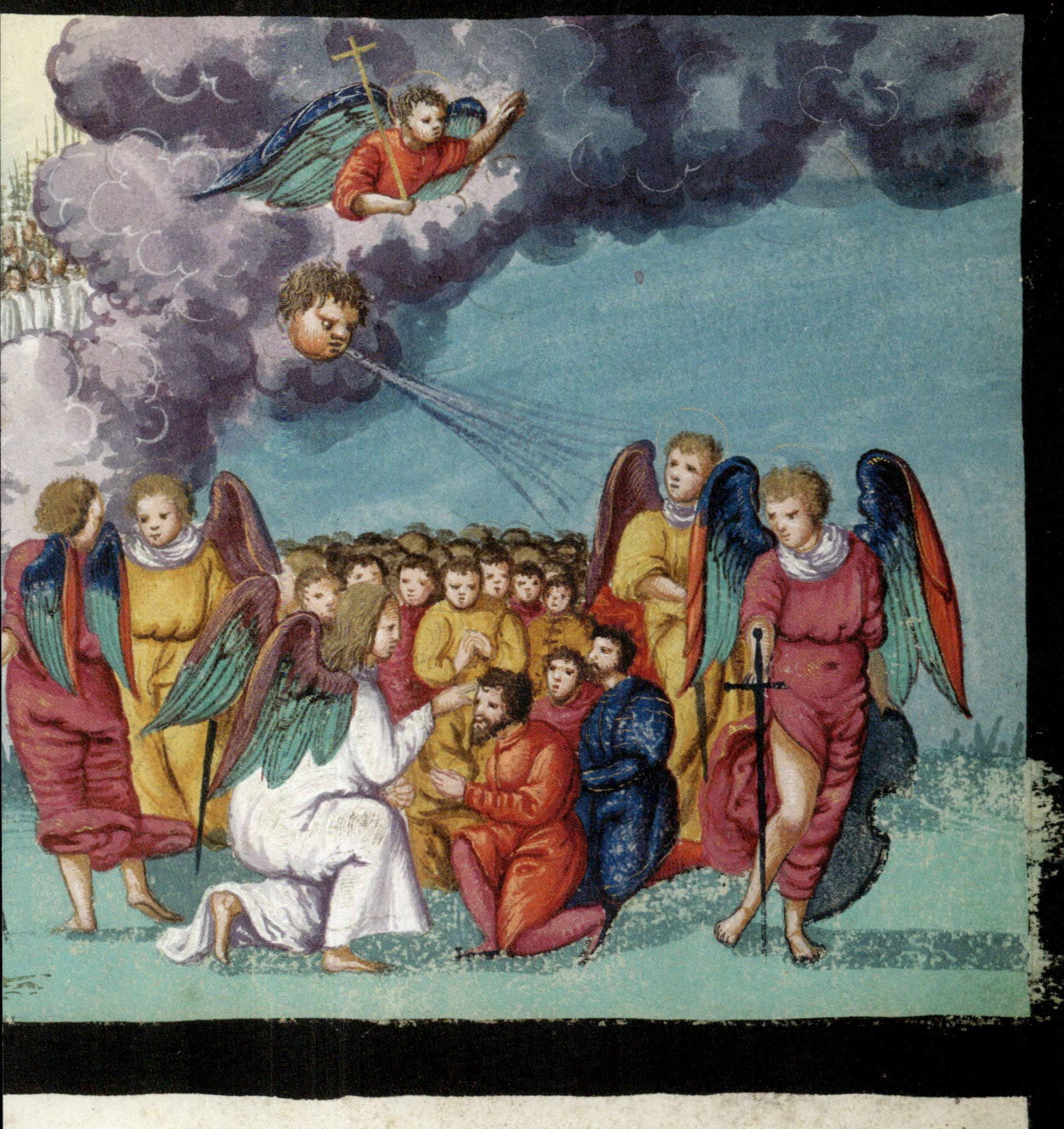

as kain wind vber die erden blies noch vber das meer noch vber ennigen.
fgang der hatte das warzeichen des lebendigen gottes vnnd schray mit
e erden vnnd das meer vnnd er sprach beschediget die erden nit noch
nsers gottes an iren stirnen

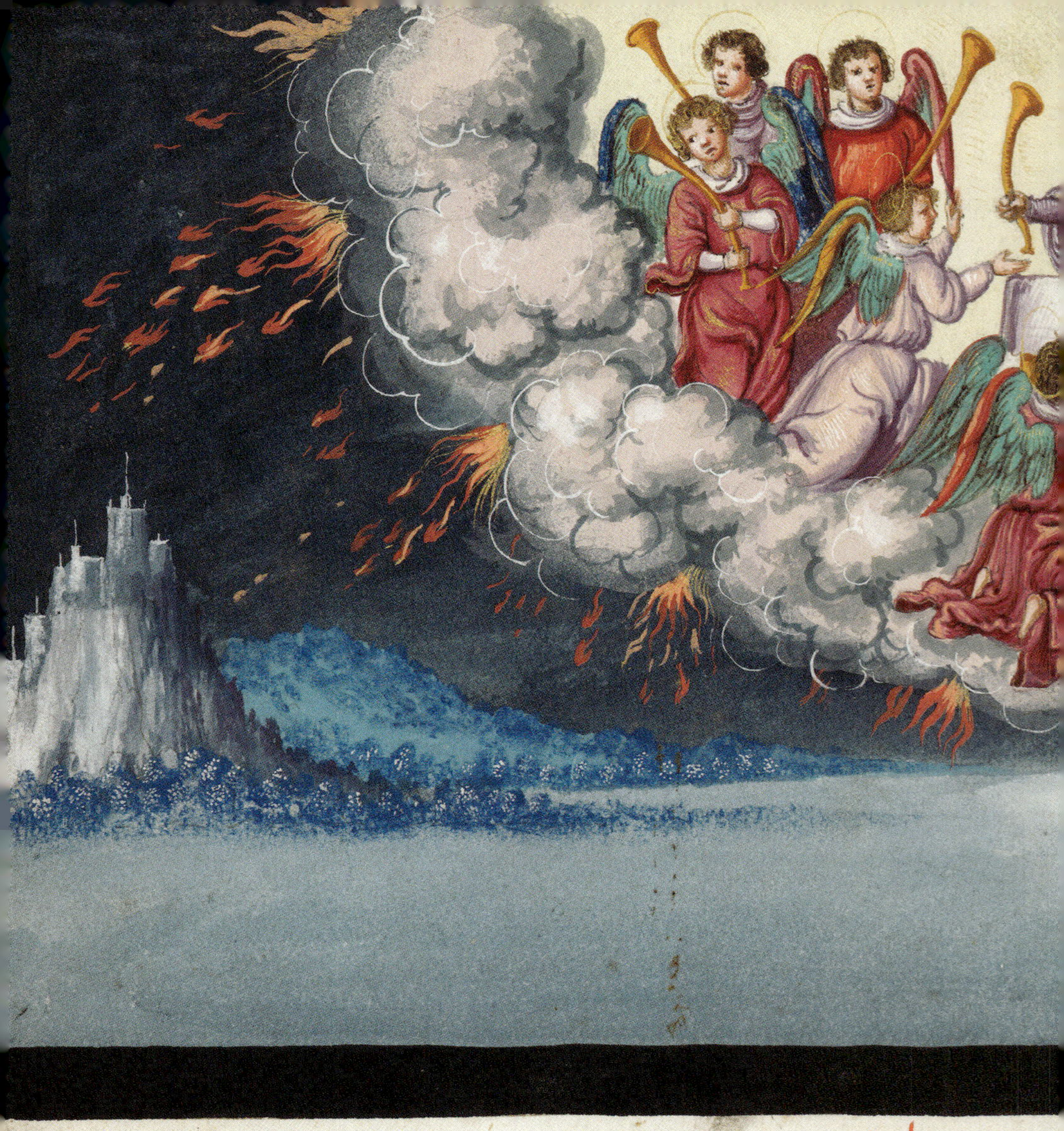

am viii capitel

Dn da es das siebend siegel auff thet/ ward ein stille in dem Himel bei einer
gegeben/ vnd ein ander engel kam vnnd trat bey dem altar/ vnnd hat
den gebeten aller heiligen auff den altar vor dem stul/ vnnd der rauch des
gott/ vnnd der engel nam das reuchfaß/ vnnd fulet es mit feiwer vom
vnnd erdbebung

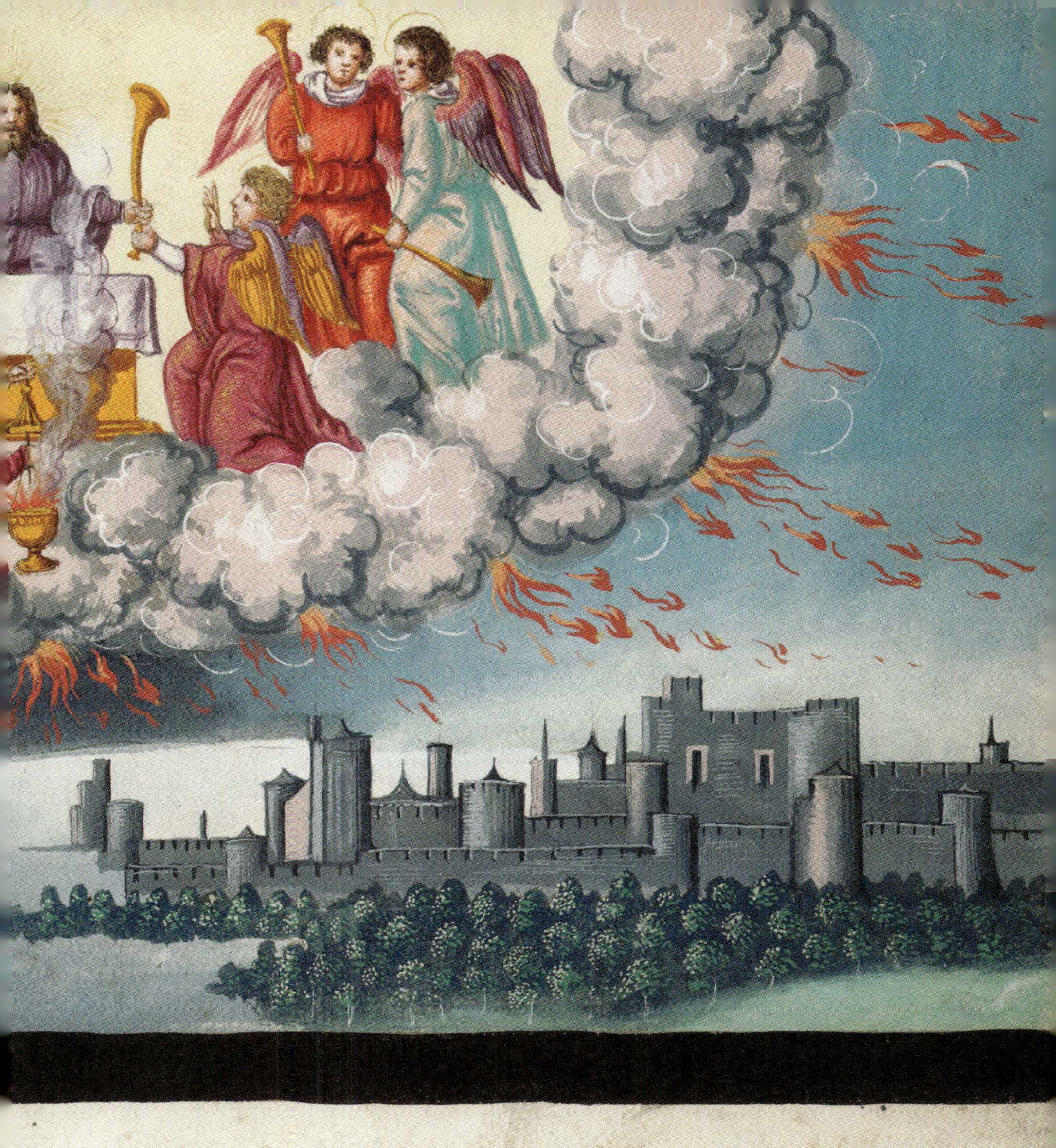

en stunde vnnd ich sahe syben engel/ die tratten für gott/ vnnd sieben posaunen
guldenen reüch fass vnnd jhm ward vil reüchwerckes gegeben/ das er gebe vonn
wercks von den gebeten der hailigen gieng auff von der handt des engels vor
r vnnd warffs auff die erden/ vnnd dagesschahen stimmen vnd donner vnnd blitz

FOL. 177

Four angels staying the winds and marking the chosen ones
Vier Engel halten die Winde fest und kennzeichnen die Auserwählten
Quatre Anges retiennent les vents et marquent les élus

Revelation 7:1–3 – 1 After this I saw four angels standing at the four corners of the earth, holding back the four winds of the earth, that no wind might blow on earth or sea or against any tree.
2 Then I saw another angel ascending from the rising of the sun, with the seal of the living God, and he called with a loud voice to the four angels who had been given power to harm earth and sea,
3 saying, "Do not harm the earth or the sea or the trees, until we have sealed the servants of our God on their foreheads."

Offenbarung 7,1–3 – 1 Danach sah ich vier Engel stehen an den vier Ecken der Erde, die hielten die vier Winde der Erde fest, damit kein Wind über die Erde blase noch über das Meer noch über irgendeinen Baum. 2 Und ich sah einen andern Engel aufsteigen vom Aufgang der Sonne her, der hatte das Siegel des lebendigen Gottes und rief mit großer Stimme zu den vier Engeln, denen Macht gegeben war, der Erde und dem Meer Schaden zu tun: 3 Tut der Erde und dem Meer und den Bäumen keinen Schaden, bis wir versiegeln die Knechte unseres Gottes an ihren Stirnen.

Apocalypse 7:1–3 – 1 Après quoi je vis quatre Anges, debout aux quatre coins de la terre, retenant les quatre vents de la terre pour qu'il ne soufflât point de vent, ni sur la terre, ni sur la mer, ni sur aucun arbre. 2 Puis je vis un autre Ange monter de l'orient, portant le sceau du Dieu vivant ; il cria d'une voix puissante aux quatre Anges auxquels il fut donné de malmener la terre et la mer : 3 « Attendez, pour malmener la terre et la mer et les arbres, que nous ayons marqué au front les serviteurs de notre Dieu. »

FOL. 178

The seven trumpets given to the angels
Die sieben Posaunen werden den Engeln übergeben
Les sept trompettes sont remises aux Anges

Revelation 8:1–5 – 1 When the Lamb opened the seventh seal, there was silence in heaven for about half an hour. 2 Then I saw the seven angels who stand before God, and seven trumpets were given to them. 3 And another angel came and stood at the altar with a golden censer, and he was given much incense to offer with the prayers of all the saints on the golden altar before the throne, 4 and the smoke of the incense, with the prayers of the saints, rose before God from the hand of the angel.
5 Then the angel took the censer and filled it with fire from the altar and threw it on the earth, and there were peals of thunder, rumblings, flashes of lightning and an earthquake.

Offenbarung 8,1–5 – 1 Und als das Lamm das siebte Siegel auftat, entstand eine Stille im Himmel […] 2 Und ich sah die sieben Engel, die vor Gott stehen, ihnen wurden sieben Posaunen gegeben.
3 Und ein anderer Engel kam, trat an den Altar und hatte ein goldenes Räuchergefäß; ihm wurde viel Räucherwerk gegeben, dass er es darbringe mit den Gebeten aller Heiligen auf dem goldenen Altar. 4 Und der Rauch des Räucherwerks stieg mit den Gebeten der Heiligen von der Hand des Engels hinauf vor Gott. 5 Und der Engel nahm das Räuchergefäß und füllte es mit Feuer vom Altar und schüttete es auf die Erde. Und da geschahen Donner und Stimmen und Blitze und Erdbeben.

Apocalypse 8:1–5 – 1 Et lorsque l'Agneau ouvrit le septième sceau, il se fit un silence dans le ciel, environ une demi-heure. 2 Et je vis les sept Anges qui se tiennent devant Dieu ; on leur remit sept trompettes. 3 Un autre Ange vint alors se placer près de l'autel, muni d'une pelle en or. On lui donna beaucoup de parfums pour qu'il les offrît, avec les prières de tous les saints, sur l'autel d'or placé devant le trône. 4 Et, de la main de l'Ange, la fumée des parfums s'éleva devant Dieu, avec les prières des saints. 5 Puis l'Ange saisit la pelle et l'emplit du feu de l'autel qu'il jeta sur la terre. Ce furent alors des tonnerres, des voix et des éclairs, et tout trembla.

FOL. 179

The first angel blowing his trumpet

Der erste Engel bläst seine Posaune | Le premier Ange sonne sa trompette

Revelation 8:6–7 – 6 Now the seven angels who had the seven trumpets prepared to blow them. 7 The first angel blew his trumpet, and there followed hail and fire, mixed with blood, and these were thrown upon the earth And a third of the earth was burned up, and a third of the trees were burned up, and all green grass was burned up.

Offenbarung 8,6–7 – 6 Und die sieben Engel mit den sieben Posaunen hatten sich gerüstet zu blasen. 7 Und der erste blies seine Posaune; und es kam Hagel und Feuer, mit Blut vermengt, und fiel auf die Erde; und der dritte Teil der Erde verbrannte, und der dritte Teil der Bäume verbrannte, und alles grüne Gras verbrannte.

Apocalypse 8:6–7 – 6 Les sept Anges aux sept trompettes s'apprêtèrent à sonner. 7 Et le premier sonna... Il y eut alors de la grêle et du feu mêlés de sang qui furent jetés sur la terre : et le tiers de la terre fut consumé, et le tiers des arbres fut consumé, et toute herbe verte fut consumée.

FOL. 180

The third angel blowing his trumpet

Der dritte Engel bläst seine Posaune | Le troisième Ange sonne sa trompette

Revelation 8:10–11 – 10 The third angel blew his trumpet, and a great star fell from heaven, blazing like a torch, and it fell on a third of the rivers and on the springs of water. 11 The name of the star is Wormwood. A third of the waters became wormwood, and many people died from the water, because it had been made bitter.

Offenbarung 8,10–11 – 10 Und der dritte Engel blies seine Posaune; und es fiel ein großer Stern vom Himmel, der brannte wie eine Fackel und fiel auf den dritten Teil der Wasserströme und auf die Wasserquellen. 11 Und der Name des Sterns heißt Wermut. Und der dritte Teil der Wasser wurde zu Wermut, und viele Menschen starben von den Wassern, weil sie bitter geworden waren.

Apocalypse 8:10–11 – 10 Et le troisième Ange sonna... Alors tomba du ciel un grand astre, brûlant comme une torche. Il tomba sur le tiers des fleuves et sur les sources ; 11 l'astre se nomme « Absinthe » : le tiers des eaux se changea en absinthe, et bien des gens moururent, de ces eaux devenues amères.

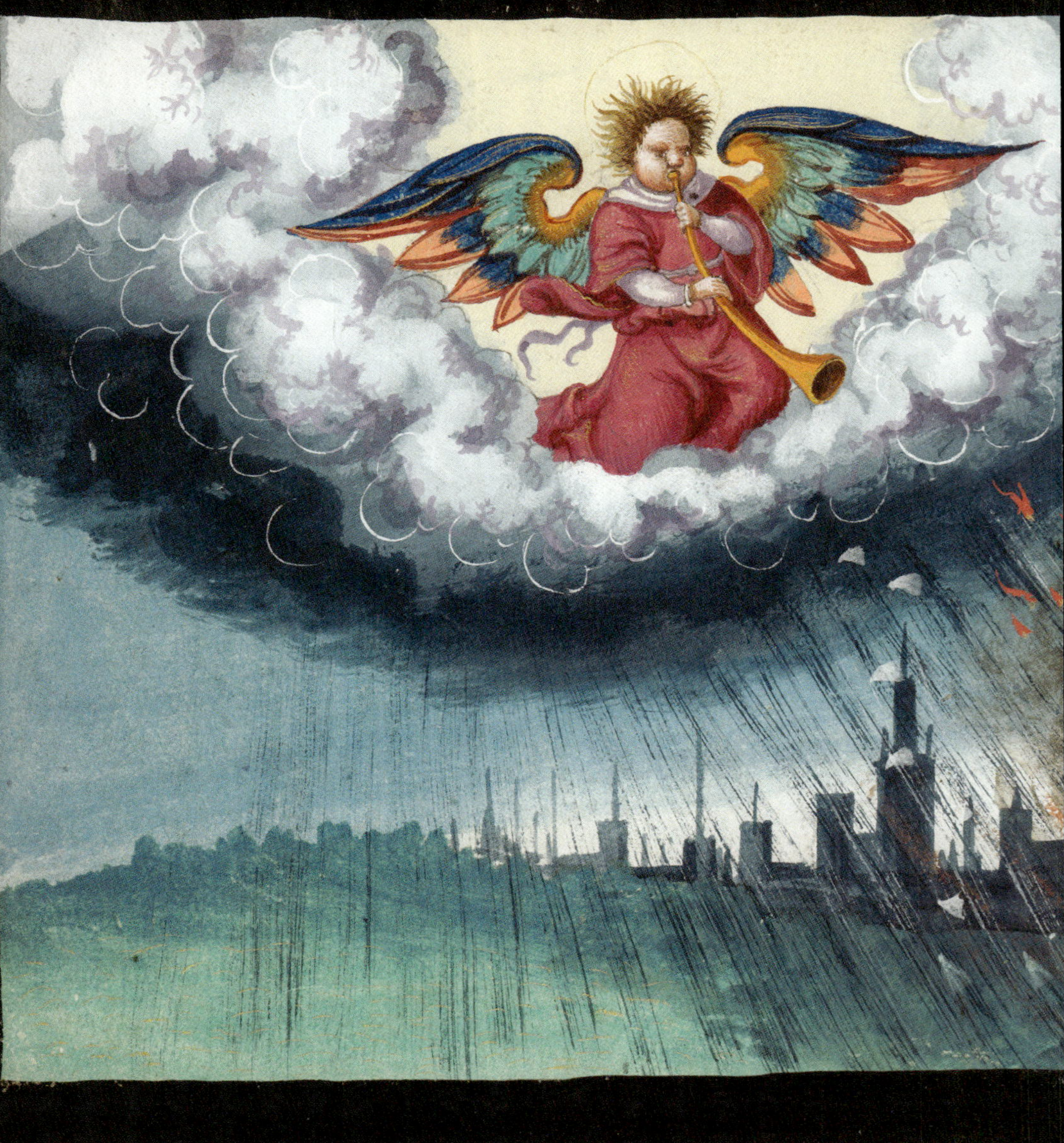

Vam viii capitel

Vnnd die ſieben engel mit den ſieben poſaunen hatten ſ

vnnd es waſs ein hagel vnnd fewer mit blut gemeng

verbrante / vnnd alles grüenne graſs verbrante

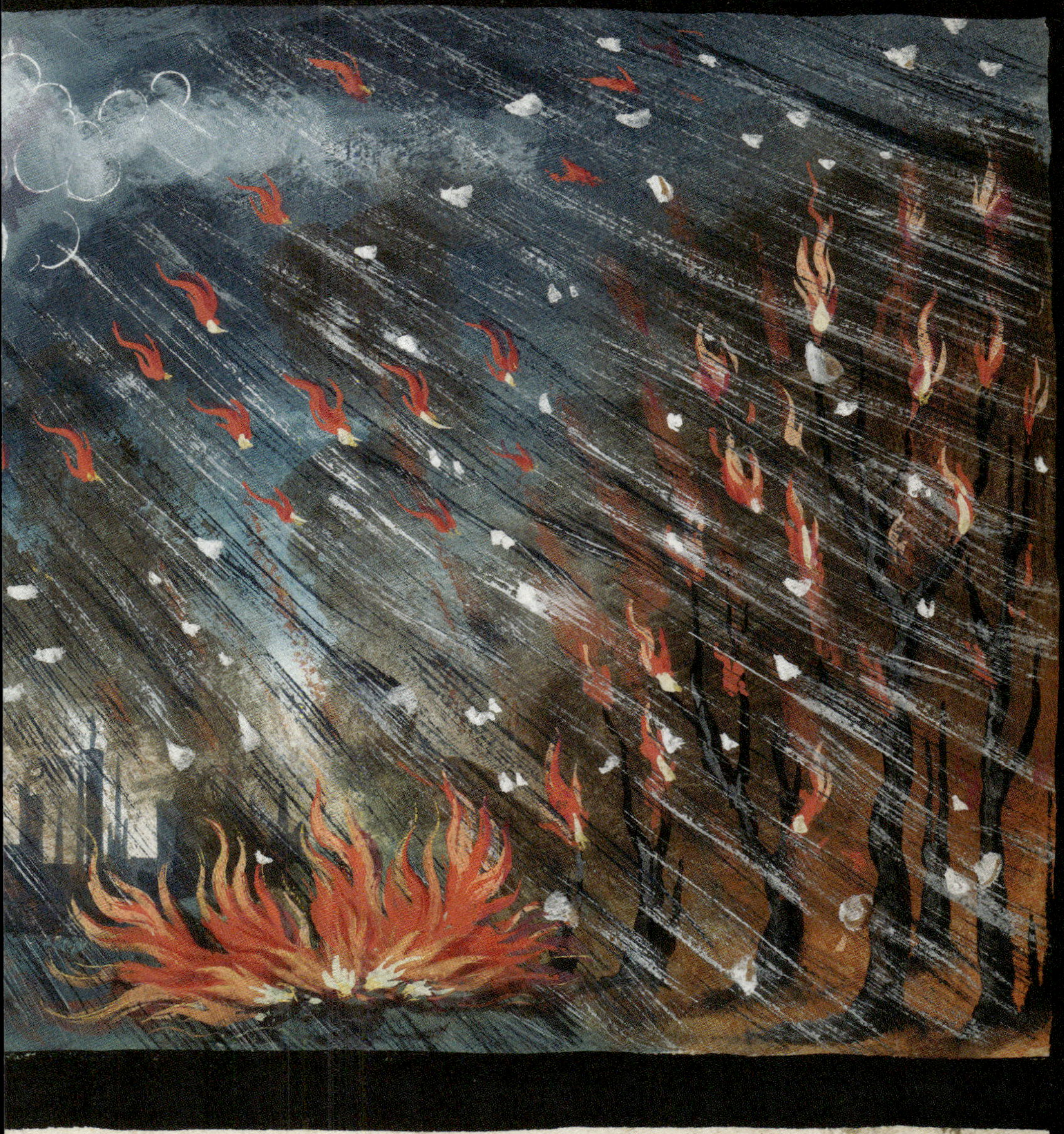

raitter zů posaunen: vnnd der erst engel posaunete:

vnnd fiel auff erden: vnnd das dritte tail der bäumes:

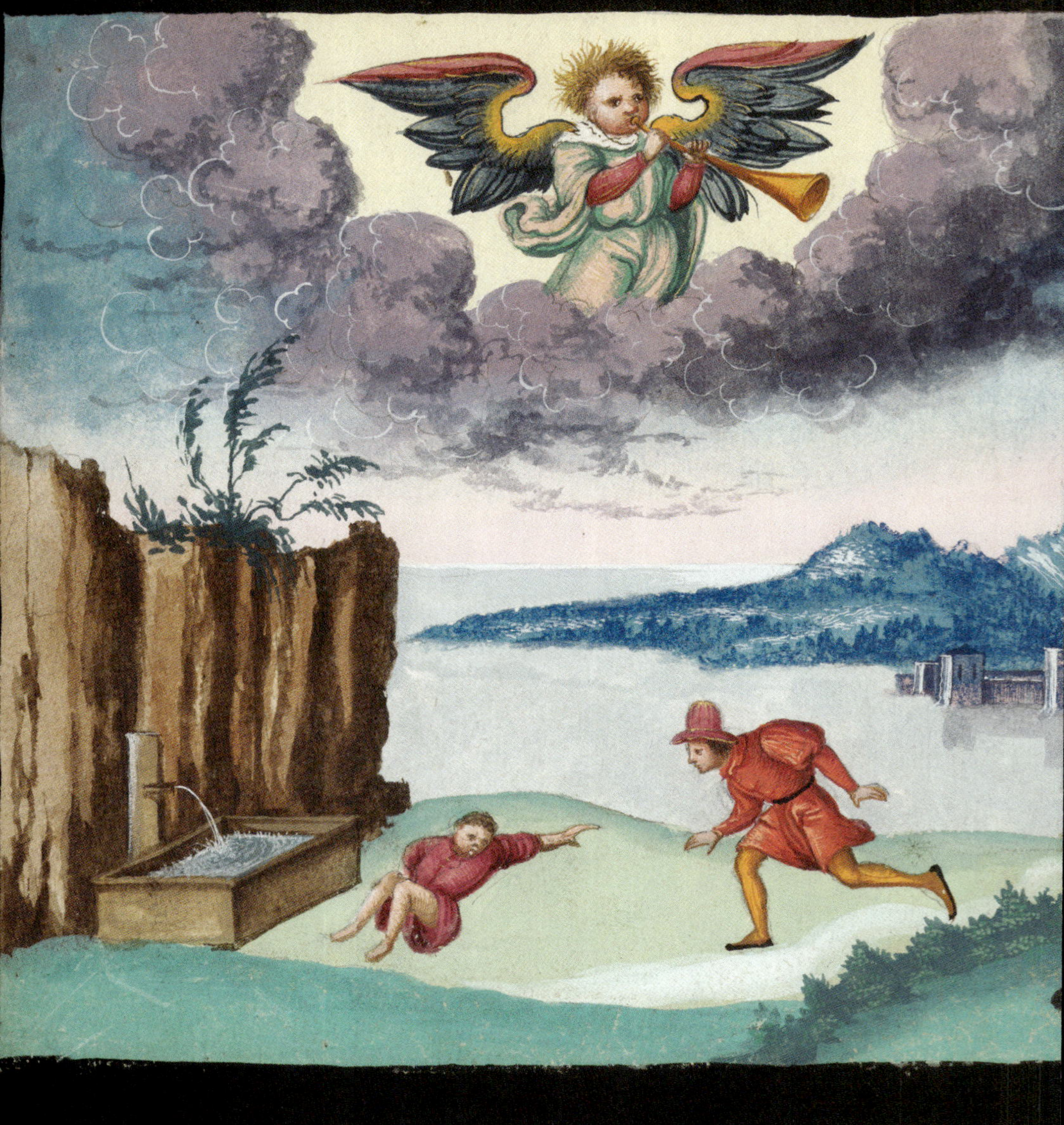

am viii capitel

Vnnd der dritte engel posaunete vnnd es fil ein grosser stern vom hiemel de
die wasser brunen vnnd der nam des sternen heist wermut vnnd
das sie so pitter waren worden.

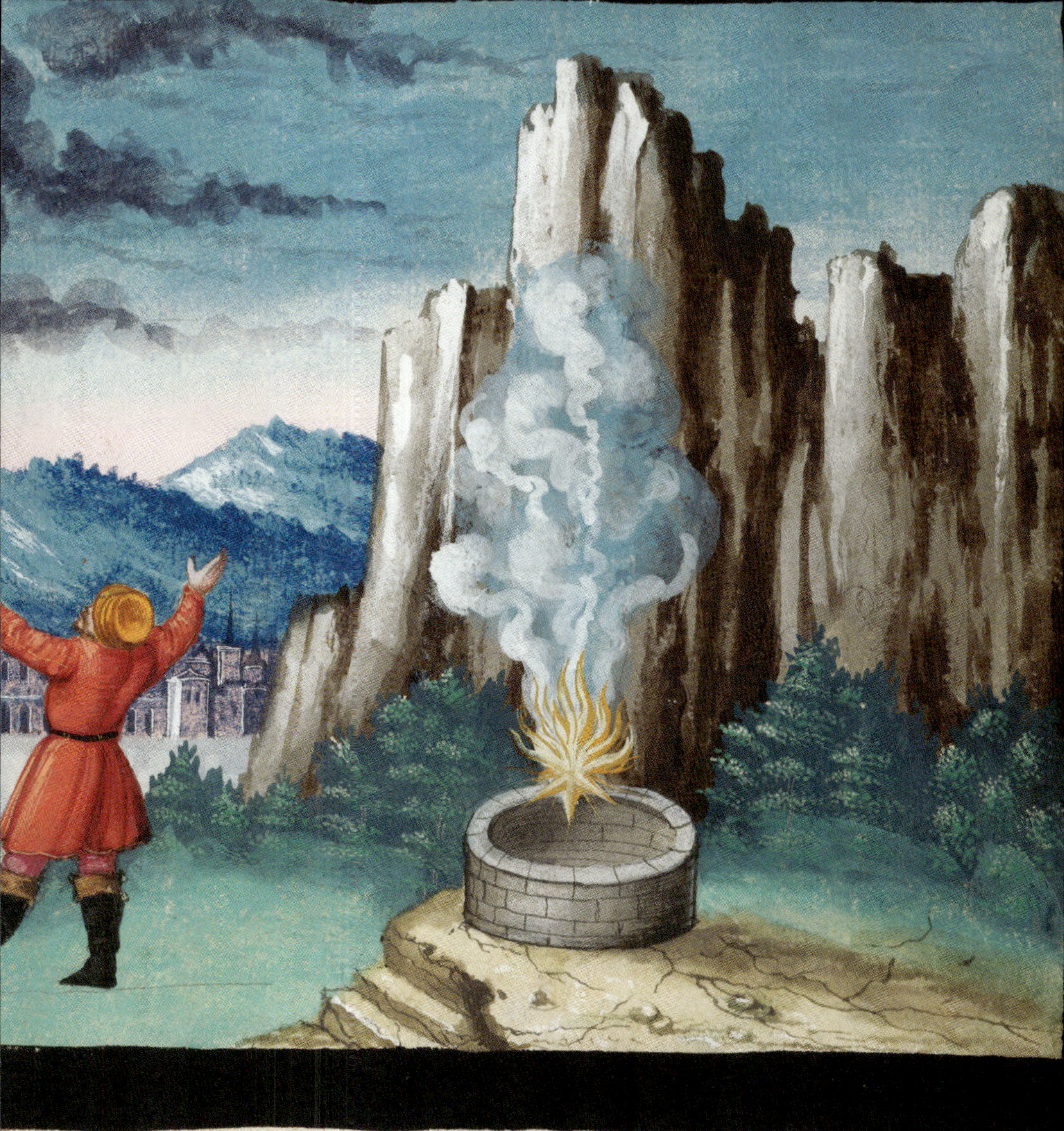

nte wie ein fackel, vnnd fiel auff das dritte tail der wasser strome vnnd vber
ritte tail war wermůt vnnd vil menschen sterben von den wassern

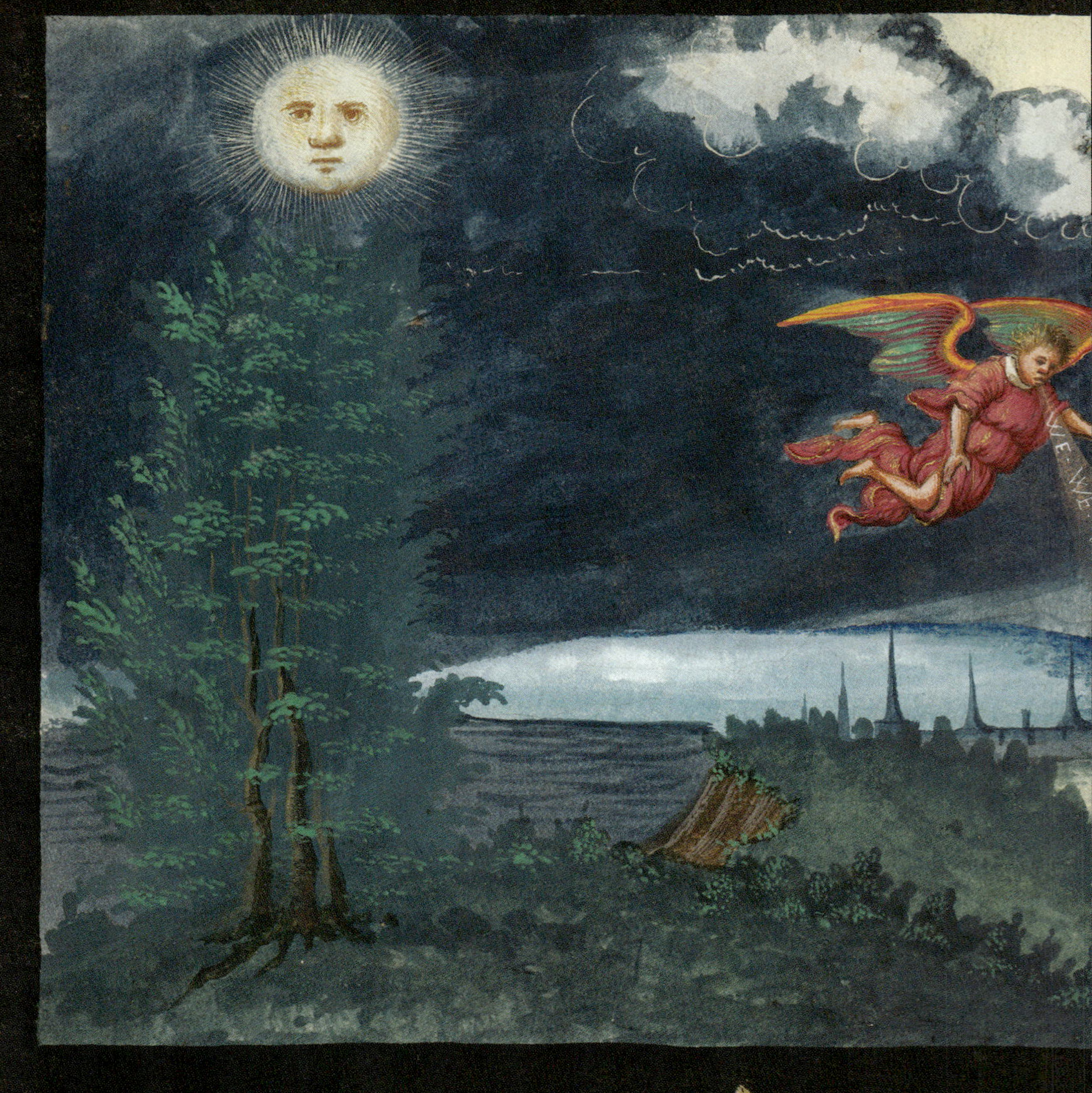

am viii capitel

Vnnd der vierte engel posaunete vnnd es ward geschlage
monden vnnd das dritte teil der sternen das ir dritte t
schein vnnd die nacht desselbigen gleichen vnd ich sahe
vnd sagen mit lauter stim weh weh weh denen die ar

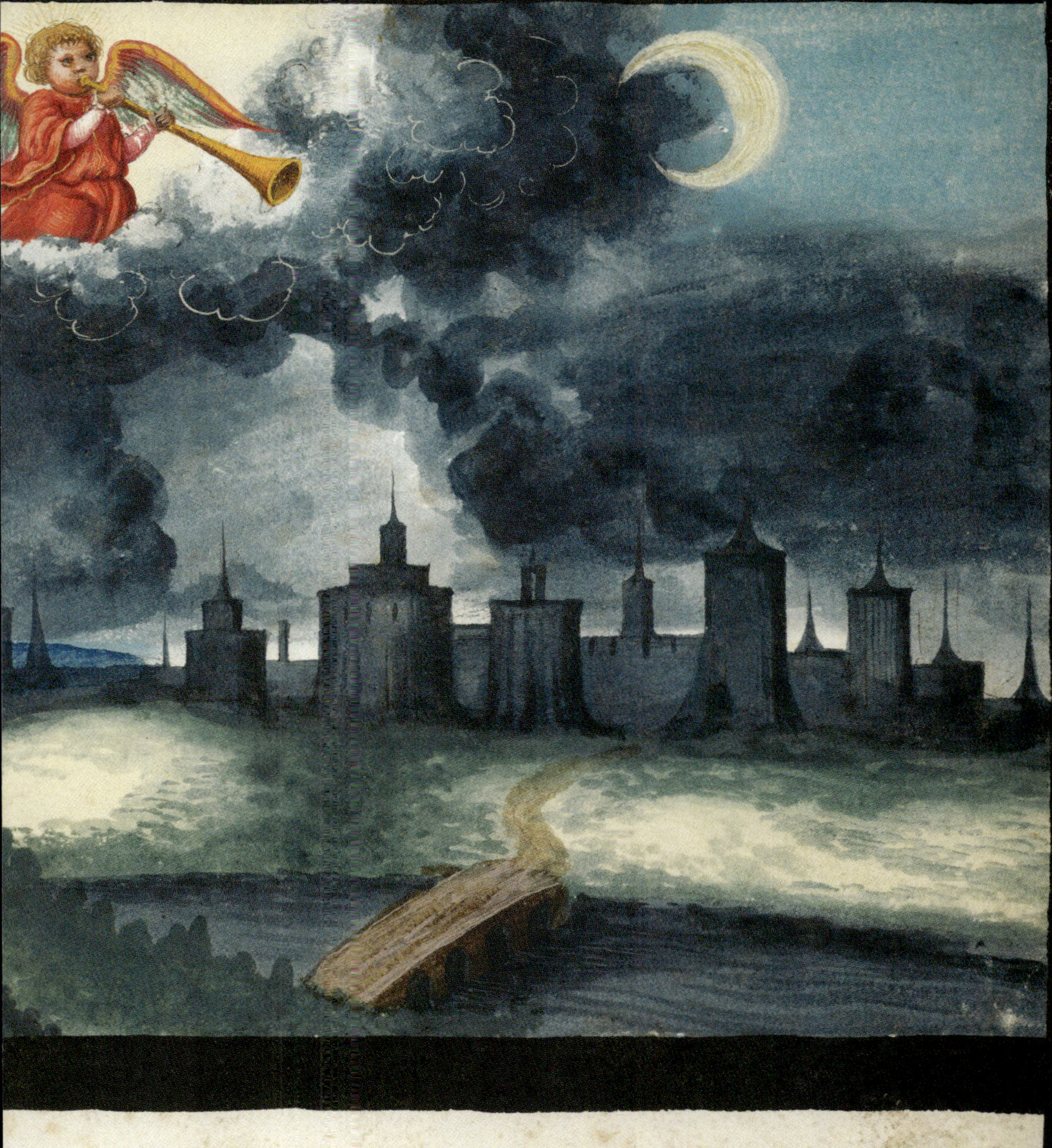

s dritte tail der sonnen vnnd das dritte tails des S
erfinstert ward· vnnd der tag das dritte taill nicht
horet einen engel fliegen mitten durch den himl
en wonen vor andern stimmen der posaunen:

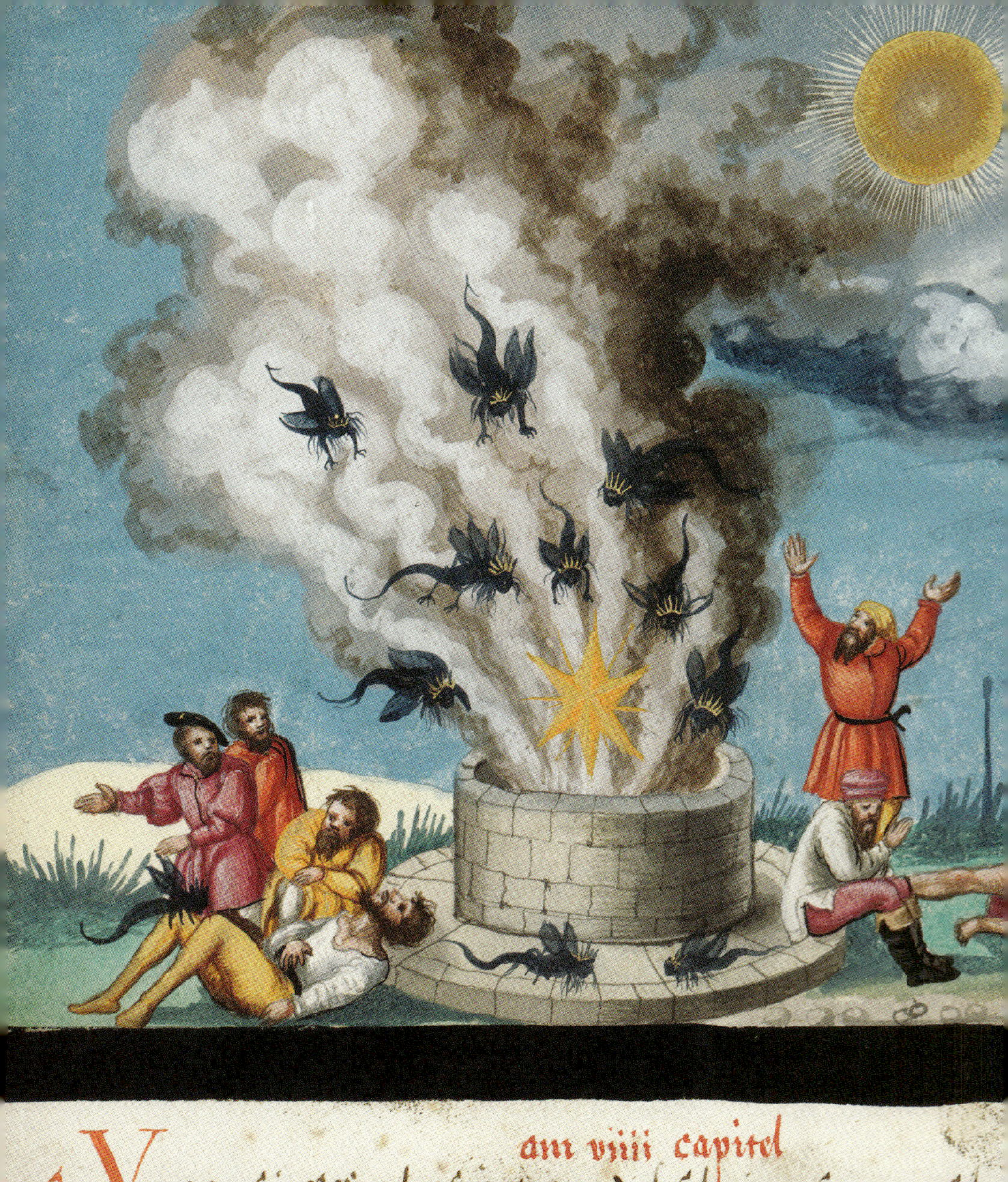

am viiii capitel

Vnnd der fünfft Engel posaunete vnnd ich sahe einen sternen gefalen
abgründs gegeben vnnd er thet den brunnen des abgrunds auff/ v
die sonne vnnd die lufft von dem rauch des brunnen/ vnd auff
geben wie die hewschrecken auff erden macht haben/ vnnd es w
kain grünes noch keinen baum sonder die menschen die haben

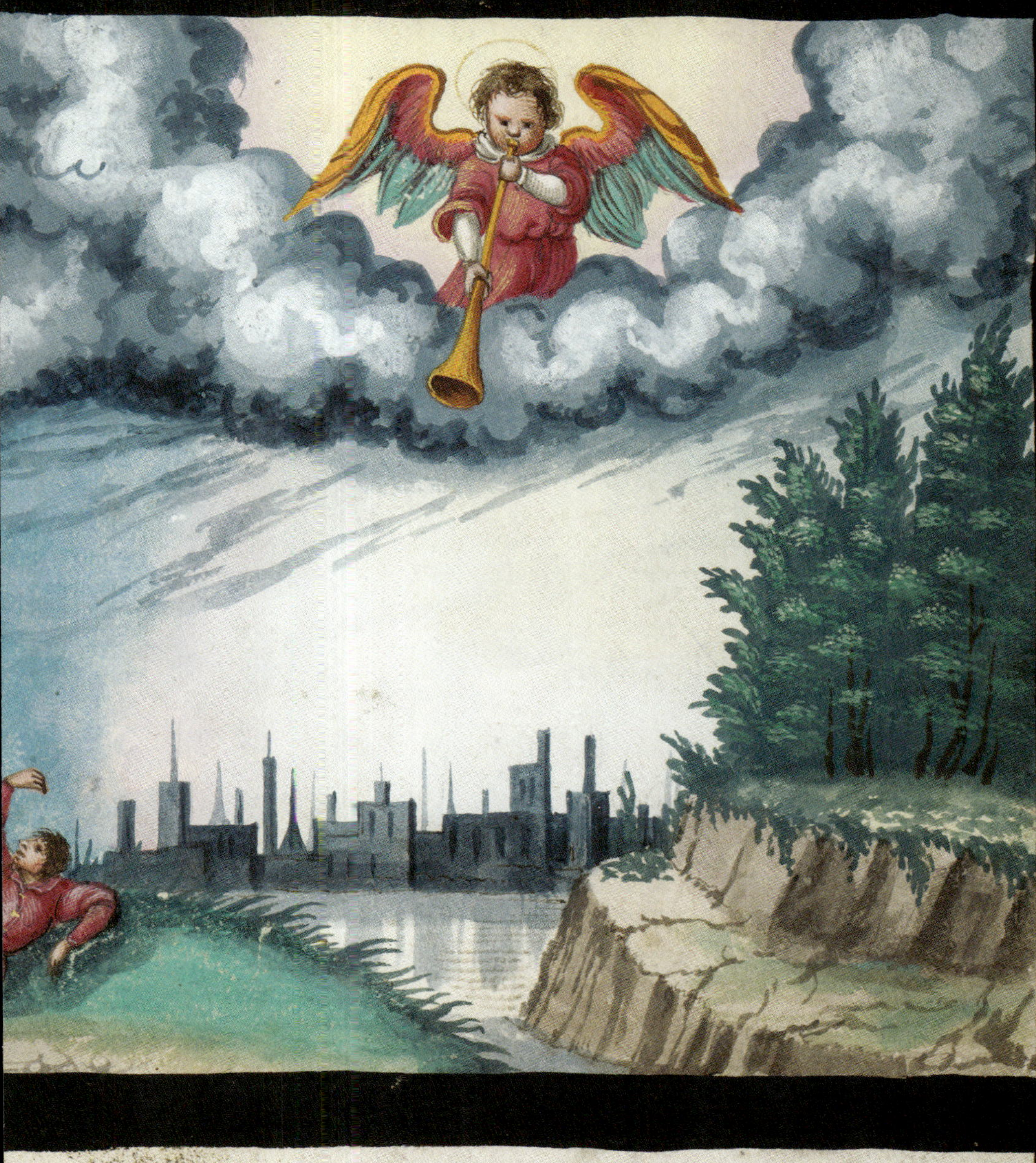

himel auff die erden vnnd im ward der schlüssel zum brunnen des
s ging auff ein rauch eins grossen offen vnnd es ward verfinstert
rauch kamen hew schrecken auff die erden vnnd in ward macht
n inen gesagt das sie nicht belaidigten das grass auff erden noch
ngel gottes an iren stiernen

FOL. 181

The fourth angel blowing his trumpet
Der vierte Engel bläst seine Posaune
Le quatrième Ange sonne sa trompette

Revelation 8:12–13 – 12 The fourth angel blew his trumpet, and a third of the sun was struck, and a third of the moon, and a third of the stars, so that a third of their light might be darkened, and a third of the day might be kept from shining, and likewise a third of the night. 13 Then I looked, and I heard an eagle crying with a loud voice as it flew directly overhead, "Woe, woe, woe to those who dwell on the earth, at the blasts of the other trumpets […]".

Offenbarung 8,12–13 – 12 Und der vierte Engel blies seine Posaune; und es wurde geschlagen der dritte Teil der Sonne und der dritte Teil des Mondes und der dritte Teil der Sterne, sodass ihr dritter Teil verfinstert wurde und den dritten Teil des Tages das Licht nicht schien und in der Nacht desgleichen. 13 Und ich sah, und ich hörte, wie ein Adler mitten durch den Himmel flog und sagte mit großer Stimme: Weh, weh, weh denen, die auf Erden wohnen wegen der anderen Posaunen […].

Apocalypse 8:12–13 – 12 Et le quatrième Ange sonna… Alors furent frappés le tiers du soleil et le tiers de la lune et le tiers des étoiles : ils s'assombrirent d'un tiers, et le jour perdit le tiers de sa clarté, et la nuit de même. 13 Et ma vision se poursuivit. J'entendis un aigle volant au zénith et criant d'une voix puissante : « Malheur, malheur, malheur aux habitants de la terre, à cause de la voix des dernières trompettes […]. »

FOL. 182

The fifth angel blowing his trumpet
Der fünfte Engel bläst seine Posaune
Le cinquième Ange sonne sa trompette

Revelation 9:1–4 – 1 And the fifth angel blew his trumpet, and I saw a star fallen from heaven to earth, and he was given the key to the shaft of the bottomless pit. 2 He opened the shaft of the bottomless pit, and from the shaft rose smoke like the smoke of a great furnace, and the sun and the air were darkened with the smoke from the shaft. 3 Then from the smoke came locusts on the earth, and they were given power like the power of scorpions of the earth. 4 They were told not to harm the grass of the earth or any green plant or any tree, but only those people who do not have the seal of God on their foreheads.

Offenbarung 9,1–4 – 1 Und der fünfte Engel blies seine Posaune; und ich sah einen Stern, gefallen auf die Erde; und ihm wurde der Schlüssel zum Brunnen des Abgrunds gegeben. 2 Und er tat den Brunnen auf, und es stieg auf ein Rauch aus dem Brunnen […], und es wurden verfinstert die Sonne und die Luft von dem Rauch des Brunnens. 3 Und aus dem Rauch kamen Heuschrecken auf die Erde, und ihnen wurde Macht gegeben, wie die Skorpione auf Erden Macht haben. 4 Und es wurde ihnen gesagt, sie sollten nicht Schaden tun dem Gras auf Erden noch allem Grünen noch irgendeinem Baum, sondern allein den Menschen, die nicht das Siegel Gottes haben an ihren Stirnen.

Apocalypse 9:1–4 – 1 Et le cinquième Ange sonna… Alors je vis un astre qui du ciel avait chu sur
la terre. On lui remit la clef du puits de l'Abîme. 2 Il ouvrit le puits de l'Abîme et il en monta une
fumée, comme celle d'une immense fournaise – le soleil et l'atmosphère en furent obscurcis – 3 et,
de cette fumée, des sauterelles se répandirent sur la terre ; on leur donna un pouvoir pareil à celui
des scorpions de la terre. 4 On leur dit d'épargner les prairies, toute verdure et tout arbre, et de s'en
prendre seulement aux hommes qui ne porteraient pas sur le front le sceau de Dieu.

FOL. 183

The battle of the angels
Der Kampf der Engel | Le combat des Anges

Revelation 9:13–17 – 13 Then the sixth angel blew his trumpet, and I heard a voice from the four
horns of the golden altar before God, 14 saying to the sixth angel who had the trumpet, "Release the
four angels who are bound at the great river Euphrates." 15 So the four angels, who had been prepared for the hour, the day, the month and the year, were released to kill a third of mankind. 16 The
number of mounted troops was twice ten thousand times ten thousand; I heard their number.
17 And this is how I saw the horses in my vision and those who rode them: they wore breastplates
the colour of fire and of sapphire and of sulphur, and the heads of the horses were like lions' heads.

Offenbarung 9,13–17 – 13 Und der sechste Engel blies seine Posaune; und ich hörte eine Stimme
aus den vier Ecken des goldenen Altars vor Gott; 14 die sprach zu dem sechsten Engel, der die Posaune hatte: Lass los die vier Engel, die gebunden sind an dem großen Strom Euphrat. 15 Und es
wurden losgelassen die vier Engel, die bereit waren für die Stunde und den Tag und den Monat und
das Jahr, zu töten den dritten Teil der Menschen. 16 Und die Zahl des reitenden Heeres war viel-
tausendmal tausend; ich hörte ihre Zahl. 17 Und so sah ich in dieser Erscheinung die Rosse und die
darauf saßen: […] die Häupter der Rosse waren wie die Häupter der Löwen.

Apocalypse 9:13–17 – 13 Et le sixième Ange sonna… Alors, j'entendis une voix venant des quatre
cornes de l'autel d'or placé devant Dieu ; 14 elle dit au sixième Ange portant trompette : « Relâche
les quatre Anges enchaînés sur le grand fleuve Euphrate. » 15 Et l'on relâcha les Anges qui se tenaient
prêts pour l'heure et le jour et le mois et l'année, afin d'exterminer le tiers des hommes. 16 Leur armée comptait deux cents millions de cavaliers : on m'en précisa le nombre. 17 Tels m'apparurent en
vision les chevaux et leurs cavaliers : ceux-ci portent des cuirasses de feu, d'hyacinthe et de soufre ;
quant aux chevaux, leur tête est comme celle du lion […].

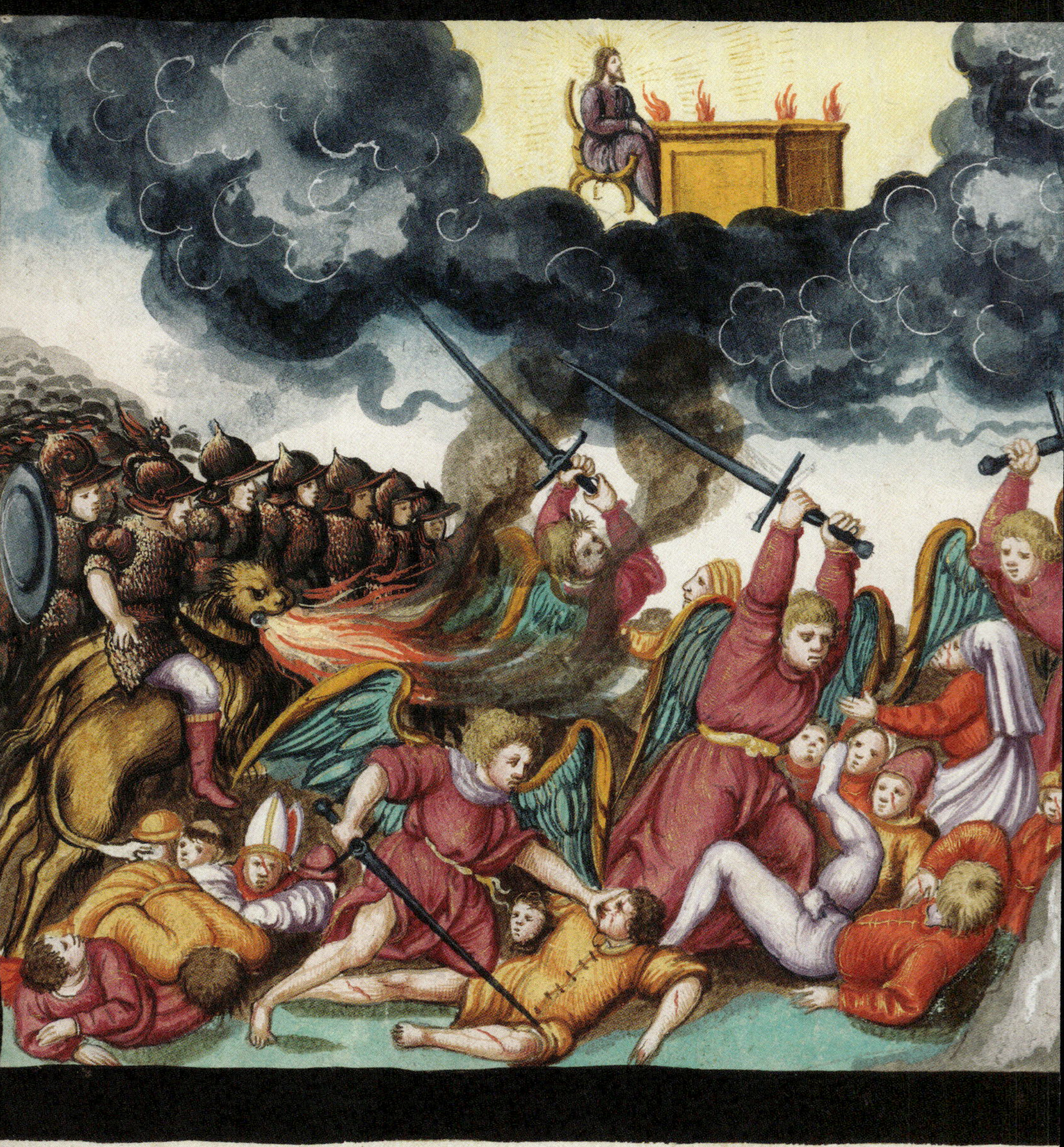

am viiii capitel

Vnnd der sechste engel posaunet vnnd ich horet eine stimme aus
der die posaunen hatte, löse auff die vier engel gepunden an
loß die berait waren auff eine stunde, vnnd auff einen tag, vn
menschen, vnnd die zal der reüterischen krieger war vil tausent
vnnd die drauff sassen das sie heten fewrige vnd gele vnnd schw

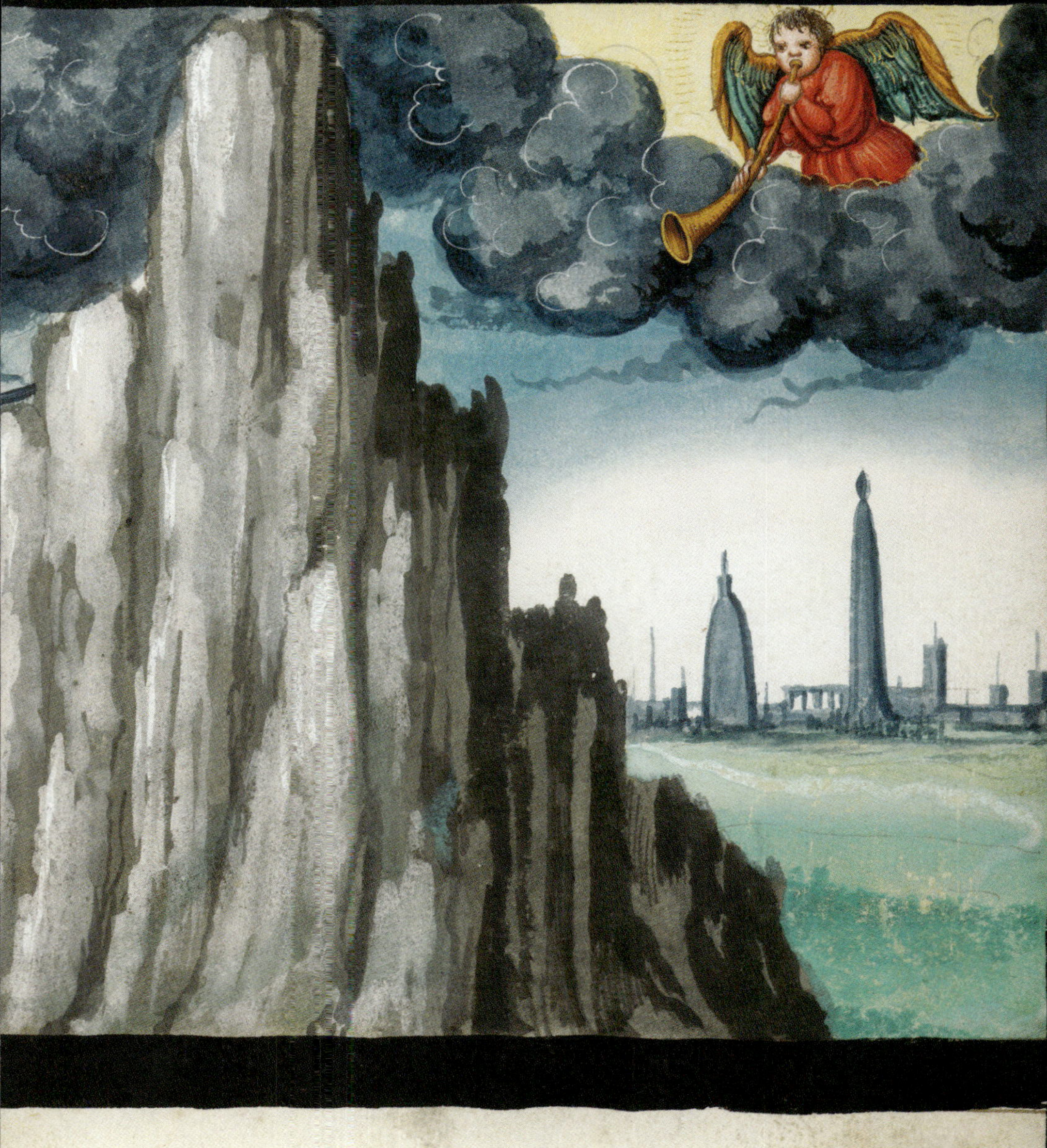

n vier ecken des gulden altars vor gott/ die sprach zu dem sechsten engel
n grossem wasser strom Euphrates vnnd es wurden die vier engel
ff einen monden vnnd auff ein iar/ das sie todten das dritte tail der:
tausent vnnd ich horet ir zal/ vnd also sahe ich die ross im angesicht:
che panzer vnnd die haubt der ross wie die haubt der lewen

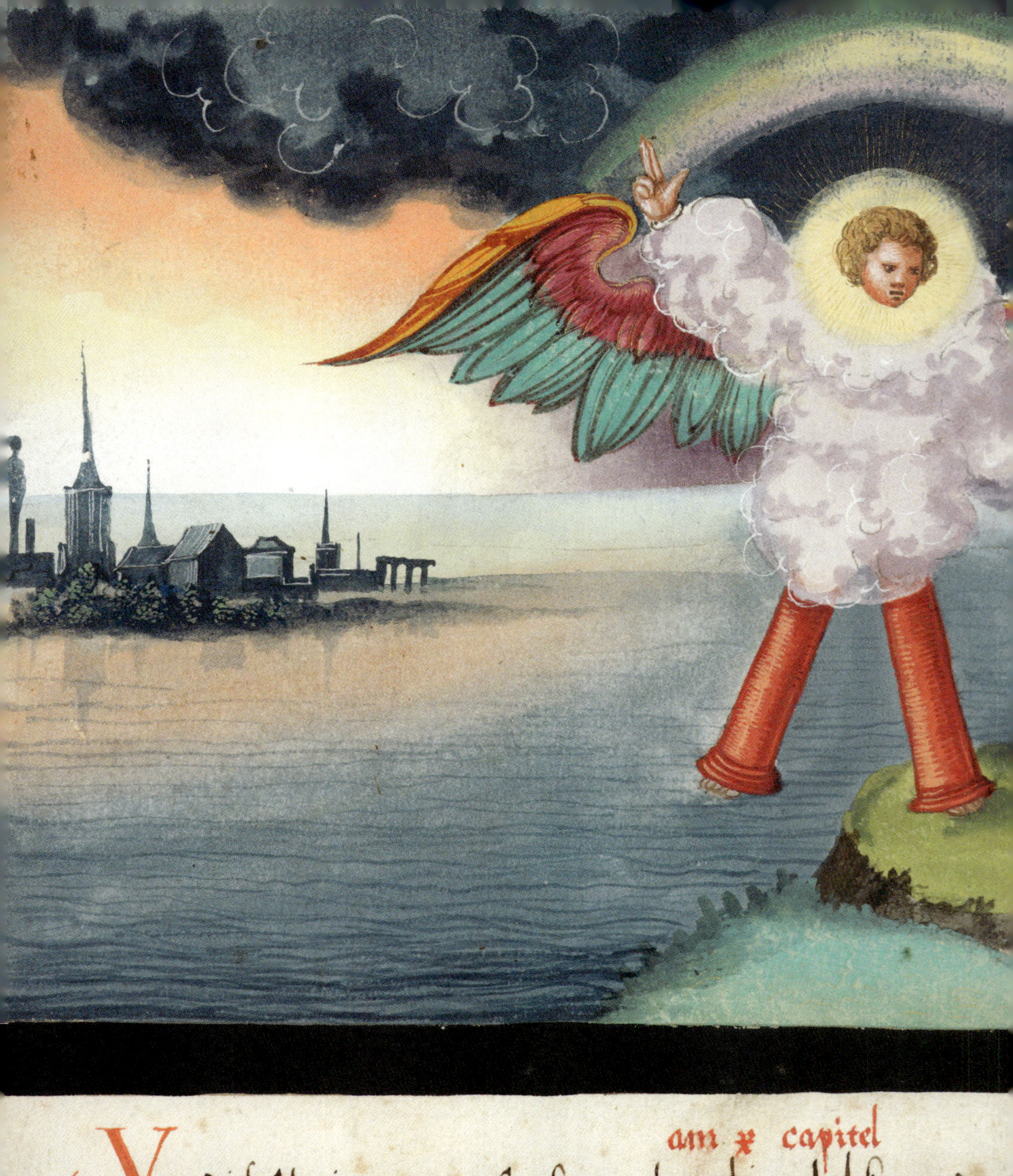

am x capitel

Vnnd ich sahe einen andern starcken engel vom hiemel ab komen/ der v
haubt vnnd sein antlitz wie die Sonne vnnd seine füsse wie feuer
X vnnd er setzet seinen rechten fuss auff das meer vnnd den li
lewe brüllet/ vnd da er schraÿ redeten sieben doner yrhe stim
sagen zu mir versigel was die sieben donner geredt haben die

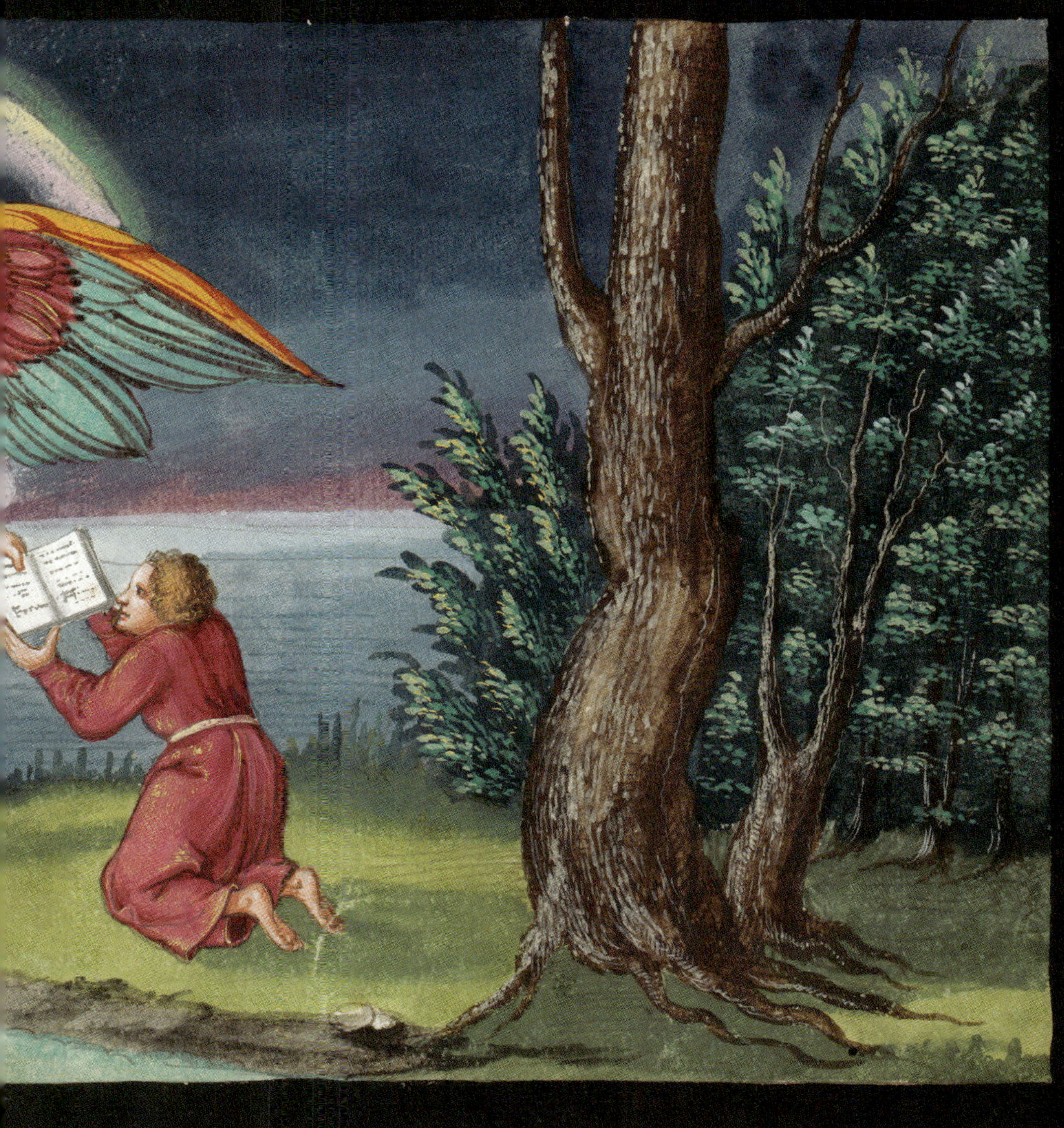

mit einer wolcken beklaidet vnnd ein regen bogen auff seinem
ülen vnnd er hatte in seiner hand ein büchlein auff gethan:
n auff die erden vnnd er schray mit lautter stim, wie ein
nd ich wolt sie schreiben da horet ich ein stim von himell:
den schreib nicht

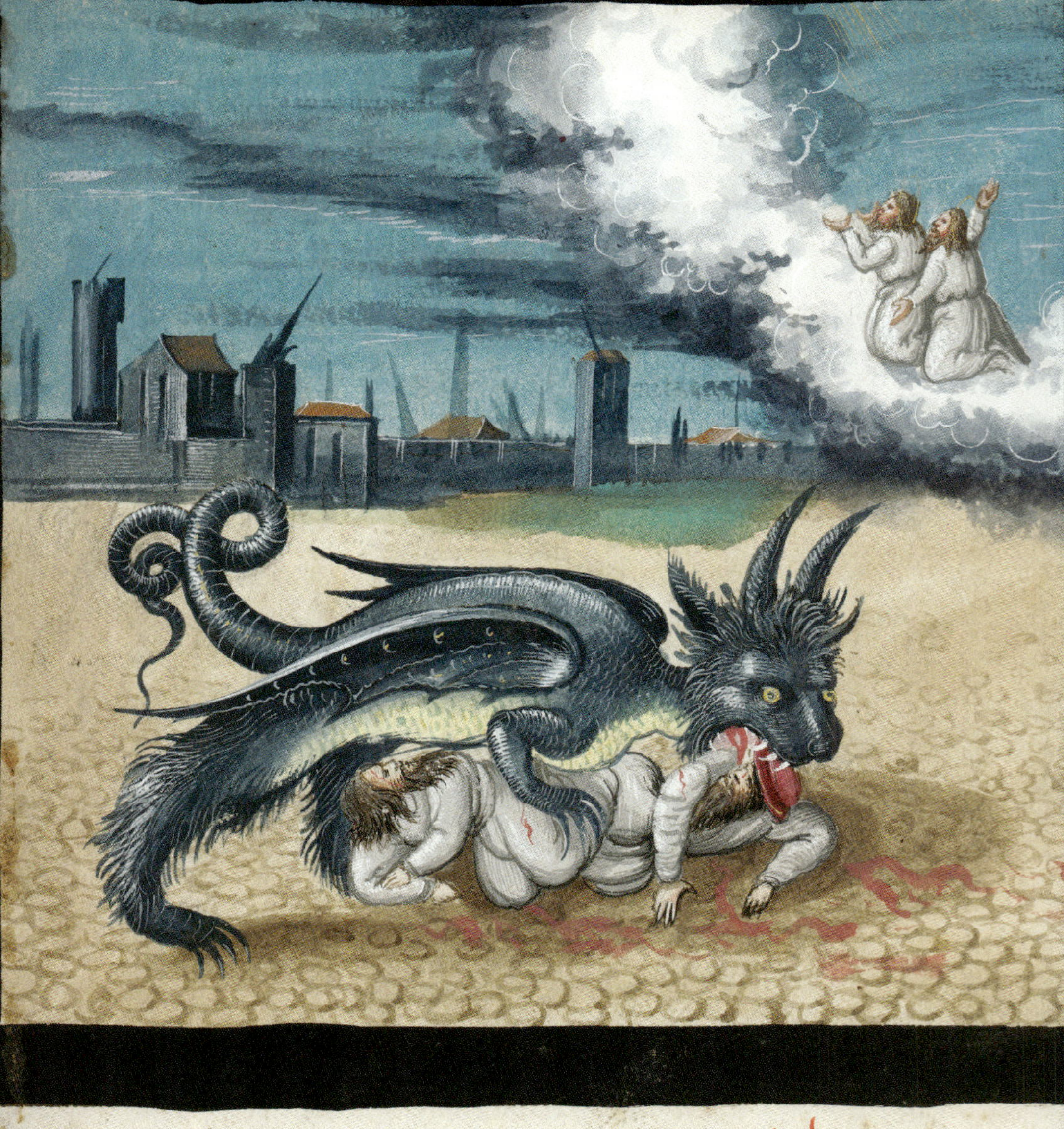

am xi capitel

Vnnd so yemand sie will belaidigen so gehet das fewer auſs irhem mu
der muſ alsô getodtet werden/ dieſe haben macht den hiemel zu ner
haben macht vber daſs waſſer zů wandlend in blůt vnnd zů sch
sie ir zeugnus geendet haben so wirt das thier das auſs dem abgr
winden/ vnnd wiert sie todten vnnd irhe leichnam werden liege

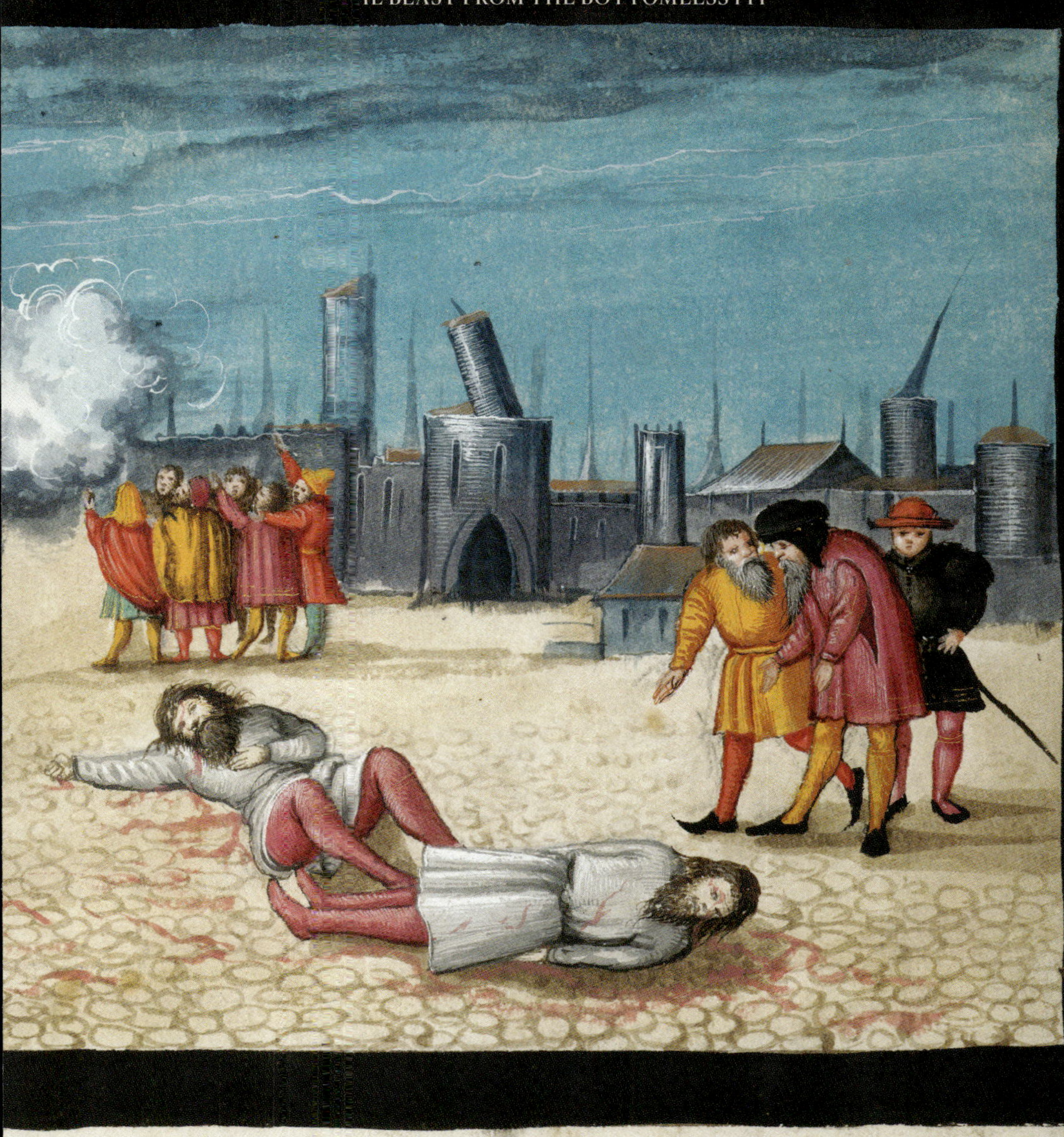

e vnnd verzeret yrhe feinde vnnd iemant sie will belaidigen:
hliessen das es nit regne in den tagen irer weyssagung vnnd
en die erden mit allerley plage so offt sie wollen vnnd we
dt auff steyget mit im einen streyt halten vnnd wirt sie vber
uff der gassen der grossen stat

FOL. 184

St John and the angel

Johannes und der Engel | Saint Jean et l'Ange

Revelation 10:1–4 – 1 Then I saw another mighty angel coming down from heaven, wrapped in a cloud, with a rainbow over his head, and his face was like the sun, and his legs like pillars of fire. 2 He had a little scroll open in his hand. And he set his right foot on the sea, and his left foot on the land, 3 and called out with a loud voice, like a lion roaring. When he called out, the seven thunders sounded. 4 And when the seven thunders had sounded, I was about to write, but I heard a voice from heaven saying, "Seal up what the seven thunders have said, and do not write it down."

Offenbarung 10,1–4 – 1 Und ich sah einen andern starken Engel vom Himmel herabkommen, mit einer Wolke bekleidet, und der Regenbogen auf seinem Haupt und sein Antlitz wie die Sonne und seine Füße wie Feuersäulen. 2 Und er hatte in seiner Hand ein Büchlein, das war aufgetan. Und er setzte seinen rechten Fuß auf das Meer und den linken auf die Erde, 3 und er schrie mit großer Stimme, wie ein Löwe brüllt. Und als er schrie, erhoben die sieben Donner ihre Stimme. 4 Und als die sieben Donner geredet hatten, wollte ich es aufschreiben. Da hörte ich eine Stimme vom Himmel zu mir sagen: Versiegle, was die sieben Donner geredet haben, und schreib es nicht auf!

Apocalypse 10:1–4 – 1 Je vis ensuite un autre Ange, puissant, descendre du ciel enveloppé d'une nuée, un arc-en-ciel au-dessus de la tête, le visage comme le soleil et les jambes comme des colonnes de feu. 2 Il tenait en sa main un petit livre ouvert. Il posa le pied droit sur la mer, le gauche sur la terre, 3 et il poussa une puissante clameur pareille au rugissement d'un lion. Après quoi, les sept tonnerres firent retentir leurs voix. 4 Quand les sept tonnerres eurent parlé, j'allais écrire mais j'entendis du ciel une voix me dire : « Tiens secrètes les paroles des sept tonnerres et ne les écris pas. »

FOL. 185

The beast from the bottomless pit

Die Bestie aus dem Abgrund | La Bête de l'Abîme

Revelation 11:5–8 – 5 And if anyone would harm them, fire pours from their mouth and consumes their foes. If anyone would harm them, this is how he is doomed to be killed. 6 They have the power to shut the sky, that no rain may fall during the days of their prophesying, and they have power over the waters to turn them into blood and to strike the earth with every kind of plague, as often as they desire. 7 And when they have finished their testimony, the beast that rises from the bottomless pit will make war on them and conquer them and kill them, 8 and their dead bodies will lie in the street of the great city.

Offenbarung 11,5–8 – 5 Und wenn ihnen jemand Schaden tun will, so kommt Feuer aus ihrem Mund und verzehrt ihre Feinde; und wenn ihnen jemand Schaden tun will, muss er so getötet werden. 6 Diese haben Macht, den Himmel zu verschließen, damit es nicht regne in den Tagen ihrer Weissagung, und haben Macht über die Wasser, sie in Blut zu verwandeln und die Erde zu schlagen mit Plagen aller Art, sooft sie wollen. 7 Und wenn sie ihr Zeugnis vollendet haben, so wird das Tier, das aus dem Abgrund aufsteigt, mit ihnen kämpfen und wird sie überwinden und wird sie töten. 8 Und ihre Leichname werden liegen auf dem Marktplatz der großen Stadt.

Apocalypse 11:5–8 – 5 Si l'on s'avisait de les malmener, un feu jaillirait de leur bouche pour dévorer leurs ennemis ; oui, qui s'aviserait de les malmener, c'est ainsi qu'il lui faudrait périr. 6 Ils ont pouvoir de clore le ciel afin que nulle pluie ne tombe durant le temps de leur mission ; ils ont aussi pouvoir sur les eaux, de les changer en sang, et pouvoir de frapper la terre de mille fléaux, aussi souvent qu'ils le voudront. 7 Mais quand ils auront fini de rendre témoignage, la Bête qui surgit de l'Abîme viendra guerroyer contre eux, les vaincre et les tuer. 8 Et leurs cadavres demeurent exposés, sur la place de la Grande Cité.

FOL. 186

The woman clothed with the sun and the seven-headed dragon
Die mit der Sonne bekleidete Frau und der siebenköpfige Drache
La femme enveloppée du soleil et le Dragon à sept têtes

Revelation 12:1–4 – 1 And a great sign appeared in heaven: a woman clothed with the sun, with the moon under her feet, and on her head a crown of twelve stars. 2 She was pregnant and was crying out in birth pains and the agony of giving birth. 3 And another sign appeared in heaven: behold, a great red dragon, with seven heads and ten horns, and on his heads seven diadems. 4 His tail swept down a third of the stars of heaven and cast them to the earth [...].

Offenbarung 12,1–4 – 1 Und es erschien ein großes Zeichen am Himmel: eine Frau, mit der Sonne bekleidet, und der Mond unter ihren Füßen und auf ihrem Haupt eine Krone von zwölf Sternen. 2 Und sie war schwanger und schrie in Kindsnöten und hatte große Qual bei der Geburt. 3 Und es erschien ein anderes Zeichen am Himmel, und siehe, ein großer, roter Drache, der hatte sieben Häupter und zehn Hörner und auf seinen Häuptern sieben Kronen, 4 und sein Schwanz fegte den dritten Teil der Sterne des Himmels hinweg und warf sie auf die Erde [...].

Apocalypse 12:1–4 – 1 Un signe grandiose apparut au ciel : une Femme ! le soleil l'enveloppe, la lune est sous ses pieds et douze étoiles couronnent sa tête ; 2 elle est enceinte et crie dans les douleurs et le travail de l'enfantement. 3 Puis un second signe apparut au ciel : un énorme Dragon rouge feu, à sept têtes et dix cornes, chaque tête surmontée d'un diadème. 4 Sa queue balaie le tiers des étoiles du ciel et les précipite sur la terre [...].

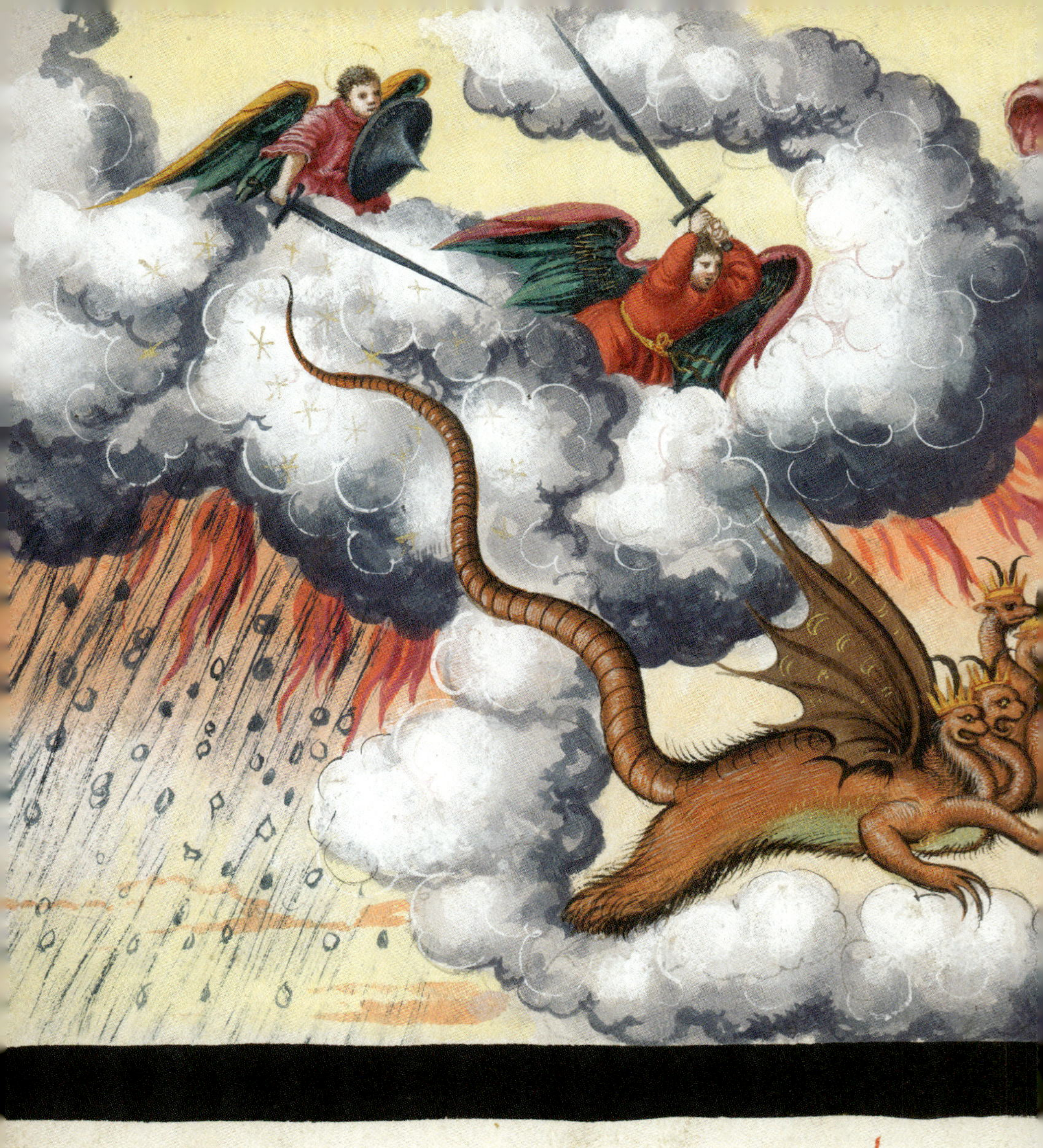

am xii capitel

Vnnd es erschein ein gros zeychem im hiemel/ ein weib mit der
yrem haubt ein krone von zwolff sternen/ vnnd si ward sch
das sie gepare/ vnnd es schein ein ander zeychen im hiemel/ v
zehen horner/ vnnd auff seinem haubte sieben kronnen vnd sein

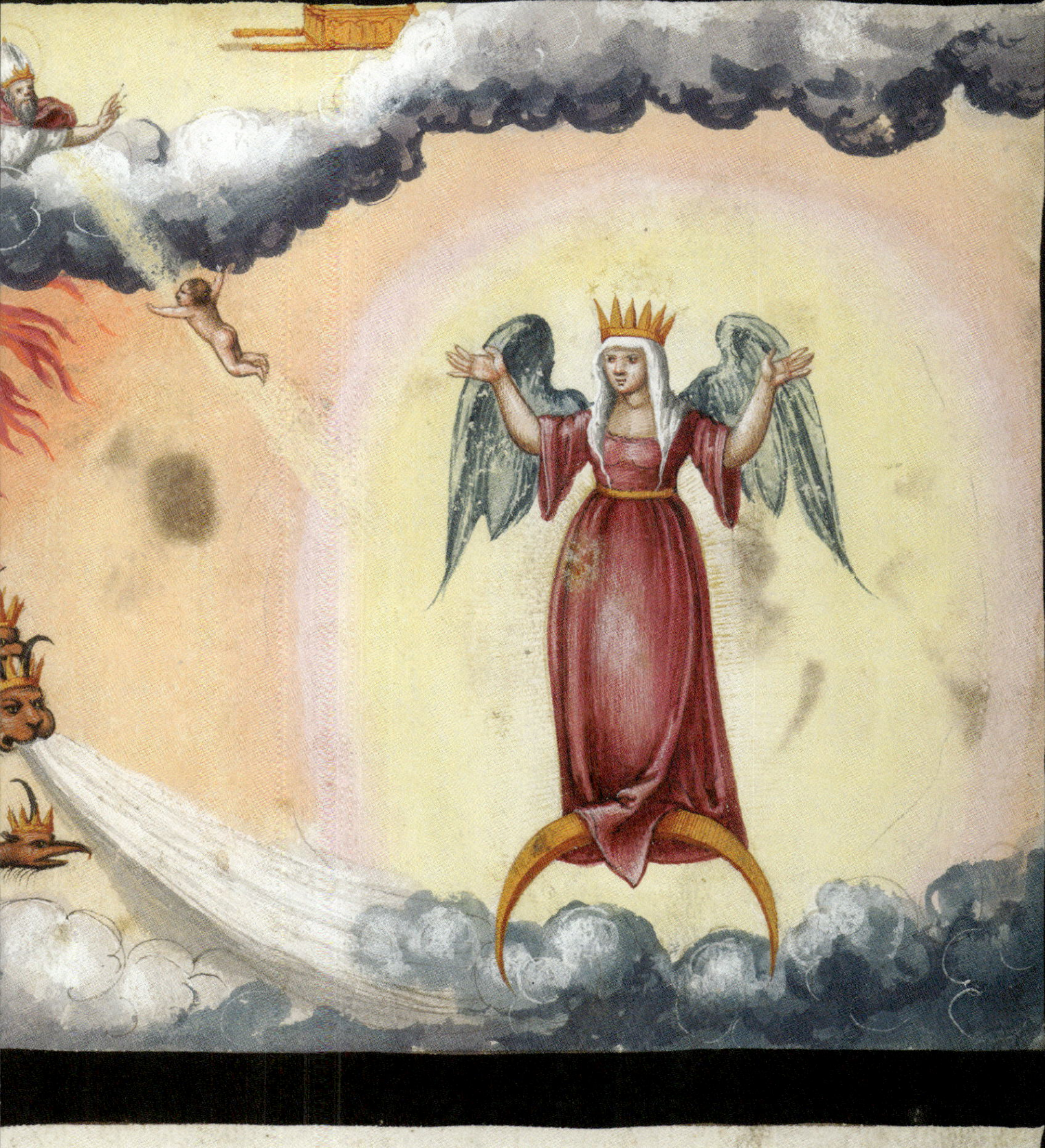

nen beklaidet / vnnd der mond vnder irhen füssen vnnd auff
nger vnd schray / vnnd war in kinds notten vnnd gequelet
sihe ein grosrer roter drache / der hatte sieben häubter vnnd
hwantz zog den dritten tail der sternen vnd warf sie auf die erden

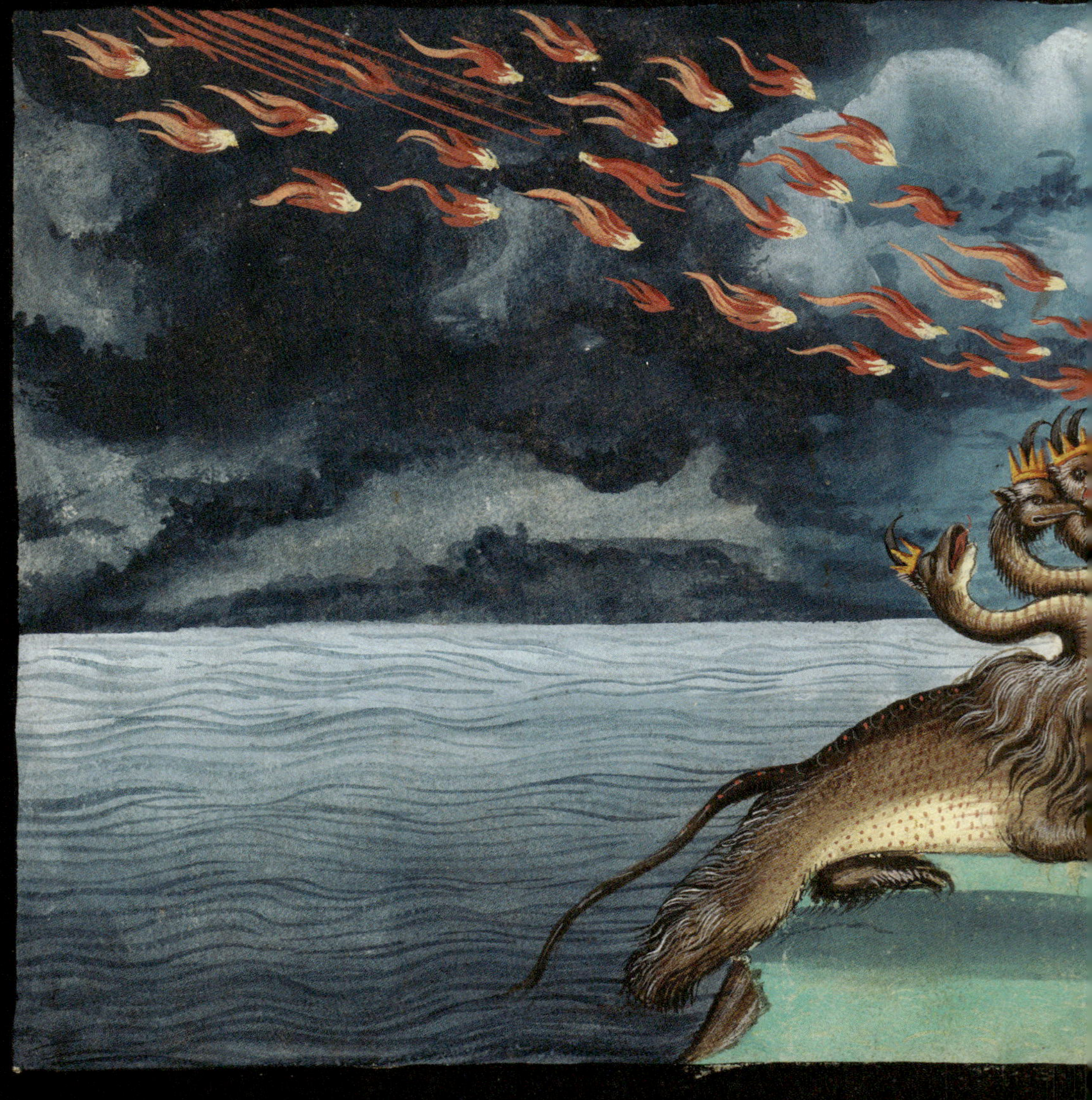

am xiii capitel

Vnnd ich sahe ein thier vss dem meer steigen das hatte sieben haubter vn
haubten namen der lesterung / vnnd das thier das ich sahe war gle
munnd / vnnd der drach gab im seine krafft vnnd sein stul vnnd
seine todliche wunde ward heil / vnnd der gantzen erboden ver wi
gab / vnnd betten das thier an vnnd sprachen wer ist dem thier

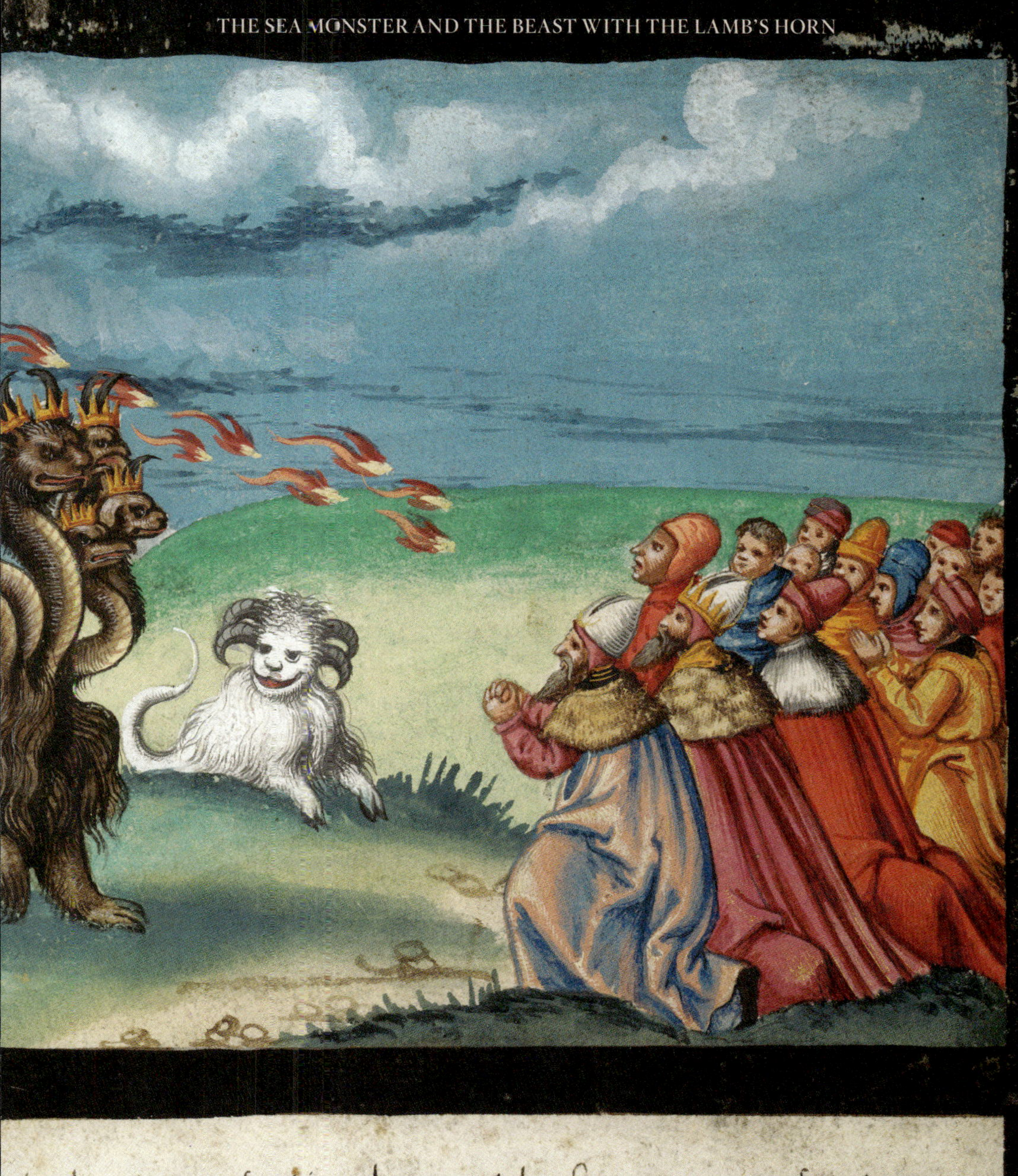

zehen hörner vnnd auff seinen hörnern sieben kronnen / vnnd auff seinem
einem pardel / vnnd seine füsse als beren füess / vnnd sein mund eines lewen
osse macht: vnnd ich sahe seiner haubt eins als were es todtlich wundt vnd
vert sich des thiers vnnd betenden den trachen an der dem thier sein macht
che / vnnd wer kan mit im kriegen

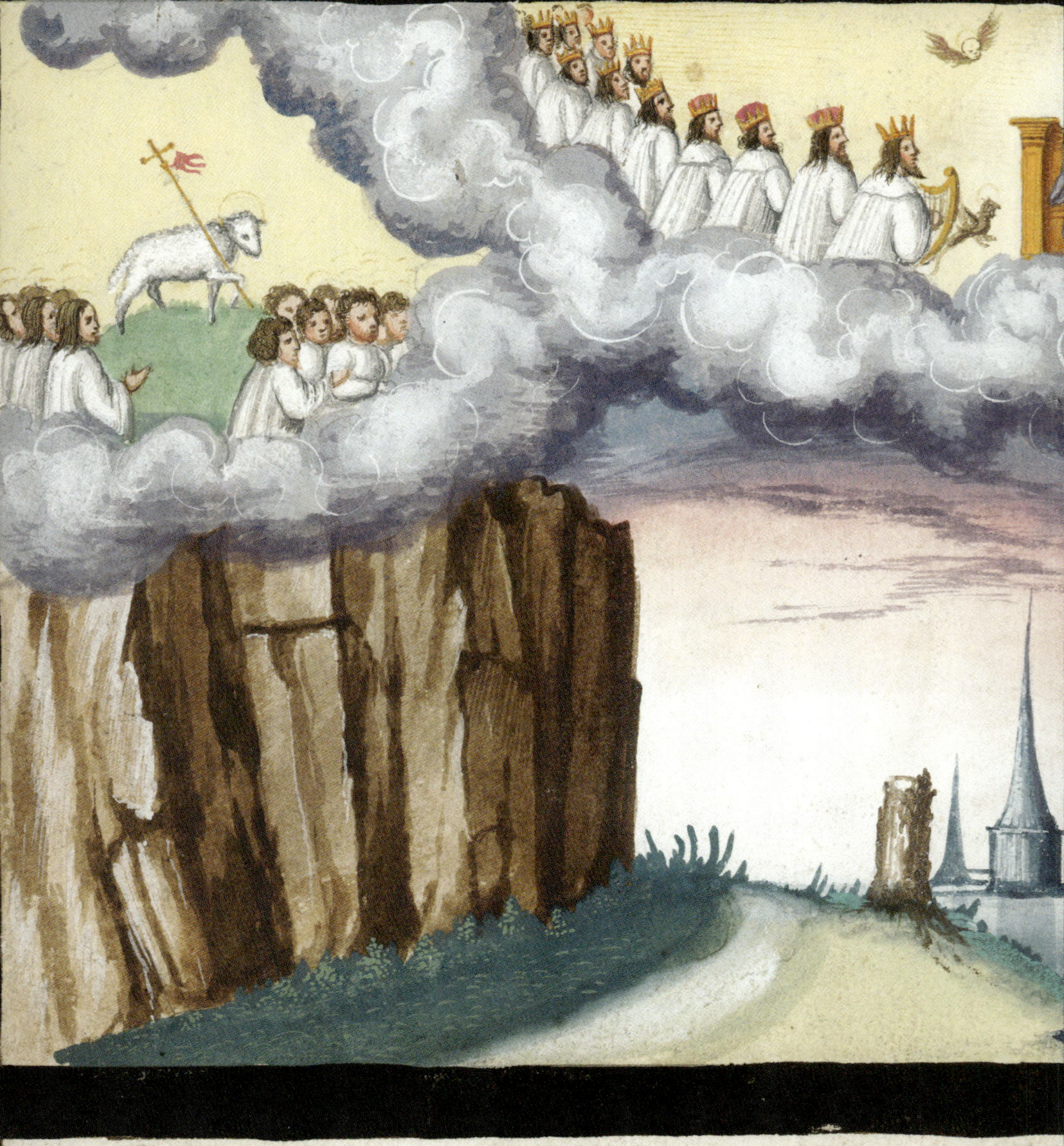

am xiiii capitel

Vnnd ich sahe ein engel fliegen mitten durch dem hiemel der hat ein ew
vnnd allen haiden vnnd geschlechten vnnd zungen vnnd volcker
seines gerichts stunde ist kumen vnnd bettet an/den der gemacht
ander engel folget nach der sprach sie ist gefallen/sie ist gefallen b
heyden getrenckt

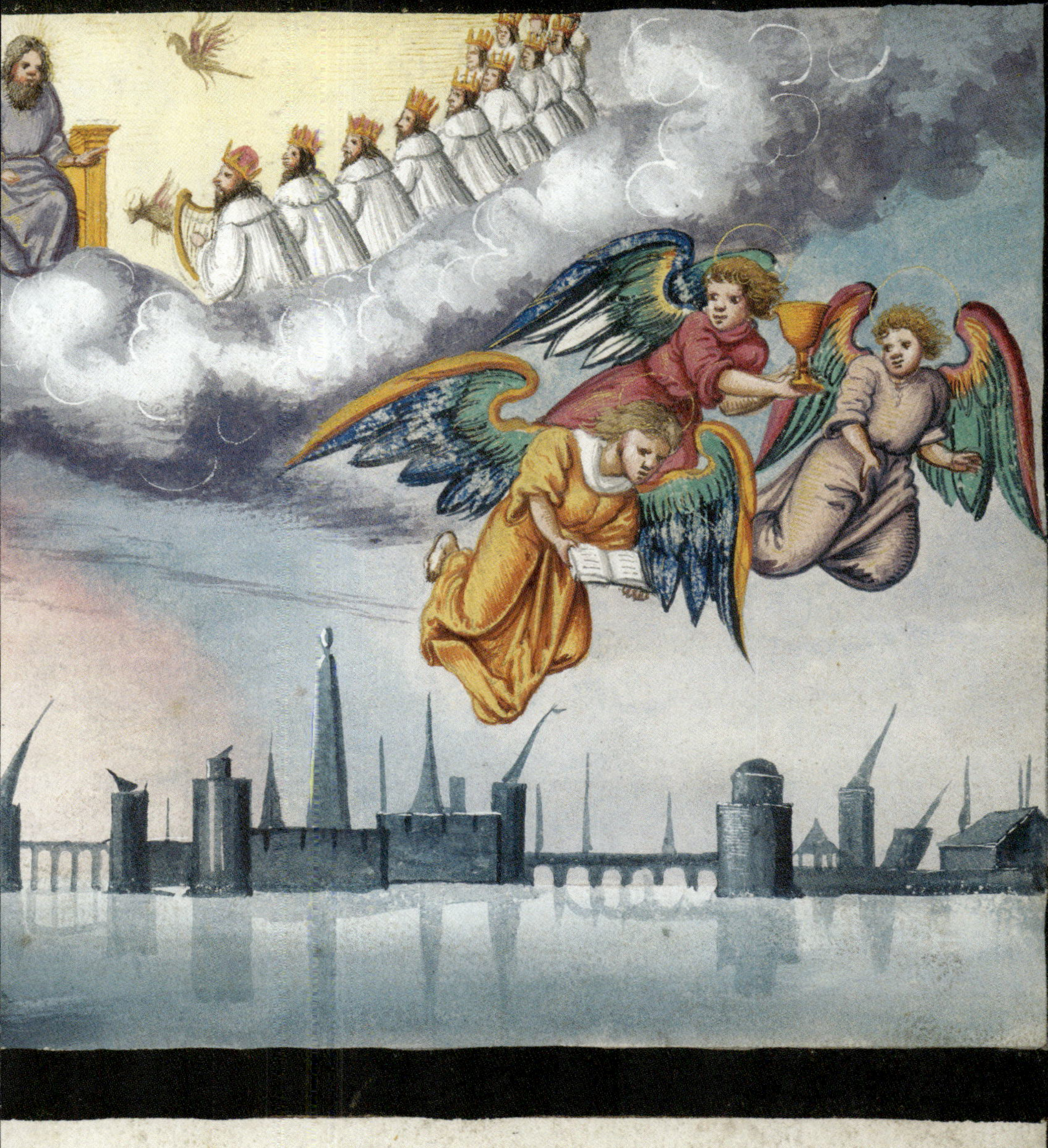

Euangelion/ zuuerkündigen denen die auff erden sietzen vnnd wonnen
vnnd sprach mit lautter stim/ forchtet gott vnnd gebt im die ehre/ den
s himel vnnd erden vnnd meer vnnd die wasser brunne/ vnnd ein:
lonia die grosse stat den sie hat mit dem wein irer hurerey alle:

FOL. 187

The sea monster and the beast with the lamb's horn
Das Meerungeheuer und die Bestie mit zwei Hörnern wie ein Lamm
La créature marine et la Bête à la corne d'agneau

Revelation 13:1–4 – 1 And I saw a beast rising out of the sea, with ten horns and seven heads, with ten diadems on its horns and blasphemous names on its heads. 2 And the beast that I saw was like a leopard; its feet were like a bear's, and its mouth was like a lion's mouth. And to it the dragon gave his power and his throne and great authority. 3 One of its heads seemed to have a mortal wound, but its mortal wound was healed, and the whole earth marvelled as they followed the beast. 4 And they worshipped the dragon, for he had given his authority to the beast, and they worshipped the beast, saying, "Who is like the beast, and who can fight against it?"

Offenbarung 13,1–4 – 1 Und ich sah ein Tier aus dem Meer steigen, das hatte zehn Hörner und sieben Häupter und auf seinen Hörnern zehn Kronen[...] 2 Und das Tier, das ich sah, war gleich einem Panther und seine Füße wie Bärenfüße und sein Rachen wie ein Löwenrachen. Und der Drache gab ihm seine Kraft und seinen Thron und große Macht. 3 Und ich sah eines seiner Häupter, als wäre es tödlich verwundet, und seine tödliche Wunde wurde heil. Und die ganze Erde wunderte sich über das Tier, 4 und sie beteten den Drachen an, weil er dem Tier die Macht gab, und beteten das Tier an und sprachen: Wer ist dem Tier gleich und wer kann mit ihm kämpfen?

Apocalypse 13:1–4 – 1 Alors je vis surgir de la mer une Bête ayant sept têtes et dix cornes, sur ses cornes dix diadèmes, et sur ses têtes des titres blasphématoires. 2 La Bête que je vis ressemblait à une panthère, avec les pattes comme celles d'un ours et la gueule comme une gueule de lion ; et le Dragon lui transmit sa puissance et son trône et un pouvoir immense. 3 L'une de ses têtes paraissait blessée à mort, mais sa plaie mortelle fut guérie ; alors, émerveillée, la terre entière suivit la Bête. 4 On se prosterna devant le Dragon, parce qu'il avait remis le pouvoir à la Bête ; et l'on se prosterna devant la Bête en disant : « Qui égale la Bête, et qui peut lutter contre elle ? »

FOL. 188

The adoration of the lamb and the hymn of the chosen
Die Anbetung des Lammes und das Lied der Auserwählten
L'adoration de l'Agneau et le cantique des élus

Revelation 14:6–8 – 6 Then I saw another angel flying directly overhead, with an eternal gospel to proclaim to those who dwell on earth, to every nation and tribe and language and people. 7 And he said with a loud voice, "Fear God and give him glory, because the hour of his judgement has come, and worship him who made heaven and earth, the sea and the springs of water." 8 Another angel, a second, followed, saying, "Fallen, fallen is Babylon the great, she who made all nations drink the wine of the passion of her sexual immorality."

Offenbarung 14,6–8 – 6 Und ich sah einen andern Engel fliegen mitten durch den Himmel, der hatte ein ewiges Evangelium zu verkündigen denen, die auf Erden wohnen, allen Nationen und Stämmen und Sprachen und Völkern. 7 Und er sprach mit großer Stimme: Fürchtet Gott und gebt ihm die Ehre; denn die Stunde seines Gerichts ist gekommen! Und betet an den, der gemacht hat Himmel und Erde und Meer und die Wasserquellen! 8 Und ein zweiter Engel folgte, der sprach: Sie ist gefallen, sie ist gefallen, Babylon, die große Stadt; denn sie hat mit dem Zorneswein ihrer Hurerei getränkt alle Völker.

Apocalypse 14:6–8 – 6 Puis je vis un autre Ange qui volait au zénith, ayant une bonne nouvelle éternelle à annoncer à ceux qui demeurent sur la terre, à toute nation, race, langue et peuple. 7 Il criait d'une voix puissante : « Craignez Dieu et glorifiez-le, car voici l'heure de son Jugement ; adorez donc Celui qui a fait le ciel et la terre et la mer et les sources. » 8 Un autre Ange, un deuxième, le suivit en criant : « Elle est tombée, elle est tombée, Babylone la Grande, elle qui a abreuvé toutes les nations du vin de l'immoralité. »

FOL. 189

The seven plagues | Die sieben Plagen | Les sept fléaux

Revelation 15:1–3 – 1 Then I saw another sign in heaven, great and amazing, seven angels with seven plagues, which are the last, for with them the wrath of God is finished. 2 And I saw what appeared to be a sea of glass mingled with fire — and also those who had conquered the beast and its image and the number of its name, standing beside the sea of glass with harps of God in their hands. 3 And they sing the song of Moses, the servant of God [...].

Offenbarung 15,1–3 – 1 Und ich sah ein andres Zeichen am Himmel, das war groß und wunderbar: sieben Engel, die hatten die letzten sieben Plagen; denn mit ihnen ist vollendet der Zorn Gottes. 2 Und ich sah, und es war wie ein gläsernes Meer, mit Feuer vermengt; und die den Sieg behalten hatten über das Tier und sein Bild und über die Zahl seines Namens, die standen an dem gläsernen Meer und hatten Gottes Harfen 3 und sangen das Lied des Mose, des Knechtes Gottes [...].

Apocalypse 15:1–3 – 1 Puis je vis dans le ciel encore un signe, grand et merveilleux : sept Anges, portant sept fléaux, les derniers puisqu'ils doivent consommer la colère de Dieu. 2 Et je vis comme une mer de cristal mêlée de feu, et ceux qui ont triomphé de la Bête, de son image et du chiffre de son nom, debout près de cette mer de cristal. S'accompagnant sur les harpes de Dieu, 3 ils chantent le cantique de Moïse, le serviteur de Dieu [...].

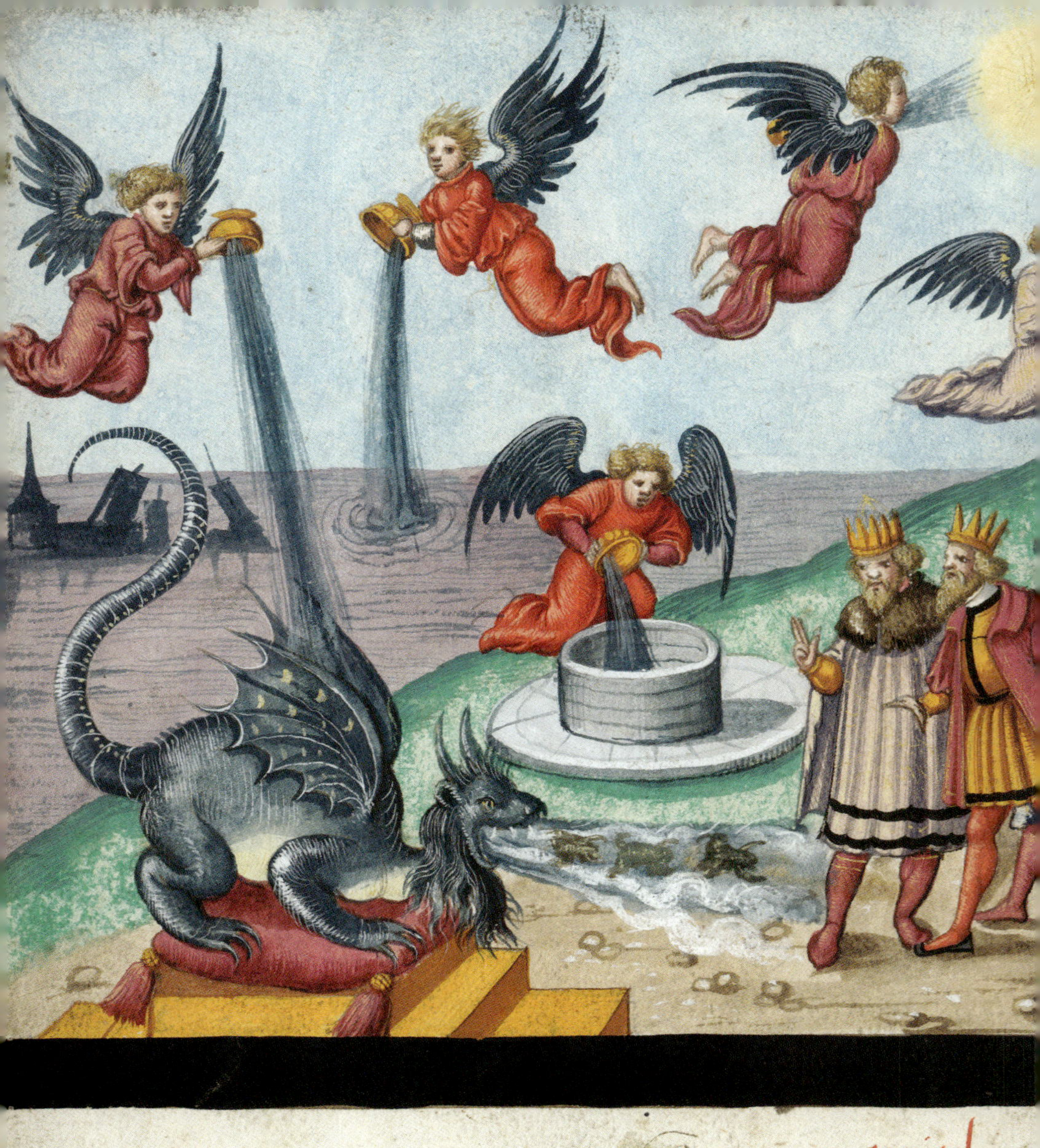

am xv capitel

Vnnd ich sahe ein ander zeichen im hiemel/ das wass gros vnnd wun
ist volendet der zorn gottes/ vnnd sahe als ein glasern meer
iij seinem bild vnnd seineinem mal zeichen vnnd seines na
harpffen vnnd singen das lied mosij des knechts gottes

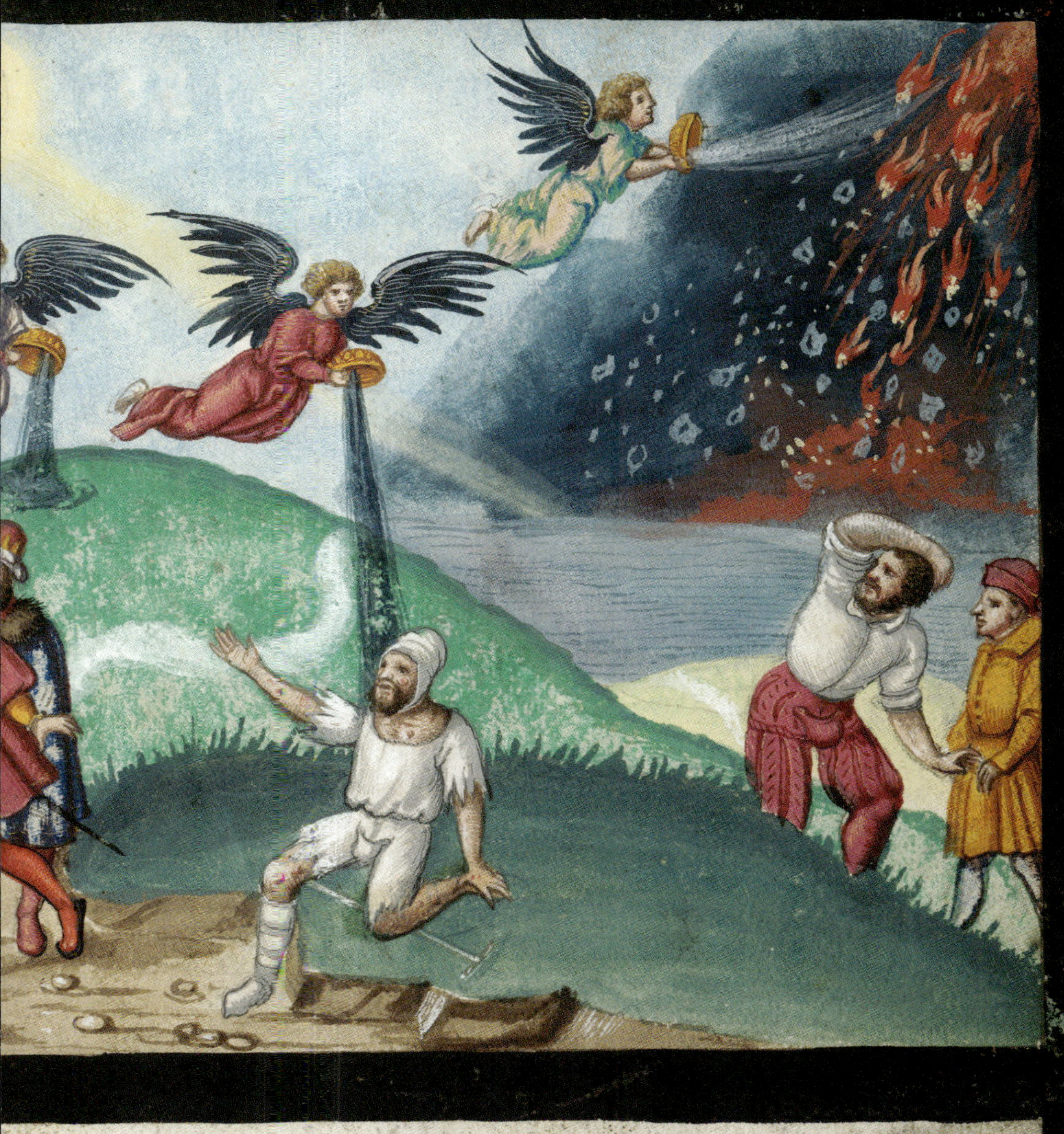

erſam ſieben Engel/ die hatten die leſʒten ſyben plagen/ den mit den ſelbigen
it feuer gemenget/ vnnd die den ſig behalten hatten an dem thier vnnd
ens zal/ das ſie ſtunden an dem gleſeren meer vnnd hatten gottes :

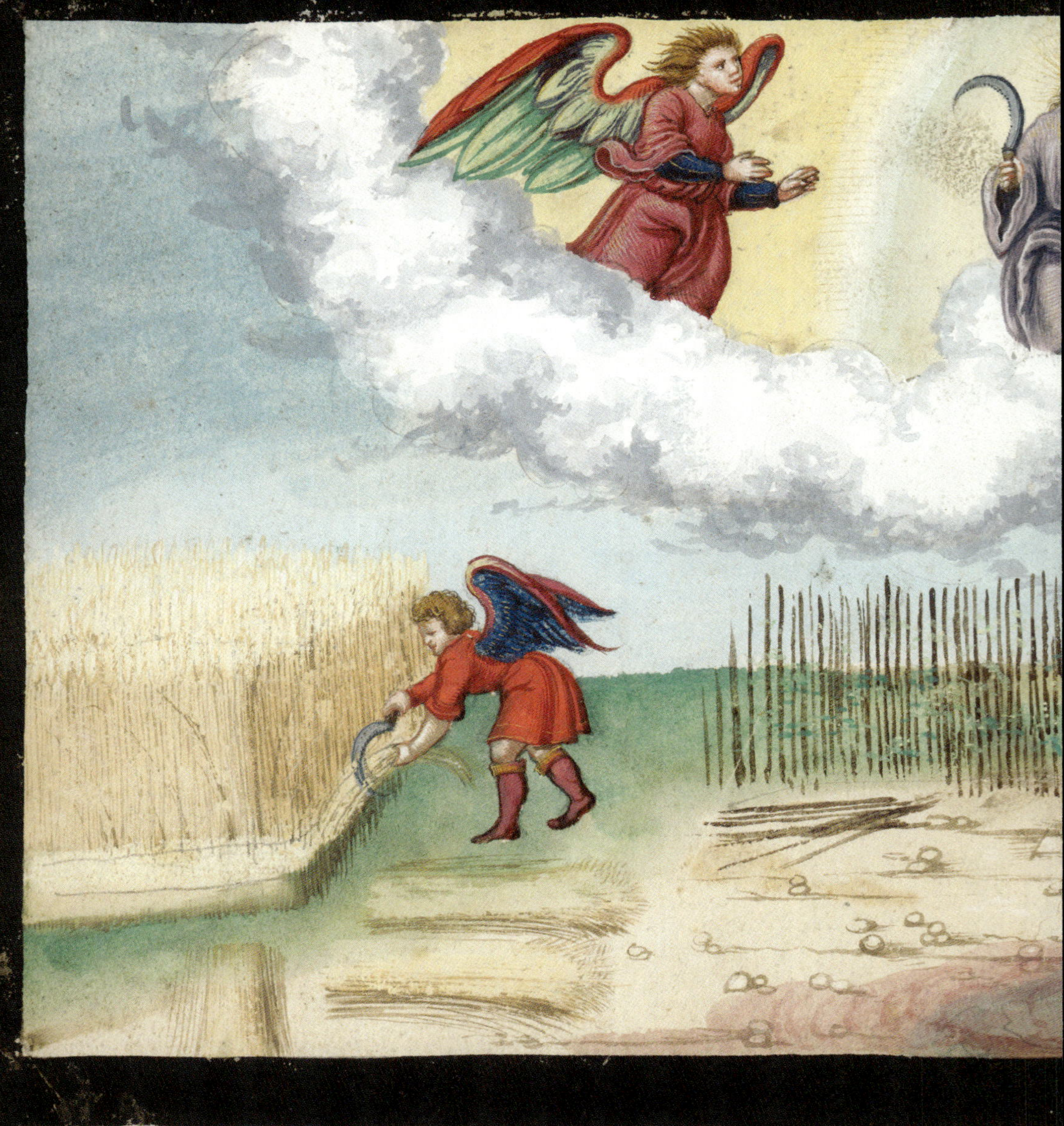

am xiiii capitel

Vnnd ich sahe vnnd siehe/ ein weisse wolcke/ vnnd auff der wolck
kron auff seinem haubte/ vnnd in seiner hannd ein scharpff
lautter stim zů dem/ der auff der wolcken sass/ schlag an
den die Erndte der erden ist dürre worden

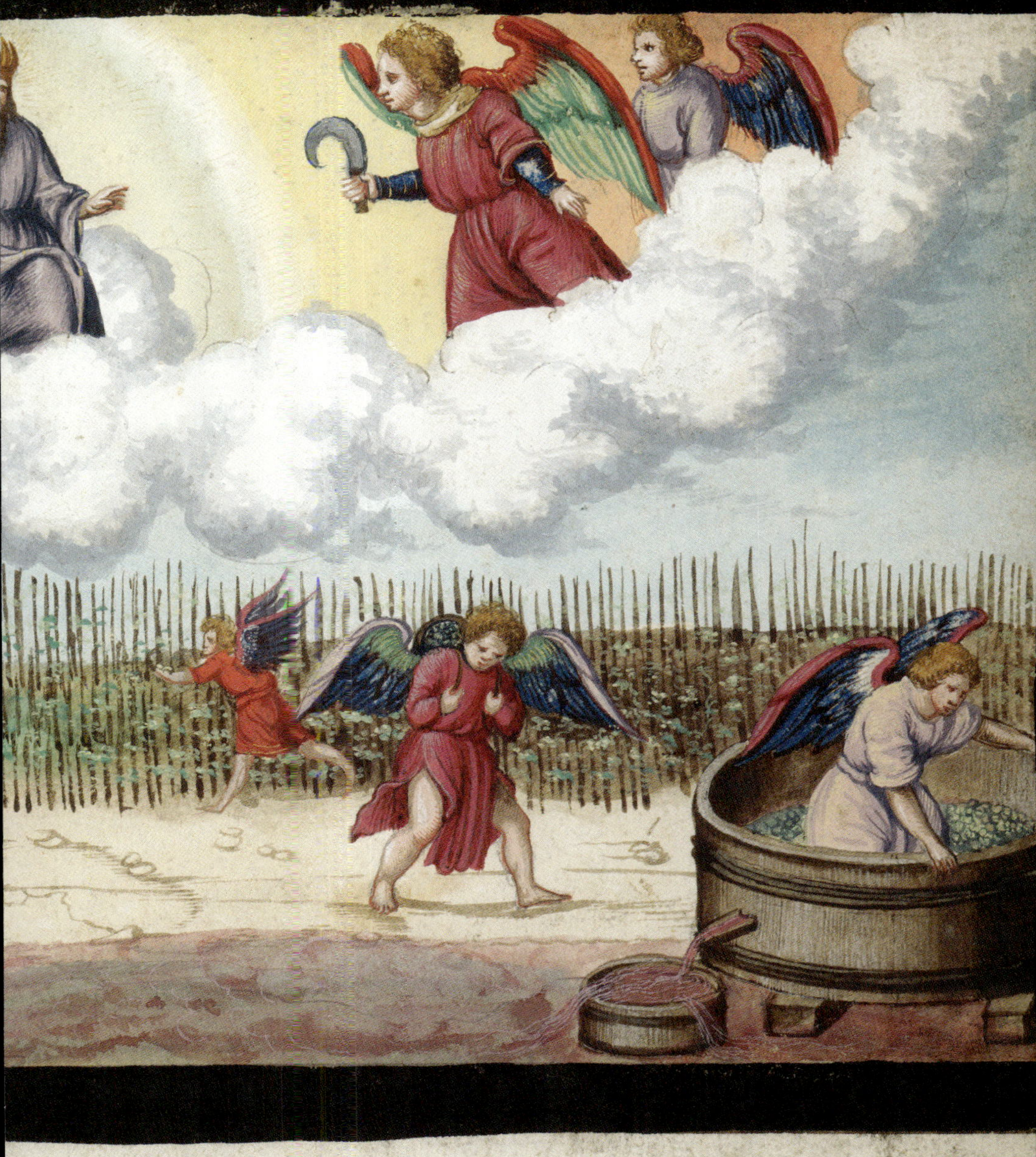

sitzen einen der war gleich eines menschen son/der hatte ein guldene/
ichel vnnd ein ander Engel gieng auß dem tempel/der schrey mit
t deiner sicheln vnnd erndete den die stunde zu erndten ist komē

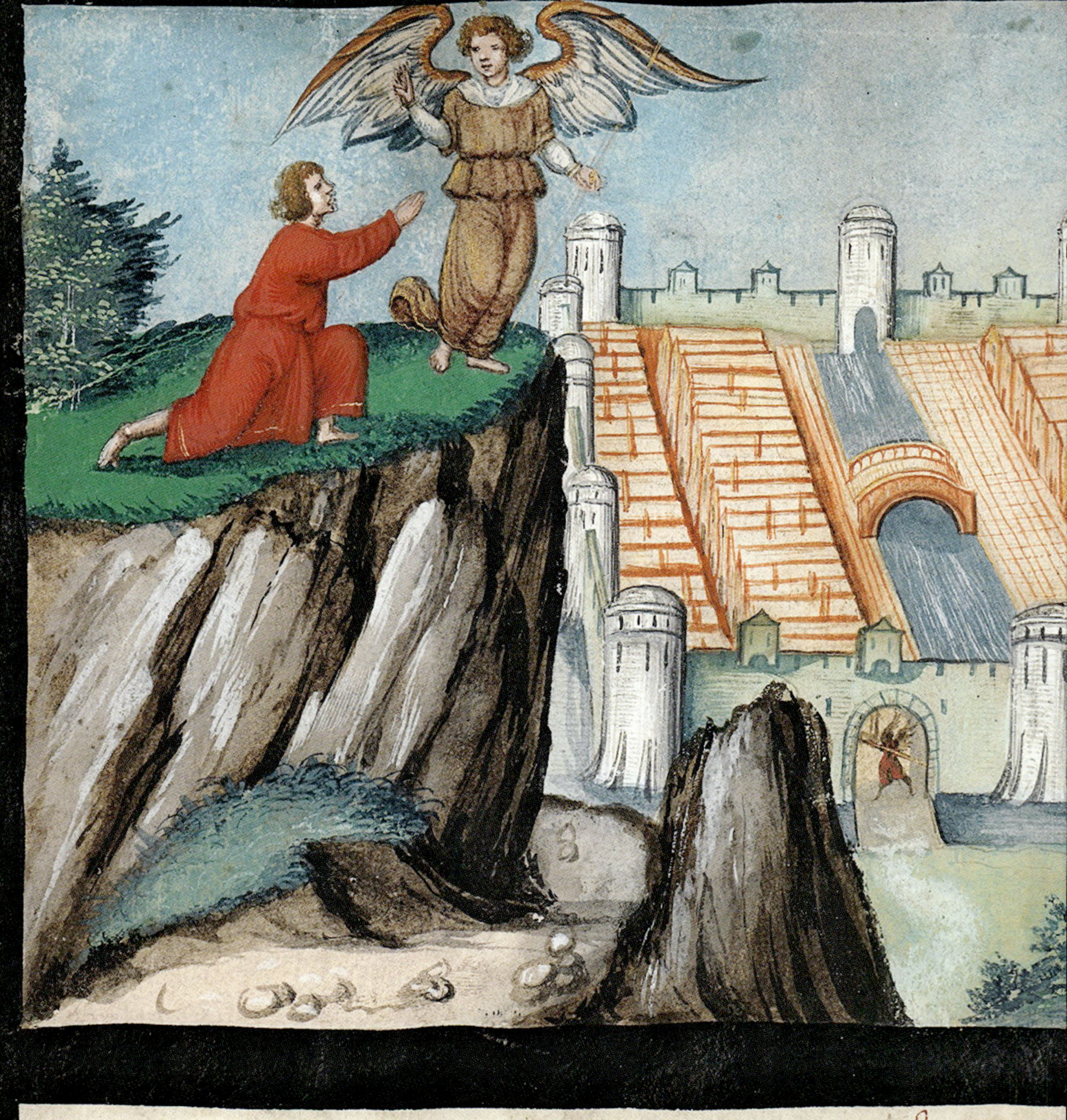

am xxi capitel

nd es kam zu mir einer von den sieben engeln welche die sieben schal
will dir das weyb zeigen die braut des lambs vnnd füeret mich hin
das heilige Jerusalem er nieder faren vom himel von gott vn
edlisten stain Jaspis vnnd dem Cristalligen vnnd hatte gros

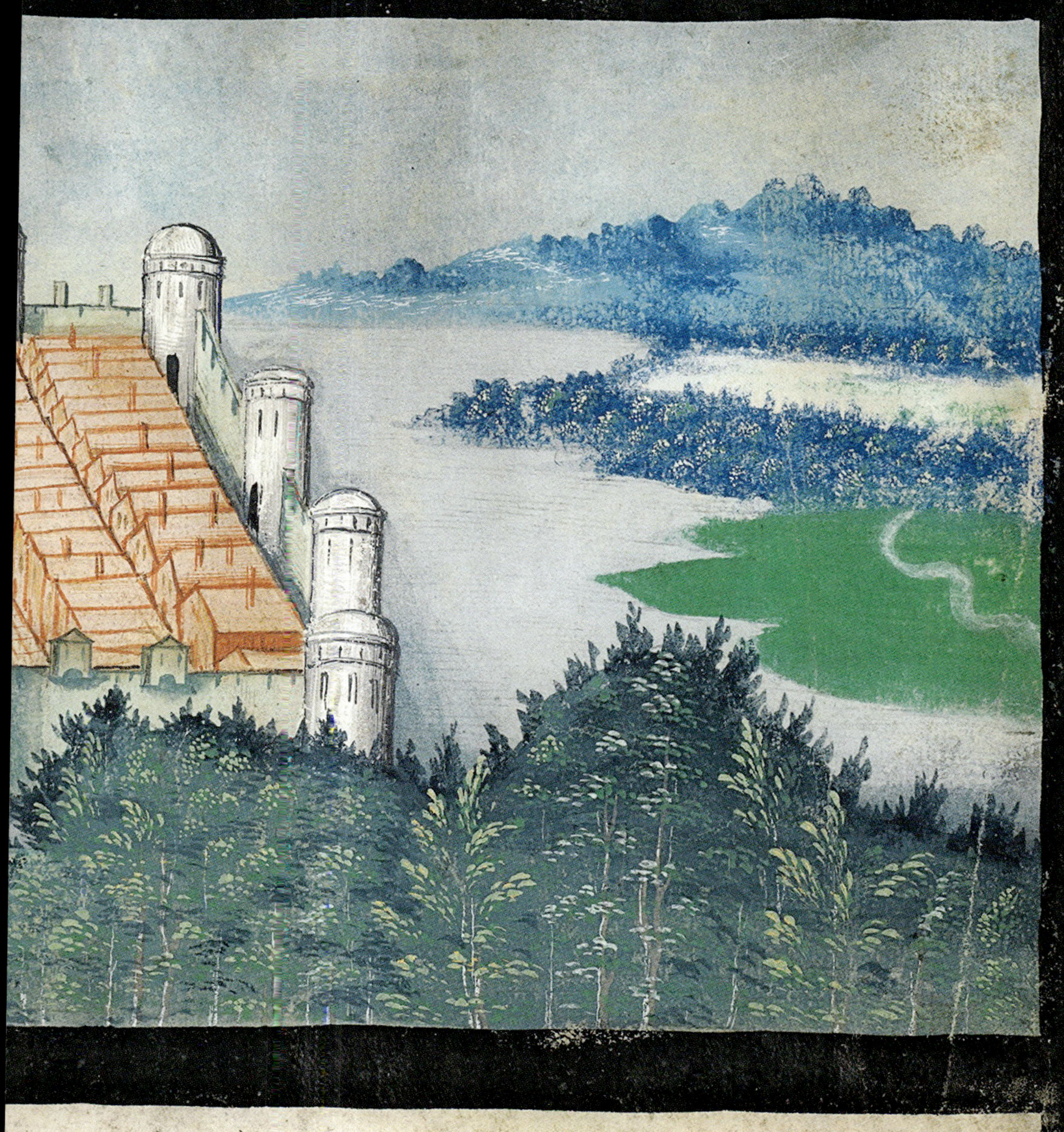

voll hatten der letzsten sieben plagen vnnd redet mir vnnd sprach/kum ich
gaist auff einem grosen vnnd hohen berg vnnd zeiget mir die grose stadt
hatte die herlichkait gottes vnnd yrhe liechte stat ward gleich dem aller:
vnnd hohe mauren:

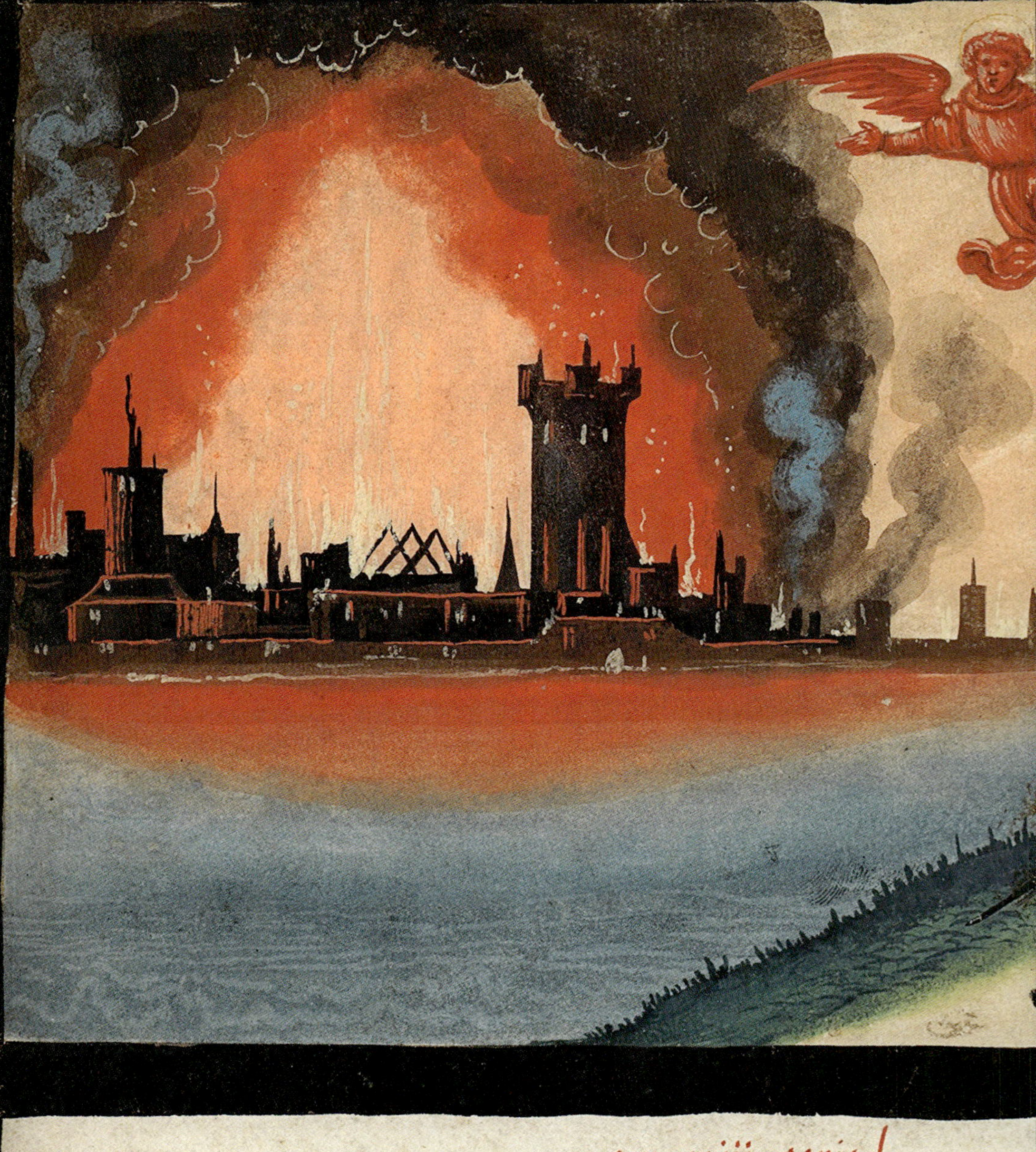

am xviii capitel

Vnd darnach sahe ich ein andern Engel nieder faren vom him
klarheit / vnnd schrey vss macht mit lauter stim vnnd sp
behausung der teuffel worden / vnd ein behaltnus aller
vogel / den von dem wein des zorens irer hurerey haben

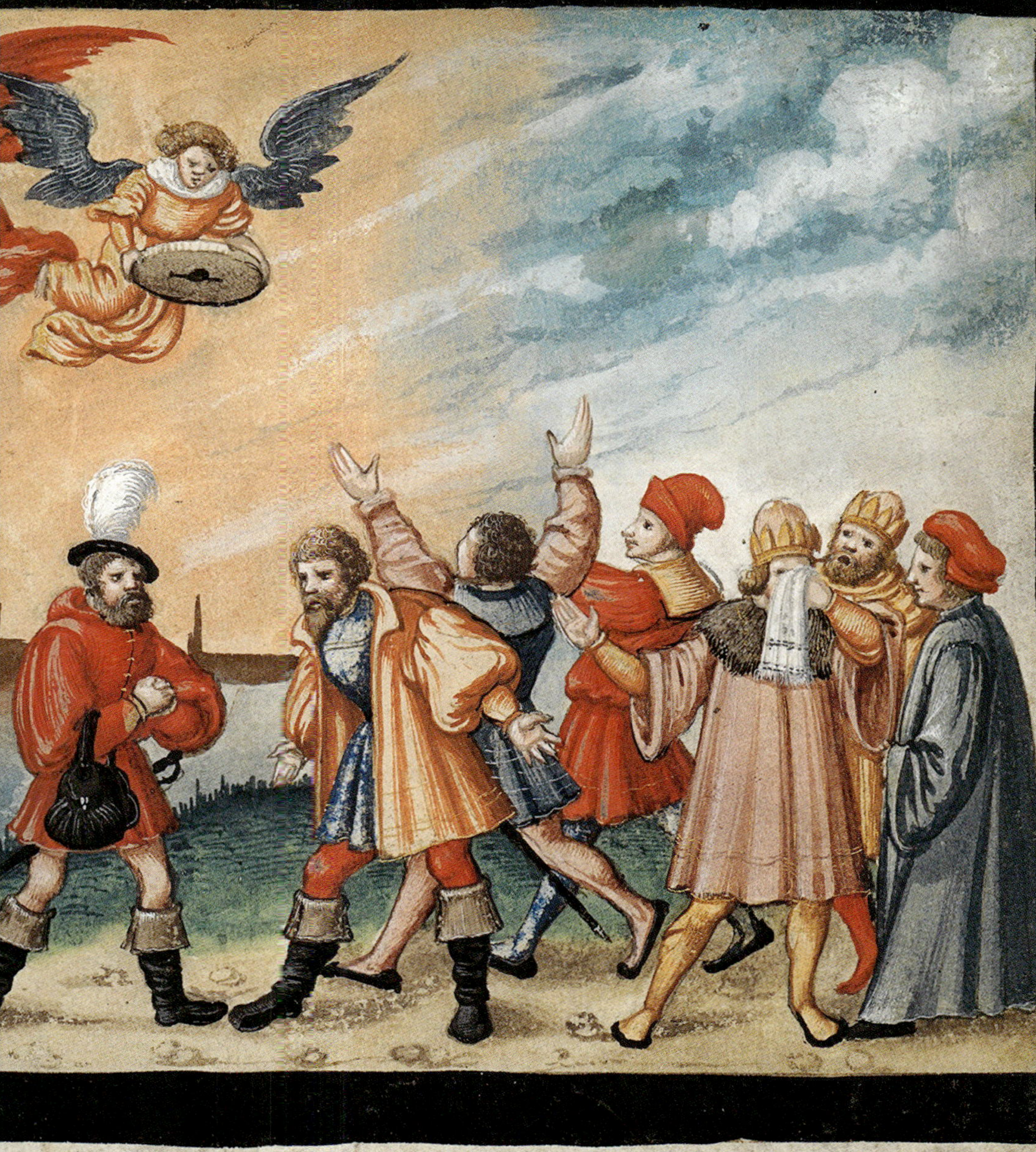

der hatte ein grose macht/ vnnd die erden ward erleucht von seiner
ch Sie ist gefallen Sie ist gefallen Babylon die grosse/ vnnd ein
reiner geister vnd ein behaltnis aller vnreiner feindseliger :
heyden getruncken vnd die könig vff erden haben mit ir hůrerey

FOL. 190

The heavenly harvest | Die himmlische Ernte | La récolte céleste

Revelation 14:14–15 – 14 Then I looked, and behold, a white cloud, and seated on the cloud one like a son of man, with a golden crown on his head, and a sharp sickle in his hand. 15 And another angel came out of the temple, calling with a loud voice to him who sat on the cloud, "Put in your sickle, and reap, for the hour to reap has come, for the harvest of the earth is fully ripe."

Offenbarung 14,14–15 – 14 Und ich sah, und siehe, eine weiße Wolke. Und auf der Wolke saß einer, der gleich war einem Menschensohn; der hatte eine goldene Krone auf seinem Haupt und in seiner Hand eine scharfe Sichel. 15 Und ein andrer Engel kam aus dem Tempel und rief dem, der auf der Wolke saß, mit großer Stimme zu: Setze deine Sichel an und ernte; denn die Zeit zu ernten ist gekommen, denn die Ernte der Erde ist reif geworden.

Apocalypse 14:14–15 – 14 Et voici qu'apparut à mes yeux une nuée blanche et sur la nuée était assis comme un Fils d'homme, ayant sur la tête une couronne d'or et dans la main une faucille aiguisée. 15 Puis un autre Ange sortit du temple et cria d'une voix puissante à celui qui était assis sur la nuée : « Jette ta faucille et moissonne, car c'est l'heure de moissonner, la moisson de la terre est mûre. »

FOL. 191

The new Jerusalem | Das neue Jerusalem | La nouvelle Jérusalem

Revelation 21:9–12 – 9 Then came one of the seven angels who had the seven bowls full of the seven last plagues and spoke to me, saying, "Come, I will show you the Bride, the wife of the Lamb." 10 And he carried me away in the Spirit to a great, high mountain, and showed me the holy city Jerusalem coming down out of heaven from God, 11 having the glory of God, its radiance like a most rare jewel, like a jasper, clear as crystal. 12 It had a great, high wall, [...].

Offenbarung 21,9 -12 – 9 Und es kam zu mir einer von den sieben Engeln, die die sieben Schalen mit den letzten sieben Plagen hatten, und redete mit mir und sprach: Komm, ich will dir die Frau zeigen, die Braut des Lammes. 10 Und er führte mich hin im Geist auf einen großen und hohen Berg und zeigte mir die heilige Stadt Jerusalem herniederkommen aus dem Himmel von Gott, 11 die hatte die Herrlichkeit Gottes; ihr Licht war gleich dem alleredelsten Stein, einem Jaspis, klar wie Kristall; 12 sie hatte eine große und hohe Mauer [...].

Apocalypse 21:9–12 – 9 Alors, l'un des sept Anges aux sept coupes remplies des sept derniers fléaux s'en vint me dire : « Viens, que je te montre la Fiancée, l'Épouse de l'Agneau. » 10 Il me transporta donc en esprit sur une montagne de grande hauteur, et me montra la Cité sainte, Jérusalem, qui descendait du ciel, de chez Dieu, 11 avec en elle la gloire de Dieu. Elle resplendit telle une pierre très précieuse, comme une pierre de jaspe cristallin. 12 Elle est munie d'un rempart de grande hauteur [...].

FOL. 192

The fall of Babylon | Der Untergang Babylons | La chute de Babylone

Revelation 18:1–3 – 1 After this I saw another angel coming down from heaven, having great authority, and the earth was made bright with his glory. 2 And he called out with a mighty voice, "Fallen, fallen is Babylon the great! She has become a dwelling place for demons, a haunt for every unclean spirit, a haunt for every unclean bird, a haunt for every unclean and detestable beast. 3 For all nations have drunk the wine of the passion of her sexual immorality, and the kings of the earth have committed immorality with her […]."

Offenbarung 18,1–3 – 1 Danach sah ich einen andern Engel herniederfahren vom Himmel, der hatte große Macht, die Erde wurde erleuchtet von seinem Glanz. 2 Und er rief mit mächtiger Stimme: Sie ist gefallen, sie ist gefallen, Babylon, die Große, und ist eine Behausung der Teufel geworden, ein Gefängnis aller unreinen Geister und ein Gefängnis aller unreinen Vögel und ein Gefängnis aller unreinen und verhassten Tiere. 3 Denn von dem Zorneswein ihrer Hurerei haben alle Völker getrunken, und die Könige auf Erden haben mit ihr Hurerei […].

Apocalypse 18:1–3 – 1 Après quoi, je vis descendre du ciel un autre Ange, ayant un grand pouvoir, et la terre fut illuminée de sa splendeur. 2 Il s'écria d'une voix puissante : « Elle est tombée, elle est tombée, Babylone la Grande ; elle s'est changée en demeure de démons, en repaire pour toutes sortes d'esprits impurs, en repaire pour toutes sortes d'oiseaux impurs et dégoûtants. 3 Car au vin de ses prostitutions se sont abreuvées toutes les nations, et les rois de la terre ont forniqué avec elle […]. »

Pages 506–507

1531 – Comet / Komet / Comète

in: *Book of Miracles*, Augsburg, *c.* 1550–1552, fol. 122r (detail)

Private collection

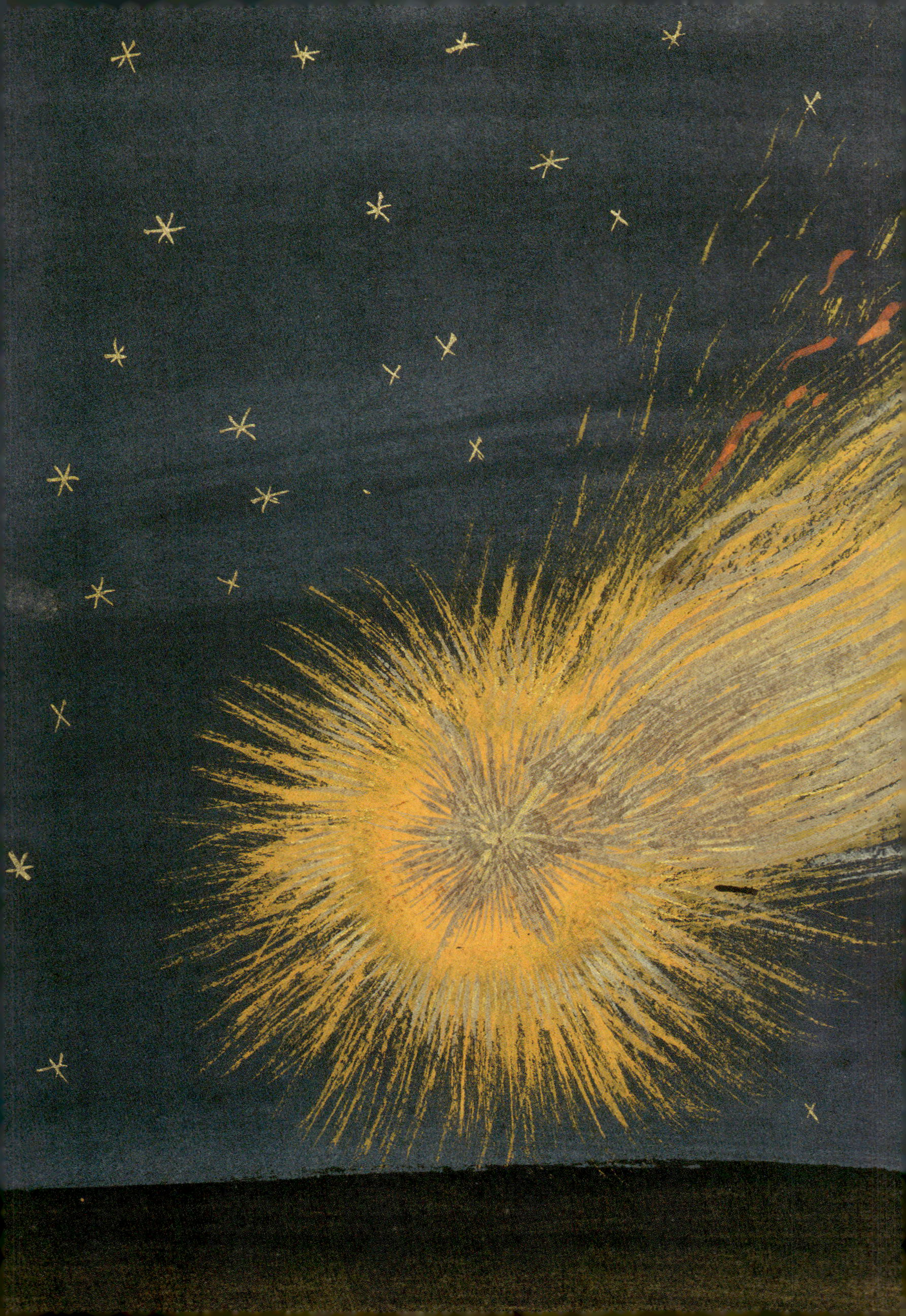

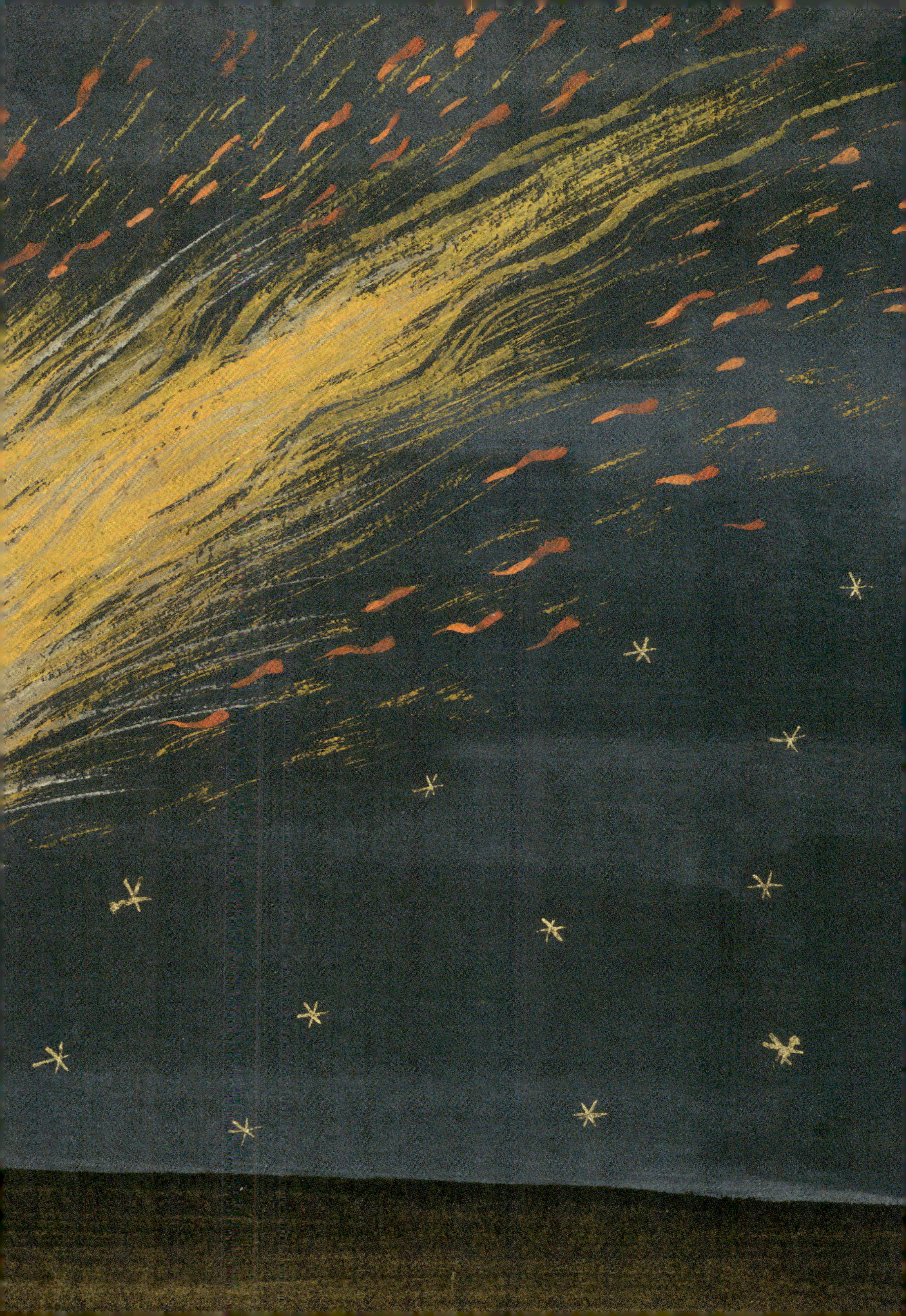

Bibliography

Augsburg 2011: *Bürgermacht und Bücherpracht: Augsburger Ehren- und Familienbücher der Renaissance*, exh. cat. Maximilianmuseum Augsburg, ed. Christoph Emmendörffer and Helmut Zäh, Lucerne 2011.

BARNES, ROBIN BRUCE, *Prophecy and Gnosis: Apocalypticism in the Wake of the Lutheran Reformation*, Stanford 1988.

BOWER, PETER, "The Augsburg *Wunderzeichenbuch:* the papers used in a sixteenth century *Book of Miracles*", in: *The Quarterly* 71, July 2009, pp. 21–28.

Day & Faber 2010: *Das Wunderzeichenbuch: The Augsburg Wunderzeichenbuch, a mid-sixteenth century book of miracles,* London 2010.

FALK, TILMAN, *Hans Burgkmair: Studien zu Leben und Werk*, Munich 1968.

FALK, TILMAN, "South German School: The Comet", in: *Master Drawings: Recent Acquisitions*, Thomas Le Claire Kunsthandel 17, Hamburg 2005, s.p., no. 1.

GREEN, JONATHAN, *Printing and Prophecy: Prognostication and Media Change, 1450–1550*, Cultures of Knowledge in the Early Modern World, Ann Arbor 2012.

HARMS, WOLFGANG/SCHILLING, MICHAEL, *Die Sammlung der Herzog August Bibliothek in Wolfenbüttel: Kommentierte Ausgabe*, 3 vols., Deutsche illustrierte Flugblätter des 16. und 17. Jahrhunderts 1–3, Munich/Tübingen 1980–1989.

HARMS, WOLFGANG/SCHILLING, MICHAEL, *Die Sammlung der Zentralbibliothek Zürich: Kommentierte Ausgabe: Die Wickiana*, 2 vols., Deutsche illustrierte Flugblätter des 16. und 17. Jahrhunderts 6/7, Tübingen 1997–2005.

HESS, WILHELM, *Himmels- und Naturerscheinungen in Einblattdrucken des XV. bis XVIII. Jahrhunderts*, Leipzig 1911.

KRAUSE, KATHARINA, *Hans Holbein der Ältere*, Munich/Berlin 2002.

LEPPIN, VOLKER, *Antichrist und Jüngster Tag: Das Profil apokalyptischer Flugschriftenpublizistik im deutschen Luthertum 1548–1618*, Quellen und Forschungen zur Reformationsgeschichte 69, Gütersloh 1999.

LUDWIG, WALTHER, "Zukunftsvoraussagen in der Antike, der frühen Neuzeit und heute", in: Bergdolt, Klaus/Ludwig, Walther, *Zukunftsvoraussagen in der Renaissance*, Wolfenbütteler Abhandlungen zur Renaissanceforschung 23, Wiesbaden 2005, pp. 9–64.

MASSING, JEAN-MICHEL, "A Sixteenth-Century Illustrated Treatise on Comets", in: *Journal of the Warburg and Courtauld Institutes* 40 (1977), pp. 318–322.

MAUELSHAGEN, FRANZ, *Wunderkammer auf Papier: Die "Wickiana" zwischen Reformation und Volksglaube*, Frühneuzeit-Forschungen 15, Epfendorf 2011.

MULLER, FRANK, *Heinrich Vogtherr l'Ancien. Un artiste entre Renaissance et Réforme*, Wiesbaden 1997.

Munich 2010: *Die Fugger im Bild: Selbstdarstellung einer Familiendynastie der Renaissance: Begleitbuch zur Schatzkammerausstellung anlässlich der Erwerbung des* Ehrenbuchs *der Fugger (Cgm 9460) und der* Fuggerorum et Fuggerarum ... imagines *(Cod.icon. 380)*, Bayerische Staatsbibliothek Munich, Lucerne 2010.

Nuremberg 2011: *Die gottlosen Maler von Nürnberg: Konvention und Subversion in der Druckgrafik der Beham-Brüder*, exh. cat. Albrecht-Dürer-Haus, ed. Jürgen Müller and Thomas Schauerte, Emsdetten 2011.

REUTER, MARIANNE: "'Maximilianj Römischen Kayssers hochloblichester gedechtnus Ritter Spyl' – eine Blütenlese", in: *Rondo: Beiträge für Peter Diemer zum 65. Geburtstag*, ed. Wolfgang Augustyn and Iris Lauterbach, Munich 2012, pp. 70–80.

ROWLANDS, JOHN, *Drawings by German artists and artists from German-speaking regions of Europe in the Department of Prints and Drawings in the British Museum, the fifteenth century, and the sixteenth century by artists born before 1530*, 2 vols., London 1993.

RÜMELIN, CHRISTOPH, "Hans Holbeins 'Icones', ihre Formschneider und ihre Nachfolge", in: *Münchner Jahrbuch der bildenden Kunst* 3. Folge, 47 (1996), pp. 55–72.

SCHENDA, RUDOLF, "Die deutschen Prodigiensammlungen des 16. und 17. Jahrhunderts", in: *Archiv für Geschichte des Buchwesens* 4 (1963), cols. 637–710.

SCHILLING, MICHAEL, *Bildpublizistik der frühen Neuzeit: Aufgaben und Leistungen des illustrierten Flugblatts in Deutschland bis um 1700*, Studien und Texte zur Sozialgeschichte der Literatur 29, Tübingen 1990.

SCHWEGLER, MICHAELA, *"Erschröckliches Wunderzeichen" oder "natürliches Phänomenon"?*

Frühneuzeitliche Wunderzeichenberichte aus der Sicht der Wissenschaft, Bayerische Schriften zur Volkskunde 7, Munich 2002.

Vienna 2012: *Kaiser Maximilian I. und die Kunst der Dürerzeit*, exh. cat. Albertina Vienna, ed. Eva Michel and Maria Luise Sternath, Munich 2012.

WUTTKE, DIETER, "Sebastian Brants Verhältnis zu Wunderdeutung und Astrologie", in: *Studien zur deutschen Literatur und Sprache des Mittelalters: Festschrift für Hugo Moser zum 65. Geburtstag*, ed. Werner Besch, Berlin 1974, pp. 272–286.

Bibliography of the reference sources

BEHAM, HANS SEBALD, *Biblicae historiae artificiosissime depictae. Biblische Historien, figürlich fürgebildet*, Frankfurt am Main 1537 (2nd ed.).

BEHAM, HANS SEBALD, *Typi in apocalypsi Ioannis depicti*, Frankfurt am Main 1539.

Biblia 1545: *Biblia: Das ist: Die gantze Heilige Schrifft, Deudsch, Auffs new zugericht*, trans. Martin Luther, Wittenberg 1545 (facsimile edition with afterword by Wilhelm Hoffmann, Stuttgart 1983).

Chronica 1528: *Chronica New: Manicherlay Historien unnd besondere geschichten Kürtzlich begreyffend, Von dem Jar der geburt unsers seligmachers Jesu Christi biß in das M.D und. xxviij. Erlengeret*, Augsburg 1528.

Chronica 1531: *Chronica Darinn auff das kurtzest werden begriffen die Namhafftigsten geschichten so sich under allen Kaysern von der geburt Christi biß auff das M.D. und xxxj. Jar verlaffen haben*, Augsburg 1531.

Chronica 1542: *Chronica Darinn auff das kürtzest begriffen die namhafftigsten geschichten so sich von der geburt Christi under allen Römischen Kaisern sonderlich inn Teütscher Nation biß auf diß gegenwürtig M.D. und XLII. Jar verlauffen haben*, Augsburg 1542.

ECKER, GISELA, *Einblattdrucke von den Anfängen bis 1555: Untersuchungen zu einer Publikationsform literarischer Texte*, Göppinger Arbeiten zur Germanistik 314, 2 vols., Göppingen 1981.

FAUST, INGRID/BARTHELMESS, KLAUS/STOPP, KLAUS, *Zoologische Einblattdrucke und Flugschriften vor 1800*, 6 vols., Stuttgart 1998–2010.

FRANCK, SEBASTIAN, *Chronica, Zeytbuch und geschychtbibel von anbegyn biß inn diß gegenwertig M.D.xxxj. jar*, Strasbourg 1531.

FRANCK, SEBASTIAN, *Chronica, Zeitbuch unnd Geschichtbibel von Anbegyn biss in diss gegenwertig M.D.L. Jar verlengt*, Bern 1550/51 (4th ed.).

HARMS, WOLFGANG/SCHILLING, MICHAEL, *Die Sammlung der Zentralbibliothek Zürich: Kommentierte Ausgabe: Die Wickiana*, 2 vols., Deutsche illustrierte Flugblätter des 16. Jahrhunderts 6/7, Tübingen 1997–2005.

HELLMANN, GUSTAV, *Die Meteorologie in den deutschen Flugschriften und Flugblättern des XVI. Jahrhunderts: Ein Beitrag zur Geschichte der Meteorologie*, Abhandlungen der preussischen Akademie der Wissenschaften 1921, Physikalisch-Mathematische Klasse 1, Berlin 1921.

Holbein 1538: Hans Holbein the Younger, *Historiarum Veteris Instrumenti icones ad vivum expressae*, Lyons 1538.

Josephus 1531: Josephus, Flavius, *Josephuß Teütsch*, trans. and ed. by Caspar Hedio, Strasbourg 1531.

Schedel 1493: Schedel, Hartmann, *Chronicle of the World: The Complete and Annotated Nuremberg Chronicle of 1493* (facsimile edition with introduction and appendix by Stephan Füssel, Cologne 2001).

STOPP, KLAUS, *Botanische Einblattdrucke und Flugschriften vor 1800*, 2 vols., Stuttgart 2001.

Texts of the Bible / Acknowledgements / Photo credits

Texts of the Bible

The Holy Bible, English Standard Version (ESV). © 2001 by Crossway, a publishing ministry of Good News Publishers, Wheaton IL, USA

Lutherbibel, revidierter Text 1984, durchgesehene Ausgabe. © 1999 Deutsche Bibelgesellschaft, Stuttgart

La Bible de Jérusalem. La Sainte Bible traduite en français sous la direction de l'École biblique de Jérusalem. Texte de la nouvelle édition entièrement revue et augmentée. © Les Éditions du Cerf, Paris 1998

Acknowledgements

The present reprint of the Augsburg *Book of Miraculous Signs* is based on the copy in the collection of Mickey Cartin. We would like to thank him for his generous co-operation and for his trust in allowing us to publish this important and valuable manuscript. We would also like to express our warmest thanks to curator Steven Holmes for his energetic support in the production of this book. The digital reproduction of the original was carried out by the Centre for Retrospective Digitisation (GDZ) at the Göttingen State and University Library, Germany. We wish to thank Martin Liebetruth of the GDZ for his invaluable collaboration.

Photo credits

Re-inserted folia / wieder eingefügte Folia / Feuilles réinsérées: 93r, v, 111r, v, 191, 192.

Basel, Kunstmuseum, Martin P. Bühler: pp. 8, 40; Berlin, bpk | The Trustees of the British Museum: pp. 30, 54, 57; Göttingen, Niedersächsische Staats- und Universitätsbibliothek: pp. 38, 79; Karlsruhe, Staatliche Kunsthalle: p. 71; London, The Warburg Institute: p. 49; Munich, Bayerische Staatsbibliothek: pp. 9, 10, 24, 29, 32, 62, 74, 81, 82, 85, 89; Munich, Karl & Faber Kunstauktionen/Photo Courtesy of The Museum of Everything: fols. 191, 192; Nuremberg, Germanisches Nationalmuseum, Graphische Sammlung: pp. 19, 50; Paris, Bibliothèque nationale de France: pp. 15, 73; Paris, RMN-Grand Palais (Musée du Louvre) / Michèle Bellot: p. 86; Private collection: folio 111r; Stuttgart, Staatsgalerie Stuttgart, Graphische Sammlung © Photo: Staatsgalerie Stuttgart: folio 93r, v, 129; Vienna, Österreichische Nationalbibliothek: p. 39; Weimar, Herzogin Anna Amalia Bibliothek: pp. 13, 23, 43, 68; Zurich, Zentralbibliothek, Graphische Sammlung und Fotoarchiv: pp. 16, 20, 27, 45, 53, 58, 61.

Imprint

Hohenzollernring 53, D–50672 Köln
www.taschen.com

English translation: Johanna Hörning (plates); Karen Williams, Rennes-le-Château (essay)
French translation: Jean-François Cornu (plates); Michèle Schreyer, Cologne (essay)
German translation: Rebekka Elsäßer (plates)

Printed in Bosnia-Herzegovina
ISBN 978-3-8365-9995-5

Pages 2–3
1009 – Burning torch
Brennende Fackel
Torche enflammée
fol. 35r (detail)

Pages 4–5
1520 – Parhelia over Vienna
Nebensonnen über Wien
Parhélies dans le ciel de Vienne
fol. 102r (detail)

Pages 92–93
Celestial fire over Augsburg
Himmelsfeuer über Augsburg
Incendie céleste dans le ciel d'Augsbourg
fol. 144r (detail)

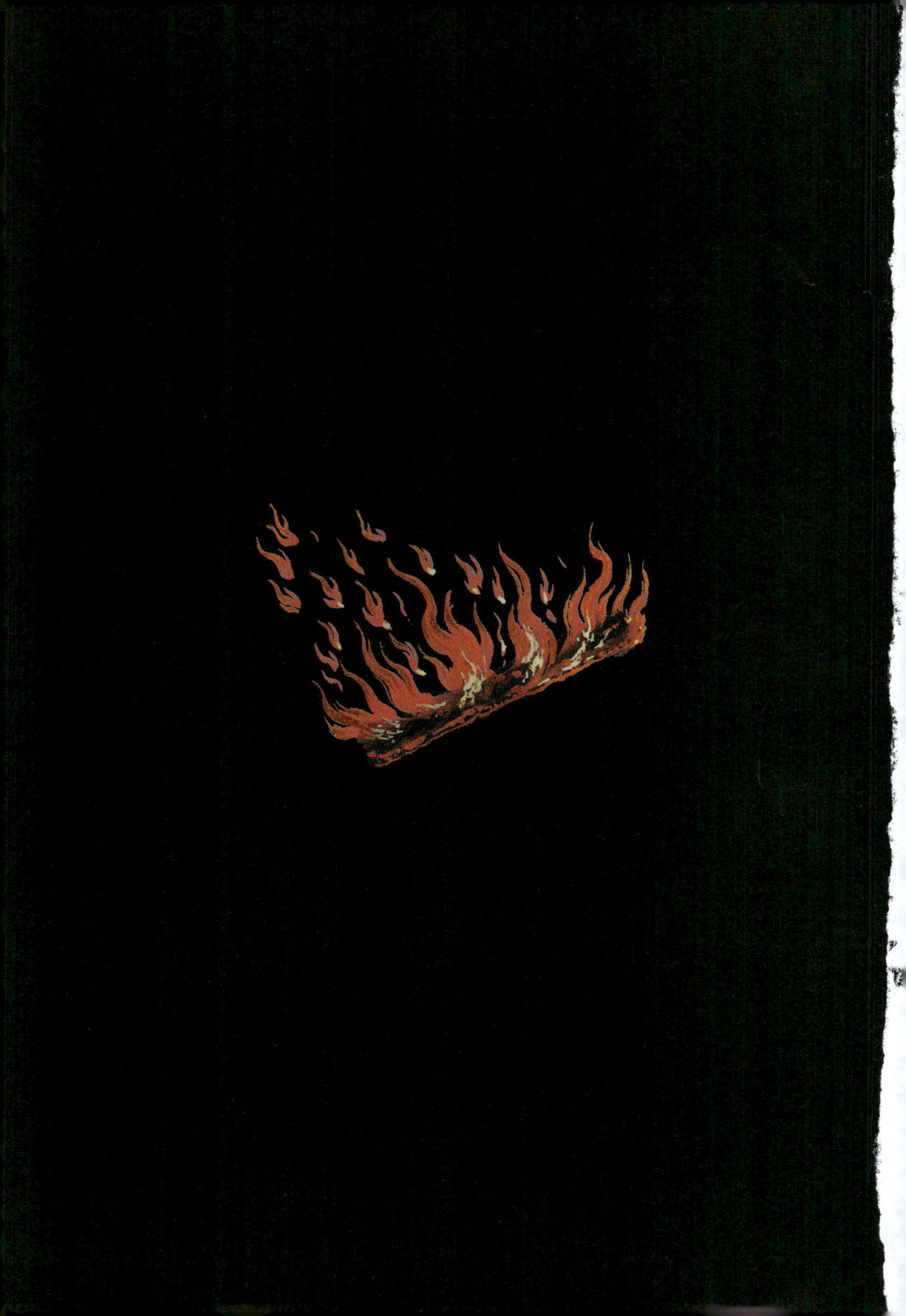

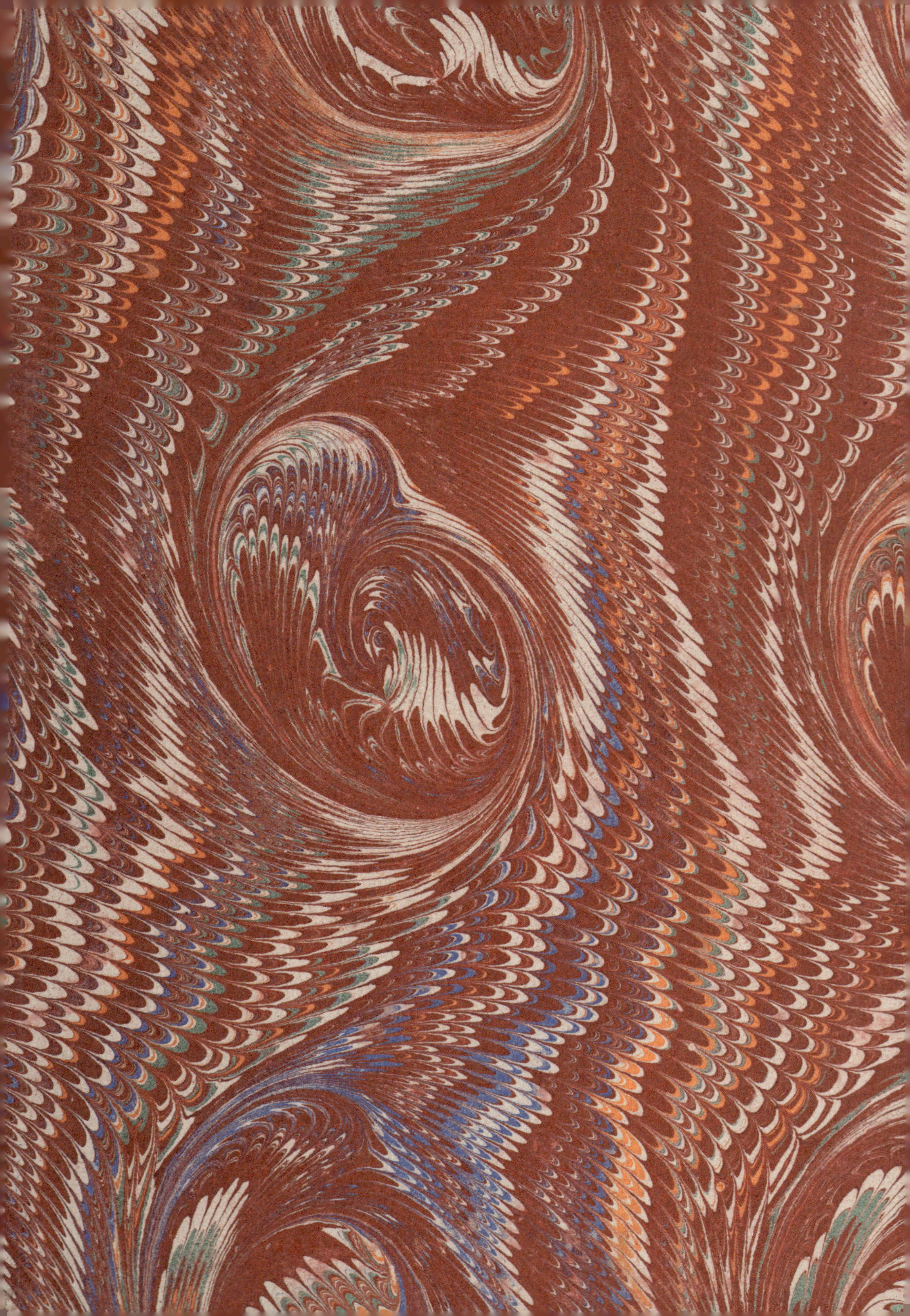